INSIDE New York 2003

the ultimate guidebook

2960 Broadway, MC 5727
New York, NY 10027
Phone: (212) 854-2804
Fax: (212) 663-9398
www.insideny.com

Publisher	Joshua S. Hundert
Editor-in-Chief	Carla Sapsford
Graphic Designer	Lisa R. Margulies
Photography Editor	Michael Pymm

EDITORIAL

Neighborhoods Editor	Imogen Rose-Smith
Shopping Editor	Esti Tambay
Arts Editors	Ann Gookin and Esti Tambay
Dining Editor	Jason Parsont
Nightlife Editor	Michael Levitin
Leisure Editor	Ann Gookin
Fact Checker	Stuart Weinstock
Assistant Fact Checker	Bridget Geibel
Writers	Noriko Akashi
	Lucia Aniello
	Rachel Aviv
	Daniel Goldman
	Ricky Gratz
	Julia Morelli
	Avi Olitzky
	Ted Phillips
	Catherine Reinhard
	Ben Widlanski
Cover Design	Lisa R. Margulies and Michael Pymm

SALES

Sales Representatives	Brian Cabezas
	Daniel Jacobs

Special thanks to: Erika Rosek, Susan Chang, Ana Astol, Pat Macken, Francine Bard and the Columbia University Center for Career Education, Sharon Brumbaugh, Maureen Peterson, Tim Firkin, Bob McKenzie, Jerry Messerley, John Reichard, Hanne Lauridsen, Michael Pymm, Jon Schalit, Rob Polsky, Elizabeth Sosnov, Amy and Michael Hundert, Bonnie and Alfred Margulies, Marilyn Sapsford, Rachel Harkins, Jaime Schwartz, Gerald Sherwin, John Grogan, Jeff Woodbury and the staff of Columbia Information Technology, Columbia Security, Columbia Campus Pages, Columbia Bartending Agency, Columbia Tutoring and Translation Agency and the stellar staff of INY 2003.

For sales or advertising information, call 212-854-2804, email *sales@insideny.com* or visit *http://www.insideny.com* Please contact BookWorld Companies at 1-800-444-2524, or Ingram Book Company, if your bookstore would like to carry *Inside New York*.

TOC table of contents

city living
page 7

neighborhoods
page 35

shopping
page 117

table of contents | TOC

arts page 145

restaurants and cafes page 195

nightlife page 239

leisure page 273

resources page 295

city
living
THE NET   THE NET   THE NET   THE NET   THE NET   THE NET   THE NET

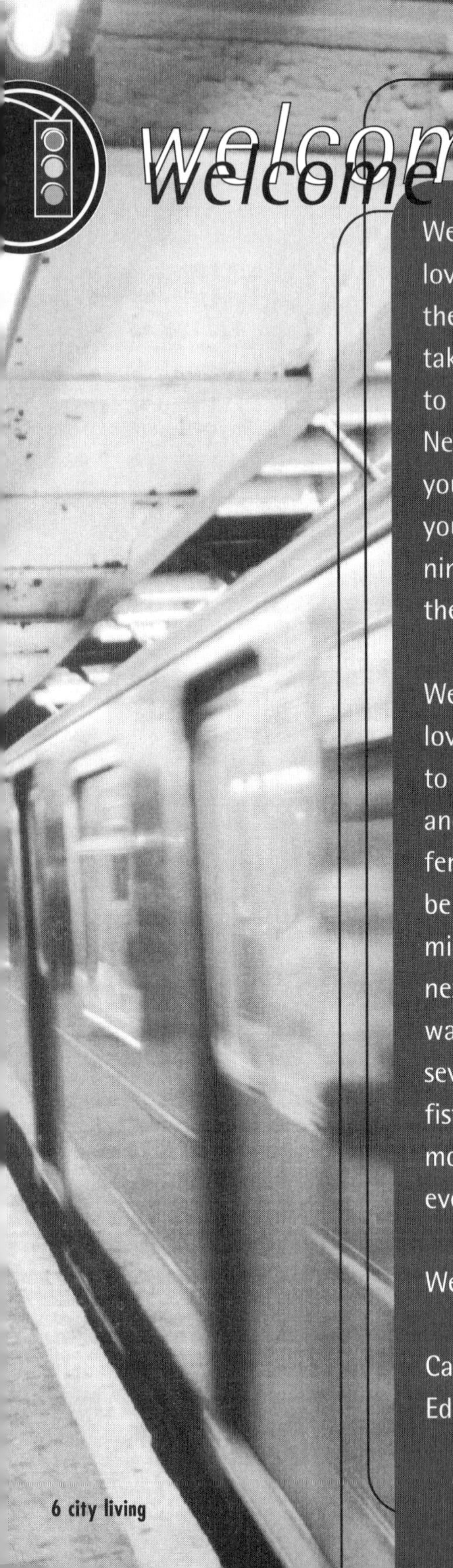

welcome

welcome

Welcome to our city, one of the craziest, loveliest, jam-packed capsules of humanity the world has ever seen. Deciphering this city takes guts, adventurousness and a willingness to be somebody you've never been before. New York is one of the best places to drop your old skin, your old lifestyle and perhaps your old friends. Every day is a new beginning here, and for every mistake you make there is an opportunity to start anew.

We invite you to explore this city that we love – its beauties and its inhumanities - and to become fully versed in all of its boroughs and villages. Every neighborhood here is different, and no two blocks are alike. You can be in SoHo, noshing with celebrities one minute, then sitting down outside to smoke next to a homeless man, then taking a subway home with b-boys. As the city is about seven miles long, everyone is piled hand over fist on top of each other, and you'll learn more about how the other half lives than you ever thought possible.

We hope you fall in love with New York too.

Carla Sapsford
Editor-in-Chief

SUBWAYS

New York's transportation system is one of the oldest and most comprehensive in the world. Somehow, in the chaos that is New York, it transports over 8 million people a day. For a mere $1.50, you can go anywhere in New York. And most agree that New York's subways, buses and trains are improving all the time. Despite recent budget cuts, most subway booths have remained open, and the MTA (Metropolitan Transportation Authority) has been hiring more car cleaners to clean up their act. More people are riding the subway than ever before.

On the negative side, the century-old age of the system translates into frequent repairs, delays and track changes (check out www.mta.info or www.mta.nyc.ny.us to find out what's going on). Even seasoned New Yorkers can

barely figure out all the service alterations. And then, there is the smell.

The smell of a New York City subway station is pungent. Stark, a fleshy mix of oil, grime and collective sweat. Some call this gross. Others liken it to a wake-up call in the morning-a reminder that they are in the greatest,

baddest city in the world. It reeks so terribly in some stations, especially during the long, hot summers, that the MTA has started spraying pine scent through some of its ventilation systems. We kid you not.

As for the sound of a subway-they give construction workers earplugs to protect

In order to find the cross street of an address, follow these simple steps:

NORTH-SOUTH AVENUES

1. Cancel the last digit of the house number
2. Divide the remaining number by two
3. Add or deduct the key number (list follows)

*On street or address numbers preceded by an asterisk, omit step 2.

For example, take 1100 Broadway:
1. Cancel the last digit so you are left with 110
2. Divide 110 by two, leaving you with 55
3. Subtract 31, the key number for Broadway addresses over 1000. Thus, 1100 Broadway is at 24th Street.

Avenues A, B, C, D	Add 3
First Avenue	Add 3
Second Avenue	Add 3
Third Avenue	Add 10
Fourth Avenue	Add 8
Fifth Avenue	
1-200	Add 13
201-400	Add 16
401-600	Add 18
601-775	Add 20
*776-1286	Subtract 18
Sixth Avenue	Subtract 12
Seventh Avenue	
1-1800	Add 12
1800 + above	Add 20
Eighth Avenue	Add 9

Ninth Avenue	Add 13
Tenth Avenue	Add 13
Eleventh Avenue	Add 15
Amsterdam Avenue	Add 59
Broadway	
1-754	= All below 8th Street
754-858	Subtract 29
859-958	Subtract 25
1000 + above	Subtract 31
*Central Park West	Add 60
Columbus Avenue	Add 59
Lexington Avenue	Add 22
Madison Avenue	Add 27
Park Avenue	Add 34
Riverside Drive	
*1-567	Add 73
*567 + above	Add 78
West End Avenue	Add 59

EAST-WEST

Addresses for any east-west street begin at the avenue listed below

East Side:

1	Fifth Avenue
101	Park Avenue
201	Third Avenue
301	Second Avenue
401	First Avenue
501	York or Avenue A
601	Avenue B

West Side:

1	Fifth Avenue
101	Sixth Avenue
201	Seventh Avenue
301	Eighth Avenue
401	Ninth Avenue
501	Tenth Avenue
601	Eleventh Avenue

scowl that makes you look like you just sucked on a sardine. Overall, the New York City subway system does a great job. New Yorkers will complain about anything and everything, and the subway takes a verbal beating. But the subway is vital to the daily life of city, and the city grinds to a halt without it.

Unwritten Rules

The subway lines aren't easy to make out. And this isn't like Washington or Boston, where you can just say "Red Line" and people will understand what you're talking about. Learn the numbers, learn the intricacies. Like remembering that the 7 is a crosstown train that is often faster than the S shuttle during rush hour. So take the time to decipher the system. Spend a day every weekend exploring. Get out at a random stop, and walk around. If you have just gotten a new job, time your commute, find an alternate route, and then tack on fifteen minutes for delays.

them from the kinds of screeches and howls you will hear on a daily basis. Forget about talking on your cell phone below ground. Forget about having a conversation uninterrupted. The subway's screechy rhythm will soon have you bringing a paper and adopting that New York

Fares

Until recently, the coin token was the currency of the MTA, but the invention of the MetroCard Gold has revolutionized the New York City subway system. It is now possible to buy your MetroCard from a machine with cash or a credit card, a change in the last few years. Bulk buying pays off: if you buy a $15 pay-per-ride card, you can get a free ride, $30 gets you two. Many other options exist: there are one-time cards, and there is an unlimited Fun Pass for $4 that allows you to ride the subway as many times as you like for one whole day. 7- and 30-day MetroCards are also available for $17 and $63, respectively, and allow unlimited usage for that time period. But beware the time delay on an unlimited MetroCard: when a card is swiped, it cannot be swiped again for 18 minutes, so you can't get your friends in for free right after you.

Transfers

New York's transit system is connected by the universal MetroCard, which allows transfers. Stations that service more than one line (for example, Times Square) allow free transfers between the different lines. Transfer points are marked by an empty white bubble on the subway map. Also, after you use a MetroCard on a subway, you have two hours to use a free transfer for a bus. The same is true from bus to subway and bus to bus. So, when you are headed out for a quick errand, take the subway one way and the bus on the return trip - the trip becomes half price.

Disabilities

Subway riders with disabilities are largely out of luck. Unlike the Washington, DC metro, New York's system is largely free of the escalators and elevators that would make a subway trip comfortable for those on crutches or in a wheelchair. We wish we had better news for those who have special physical needs, but essentially New York is more expensive for those who are disabled. On its website, the MTA does point out wheelchair-accessible transfer points for subways. Many disabled residents take cabs or buses, which are usually equipped with a working lift that will hoist a wheelchair up via the back window. Hailing the attention of the bus driver to lower the bus and ramp is usually the hard part. There are city buses for the disabled: Access-a-Ride and other charter buses are available for some who qualify. Call (877) 377-2017 or see www.mta.info for further information.

Recent Changes

The V train is a new express train that runs along part of the way of the B, D, and F routes. The 9 train is out of commission until a new station can be built under the former World Trade Center, and the 1 no longer goes to South Ferry. It now ends at the Brooklyn Bridge. The 2 train is now a local in Manhattan until 96th Street, where it becomes express again. Grand Central Station, upstairs, has a large information booth with detailed maps, or you can get a general service map from any token booth operator. Pick up a subway map in a station or call (718) 330-1234 for the most up-to-date changes.

Directions

"Uptown" means Bronx- or Queens-bound. "Downtown" similarly means Brooklyn-bound. If you accidentally swipe your card and get onto the wrong direction-bound train, try and find an underground passageway if you can. If not, suck up the $1.50 and exit, cross the street and start over.

A local train makes all stops, an express train will only stop at the major thoroughfares, marked by a big white bubble on your subway map (enclosed in this book). Express trains are often super-crowded, and sometimes are not much faster than locals in Manhattan, so think twice

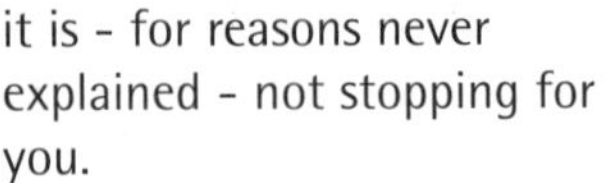

before you take one during rush hour.

Subway Etiquette

✔ Subways have their own unwritten rules:

Know where you are going. There's no chump like the cheesy newcomer who keeps whipping out their map and asking people where the Met is. Thieves know whom to roll, and that would be you if you do this. So always look like you

it is - for reasons never explained - not stopping for you.

✔ Always check the train number in the window to make sure it is the right one. Since September 11, some trains aren't running, or are running on different tracks. Again, you will never get an explanation. We've ridden the 5 train on the 3 track (not supposed to happen).

✔ Always pay attention to those signs posted next to the subway booth, that tell

✔ When you get to a station, head to one of the two far corners of the track - there are less people there. Don't do this at night.

✔ When you get into a train, if there are absolutely no seats, head for the doors between the cars - there are fewer people scrunched up in the corners and you have something to lean into when the car jerks around.

✔ Count on delays. With the system in constant repair these days, anticipate your journey taking an extra 15 minutes. There are more "police activity" episodes these days. You just can't count on a steady train like you used to.

Subway Safety

There are a few unwritten rules about subway safety. If you are a woman traveling alone, watch your back at night, no matter your neighborhood.

know where you are going, even if you don't.

✔ Always look at the seat before you sit down. You really don't know where that paper, cup or fluid has been.

✔ Stand up if you see a pregnant lady standing. If you see a lady struggling to take her baby carriage on or off a train, or up or down those stairs, help her. Few will.

✔ If a subway car is blowing their horn as they barrel down your track, that means

of delays and late-night construction. It will make your life miserable if you're out partying till 3, then wait two hours for a train with the mind-numbing sound of jackhammers.

✔ Whip out that MetroCard before you get to the turnstile. Halting and fumbling around your bag for your card not only makes everyone around you immensely teed off, but you'll get jostled and possibly cursed at.

Ask your female neighbors how safe they feel walking late at night. And if possible, when coming home late, spring the money for the cab. Your safety is worth it. Although the subways and neighborhoods of New York have been getting safer, the city is currently in a budget crunch, and all bets are off now that the city's police force has been reduced under Mayor Bloomberg. Although there is still the occasional Guardian Angel [see sidebar] or Metro Police in the subway, you can't count on them being around if you get in a pinch. If you must take the train late, wait in the after-hour train waiting area. Avoid walking through long underground tunnels at major train stations after dark. Always avoid subway entrances with no token booth operators-they are supposed to have a red light above-ground. Keep your wallet deep inside your bag, and never in a back pocket. Hold your bags close, and if you put them down, keep one strap in your grip at all times.

BUSES

Buses are definitely slower than the subway, but you'll see more of your city than being stashed underground in the subway. Most buses stop every few blocks along major streets or avenues. Stops are marked by a glass shelter. Be forewarned, however, that many posted schedules aren't valid. Often, buses will not run for a long period of time, and then they will come clumped together. This herding effect is most noticeable during rush hour.

This private group of security volunteers wears satin red berets and jackets, patrolling the underground caves and tunnels of New York for no pay. Their security details, called "24-7s" for their round-the-clock patrols, have been alternately lampooned and praised by the city's residents and police department. Started in 1979 in the Bronx, their motto is "dare to care." Its founder, Curtis Sliwa, now a radio personality on WABC, was a McDonald's manager when he enlisted thirteen friends and employees to start cleaning up the Bronx. What started out as a sanitation committee became an abiding commitment to public safety, in a time when gangs, drugs and violence ran rampant in the streets, buses, and subways of New York. Only one of the "Magnificent Thirteen" still works for the Angels, Arnaldo Salinas, and he sports the scars from numerous stabbings to prove it. From a group initially snickered at, to a group that recently toasted Mayor Bloomberg at their annual dinner, the Guardian Angels have a visible presence in New York, and many feel safer as a result.

All buses flash their numbers on the screen above the front window. They always begin with a letter, then a number. M is for Manhattan, Q for Queens, B for Brooklyn and Bx for the Bronx. Most buses run continuously from 7 am to 10 pm. After that, service is slow. After midnight, many lines only run once an hour or so. Most bus lines run north to south, though there are some cross-town buses, especially traversing the roadways cutting through Central Park. To switch bus lines, ask the driver for a transfer if you've paid in quarters. If you've paid by MetroCard, the transfer is saved on your card.

The seats nearest the driver are reserved for the handicapped, so try not to sit there unless the bus is full and there are no elderly, pregnant or otherwise child-encumbered people standing. Try to use the back of the door when exiting, for new passengers tend to crowd the front door. Finally, it is important to let passengers off before you board.

Express buses are the bus of choice for most New Yorkers who live further out - they can decrease a typical commute from an hour and a half to 45 minutes. Many run between boroughs, and they are subsequently notated by a lower-case x. The fare for an express bus is $3 each way. *For more information, refer*

Philadelphia. Once you master these rail systems, you will uncover dozens of destinations you can access for very little money. A weekend vacation will no longer be out of reach. *SEPTA Information (215) 580-7800.*

PATH
The PATH, or Port Authority Trans Hudson, trains are a fast and cheap way to visit New Jersey's major cities. The largest portal for PATH trains is now at the Manhattan Mall Station, located at 33rd Street and Sixth Avenue, a block east of Penn Station next to Macy's. The station at the former World Trade Center is currently under renovation. The trains also stop at Christopher St., which is the last stop before exiting Manhattan. Although there has been a recent fare increase, from $1 to $1.50 each way, the PATH remains the most efficient way to access Jersey's biggest cities. Ⓦ Ⓥ Ⓠ Ⓝ Ⓡ Ⓑ Ⓓ Ⓕ *www.panynj.gov/ path/*

Metro North
Metro North is the most well-heeled commuter line, with train connections to Westchester, upstate New York and Connecticut. These trains aren't cheap, and most destinations run around $6, but the ride will

to www.mta.info.
TRAINS

LIRR
The LIRR, or Long Island Railroad, is based out of 34th Street-Penn Station, and feeds almost all of Long Island with regular service. Be sure to buy tickets either at the ticket window or from the automated machines, as a surcharge is added for onboard purchases. There are many wonderful beaches and lovely destinations for the weekend warrior, not to mention shopping malls and an IKEA store. *Penn Station at 34th St. (bet. 7th and 8th Aves.), (718) 217-LIRR or (516) 822-LIRR, Lost Articles (212) 643-5228,* ❶❷❸Ⓐ ⒸⒺ *to 34th St.-Penn Station.*

New Jersey Transit
New Jersey Transit is another extensive rail network that delivers hundreds of thousands of commuters a day into New York from the suburbs. The line is based out of Penn Station, on the same level as Amtrak. Both train systems are listed on the huge train board that hovers over the middle of the station, and finding the right train can be confusing. The trick here is to listen to the announcements closely, for they usually don't announce a train's track until minutes before it is to depart. Then the race is on. *Penn Station at 34th St. (bet. 7th and 8th Aves.), (973) 762-5100, Lost Articles (212) 630-7389,* ❶❷❸Ⓐ ⒸⒺ *to 34th St.-Penn Station.*

Jersey Transit also feeds into SEPTA, which is the rail system for Pennsylvania, and the cheapest way to get to be fairly quiet and comfortable, and the scenery can't be beat in most cases. The 125th Street station is another way to hop on Metro North's lines that run up the east side without having to travel all the way down to Grand Central. *Grand Central Station at 42nd Street (at Park Ave.), (212) 532-4900 or (800) METRO-INFO, Lost Articles (212) 340-2555,* ❹❺❻❼ ❺ *to 42nd Street-Grand Central Station or* ❹❺ ❻ *to 125th St.*

TAXIS

Taxis are well-regulated these days. At the major transit points, such as Grand Central and Penn Stations, you must join a queue like a nice orderly person to catch a cab. Otherwise, in the street you're on your own, just like old times. Only the cabs with a light on the top of their roof will be available. If you're serious about getting a cab, go to the center of the block to hail one, because frequently other people will jump into your cab even if they've arrived later.

Rates include $2 just to turn the meter on, then 30¢ for each additional fifth of a mile and 20¢ for sixty seconds of stop time. There is an additional 50¢ charge after 8 pm. Legally, the driver can take up to four passengers, although if you charm him you can negotiate up to five. There are the occasional female cab drivers, but the overwhelming majority are men. Under the Taxi and Limousine Commission guidelines, if you get bad service, you can take the medallion number of the car (also located on the visor in the front passenger seat) and call (212) NYC-TAXI. Drivers are not allowed to refuse a ride to any destination. You are also entitled to a smoke and incense-free environment, a quiet ride (sans music), and air conditioning if you ask for it. Tipping 10-15% is customary.

Gypsy Cabs

These cabs proliferate in the outer boroughs, but essentially they are rent-a-wrecks, not yellow cabs with medallions. Note, they are illegal and unlicensed. They do, however, take you to areas that yellow cabs won't. The number of gypsy cabs has fluctuated, as New York has experienced in the last five years a few limousine driver murders and robberies. Always agree on a price if you get into one of these.

FERRIES

The Staten Island Ferry is free, and leaves from the tip of Battery Park. If you've seen the movie "Working Girl," you'd remember the shots of Melanie Griffith leaning over the rail every day, plotting her corporate coup. The ferry connects lower Manhattan with the only borough that doesn't have a subway connection. The ferry is old and the concession stand is out of another era, but the experience is classic NY. You'll have some great views of Ellis and Liberty Islands and Manhattan. *South Ferry, (718) 815-BOAT,* ❹❺ *to Bowling Green or* ❶❷ *to South Ferry.*

CARS

Owning a car is a bad idea in New York, ask anybody who has one. Not only will your insurance rates skyrocket, but if you live in an area that has a high rate of car break-ins you'll need to pay a garage fee (check with your local precinct or go online to *www.nyc.gov/html/nypd/ home.html* and check out "Compstat" crime rates in your area). Not to mention that finding gas stations in New York can be inconvenient, and it can take up to an hour to get on a bridge out of the city. Repairing your car will cost more here too.

Even with the most highly developed mass transportation system in the world, New York's traffic is infamous. Subject to heavy abuse, the older roads of New York are deteriorating rapidly. For commuting from New Jersey, Westchester and Long Island, it is best to use the commuter rails which are definitely faster than driving to and from the city. Since September 11, many of the East and Hudson River Crossings have new limitations on carpools. Tolls are $3.50 each way on East River Crossings, except for the Queensborough and Downtown Bridges. New Jersey tolls are $4.00 round trip. Street parking is rare. If you are so lucky to find a street space, always check for signs about parking limitations and meters. Cars are extremely luxurious, but trust us, use mass transit. Not only will you save money, time, and aggravation, but you won't have to worry about coming back to an empty parking space.

RENTING A CAR
New Yorkers, smart New Yorkers, rent a car when they want to escape the city. Try Zipcars (www.zipcar.com) if you only need a car for a few hours on a regular basis. They're perfect for picking up a lot of shopping or making a quick trip to an outlet mall. Otherwise, New York Rent-a-Car has better rates on average than Hertz or the national chains. Aamcar is another New York local chain (www.aamcar.com). If you are moving, there are the usual U-Haul type companies. But be forewarned on all car rentals in New York: not only do they usually favor an in-state driver's license, but they'll ask you for about $500 in cash or a credit card (NOT a debit card) with that amount reserved on it. So if you're broke, you're probably out of luck. If you need to move, it is often cheaper in terms of up-front costs, to get a "man with a van." These men advertise all over the city, usually on signposts.

LONG-DISTANCE BUSES

Unfortunately, Peter Pan Trailways and Greyhound are now basically one big monopoly, but their nationwide access can't be beat. Students get a 15% discount with a Student Advantage Card (*www.studentadvantage.com*). Don't try waving a student ID, they won't honor it. The buses now ask for identification when you buy your ticket, and security is tight everywhere. You can still visit those high school or college friends for affordable prices. For instance, a one-way to Washington or Boston will run about $40. Both companies leave from Port Authority Bus Terminal at 42nd Street and Eighth

Avenue. Expect long lines to get tickets and to board the buses. All lines now require that passengers check all luggage bigger than a pocketbook. Buses are known for odd passengers and bathrooms that have no water for washing hands, but that's part of their charm. *Port Authority at 42nd St. (at 8th Ave.), (212) 564-8484, Greyhound Information (800) 231-2222, Peter Pan Information (800) 343-9999,* ❶❷❸❼Ⓐ🅒 🅔🅝🅡🅢🅦🅠 *to 42nd St. -Times Sq.*

LONG-DISTANCE TRAINS

Amtrak isn't a cheap option, but for traveling the Northeastern Corridor, it is cheaper than flying and much more comfortable than waiting in an airport or riding the bus. The much-touted Acela trains are expensive and don't lop off much time between NY and Washington (from four hours to about three), but they are more fun. MetroLiner trains still run to Philadelphia and some New Jersey destinations on weekdays, reservation required. And if you travel between New York and Boston, expect that the train will stop midway to switch power sources (it's a long story, but it's very inefficient). If you are traveling to Philadelphia or destinations in Connecticut, Pennsylvania or Delaware, the bus or local trains are much less expensive. *Penn Station at 34th St. (bet. 7th and 8th Aves.), (800) USA-RAIL,* ❶❷❸Ⓐ🅒🅔 *to 34th St.-Penn Station.*

TRAVEL TO AND FROM AIRPORTS

All three airports can be accessed by an (*www.super-shuttle.com* or (212) BLUE-VAN) where

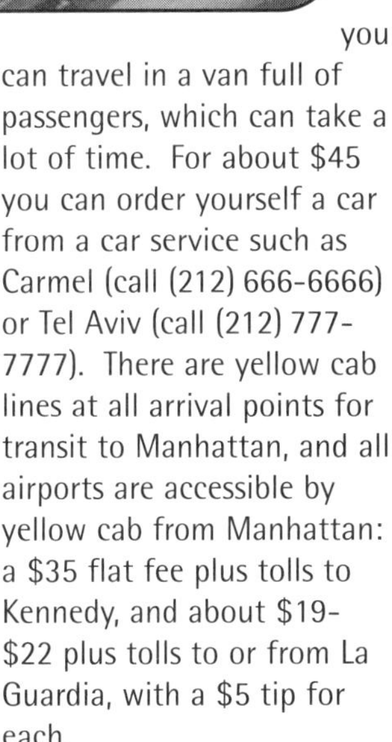

you can travel in a van full of passengers, which can take a lot of time. For about $45 you can order yourself a car from a car service such as Carmel (call (212) 666-6666) or Tel Aviv (call (212) 777-7777). There are yellow cab lines at all arrival points for transit to Manhattan, and all airports are accessible by yellow cab from Manhattan: a $35 flat fee plus tolls to Kennedy, and about $19-$22 plus tolls to or from La Guardia, with a $5 tip for each. *www.airportservice.com*

La Guardia Airport
The M60 bus, for $1.50 (exact change, coins only or a MetroCard), is the cheapest way to and from La Guardia, taking riders from Columbia University/Harlem to the airport in about an hour's time. Expect the trip back to take longer. Or take the NY Airport Service Express bus from Grand Central station for about $10-$12.

JFK International Airport
Kennedy airport is further from Manhattan than La Guardia, but it is serviced by the A train. Exit the A train at the Howard Beach-JFK stop, where a free shuttle bus to all terminals comes every 15 minutes. Allot at least two hours for this route, plus the time for check-in. The NY Airport Service Express bus from Grand Central Station goes to JFK airport, too.

Newark International Airport
Newark can be accessed by taking a PATH or NJ Transit train to Newark, then taking a cab or bus. Also, an Olympia Airport Express shuttle runs from Port Authority, $11 one-way and a $21 round-trip.

new york city's neighborhoods

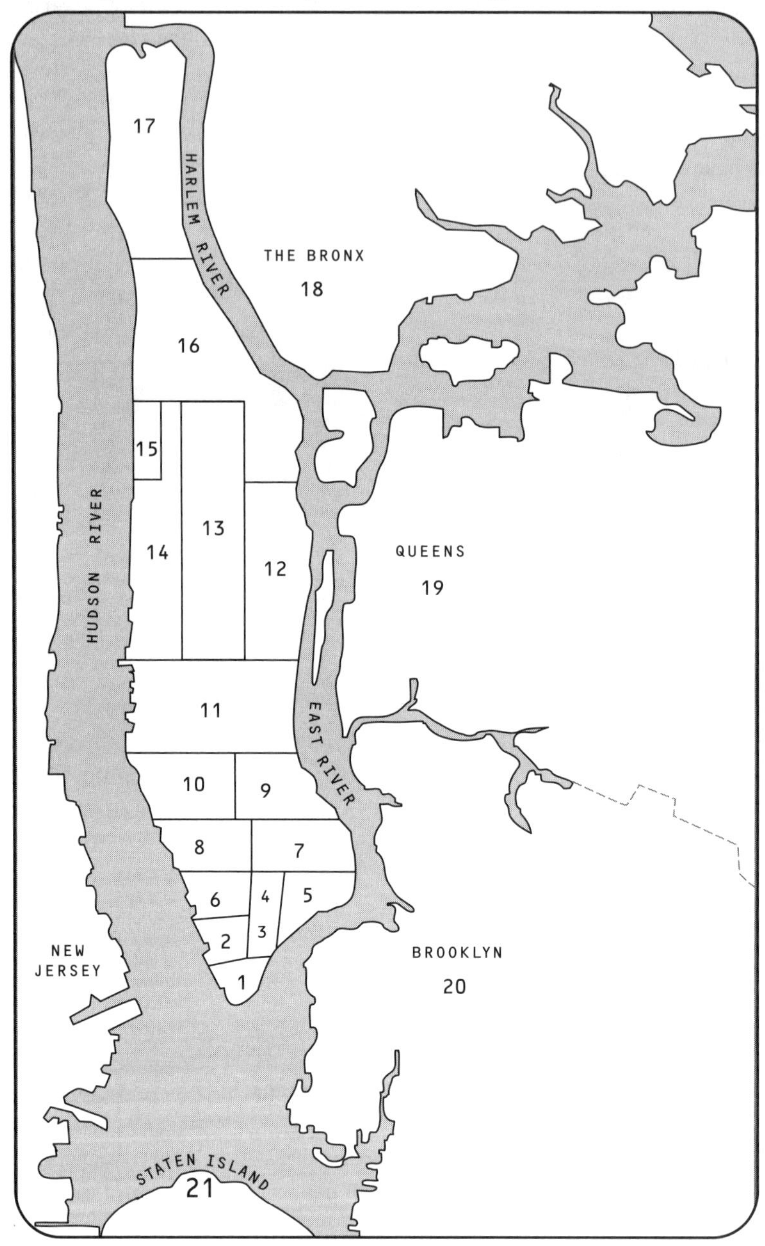

1. Financial District
2. TriBeCa
3. Chinatown
4. Little Italy
5. Lower East Side
6. SoHo
7. East Village
8. Greenwich Village
9. Gramercy
10. Chelsea
11. Midtown
12. Upper East Side
13. Central Park
14. Upper West Side
15. Morningside Heights
16. Harlem
17. Washington Heights
18. Bronx
19. Queens
20. Brooklyn
21. Staten Island

Banking in New York is light years ahead of what it was in the '90s. With more and more banks realizing that customers defect when faced with long lines, bad service and lost deposits, the customer is again king. The best banks for newcomers seem to be DIME, Greenpoint and Commerce Banks. There are many more local options in the New Jersey, Pennsylvania and Connecticut suburbs, but New York's banks are coming along.

The monolithic banks in New York are Citibank and Chase, and they both have branches near every university in New York. There are advantages to banking with a company that has literally thousands of ATMs, as you will save yourself withdrawal fees, but the main drawbacks include what many consider to be abysmal customer service, long wait times in branches, and very high over-limit fees.

The Basics

What you are entitled to: free checking, with low or no minimum balance. All of the above banks have programs like this. If you are a student, you can also get this option at Citibank and Chase, but they sometimes require that your payroll be direct deposited. You are also entitled to receive a free starter set of checks.

Things to be aware of: be careful of the fine print, especially for terms regarding ATM usage, and a cap on the number of checks you can write per month. For most New Yorkers, check writing is limited to utilities and rent because most merchants don't accept checks anymore. Also be aware of any minimum balance requirement, because if you fall below a certain amount, these types of accounts will usually charge you a hefty fee. Many banks now shut down accounts that exceed a certain amount of bounced checks, so watch your balance carefully.

Overdraft Protection

If you tend to scrape bottom every month, you might consider asking for a line of credit from your bank, or overdraft protection. This service requires stellar credit and is not free to use - they charge a percentage on any amount that you dip into. But it can be a lifesaver for those distracted souls too busy to keep their bank balance straight, or those who always run short near payday.

Online Banking

A lot of younger New Yorkers do their banking, and bill-paying, online. This alleviates the need to write checks at all, and often this feature will reconfigure your balance to factor in checks written. This can be a godsend to people with tiny apartments who have little space for a bunch of paper bills cluttering their precious counter space. Basically, you set the account up so that your utilities, cable and other basic expenses are sent electronically to your bank, so that they show up when you log in. Then you tell the bank to either automatically pay them, or you can designate when you want them paid (if you are strapped for cash).

There are growing numbers of New Yorkers who are using non-bank affiliated bill paying services, such as Paytrust (*www.paytrust.com*). These services allow the user to set up all kinds of accounts. For instance, you can send Aunt Millie a birthday check with a personalized note. The bill paying service will also have all bills sent to their bill processing center, and will scan them and then place the bills online for you to view. You can also designate whether you want your bills to be paid automatically (they issue a check through the mail, with your signature "on file"). You know to login because the service sends you an e-mail when a bill comes. Paper-free is the wave of the bill-paying future, and at $12.95 a month, this can be a bargain for those looking to simplify their lives.

Check Cashing Services

These services, for a hefty fee, will cash your payroll taxes if you live or work in the area they service. Usually low- or middle-income New Yorkers go to these stores to get their money quick. Either they don't have a normal bank account or don't wish to wait a week for their checks to clear. Lines are usually long, even during non-peak hours. These stores also carry metro cards and stamps, also at a profit. The check cashing services are only for those so cash-strapped that they cannot afford banking fees, don't have good credit to get an account, or who must pay bills right away without waiting for a check to clear. These stores also let you pay a utility, phone or cable bill, also for a charge and usually only for customers who have had their service interrupted. Otherwise, these stores are not recommended.

Credit Cards

Ask your credit card company for a lower interest rate: they pay about $140 to find and gain you as a customer, so they usually don't want to lose you. Say, 'hey, I've been good so please lower my rate from 18% (or whatever yours is) to 12% (or less). ' Negotiate. Also ditch cards that carry an annual fee, unless you have bad credit. For good rates, try www.bankrate.com to find a card that is free.

Income Taxes

If you've lived in New York even part of a fiscal year, you need to file a New York City tax return, a New York State tax return, a federal return of course, and returns from any other state you lived in. The IRS will find you, if you try and avoid filing in more than one state, and then the onus is on you to prove that you don't owe them. For the first year you are here, it may be beneficial to either file online with a service like TurboTax.com (it's free if you earn under $20,000 or so) or go to H&R Block. If you are a student or have a lot of student loans, it behooves you to get good advice on deductions. If you are self-employed, save your receipts as you can deduct a portion of your apartment rent as a work expense. You can get all tax forms online or in your local public library. File early, as the post office is a mess around April.

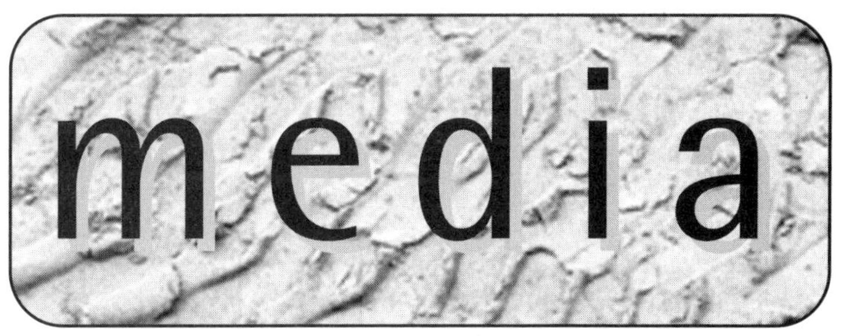

New York is the media mecca, and you will find the best selection of magazines and newspapers at your corner newsstand than anywhere in the world. If you read a foreign language, you can find a newspaper in that language somewhere in the area - the minority press here is fabulous. Reading outside the normal one paper a day can open up a whole other side to New York. One caution about subscriptions: if you live in a sketchy neighborhood without a doorman, your subscription will most likely disappear. Either get a subscription delivered to work or do like everybody else, and buy it on the street corner. If you do get a subscription, try Mitchell's Newspaper Delivery at (212) 594-6397.

BASIC NEWSPAPERS

The New York Times. The *Times* isn't called "the Gray Lady" for nothing. It's fuddy duddy, sometimes considered elitist, but you will find a wide variety of world and local coverage that other papers can't match. The *Times* has a huge budget, and they can afford to have reporters all over the place, and it shows.

The Wall Street Journal. The *Journal* is geared towards the finance types, but it has undergone a transformation lately, now printing in color with more personal stories.

Daily News and *the New York Post.* These are the tabloid-style papers of New York. They often break scandals and pride themselves on having the pulse of working-class New York. Their local political coverage is generally better, and they gleefully publish rumor, gossip and innuendo. Overall, a good read. The *Post* is notorious for its front page and gossip columns on page 6. Most New Yorkers, whether or not they read these papers, snicker over their headlines.

El Diario/La Prensa and Hoy. These are the two largest Spanish-language papers in New York. *El Diario* started out as a Puerto Rican paper while *Hoy* is more a Spanish version of the *Daily News*, which publishes it. They both have consistently good reporting on immigration and Latino politics.

There are many other local papers. For instance, in Washington Heights and Manhattanville, you'll find Dominican papers, in Flushing you'll find Haitian and Caribbean papers. Pick

them up, you'll be surprised at what's going on underneath the news radar.

Amsterdam News. This is a paper out of Harlem, chronicling the African-American communi-ty. This has a lot of local political coverage, and you'll read about the changing dynamics of Harlem and other historically black neighborhoods facing gen-trification.

New York Observer. This is a high-end tab, slinging barbs and arrows at the city's elite with glee. The cartoons and headlines alone are worth a look. Those unfamiliar with the inner workings of the gov-ernment, fashion industry and business communities

radio station guide

AM

Adult Standards	WVNJ 1160
Adult Standards	WFAS 1230
Barnard College	WBAR 1680
Caribbean/R&B Oldies	WWRL 1600
Children's (Disney)	WQEW 1560
Chinese (Mandarin)	WGBB 1240
Chinese	WZRC 1480
Christian	WWDJ 970
Christian	WMCA 570
Easy Listening	WHLI 1100
Multi-Ethnic	WPAT 930
News	WBBR 1130
News/Yankees	WCBS 880
News	WINS 1010
News/Islanders	WEVD 1050
NYU	WNYU 800
Pop	WMTR 1250
Spanish/Christian	WWRV 1330
Spanish/Talk	WADO 1280
Spanish/News/Talk	WKDM 1380
Sports	WFAN 660
Talk/Jets, NJ Devils	WABC 770
Talk/NJNets	WOR 710

FM

Contemp.	WALK 97.5
Contemp.	WHUD 100.7
Contemp.	WEBE 107.9
Contemp.	WFAS 103.9
Contemp.	WLTW 106.7
Contemp. (Spanish)	WPAT 93.1
Barnard College	WBAR 87.9
Big Band/Nostalgia	WRTN 93.5
CCNY	WHCR 90.3
CW Post Campus	WCWP 88.1
Classic Rock	WAXQ 104.3
Classical	WQXR 96.3
Columbia U	WKCR 89.9
Community Services	WNYE 91.5
Contemporary Jazz	WQCD 101.9
Easy Listening	WEZN 99.9
Fordham U.	WFUV 90.7
Freeform Music	WFMU 91.1
Hofstra U.	WRHU 88.7
Jazz	WBGO 88.3
News/Arts/Music	WBAI 99.5
News/Talk	WNYC 93.9
NYU	WNYU 89.1
Nassau Comm. College	WHPC 90.3
Oldies	WCBS 101.1
Oldies	WKHL 96.7
Oldies	WLNG 92.1
R&B	WBLS 107.5
Rap/R&B	WFSH 106
Rock	WXRK 92.3
Rock	WEHM 96.7
Rock	WLIR 92.7
Rock	WBAB 102.3
Rock	WDHA 105.5
Rock/Talk	WNEW 102.7
Seton Hall U.	WSOU 89.5
Spanish	WSKQ 97.9
Spanish	WNWK 105.9
Spanish	WYNY 107.1
Top 40	WHTZ 100.3
Top 40	WDAQ 98.3
Top 40	WBLI 106.1
Top 40	WPLJ 95.5
Top 40/Urban	WQHT 97.1
Top 40/Urban	WWPR 105.1
Top 40/Dance	WKTU 103.5
Urban Contemp.	WRKS 98.7

might be a bit confused at many of the insider references. The *Observer* is easily recognized by its salmon-colored paper.

The Sun. The *Sun* is the latest addition to the New York paper scene, claiming to be a truly New York-centered paper. Its reporting is trying hard to appeal to a broad cross-section of New Yorkers. The *Sun* faces a lot of competition.

Newsday. This paper is based on Long Island, and is known for its investigative reporting and great New York City political coverage and thorough touch with immigration, city government and school issues.

FREE NEWSPAPERS/ WEEKLIES

The Village Voice. The *Voice* is still the liberal bastion of New York's papers. Fans say it has the best investigative pieces on politicians. Critics say its sometimes histrionic writing is all over the place. You be the judge.

New York Press. This is a paper about things to do in New York, mainly for singles. Fans say it has the best personals section and fun features in New York, critics say the writing is incomprehensible.

Manhattan Spirit. This is an Upper West Side paper,

heavy on neighborhood politics. It is a true Manhattan insider paper.

The Onion. This is a satire paper, and its distribution is spotty, but it has a huge cult following. Most New Yorkers read it every Wednesday on the Internet (theonion.com).

Resident. There are different, neighborhood-specific versions printed throughout Manhattan, look for them in your bank lobby or on streetcorners. They offer a microscopic look at each small slice of New York.

For listings of Brooklyn papers, go to *www.brooklyn papers.com*

MAGAZINES

The New Yorker. This is the grande dame of the New York magazines, never profitable but usually lauded as having smart, sassy writing that covers everything from world events to local controversies. Its content is widely followed and if you'd like to keep a finger on the pulse of what New York is thinking about these days, a subscription is worth the price.

New York Magazine. This is the magazine for the Hamptons set, with stories like how to get your kids into the best private schools. It's entertaining, but most of us can only afford to read about how the other half lives.

Time Out New York. This is the bible for party animals. They have fun covers, witty articles on everything from the best S&M clubs to the cheapest Asian eats. It's written with the twenty- and early thirty-something in mind.

Paper. The shiny bible of the downtown scene, dishing out weekly pronouncements on the latest in fashion, entertainment and lifestyle. The perfect accessory for every hipster's coffeetable. (212) 226-4405

RADIO

Radio in New York has been undergoing many changes after the many antennas atop the World Trade Center were destroyed. Many stations got the picture that New Yorkers wanted more news and relevant talk radio since September 11, and the format of many stations has shifted. In mainstream radio, you'll find the usual contests and morning zoos, but the ethnic and public radio scene is increasingly relevant to this city.

Public Radio
Since September 11, public radio has undergone a transformation in New York. No longer the realm of the stuffy classical music afficionado, it is now chock-full of talk radio for the thinking crowd. **WNYC** (93.9 FM or AM820) now has the Diane Rehm Show from Washington, Fresh Air with Terry Gross, Brian Lehrer's local news show, Leonard Lopate's talk local show,

among many others. **WFUV**, based out of Fordham University, has a steady stream of folksy music interspersed with hourly updates from National Public Radio.

College Radio
WNYU, 89.1, New York University. WNYU shares its frequency with **WFDU**, Fairleigh Dickinson University in NJ. Its format varies from hard rock to jazz, and their new music show is every afternoon. WFDU plays alternative music.
WSOU, 89.5, Seton Hall University in South Orange, NJ: they play metal, punk and various hard core stuff.
WKCR, 89.9, Columbia University: This is the most classical of college radio, programming also jazz, world music and an evening news broadcast.
WFUV, 90.7, Fordham University. See above, under public radio.
WNYE, 91.5, New York public schools. They program Radio France Internationale late night and early weekday mornings. On weekends, the

station programs a Greek show and various talk shows.

CABLE SHOWS

Check out the Metro Channel on cable (see your local cable listings). It is basically the *Time Out New York* of cable, and you will see and hear more about New York here than any other station, mostly on the fashion and entertainment scenes. NY1 (channel 1 for digital subscribers, 10 for basic cable) is an all New York news channel, all the time. They cover New York politics and City Hall well.

<table>
<tr><td colspan="2">Television Guide</td></tr>
<tr><td>ABC</td><td>Channel 7</td></tr>
<tr><td>CBS</td><td>Channel 2</td></tr>
<tr><td>FOX</td><td>Channel 5</td></tr>
<tr><td>NBC</td><td>Channel 4</td></tr>
<tr><td>PBS</td><td>Channels 13, 21</td></tr>
<tr><td>UPN</td><td>Channel 9</td></tr>
<tr><td>WB</td><td>Channel 11</td></tr>
</table>

PUBLIC ACCESS

Public access in New York means what it says, and anything goes. This includes shows with a guy asking freaked-out New Yorkers to do crazy stuff in subway stations like throw paint at a canvas or dress up like Revolutionary War heroes, or Robin Byrd, who interviews local porno celebrities who strip on stage. Usually the production values are, shall we say, below par. But you will usually be laughing, most likely in horror.

Searching

for a job in NYC is more challenging than ever. If you don't have one when you arrive, consider temping, contracting out or taking on a backup profession till you do. Life is very expensive here while you look, so have a back-up plan. There are over a hundred temp agencies, and if you think your college degree makes you too good for answering phones, think again. Even Jennifer Lopez worked in a law office before becoming a Fly Girl, and Madonna worked in Dunkin' Donuts while living in the East Village.

Job Hunting Strategies

1. Subscribe to the Village Voice Classifieds notification service. For a fixed fee, they will email you new job listings as they get posted, which gives you an advantage. Check the New York Times and every other classified section online, and have them email you notifications for free.

2. Post your resume all over Web job boards. Most people say this is a waste of time, but what do you have to lose? Also subscribe to their free job notification services, tailored to fit your job search criteria. Popular websites include *monster. com, job-hunt.com, jobweb. org, headhunter.net, flipdog.com* and *hotjobs.com.*

3. Visit headhunters. A lot of them. It is their job to look for you. If this means finding an agent, if you're in a creative field, do your homework and find out who has the clients you want. This will involve a lot of legwork, but can pay off big.

4. Know your job market, and what is and isn't realis-

tic. Not that you can't make it big here, but it's harder when you have so much competition. Know your salary range, for they will ask you and if you aim too high you might place yourself out of a job.

5. Network like crazy. Unearth the schmoozefests in your field. Almost every profession has a professional association, and go to every cocktail, luncheon and lecture they offer.

6. Brush up on your computer skills. This doesn't hurt for most professions. Have somebody teach you Quark, or PowerPoint, or whatever software you might be called upon to use. The New York Public Library offers free classes.

7. Call all your friends, have them call friends, etc. Most jobs are found by word of mouth, and use whatever ins you have. Use your alumnae

networks, and find out your alma mater's password to log into *monstertrak. com.*

8. Spiff up your image. New York has a look, and you'll have a better chance at getting a job if you don't show up for an interview in khakis and penny loafers. Ask friends in the field you'd like to break into what they wear, and more importantly, what their bosses wear.

9. Don't be shy. If you'd like to be the next best thing to the star in your field, then try and contact that person or someone on a lower rung who might meet with you. Just say, 'I'm not looking for a job from you, but would love to have an informational interview on how you got to be where you are.' Most people like to talk about themselves, so let them. Don't ask more than once, however.

10. Go to as many parties as you can. This is a hard job, but someone has to do it. The more you mingle, the

top *new york job scams*

New York has got its share of cons and dubious work, so watch out for these:

✗ *Envelope stuffing.* When an advertisement says you can work from home, such as stuffing envelopes, beware. Most of these have you paying a fee to do supposed work from home, but usually these aren't valid business opportunities.

✗ *Promises of fortune.* When a company swears you will make $20,000 a month, don't believe it. Nobody can make that much a month on commission without some illegal stuff going on. If it sounds too good to be true, it is.

✗ *Lose weight! Make money!* These are the top two cons of all time, and the combination of the two is major trouble. Nobody is going to pay you to lose weight, unless you're the Princess of York.

✗ *Nanny.* Like the book "Nanny Diaries" explains, babysitting kids for the Park Avenue crowd is no bargain, and you will usually be working for slave wages for long hours. Exchanging your life for free housing and a small stipend is no bargain.

✗ *Clinical Trials.* Do you really want to sign your life over for the sake of medicine? Think needles, think hospital stays, think major inconvenience.

✗ *Artistic modeling.* Many of these opportunities are really ploys by major perverts to take nude photographs of young men and women, either for private viewing or for publication.

✗ *Travel companion.* When an older, single man offers free travel to young women and men you know there's a catch. Don't fall for it.

✗ *Personal helper.* There are many people in NYC who need nursing care, and sometimes this is put under the guise of a "helper." Be clear what your duties would and wouldn't be.

✗ *Freelance writer/producer.* Beware guidebooks, television production companies or sundry publications which promise riches down the line when they "make it big." You will need a contract stipulating how much and when you would get paid, and don't fall for promises of future riches.

greater chance you will have to meet the employer of your dreams, and have Job Charming. Always bring your business cards. If you don't have them, get them soon.

11. Consider an internship. This is for those who can afford to do unpaid labor for a while, or have night/weekend jobs. The experience can really be worth it and many interns get hired.

12. Use any specialty skills you have. If you are a Mac person, try Aquent, a temp agency. If you know wine, try a high-end wine store or apply to be a maitre'd.

13. If you are bi- or tri-lingual, consider translating. Check out all the translation agencies in the yellow pages. You usually have to have some experience or language certification.

There's one main fact you should know: no matter what you do, you will probably end up shelling out several thousand dollars to a broker before you land the apartment of your dreams. Finding an apartment is a dramatic rite of passage for many, up there with your first date or getting your driver's license.

Top Ten Tips

1. Do make sure you have a realistic view of your credit history. In New York, if you want to live anywhere in or near Manhattan, you need to have sterling credit if you don't want to go through the sometimes humiliating process of getting a guarantor for your lease. You will probably have to pay the broker about $50 to run a credit check on you. Not only do you pay them to do their job, but if you don't pass it you don't get your money back. So don't fill out that paperwork on a fabulous apartment if you know you've had a string of late marks on your credit report. Every little mark counts against you. Landlords have dozens of sterling applicants, why should they take you?

2. Landlords expect you to make approximately 28 times your monthly rent, unless you are in an apartment share situation. If you need a guarantor, they need to make approximately 50 times your monthly rent. You will need to prove your income in most cases, so prepare pay stubs and ask your employer, if you have one, to write a letter stating how much you make and that your future employment prospects look outstanding.

3. Be prepared to plunk down a check, cash or cashier's check on the spot after looking at an apartment and sometimes even before clearing a credit check. Even five minutes can make or break whether or not you get that deal.

4. Try and visit the neighborhood at night before you look at the apartment, to get a realistic assessment of how safe you FEEL there. If you're serious about safety, go to the Compstat page of the NYPD's webpage (*www.nyc.gov/html/nypd/ home.html*) and look up crime statistics, or visit the local precinct to get the real deal (see car section). Trust your instincts, and if they say 'no way' then don't do it, no matter how low the rent is.

5. Do your research about the neighborhoods you are interested in. Don't waste your or your broker's time looking at places you would hate to live in. Be realistic about what you can afford, too, and go to broker websites or look in the Village Voice to see what apartments in certain neighborhoods are going for.

6. Be clear what you can and can't live with. If you MUST have a bathtub in your apartment, don't look at apartments with showers.

7. Draw up a budget, considering your expenses and anticipated salary. Just remember that about a third to 40% of your paycheck will be swallowed up by city, state and federal taxes so that your take-home will be much less than you expected. Then subtract your rent from the monthly take. The remainder is how much you have to live on. After you factor in, say, $50 a month in utilities, about $50 for cable, $50 for phone, $250-400 for groceries, $60 in subway cards and however much you spend on entertainment, beauty, dating or eating out, you may not have any money to party in that neighborhood. A trip to the local Duane Reade pharmacy will put you out $50, easy. So remember, high rents mean house-poor people. Low rents mean you can party like an animal and not scrimp every penny. New York is always handing you expenses you hadn't counted on, and as any long-timer will tell you, money will fly out of your wallet at an alarming pace. Ideally, try not to spend more than a third of your

take-home on rent, although for most of us that is not a realistic assessment.

8. If you decide to get a roommate, check out their references carefully if you

don't know them well. There can be some messy situations if things don't work out, such as losing deposits, being stiffed on rent and utility bills and the hassle of finding someone new. There are many roommate finder services in New York, such as www.room-mateaccess.com. Look in the classified section of the *Village Voice* or *New York Times*. If you do have a roommate, try and have them put their expenses under their name, such as

their phone jack. You don't want to be left with the bill should they decide to move out in the middle of the night.

9. When choosing a broker, be sure that they are accredited and have lots of listings in the neighborhoods you are looking for. And check out their fees first. How much will they charge for you to submit an application and get a credit check? What are the broker's fees? The standard fee is 12-15% of the yearly rent. And that is up front, before you pay your deposit and last month's rent.

10. Budget how much it will cost to move into your apartment, as well as the money it will take to get your electricity, phone and cable up and running. Moving in New York costs about $3,500, even if you rent the van yourself. If you go to a neighborhood around NYU or Columbia or the New School, you will see posters tacked onto poles advertising "Man with a Van." These men may be cheap, but they aren't registered anywhere so use your judgment when trying to save a few bucks. If you rent a van, you have to put down a sizeable deposit to put the key in the ignition.

After all that, enjoy your New York bite-sized apartment.

New York's politics are entertaining, and if you pay attention and vote you might actually make a difference. Most New Yorkers don't vote. With elections coming under heavy scrutiny since Gore lost the presidential election and the city's archaic voting machines came under fire, the Election Board has had its hands full. The school board in particular is very active as well. Talk radio, the local papers and NY1's debates are good ways to keep track of who is doing what to whom.

New York is unique in that as a city, it contains five counties. Nearly everywhere else in the United States cities are within counties and not vice versa. Each borough is its own county: Manhattan is New York County; Brooklyn is King's County; Staten Island is Richmond County; the Bronx is Bronx County; and Queens is Queens County. An 1898 charter established the office of borough president in hopes of preserving borough pride despite consolidation into one city. Each borough president ("beep" for short) serves as a cheerleader, spokesperson and advocate for his or her own borough. Large, well-funded offices allow borough presidents to hold investigations and commissions, and issue reports and recommendations, but nothing is binding and they possess little real power aside from the fact that the press will quote them regularly. The borough presidents also appoint members of local community boards, neighborhood citizen bodies which deal with zoning issues. Community boards can raise objections to building projects, thereby stopping them permanently. (See *www.nyc.gov* to find the contact information for the nearest community board.) Meetings can range from a real snooze to a royal battle: one meeting once in the East Village had squatters hurling cat feces at board members unsympathetic to their plight.

The city's legislative branch, City Council (and its 51 members), share power with the mayor. The Council votes on everything regulated by city government, including zoning, sanitation, quality-of-life issues, recycling and setting city-wage taxes. Also, the Council investigates the actions of the executive branch. Traditionally, the Council has been monopolized by Democrats. Representation in the Council is roughly proportional to a district or borough's population. In 2000, Brooklyn had the largest population at roughly 2.5 million, followed by Queens at 2.2 million, Manhattan at 1.5 million, the Bronx at 1.3 million and Staten Island at 443,728.

Political History
Political involvement in the city can start with a political club. NYC Democratic political clubs are a holdover from Tammany Hall, New York's legendary Democratic political machine, which controlled city government from the late 19th century through the early 20th. Initially organized by local district leaders who were part of Tammany, the clubs gave the machine its

strength by providing constituent services and favors, particularly to immigrant populations.

In 1933, Mayor Fiorello La Guardia won a three-way race as a fusion candidate who opposed Tammany, and after his three terms the institution was powerless.

Despite its early demise, the clubs still exist today. Each club covers sets of election districts based on groupings of several city blocks. Particularly thriving are the five clubs on the Upper West Side, a traditionally intellectual, liberal area. The four Democratic and one Republican clubs keep West Siders the "most politically active in the city." To find the name and number of a club near you, call Manhattan's Democratic County Committee at (212) 687-6540 for more information, or the Republican County Committee at (718) 351-4800.

Students may register to vote in New York after they have been in the city for 30 days. After you register here, you may be called for jury duty, since the many federal, state, and civil court cases in the city necessitate lots of jurors. While school is in session, you can postpone jury duty by responding to summonses with a letter

A 2000 Ad by a pro-marijuana group, featuring a quotation by Mayor Bloomberg

explaining your status. Students who change housing each year need to update their address to vote. If you are attending school here and prefer to continue voting at your permanent address, contact your home state Board of Elections and request an absentee ballot. For more information about voting call (800) 367-8683.

City Tips
How to beat the housing market:
If an apartment is rent stabilized, these conditions must be met: rent must be lower than $2000; the apartment building must have been built before 1974, must contain six or more units, and must not be owned by a hospital, university, or other institution. To research an apartment's rent regulation status, call the DHCR's information line (718) 739-6400. See if a landlord is raising the rent above the legal limit, though DHCR won't reveal an apartment's rental history unless you live in that apartment.

How to stop a noisy neighbor:
With regard to irritating, noisy neighbors, the City Council doesn't enforce noise pollution laws enough to help punish offenders. First, try contacting your local community affairs office. Or, get your noisy neighbor to agree to an impartial mediation with the Community Disputes Resolution Program office. Police will then serve the offending neighbor with a summons. Once resolutions are signed by both parties, peace and quiet can be had by all. New York Police Department: (212) 374-5000.

How to get your pay phone quarters back:
Most pay phones are run by companies. If a pay phone steals your quarter, call either the DoITT Street payphone complaint line (718-403-8216) or State Public Service Commission comment line (800-335-2120).

Converting an out-of-state driver's license to a New York license:
As long as a license has been expired for less than a year and was active for more than six months, the defunct piece of plastic can be the ticket to get a New York license. *See Resources for DMV listings.*

The bronze plaque outside 53 Christopher Street commemorates the dramatic event that launched the gay rights movement in the United States almost three decades ago. On the night of June 27, 1969, more than 100 men, patrons of a gay bar called the Stonewall Inn, stood their ground in defiance of policemen who raided the establishment as part of an ongoing bullying tactic to intimidate and threaten homosexuals. The confrontation was violent and lasted several nights as word and outrage spread through the community, but it was a defining moment for gay men and women in this country.

In the early days of the 20th century, a burgeoning community established itself in the West Village. Stewart's and Life Cafeterias, formerly situated on Sheridan Square, were well-known gay hangouts, serving essentially as halfway houses where young gays could "come out" and gather with others.

The East and Greenwich Villages became magnets for artists eager to make their mark. The numerous gay playwrights, actors, painters, sculptors, novelists, poets, photographers and musicians who flooded into the Village contributed to the area's bohemian flair and intellectual prowess, and made them the city's most famous gay enclaves.

Famous Residents

Before emigrating to Paris, a young James Baldwin penned Giovanni's Room while living in a $100 per month apartment on Horatio Street. Playwright Edward Albee, very much a part of the Village gay scene in the late 1950s, walked into the restroom at The Ninth Circle, a bar he frequented, and found "Who's Afraid of Virginia Woolf?" scrawled across the mirror. He later used the question as the title for his most famous play. Djuna Barnes, best remembered for her novel *Nightwood*, lived the last reclusive years of her life in a small apartment at Patchin Place, and some of the century's most accomplished poets, Allen Ginsburg, Frank O'Hara, and W.H. Auden, lived in the perennial non-conformist East Village.

In recent years, the West Village has remained as much the core of the gay community as it was almost one hundred years ago. Many political organizations have offices in the area, and help organize local goings-on. Chelsea has also become a predominately gay area, with many young gay professionals. Every June is Gay History Month. In addition to two popular film festivals, the most anticipated event is the pride march.

Every year, on the last weekend in June, the march begins with "Dykes on Bikes." The motorcycles are lined up in alternate rows of three and four. The march culminates in a huge street fair around the Stonewall Inn, and at night, the top of the Empire State building is illuminated in lavender and white. In the mid '90s, the hit Broadway musical "Rent" brought a gay couple back on stage, as well as AIDS.

There are plenty of queer dating services in NYC, although the bar scene alone could fill up your dance card. Check out the classified section of the *Blade*, or the *Voice*, or any other queer magazine you like. The bisexual community here is very large. There are plenty of online resources for gay life here, and dating services (such as *malebox.com*). Check out the queer bookstore *A Different Light* for all your dating/outing books and magazines.

RESOURCES

Plug yourself into the most diverse gay and lesbian community in America. The following publications will keep you up to date with local and city-wide gay events, usually in enough time for you to plan the perfect date:

The New York Blade, 268-2701
A relatively popular addition to the growing number of gay and lesbian New York publications, this free weekly can be found throughout the city.

MetroSource, 691-5127.
A comprehensive listing of community businesses, this quarterly also features articles on various gay-related topics.

Time Out New York, 539-4444.
An essential guide to everything that's happening in the city, it's a must for everyone and includes a special gay and lesbian section in every edition.

The following organizations can provide help and counter discrimination and homophobia:

The Gay + Lesbian Switchboard, 989-0999.
If you have a question about almost anything gay-related, or don't know where to turn for help, it can provide answers.

Lesbian + Gay Community Services Center, 208 West 13th St., www.gaycenter.org, 620-7310.
Founded in 1984, the center sponsors many activities, including lectures and dances. It houses an extensive gay historical archive.

Gay + Lesbian Alliance Against Defamation, 150 West 26th St., Suite 505, www.glaad.org
GLAAD is a media advocacy organization established to ensure fair and accurate reportage of issues and events concerning the homosexual community.

gay religious groups

Gays and lesbians and organized religion are far from mutually exclusive. The many gay and gay-friendly congregations that march every year in the Gay Pride Parade signal not only their existence, but the need that many gays and lesbians have for a spiritual community. The following is a modest sampling of these organizations.

Contact the Lesbian and Gay Community Center (see Resources) for additional information and a comprehensive list.

Metropolitan Community Church, 629-7440.
Founded in the early 1970s by Troy Perry, the MC is an amalgamation of the Catholic, Anglican and Lutheran Churches.

Congregation Beth Simchat Torah, 929-9498.
This lesbian and gay synagogue lies in the heart of the West Village.

Dignity, New York, 627-6488.
The largest Catholic gay organization is vocal in its opposition to the faith's traditional position on gays and lesbians. Its

Episcopalian counterpart is called Integrity, 691-7181.
West Park Presbyterian Church, 362-4890.
The day after the official Presbyterian Council struck down amendments that would have sanctified same-sex relationships, this progressive church defiantly flew the rainbow flag.
Saint Paul's, 265-3495.
This Roman Catholic Parish is always in hot water with the Archdiocese for sponsoring a very active gay and lesbian congregation.

city calendar

JANUARY/FEBRUARY

Chinese New Year
Celebrate the New Year in Chinatown during the first full moon. Parades, fireworks and food make it worth the crowds. *Information at Chinatown Visitor's Center, 484-1222,* J M Z N Q R W 6 *to Canal St.*

Tisch School of the Arts Theater
Free theater in February from this talented student theater group. *New York University-Tisch School, 998-1850 for reservations,* A B C D F Q *to West Fourth St.*

Black History Month
Black History Month is celebrated throughout the city throughout the month of January, with readings, concerts, theater events, etc. *Consult the* New York Times *and call museums for more information.*

Empire State Building Run Up
26th annual mad dash to the 86th floor, for those who have something to prove. Every February. Contact New York Roadrunners Club for more information. *Fifth Ave. (bet. 33rd and 34th Sts.), 860-4455 or nyrrc.org,* A C E 4 5 6 *to 34th St.*

MARCH/APRIL

Art Expo NY
The world's Largest Show of Pop Art comes to the Javits Convention Center featuring landscapes, posters, sculptures, decorative arts and more. *Javits Center - Eleventh Ave. (bet. 34th and 39th Sts.), (212) 216-2000 or javitscenter.com for information.*

St. Patrick's Day Parade
An annual political event featuring the wearin' o' the green', baby-kissing and gay and lesbian protesters. *Fifth Ave. (at 44th St.),* B D Q *to 42nd St. or* 7 *to Fifth Ave.*

Symphony Space's "Wall-to-Wall" Marathon
Second or third Saturday in March. The 24-hour music marathon features a multitude of performers and a different theme each year. It's always fun. *2537 Broadway (at 95th St.), 864-5400 or symphonyspace.org,* 1 2 3 *to 96th St.*

Annual English Handbell Festival
Features 100 ringers from New York plus guest choirs. *Riverside Church on Riverside Dr. (at 122nd St.), call for date at (212) 870-6722,* 1 *to 125th St.*

Easter Day Parade
Easter Sunday. The annual exhibit on 5th Ave. of the good life has become more interesting since it has become a drag-rehearsal for Wigstock. *Fifth Ave. (bet. 49th and 59th Sts.)*

Opening Day at Yankee Stadium
A few baseball legends always show up. *Yankee Stadium at 161st St., 718-293-4300 or TicketMaster,* B D 4 *to 161st St.*

Cherry Blossom Festival
A great reason to see what's in bloom at the Brooklyn Botanical Gardens. *Brooklyn Botanical Garden, 718-623-7200,* 2 3 *to Easten Pkwy./Brooklyn Museum*

Bike NY: Great 5 Borough Bike Tour

First weekend in May. Don't worry about a near death cab experience because the city closes off streets so you can bike all five boroughs. *Call (212) 932-0778 or visit bikenew york.com for more information.*

AIDS Walk NY

Third Sunday in May. This annual walk raises money to fight AIDS and for the Gay Men's Health Crisis. *Call (212) 807-WALK for information.*

Martin Luther King Jr. Parade

Celebrate the legacy of Dr. King in May. *Fifth Ave. (bet. 60th and 86th Sts.)*

Ninth Ave International Food Festival

Mid-May. International food galore-pick what you eat carefully because there is a huge amount to choose from. *Ninth Ave. (bet. 37th and 57th Sts.)*

Memorial Day Concert at the Cathedral of St. John the Divine

Memorial Day at 8pm. The Philharmonic performs at the Cathedral of St. John the Divine on Amsterdam Ave, but the lines start at 3pm. *Amsterdam Ave. (bet. 110th and 113th Sts.), ❶ to 110th St. - Cathedral Pkwy.*

Fleet Week

On Memorial Day weekend, the city's harbors fill up with naval vessels while the streets and bars fill up with sailors. Land ho!

Belmont Stakes

Early June. A circus of high stakes and fun at the longest, and final, Triple Crown leg. *Call (718) 641-4700 for more information.*

Puerto Rican Day Parade

Sunday in early June. Salsa music, food, and pride in Puerto Rican culture. *Fifth Ave. (at 86th St.)*

Met Opera in the Parks

Begins in June. The Metropolitan Opera gives performances in the city parks; call for a schedule. *Call (212) 362-6000 ext. 4.*

HBO/Bryant Park Film Festival

Dance, food, comedy, music, films! What could be better? *Sixth Ave. (at 42nd St.), 512-5700, ⓑⓓⒻ❼ to Fifth Ave.-42nd St. or ❶❷❸❼ⒶⒸⒺ ⓃⓇⓈⓌⓆ to Times Square.*

Mermaid Parade

Late June. Celebrate Coney Island boardwalk's season opening. Some nude women have been arrested. Marvel at the innovative ways women dress up as mermaids, waddling down the boardwalk. *Coney Island, ⓑⓓⒻ to Stillwell Ave./Coney Island.*

Lesbian and Gay Pride March

Late June. The annual parade gets bigger and better each year. *Columbus Circle to Greenwich Village.*

Midsummer Night Swing Dance Festival

June-August. Dance the night away under the stars and tango around the Lincoln Center fountain; also jazz, zydeco, swing-all for $8. Free dance lessons at 6:30. *Lincoln Center, lincolncenter.org for information, ❶ to 66th St.-Lincoln Center.*

New York Philharmonic/Time Warner Concerts in Parks

The New York Philharmonic gives concerts in city parks. Call for a schedule. *Various city parks, call 875-5709 for more information.*

Macy's Fourth of July Fireworks

Ooh and Aah at the gala fireworks on display over New York Harbor. Find a spot in Battery Park or call a friend with a 20th floor penthouse with a downtown view. *Battery Park, check local papers for specific information.*

Harlem Week

A slew of cultural activities, including concerts, outdoor fairs and educational workshops. *Check media for dates.*

US Open

The drama of championship tennis makes its way to Queens every year. *Arthur Ashe Stadium, Flushing, Queens, (718) 760-6200 or usta.com, ❼ to Willets Point/Shea Stadium.*

Washington Square Outdoor Festival

Early in September. Great art outdoors for free! What could be better? *Washington Square Park, ⒶⒷⒸⒹⒺⒻⓆ to West Fourth St./Washington Square Park.*

Broadway on Broadway

Noon-2pm, first weekend in September. See Broadway stars belt out their signature tunes. *Broadway and Seventh Ave. (bet. 43rd and 48th Sts.),* ❶❷ ❸❼ⒶⒸⒺⓃⓇⓈⓌⓆ *to Times Square.*

Medieval Festival in Fort Tryon Park

Fort Tryon Park transforms into a New York that never was with falconers, jesters, knights, fair maidens and medieval food. *Fort Tyron Park, 923-3700 for information,* Ⓐ *to 190th St.*

West Indian-American Day Carnival & Parade

Eastern Parkway from Utica Ave. to the Brooklyn Museum is lined with food, floats and shopping. The parade begins at 8am on September 1st. *Crown Heights,* ❷❸ *to Eastern Pkwy./Brooklyn Museum.*

Downtown Arts Festival

Art education, events, and performances at NYC galleries and performance spaces. Contemporary and experimental performances. *For information, call (212) 243-5050 or visit simonsays.org.*

San Gennaro Festival

Little Italy's yearly bash, with or without Vinnie the Chin. *Little Italy,* ⒷⒹⓆ *to Grand St.*

Atlantic Avenue Antique Festival

Vast street fair in Brooklyn in September. *Call 875-8993 for more information.*

Columbus Day Parade

Every October. Cheer on Christopher's "discovery." *Fifth Ave. (from 44th to 48th Sts.)*

Village Halloween Parade

What used to be a carnival of subversion has become a parade of drunken innocents, but it is Halloween after all and the goblins turn out in all their fabulous glory. *Greenwich Village, Broadway (from Spring St. to Union Sq.),* ❶❾ *to 14th St or 456LNR to Union Sq.*

NOVEMBER/DECEMBER

New York City Marathon

20,000 runners take over the city. It's fun to watch them don insulated, silver shawls so they don't die from exhaustion. *Call 423-2240 or visit nyrrc.org for more information.*

Macy's Thanksgiving Day Parade

Thanksgiving Day. Beware of giant Rocky and Bullwinkle, and wear your mittens. Other than that, it's the kind of PG-13 fun you never get over. *Fifth Ave.*

George Balanchine's "The Nutcracker Suite"

Late November. NYC Ballet and the School of American Ballet unite to perform this Christmas classic. *New York State Theater, call 870-5570 for information.*

Holiday Windows on Fifth Avenue

New York outdoes itself with whimsy and holiday cheer, especially Saks Fifth Ave. and Bergdorf's. *Fifth Ave. (bet. 50th and 59th Sts.)*

Rockefeller Center Tree Lighting

Gather around the tree for the ceremonial lighting and celebrity ice-skaters at the ice rink. *Rockefeller Center,* ⒷⒹⒻⓆ *to 47th-50th Sts.-Rockefeller Center.*

Marathon Reading of a Literary Classic

The reading begins on December 31st and ends in the wee hours of January 1st when the book is finished. A few years ago, Nabokov's Lolita was read. *21st St. (bet. Tenth and Eleventh Aves.), (212) 255-1105,* ❶ *to 23rd St.*

Times Square New Year's Eve Countdown

Dick Clark is ageless, New Yorkers become warm and fuzzy, and the City counts down in delirious unison waiting for that ball to drop. *Times Square,* ❶❷❸❼ⒶⒸⒺⓃⓇⓈ ⓌⓆ *to 42nd St.-Times Square.*

YEAR 'ROUND FUN

Tour Grand Central

Learn all about one of the nation's most important landmarks. *Grand Central Station, 935-3960, 4567S to 42nd St. - Grand Central Station.*

Moonlight Bike Ride

First Friday of each month at 10pm. Join other bikers for a safe ride through Central Park. *Meet at Columbus Circle entrance to Central Park, 59th St. and 7th Ave., 802-8222,* ⒶⒷⒸⒹ❶❷ *to Columbus Circle.*

Urban Park Rangers

Saturdays and Sundays at 11am and 2pm. Walk with the Urban Park Rangers in NYC Parks for entomology, ecology, ornithology, and plain old fun. Who knew there was nature in NYC? And it's never been more interesting. *Saturdays and Sundays, 11am and 2pm, 800-201-PARK.*

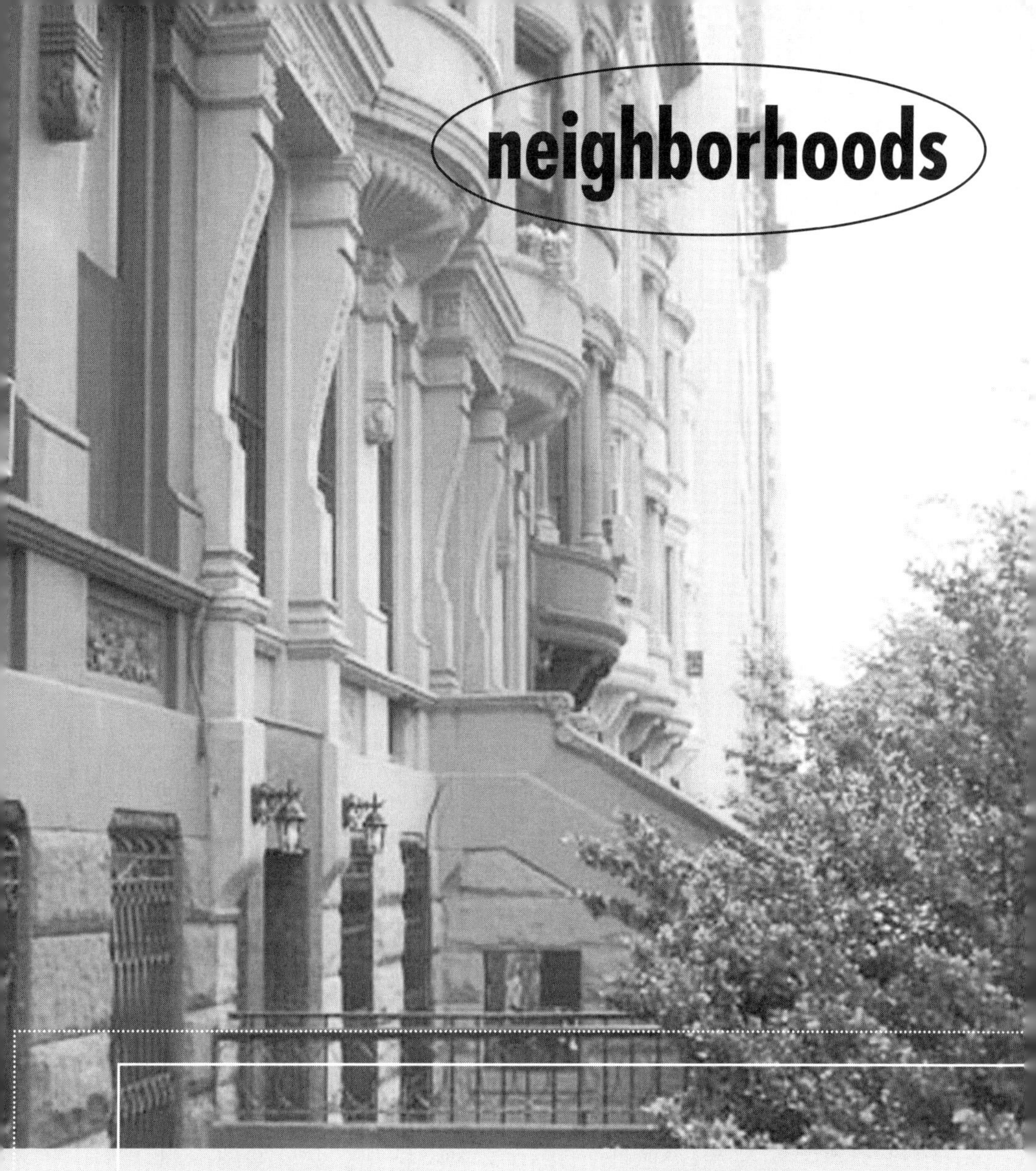

neighborhoods

financial district

The landscape of New York's financial district will never be the same after the events of September 11. The Twin Towers were the lodestar of southern Manhattan, and New Yorkers from all boroughs looked to them as reassurance that New York was the grandest city on earth.

Whatever is eventually built to memorialize that day, the ongoing hustle on Wall Street, through security checkpoints and barricades, will be a constant reminder of that day. That day, when so many people doing nothing more heroic than going to work lost their lives. Today, the sight where the Twin Towers were literally a gaping hole - in some ways a testament to the wound inflicted on the city.

Yet in so much as the financial district was battered by the destruction on that September day, it is now very much back on its feet. Walking down Wall Street on a weekday is still to experience the epicenter of American commerce. Gawking tourists look even more ungainly than usual standing against the impeccably-

groomed business men and women as they hustle from power meeting to power meeting. Somewhere under the street noise is the constant hum of money being made and deals getting done.

Not all of the financial district is at work. Battery Park City, the upscale housing development and park on the island's tip, is a testament to its love of (occasional) leisure. The apartments, most newly built, cater mainly to the up-and coming players of Wall Street who can't quite afford that mid-

town duplex and would rather spend their evenings playing in the city than commuting. While there are few bars or restaurants in the neighborhood of any distinction, it is only a short way to the wonders of Tribeca, SoHo and Little Italy. The park itself is popular with tourists and locals alike. On weekends expect to be knocked sideways by avid rollerbladers or joggers. Still, the Atlantic and views of Ellis Island and the Statue of Liberty are enough to warm the heart of even the most hardened New Yorker.

Battery Park

A gun battery in colonial times, later an entrance point for millions of immigrants, the park's river view calms tourists waiting in line for a ferry to Lady Liberty. *South of State St., ❹❺ to Bowling Green*

Battery Park City

This park's remarkable cleanliness seem transplanted from a kinder, gentler city. Meander alongside the Hudson on this well-maintained esplanade and pretend you're somewhere more nature-friendly than Manhattan. *Bounded by Chambers St., West St., Pier A and the Hudson River, ❹❺ to Bowling Green*

Bowling Green

The oldest extant public park in the city, this spot where Pieter Minuit supposedly "purchased" Manhattan once boasted the famous statue of George III that irate Revolutionary patriots toppled and used for bullet metal. *Broadway and Battery Place, ❹❺ to Bowling Green*

Ellis Island

The city's first immigration center, in use from 1892-1932. A single fee covers the ferry ride and admission to both Ellis Island and the Statue of Liberty. Visitors can trace the immigrant's path from the baggage registry rooms and view the American Immigrant Wall of Honor. "Your tired, your poor, you huddled masses" also applies to the bedraggled tourists lugging around kids. Ferries depart from Castle Clinton in Battery Park every 30 minutes during the summer. *(212) 269-5755, Admission and Ferry $10, ❹❺ to Bowling Green.*

New York Stock Exchange

The world's largest security exchange and the site of some of the greatest financial disasters in U.S. history. Watch the frenzied activity from a distance at the viewing gallery, but please, don't feed the traders. *20 Broad St. (bet. Exchange and Wall Sts.), (212) 656-5168, Admission Free, ❶❷ to Wall St.*

history

One of the most famous real estate scams in history occurred here in 1626. For the equivalent of $24, Pieter Minuit, the Director General of New Netherlands, bought the island of Manhattan from its inhabitants. This was pushed through under the justification that Native Americans could not conceive of private property. So, the modern Island of Manhattan was born, or bought, and the Native Americans were duped out of what is now among the most prime real estate in the world.

The Dutch had been moving in on the action long before they actually owned the Island, however. As early as 1609 Henry Hudson showed up, hired by the Dutch East India Company to find a passage from India to China. Instead what he discovered, and gave his name to, was a river and a harbor. As news of the harbor's easy access to America's mainland spread, settlers started arriving.

The Island quickly developed into the biggest center of commerce in America. Shipping gave way to finance at the turn of the century, and with advances in architecture, the skyscraper was born. The Woolworth building was one of the first of these colossal structures. Ironically, many of the city's construction crews were and are Mohawks, strangers to vertigo.

The skyline of downtown was forever transformed as monumental buildings rose into the sky. For some time, the Twin Towers were the tallest buildings in the world. Not everyone was impressed, however. Viewing Manhattan's transformed skyline from the river, Henry James sighed, "there should have been wonder in it."

In the 1970s the World Trade Center was built. The imposing Twin Towers transformed the city's skyline once again, becoming an icon in their own right. It remains to be seen what will be built in their place, but no matter what comes to the Financial District, the buildings will not be forgotten.

A Saturday in the Financial District

While Ground Zero springs to mind in terms of visiting this area, New Yorkers do not tend to be the ones lining up at South Street Seaport to get tickets for the viewing platform. While we don't list this site below, the viewing platform is open to the public, and tickets can be bought adjacent to the South Street Seaport. Many New Yorkers here that day have not yet seen the cleaned-up version of Ground Zero.

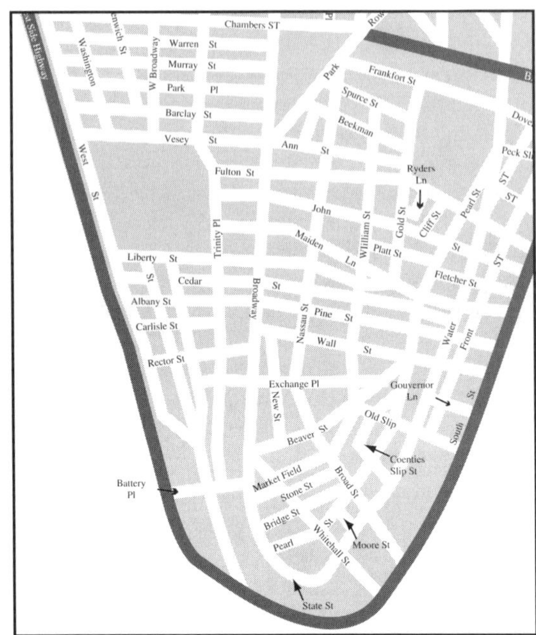

9 am

A Wake-Up Walk

Begin the morning with a brisk walk or roller blade in Battery Park City. A favorite recreational activity for residents in the Battery Park apartment complex, it is a good place to get a workout and a real feel for who lives in this neighborhood.

11 am

Shop 'til you Drop

It is still early, so head to Century 21 at Court Street. Many New Yorkers have been known to get lost here, sorting though the discounts on designer clothing at this retail institution. Best to get here before the crowds though, otherwise you risk ending up in a catfight over that DKNY number going for a song.

12 pm

Brownbag Lunch

A good two hours of shopping will make even supermodels hungry. Eating in the financial district on weekends, however, is something of a pain. So why not brownbag it? Bring a lunch or order a gyro from a lunch cart and sit out by the water enjoying the view of Staten Island, the Statue of Liberty, and Ellis Island.

1 pm

Museum Hopping

Walk over to the beautiful Alexander Hamilton Customs House and visit the National Museum of the American Indian at Bowling Green on lower Broadway. Part of the Smithsonian, its revolving collection consists of over 10,000 Native American artifacts. There is also the Museum of Jewish Heritage in Battery Park itself. Or just take a walk round enjoying the sculptures in Battery Park and Battery Park City.
*See Museum Listings
in the Arts Section.*

5 pm

Eat Up!

Bridge Café is an unpretentious and relatively inexpensive place to enjoy some seafood and relax at the end of a long day.
279 Water St. (at Dover St.), (212) 227-3344

The Day that Changed Everything

Sept. 11 was a memory all New Yorkers clutch deep in that place where our collective fears lie. No matter your age, income or occupation, the day was filled with terrifying smoke, noise and grief. Suddenly, many in this city felt like they were living on a floating target. The news didn't provide any answers, the phones were dead and sirens were everywhere. People walked the streets looking for attacking airplanes, the latter-day kamikazes. People cried, people screamed, people went into shock for weeks. The city ground to a virtual halt.

So, for those new to New York, it may be hard to understand the profound shifts, great and small, that have overtaken this city since that day. Although New Yorkers may be kinder and more human as a result, we are also more fearful as a rule, and some of our self-assuredness has rubbed off. We know we are no longer invincible.

The city collectively regrouped for months, absorbing what had happened to us. When New Yorkers look south now, we still involuntarily look for the silhouette of those downed buildings. We aren't used to our new skins yet, for the most part, and we aren't used to that feeling either.

The effects rippled into everyday life here. Restaurants and businesses were closed for months. Missing posters were plastered onto every square foot of space, for weeks. Many lost their jobs, especially those in the service professions and immigrants. New Yorkers stopped spending so much, stopped eating out, stopped traveling. Layoffs have been rampant.

Life has gone on, as this book will attest. People have moved back down to Battery Park City, thanks also to generous government subsidies. People have returned to eating, drinking, smoking and romancing. If anything, we are doing all of the above more often. But we are changed as a city and as people. We hope you like and appreciate our city, our changed city. We love New York more than ever.

September 11, 2001

...nd coming neigh-
...d in the mid
...s, these handful of
...y blocks kicked and
scratched their way
into the
Manhattan elite.
The rapid ascent
of this "Triangle
below Canal"
Street area (of which
TriBeCa is an acronym)
was assisted by the num-
ber of celebs rallying to
the cause.

It was Robert De Niro
opening the Tribeca Film
Center and Tribeca Grill on
Greenwich Street and
Franklin that really pushed
the area into the lime-
light. John F. Kennedy, Jr.
lived here in the years before
his death. Harvey Keitell, Tim
Robbins and Susan Sarandon
are among the established New
York entertainment elite likely
to be spotted sipping at a bar
or dining at one or another of
the high-class bistros.

Mostly, though, the crowd is a
more pedestrian mixture of
young Wall Streeters who have
drifted up from the financial
district. Tribeca on a Saturday
night is living proof that the
yuppie is not dead.

It was not always like this.
Tribeca, like its more artsy elder
sister SoHo, had been a quiet
backwater of cobbled streets
and disheveled warehouses. The
sharp transformation in
Tribeca's fortunes is yet another
example of Manhattan's ruth

less process of gentrification -
artists discover a run-down
cheap neighborhood, only to
have the wealthier crowed run
in after them jacking up rents
and opening cute little stores.

The results in Tribeca's case
have been mixed. The area well
deserves its reputation for being
both expensive and hip, with
restaurants like Nobu and
Danube as well as a smattering
of crowd-pleasing bars including Naked Lunch (named after
the Burroughs book and decorated accordingly) and Church
Lounge in the Tribeca Grand
Hotel.

The apartments, housed as
many of them are in old industrial buildings, are amazing but
rents are generally exorbitant.
There are still a number of
empty blocks throughout the

neighborhood, and at night it
can feel quite spooky away
from the crowds. Yet for those
in the know, there are still also
other, less chi-chi highlights
such as the humble Knitting
Factory, which offers some of
the best live music in town. For
some reason shopping has not
really taken off in Tribeca and it
is not glutted with the small
ritzier stores that are SoHo's
stock in trade.

The neighborhood has also been
affected by the events of
September 11, as it is so close
to the Financial District. A lot of
the smaller businesses are
struggling to survive because of
the dramatic dip in customers
following the attacks. But, on
the bright side, there is more
elbow room and no lines at
your Tribeca neighborhood
favorites.

White Street

Take a walk down White Street, between West Broadway and Broadway, to glimpse some of Tribeca's most renowned architecture. Numbers 10 and 8 are particularly striking, 10 for its interesting stone work, and both for their small top story designed to give the illusion of additional height. *White Street (bet. Church St. and West Broadway),* ❶ *to Franklin*

AT&T Long Lines Building

One of the most bizarre buildings in the city, local legend has it that this strange structure is really a secret government center designed to resist nuclear attack. The phone company has never come up with an adequate explanation of what exactly does go on inside this imposing-looking building with its somber granite windowless exterior. It looks like a leftover movie set from Batman. *Church Street (bet. Thomas and Worth Sts.),* ❶ *to Franklin St.*

Tribeca Film Center

The heart and soul of the new Tribeca is the film center, which contains screening rooms and production offices. Film buffs may salivate at the mere thought of bumping into Wes Anderson. However, the actual structure is rather uninteresting. Downstairs is DeNiro's Tribeca Grill and across the street his Tribeca Deli which offers less expensive but equally delicious sandwiches. *325 Greenwich St. (bet. Franklin and North Moore Sts.), 212-941-4000. Open M-F 9am-6pm* ❶ *to Franklin*

Duane Park

The second oldest park in New York, it was once a part of a Dutch farm from 1636. The future King James II seized it in 1674 and later it was given to the still-extant Trinity Church in 1705. Parsons and Vaux designed the present-day park in 1887 on Duane at Hudson. ❶❷ *to Canal St.*

history

This small slice of Manhattan has its humble origins in commerce. Tribeca made a name for itself in fruit with the opening of Bear Market in 1813 where Gotham residents would come sift through produce. By the mid nineteenth century, the area was a major point of transfer for the huge volume of commerce that made its way through the city on a daily basis. As entrepreneurs and merchants moved in, the neighborhood started to manufacture. Vast warehouses and factories sprung up, increasing in scale as they moved closer towards the river. The buildings, many of which still exist today, were built in the wrought iron style popular here and in SoHo at the time. This style made to spacious loft apartments. In 1939 Bear Market and the nearby area were renamed Washington Market.

It wasn't until the mid-60's, with the abandonment of downtowns all across America, that the market types started leaving the area in significant number. They were soon replaced by savvy realtors who could spot a bargain in those large and spacious buildings, so much easier to hawk than the cramped tenements which make up the real estate below 14th Street.

The area was renamed Tribeca in the 1970's by an inspired realtor looking to boost its marketability. His efforts and that of others certainly played off, Tribeca's population spiked from 243 at the beginning of the 1970's to 5,000 by the decade's end. Development continued into the 1990's and beyond. As prices

rose, the demographic of the residents began to shift. In 1993 Stuyvesant High School opened its doors in Tribeca, one of the city's most competitive and well-known public high schools.

Last year De Niro launched the Tribeca film festival. Expected to be an annual celebration of New York film in the second week of May, the festival culminated in 2002 with free music and comedy in Battery Park City.

A Saturday in Tribeca

9 am
Brunch at Bubby's

Expect to wait in line behind the trendier-than-thou hipsters at this local eatery, but the food and atmosphere make up for it. It is always possible to mill around outside and people watch. A tip for beating the crunch, however, is to get there early. No resident of Tribeca would dream of rising before noon on a Saturday.

See Dining Section

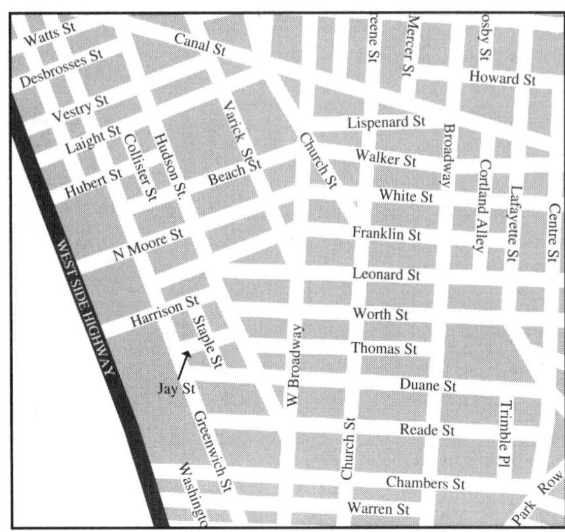

11 am
Sight Seeing

Check out the sights in the neighborhood. With the old industrial warehouses and the AT&T building (see Sights and Parks), Tribeca is a real architectural feast. Walk over to the river to get some perspective on how the area used to be. Don't forget the real sightseeing, people watching. When your feet can't take it anymore, chill out on the grass in Washington Market and watch as the world walks by.

Best Celebrity-Spotting
Greenwich Street
Camp out on Greenwich Street and look for interesting and famous people. Robert DeNiro, Kurt Loder and Christopher Walken are all known to make appearances.
Greenwich St. (bet. Duane and Moore Sts.), ❶ *to Franklin St.*

Most Affordable Good Breakfast
Kitchenette
Low prices and the cute setting keep this Tribeca restaurant hopping. For lunch, try the Soup Pot across the street, owned and operated by the same people.
80 W. Broadway (at Warren St.), (212) 267-6740, AmEx, ❶❷ *to Chambers St.*

2 pm

Get Liquored Up

Grab a few drinks at this charming local bar, The Liquor Store, on White and West Broadway. In its previous life this bar was, naturally, a liquor store and it still has the sign to prove it. It is small, friendly and earlier in the day not to crowded. In summer you can sit at a table outside while you sip your beer.
See Nightlife Section

5 pm

Dinner and a Movie

Not only is The Screening Room one of the best independent movie theaters in the city, it also looks the part with its great art deco design and its classy restaurant is just about inexpensive enough not to provoke the wrath of the credit card company. For around $40 you and a date can enjoy dinner and a movie, indulging in Tribeca's two greatest passions - film and food.
See Arts Section

8 pm

Rock The Night Away

Not done for the night yet? Walk around to Leonard and Church Street to The Knitting Factory. Check out one of the indie bands rocking it on one of the stages, catch some experimental theater or comedy on one of the smaller rooms, or just grab a drink at the friendly and reasonably priced bar.
See Nightlife Section

Looking for an essential electrical part? A tattoo? A gold necklace? Fish eyes? Anything and everything can be bought in Manhattan's Chinatown for those who know where to find it. A claustrophobic's nightmare, the streets teem with people from morning to night. On the sidewalks along Canal Street vendors vie to outbid one another. Look no further for that Prada handbag - so long as you don't mined touting one made by Pruda.

Home to the largest Chinese-immigrant community outside Asia, Chinatown is distinctive for a Manhattan immigrant neighborhood in that it is still rapidly growing. Officially the boundaries are Canal Street to the north, Worth Street to the south, the Bowery to the east and Church Street to the west. Chinatown has long since disregarded these restrictions, however, and continues into space on the Lower East Side and Little Italy. The city's four other Chinatowns (two in Brooklyn and two in Queens) are also on the up and up, but Manhattan's district remains the most popular and the most renowned.

But it is down the side streets that the real treats are hidden. Restaurants offer vast selection of Asian delicacies. Stores blast Asian soft rock out onto the streets and sell an elaborate variety of unusual goods. Ancient tea parlors and barber shops still exist, along with countless ginseng sellers. Right next to the older tea shops are gourmet tea

vendors selling Chinese bubble tea, complete with tapioca balls.

On Sundays vendors hawking Chinese-style crullers, warmed soy milk, fresh tofu and bean sprouts congregate under the Manhattan Bridge. The drugstore on Grand Street still weighs out deer antlers and "dragon's eyes" with brass hand scales the way they did in China a century ago.

The area is a riot of gold and deep scarlet, where even the McDonald's has been designed to blend in. Aromas of cooking mix in the air with the scent of rotting fruit and dead fish. The sensual overload and hustle means that this neighborhood gives the impression of existing in perpetual chaos. Take the time to scratch the surface and an organized community is revealed. The problem is that those not fluent in Mandarin will be hard pressed to figure out the logic. Chinatown remains very community-oriented.

There is a dark side to the neighborhood too. Despite ongoing and well-organized community efforts to stamp out the practice, sweatshops still exist. Be especially careful here walking alone at night. As long as you are cautious, though, exploring Chinatown is a great adventure.

Eastern States Buddhist Temple

The devout flock here daily to kneel and burn incense before the imposing porcelain Buddha. Pick up trinkets at the gift shop. *64 Mott St. (at Mulberry St.), (212) 966-6229, Open M-Su 9am-6pm.* **A C E** *to Canal St.*

H.T Dance Company

Since 1978, the company's small black-box theatre has hosted the Arts Gate Center, which offers dance classes to children and adults, and commissioned other contemporary choreographers. *70 Mulberry St. (at Bayard St.), (212) 349-0126,* **N R Q W J M Z 6** *to Canal St.,* **S** *to Grand St.*

Chatham Square Library

Four stories of books, including an impressive Chinese Heritage Collection featuring the classics, keep Chinatown's avid readers busy. Available resources include free computer workshops, art, poetry, pre-college information sessions, live performances, magazines, popular fiction, videos, and Friday-night Internet training classes. *33 East Broadway (near Catherine St.), (212) 964-6598,* **F** *to East Broadway*

Columbus Park

There's more asphalt than grass at this park, but that doesn't stop anyone from coming. Pick-up basketball games and bladers share space with Chinatown's elderly, who gather to play cards, gossip and sun themselves. *Between Bayard and Worth Sts. (north and south borders), and Mulberry and Baxter Sts. (east and west borders),* **N R Q W J M Z 6** *to Canal St.*

The Museum of the Chinese in the Americas

No Chinatown experience is complete without a visit to this wonderful community-oriented museum, the first ever dedicated to the history of Chinese in the Americas. The award-winning permanent exhibition entitled, "Where is Home?" features a moving collection of photographs, memorabilia and commentary exploring the diverse identities and experiences of Chinese Americans. *70 Mulberry St. (at Bayard St.), (212) 619-4785. Open T-Su 12pm-5pm. Admission $1,* **N R Q W J M Z 6** *to Canal St.*

history

Volumes have been written on the history of this complex neighborhood. Chinatown sprang up in the mid-to-late 19th century, with the first wave of immigration to this country. Prior to the Chinese immigration, the area now regarded as Chinatown was part of the notorious Five Points district. Residents at the time characterized the neighborhood as a lawless place, notorious for its vice, violence and prostitution.

The first recorded Chinese resident was a merchant from Kwantung who moved into 8 Mott Street in 1870. Migration had not been easy for the Chinese. Isolationist leaders had not allowed them to leave their homeland, and immigrants were greeted with fear and even hatred when they arrived in the United States. Most settled in California, working in mining and railroad construction, and were dubbed the "Yellow Menace." After the Chinese Exclusion Act of 1882, many moved to larger cites and urban Chinatowns began to grow across the country.

Immigrants were restricted to a few types of businesses, but soon their shops began to attract visitors. In New York, the population grew and restrictions and prejudices began to wane. In the late 1960's Manhattan's Chinatown expanded into the Lower East side and Little Italy, making it the largest Chinatown in the country. Today, the population is at around 150,000 legal residents. In recent years, many Vietnamese, Indonesian, Malaysian and Thai immigrants have been moving into the area.

A Saturday in Chinatown

8 am

Wake Up, Time for Exercise!

Head for the Forsyth Conservancy Garden in the Sara D. Roosevelt Park. Join in, if you know what you're doing, with the older folks doing tai chi or listen to their pet wah mei birds singing to the morning sun. *Delancy and Forsyth Sts. (off Canal St.)*

10 am

A Dim Sum Snack

After all that warming and stretching, head over to The Golden Unicorn on East Broadway for some of the best dim sum imaginable. Be adventurous and try one of everything. Just be careful not to get run over by one of the food carts being bustled out onto the streets for the busy day ahead. *See Dining Section*

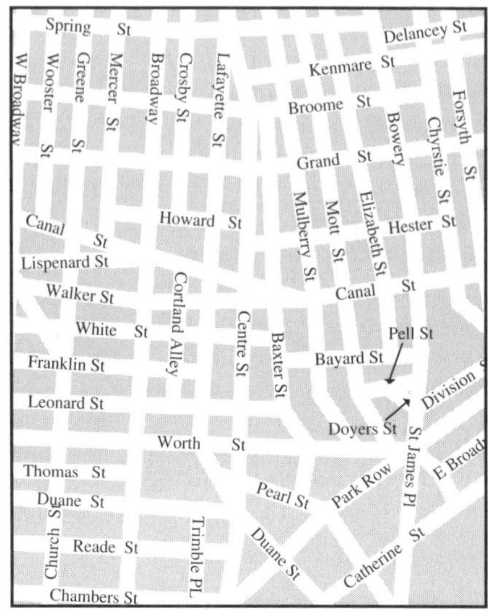

12 pm

Shop Till You Drop

Over in the commercial center of Chinatown, between Mott and Pearl, you will find everything imaginable. Wonder into the two story Pearl River Mart and dig through an array of merchandise. It is as good a place to stock up on kitchen supplies as it is to pick up new shoes or a video. Back out on the street see what the vendors have on sale today. Be careful though, just because the Walkman says Sony, doesn't mean it was made in Japan. *See Shopping Section*

Most Informative Wall
Wall of Democracy
A mind-collage of posters, news articles, and hand-lettered statements on current events in China are pasted on this giant wall. *Bayard St. (bet. Mulberry and Mott Sts.),* ⓙⓜⓩⓝⓡⓠⓦ❻ *to Canal St.*

Most Museum for One Dollar
The Museum of the Chinese in the Americas
Learn all about the heritage of one of the city's largest ethnic populations for only $1. *70 Mulberry St. (at Bayard St.), (212) 619-4785,* ⓙⓜⓩⓝⓡⓠⓦ❻ *to Canal St.* *See Sites + Parks*

3 pm

Tea Time

With so much to eat and drink, why stop at ice cream? On of the latest Asian fads which is now making a showing in the U.S. is Taiwanese-style tea at a teahouse such as St. Alps. Dark tapioca pearls decorate the bottom, waiting to be sucked up through a fat straw. In true Asian pop culture fashion this tea comes in a rainbow of pastel colors and is ultra sweet and frothy.
51 Mott St., (212) 766-9889

4 pm

Just Playing Around

While those who are not video fanatics may run in horror at the idea of going to an arcade, the Chinatown Fair situated at 8 Mott Street will win over even the most grudging of skeptics.
www.chinatownfair.com, (212) 964-1542.

6 pm

Discount Dining

It would be criminal not to end the evening with a meal in one of Chinatown's countless restaurants. Bo Ky at 80 Bayard Street is one of the best Vietnamese spots going. Its noodle soup is to die for and its menu is satisfyingly inexpensive.
See Dining Section

Most Noodle for Your Buck
Noodle Stands

For less than it costs to do your laundry, you can enjoy a big container of lo mein or a handful of egg rolls bought at one of the food carts lining Canal Street.
Canal St. (bet. Lafayette and Mulberry Sts.), Cash Only,
Ⓙ Ⓜ Ⓩ Ⓝ Ⓡ Ⓠ Ⓦ Ⓖ *to Canal St.*

{cheap *thrills*}

It has become something of a running joke by now that the last people to be found on the few blocks that make up Little Italy these days are Italians. While the four north-south streets that make up neighborhood - Mott, Mulberry, Elizabeth and Baxter - are crammed with Italian eateries and the red white and green of the Italian flag, most of the local Italians have fled for the suburbs leaving the streets for tourists and the curious. While Little Italy used to stretch from Canal Street to Houston Street, it now occupies barely four blocks in length. The Italians have not forgotten the old 'hood, though. They flood back in from Queens and Brooklyn to show their pride at the feast of the San Gennaro every September.

This evolution into something resembling the Italian section of Epcot Center at Disneyworld has not made the area unpleasurable. After all, only the most reckless of sightseers would have freely wandered the streets back in the 1920's when the mob ruled the roost. The beautiful brick buildings and cobbled streets are the charm-ing site of many a movie shoot. It is still possible to get a feel for the old neighborhood by stepping into one of the local old school grocery stories, like DiPalo's Fine Foods at 206 Grand (at Mott St.), where old Italian residents still go to buy their olive oil. Those in search of the good old bad days should stop by Umberto's Clam House on Broome Street (see Restaurant Section). This is where mobster Joey Gallo was mown down in 1972 while celebrating his birthday. The killing was apparently in retaliation for Gallo's bad-mouthing a rival family. Even more recently, the site now occupied the Amy Chan boutique, off Prince Street, used to be the Ravenite Social Club and Dapper Don John Gotti's headquarters.

The Police Building

The domed edifice built in 1909 served as the city's main police headquarters for nearly 65 years. Its new copper dome was crafted by the same French artisans who restored the Statue of Liberty's flame and now shelters 55 co-op apartments. *240 Centre St. (bet. Grand and Broome Sts.),* **N R** *to Prince St.*

Elizabeth Street Company Garden Sculpture

Most Manhattanites couldn't fit these sculptures in their living rooms, let alone a garden to which they may have access. However, this patch of green off of Elizabeth Street is the perfect place to escape to dream of the countryside. *210 Elizabeth St. (at Spring St.),* **6** *to Spring St.*

St. Michael's Russian Catholic Church

With its rosy-pink façade and onion domes, this Orthodox church adds a distinctively Eastern flavor to the area, complementing its better-known Catholic neighbor. *266 Mulberry St. (bet. Prince and Houston Sts.), (212) 226-2644* **N R** *to Prince St.*

Old St. Patrick's Cathedral

Though it's difficult to tell now, the church was New York's oldest Roman Catholic Church, built in 1815 by Joseph Mangin. A fire in 1866 destroyed the historic façade, necessitating Henry Englebert's 1868 renovation. *Mott St. (bet. Prince and Houston Sts.), (212) 226-8075,* **N R** *to Prince St.,* **F V S** *to Broadway-Lafayette St.*

history

Beginning with the explorer Giovanni da Verrazzano's 1524 arrival in Manhattan's bay, Italians have been an important part of New York City's history. Immigrants from Northern Italy arrived in the early 17th century, but their numbers were dwarfed by larger waves of Southern Italians, who came in the late 19th century. From 1880 to 1900, the number of Italians in New York rose from 12,000 to 545,000 by 1910. Most of the Italian immigrants settled in lower Manhattan, an area packed with poor immigrant families living in crowded, unsanitary tenements in neighborhoods dotted with religious institutions. Immigrants tended to cluster according to their relations in the Old World, with Genoans, Calabrians and Sicilians living on the east side, and Piedmontese, Tuscans and Neopolitans living on the west side. This was the era chronicled by Francis Ford Coppola in *The Godfather II* when Sicilian Vito Corleone established himself as the benefactor of his small community.

However, by the mid-20th century, like the fictional Corleone, most Italians had moved out of the old neighborhood to greener places, such as Staten Island, Brooklyn, Long Island and New Jersey. Despite Little Italy's romance, most Italians now consider the Italian section of the Bronx to be the real "Little Italy."

A Saturday in Little Italy

10 am

Shopping Just Like Mama Used To

Walking into this gourmet Italian market is the closest thing to an Italian shopping experience this far from the Mediterranean. The selection of food is almost overwhelming. DiPalo's is the perfect place to pick up fresh mozzarella, mascarpone, ricotta and home-made sausage. Cooking fanatics will be in seventh heaven. *206 Grand St. (bet. Mott and Elizabeth Sts.), (212) 226-1033,* **S** *to Grand St.*

Make sure to pick up some freshly baked crusty bread from the Vesuvio Bakery on Prince St. (off W. Broadway). No Italian meal would be complete without some fresh pasta. Fortunately Piemonte Ravioli Company is at hand at 190 Grand St., selling home made pasta of every description.

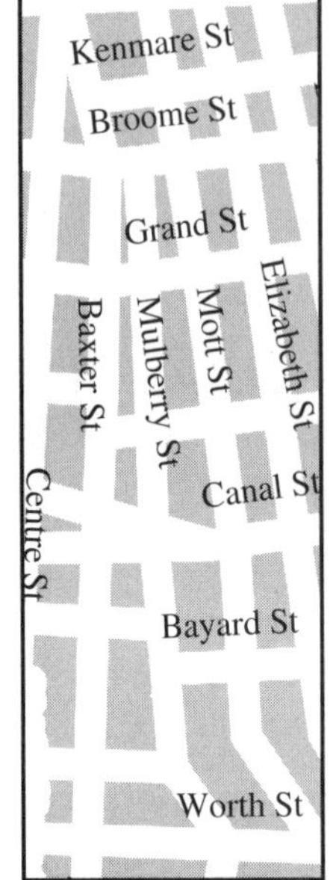

Most Sidewalk Lunch Carts on Parade
The San Gennaro Festival
Get yourself a huge Italian ice and watch at the men trying to win oversized stuffed animals for their girlfriends. Mingle with tourists, natives and dancers along Mulberry Street. Food is overpriced but delicious, so make sure you eat something beforehand, or you won't be able to resist the aromas from the stands.
Second week in September, Mulberry St. (bet. Canal and Grand Sts.), Cash Only, **N** **R** *to Prince St.*

12 pm Hasta la Pasta

A lot of the eateries that cowed onto Mott and Mulberry are poor quality and overpriced. Avoid the aggressive louts anxious to get you into their restaurant and head into Il Cortile at 125 Mulberry Street between Canal and Hester. The food is reasonable and bound to leave you inspired to put all those recently purchased ingredients to good use.
(212) 226-6060, **J M Z N Q R W** *to Canal St.*

2 pm

One For Old Blue Eyes

After a leisurely lunch finish off with an espresso and a cannoli from Ferrara, an Italian pastry shop and local institution. *195 Grand St. (bet. Mulberry and Mott Sts.), (212) 226-6150*

Or, for those in the need of something stronger, grab an aperitif from Mare Chiaro at 176 Mulberry St. The photos on the wall reveal that this bar, now being cottoned to by a new generation, was once a popular haunt of Rat Pack crooner Frank Sinatra. *Between Broome and Grand Sts., (212) 226-9345.*

lower east side

Every year, the press searches frantically for a neighborhood to tag as "the new hip thing." More often than not in the past five years this has tended to be some place in Brooklyn. A recent surge in popularity, however, has forced The Lower East side onto the scene, causing the gentlemen of the press to ponder: "The Lower East Side: The New Brooklyn?" In reality, young New Yorkers have been coming to this stretch of land below the East Village and east of Chinatown for quite a while now. Evidence of their presence can be seen in the number of art galleries, bars and boutiques that have sprung up, as well as the high volume of hipsters who for the most part have replaced the heroin addicts that used to frequent the sidewalks.

What is true is that more people are moving into this neighborhood. In a city where a studio apartment with the bath in the kitchen for under $1,000 a month is regarded as the deal of a lifetime, on the Lower East Side it is still possible to find an apartment without going bankrupt. Some of the spaces, par-

ticularly if they are lofts, are even quite spacious by Manhattan's standard of scale. Be warned, however, because a lot of these buildings are old tenements and the area is only just emerging from the deep neglect into which it sunk from the 70's through to the 90's, a lot of the buildings are in a bad state of repair. Landlords will often try and get away with renting out hovels to the desperate.

The area still wants for conveniences, and the lack of good subway connections is a constant complaint from those who live here. Not everyone on the

streets is a 20-something, there are still a lot of older residents. In particular the Hispanic and Puerto Rican working classes moved into the neighborhood in the 1980's. It was this community that banded together, forming block associations such as Centro Cultural Celmente Soto Velez. The streets had been notorious for their high volume of drugs and crime before local residents fought to get the situation in hand. It was their efforts that allow the in-crowd to feel at home here. The community still thrives, however, giving the area a more diverse, family atmosphere then it might otherwise have had.

Eldridge Street Project/Synagogue

Eastern European Jews erected the Lower East Side's first large-scale building in 1887. With its multihued stained glass windows, brilliant frescoes and intricate woodwork, the synagogue stood out for years amidst the notorious tenements. It fell into disrepair during hard times, but in recent years, the Eldridge Street Project has made significant renovations. *12 Eldridge St. (bet. Canal and Division Streets), (212) 219-0888, Admission $3. Call for more information, ⒡ to East Broadway.*

Lower East Side Tenement Museum

These are permanent, interactive exhibits on sweatshops and old-time tenements. The Confino apartment is the exhibition of a Sephardic-Jewish immigrant family in 1916 and the others were restored to look like they did in 1870 and 1935. *90 Orchard St. (at Broome St.), (212) 431-0233. Open M-Su 11am-5:30pm, ⒥ⓜⓩ to Essex St.*

East River Park

Every Saturday and Sunday in the warmer months, this park fills up with families from the nearby buildings who come up here to barbecue, fish, play ball, bike, or just hang out in the shadows of the Williamsburg Bridge. A walk through this riverside park reveals romantically derelict urban landscapes of industrial Brooklyn. Don't venture here after dusk or on rainy days, when it can get a little sinister. *Jackson-15th Sts. (east of the FDR Drive), ⒥ⓜⓩ to Essex St.*

Hamilton Fish Pool and Recreation Center

Just $25 per year buys membership to this and many other municipally-run pools and fitness centers around the city. The pools are generally clean, the gyms basic but friendly. Don't expect state-of-the-art equipment or classes; just a workout without an attitude. *127 Pitt St. (off Houston St.), (212) 387-7687, ⒡ to Second Ave.*

history

For immigrants traveling from the provincial areas of Europe, the tenements which dominated the landscapes of the Lower East Side must have been a chilling sight. Infamous for providing the worst housing conditions in the city, these five-story firetraps absorbed most of the first major wave of immigrants who passed through Ellis Island and could not afford anything better. During the last two decades of the 19th century, the largely Irish population was joined by Italians and Eastern European Jews who crowded in by the thousands.

New laws and housing plans failed to alleviate the situation. The first city housing project, built in 1936 as a last-ditch effort, portended the limited success of projects in general. But great spirit arose out of poverty and the neighborhood soon became as well known for its wealth of intellectual and artistic life as for its overcrowding.

During the early part of this century, Yiddish theater flourished along Second Avenue, where newspapers grew into forums for intellectual debate and performers like George Gershwin, Irving Berlin and the Marx Brothers cut their teeth. The '50s and '60s saw revolutionaries, writers and musicians population the northern boundaries, an area that later expanded and later became known as the East Village.

The Lower East Side fell into decline as rents once again decreased and crime, drugs and dilapidated housing became prominent neighborhood features. In the '80s, the area stabilized somewhat after an influx of Latinos who dubbed the area "Loisaida."

A Saturday in the Lower East Side

9 am

Saturday In The Park

If the weather is fine, take a walk through the East River Park. Enjoy some dramatic views of Brooklyn and hang out with the local families, who are enjoying their weekend in the time-honored tradition of Lower East Side residents. *See Sites + Parks*

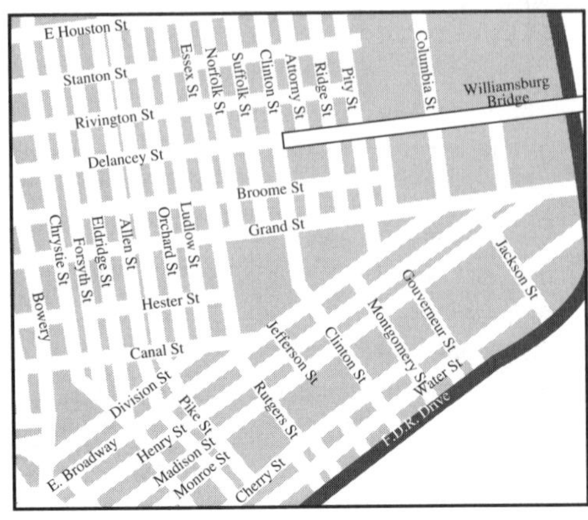

12 pm

Lunch With History

Load up with a pastrami on rye sandwich at Katz's Delicatessen at 205 E. Houston St.. The legendary old-school deli has hardly changed since it was opened back in 1888. Grab a ticket at the front and walk over to the counter, where the server will cut you a sumptuous meaty sandwich. *See Dining Section*

1 pm

A Walk On The Wild Side

Shop till you drop. There are still some great vintage clothing shops, especially on Orchard and Ludlow Streets. Revamp your image or just get some new threads.

3 pm

Learn A Little

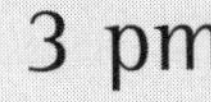

Take a visit to the Lower East Side Tenement Museum on Orchard Street. The video is free, but for $8 ($6 for students) you can get an excellent guided tour that really evokes what it must have been like for the thousands who lived here at the turn of the century. The cramped living conditions will humble those who grumble about the size of their Manhattan apartment. *See Sights + Parks*

Most Hip Kosher Lounge
Lansky Lounge

Named after Jewish Mafia Don Meyer Lansky, this hot nightspot (located in Ratner's Delicatessen) channels the spirit of the celebrated speakeasy whose site the club now occupies. *104 Norfolk St., follow the lights up the staircase to the unmarked door, MC, V, AmEx, Entrées: $9,* **F J M Z** *to Delancey St. (212) 677-9489, Open 6 pm –dawn.* www.lanskylounge.com

Best Casual Deals
Delancey St.

Stores offering cheap but cheerful shoes and hip-hop gear crowd along vibrant, if somewhat derelict, commercial stretch. **F J M Z** *to Delancey St.-Essex St.*

5 pm Dining In Style

Slip into one of the half-booths at Torch on Ludlow Street. Sip on a Martini and have a fabulous, leisurely meal. This sexy '40s-style supper club is perfect, right down to the tasty entertainment.
See Nightlife Section

7 pm Coffee and Cool

Hang out at the Pink Pony at 176 Ludlow St.. This mildly skuzzy coffee shop is one of the more established hipster locals. Expect the mug to be chipped and the server to be more intent on talking with his friends. Once that ordeal is over with, sit back and enjoy the atmosphere.
Between Houston and Stanton Sts., (212) 529-3956

8 pm And Now, For Something Completely Different

Pop into Tonic, a cavernous performance space at 107 Norfolk St. This bar is host to some of the cities best avant-garde musicians and artists. If you find this evening's sounds unlistenable, wander downstairs to the subtonic lounge. That booth you're sitting in is an old wine cask from when this building used to be a kosher winery.
At Delancey St., (212) 358-7501, www.tonic107.com, F to Delancey St.

10 pm Bar Crawl

The night is still young, and there are plenty of bars to be discovered on the Lower East Side. Some of the most notable include the inexpensive retro theme bar Welcome to the Johnsons, the menacing but tempting Motor City Bar on Rivington Street and for those who want to dance, DJs spin great live music at Sapphire on Elridge Street.
See Nightlife Section

soho

The area, which forms a more or less perfect square in the middle of downtown Manhattan, is bordered by Houston to the north, Canal Street to the south, 6th Avenue and Crosby Street to the west and east. It is known for its charming industrial style architecture and cobbled streets. Particularly striking are the old cast iron buildings - formerly factories and sweat shops - along Green Street. Apartments, for those lucky enough to live here, are often wonderful and expansive lofts - which artists loved.

Today, any Wall Street type worth his suspenders knows SoHo like the back of his hand, and he would hardly feel out of place in this credit card friendly environment. Most of the artists who built up the neighborhood in the '60s through the '80s have long since decamped as rents skyrocket and supermodels moved in. This is the neighborhood that became a case study for New York's never-ending process of gentrification.

Shopping is the name of the game here. On almost any given day the sidewalks are filled with glamorous-looking Manhattanites and tourists, their arms laden with bags from a handful of the countless boutiques crowding the streets. Models in hip-hugging capris flounce by and locals dine leisurely at one or another of the charming little restaurants. There is still a smattering of galleries, as well as museums including the Museum of Contemporary Art and the Museum of African Art. Mired by financial troubles, the Guggenheim recently closed its swishy SoHo location. The many of beautiful people who inhabit this area make it clear that in their view by far the best art is not in the galleries but out walking the streets.

New York Open Center

A holistic learning center which offers lectures, workshops, and weekend retreats on topics ranging from screenwriting to yoga to flamenco dancing. Call for a catalogue. The meditation room is open to the public free of charge, pillows provided, if you forgot to bring your own. *83 Spring St. (between Broadway and Lafayette Sts.), (212) 219-2527, NR to Prince St., 6 to Spring St.*

The Puck Building

Erected in 1886, this building was originally a printing plant for Puck, America's first humor magazine. Today, the first floor hosts galas and the upper floors are apartments and offices, including those of the NY Press. Puck still grins from the northeast corner of the building. *295 Lafayette St. (at Houston St.), (212) 274-8900, FVS to Broadway/Lafayette St.*

Poet's House

This free reading room and resource center houses the largest collection of poetry books in the country (40,000 volumes). Current poetry and literary periodicals are available for browsing, and Walkmen are provided for listening. Call for information about live readings. *72 Spring St. (bet. Broadway and Lafayette St.), (212) 431-7920, FVS to Broadway/Lafayette St.*

history

In the early '60s before SoHo had its name (South of Houston), it was an abandoned commercial slum known as "hell's hundred acres." By the late '60s and early '70s, artists with little money and a greater vision for both themselves and these desolate streets, took a risk, and on the sly packed up their drawing tables, canvasses and paint brushes to invade these vacant and decrepit, but large and light-filled commercial warehouses. They converted them into combined studios, galleries and homes. This powerful colony of artists fought to make their presence legal in the neighborhood and began community board meetings to convince the New York City Landmarks Commission to designate an area of 26 blocks in SoHo as a Historic District by 1973. Their passionate dedication led to the preservation of the elaborately ornamented, wonderfully spacious cast-iron buildings, which define SoHo's unique architectural style. SoHo is going the way of Greenwich Village in transforming from a hotbed of cultural revolution to a more staid standard-bearer of respectability. As rents climb into the stratosphere, expensive boutiques and galleries populate the creaky warehouses. Designers and the models who don their wares hold court at the bars and restaurants which line Mercer, Prince, Lafayette and Spring Streets. While visitors may never achieve a real intimacy with SoHo, they can at least enter into the orbit of SoHoites by poking into one of the galleries lining Greene and Wooster Streets.

A Saturday in Soho

10 am

Brunch French

Start the day of with a little bit of Euro style, by brunching at Country Café at 69 Thompson Street. Small and intimate (so expect to be waiting in line forever) serving French Moroccan fusion food. Shockingly, this restaurant manages to pull of chic without being snooty.

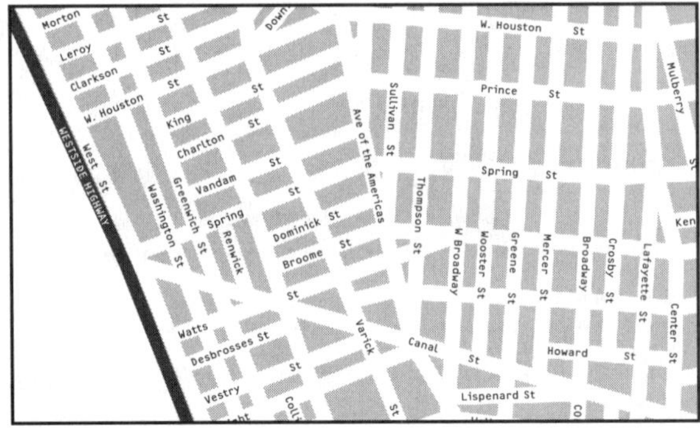

12 pm

Seeing Stars

Watch the Saturday matinee at Film Forum on Hudson off Sixth Avenue. There is something deliciously decadent about wasting away the afternoon in a movie theater, and nobody does it better then this institution. More often then not there is some restored flick from Hollywood's golden years. Enjoy and bask in the glamour.

2:30 pm

Art Today

Art galleries in SoHo have fallen by the wayside in recent years, as the neighborhood has turned more and more towards shopping and entertainment. Some, however, are still worth a look. Check out Andrea Rosen Gallery on Prince Street and Wooster. This is one place at least that still supports new talent.

4 pm

Shopper Heaven

Oh for an extended credit limit and someone else to foot the bill. Shopping is SoHo's forte. Almost every designer in the known universe can be found here. Those looking for upscale fashion at relatively affordable prices could do worse than to check out Flying A on Spring Street and Thompson. The really committed just strap on a pair of sensible shoes and roam the streets. Try Kate Spade, MAC, French Connection and Armani.

7 pm

Cocktails and Dreams

Haven't spotted enough stars yet? Grab a $15 Cosmopolitan at the hotel bar of Mercer Hotel - always crawling with celebrities. While the drinks may be pricey, it is a cheap way to at last have a window into the lifestyles of the rich and famous.

8 pm

Cuban Class

Eating well here is not a problem, though finding something affordable might be in SoHo. Café Habana on Elizabeth and Prince Streets manages to buck the trend, being inexpensive, funky and tasty. It is a fitting location to unwind and dine after a tough day trawling SoHo's cobbled streets.

{ cheap *thrills* }

Most Passionate Flamenco Night

ñ

Flamenco dancers perform every Wednesday night and make it easy to order one more pitcher of sangria. *Weekdays 5 pm-1:30 am, Fr/Sa 5 pm-3:30 am. 33 Crosby St. (bet. Broome and Grand Sts.), (212) 219-8856, Cash Only,* J M Z N R Q W 6 *to Canal St.*

east village

Welcome to The East Village - responsible for many a lost weekend. Much of its hype though is really just self-mythologizing fiction.

Situated on the far east side of downtown Manhattan, this neighborhood boasts a very diverse street life. Artists straggle in from Cooper Union to spend hours nursing one cup of coffee in one of the handful of hang-outs along Avenue A.

In the avenues known as Alphabet City, Puerto Rican kids play out on the streets until late into the night. The homeless sit on benches in Tompkins Square Park, drinking and bickering. High school kids playing hookey shop for the latest in offensive fashion or cheap CD's. Large Russian men steam in the Russian bathhouses. The aroma of food wafts from the mediocre Indian restaurants along Little India on 6th Street. Poets read their works at the 27 year-old The Nuyorican Poets Café - one of the few institutions to actively support minority poets and spoken word artists.

Like many of the neighborhoods in this area, The East Village fell into disrepair in the 70s. Up into the early 1990's, it was known to be a labyrinth of vice and despair. It was brought down by drug addiction, poverty and crumbling houses owned by negligent landlords. Typically, the artists found the low rents

more than made up from the possibility of being mugged and moved in. The scene and sense of the atmosphere here in the 1980's has been chronicled - often badly - in many of the artwork produced during that time.

Madonna lived here when she first came to NY, as did the artist and her one-time lover Jean-Michel Basquiet. Some of the gritty urbanity still survives, particularly on the more easterly avenues. There are still local characters. That woman clad in pink latex, picking up some shampoo at the corner grocery, might be The Baroness, a renowned fetishist who won't wear anything but the latex clothing she designs.

In general though, the ridiculous rent prices have meant that the majority of residents these days are young urban professionals. For old-timers, however, the East Village was and is a place that values creativity and fringe voices.

Those thinking of making a move to this area should be careful. A lot of the buildings are old and practically falling over. It is easy to end up living in a windowless shoebox, too broke from paying the exorbitant rent to enjoy the treats on the streets.

Community Gardens

Explore the nooks and crannies of Alphabet City, and you'll be sure to come upon at least one of a number of community-owned-and-operated gardens, such as the lovely retreat on 6th Street and Avenue B, where poetry readings, performances, and festivals are frequently held. When it's open during the day, take advantage of the shade. *Throughout Alphabet City,* **F** *to Second Ave., L to First Ave.*

Cooper Union

A subsidized college specializing in art, architecture, and engineering education, Cooper Union's standards are some of the highest in the country. The school houses the Houghton Art Gallery and the Great Hall, the site of an 1860 speech by Abraham Lincoln. *51 Astor Pl., (212) 353-4000, www.cooper.edu,* **6** *to Astor Pl.*

Tompkins Square Park

Major renovations in 1992 improved the park's facilities and safety, and the recreational courts, working bathrooms and open green space attract families, tourists, and local oddballs alike, enlivening the park year-round. On any given weekend, you may stumble across a free concert or arts-and-crafts festival in the park, but the best events are spontaneous, like the drum circles, impromptu chess marathons and the endless parade of East Villagers walking their dogs. *7th to 10th Sts. (bet Aves A and B),* **F** *to Second Ave.,* **L** *to First Ave.*

history

As with most downtown areas, urban decline hit the East Village hard. Pockets of old immigrant communities held out against the rising tide of crime. In particular the Puerto Ricans and Hispanics who moved into the area in the 1980's worked hard to create a sense of community in these bleak times. Evidence of the strong local spirit can be spotted in the often eccentric and beautifully bizarre community gardens that are particularly popular in the outer avenues.

In the early 1990's the East Village was the sight of a dramatic example of the gentrification process. The neighborhood's new-found popularity, bought as a result of the hard efforts of the local residents and artists and the growth of New York University, piqued the interest of the previously negligent landlords. Since a lot of these apartments are rent stabilized, the only way the renters could raise prices was to evict the existing residents. Many people had been living in their apartments for years, and as a result, they were certainly in no mood to move.

Undeterred, however, landlords launched a charm offensive, turning off basic necessities like heating and water, refusing to do even the minimal maintenance they had been performing previously, and generally behaving in a manner designed to force these tenants out onto the streets. That is exactly how many of them ended up: too poor to find housing in a real estate market that was spiraling out of control. The result was that they, along with others of the city's homeless (many of whom had been evicted from mental homes when these institutions closed down), descended upon Tompkins Square Park. A shantytown grew up almost over night. Its appearance and activist nature did little did little to please the police or the landlords, who were finding these now vacant apartments were tougher to rent out. After a stand off of a few weeks, the police moved in by ground and helicopter in the middle of the night and pulled these people out from their makeshift homes. The raid was captured on camera and broadcast by the New York news stations.

In the last few years, the previous problems of the East Village have subsided, but gentrification has continued. The neighborhood has become a hotspot for college students and recent graduates working in the city.

A Saturday in the East Village

9 am

A morning pick me up

Grab a dog-eared paperback or the morning paper and stop at Pick Up Café, on 9th Street and Avenue A, for a light bite, a long coffee and a quiet read. Despite the suggestive name, this European-flavored coffee shop is not a dating switchboard. For the most part it tends to be populated by intellectual types who would rather wax lyrical about the tortures of romance than actually go out there and pick someone up.

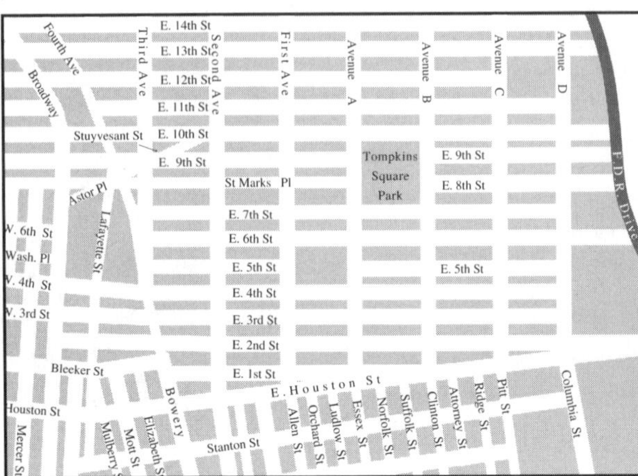

11 am

Sounds of the City

East Eighth Street has some of the best CD stores in the city. Alternative, electronica, hip-hop, jazz – almost all tastes can be accommodated. Those with patience should spend some time hunting for bargains on St. Marks Place between First and Second Avenues. The music department at Kim's Video and Music on the same block has top-notch new releases for anyone whose tastes run outside of the top 40.

12 pm

The Art of Gardening

Saunter down to Avenue B and admire the host of charming and often crazy community gardens. In typical East Village style, some of them more resemble avant-garde artworks in progress than perfectly groomed back lots.

3 pm

Pretty in Pink....or Purple, or Lime, or ...

For all trashy and tacky beauty needs pop into Ricky's on Broadway and West 4th Street. Duane Reade this is not. Walk in a regular mortal and walk out a superstar. Rainbow colored eye shadows, to fancy full wigs, Betty Page babydoll shirts, lunch boxes and sex toys – shopping for toiletries should never be this fun.

Most European Fries
Pommes Frites
Pretend you are in Amsterdam for dinner and you have French Fries slathered in vinegar with a side of garlic mayo. A lucky few can fit inside, the rest get theirs to go. *123 Second Ave.,* **F V** *to Second Ave. Cash only. 11:30 am – 1 am weekdays, till 2 am weekends. (212) 674-1234*

{cheap *thrills*}

5 pm

The Loisaida Vibe

Walk over to The Nuyorican Poets' Café, the cultural hub of Loisaida. Check for listings before going, but performances range from poetry slams to live hip-hop and spoken word. If there is nothing going on, head to Good Old Lower Eat Side on Avenue B and First. This thrift store was started to help residents fight local landlords seeking to kick out old-time Puerto Rican tenants to make way for yuppies. *See Arts Section*

7 pm

Classic Cinema

Sick of pounding the pavements? Time for a move to Cinema Classic on East 11th Street between First and Second Avenues, which had the inspired idea of combining a coffee shop with a movie theater. The taste in films tends to be excellent if a little out there. Those looking for something more contemporary but still alternative should check out The Pioneer Theater on East Third Street and Avenue A.

9 pm

Drink Up, It's Time

Now hit the bars and experience what the Village has become notorious for – its drinking scene. Every group has their favorite haunts, but most bars offer some combination of cheap drinks, dark lighting, loud music, seedy furniture and increasingly intoxicated 20-somethings.

4 am

Breakfast?

For those still standing. The décor at Yaffa Café on St. Marks Place between Avenue A and First Street might evoke nausea at this point, but the food is good and sobering after a long night out.

To the untamed eye, this neighborhood might disappoint. Steeped as it is in a history of counter culture and bohemian chic, the Village at first sight looks as though it has been usurped by the ubiquitous Starbucks and an endless onslaught of dog-walking upwardly mobile couples. Monica Lewinsky lives in an apartment here. Ethan Hawke and Urma Thurman have taken up residence somewhere in the vicinity of Bleecker and West 10th. These facts alone might be enough to send the average Jack Kerouac-spouting rebels running as fast as humanly possible eastwards, towards a village (the East Village) which touts itself as the real deal in urban decay. The Village has a special charm all of its own.

While the same apparent hodge-podge of boutiques, bistros, bars, fitness centers and galleries are on display here as in other chi-chi areas, their existence far from completes the picture. Diversity is the name of the game. In the West Village, the neighborhood stretching from 6th Avenue to the river down to Houston and up to Fourteenth Street, gay couples, young and old, male and female, walk arm-in-arm.

The northernmost segment of the West Village, known as the Meat Packing District, still functions as a working neighborhood – as the somewhat pungent stench of flesh in the

air will testify.

Back in the area traditionally known as Greenwich Village, below 14th Street to Houston Street and between 6th Avenue and Broadway, New York University students, hippies and hobos waste time in Washington Square Park. The park is being cleaned up with ongoing renovation on the well-known arch. The park is central to NYU's main undergraduate campus, and most of the surrounding buildings sport the NYU purple flag. Check out the chess games that are played at all hours of the day.

The key to understanding the Village is realizing that the people responsible for the yuppie flavor are also the very same people who give this area its cultural edge. Artists, rebels and other social outlaws have been moving into the Village since the 1920's. And unlike later post 1970's artist pioneers in communities such as SoHo, many of them did not leave. Instead, they grew older, more successful. The upshot is a community which accepts more or less any lifestyle, but which also likes to buy its groceries from stores with "gourmet" in the title.

The Jefferson Market Library

High Victorian Gothic pinnacles and a patterned slate roof crown this former courthouse, erected near the site of the former produce market for which it is named. Voted as one of the country's most beautiful buildings in 1885, it served as a Women's Detention Center, Police Academy annex and temporary housing for the Census bureau until the city decided to landmark it and convert it into a branch of the New York Public Library. *425 Sixth Ave. (at 10th St.), (212) 243-4334,* **F L** **1 2 3** *to 14th St. Call for hours.*

Stonewall Memorial Statues General

Sheridan gazes down upon a standing gay male couple and a sitting lesbian couple that commemorate the 1969 gay riots at the Stonewall Inn. *At Sheridan Square,* **1 2** *to Christopher St.*

St. Lukes in the Fields

A church that remembers a time when there were fields. The grass has given way to The Gap, but you can still get a taste of old-time Village life within the church. *487 Hudson St. (bet. Grove and Christopher Sts.), (212) 924-0562, Open Sa-R 9am-5pm, F 9am-12pm.* **1 2** *to Christopher St.*

Washington Square Park

The park is now almost unrecognizable as the public gallows and potters field of its 1780 origins. Most of the surrounding 19th century Federal-style brownstones have been taken over by NYU. The elegant houses known as "the Row" on Washington Square North once housed such talent as Henry James. **A C** **E F V S** *to W. 4th St.*

Judson Memorial Church

King Juan Carlos II of Spain provided funds for the renovation of this Romanesque church designed by McKim, Mead, and White in 1892. Originally constructed to unite the poor living on the south side of the square with their upscale northern counterparts, the building now houses NYU academic departments, including the new King Juan Carlos II of Spain Center. *55 Washington Square South (bet. Thompson and Sullivan Sts.), 477-0351,* **N R** *to 8th St.*

history

In the mid-19th century, as New York University was built around Washington Square and beautiful churches sprang up, the neighborhood became host to art clubs, private galleries, literary salons, hotels, shops and theatres.

As the art scene increased in importance, the Village's removal from the financial constraints of Midtown Broadway theaters resulted in the development of a phenomenon for which the neighborhood would become world-famous: the Bohemian lifestyle. Experimental theater, galleries specializing in avant-garde art, and irreverent "little magazines," exploded onto the scene. Wild parties, candle-lit tea-rooms, novelty nightclubs, and bizarre boutiques soon followed suit.

Just prior to the Depression, "artistic flats" became the era's local euphemism for luxury apartments that displaced the longtime residents that had spawned the artistic revolution and first put the neighborhood on the map.

Following the Depression's end, the Beat Generation arrived and the village saw the first stirrings of gay culture. Again, writers and artists of all kinds congregated here, fueling the genesis of the hippie movement and the gay revolution. Novelist Norman Mailer started the Village Voice in 1955. The paper remains a leading organ of the left wing throughout the city and beyond.

Near the Village's still bustling Sheridan Square, a 1969 police raid on a local gay bar resulted in the Stonewall Rebellion, a seminal

moment in the developing movement for gay and lesbian rights. During the '80s came the AIDS epidemic, which hit the Village community very hard. AIDS sparked political and social activism that still continues in the Village today.

A Saturday in Greenwich Village

9 am

Coffee and Cupcake

Grab a coffee and a cupcake from Magnolia Bakery on Bleecker and 12th Street. The pastel shades of icing on these bite-sized cakes are so charming they almost seem a shame to tuck in. Almost.

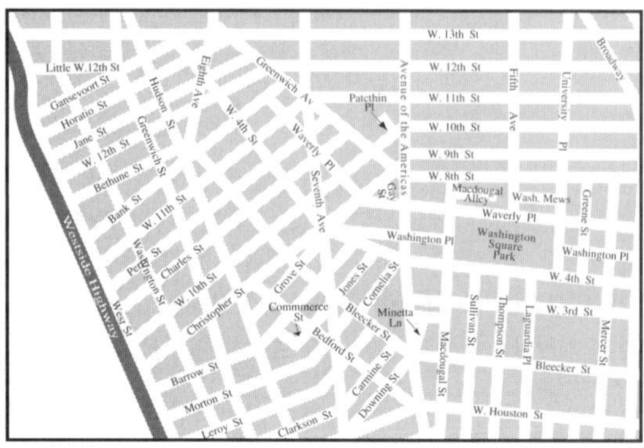

9:30 am

Work off that Cupcake

Head over for an early yoga session at the Integral Yoga Institute on West 13th Street between Seventh and Eighth Avenues. Yoga has become a hot trend amongst stressed-out workaholics in this neighborhood, and the institute offers a flexible schedule for anyone from beginners to Zen masters.

12 pm

People-Watching

Grab another cup of Joe from one of the plentiful coffee spots in the neighborhood. Take it to go, sit out in Washington Square Park and enjoy the show. Goth kids make out, homeless people holler, dogs howl, NYU students look sultry and there is almost always some type of entertainment provided by a local eccentric. For those who can't find sufficient entertainment at the park, wander over to the basketball courts on 6th Avenue and West 4th and watch the future stars of the NBA strut their stuff.

2 pm

A Slice of Life

If the effects of the cupcake have worn off, then it must be time for a snack. Pick up a slice of pizza from Mona Lisa's on Bleecker and 6th Avenue. One of the best pizza joints in the village, it beats any Ray's around.

8 pm

Would You Like Fries With That?

Make a beeline for Le Frite Kot, the Belgium fry and mussel place on 148 West 4th off 6th Avenue. Grab a table in the friendly dimly lit bar out back. Two small servings of fries and one order of mussels should be more then enough for even the hungriest of couples. Don't forget to order some funky sauces (like peanut or mayonnaise) to dip those fries in. After dinner, relax with the student crowd and knock back a few beers.
(212) 979-2616

11 pm

Hello Spice Girls!

Those with a hankering to make a night of it, need look no further then the notorious Brit pop night at Don Hills, on Spring and Greenwich Streets. While this is technically Tribeca, the wall-to-wall hipsters dressed up like mods and aggressively not dancing to the Rolling Stones and Blur seem more part of the Village scene than the Tribeca. Make sure not to trip over someone's Vesper as you struggle outside at 4:00 am.

4 am

Breakfast?

For those still awake, hop into a cab or walk up to Florent on 69 Gaansevort Street off Greenwich. For years this has been the place to come for that post-clubbing breakfast. Not only is the food great, but at the right time of night you are almost guaranteed to be dining next to one of the Meat Packing District's (ahem) ladies of the night stopping in for a snack.

gramercy

The number of different neighborhoods clamoring for attention in New York can often feel overwhelming. It comes as something of a relief to come across a space in the midst of Manhattan that could almost be considered pedestrian.

Gramercy and the Flatiron District, while laboring under their fair share of history and offering a large number of distractions, seem relatively subdued compared to their flashy neighbors. If they were people, they would be the sensible type. They would be the friends who don't particularly enjoy going to parties, but go dutifully if invited and always help clean up the carnage the next morning.

Taking up the swathe of land between 20th Street, 34th Street, First Avenue and Park Avenue South, Gramercy is mostly known for its park by the same name. The serene square of green stands out like a tempting oasis. One of the only private parks in the city, this landscaped idyll is only open to residents and those lucky enough to stay at the exclusive Gramercy Park Hotel. Paparazzi-shy models and movie stars are drawn to this quiet district.

Across the way, the Flatiron District is more industrial than residential. It too, takes its name from its most distinguishing landmark - the majestic Flatiron Building, which stands

on the intersection of Broadway, Fifth Avenue and 23rd Street (and is featured on our cover). Built in 1902, the building was immortalized in a famous picture by the photographer Alfred Steiglitz. In the late 1990's it attempted to reinvent itself as Manhattan's answer to Silicon Valley - a move that lead to predictably rocky results.

Sandwiched between Gramercy and the Flatiron District, lies Union Square. The uncouth interloper in this group, Union Square and the surrounding area injects a little of the "below 14th street" vibe into an area which splits the hairs between midtown and downtown.

The farmers' market which sets up residence three days during the week and on Saturdays is known to be the best in the city. The ultra swank W Hotel has become the home away from home for music types from out of town. In summertime it is possible to relax on the grass, drink at the bar or sit at the terrace at the swanky Coffee Bar sipping a mojito.

Flatiron Building

While 20 stories barely constitutes a skyscraper in modern parlance, this triangular office building at the intersection of Fifth Avenue and Broadway, erected in 1902 by Daniel H. Burnham, certainly impressed turn-of-the-century tourists. The men were especially eager to see if the unusual flow of air created by the building's angle really did lift ladies' skirts above their ankles. For many, its rusticated limestone façade and steel frame symbolized the dawn of the skyscraper era. *23rd St. and Broadway,* **N R 6** *to 23rd St.*

Theodore Roosevelt's Birthplace

Saturday afternoons are the best time to visit the birthplace of our 26th President. See a couple of museum galleries and a chamber music concert. Ask about Roosevelt's playboy uncle Robert, who lived in the brownstone next door. *20th St. (bet. Park Ave. and Broadway), (212) 260-1616, Admission $2,* **6** *to 23rd St.*

Madison Square Park

Dog walkers and baby-sitters bask in the serenity, just as Edith Wharton and Theodore Roosevelt once did, on the site of the original Madison Square Garden. *23rd to 26th Sts. (bet. Fifth and Madison Avenues),* **N R 6** *to 23rd St.*

Gramercy Park

Only the crème de la crème of Gramercy possess a rusty key to this private park, where time seems to stand still. It is opened only once a year to the general public. *20th Street and Irving Pl.,* **6** *to 23rd St.*

Union Square Park

On Mondays, Wednesdays, Fridays and Saturdays, one of the city's largest-though not cheapest-greenmarkets, chock-full of farm-fresh produce and nongreen goods like pretzels and books, takes over. *14th to 17th Sts. (bet. Broadway and Union Square W.),* **L N R Q W 4 5 6** *to Union Sq.*

history

Although originally a swamp, the area surrounding Gramercy Park has long been one of the most fashionable addresses in New York. Thanks to its intellectual residents at the turn of the century, the historical Gramercy has been called an "American Bloomsbury." Past residents include James Harper, founder of the Harper Collins publishing house, Theodore Roosevelt, Edith Wharton, Eugene O'Neill, and O. Henry, who wrote *The Gift of the Magi* in a local restaurant, Pete's Tavern.

In 1831, Samuel Ruggles, longtime trustee of Columbia College, drained the swamp and laid out 66 English-style lots around a private park, still standing as the neighborhood's famed Gramercy Park. In the 1920s, the development of high-rise apartment buildings, the extension of the Third Avenue L, and the onset of the Depression meant that an address around Gramercy Park was no longer as desirable as it once was. The neighborhood's majestic mansions crumbled a bit, and the turn-of-the-century elite shopping mecca dubbed "Ladies' Mile" became a "temple of love" after an influx of brothels. On the heels of a capital flight came a vibrant population of leftists and artists, including Andy Warhol, who instituted his legendary Factory. Gramercy became an enclave for groups of rebels, ranging in identity from communists to junkie divas, and heavy drug traffic and drifters plagued the area.

Today, the revitalization that has spurred development in most of the downtown area has returned some of the old panache to Gramercy, and a Union Square address is desirable once again.

A Saturday in Gramercy

11 am

Feeding Time

Get that monthly quota of carbohydrates in just one sitting by ordering a colossal brunch at Friend of a Farmer at Irving Place between 17th and 18th Street. New Yorkers like their brunches big and this place certainly delivers.

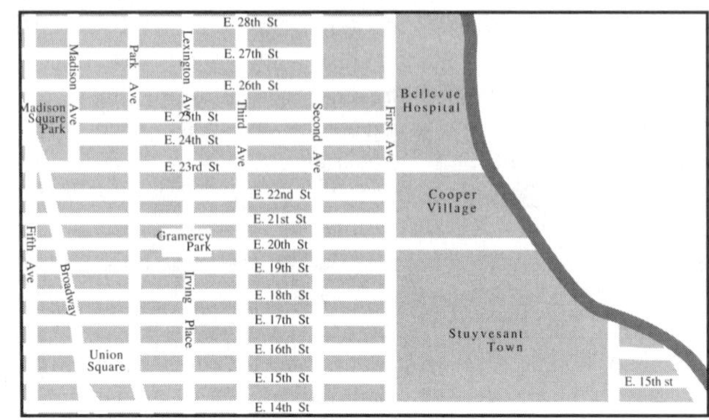

12 pm

Fruit and Veggie

Walk off that meal by exploring the farmers market at Union Square. In this city it is a rare treat to find affordable produce that is already half rotting, but the sellers here bring their fruit and vegetables in fresh off the farm.
See Sights and Parks

3 pm

Looking Good

Now get an architectural eyeful by taking a look at the Flatiron Building. Even though so many bigger and better structures came after, there is still something in the design of this building which makes on lookers catch their breath. Don't forget to take some time sitting in the park.

7 pm

Sexy Bowling – Strange But True

Now waste a few hours at Bowlmor Lanes – the crème de la crème of the city's decidedly hip bowling establishments. How many other bowling alleys are there in the world which provide an exclusive elevator ride up to the lanes? And run an ad campaign which consists of a girl dropping her panties on the lanes? This is where Madonna and artist Basquiet used to bowl back in the 1980's. On Monday night for $20 there is unlimited bowling from 10:00 pm onwards. Then, the lights go out, the pins are glow-in-the-dark neon and there is a live DJ spinning the latest. Saturday's aren't quite such a great deal – but still enough fun to warrant the lane fee. Upstairs from the lanes is an amazing new pool hall that looks more like an aircraft hangar than a traditional pool establishment. Watch out though, the mixed drinks are expensive.
See Nightlife Section

4 pm

Caffeine and Attitude

It might pretend it is aspiring to be nothing more then a diner with frills, but Coffee Shop on Union Square is hip and it knows it. Watch as the hostess gives the model types the nice seats, leaving lowlifes to scramble for what remains. Still, this is the price common people must pay for some iota of street credit.

chelsea

Other areas of the city, most notably the West and East Villages, have a thriving gay scene. Yet Chelsea, which stretches from the Hudson river to Broadway spanning from West 14th Street to West 28th, spent the 1990's building a reputation as the city's gay hub.

Back in the day, the neighborhood was down and out with very little going for it in terms of culture or convenience. Its industrial feel and blocks of vacant warehouses attracted prostitution in alarming numbers. As a result, real estate was cheap. Gay, primarily male, couples and singles began moving into the area, and with the combined effort of their cultural and economic zeal, began transforming Chelsea into what it is today.

Chelsea is all about the new Adonis. Biceps budge, six packs glisten and many of the men look ready to bust out of their tight muscle shirts. For a lot of Chelsea residents, working out is a lifestyle. Some might say that fitness here has reached the level of performance art. But, for most at least, there is more to life than beefcake. The streets are full of interesting bars, coffee shops, restaurants and stores.

Looking for love? The nightlife offers venues to fit every persuasion - leather lovers, club kids, drag queens or couples in search of a romantic drink. Dining is another of the neighborhood's fetishes. Chow down in one of the area's upscale eateries, Cafeteria (*119 Seventh Ave. at 17th St., (212) 414-1717*), which is still a hot favorite with the in crowd, or just waste a few hours at one of the friendly sidewalk restaurants.

An integral part of Chelsea's renaissance has been the art galleries which have sprung up mainly in the old warehouses towards the river. Check out Damian Hearst's latest, or seek out the next new up and coming darling.

There is no need to have a bank account to rival a Saudi oil tycoon to enjoy these spaces. Galleries tend not to mind people who are just there to browse. Cruise the amazing flower market on 28th Street, as fresh roses can add beauty to even the tiniest apartment and can be bought for wholesale prices.

The Chelsea Hotel

From its opening, the residential hotel has lured literati and pop-culture icons to its fabled halls. Mark Twain, Dylan Thomas, William S. Burroughs, Vladimir Nabokov and Arthur Miller all crashed here at some point. Even sometime girlfriend of Sex Pistols front man Sid Vicious, Nancy Spungen, met her untimely end here, allegedly at the hands of hunting-knife-wielding Sid himself. *222 W. 23rd St. (bet. Seventh and Eighth Aves.), 243-3700, ❶❷ to 23rd St.*

Little Spain

Though the population of Spanish sailors that burgeoned after the Civil War has died away, snatches of Spanish still drift by on the streets, salsa music pours from the windows, and a few bookstores and restaurants persist as remnants of the past. *14th St., west of Sixth Ave. ❶❶❶ ❷❸❾ to 14th St.*

Chelsea Piers

Restless New Yorkers recreate at this insular arena of sports and recreation facilities. Indoor soccer, the sky rink, and an open-air roller rink help city-dwellers relive starry-eyed junior-high romance. Boutiques galore, too. *Piers 59-60, near 23rd St., ❸❸ to 23rd St.*

General Post Office

A beautiful example of McKim, Mead and White architecture, circa 1913, this imposing, columned structure on the cusp of Chelsea and Clinton bears the famous postal slogan. *Eighth Ave. at 30th St., ❶❸❸ to Penn Station*

Chelsea Flower District

Sunrise heralds the aroma of roses and snapdragons wafting along this stretch of Sixth Ave., where vendors meet the horticultural needs of every urban green thumb. *Sixth Ave. and 27th St., ❶❷ to 28th St.*

history

Number one on any self-respecting tour of New York's sordid past must be The Chelsea Hotel. Opened in 1884, on 23rd Street between 7th and 8th Avenues, it continues to bask in its well-earned rep as an underground Mecca.

Back in 1912 survivors from the Titanic spent a night here, but their brief stay has nothing on some of the hotel's more long-term residents. This was where Welsh poet Dylan Thomas lived before he died of alcohol poisoning after having had a few too many a few too many times at the West Village's White Horse Tavern. Leonard Cohen, Mark Twain, Tom Wolfe, O. Henry, and Arthur C. Clarke all lived here. Its trash-tastic Benzedrine-riddled vibe was immortalized by Andy Warhol's film Chelsea Girls.

One of the hotel's most notorious moments of celebrity history came when ex-Sex Pistol Brit psycho Sid Vicious and his then girlfriend Nancy Spungen forked over the deposit for a room key back in 1978. Vicious was always the most unhinged of the Sex Pistols. "He was called Vicious because he was such a wanker. He couldn't fight his way out of a crisp bag," said Johnny Rotten in an interview. After the Sex Pistols broke up, Vicious found himself at loose ends, with a mounting heroin addiction.

On October 12, 1978, Nancy was found dead in her room at the Chelsea hotel. She had been stabbed several times in the stomach. There were no witnesses but Vicious looked like the likely and only suspect. He never confessed to the murder. Two months later - out on bail for knifing Patti Smith's brother in a bar brawl- he died of a drug overdose.

Another relic from Chelsea's days of old is the Vanderbilt YMCA at 224 East 47th Street. Remember the Village People song "YMCA"? Well, this community center was its prime inspiration. In the 1970's it became a well-known dose house and pick-up joint. All in all, Chelsea has flavor for the naughty .

A Saturday in Chelsea

8 am

Antique Hunting

Get up early and explore the famous outdoor antique markets scattered between 26th and 28th Streets along 6th Avenue. Countless gems can be picked up wondering through the sales, and riffling through their stashes. Fancy a retro sofa, or perhaps an antique watch? Prices are a little higher than they would be outside of the city.

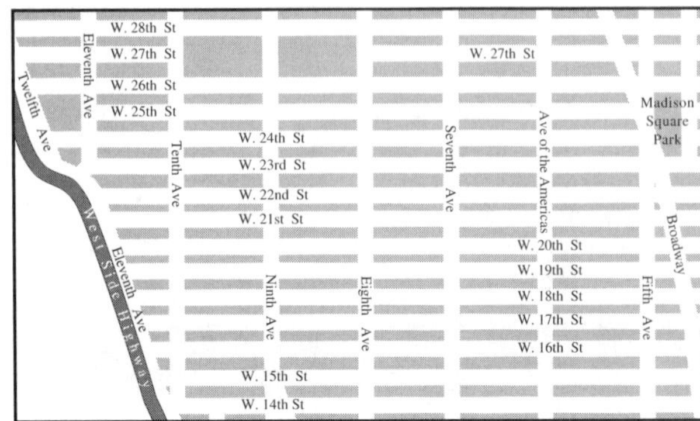

10 am

Diner Dining

After hours of shopping, stop in for brunch at the art deco Empire Diner on 10th Avenue and 22nd Street. Service (usually) comes with a smile, and the jazz tunes coming from the piano add that extra touch of class. Also, their onion flakes might not sound too appetizing, but once tried there is no turning back. *(212) 243-2736*

12 pm

Pamper Yourself

Boys – Head over to Nickel, the new fancy schmancy, all- male day spa on 14th Street at 77 8th Avenue. It is so chic it is French, and so sensuous that a visit will leave you tingling for days. It will also leave you wondering what happened to that extra $ in your bank account.
(212) 243-3203

Girls – Try Juvenex, a new 24-hour spa at 25 West 32nd Street. Try the crushed jade scrub and check out their Korean Igloo.
(646) 733-1330

People-watching at Big Cup
Nurse a cup of joe from behind one of the gigantic windows of the ever-hip coffee shop. *228 Eighth Ave. (bet. 21st and 22nd Sts.), 206-0059, Cash Only,* Ⓒ Ⓔ *to 23rd St.*

Enjoying Some Silence
Read amidst General Theological Seminary's greenery. *Ninth Ave. at 20th St. Admission: free,* Ⓒ Ⓔ *to 23rd St.*

{cheap *thrills*}

Blading by the Hudson
The outer rink on the water is fun, but avoid crowded times when the slow-moving, flat-footed folk turn into so many bowling pins. *23rd St. at the Hudson River,* Ⓒ Ⓔ *to 23rd St.*

3 pm

Fun and Games

Now it's time to bowl. Hit the lanes at Chelsea Piers. Because this is Manhattan, everyone dances to disco beats and sips on drinks as they go for the strike. Even bowling shoes manage to look cool here. *See Sites and Parks*

5 pm

French Fare

Head over to one of Chelsea's many pleasant French-style bistros. The decibel level at The Red Cat, at 227 Tenth Avenue between 23rd and 24th Streets, might be too high for dining, but no one is going to quibble with the reasonably priced menus and delicious fare.
This "cauldron of creativity" is one-of-a-kind.
(212) 242-1122

7 pm

Martinis and Nostalgia

Stop into the subterranean bar at the Chelsea Hotel, a rest stop for rare individuals, to end the evening with a quick Martini and a bit of nostalgia. Ask the bartender about the hotel's murders, suicides, and loomy geniuses. *See Sites and Parks*

midtown

When midwestern suburbanites dream about New York, Midtown is what they are thinking about. For them the area of Manhattan from 32nd Street to 60th has it all. On weekdays the streets are populated with frazzled-looking business types tripping over befuddled tourists as they rush to their next high powered meeting. Well-heeled shoppers stop in at Saks and wear a groove in their platinum card in the designer stores on Madison Avenue.

Professionals and socialites power lunch, or harried office types pick up something to go from the old school delis, particularly on the east side. Die-hard fans and out-of-towners stand in line for hours to grab tickets to the latest Broadway hit show. Those with a hankering for low culture wait hopefully to be picked as audience members for Ricky Lake, David Letterman, Conan O'Brian or Saturday Night Live.

The heart of midtown remains Times Square. New Yorkers like to kvetch about the Disneyfication of the area around 42nd Street. They miss the time when Times Square looked more like "Bring Out the Dead" than "42nd Street," the musical. Out went the strip clubs, sex shops and hobos that use to call Time Square home, and in came *The Lion King*, Madame Tussaud's and many themed restaurants. Remains of the old neighborhood remain, particularly out on 8th Avenue

where it is still possible to find rather bedraggled looking go-go dancers.

The area's distinctive edginess has been subsumed by a cookie-cutter vision of what passes for entertainment. Most people, however, don't really find being mugged all that desirable an experience and women everywhere have breathed a collective sigh of relief at being able to walk down the street without being subject to a rousing round of cat calls. A more serious issue is the fact that so many of the small business owners and entrepreneurs, who gave the area its charge, were pushed out to make way for the trappings of Walt Disney and corporate America.

Unlike the rest of the city, much of midtown is nonresidential. Those looking to set up home here tend to cluster in the once infamous Hell's Kitchen on the west side or Murray Hill on the east. For a while now Hell's Kitchen residents and realtors have been telling anyone who will listen that the neighborhood is really called Clinton. The campaign is part of an effort to surgically remove the area from its rough and tumble past when it was known as an Irish and Italian enclave notorious for violence. While this rechristening has proven fairly unsuccessful, Hell's Kitchen has become a lot more habitable - and more expensive. Home of some of the most impressive brownstones around, Murray Hill has never suffered from its neighbor's image problem. For the most part it is populated by yuppies who enjoy the quieter things in life and can afford its astronomical housing costs.

Bryant Park

Strangely enough, in a city where everything not bolted down disappears, the elegant movable chairs never stray far from their designated spots. Walk around and note the funky statues. Gertrude Stein's is one of the city's few statues of historical females. Summers, classic movies projected onto a large screen draw after-work crowds toting cheap wine and blankets. *40th to 42nd Sts. (bet. Fifth and Sixth Aves.), behind the New York Public Library,* **B D F Q** *to 42nd St., 7 to Fifth Ave.*

Rockefeller Center

The 19 commercial buildings and a subterranean network of shops and tunnels are dwarfed by attractions immortalized in the popular lore of New York: seasonal highlights include the ice rink and the tree lighting. Also, in the winter slip and slide among twirling would-be Ice Capades at the skating rink or just park yourself on the sidelines and take in the scene while sipping a cup of hot cocoa. *49th to 52nd Streets (between Fifth and Seventh Aves.)*

Pennsylvania Station

McKim, Mead, and White modeled the original station on the Baths of Caracalla in Rome, intending to upstage Grand Central and put another feather in the City Beautiful movement's cap. Today's Penn Station recently got a facelift and is as busy as ever, serving up to one thousand passengers every 90 seconds. *Between 30th and 34th Sts. (bet. Seventh and Eighth Aves.),* **1 2 3** *to Penn Station*

Grand Central Station

With its soaring ceilings, leaded lunette windows, and stolid, ornamented façade, this cathedral to industrialization is also one of the world's busiest and most spectacularly efficient train stations. Designed in 1889 by Reed and Stem, Grand Central Terminal has thus far eluded the sinister machinations of real estate speculators. A recent facelift restored some of the twinkle to the constellations painted on the vaulted blue ceiling. *42nd St. (bet. Park and Lexington Aves.),* **S 4 5 6 7** *to 42nd St. Grand Central Station.*

---

history

Much of the literature written on the history of midtown centers around its hub, Times Square. Originally called Long Acre Square, it was renamed when the New York Times moved its headquarters there in the 1890's. In part because the area was close to so many of the city's entrance and exit points, it quickly got a reputation as a home of sin and vice. During the 19th century its brothels were world-renowned. By the first World War the area had attracted many theaters, which moved up here from the Bowery in the Lower East Side.

Its dirty reputation increased in the 1940's as GI's on leave arrived, spilling from Grand Central and Penn Stations, looking for a good time and loose women. In the 1970's it became home to a revolution in pornography when some of the era's classic smut flicks debuted at its porn theaters.

The Vicious Circle

"As only New Yorkers know, if you can get through the twilight you'll live through the night." -- Dorothy Parker

Not all of midtown's history is tied up in sex. During the 1920's the Algonquin Hotel, at 59 W. 44th Street between Fifth and Sixth Avenues, was home to the heavy drinking, fast-talking group of Mahattanite intellectuals whose informal salon became known as the Algonquin Round Table. Made up of a tight-knit group of friends, many of whom wrote for the fledgling New Yorker, their irreverent and often manic antics came to personify an era and the city. F. Scott Fitzgerald would later write, "Who could tell us any longer what was fashionable and what was fun?" The star of the group was Dorothy Parker, known for her caustic wit and self-destructive streak, and intellectuals are still dropping Parker witticisms. She is reported to have said of a party the night before: "I drank so much I was under the host." Not only did Parker and her group frequent the bar of the Algonquin, but she spent years living there. Apparently she never paid any rent because she believed the 'Gonk' should be pleased just to have her there, though the hotels owners probably failed to agree.

A Saturday in Midtown

9 am

Morning Joe

Start the day with a well-brewed cup o' Joe at Café Europa on West 57th Street and Seventh. Try one of their European-style pastries.

10 am

Big Fun

Check out FAO Schwartz in the former GM Building at 767 Fifth Avenue off East 59th Street. Play like it's going out of style, as Tom Hanks did in *Big*. The din will wake you up, if the coffee didn't.

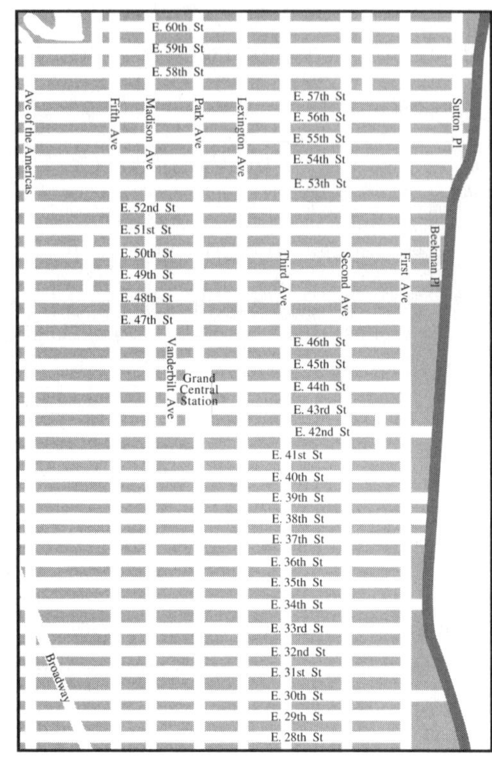

east midtown

11 am

Tanga

Stop over at West 46th Street between Fifth and Six Avenues, and try on some Brazilian tangas at Buzio's Rio De Janeiro.

12 pm

Hungry after all that Dancing?

Now that you've gotten comfortable with seeing
yourself bared in a whole new way, grab some fab
Brazilian fare at Emporium Brazil at 15 West 46th
Street. Try the feijoada or the fish casserole, and
try the lime drink caiparinha if you dare. Roll
yourself out of the restaurant with the intention
of pounding the pavement some more.

west midtown

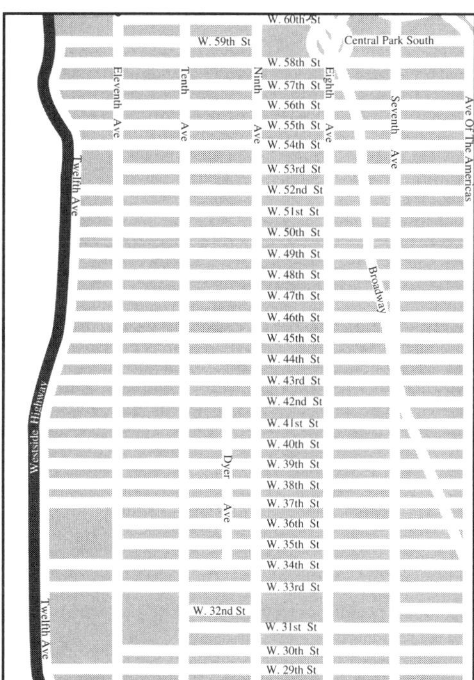

3 pm

See the City from Above

Head down to the Empire State Building
on Fifth Avenue and head up to the
observation deck. It was built in 1931.
350 Fifth Ave. (at 34th St.)

upper east side

Woody Allen immortalized it, Tom Wolfe parodied it, *Sex and the City* reveled in it and the tell-all book "The Nannies" scandalized it. The Upper East Side is the first and last word in old school money, style and aristocracy.

The stretch of land along Fifth Avenue fronting onto Central Park and known as Museum Mile boasts some of the most expensive real estate in the world and runs from 60th to 96th Street between Central Park and the East River. The neighborhood still beats Beverly Hills 90210 as the nations classiest zip code.

With its classic doormen, in their bleached white gloves and pill box hats, the Upper East Side evokes a bygone era. Mayor Bloomberg still calls it home. Marilyn Monroe and Lauren Bacall had it right in the 1960's film *How To Marry A Millionaire*, when they set up house here and devoted their considerable energies to snagging a blue blood spouse. New York's Mayor is also a resident of the Upper East Side, living in Gracie Mansion.

The East Side is also home to the city's literary and artistic old-guard, many of whom remain regulars at Elaine's, the legendary salon on Second Avenue and 88th Street. Are you a fan of Norman Mailer or Michael Douglas? They hang out here. Don't bother trying to get inside though - Elaine is very picky about who gets through her doors and gawkers are certainly not invited.

The Upper East Side houses the highest number of the city's museums, including the Metropolitan Museum of Art, the Whitney Museum, the Frick Collection, and the Cooper-Hewitt. Fortunately, these spectacular institutions, home to some of the most famous pieces of art in the world, are open to one and all for a small fee. Your last name doesn't have to be Rockefeller or Guggenheim for you to enjoy the pleasures this neighborhood has to offer, so take time to explore this interesting and exciting area.

Carl Schurz Park

Picturesque views of the East River, Queens and the Triboro Bridge are the draw of this green locale, not to mention Gracie Mansion. Get a feel for the east side amidst the rollerbladers, and joggers and well-groomed dogs who frequent this site. *East End Ave.(bet. 84th and 90th Sts.),* **4 5 6** *to 86th St.*

Gracie Mansion

Constructed in 1799 by merchant Archibald Gracie, this retreat from the urban gridlock of the city continues to stand as an elegant reminder of a bygone NY elite. Bought by the city in 1887, it became part of Carl Schurz Park and housed the Museum of the City of New York from 1923-32. Since the 1940s it has been the official residence of New York mayors. Tours are conducted Wednesdays; call in advance for times and reservations. *East 88th Street (at East End Ave.), (212)570-4751, suggested admission $4,* **4 5 6** *to 86th St.*

Henderson Place

Rumor has it that the 24 Queen Anne-style townhouses built in 1882 by fur importer John Henderson are haunted, either by ex-residents or by vengeful beavers. *86th St. (bet. East End and York Aves.),* **4 5 6** *to 86th St.*

Museum Mile

Fifth Avenue along the length of Central Park houses many of the city's best museums. Here are a few (*also see the Arts section*):

• **The Metropolitan Museum of Art** contains an impressive collection of Western and non-Western art; it is the most comprehensive art museum in the western hemisphere.

• **The Solomon R. Guggenheim Museum,** designed by Frank Lloyd Wright, is an architectural wonder that exhibits works of modern art along its curved central ramp and galleries.

• **The Museum of the City of New York,** which inhabits a Georgian East Side mansion, holds artifacts from old New York.

• **El Museo del Barrio,** located in a former public school building, displays art exhibits dedicated to preserving and documenting the heritage of Puerto Rico and Latin America.

• **The Whitney Museum of American Art** exhibits a collection of modern works by American artists.

• **The Frick Collection** displays great European works from the Renaissance to the end of the 19th century.

• **The Cooper-Hewitt Museum,** located in the former Carnegie Mansion, exhibits decorative arts.

history

Until Central Park opened in the 1860s, much of the uptown landscape resembled an affluent countryside. However, as the city expanded northward, the Upper East Side was settled and built up.

The eastern section of the area developed rapidly as the Second and Third Avenue elevated lines, completed in 1879, facilitated transportation between the urban center and outlying regions, attracting Irish and German immigrants who settled in the brownstones and tenements lining the area that would become Yorkville. The development that earned the area its elite reputation, however, was construction alongside Central Park. These streets would become the luxurious Fifth, Madison and Park Avenues. From Astor to Tiffany, New York's wealthiest barons erected park-side mansions. Although most were later demolished, the Carnegie and Frick survive as the Cooper-Hewitt Museum and the Frick Collection, respectively.

Park Avenue's glamorous reputation developed after the New York Central Railway buried its above-ground tracks. Elegant and spacious apartment buildings lined the newly cleared blocks while Madison Avenue's wealthy inhabitants attracted opulent boutiques to the ground floors of the street's row houses.

The Upper East Side cemented its reputation for both ethnic diversity and upscale living with the construction of high-rises like Rupert Towers at East 91st Street, as even the former working-class, immigrant-packed Yorkville area became desirable in the 1950s. Upper-class immigrants from Europe and Asia continued to arrive in the '80s, making the area one of the most exclusive in the United States.

A Saturday in the Upper East Side

9 am

The Regency

If you have never seen a big business deal conducted before regular business hours, rest assured, you will here. This is where corporate brass butter their muffins and sip mimosas at 9am. City regulars may feel more than at home here if they dress smartly. *540 Park Ave. (at 61st St.), (212) 759-4100.*

11am

Carl Schurz Park

Small but picturesque, this is a nice place to relax after your ritzy meal at Regency. The Park also affords the best views of the East River. *E. 86th St. (at the East River)*

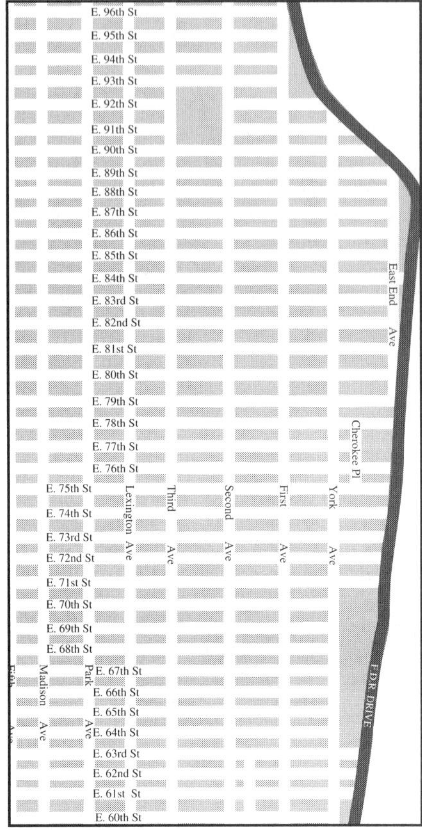

1 pm

Gracie Mansion

The New York mayor's private residence since 1942 is in Carl Schurz Park. There are tours only on Wednesdays, but you can photograph the building anytime. *See Sites and Parks*

Most Marvelous Marzipan
Elk Candy Company
More than 60 years have gone by since this Yorkville landmark opened its doors. *240 E. 86th St.,* **4 5 6** *to 86th St.*

Most Overpriced Clothing
57th Street bet. Sixth and Park Aves.
Unless you belong to the Knickerbocker Club, you probably can't afford anything on this street of fantasy. **B Q** *to 57th St.*

Most Exclusive Club
Knickerbocker Club
Knickerbocker Club is inclusive only to those whose ancestors were present in America during colonial times. *2 E. 62nd St.,* **4 5 6** *to 59th St.*

2 pm

Serendipity III

Known for its frozen hot chocolates and other goodies, Serendipity also serves great hamburgers. The lines are long, but thankfully, there are tons of toys to play with in the Serendipity General store while you are waiting for a table. *225 E. 60th St. (bet. Second and Third Aves.), (212) 838-3531.*

3 pm

Museum Mile

Some of the best addresses in the city are along this stretch of Fifth Avenue, and many of the museums, including the Cooper-Hewitt and the Frick Collection were the former private residences of the richest men in America. You could either walk the mile or spend the whole day in any one of these world-class museums. They will not disappoint.
See Sites and Parks and Arts Section

8 pm

Match Uptown

Lively and candlelit, this uptown twin of the popular SoHo restaurant serves excellent, eclectic New American cuisine and is a place to see and be seen. Dress up and walk in with attitude.
See Restaurants Section

10 pm

Manny's Car Wash

Reserve your table early for the nightly blues fests at this hot nightspot. *1558 Third Ave. (bet. 87th and 88th Sts.), (212) 369-BLUES*

upper west side

The Upper West Side is where the urban hipsters who define the neighborhoods below 14th Street come to grow up, settle down and perhaps reproduce. As such it combines the trappings and comforts of suburbia the city's more alternative edge.

It differs from the Upper East Side in that its residents, while still well off, have a reputation for being younger and more liberal. Babies and the occasional poodle still make a showing, but so too do bookstores, coffee shops and shaggy-haired academics. Culture lovers cluster around Lincoln Center, feeling their IQs rise as they stand in line for tickets to the opera. The West Side is also home to numerous upper crust private schools.

Older neighbors love the area for its open parks. Not only is Central Park on the doorstep but so is the less popular Riverside Park.

Anyone who is wondering whatever happened to Generation X - need look no further. The area, which runs up the west side of Central Park from 60th to 96th Street, was the fictional home of Jerry Seinfeld in his hit TV show, and he can be seen as a founding

father. Critics of the neighborhood say that Upper West Siders have never found a cause they didn't like.

Upper West Side residents also have rarely found a trend that they don't rush to adopt, as the area's other fictitious inhabitants - the cast of *Friends* - can testify to. The fad of choice for the last few years has been yoga - perfectly suited to the stressed out Generation Xer. Other fitness fads, mainly originating at Reebok Gym on Columbus Avenue, have included spinning, rock climbing and kick boxing.

When not working out, many Upper West Siders who have not tied the knot are looking for love. Yes, it's *Sex and The City* but with far smaller apartments and much less extensive wardrobes. The cafe Drip has made a name for itself as a

place where local residents can sit down and flip through a book of available singles. It is a good place to hang out for anyone looking for something besides the coffee to pick them up, and the advent of Internet dating services like Match.com has made blind dates de rigeur for young urbanites.

Those who prefer to get a date the old fashioned way can find plenty of bars to chose from. College kids trickling down from Morningside Heights mix with the locals on Saturday nights at the plethora of bars along Amsterdam Avenue, Broadway and surrounding streets.

The Upper West Side caters to a variety of groups including both individuals and families. While it is quieter than other neighborhoods downtown, there is usually something for everyone.

The Ansonia

Completed in 1904 with the intention of bringing Parisian architecture to the Upper West Side, the building's interior has since been drastically altered. Most of the grand, irregularly shaped oval rooms have been subdivided. The ornate exterior is still intact. *2109 Broadway (bet. 73rd and 74th Sts.),* ❶❷❸ *to 72nd St.*

Lincoln Center

San Juan Hill, the setting for *West Side Story*, was leveled in the '60s to make way for the city's cultural heart. The New York State Theater, Avery Fisher Hall, the Metropolitan Opera House, the Juilliard School, the Performing Arts branch of the New York Public Library and the Walter Reade Theater are all housed within the complex, designed by Robert Moses and funded largely by the Rockefellers. To the left of the Met, Damrosch Park hosts free summer performances outside. *62nd to 66th Sts. (bet. Columbus and Amsterdam Aves.), (212) 875-5030* ❶ *to 66th St.*

The Apthorp

Commissioned by William Waldorf Astor, who dreamed of a new, monumental style of building in New York, this enormous limestone structure was built around an elegant courtyard which is only open to tenants. *2111 Broadway (bet. 78th and 79th Sts.),* ❶ *to 79th St.*

history

The area that is now the Upper West Side was once viewed as a distant suburb of New York. Known as Bloomingdale, it was a popular refuge from the hustle and bustle of Manhattan's bustling center. The famous Westside apartment complex, once the backdrop for *Rosemary's Baby* and the site of John Lennon's assassination, was christened The Dakota because residents felt it was so far away from the city's hub that it might as well have been in the Dakotas.

It took the building of the elevated train line in 1879 for this neighborhood to make it onto street Manhattan's map. Yet, as with the Upper East Side, it wasn't until the completion of Central Park that things really took off. The advent of the park spurred a wave of construction that resulted not only in residential housing but a number of cultural institutions, most notably the American Museum of Natural History.

More ethnically diverse then its easterly neighbor, the area between Columbus and Amsterdam Avenue is still home to a Latino community. This part of the neighborhood underwent a cultural facelift of sorts in the 1960's when Lincoln Center was built. While people still debate the aesthetic merits of the Center, many arguing that it's an ugly blot on the landscape, few deny its contribution to the arts. Other architecture projects are in the works.

A Saturday in the Upper West Side

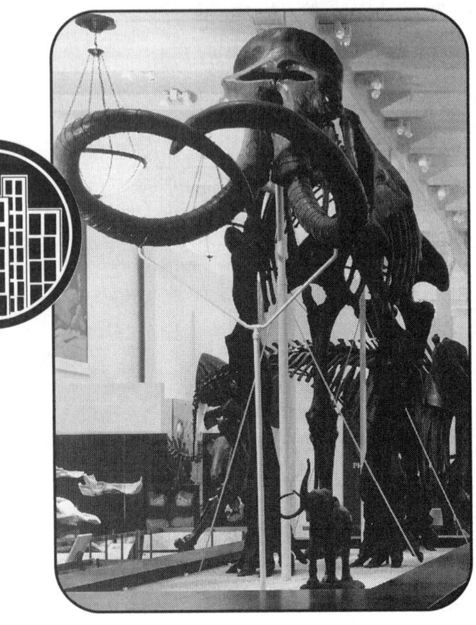

9 am

American Museum of Natural History

Dinosaurs aren't just for kids anymore. The impressive collection of animals, oceanography, IMAX pictures and environmental displays will keep even the most jaded New Yorker occupied. *West 79th Street and Central Park West.*

1 pm

Yum!

You've walked your tootsies off in the museum. Now it's time to have lunch at Café Lalo, at 201 W. 83rd St. (bet. Amsterdam Ave. & B'way). Famous for being in *You've Got Mail*, this quintessential café is packed with people, all the time, eating sweets that are sure to give a buzz.

Most Delectable Window Display
Zabar's and *Citarella*

These two gourmet shops lining Broadway have gourmet foodstuffs you won't find in your neighborhood Safeway. Citarella is on West 75th Street, Zabar's on West 80th. Check out their olives, foreign pastries, cheeses and fish. Great for that Tuscan dinner you always wanted to make.

"

2 pm
Rollerblading in Riverside or Central Park

If you happened to take your rollerblades in your backpack, whip them out and get some fresh air today. Get used to pockmarked cement and hordes of strollers. Think of it as an obstacle course.

4 pm
Drip

Interrupt your day in the café-cum-matchmaking spot famous for its book of eligible singles. Peruse the possibilities, if you like someone(s) tell the barista and they will make the phone call for you. If the other person digs the idea, you have a blind date. It's the next step beyond Internet dating. *489 Amsterdam Ave. (bet 83rd and 84th Sts.), (212) 875-1032*

8 pm
Beacon Theatre

Check out this eclectic concert hall with names big and small. Call for listings.
See Nightlife Section

{cheap *thrills*}

Most Transporting Way to Spend an Afternoon
Matinee at Lincoln Center
You've had enough exercise, now it's time to grab an indie movie at a film festival or at the Lincoln Center Cinemas across the street on Broadway and West 65th Street. Shell out $10 and enjoy a film you can't see in Cincinnati.

morningside heights

Better known as "that area around Columbia," Morningside Heights offers more than a place to get an Ivy League degree while destroying your credit rating. Aside from the tour buses in front of the Cathedral of St. John the Divine, the neighborhood has a distinct lack of out-of-towners. Many of New York's trendier types, if pressed, admit there is life north of Central Park, but damned if they know anything about it. This is all for the good, since crammed into this narrow stretch are more than a few cultural and architectural feasts.

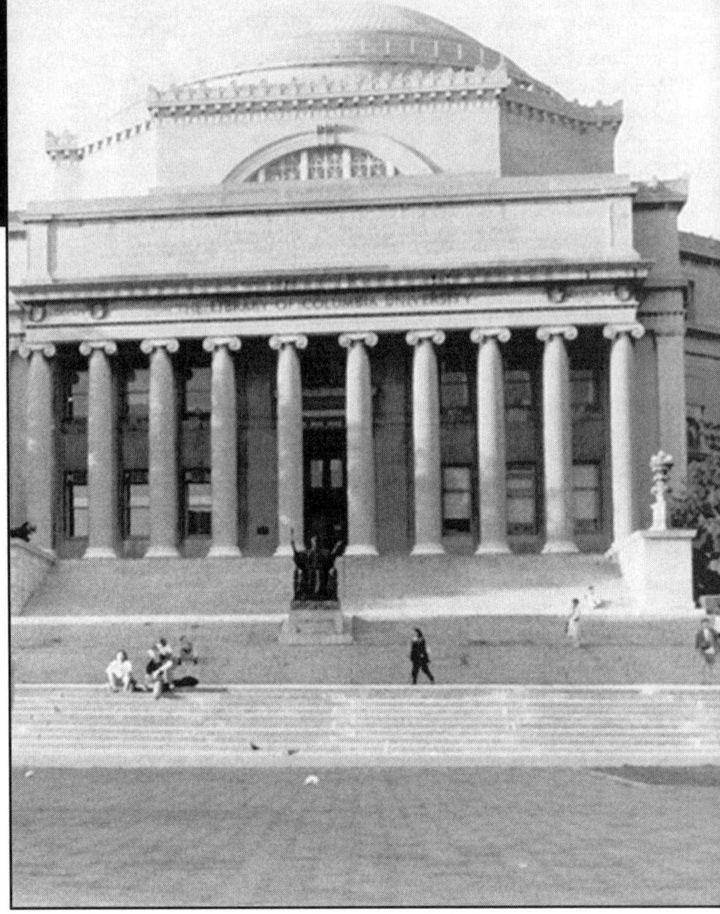

Morningside Heights, once known as Vandewater Heights, takes its name from Morningside Park, named for the fact that it slopes toward the morning sun. The name Cathedral Heights was once pushed, but didn't stick.

In the post-boom 00's, the neighborhood is defined by academics, joggers, jogging academics, and a few serious drinkers. Just like any college town, the streets support their share of new and used booksellers. Broadway between 112th and 113th is the place to hang out in warm weather when the bistros, cafes and eateries fill the block with their sidewalk tables. The West End Café, once a hang out for Kerouac, Ginsberg and Burroughs, still attracts academics. The local restaurants are full of pimply students and grizzled absentminded professor types, together with old neighborhood standbys, mommies with strollers. Restaurants here are not known for their food. Bars aren't known for their beer either, but high taste doesn't run rampant here and most residents come and stay here to let their hair down.

The area has a bi-polar personality: Riverside Drive has some of the highest-rent condos in the city, while Cathedral Parkway (West 110th Street) has some run-down looking apartments. The neighborhood borders Harlem and reflects that crossover. The southern end of the district, Manhattan Valley, has traditionally been a haven for Puerto Rican and Dominican New Yorkers.

The brambles and well-worn paths of Riverside Park are a pleasant if not exactly quiet respite from city life- Riverside Drive and the Westside Highway kick up some serious noise. The views, though, are spectacular. Residents tell you this park is far preferable to Morningside Park, which is known as a dangerous area. The flavors of this neighborhood make for a varied experience.

Cathedral of St. John the Divine

The largest Gothic cathedral in the U.S. and principal church of the Episcopal Diocese of New York, it is both a place of worship and a host to a multitude of community events, including an all-night recitation of Dante's Inferno and traditional chamber music and candlelight vespers. *1040 Amsterdam Ave. (at 112th St.), (212) 316-7540, ❶ to 110th St.*

Columbia University

This heavily symmetrical creation of McKim, Mead and White appears uncannily like a walled city from the outside. Recent construction and renovation projects solidify this Ivy's presence just below Harlem. Low Library was once voted one of the most beautiful buildings in North America. The 'Steps,' recognized as one of the best hangouts in NY, is a great spot for people-watching and lazing in the sun. The plaza below is a grassy playground for co-eds and families alike. *From 114th to 120th Sts. (bet. Broadway and Amsterdam Aves.), 854-1754, ❶ to 116th St.*

Grant's Tomb/Sakura Park

Pay your last respects to the General and his wife at America's second-largest mausoleum. The tomb, once plagued by spray-paint-wielding youths, is now in prime condition to celebrate its legacy as one of America's most highly acclaimed buildings. Sakura Park, located across the street, is a favorite family retreat. Don't mind the exhibits with typos. *Riverside Drive (at 122nd St.), 666-1640, Admission Free, ❶ to 116th St.*

New York Buddhist Temple

This branch of the Japanese Buddhist sect Jodo Shinshu welcomes visitors to the Sunday services, which are conducted in Japanese and English, and to meditation workshops. *331-332 Riverside Drive (bet. 105th and 106th Sts.), (212) 678-0305, ❶ to 110th St.*

Riverside Church

Based on the Cathedral at Chartres, this interdenominational church boasts spectacular stained-glass windows, the world's largest carillon (bells) and an impressive view of the city from its tower. Take a free ride to the top on Saturdays. Lectures and concerts held regularly. *120th St. (bet. Riverside and Claremont), (212) 222-5900, ❶ to 116th St.*

Riverside Park

Walk along this two-mile stretch for pleasant views of the river and the European-style apartment buildings along Riverside. Playgrounds and tennis courts lie alongside landmarks such as the Soldiers' and Sailors' monument, Grant's Tomb, and the Firemen's Memorial. *Riverside Drive (bet. 72nd and 125th Sts.)*

history

The Battle of Harlem Heights took place here (around 119th and Broadway) on September 16, 1776. The Yanks pushed the Brits back that day, but soon abandoned the city to the British laddies (in a pattern that has repeated itself in music, art and men's magazines ever since). Through much of the 19th century the neighborhood was home to an insane asylum and an orphanage.

After Morningside Park opened in 1887 and Riverside Drive in 1890, the neighborhood saw most of its landmark buildings built in the following two decades. The Interborough Rapid Transit (IRT) opened in 1904 connecting uptown to downtown. Suddenly it was okay to live in the suburbs. The building boom wouldn't survive the market crash of 1929, but the neighborhood had taken shape by that time and Morningside Heights was no longer the boonies.

Just before the turn of the century the area was still a backwater, though development was encouraged by the paving of area roads, the construction of Riverside Drive and the promise of subway accessibility. The Anglican Church began construction on the world's largest cathedral, St. John the Divine, which remains unfinished to this day; its bizarre hybrid of architectural styles reflects the varied visions of its several collaborators over a century. Grant and his wife were reburied in Grant's Tomb, constructed in 1897, by which time Columbia University was busily moving into its present location, soon to be joined by Barnard College, and the Jewish and Union Theological Seminaries. Today it is an intellectual bastion and a neighborhood on the rise.

A Saturday in Morningside Heights

9 am Hungarian Pastry Shop

Start the day with dark, heady sludge coffee with Manhattan's only free refills. Try the prune danish or poppyseed strudel – the desserts and pastries here are the real deal. Watch the various unemployed-looking students wander in and out, looking shell-shocked from their latest tuition bill. Get off the ❶ train at 110th Street, walk away from Riverside Drive on Cathedral Parkway. Make a left on Amsterdam, stroll up half a block.

10 am Riverside Park

Head down 110th toward the river, and let your greasy lunch settle in your stomach as you stroll down this long finger of a park. During the summer, there is a café halfway down under one of the major arches, which serves burger fare next to the volleyball pits. Check out the enclosed dog-walking park, where owners chat each other up as their dogs sniff away. The park stretches four miles from 72nd to 158th Streets along the Hudson, and designed by Fredrick Olmsted (of Central and Prospect Park fame). The 79th Street Boat Basin has a fabulous restaurant during the balmy summer months, overlooking the water amidst Roman-like archways (a good date place).

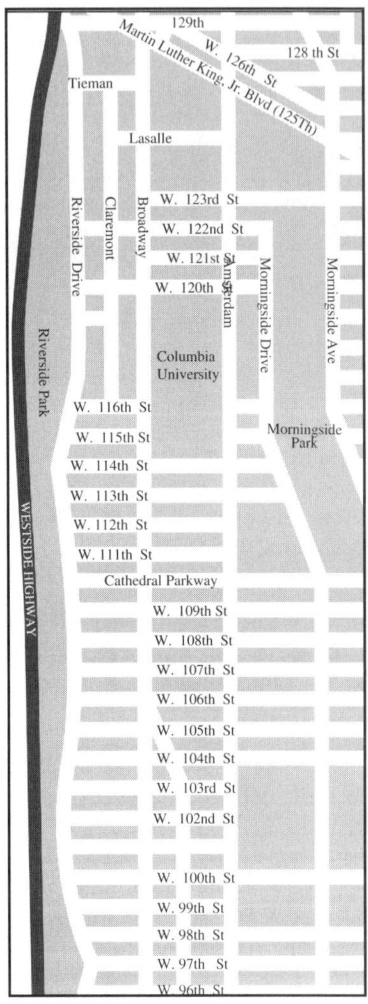

12 pm

Tom's Restaurant

This was the restaurant where the *Seinfeld* gang supposedly got together to shoot the breeze, in true New York sitcom style (where nobody seems to work). The Kramer guy who was the inspiration for the character on the show, gives tours that leave from this greasy spoon. Eat here, just don't expect more than a diner can deliver.
2880 Broadway (at 112th St.)

5 pm

The West End

This is a Morningside institution, ever since the Beat Generation made this one of their hangouts. Now reportedly owned by a Columbia Journalism School grad, the bar and restaurant features heartburn-inducing food and big pints. A fave of the college set, although on weekends the noise can be deafening.
Broadway at 114th St.

Most Interesting Tomb
Grant's Tomb
Bypass the often-misspelled exhibits upstairs and head down to the base of this neoclassical mausoleum to look at the crazy-quilt tile mosaic structure.
Admission is free.
Riverside at 122nd St.

Best Free Folk Music
Postcrypt
Every Thursday night, the university chapel hosts a free folk music and popcorn night in its basement café. Get there around 9 pm, call before you go.
See Nightlife Section

harlem

In a city stricken by chronic amnesia, Harlem is distinctive for remembering its past. A visit to the Cotton Club, one of the old school jazz haunts (though now at 125th Street), or Showman's, can feel like stepping back in time. Yet hanging with the kids on the stoops of Spanish Harlem is like catching a wave of the city's Latin future.

More than anything, music defines this neighborhood - old school jazz mixes with hip hop, R&B and the sounds of salsa, pop and world music, in an infusion not found anywhere else in the world. There on 125th Street and Seventh Avenue is the Apollo Theater - a touchstone for big bands of the 1930's, the venue that has launched countless African-American stars from Ella Fitzgerald to Michael Jackson to Lauryn Hill. The disheveled theater is now home to the always riotous amateur night on Wednesdays at the Apollo.

Harlem is and was the mecca of black culture in New York. Take a walk along 125th Street, Harlem's main drag, to feel the tingling of this, the biggest and baddest of America's cities. At almost any hour of the day the street teems with life. The street is a mix of old-style merchants and the encroaching corporate America - Starbucks and Walt Disney are making themselves right at home. Not

to mention the office of Harlem's newest resident, ex-President Bill Clinton. "America's first black President," to quote Toni Morrison. No one has yet seen Bill handing out at the equally new Harlem USA movie theater just across from his digs. Word is that he has been known to sneak the odd plate of greens round the corner on 127th Street at Sylvia's, the city's best known soul food restaurant.

This neighborhood was born out of conflict. Here, in the early 17th century, the original Dutch settlers and local native tribe members began killing each other off as the Europeans began homesteading. Enslaved Africans helped build this area beginning in 1626. After the Civil War, the neighborhood became home to the white middle class, but by 1930 Harlem was two-thirds black. Harlem boasts some of the

city's most impressive brown-stones. As housing prices quadrupled downtown, it was not long before the city's wealthy, predominantly white residents started moving up, many shelling out up to six fig-ures to renovate these build-ings.

Many older residents lost out, but the experience of gentrifi-cation here has not followed the path of downtown. On one level, the process has allowed for restoration that the area as a whole might not have been able to afford. At the same time the existing residents have always been very active in pre-serving their own neighbor-hood.

For years now, a lively Hispanic neighborhood has been grow-ing east of Fifth Avenue above 86th Street. This community has breathed its own distinctive life and culture into the area.

Abyssinian Baptist Church

Pastor Adam Clayton Powell, Sr. built this church in 1921 to serve the needs of the growing numbers of blacks settling on the Upper West Side. The church is named for its first worshipers, Abyssinian merchants who wanted to maintain their connection with Africa. The congregation has grown to over 4,000 to date. *132 West 138th St. (bet. A.C. Powell and Malcolm X), (212) 862-7474, ❷❸ to 135th St.*

Jackie Robinson Park

Oak-lined walkways, an Olympic-sized pool, band-shells and pick-up basketball make this oasis in Harlem's St. Nicholas district one of the area's best-equipped parks. *145th to 152nd Sts. (bet. Edgecombe and Bradhurst), (212) 234-9607, ❹ ❺❻❼ to 145th St.*

Langston Hughes House

Writers have inherited the former home of this Harlem Renaissance poet; his memory is kept alive through regular readings. Tours by appointment. *20 East 127th St. (bet. Madison and Fifth Aves.), (212) 862-9561, Suggested Admission $3, ❷❸ to 125th St.*

Marcus Garvey Park

The "Back to Africa" spokesman and noted civil rights leader was honored thus in 1973. The park boasts an iron frame belltower built in 1956, as well as one of the city's best vistas. *120th to 124th Sts. (bet. Fifth and Madison Aves.), (212) 410-2818, ❷❸ to 125th St.*

Schomburg Center for Research in Black Culture

World-famous for its extensive research facilities, this branch of the New York Public Library is an invaluable resource for scholars of black history and culture. *515 Malcolm X Boulevard at 135th St., 491-2200; ❷❸ to 135th St.*

The Hispanic Society of America

One of the city's hidden gems, the museum focuses on the art, literature, and cultural history of Spanish and Portuguese Americas. It also offers a reference library open to the public. *Broadway and 155th St., (212) 690-0743, open T-Sa 10am-4:30pm, Su 1-4pm, Admission free; ❶ to 157th St.*

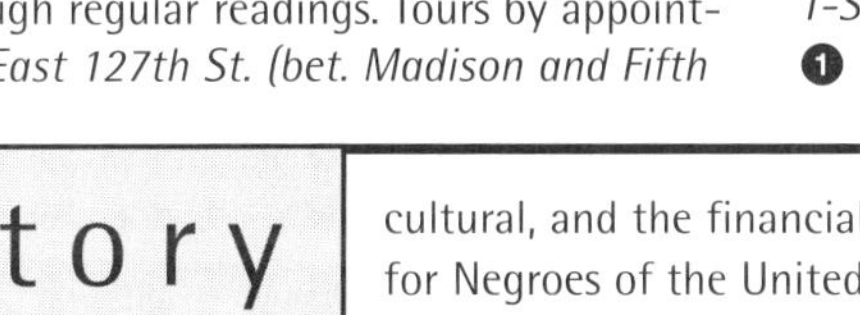

history

In 1925, when Alain Locke edited *The New Negro*, an anthology of poetry and prose by up-and-coming black artists, he wrote, "I believe that the Negro's advantages and opportunities are greater in Harlem than in any other place in the country, and that Harlem will become the intellectual, cultural, and the financial center for Negroes of the United States. The Harlem Renaissance of the late 1920s proved Locke correct, but Harlem's population in the early part of that decade was by no means entirely black.

Many immigrants from Ireland and Germany settled around 125th Street. As more and more blacks moved into the area, however, whites began to leave. The combined effect of white flight and black migration from southern Manhattan helped solidify the development of black Harlem.

This new concentration of blacks spurred the Harlem Renaissance as many wealthy Harlemites began entertaining and organizing literary and social clubs. At these gatherings, authors and poets such as Countee Cullen, Langston Hughes and Zora Neale Hurston read from their work.

The Depression sent the area into decline, and racial tensions erupted in several large-scale riots. Today, business and rebuilding efforts from within the community are helping restore Harlem to its former glory and prominent members of the black community live in the area. Perhaps that's why Nelson Mandela called Harlem "the capital of the Black world."

A Saturday in Harlem

10 am

Let us Pray!

This is now a major tourist destination, but go attend a service by the Abyssinian Baptist Church, NY's oldest surviving African-American Church, founded in 1808. Services are held at 9 am and 11 am. *132 Odell Clark Place at West 138th Street between Malcolm X Boulevard and Adam Clayton Powell Boulevard. www.abyssinian.org*

11:30 am

True Grit

Start your day off right at one of Harlem's best breakfast stops. Don't miss the grits!

12 pm

La Comida

El Fonda Boricua is the real deal in Puerto Rican cooking. For homestyle chicken and rice, plaintains, etc. this café has the competition beat. *169 E. 106th Street, (212) 410-7292.*

1 pm

Sugar Hill

Take a stroll down Convent Avenue. The stretch between 145th Street and the City College campus on 137th is lined with beautiful, historic brownstones. Think the Huxtables.

4 pm
International Museum of Salsa

In "El Barrio," as this area around the East 100s is known, the Puerto Rican beat may be fading to the Mexican tejano, but the salsa legends live on in this lovingly cared-for museum. Take a tour, see items from Celia Cruz, Ray Barreto, Eddie Palmieri and Tito Puente. Then buy some fried plantain chips and get souvenirs before moving on. *2127 Third Ave. (at 116th St.), (212) 289-1368. www.intlsalsamuseum.homestead.com*

5 pm
El Museo del Barrio

Explore East Harlem's history and art in this often overlooked yet wonderful museum. This museum has over 8,000 pieces of Latino and Caribbean art, including pre-Colombian art.
1230 Fifth Ave., (212) 831-7272

10 pm
Lenox Lounge

Catch a great jazz act at this historic Harlem mainstay.
288 Malcolm X Blvd., (212) 427-0253

{cheap *thrills*}

Most Wave of the Future
Magic Johnson Harlem USA

This multiplex has the latest and greatest movies, and the matinees are actually affordable. Much grumbling accompanied the arrival of this mall-looking complex, replete with Old Navy next door and a Starbucks down the block. But still the customers come, so Harlem USA is here to stay.

washington heights + inwood

You don't have to speak Spanish to get by in Washington Heights and Inwood, but it helps. Salsa and merengue rhythms mingle in the streets with hip-hop beats and car horns. Extended families sit in grassy parks on weekends and evenings for barbeque, dominoes and soccer. This area might be the last part of Manhattan to be conquered by concrete. It's been "discovered" numerous times by people searching for a break on rent, yet remains a Dominican enclave nonetheless.

Washington Heights gets attention outside the city because of Columbia's Health Sciences campus in the mid 100s. Yet the crowds that work, study and research here usually fade by nightfall - surrendering the neighborhood to its real Latino origins.

The Heights has a sometimes deservedly rough reputation - the area has been notorious for drug dealing. On select corners young men still hang out, but the effects of gentrification can be felt here as well. The neighborhood is often overlooked by Manhattanites, but contains a tremendous number of interesting, diverse neighborhoods within its borders.

In the upper reaches of Washington Heights and into Inwood, enclaves of Orthodox Jews, students and yuppies have moved in. For cheap rents they find a lot of space and plenty of nature. And all along the perimeter of Riverside Drive, residents get spectacular views of the city's bridges and waterways heading into Queens. The area is rapidly escalating in price, but for old-timers, they figure they have found paradise: cheap rents, great views, fabulous parks and an escape from the city. Many residents prefer that their neighborhood remain undiscovered.

Baker Field

After student rioters in the '60s effectively canceled plans for a massive recreational facility in Morningside Park, Columbia built here. The complex also includes tennis courts and a baseball diamond located in the midst of a neighborhood of beautiful brownstones. *Broadway at 218th St., (212) 942-0431,* ❶ *to 215th St.*

Dyckman Street Marina

Self-described "boat bum" John Boldt has toiled for years to save money for a marina at the western end of Dyckman Street, the only point above 145th Street where river access isn't blocked. This is one of the latest steps in recent revitalization plans for the waterfront. *Dyckman St. on the Hudson River,* ❶ *to Dyckman-200th St.*

George Washington Bridge

Othmar H. Ammann's original design called for granite sheathing, but the onset of the the Great Depression forced him to leave it out. Le Corbusier called it the most beautiful bridge in the world, and it is the only bridge connecting New Jersey to New York City. ⓐ *to 175th St.*

Fort Tryon Park and Cloisters

Home to the Cloisters, the entire park sparkles. A park ideal for picnicking, lounging, and relaxing. There is also a museum with a very large collection of Medieval works. *Entrances at 191st and 200th Sts., 360-8111,* ⓐ *to 190th St., M4 directly to Cloisters. See Museums section*

Inwood Hill Park

This uptown expanse of woodland boasts cross-country ski trails, caves once inhabited by a local tribe, and the island's last remnant of primeval forest. Park Rangers organize tours of the caves during the summer. Safety concerns dictate that you not explore them alone. *Entrance at 207th St. and Seaman Ave. 360-8111,* ⓐ *to 207th St.*

history

Present-day Washington Heights is quite a change from a neighborhood that was once farmland and country estates. When George Washington wanted to survey his New York revolutionary headquarters—the estate now called the Jumel-Morris Mansion - he'd have to walk from the Hudson to the Harlem. The estate had to shrink a bit to make way for a few thousand apartments that now stand in its place.

The first woman ever to fight as an American soldier is memorialized at Fort Tryon, where the Patriots battled Hessian troops in 1776. The original Fort Washington, however, is gone.

In 1811, when the city designed the grid they saw no need for the streets to extend past Trinity Cemetery at 155th Street. Just like the rest of upper Manhattan, the IRT changed all that when it reached Dyckman Street in 1906, and the neighborhood soon followed. The area was once predominantly Irish, but with time and migration it gave host to German-Jewish refugees, Greeks, Armenians, Africans and Latinos.

Most people know Inwood only in relation to the Cloisters. A lesser known secret is that Inwood's beautiful parks are vast and very quiet. Though Highbridge Park seems to have missed out on the infrastructure projects of the 90's, trips to Inwood, Fort Tryon and Isham Parks are the closest you can get to leaving Manhattan without actually doing so. And if taking some time in the parks doesn't totally fulfill your mental-health needs, there's always the stylishly designed Psychiatric Institute on Riverside Drive at 165th Street for a real escape from New York.

A Saturday in Washington Heights

10 am

Fort Tryon Café

Delicious pastries, divine coffee

and heavenly soups are standard

fare at this charming cafe conve-

niently located near the Cloisters.

see Restaurants Section

12 pm

Cloisters

Enjoy the art and atmosphere

at one of the city's most peaceful (and

medieval) spots.

Why go out for lunch

when the Cloister's lush lawns

beg for a picnic?

See Sites and Parks and Museum

Listings in Arts Section

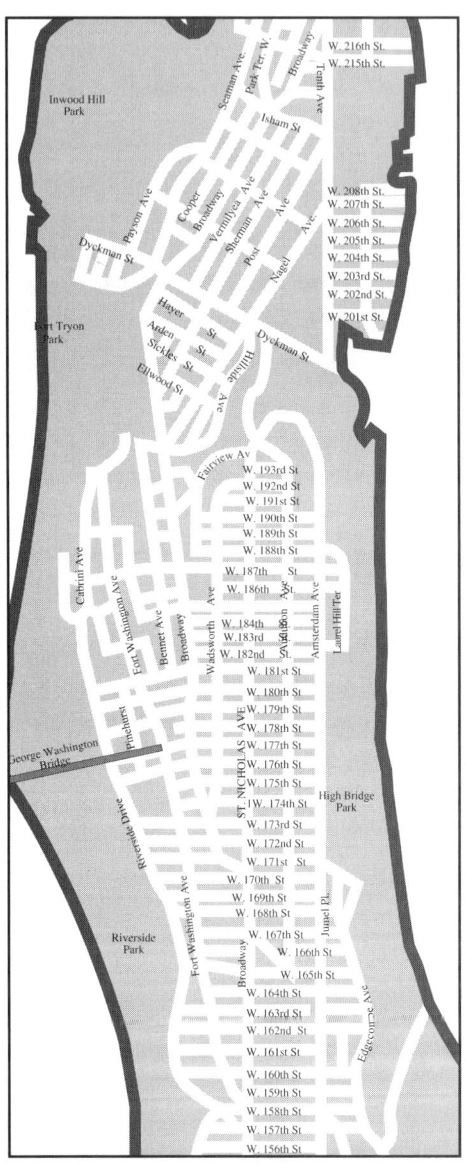

{cheap *thrills*}

3 pm

George Washington Bridge

Follow the sun toward Jersey and watch the tugboats steaming along the Hudson River. After your leisurely afternoon, a walk across "the most beautiful bridge in the world" will work up an appetite and prepare you for venturing back into modernity.

see Sites and Parks

6 pm

Bleu Evolution

The food and setting will justify the trek uptown, if the other sites you've seen today haven't. There's a lovely garden to eat in and a lounge that stays open long after the kitchen closes. Some say it's the best part of the neighborhood. *806 W. 187th St. (at Fort Washington Ave.), (212) 928-6006.* **Ⓐ** *to 181st St., elevator to Ft. Washington*

see Restaurants Section

Ropa	99¢ World
If you're patient enough to sort through acres of vintage clothes, you'll leave with some of the best deals in the city. *see Shopping Section*	A subway token uptown costs more than anything you'll find at this well-stocked enclave of snacks and household items. Nothing over a dollar (plus tax). *655 West 181st St. (bet. Broadway and St. Nicholas Ave.), 981-1064, Cash Only,* **❶Ⓐ** *to 181st St.*

The uninitiated tends to envisage this outer borough as an urban labyrinth. In short, the Bronx gets a bad rap. True, the South Bronx is still unsafe despite ongoing, and often successful, local efforts to revive the area. But this most northerly New York borough is a neighborhood defined by contrasts. Riverdale, to the north, is one of the most fancy New York addresses.

The extremes of this borough don't stop at the doorstep of Riverdale. The adventurous who roam as far as City Island will be likely to experience the equivalent of cultural whiplash. In the northern end of the Bronx, a little piece of New England. And the maritime aesthetic and small-town feel of this village within the city do give it a certain clam chowder vibe.

The neighborhood responsible for the South Bronx is also New York's second greenest borough. If a trip to Little New England fails to rock your boat, then check out the Bronx Botanical Garden, or better still the Bronx Zoo. By far the largest and the best of the city's zoos, this zoo is likely to deliver. Those in the know come on weekdays to avoid the crowds and children. For cheapskates, admission on Wednesdays is free.

Just outside of the zoo is the

Bronx's bigger and more authentic answer to Manhattan's Little Italy. Belmont boasts an array of fine bakeries, butcher shops, restaurants and produce markets. Locals bicker about soccer games, while elderly women carry fresh-made mozzarella and prosciutto home for dinner. Italians, of course, are not the only ones who settled in the Bronx.

The ethnic diversity of the borough is most clear in the area around Fordham University. Here, Latinos, African-Americans and Afro-Caribbeans hang out, and the area is infused with a hip-hop vibe that sets the tone for the trendy bars and shops.

Certainly, those whose only experience of the Bronx is to yell "go Yankees" at Yankee Stadium are missing out on one of the city's most exciting areas. Go explore this untapped resource, and you won't be disappointed!

Bronx Zoo/Wildlife Conservation Park

Four thousand animals observe visitors with an air of profound boredom as they whistle, wave, and gesticulate. The monorail brings you within feet of these animals. Many exhibits are individually ticketed, even on "free" Wednesdays, so be prepared to spend $7 or $8 per person over the regular price of admission. *Bronx River Parkway and Fordham Road, (718) 367-1010. Open 10am-5pm. Admission $11 regular, $4 children and seniors, free on Wednesdays, &, ❷ to Pelham Parkway Station*

Bronx Botanical Garden

New York's largest and most magnificent gardens include both cultivated exhibits and 40 acres of pristine forest. An extensive botanical library is available to the public, and classes, sales and events fill the calendar year-round. Weekdays afford remarkable quiet and solitude. The Garden Cafe offers sandwiches and snacks, but visitors are welcome to bring a picnic basket. *200th St. and Southern Blvd., (718) 817-8705, Passport ticket which includes tram tour is $15 for adults, $12 for seniors and students, $4 for children 2 to 12, ❹❹ to Bedford Park Blvd., then Bx26 to Gardens; on-site parking $4*

Van Cortlandt Park

The Bronx's answer to Central Park, "Vannie" is overwhelmingly huge, occupying 1,146 acres near Riverdale, which serve as a massive center for recreation and nature. The main parade ground hosts numerous soccer, softball, cricket and football games but is just as nice for playing Frisbee and sitting on a blanket. There are plenty of trails for nature hikes and biking, as well as one of the nation's best cross-country courses. Play a round at the Van Cortlandt Golf Course, the first municipal course in the country, ride a horse at the bridle path, visit the Van Cortlandt Historical Mansion, take a swim in the pool, stroll the gardens, and then take a nap in the grass. *(718) 430-1890; (718) 543-4595 golf course; ❶ to W. 242nd St.*

---

history

The Bronx is the only borough named after a person: Jonas Bronck, a Swedish sailor who cleared 500 acres and built a farmhouse. By 1700, Bronck's farm was destroyed and most of the land was split between four large manors: Pelham, Morrisania, Fordham and Phillipsburg.

The Bronx became famous for its landscaping and attractions. In the late 19th century, the Grand Concourse was built, modeled after tree-lined French boulevards. In 1891, the New York Botanical Gardens opened, followed by the Bronx Zoo. At 2764 acres, Pelham Park is still the city's largest oasis.

The borough was consolidated into New York City in 1898, and immigrants flocked there after 1904, when the first subway connecting the Bronx with Manhattan was completed. Droves of Yugoslavians, Armenians and Italians arrived, as well as many Jews from central and eastern Europe. Business in the borough took off, with the Hub and Fordham Road becoming major shopping centers. Yankee Stadium was opened in 1923 and the Bronx Bombers soon became the world's most famous baseball team.

After World War II, wealthier residents moved to luxury apartments or toward the suburbs in Westchester. An influx of poor people, displaced by urban renewal in Manhattan, moved to the southern neighborhoods, and poverty grew. While other parts of the Bronx continued to prosper as residential communities, the South Bronx declined.

A *Saturday* in the Bronx

9 am

Royal Coach Diner

Have a filling, tasty brunch
in this Bronx classic.
See Restaurant section

11 am

Bronx Zoo

After you've checked out the
flora, find out where the wild
things are. The world-renowned
zoo tries its best to give the animals a natural habitat.
See Sites + Parks

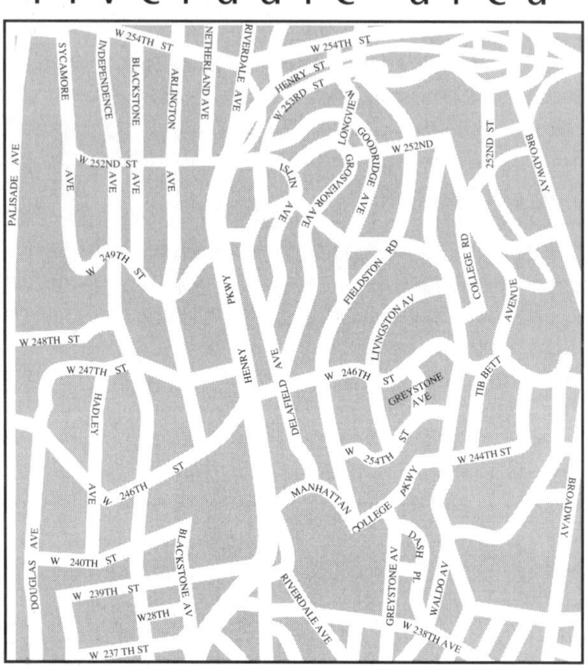

1 pm

Yankees Game

Root for the Yankees, and try to catch a Subway
Series game against Queens' Mets.
See Sites + Parks

3 pm
Botanical Gardens

Bring a thermos and a newspaper to relax in the gardens, then spend a few hours soaking up the gorgeous flora. *(see Sites + Parks)*

5 pm
Little Italy

Walk around the Bronx's authentic Little Italy, then celebrate the Yankees' win or console yourself for their loss with dinner and drinks at an authentic Italian restaurant.

7 pm
Key Skating Center

Old school fun. Gives visitors the chance to throw on the skates and race, hold hands and skate to hip hop and Latin. 220 E. 138th St, (718) 322-0203, www.keyskate.com

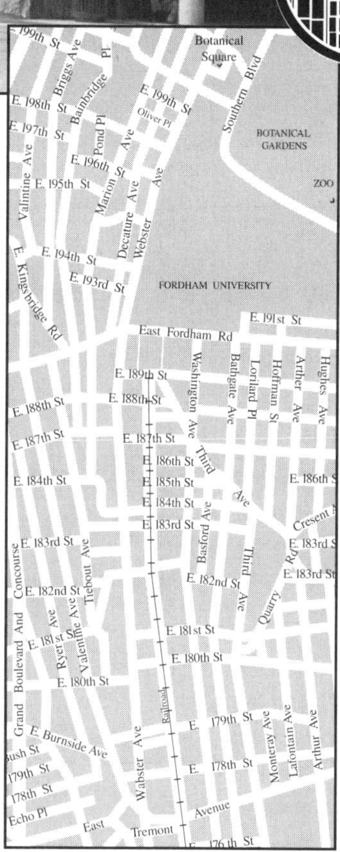

f o r d h a m   a r e a

Of all the boroughs in New York, Queens is the most all-American. Queens is home to over 100 different ethnic groups speaking over 120 distinct languages, and holds the honor of being the most ethnically diverse slice of the world there is.

Unlike Manhattan or Brooklyn, Queens was and remains a suburb. Its basic demographic group is the family, large or small, and its basic interests are family interests. While the rest of the city might be staying up until the early hours, Queens residents tend to stay closer to home. This is not to say that they can't get wild with the best of them. Many in Queens party in New York City every weekend, but the borough overall has a quieter tempo to it.

The residents of Queens love its relative quiet and diversity. Each area has its own charms, and residents will forever be haggling good-naturedly over where the best area of Queens is to live. Nature lovers root for Kew Gardens or Flushing Meadow, with their acres of green open space. Strong contenders too are Astoria and Long Island City, with their smattering of funky bars, delightful museums and view of the Manhattan skyline. The MoMA has recently moved into temporary accommodation in Long Island City. Art aficiona-

dos have long been a fan of PS1, the modern art wing of MoMA which is a Queens institution. Nothing, however, beats the secluded Isumu Noguchi Garden Museum, one of the city's best untapped cultural gems.

The mix of cultures in this borough is clear in the array of restaurants. Home to the city's largest Indian community, Jackson Heights has some of the best Indian food this city has to offer. Those with a hunger for something more Mediterranean could do worse then to take a walk through Astoria, stopping in at one of its Greek eateries or grabbing a slice of pizza at Sac's.

King Manor

Home of Rufus King, delegate to the Constitutional Convention. The oldest house in southeast Queens has been restored to reflect the early 19th century. Guided tours are available in English and Spanish. Exhibit galleries are devoted to local history and to village life during the early 1800s. *15003 Jamaica Ave. (bet. 150th and 153rd Sts.), (718) 206-0545, Admission $2 for adults, $1 for children, Cash Only,* (E)(J)(Z) *to Jamaica Center*

Weeping Beech Tree

Created in 1847 by Samuel Parsons, this neatly landscaped park, located in a residential section of Flushing, is a New York City "living landmark." The original beech from 1847 died but is survived by several "sons of a beech." *143-35 37th Ave. (bet. Parsons and Bowne), (718) 939-0647,* (7) *to Main St.*

World's Fair Ice Skating Rink

Near the Unisphere at Flushing Meadow Park, this is a popular attraction for kids of all ages. Great skating music, but the snack bar and vending machine food are pricey. *Open Oct. - March. Flushing Meadow Park, (718) 271-1996, $7 adults w/ $4 skate rental,* (7) *to Shea Stadium*

Bowne House

Historic home of John Bowne, whose trial for holding Quaker meetings helped establish religious freedom in America. The oldest building in Queens, it dates back to 1661. *37-01 Bowne St., Flushing, (718) 359-0528, Admission $2 adults, $1 students/children;* (7) *to Main St., walk two blocks east to Bowne, then one block north*

Cunningham Park

Open seven days a week from 6am to sunset, this park boasts two bocce courts, 25 baseball fields, 20 tennis courts, bike paths, a running path and two soccer fields. Also a popular site for picnics, summer concerts and operas. *196-00 Union Turnpike, (718) 217-6452,* (F)(R) *to 179th St., left at Midland Parkway, left on 188th St., right on Union Turnpike*

history

Queens was "sold" by the natives to the Dutch around 1683 and later named after their Queen. When Queens was consolidated into New York in 1898, much of it was still fenced off into farms, and in the eastern section of Queens, there was little desire to become a part of any city. A nonbinding referendum introduced to voters in 1984 found Flushing, Hempstead and other outlying areas solidly opposed to consolidation. This lack of a distinct borough community was mitigated by the secession of far eastern areas toward Nassau County as well as increasing urbanization, much of the original identity crisis remains today. This is neatly symbolized by Northern Boulevard, laid over old country pathways which led to once-rural eastern areas of Long Island. By the '20s and '30s, Queens was beginning to develop its current character, with tree-lined rows of modest brick and wood-frame houses.

Queens was well on its way to development, but it was the 1939 World's Fair that solidified its role as New York's primary locale for recreation, arenas and beautiful parks. Preparation for the Fair converted Flushing Meadows/ Corona Park from a dumpsite to the city's second largest landscaped recreation area. LaGuardia Airport and bridges were built, streets were widened and sports stadiums were constructed.

Queens has become the borough of choice for immigrants since the '60s, a place where newcomers can solidly establish themselves. In 1990, first-generation immigrants made up more than one-third of the two-million plus population of Queens, the greatest percentage in the five boroughs. Queens is also the most ethnically diverse borough. Although certain neighborhoods are identified with predominant ethnic groups, the extent to which these areas interact demonstrates that there is unity in diversity.

A Saturday in Queens

10 am

Get Some Grub

Get on the Queens-bound **R** train and ride it out to Steinway. Be warned, the subway ride to Queens is notorious for making unexplained changes on weekends. Walk up the street to an inexpensive cafe and gorge on the cheap.

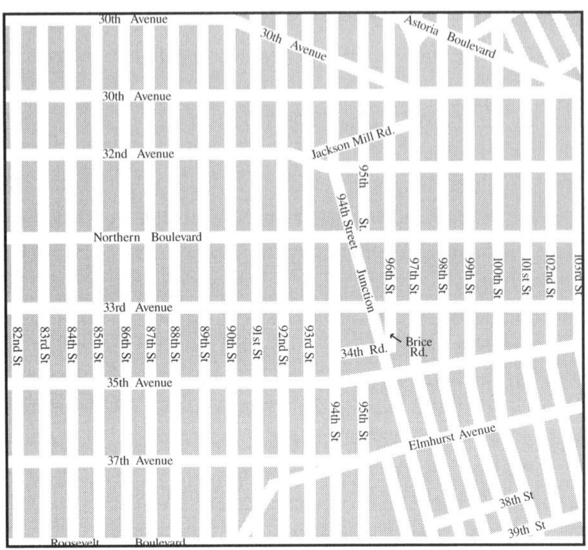

jackson heights area

12 pm

Watch Some Movies

Stroll across the street to the American Museum of the Moving Image, the only museum of its type in the country. For the price of an entry ticket on weekends, patrons can wander through the interactive exhibits on filmmaking and watch two retro flicks.
(See museum section)

2 pm   Oasis

Head over to 43rd Ave. The Noguchi Garden Museum is an island of tranquility in the bustling metropolis and perhaps the best small museum in the outer boroughs. It hosts an impressive collection of sculptures and art from the artist's long and auspicious career.
(718) 204-7088, www.noguchi.org

The Socrates Sculpture Park
Large-scale outdoor sculptures by artists from all over the world are free as well as public concerts, performance art, etc.
B'way (at Vernon), Long Island City,
(718) 956-1819, www.socratessculpturepark.org, Open 10am-sunset year-round, **N** *to Broadway*

The Unisphere
Created for the 1964 World's Fair, the Unisphere is an impressive model of our planet; its fountains provide welcome relief on a hot day. It was destroyed by a flying saucer in the film *Men in Black*.
Flushing Meadows/Corona Park, **7** *to Willets Point*

4 pm

Hungry?

Walking back along Broadway, stop into Sac's Pizza Place for some delicious thin crust pizza. Foodies should also spend some time shopping at the handful of ethnic delis that line this street. Greek and Italian delicacies are particularly plentiful. *7541 Broadway, (718) 204-5002*

6 pm

A Bollywood Flick

Stop in at the multiplex on Broadway at 36th Avenue and watch the latest, undoubtedly epic, Bollywood film. If the plot doesn't captivate, the singing and dancing numbers certainly will. Check out the star-crossed lovers darting in and out of tree groves playing peek-a-boo. In some ways it is like stepping back into the good old days of the Hollywood studios.

6 pm

Winding Down

Now walk back up to 36th Street and drink the night away at Tupiloe's to the late Goth sounds. This is a lively bar where the local artistes gather to party the night away far from the madding Manhattan crowd. *34-18 34th Avenue, (718) 707-9588,* **N** *to Broadway,* **R** *to Steinway*

astoria area

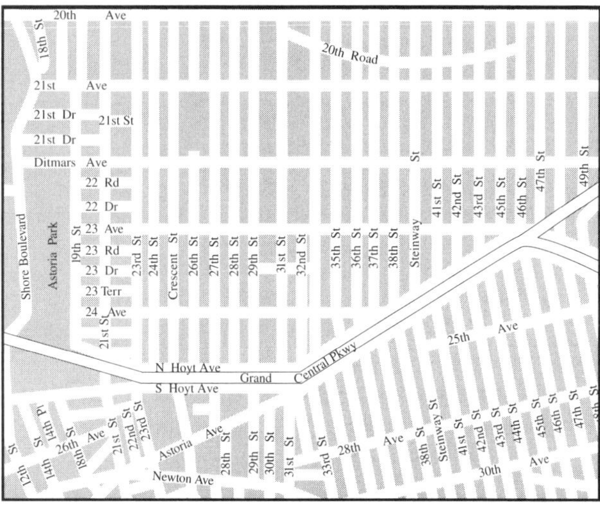

brooklyn

Some diehard Manhattanites still turn pale at the suggestion of crossing over the river into Brooklyn. Most discover that they do not automatically implode once in the outer boroughs. Hypnotized by the seductive Brooklyn whispers of lower rent, more space and hardwood floors, many awaken to find they have moved into the neighborhood. More and more of these converts can be found these days. For them and many others, Brooklyn has become the new Manhattan.

When most outsiders refer to Brooklyn, however, what they are really taking about is a handful of neighborhoods that have become popular over the past five years or so. Williamsburg, Fort Green, Park Slope, Brooklyn Heights, Cobble Hill, Carroll Gardens, DUMBO and Prospect Heights have all undergone a transformation of sorts. Manhattanites realized that their humanities educations and subsequent salaries meant they could no longer keep themselves in micro beer and take-out Thai food to which they had become accustomed.

They discovered the cheaper rents of Brooklyn and started moving across the river in droves. With them came the requisite hip bars, restaurants, fashionable stores and entertainment venues. The result is that many living out here now find very little to miss in Manhattan - and housing prices have soared accordingly. Each of these areas now specializes in their own particular brand of hipsters. Emaciated indie kids who haven't read Kafka but act as though they might are a dime a dozen in Williamsburg. The lure of Prospect Park and old brownstones drew the late 20's latté sipping yuppies to Park Slope. Dumbo is making a name for itself amongst artistes.

This new found image of Brooklyn as the hipster's playground is only one facet of the borough. Those with the patience and inclination will find much more that appeals in Brooklyn than just the latest retro-fit drinking hole. A trip out to Coney Island is always worth the lengthy subway ride, particularly on Friday nights in summer when the treats include margaritas, fair rides and a free fireworks display.

Brooklyn Bridge

Bike, blade or walk across the bridge on the well-maintained pedestrian path high above the traffic. **2 3** *to Clark St.,* **A C** *to High St.*

Coney Island Boardwalk

A stroll down the famous boardwalk presents a stunning view of the Atlantic shore and visions of scantily clad women in heels, wizened Russian card-players and children waving corn dogs. Walk out onto the pier, where fishermen haul in ocean fish and spiny crabs. The beach is passable, but trash mars the effect on busier days. *www.coney-island.com* **B D F** *to Stillwell Ave./Coney Island*

Brooklyn Heights Promenade

Playgrounds, room for rollerblading and benches draw crowds of all ages, but the main attraction is the stunning view of Manhattan. *Montague Terrace,* **M N R** *to Court St.,* **2 3** *to Clark St.*

New York Aquarium

Various exhibits and habitats present marine life in both indoor tanks and outdoor pools. *www.nyaquarium.com,* **D F** *to West 8th St./New York Aquarium*

Prospect Park

Brooklyn's expansive central park borders many different neighborhoods whose residents fill the park for cookouts, sports, fishing, and tailgating. In June, the "Celebrate Brooklyn" festival holds weekend events in the Prospect Park bandshell, where a $3 "contribution" grants admission to concerts by the likes of Dee Dee Bridgewater, Allen Toussaint, and Don Bryan. *From Grand Army Plaza to Fort Hamilton Parkway, (718) 965-8951, www.prospectpark.org,* **2 3** *to Grand Army Plaza,* &

Botanic Gardens

Unwind at one of the many gardens situated on the 52 acres, including the Shakespeare and Conservatory Garden, the Pond Garden, and Celebrity Park's Herb Garden. *Entrances at Flatbush Ave. and Empire Blvd. and at Washington Ave. and Eastern Parkway, (718) 623-7200, www.bbg.org, Admission $3,* **2 3** *to Eastern Parkway*

Fort Greene Park

A trip through this park is both relaxing and historical. Visitors can view Martyr's Monument, designed by Olmstead and Vaux. The park is dedicated to Continental soldiers on British prison ships in Wallabout Bay. *Myrtle and DeKalb Aves, and St. Edwards and Cumberland Streets, Admission Free,* **D M N Q R** *to DeKalb Ave.*

history

Like Manhattan, the borough of Brooklyn was originally settled by Dutch explorers. When they purchased land from the Canarsie Native Americans and linked together three villages in 1642, the new community called itself "Breuckelen" or "Broken Land."

Brooklyn remained rural until the 1800s, when large numbers of immigrants began to settle in the area. By 1814, Robert Fulton's steamboat service established regular transportation to Manhattan and helped develop stronger commercial links between the two island communities.

In 1833, Brooklyn was asked to join New York, but refused and incorporated itself as a separate city the next year. It remained an independent city even after the opening of the Brooklyn Bridge in 1883, an event which altered Brooklyn's social and economic geography more than any other. Brooklyn became a borough of Greater New York in 1898, a decision called "The Great Mistake" by writer Pete Hamill.

Brooklyn remains New York's most populous borough and maintains its own flavor and symbolic autonomy. Brooklyn's sense of self has nonetheless been subject to many vicissitudes, exemplified by the fate of the Dodgers, who won the World Series for the first time ever in 1955 and moved to Los Angeles two years later. Brooklyn is most fondly thought of as a hometown by the millions who have grown up here.

A Saturday in Brooklyn

9 am

A Bridge Too Far

Start the day with a walk across the historic Brooklyn Bridge. One of the greatest architectural structures in the city, it even attracted the attention of Walt Whitman. The opening of the bridge heralded the death of Brooklyn as an independent city, as it bowed under the weight of Manhattan's commercial might.

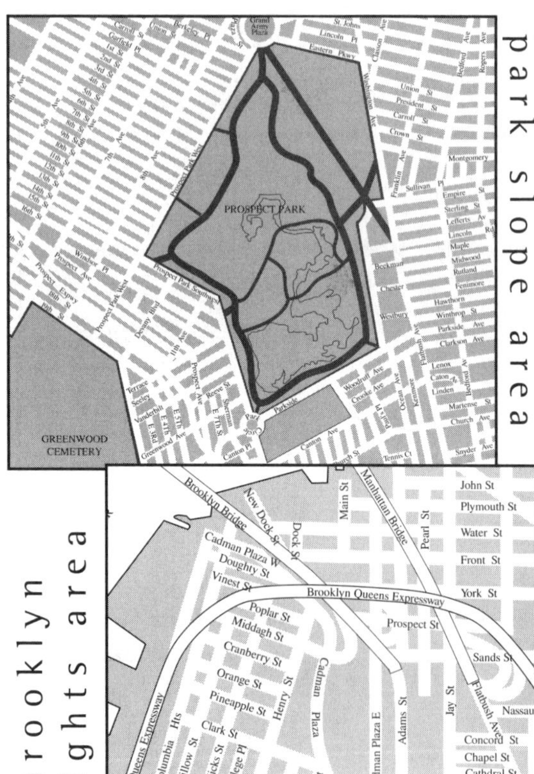

10 am

Shmeared

Stop for coffee and a bagel in the historic Brooklyn Heights. Take your food to go and walk along along the river enjoying the scenic views of Manhattan's skyline.

11 am

Your Cup Runneth Over

Head over to Jay Street - Borough Hall, and jump on the **F** train heading further into Brooklyn. Get off at the 7th Avenue stop, and walk out onto the main drag of Park Slope. Spend some time in this area browsing through local bookstores. This tends to be a literary neighborhood, so there are plenty of books to be found, although they can be on the pricey side.

3 pm

Get Cultured

Culture buffs should stop off at the Brooklyn Museum of Art. One of the best art museums in the outer boroughs, there is always some interesting new exhibit, and the permanent collection alone is worth the price of admission.
(718) 638-5000 x234, www.brooklynart.org, ❶❷ *to Eastern Pkwy*

brighton beach area

5 pm

Pucker Up at Black Betty

Known for its swinging and non-seedy singles scene, this bar also has a great restaurant attached. Then stop in the bar for one of the best margaritas this side of the border.
366 Metropolitan Ave., (718) 599-0243

7 pm

Brooklyn in the House

Check out the nightlife in Williamsburg. There is plenty to be found, and it would be foolish to limit intrepid explorations to one location. Some may choose to hang with the hipsters at Enid's. Others will enjoy the quieter pleasures of the Turkeys Nest (*94 Bedford Ave., no phone*). Those who are in the mood to dance the night away might want to check out the Luxx bar (*256 Brand St., (718) 599-1000*). Whatever your tipple, Williamsburg is bound to provide. Remember the ❶ train is your ticket back to Manhattan.
(See Nightlife Section)

{cheap *thrills*}

staten island

As the neglected borough of New York, Staten Island has a lot to grumble about. Not only was it the dumping ground for the city's garbage for years but, despite its 400,000 plus population, the majority of the city insists on acting as though no one in their right minds would live there. For locals, Staten Island offers proximity to yet isolation from the city.

Staten Island has been fighting a long and largely unsuccessful battle for succession from the city. Predominantly Irish and Italian, locals tend to come from families who have been here for years. Rare is the brave soul who actually relocates out here. "I'm thinking of moving to Staten Island," is not a popular refrain, even with the city's ongoing housing crunch. For those who do move, the area offers all the traditional advantages and disadvantages of suburbia. Communities are small, strip malls a common architectural motif and no one remains a stranger for long.

These Islanders know that their island is one of the city's untapped resources. It brims with undiscovered sights, restaurants and museums, not to mention a perfect view of the Statue of Liberty, Ellis Island and the downtown skyline.

Hipsters beware, however, the island lacks for a happening

nightlife. The few clubs that do exist tend to cater to a younger crowd, and the bars lack a Manhattan sheen. If you're looking for a brawny working man or woman, however, Staten Island has its fill of beautiful people too.

Fresh Kills, the nation's largest dump, was actually shut down years ago, although it reopened briefly after September 11 for the refuse from Ground Zero. The city has yet to come up with a new and better solution to its waste crisis.

What the area lacks for in nightlife it makes up for in recreation. Staten Island may house the best spots for day trips. When city dwellers whine about needing a break from the daily grind, most remain

unaware that their salvation is only a free ferry ride away. For those sick of cement sidewalks and dying to feel the sand beneath their feet, Staten Island offers a selection of surpassingly clean beaches. South Beach, Tottenville Beach and Midland Beach are all worth a visit. Only the supremely foolish would consider a swim or paddling in the waters, however. Sharks have nothing on the toxicity of the sea surrounding New York City.

Check out one of the island's handful of spacious and impressive gardens. The New York Chinese Scholar's Garden remains one of the city's little known secrets. A maze of rocks, fishponds, flowers and pagodas, it is a true haven for those seeking peace of mind.

Alice Austen House

This ivy-covered Victorian cottage called Clear Comfort was home to Alice Austen, the Emily Dickinson of turn-of-the-century photography. Although Austen took more than 8000 photographs of daily life from 1884-1934, she went undiscovered most of her life. The view is breathtaking. *2 Hylan Blvd., (718) 816-4506,* **S51** *from Whitehall Ferry*

Snug Harbor Cultural Center

This National Landmark is one of the city's great quiet retreats, with historical buildings, gardens and exhibition sites. The Newhouse Center for Contemporary Art is an exhibition space and concert hall. The Staten Island Botanical Garden contains butterfly gardens, a bonsai collection and a fragrance garden. Gardens are open from 9am 'til dusk and admission is free. *1000 Richmond Terrace, (718) 448-2500, www.snug-harbor.org,* **S40** *from Whitehall Ferry*

Historic Richmond Town

This exhibit documents local history and includes, among other historic buildings, the oldest surviving elementary school in America. Volunteers dress in 18th century costume to re-enact everything from candle-making to war declarations. *441 Clarke Ave., (718) 351-1611,* **S74** *from Whitehall Ferry*

South Beach

The fourth longest boardwalk in the country is packed with cyclists, but this is primarily a bathing beach for families and sun worshipers admiring the great view of the Verrazano Narrows Bridge. **S51** *from Whitehall*

Jacques Marchais Center of Tibetan Art

Housed in a two-story stone building resembling a Buddhist mountain temple and set in a terraced garden overlooking NY Bay, the center features a collection of Tibetan and Buddhist art and ethnography. The Dalai Lama came in 1991. *338 Lighthouse Ave., Wednesday through Sunday 1-5pm, (718) 987-3500, www.tibetanmuseum.com,* **S70** *to Whitehall Ferry*

history

Henry Hudson gave" Staaten Eylandt" its original name in 1609, when he sailed into the bay which now bears his name. In 1639, the Dutch opened Staten Island to colonization, but the area remained difficult to settle due to conflicts with native inhabitants. There were constant wars between Native Americans and the Dutch. Staten Island became a province of New Jersey after the British took control of NY in 1664. The island was then known as Richmond County, after the Duke of Richmond, a son of Charles II, until Manhattan won it back in a sailing race in the Lower Bay at the end of the 17th century.

Even after becoming part of NY, Staten Island was reachable only by private boat and remained largely a secluded place for fishing and farming until 1713, when a public ferry began carrying passengers to and from Manhattan and continues to do so today.

But Staten Island's independent streak has persisted even since it joined NYC in 1898 and saw the 1964 construction of the Verrazano Narrows bridge, which connects it to Brooklyn. Fed up with garbage dumps filled largely with trash from elsewhere, the citizens of Richmond voted in 1993, albeit unsuccessfully, to secede from NYC.

Staten Island has been the residence of many of Gambino family (one of NY's five mafia families), as well was the home of mobsters Paul Castellano, John Gotti and Sammy "the Bull" Gravano. Other celebrities who have called Staten Island home are Christina Aguilera, Joan Baez, Emilio Estevez, Paul Newman, Martin Sheen and rappers Wu-Tang Clan.

A Saturday in Staten Island

9 am
Island Hopping

Start out with breakfast on the ferry- a donut will do. Head over to a tour at Historic St. George, the epicenter of historic Staten Island (walking distance from the ferry terminal).

11 am
Find Culture

Next, see if the Staten Island Yankees are playing (walking distance from St. George). If not, head left (a short car or taxi ride) to Snug Harbor's Cultural Center. Usually there are kid-friendly activities and fairs year-round. *1000 Richmond Terrace (bet. Tysen and Snug Harbor Rd), (718) 448-2500, www.snug-harbor.org*

12 pm
Serenity

Hop on a bus to the Chinese Scholar's Garden midday, and enjoy the serenity and the inexpensive lunch. *Staten Island Botanical Garden, 1000 Richmond Terrace, (718) 273-8200*

2 pm
Revolution Time

Head up to the Conference House in Tottenville (on the opposite side of the island, hop on the subway) and explore the history of Staten Island. *7455 Hylan Blvd., (718) 984-2086*

4 pm
Talk Trash

Take a car to the Staten Island Expressway towards the bridge and get a glimpse of Fresh Kills Landfill, which is rumored to be visible from space.

5 pm
Tuscany on the Island

For dinner, enjoy authentic Tuscan food at Basilio Inn, a 19th century stable which is known for its fresh dishes. *Galesville Ct. (off Pond Ave.), (718) 720-6835*

The Ferry
Forget the Circle Line; the Staten Island Ferry is now absolutely free and also boasts excellent musicians below deck. *Docks at the foot of Whitehall St., 806-6940,* ① *to South Ferry,* ④⑤ *to Bowling Green, or* ⓃⓇ *to Whitehall St.*

Most Famous Ices
Ralph's Ices
From the traditional lemon to more exotic flavors like honeydew, these ices are the perfect warm weather treat. *501 Port Richmond Ave., 718-273-3675, www.ralphsices.com,* ① *to South Ferry, Staten Island Ferry to S44*

NYC shopping ⟶ 118

features:

listings:

New York is Cloud Nine for shoppers. In this fast-paced fashion metropolis, anything is available, from anywhere, for any price. Despite the growing "mallification" of Manhattan specialty shops and boutiques, they continue to thrive alongside these retail flagships. New York continues to have the greatest concentration of one-of-a-kind stores in the world. Despite September 11th and its influence on the downtown area, New York remains the pinnacle of fashion and shopping. New York strives to please all tastes and all wallet sizes. Shopping in New York is like jumping into a private fantasy world, where you can try on new clothes and personas that you probably wouldn't recognize yourself in.

Whatever the shopper's fetish, it will be indulged here. For gourmands, the food and spice shops here rival Harrod's. Shoes are incredible. Sexy or even Goth-like lingerie, no problem. Film and comic strip buffs will find stores that cater to their tastes. The world's music is on display here. The list is exhaustive, and we can't cover the spectrum here, but we guarantee you will find what you are looking for (even if you have to pay a little more for it).

Each neighborhood with its unique 'flavor' provides for New York's shopping diversity. Fifth Avenue has been nicknamed "Millionaire's Row," and the East Side represents the high end of shopping with its elegant windows and its flagship names. SoHo is Manhattan's young and hip end, while the Lower East Side embodies its bargain side. Chelsea displays the island's artsy side. NoLIta (North of Little Italy) is New York's up-and-comer: tiny boutiques have become big business in this cutting-edge shopping neighborhood. New York shopping never stops transforming to please its finicky shopaholics.

New York shopping is worth doing even with an empty wallet. Manhattan's greatest shopping lure is 'The Bargain.' Vintage and thrift stores as well as flea markets make for a fun and fruitful treasure hunt.

New York, a city without borders, has plenty of shopping not confined to four walls. Remember *9 1/2 Weeks* where Kim Basinger meets her creepy boyfriend in an open-air market? Chances are, you'll find more bargains than romantic partners, but open-air markets (a.k.a. flea markets) offer classic kitsch, bizarre Americana and designer duds. Puppets will be lying next to Persian carpets, designer make-up next to sneakers with wheels for kids on the go and D-cup bras will swing in the breeze next to bamboo shoot planters. Give a market a little time, and it will present you with a find or two.

Vintage shops have been making a comeback in recent years, with many wealthy New Yorkers throwing away classic threads that stand the test of time. Stores like Housing Works takes these throw-offs and offers them to discriminating shoppers willing to mend a loose seam or two for the chance to wear Dior. Many a star-let seeking something unique has sent her personal shopper to these stores, looking for just that detailing that will set her apart at the next Hollywood event. Vintage isn't always cheap, but it is always an adven-ture in style.

The salespeople here aren't usually pushy and once you narrow down the six outfits you want to try on, you can turn the humble dressing room into your private catwalk. Try on clothes you won't find in Columbus, try on bathing suits you can't wear in Daytona, try on shoes you can't walk more than a block in. So try on that see-through dress or that flashy muscle shirt, go ahead. Be Clooney, be Madonna for a minute. You won't have witnesses, unless you want them. Here, nobody cares and neither will you.

Best of the Best

Best Women's Clothing
1. Macy's Herald Square
2. Century 21
3. Anthropologie
4. Club Monaco
5. Urban Outfitters

Best Gourmet Grocery
1. Dean & Deluca
2. Balducci's
3. Zabar's
4. Union Square Greenmarket
5. Fairway Marketplace

Best Offbeat finds
1. Century 21
2. Daffy's
3. Betsey Johnson's
4. Urban Outfitters
5. Patricia Field's

Best Music Store
1. Other Music
2. Virgin Megastore
3. J&R Music World
4. Mondo Kim's
5. Tower Records

Best Vintage Clothing
1. Screaming Mimi's
2. What Comes Around Goes Around
3. Annex Antique Fair & Flea Market

Shopping with 4 Fashionable Gals...

For four seasons now, the women from *Sex and the City* have been the source of our fashion desires with their amazing fashion sense. Carrie (Sarah Jessica Parker), Samantha (Kim Catrall), Charlotte (Kristin Davis), and Miranda (Cynthia Nixon) each have their own individual style but always appear to be ready for the catwalk. Longtime New Yorkers know that Carrie could never afford that fabulous apartment, those fabulous shoes and that fabulous wardrobe on a columnist's salary, but then again, reality is dull. Carrie, especially, possesses every party girl's dream closet, home to her high-waist poodle skirts, flower-pinned tees, and her endless supply of fabulous accessories - and Sarah Jessica Parker gets to keep it all! Middle America may wonder where on earth they could wear such things, but millions of women envy Carrie for her dare to bare. But where do these fashion-savvy New Yorkers shop?

Jimmy Choo
645 Fifth Ave. (212) 593-0800
The London shoe designer's ultra-chic stilettos compare with Manolo Blahnik's in beauty, sexiness, and alas, price.

Intermix
125 Fifth Ave.
(212) 533-9720;
1003 Madison Ave.
(212) 249-7858;
210 Columbus Ave.
(212) 769 -9116
Since its opening in 1994, this Flatiron-based boutique has become a mini-fashion empire with satellite stores in Boston, South Beach, and Tokyo. You can find Carrie's must-have Mia & Lizzie jewelry exclusively at the Madison Ave. store.

Patricia Field Boutique
10 East 8th St. (212) 254-1699
Patricia Field, the costume designer for the show, has her own mystical Greenwich Village boutique, which has been a shopping haven for the fashion in-the-know crowd for almost 30 years. Drag queens, rock stars, club kids and New York "it" girls like Carrie flock here to get the latest outfits and must-have accessories. The Mia & Lizzie diamond horseshoe necklaces Carrie wears this season are available here on special delivery. You can find such "white trash charms" as Carrie's third season lightning bolt necklace, some "dare-to-wear" outfits that few but Carrie can pull off. Check out the Patricia Field website (www.patriciafield.com) for more info.

Furniture Company
818 Greenwich St.
(212) 352-2010
Carrie meets furniture designer and last season's love Aidan at this store tucked away in the West Village. The designs are elegant, comfortable, and absolutely fabulous.

Tiffany & Co.
727 Fifth Ave. (212) 775-8000
Trey takes Charlotte here to find her impressive wedding ring. Even though her marriage was not as flawless, Tiffany's diamonds are sure to be.

ABC Carpet & Home
888 Broadway
(212) 473-3000
The SATC women spend many shopping expeditions at this mecca of home furnishings. As you might guess, these women change apartments and décor almost as often as their men. The ten-story emporium carries an eclectic selection of unique items for any room, from 19th century Chinese wedding chests to luxurious Italian linens. ABC is the store of choice for high-end home decorators.

For more information on the women's' favorite shopping spots, check out
http://www.hbo.com/ city/cmp/city_style/address_boo k_shopping.html

Sex and the City Bus Tour

iMar and Greyhound let you follow in the fancy footsteps of Carrie & Company: where they drink, where they shop, and where they gossip. This three-hour tour twists and turns through the Sex and the City women's stomping grounds, visiting the gyms where they work out, the restaurants where they wine and dine, the shops where Carrie spends her rent money. Live the chic chick life on a bus, hopping on and off to catch a glimpse into the lives of four of New York's most eligible bachelorettes. The tour costs $30, but is well worth it.

Manolo Blahnik
31 West 54th St.
(212) 582-3007
In the dream life of foot-fetishists, Manolo Blahnik's ultra-sexy, elegant stilettos reign supreme. Despite the steep prices, shoe addicts Carrie and Charlotte indulge in a 'fab' pair on a regular basis. Carrie hits the store when needing to outshine arch-nemesis Natasha. In the third season, she even gets mugged for her favorite pair of Manolo Blahnik's (on sale for 40% off).

Decorating a tiny dorm room and adding some personal flair to the institutional walls may seem tricky, but there are many ways to maximize any room's character. The many houseware stores around the city are sure to have items that will help you get your room tidy and mirror your own decorating flavor.

Crate and Barrel (650 Madison Ave., (212) 308-0011) can be a good first stop for organizing and accessorizing. Here, you can find beautiful wicker baskets, Plexiglas organizers, and many home accessories. For about $30, one can purchase folding and stackable bookshelves, which are very practical when in need of more space (www.crate-andbarrel.com). **Pottery Barn** (600 Broadway, (212) 219-2420) holds some fancier items, such as colorful throw rugs and velvet or canvas wing chairs and sofas (*www.potterybarn.com*). If you are looking for more young and funky furniture and accessories, drop by **Dom USA** (382 W. Broadway, (212) 334-5580) where you can find inflatable furniture and some trendy neon-colored knickknacks. Check out **Organize Everything** (www.organize-everything.com) they will do just as they say: organize everything.

ABC Carpet and Home (881 Broadway, (212) 473-3000) holds ten floors of houseware items and represents the high-end houseware department stores. This emporium carries an eclectic selection of unique items for any chosen décor. Despite the high prices, a little basket or some linen might help you pull the room together. Or, after decorating your room and achieving the status of pro interior decorator, simply drop by to revel in the beauty and luxury of these items (www.abchome.com). **Bed, Bath, and Beyond** (620 Sixth Ave., (212) 255- 3550) is ABC Carpet and Home's more moderate equivalent. It holds an array of all things domestic and fits the bill for convenience by having everything in one store. If you are the one-stop-find-all type of shopper, this is the place for you (*www.bedbathandbeyond.com*).

To bring character to your room, drop by **Just Bulbs** (936 Broadway, (212) 228-7820) where you can find, as the name says it, light bulbs. These light bulbs do not compare to the 100-Watt bulbs of **Columbia Hardware** (2905 Broadway, (212) 662-2150): these bulbs are great for decorations, gifts, and specific holidays. **Fish's Eddy** (2176 Broadway, (212) 873-8819) is also home to some great finds: this shop sells commercial dishes and glasses bearing the logos of the restaurants from whence they came for cheap prices.

After getting all the items it takes to survive, freshman year comes the time to make one's room one's own, by imbuing it with one's own twist. Photos, posters, and collages are three ways to liven up your room walls. Stop by **Jerry Ohlinger's Movie Store** (242 W. 14th st., (212) 988-0869) to find old publicity shots, movie stills, posters, and playbills that would knockout any movie-buff and make for great wall decoration, or check out some Bleecker Street stores.

But no matter where you go to decorate your room, remember to make it your own. One's favorite color sheets, stuffed animal, or ripped Star Wars poster...As long as it's you, it works. Some decorators recommend following a common theme when decorating a room (retro, Asian, art-deco, spring), but YOU are the common theme.

Queens has the highest percentage of foreign-born people in the United States, and Astoria is no exception. The area south of 74th Avenue is mainly Indian and Pakistani, and the area north of 84th Avenue is largely Asian. But this stretch of Astoria is Colombian, Ecuadorian and Mexican and all their cuisines and cultures mingle in this vital borough of New York. In one block you will find trendy clothes fit for a music video, gold chains straight from a Saturday Night Fever movie, and Cuban sandwiches next to a bakery selling corn cakes (arepas). English isn't spoken everywhere, but who cares once you spot the bargains to be found here. Eat up, shop till you drop and have a great time experiencing the Other New York! Subway: ❶❷ to 74th or 80th Street

Jackson Heights Florists
81-18 Roosevelt Avenue, 718/429-1800
Jackson Heights, NY 11372-6746
8 – 6:30 Mon – Sa
9 – 5 pm Su
This flower shop has been around a long time, since the days of an all-Irish neighbor-hood. They'll even do funeral arrangements in the shape of a shamrock, a baseball diamond, a flag or a piano ($250-$900). They also have exotic plants like the zebra plant (it's yellow and green, but you get the picture).

Ilan Boutique
80-01 Roosevelt Avenue, 718/476-0122
Jackson Heights, NY 11372
10 – 7:30 pm Mo – Sa
12 – 6 pm Su
This boutique carries the cutest women's clothing for under $20.

Casa Bella Discount
40-12 82nd Street, 718/639-6669
Jackson Heights, NY 11373
10:30 – 8 every day
This is the perfect place for the shopper on lay-away. They will take any plan for any furni-ture. No money? No problem! They have everything from cribs to matresses to Murphy beds and bassinets. A couch runs $700, a bedroom set runs $1,500.

Leather Land USA
3757 82nd Street, (718) 565-1835
Jackson Heights, NY 11372
9:30 – 8:30 pm Mo – Sa
10:30 – 8 pm Su
Leather Land has a fine selec-tion of fine leather for fine women. Their goods are soft, supple and pleasing to the eye. You can't do much better in Manhattan, especially for prices as low as $140 for a full-length jacket. Their sign proclaims them Bueno, Bonito y Barato (good, cute and cheap).

Superior Pharmacy
78-14 Roosevelt Avenue, (718) 478-1135
Jackson Heights, NY 11372
8 – 8 pm Mo – Sa
9 – 6 pm Su
Superior has all types of female beauty products, gifts and tchotchkes. Their hair products are extensive, including coconut, garlic, aloe, chamomile and avocado conditioners.

Pretty Girl
37-49 82nd Street, (718) 507-6785
Queens, NY 11372
10 – 8 pm Mo – Sa
11 – 7 pm Su
Pretty Girl will make a pretty

out of any girl. Their delicate and feminine tops and jeans will have any woman feeling like a blushing teenager again.

Picanteria y Carniceria Don Alex
32-04 36th Avenue, (718) 482-7461
Long Island City, NY 11106
9 - 9 pm Mon - Sa
9 - 6 pm Su
This shop is a treasure trove of spices for cooking and meat tenderizing. It's title literally means "spicery and butcher."

Los Paisanos
79-16 Roosevelt Avenue, (718) 898-4141
Jackson Heights, NY 11372
9 - 2 am every day
Los Paisanos specializes in Central American goods, as well as Mexican, Colombian and Peruvian items such as corvine picudo. They have Cuzco beer, $30 t-shirts proclaiming national pride and various spices and sauces with names like "Inca." They have over five types of corn, three types of beans and spices such as flax seed and anise stars.

MiraCali Bakery
76-04 Roosevelt Avenue, (718) 779-7175
Jackson Heights, NY 11372
6 am - 8 pm daily
This is a pure Colombian bakery, with various sweet buns, sausages stuffed with cheese, corn biscuits, blood sausage and fried pork on a bone.

Nivel Musical
(718) 424-1230
9 - 9 Mo - Sa
10 - 9 Su
This store has mostly Colombian music, including cumbias, boleros, sonideras and rock en espanol.

Galleria Home Décor
37-54 82nd Street, (718) 335-1115
Jackson Heights, NY 11372
10 - 8 pm every day
This is the place for $10 toilet seats, curtains galore, bed covers and porcelain light fixtures. Galleria isn't Martha Stewart, but then, who is?

Don Juan Jewelry Inc.
81-07 Roosevelt Ave., (718) 651-1680
Jackson Heights, NY 11372
12 - 7 pm Mo - Sa
Don Juan specializes in diamonds, and they put them on medallions, anklets and earrings any way you like. They will also custom-make some earrings, a ring or a necklace with your name written in bold cursive script.

Plaza Dama
37-44 82nd Street,
(718) 507-5533
Jackson Heights, NY 11372
10 - 8 pm Mon - Fri and Sun
10 - 8:30 pm Sa
Plaza Dama is the cutest little shop for crop tops, baby-doll shirts and peasant skirts. Everything here will wear well in Manhattan too, and the price is right.

Botanica Caridad del Cobre
81-18 Roosevelt Avenue, 2nd Floor, (718) 639-6004
Jackson Heights, NY 11372
9 - 6:30 pm every day
Caridad is a one-stop Catholic shop. They have statues of Maria, power sprays (ask them) and incense, tarot cards, books on everything from divination to Wicca, mystic baths, floor wash, various house blessings and fresh herbs. The service is lovely and the shop is kept clean and light.

In New York there are men who throw around the names of tony designers as freely as they throw around the names of their favorite baseball players. The typical reaction of a recent male emigrant to our city is of scorn or resignation, or perhaps both; "Even if I could afford it...why would I care?" Fear not, men; you do not need the disposable income of an investment banker to make a fashion statement.

The best place to start trying to look New York is at H&M (34th St. - Herald Sq., (646) 473-1164). The most relentless designer imitator around, H&M manages to spare every expense, allowing you—for the price of a single high-end designer item at, say,

Bergdorf's, to walk out with bags full of clothes that will fool a lot of people. But H&M is not a cure-all. Sweaters, yes; t-shirts and jeans, emphatically yes; $69 "suits" that were probably made from dyed toilet paper, no. A little H&M will go a long way.

For a little more color in your palette, head not to Banana Republic but to their European counterparts, **Zara** (750 Lexington Ave., (212) 754-1120) and **Benetton** (597 E. 5th Ave., (212) 317-2501). You may remember Benetton from their ads that featured emaciated, unpressed models sporting political statements. Don't let it discourage you. If you prefer sportier outfits that will make you an 'all-American', head down to **Abercrombie and Fitch** (199 Water Street at South Street Seaport, (212) 809-9000). From Wall Street to Greenpoint, A&F is the clothier of choice for all income levels.

Accessories? For classic yet aggressively styled watches, shoes, and belts, head over to **Kenneth Cole** (130 E. 57th St., (212) 688-1670. If you are thinking cheaper and trendier (but riskier and less durable), shoes and belts are available in dozens of "Italian" leather stores along West 8th Street, while passable watches are available for $10 on the street all over midtown Manhattan. Select with care, however. If you're not feeling adventurous and would prefer a "real" store, you can get some stylish, cheap, and highly versatile sneakers at **Diesel** (770 Lexington Ave., (212) 308-0055) - the only good value in a store that gives new meaning to the phrase "sticker shock". Diesel's baggy jeans are also built to last.

For dressier clothing, start by heading over to **Filene's Basement** (620 Sixth Ave., (212) 620-3100). Since 90% of their merchandise merits Salvation-Army-style billing, this takes some patience. Yet when you find a Gianfranco Ferre dress shirt for $24 or Zegna dress pants for the absurd price of $52-all that wading through a huge collection of 1993 Reebok tracksuits will be quite worth it.

Once you've exhausted the meager offerings at Filene's, make your way over to **Century 21** (23 Cortlandt St., (212) 227-9092), the absolute top of New York discount department stores. The bargains at Century are less shocking than those at Filene's but they are far more numerous, and the merchandise on the whole is of higher quality. Here you can find a classic power suit from formalwear titans Giorgio Armani and Hugo Boss. Or, if you're looking for something sportier, seasonal selections from ultra-hip European lines like Bikkemberg and Dolce & Gabbana -all at semi-reasonable prices.

If you want the ultra-preppy jock look, you cannot be without a few Izod polo shirts from **Lacoste** (543 Madison Ave. (212) 750-8115). For the young investment banker with a Master of the Universe attitude, a new **Thomas Pink** (520 Madison Ave. (212) 838-1928) dress shirt will have the competition sweating. Even Regis Philbin wears bright shirts with matching monochromatic ties. And of course, if you want everything under one roof - the hottest of the hot - and can face prices that rise through the stratosphere, **Barney's** (660 Madison Ave. (212) 826-8900) will become your new best friend. The city is waiting for you. Start shopping.

FASHION WEEK

Every September and February, over a hundred fashion designers from all over the world gather at Bryant Park to present their latest. Traditionally, NY is the first of the four fashion capitals (NY, London, Milan and Paris) to host its Fashion Week. For September 2002, however, because New York's designated week (Sept. 12-17) conflicts with the anniversary of the attack on the World Trade Center, London has agreed to swap dates (Sept. 18-23) with NY and go first.

The show is arranged by 7th on Sixth, an association that organizes and arranges nearly all American runway shows. Since it's inception in 1993, 7th on Sixth has produced 25 seasons and over 1,000 shows. To stage a runway show, designers must pay $200 - 500 thousand dollars. With all the media coverage, 7th on Sixth producers say that one fashion show is like placing an ad in Vogue every month for a year.

Under the big, otherworldly white tents that will fill up Bryant Park this year, expect to see a return to luxury and glamour after a year of fashion austerity. Designers seem to agree: Fall 2002 is all about a celebration of new money. You'll see lavish fabrics – fur-trimmed hourglass suits, rabbit fur vests and dyed shearling coats. Despite

Prada comes to SoHo

The new SoHo Prada store, whose star-studded grand opening was on everybody in the fashion-know-know's lips, epitomizes this blend. The high-fashion store is located in the former SoHo Guggenheim. The two-floor store was designed by architect Rem Koolhaas and the Office for Metropolitan Architecture. The store includes a huge cylindrical glass elevator, a ramp leading into an amphitheater and old bookcases gliding on tracks. The Dutch architect has made the changing rooms interactive by enabling the shopper to dim a light by the touch of a finger and surf the Prada database for items that might have escaped the rack. This typifies a distinctly NY phenomenon, a shop that deserves the same awe as a museum.

the seeming frivolousness of the fashion world, this year the industry has proved itself to be more grounded than anyone thought. Expect a big emphasis on signature styles – a return to black and white, logo appreciation and uptown chic.

In a year where the fashion industry has struggled, this year's Fashion Week will bea reminder that interest in something as insignificant as clothes can still thrive. The show will go on.

LISTINGS

ART SUPPLY

Lee's Art Shop
Paints and brushes are just the beginning at this valuable resource for artists who work in all mediums. Drafting supplies, silk screens, a good selection of pens and stationery, and a framing service.
220 West 57th St. (bet. Seventh Ave. and Broadway), (212) 247-0110. Open M-F 9am-7pm, Sa 9:30am-6:30pm, Su 12pm-5:30pm. MC, V, Am Ex, (A) (C) (D) (1) (2) *to 59th/Columbus Circle, NRW to 57th* &

Pearl Paint
A labyrinthine motherlode of supplies for all media, these four crowded floors offer one-stop shopping for students and pros. Staff members will assist you in investigating nooks and crannies. The crotchety warehouse elevator serves as a reminder of the gritty conditions that once characterized everything below Canal Street.
308 Canal St. (bet. Church St. and Broadway), (212) 431-7932. Open M-f 9am-7pm, Sa 9am-6:30pm, Su 9am-6pm. AmEx, D, (N) (R) (Q) (W) (J) (M) (Z) (A) (C) (E) (1) (6) (2) *to Canal St.*

Sam Flax
Whether in search of canvas or some stylish wrapping paper, shoppers will find it all at this well-staffed store. Check out the sale section in back for some good furniture bargains.
20th St. (bet. Fifth and Sixth Aves.), (212) 620-3038. Open M-F 9am-7pm, Sa 10am-7pm, Su 10am-5pm. MC, V, AmEx, (F) (V) *to 23rd Street* &

CLOTHING

Trendy Basics: 555 Soul, Inc.
The styles here are nothing if not original. The prices on the hip-hop clothes are moderate to expensive, but most would say they're worth it. This store is a cut above the rest in hip-hop fashions.
290 Lafayette St. (at

Prince St.), (212) 431-2404. Open M-Su 11am-7pm. MC, V, AmEx, D, N R to Prince St. &

99X

This boutique sells some of the hippest threads in the city, with the usual high prices. The look is that oh-so-trendy 60's mod, featuring a large selection of British imports, from labels like Fred Perry, Lonsdale and Ben Sherman. *84 E. 10th St. (bet. Third and Fourth Aves.), (212) 460-8599, www.99xny.com. Open M-Sa 12pm-8pm, Su 12pm-7pm. MC, V, D, 6 to Astor Pl., N R to 8th St.*

Abercrombie & Fitch

Carrying women's, men's and children's "rugged, authentic" clothing, this two floor flagship A&F offers the same homogenous clothing and accessories that you will find in their other locations and in their notoriously risqué catalog. A&F has become the clothier of choice for young New Yorkers, from streetwise b-boys to preppy coeds. *199 Water St. (South Street Seaport), (212) 809-9000, www.abercrombie.com. Open M-Sa 10am- 9pm, Su 11 am-8pm. MC, V, AmEx, D, 4 5 to Fulton Street, 12ACJMZ to Broadway-Nassau*

Anthropologie

The grown-up Urban Outfitters. Created by the same people, with a simi-lar variety of housewares and clothing for men and women, the bent here is more stylish than trendy, with lots of classic and basic pieces that are of high quality, but prohibitively priced at around $70 and up. The clearance racks generally yield some good finds though, and sometimes paying full price isn't so bad, since the clothes are unlikely to either fall apart or go out of style quickly. *375 W. Broadway (bet. Spring and Broome Sts.), (212) 343-7070. Open M-Sa 11am-8pm, Su 11am-6pm. MC, V, AmEx, D, N R to Prince St., E6 to Spring St*

Antique Boutique

This trendy and lively Broadway institution shouts "very high prices!" Newer, teenage-oriented designer brands take up most of the upstairs, while downstairs is devoted to top-notch vintage coats, shirts, and jeans. Clothing in the very back room is sold by the pound. *712 Broadway (at Astor Pl.), (212) 460-8830. Open M-W 11am-9pm, Th-Sa 11am-10pm, Su 12pm-8pm. MC, V, AmEx, D, Diners, N R to 8th St., 6 to Astor*

APC

Clothes so simple and perfect that you simultaneously wonder why they cost so much and how you've lived without them for so long. Classics like jeans and button-down shirts hover around the $100 range, so clasp your credit card tightly. It's hard to resist such flawless incarnations of old standards at any price. *131 Mercer St. (bet. Prince and Spring Sts.), (212) 966-9685, www.apc.fr. Open M-Sa 11am-7pm, Su 12pm-6pm. MC, V, AmEx, FVEC6 to Spring St.* &

Banana Republic

Banana has insinuated its way into every upper-middle class neighborhood in Manhattan. If you like "earthy" colors and "classic" chic, you have come to the right place. Banana is becoming known as the place of choice for khakis and slacks. Find clothes for work and play, but always with a fancy touch. *2360 Broadway (at 86th St.), (212) 787-2064. Open M-Sa 10am-9pm, Su 10am-7pm 1 2 3 to 86th St. Additional locations in Manhattan and Brooklyn*

Betsey Johnson

In-your-face girly chic means she's not afraid to flaunt lace alongside faux leather, or pair zebra stripes with fuschia fishnets. Straightforward, sexy slip dresses are surprisingly affordable on sale. The store itself looks like some funky teenagers took a paintbrush to mom's boudoir.

138 Wooster St. (bet. Prince and Houston Sts.), (212) 995-5048. Open M-Sa 11am-7pm, Su 12pm-6pm. MC, V, AmEx, N R to Prince St.

Blue

If Cinderella was set in modern-day downtown NYC, then her gown surely would have come from here. This shop offers one-of-a kind fancy dresses that fall somewhere between little girl fairy-tale fantasy and grown up chic. Definitely worth a look if there's an upcoming ball you want to be the belle of. *125 St. Mark's Pl. (bet. First Ave. and Avenue A), (212) 228-7744. Open M-Sa 12pm-7pm, Su 12pm-5pm. MC, V, AmEx, 6 to Astor Place, NR to 8th St.* &

Calypso

Fun and funkily-printed fabrics abound in this boutique which successfully attempts to bring an international-island aesthetic to the neighborhood. While the inspiration for the clothing styles may be otherworldly, though, the prices all-too-closely mirror those of other East Side fashion boutiques. Paradise doesn't come cheap, after all, for the true fashion elite.
935 Madison Ave. (at 74th St.), (212) 535-4100. Open M-Sa 10am-6pm, Su 12pm-6pm. MC, V, AmEx, DC, 6 to 77th St. Additional location in Little Italy.

Club Monaco

This Ralph Lauren-owned chain offers a sleeker, more urban version of casual staple stores like J. Crew and Banana Republic. Some of the clothes could be mistaken for Helmut Lang or Prada but cost much less - think Eurochic.
2376 Broadway (at 87th St.), (212) 579 -2587. Open M-W 10am-8pm, Th-Sa 10am-9pm, Su 11am-7pm. MC,V, AmEx, D. 12 to 86th St. Additional locations in Manhattan.

Cynthia Rowley

Classic and simple designs, executed in extraordinary fabrics. The prices are relatively low for such an established designer, and much of the clothing comes in mix-and-match pieces, making it easy to achieve the look by integrating a splurge into your existing wardrobe.
112 Wooster St. (bet. Spring and Prince Sts.), (212) 334-1144. Open M-Sa 11am-7pm, Su 12pm-6pm. MC, V, AmEx, N R to Prince St.

Diesel

Two stories worth of youth culture in all its incarnations. Pump your system full of caffeine with a visit to the cappuccino bar before ravaging the aisles of shoes, underwear, outerwear and accessories.
770 Lexington Ave. (at 60th St.), (212) 308-0055, www. diesel.com. Open M-Sa 10am-8pm, Su 12pm-6pm. MC, V, AmEx, DC, D, N R W 4 5 6 to 59th St.-Lexington Ave. Additional location in Union Sq.

French Connection

Modish store deftly blending '70s and '80s retro and classic clean lines to produce well-tailored and pricey clothes suitable for work and play. Seasonal sales yield bargains on silk weaves, linen, and slinky, quasi-Parisian dresses.
700 Broadway (at West 4th St.), (212) 473-4486. Open M-F 11am-9pm, Sa 10am-9pm, Su 11am-8pm. MC, V, AmEx, D, N R to Prince St., 6 to Astor Pl.

Gap

For a clean, crisp look, check out this home for all the basics: khakis, whites, blacks, cotton t-shirts. This mega-chain takes a utilitarian approach to merchandising: stores are packed with folded sweaters, tees and the ever-present wall of jeans and khakis.
1212 Avenue of Americas (at 48th St.), (212) 730-1087. Open M-F 8am-9pm, Sa 9am-9pm, Su 11am-7pm. MC, V, AmEx. 1 2 to 50th St. Additional locations in Manhattan

H & M

Crowded to the point of suffocating, Euro import H & M draws hordes of fashion-hungry New Yorkers to its two Manhattan outlets with its chic clothes at ludicrously cheap prices. Of course, no one ever accused H & M of making their clothes well. But if you want to look like a million bucks and only pay wholesale, follow the Scandinavian lead.
34th St.,Herald Square (at Broadway), (646) 473-1164. Open M-Sa 10am-9pm, Su 11am-8pm. B D F V N W Q R to 34th St.-Herald Sq.

J. Crew

From Hampton chic to Wall Street sleek, this veritable Mecca of Preppy offers comfortable, classic looks for both men and women. While most of the company's business is conducted through catalog sales, the spacious Rockefeller Center location includes the added convenience of eager sales-help and fitting rooms. 30 Rockefeller Center (at Fifth Avenue and 49thSt.), (212) 765-2227. Open M-Sa 10am-8pm, Su 10am-7pm. MC,V, AmEx. B D F V to Rockefellet Center. Additional locations in Manhattan.

Living Doll

Plenty of throwbacks to the 80s chic à la Madonna at fair prices. Doll is perfect for young SoHo migrants on the east side of Broadway.
123 Crosby St. (bet. Prince and Houston Sts.), (212) 625-9410. Open M-F 11am-

*7pm, Sa 11am-8pm, Su 12pm-7pm. MC, V, AmEx, **6** to Bleecker St., **N R** to Prince St.*

Lord of the Fleas

This chain is so popular that they're currently operating several outlets within spitting distance of each other. This is the place to go to add a few trendy pieces to your existing wardrobe or to find something appropriate for a night of club-hopping. The prices and quality are generally low, ideal for stuff that's in now but probably won't be next year.
*2142 Broadway (bet. 75th and 76th sts.). (212) 875-8815. Open M-W 11am-8pm, Th-Sa 11am-8:30pm, Su 11am-7pm. MC, V, AmEx, D, **1 2 3** to 72nd St.*
Additional location in Manhattan.

Mister Roger

This place is full of Italian styles for men. Prices are steep, but the establishment has managed to maintain a beautiful selection for 14 years.
*565 W. 181st St. (bet. St. Nicholas and Audubon Aves.), (212) 795-1774. Open M-Sa 10am-8pm, Su 12am-7pm. MC, V, AmEx, D, **1** to 181st St., **A** to 181st St.* &

Original Levi's Store

A quirky, funky interior shows off Levi's complete clothing line. The selection and prices offered here are good, but not supercheap - the women's floor especially will leave you wondering if it was worth the four-flight climb. Expect to pay about $40 for a shirt and $60 for a pair of jeans. The Original Levi's Store definitely deserves a visit if you're in the area.
*3 E. 57th St. (bet.. Fifth and Madison Aves.) (212) 838-2188, 1-800-LEVI-USA, www.levis.com. Open M-Sa 10am-8pm, Su 11am-6pm. MC, V, AmEx, D. **N R** to Fifth Ave. and 59th St.* &

Patricia Field

From the woman who brings you fresh, fun fashion on HBO's Sex and the City, beloved downtown designer Patricia Field keeps her own store stocked with all the creations you love to see on Carrie, Miranda, Samantha and Charlotte. The perfect place if you want something really "funky," Patricia Field has men's and women's clothing, accessories, lingerie, suits, make-up, shoes, toys and a hair and wig salon. Work, it, girl!
*10 E. 8th St. (bet. University Pl. and Fifth Ave.), (212) 254-1699, www.patriciafield.com. Open M-Su 12pm-8pm. MC, V, AmEx, D. **N R** to 8th St.-NYU.*

Stüssy

Skater-surfer gear with a West Coast feel endures. It is worth the price to have a T-shirt that reads "Stüssy."
104 Prince St. (bet. Mercer and Greene Sts.),

*(212) 274-8855. Open M-Th 12pm-7pm, F-Su 11am-7pm. MC, V, AmEx, **N R** to Prince St.* &

TG-170

The most sophisticated of the small boutiques on the Ludlow strip features simple dresses, skirts and tops in subtle but fashionably retro designs, as well as phat Freitag bags and wallets.
*170 Ludlow St. (bet. Houston and Stanton Sts.), (212) 995-8660. Open M-Su 12pm-8pm. MC, V, AmEx, **F** to Second Ave.nue* &

Urban Outfitters

This hipster playground for the post-mall generation packs its industrial-esque interior with racks of multicolored, funky kid fashion, suitable for an array of day or evening urban outings. Weave through aisles of vintage clothing, sassy sundresses and trendy housewares while swaying to the smooth rhythms of ambient music.
*374 Sixth Ave. (at Waverly Pl.), (212) 677-9350. Open M-Sa 10am-10pm, Su 12pm-8pm. MC, V, AmEx, **A C E F V S** to West 4th St.*

Von's School of Hard Knocks

Over six years ago a father-and-son sneaker and men's sportswear business spawned the School of Hard Knocks, a men's line with a large hip-hop influence. Everything from jackets and caps, to sneakers and knapsacks, can be had for relatively low prices. Women's and children's lines are also sold here.
*Corona, Queens 106-11 Northern Blvd. (bet. 106th and 107th Sts.), (718) 898-1113, www.hard-knocks usa.com. Open M-Sa 10am-8pm. MC, V, AmEx, D, **7** to 103rd St.-Corona Plaza.* &.

Zara

This Spanish good-priced and good-looking chain is a favorite of the international crowd. Although the carbon-copy designer looks have been called "scandalous" by fashion's inner circle, shoppers find the low prices rather shocking. From one-season staples to everyday standbys, this chain is sure to please.
*750 Lexington Avenue (at 59th St.), (212) 754-1120. Open M-Sa 10am-8pm, Su 12pm-7pm. **N R 4 5 6** to 59th St.*

Flagship Designers:

agnès b.

Among the finest in smart, up-to-date women's wear, with a touch that makes you feel like Ingrid Bergman. *103 Green St. (bet. Spring and Prince), (212) 925-4649, www.agnesb.fr. Open M-Su 11am-7pm. MC, V, AmEx,* ❻ ❻ ❺ *to Spring St.* ♿

Anna Sui

Rock-n-roll style meets the runway and boutique world in this small designer outpost. Leather pants hang alongside sequined camouflage dresses and the atmosphere is relaxed enough to allow for trying it all on without feeling conspicuous. It's expensive, but markdowns are often cheap enough for a reasonable and well-deserved splurge. *113 Greene St. (bet. Spring and Prince Sts.), (212) 941-8406. M-Sa 11:30am-7pm, Su 12pm-6pm. MC, V, AmEx, Diners,* ❻ ❻ *to Prince St.*

Bally

One of the best-known leather companies in the world, this Swiss tannery sells a vast selection of high-quality leather shoes, bags, belts, and accessories. *628 Madison Ave. (at 59th St.), (212) 751-9082. Open M-Sa 10am-6:30pm, Su 12am-5pm. MC, V, AmEx, 4 5 6 to 59th St,* ❻ ❻ *to Fifth Ave.* ♿

Calvin Klein

Pay tribute to the commercial master who made a young American public hunger for androgyny and kiddie ads. Along with its refined, simple men's and women's wear, this flagship megastore boasts roomfuls of classically styled home accessories and a full staff of the predictably trendy, long-limbed sales specimens. *654 Madison Ave. (at E. 60th St.), (212) 292-9000. Open M-W, F-Sa 10am-6pm, Th 10am-7pm, Su 12pm-6pm. MC, V, AmEx, DC, D,* ❻ ❻ ❹ ❺ ❻ *to 59th St.-Lexington Ave.,* ❻ ❻ ❻ *to Fifth Ave.* ♿

Chanel

Coco would be proud. Complete with uniformed doorman, this sparkling shrine to simple elegance with a flair, sells clothing, jewelry, shoes, accessories, and of course, perfume. *15 E. 57th St. (bet. Fifth and Madison Aves.), (212) 355-5050. Open M-W,F 10am-6:30pm, Th 10am-8pm, Sa 10am-6pm, Su 12pm-5pm. MC, V, AmEx, Diners,* ❻ ❻ ❻ ❻ ❹ ❺ ❻ *to 59th and Lexington.* ♿

Comme des Garçons

High-flying artists and fashionistas frequent this airy, high-ceilinged boutique for shimmery garments from path-blazing Japanese designers Rei Kawakubo and Junya Watanabe. This is statement clothing in all its extraordinary glory. The prices here can flame like rockets, and your credit card might burn and burn. *520 W. 22nd St. (by 10th Ave.), (212) 604-9200. Open Su-M 12pm-6pm, Tu-Sa 11am-7pm. MC,V, AmEx.* ❻ ❻ *to 23rd St.*

Dolce & Gabbana

This flagship boutique, worshipped by the wealthy, carries the latest sports line from Dolce and Gabbana in all its raw vibrancy. This two floor unisex store features a variety of styles in colors like fuschia, lime green and azure blue. For the more tame at heart, there is also conservative wear like black pants and khaki blazers. If looking for accessories, they also have their own line of belts, bags and shoes. *434 Broadway, (bet. Prince & Spring Sts.), (212) 965-8000. M-Sa 11am-8pm, Su 12pm-6pm. MC,V, AmEx.* ❻ ❻ ❻ ❻ *to Spring St.,* ❻ ❻ *to Prince St.*

Emporio Armani

Cleanly cut casual suits that are a bit more accessible price-wise than Armani's main line. Just about everything looks classy in the renovated Stanford White building. *110 Fifth Ave. (at 16th St.), (212) 727-3240. Open M-W, F-Sa 11am-7pm, Th 11am-8pm, Su 12pm-6pm. MC, V, AmEx, D,* ❻ ❻ ❻ ❻ ❹ ❺ ❻ *to Union Sq.*

Givenchy

Audrey Hepburn and Givenchy helped make each other even more famous back in their heyday. Today, their designs are still very French and very chic, though there's probably no movie star today that could carry them off like Hepburn. *710 Madison Ave. (at 63rd St.), (212) 688-4338. Open M-Sa 10am-6pm. MC, V, AmEx,* ❻ ❻ ❻ *to Fifth Ave.* ♿

Gucci

Tom Ford's sleek looks find their home in this ultra-modern Fifth Avenue showcase. The quality of leather goods is excellent and the clothes upstairs are sleek. In a store that caters to "the beautiful people," be prepared for some high-end and high-attitude sales help. Walking away with that Gucci bag will make most feel like a million bucks. *685 Fifth Ave. (at 54thSt.), (212) 826-6200 Open M-W, F 10am-7pm, Th, Sa 10am-6pm. MC, V, AmEx.* ❻ ❻ *to Fifth Ave.*

Miu Miu

Prada's second break-through strikes a more contemporary look for a younger crowd.
100 Prince St. (bet. Mercer and Greene Sts.), (212) 334-5156. Open M-Sa 11am-7pm, Su 12am-6pm. MC, V, AmEx, **N R** *to Prince St.*

Prada

Chic, classic and stylish, Prada is still at the top of its fashion game. Prada's interior looks less like a store and more like a performance space with its enormous wave in the middle of the store's floor plunging into stadium seating for public events and galas. Explore the downstairs hallways and find racks of high quality (and pricey) clothing, shoes and accessories among hundreds of television screens interspersed in the racks displaying clips of movies as well as videos of old collections.
575 Broadway (between Spring and Houston Sts.), (212) 334-8888. www.prada.com. Open M-Sa 11am- 7pm, Su 12pm-6pm. MC, V, AmEx, D, **N R** *to Prince St.,* **B D F Q V** *to Broadway Lafayette. Other locations in Manhattan.*

DEPARTMENT STORES

Barney's

Power dressers and those looking for something more elegant put dents in their bank accounts at this airy, beautiful legend, which still holds its head high despite its original Chelsea store closing. Head to the top floor for the lowest prices and most casual wear. Check out Barney's Warehouse Sales in February and September to find good deals on usually pricey items.
660 Madison Ave. (at 61st St.), (212) 826-8900. Open M-F 10am-8pm, Sa 10am-7pm, Su 11am-6pm. MC, V, AmEx, D, **N** **R W F 4 5 6** *to 59th St. and Lexington Ave.*

Bergdorf Goodman

Tour the museum-quality merchandise worthy of its chandelier and marble surroundings in this home of high fashion. To actually purchase something, leave the clientele of wealthy Upper East Siders behind and travel to the fifth floor where less expensive (though still somewhat pricey) sportswear abounds. All cash and credit card transactions occur in a "back room" whose doors blend with the walls. Window displays here are among Fifth Avenue's finest.
754 Fifth Ave. (at 58th St.), (212) 753-7300. Open M-Sa 10am-7pm, Su 12am-6pm. MC, V, AmEx, D, **N R** *to Fifth Ave.*

Bloomingdale's

Although the trademark perfume arcade is usually a zoo, the upper floors are open, bright and filled with helpful salespeople eager to successfully match people with outfits bearing three-digit price tags.
1000 Lexington Ave. (bet. 59th and 60th Sts.), (212) 705-2000. Open M-F 10am-8:30pm, Sa 10am-7pm, Su 11am-7pm. MC, V, AmEx, **N R F W 4 5 6** *to 59th St. and Lexington Ave.*

Henri Bendel

One of the plushest shopping experiences around. An elegant staircase winds its way up through the many-storied townhouse, maintaining the splendor of Bendel's original boutiques while incorporating modern accents. Henri Bendel has the same type of clothing as Bergdorf Goodman or Saks, but classier.
712 Fifth Ave. (bet. 55th and 56th Sts.), (212) 247-1100. Open M-W, F-Sa 10am-7pm, Th 10am-8pm, Su 12pm-6pm. MC, V, AmEx, D, **N R** *to Fifth Ave.*

Macy's

"The Largest Store in the World" often resembles the chaos of the Thanksgiving Day parade they sponsor, especially after work and around Christmas. Most items are lower priced than other department stores, but the service and bathrooms reflect this reduction.
34th St. (at Broadway), 695-4400. Open M-Sa 10am-8:30pm, Su 11am-7pm. MC, V, AmEx, **B D F V N R Q W** *to 34th/Herald Square. Additional locations in Manhattan and Brooklyn.*

Pearl River Mart

Sort of like a Chinese Woolworth's, this two-floored department store stocks all the staples that Five and dimes used to, with a twist: bamboo mats, bedding supplies, electronics, video rentals, a minigrocery section and traditional cookware.
277 Canal St. (at Broadway), (212) 431-4770, www.pearlriver.com. Open M-Su 10am-7:30pm. MC, V, AmEx, D, **J M N R**

Z 6 *to Canal St.*

Sak's Fifth Avenue

This classy store makes for great, if somewhat dizzying, browsing. Window displays make the Fifth Ave. promenade a bit more exciting.
611 Fifth Ave. (bet. 49th and 50th Sts.), (212) 753-4000, www.saks-fifthaveneue.com. Open M-W, F-Sa 10am-7pm, Th 10am-8pm, Su 12pm-6pm. MC, V, AmEx, DC, D, **B D F V** *to 47th-50th Sts.-Rockefeller Center.* &

Takashimaya

An experience in itself, this Japanese import is synonymous with elegance and ambiance. A Barney's from the East, the fresh flower department is a favorite of urbanites craving greenery. The midtown oasis leaves shoppers with a lighter spirit, not to mention a lighter wallet. Its Asian tea and delicacies department is to die for, and Takashimaya's is synonymous with the one-of-a-kind gift or splurge item.
693 Fifth Avenue (at 54thSt.), (212) 350-0100. Open M-Sa 10am-7pm, Su 12pm-5pm. **F** *to 57th St.,* **E V** *to Fifth Ave*

Burlington Coat Factory

Why pay more? With five floors of discount coats, suits, shirts and casual sportswear, you're sure to find what you need at the right price.
707 Sixth Ave. (at 23rd St.), (212) 229-1300 Open M-Sa 9am-9pm, Su 10am-6pm. MC, V, AmEx, **F V 1 2 N R** *to 23rd St.*
Additional locations in Manhattan

Century 21

Determined shoppers will find designer items for as much as 80 percent off. The other departments attract a slightly less bloodthirsty crowd. Don't go wearing bulky clothing, as there are no dressing rooms and it's standard to try things on over what you're wearing.
23 Cortlandt St. (bet. Broadway and Church St.),(212) 227-9092. Open M-F 7:45am-8pm, Sa 10am-8pm, Su 11am-7pm. MC, V, AmEx, N R to Cortlandt St. **J M Z** **A C 1 2 4 5** *to Fulton St.*

Conway Stores

Conway is a mandatory stop-over for bargain hunters everywhere. Shoppers flock here for the incredible prices: expect to get a really big bang for your buck. Words of caution: take heed of the weekend mobs and of items that are listed as slightly irregular (i.e., underwear).
1333 Broadway (at 35th St.), (212) 967-3460. Open M-F 8am-8pm, Sa 9aM-8PM, Su 9:30am-7pm. MC, V, AmEx, D. **B**

D F V N Q R W *to 34th St. - Herald Sq.*

Daffy's

For more reasonable prices than most department stores, this heavily advertised pit stop for savvy shoppers sells clothes, shoes, lingerie, and accessories, usually by lesser known European designers.

During clearance sales, some items are slashed to fewer than five dollars.
111 Fifth Ave. (at 18th St.), (212) 529-4477. Open M-Sa 10am-9pm, Su 12pm-7pm. MC, V, D. **L** **N Q R W 4 5 6** *to Union Square.*
Additional location on Madison Ave.

Dee & Dee

Bargains galore. Everything from holiday decorations and housewares to $3 tank tops and $10 polar fleece jackets fill the racks and shelves of this cut-price warehouse. Even if you don't really need anything, with deals like this it's hard to walk away empty-handed.
97 Chambers St. (bet. Church St. and Broadway), (212) 233-3830. Open M-F 8am--7pm, Sa 9:30am-6pm, Su 11am-5pm. MC, V. **A C** *to Chambers St., NR to City Hall*

Domsey Warehouse

In this 30,000-sq. ft. warehouse, be impressed by quantity and not quality. Only the courageous sift through floors of merchandise including men's, women's and children's wear. You will find Hawaiian shirts, military uniforms, prom dresses, bridal gowns and cowboy boots all in one place. After many hours of treasure hunting, your finds will make it all well worth it.
Brooklyn, 496 Wrythe Ave. (between Broadway and 8th St.), (718) 384-6000. Open M-F 9am-5:30pm, Sa 9am-6:30pm, Su 11am-5:30pm. **J M Z** *to Marcy Ave.*

Filene's Basement

This bargain staple superstore carries Calvin Klein, Perry Ellis, Kenar and other designer names. It is worth a look for shoes, lingerie, coats, suits and evening wear. Check out the occasional clearance sales where many prices are slashed to below $5.
620 Sixth Ave. (bet. 18th and 19th Sts.), (212) 620-3100, www.filenesbasement.com. Open M-Sa 9:30am-9pm, Su 11am-7pm. MC, V, AmEx, D, **1** **2** *to 18th St.* **X** *Additional location on Upper West Side.*

Loehmann's

As legendary as Century

21 in designer junkie circles, this 5-floor Chelsea outpost rewards the shopper who makes the trek. Lots of big-name labels and high stock turnover justify frequent trips.
101 Seventh Ave. (bet. 16th and 17th Sts.), (212) 352-0856, www.loehmanns.com. Open M-Sa 9am-9pm, Su 11am-7pm. MC, V, D, ❶❷ to 18th St. ♿

Moe Ginsburg

Over 50,000 square feet of suits, overcoats, sportswear, accessories and shoes, with suppliers from Italy, Canada and here.
162 Fifth Ave. (at 21st St.), (212) 242-3482. Open M-Th 10am-8pm, F 10am-7pm, Sa 10am-6pm, Su 11am-6pm. MC, V, AmEx, D, ❶❷❸❹ to 23rd St. ♿

Strawberry

While Manhattan fashionistas may consider this store passé, there are many bargains to be had in this reasonably priced Manhattan staple. While the trendy is mixed in with the frumpy, seasoned shoppers can find stylish looks with small price tags if they look hard enough.
501 Madison Avenue (at 52nd Street), (212) 753-5008. Open M-F 8am-7pm, Sa-Su 10am-6pm. MC, V, AmEx. ❺❻ to Fifth Ave.
Additional locations in Manhattan

Syms

Originally a men's suit warehouse, today Syms offers complete lines of men's, women's and children's designer clothing at heavily discounted prices. With items from over 200 brand labels in stock, and a convenient color-coded price tag system to tell you what's in your price range, Syms is a great place for both apparel aficionados who crave the ultimate bargain and novice shoppers who just need a nice, cheap ensemble.
42 Trinity Pl. (at Rector St.), (212) 797-1199, www.syms.com. Open M-W 9am-6:30pm, R-F 9am-8pm, Sa 10am-6:30pm, Su 12pm-5:30pm. MC, V, AmEx, D, ❶❷ to Wall St.

TJ Maxx

This off-price retail department store offers clothing for the whole family as well as home furnishings, accessories, and shoes. Offering 40%-60% off brands such as Tommy Hilfiger, Ralph Lauren, DKNY and Jones NY, you will be able to find a good deal if you have the time and patience to sift through endless racks in search of it.
620 6th Ave. (bet. 18th and 19th), (212) 229-0875, www.tjmaxx.com. Open M-Sa 9:30am-9pm, Su 11am-7pm. MC, V, AmEx, D. ❶❷❸ to 14th St., ❶❷ to 18th St.

VINTAGE

Alice Underground

Behind the hippie-ish exterior is one of Manhattan's biggest and best vintage stores. Skip the bargain bins as there's usually a good reason why the items are being unloaded for so cheap, and shell out a little more for pants and jackets off the racks, where the finds can range from the fabulously unique to solid standards. An excellent selection of winter coats.
481 Broadway (bet. Grand and Broome Sts.), (212) 431-9067. Open M-Su 11am-7:30pm. MC, V, AmEx, ❶❷❸❹❺❻❼ ❻ to Canal St. ♿

Andee's Chee-Pees

Though on the expensive side, Andee's houses a large selection of mostly polyester-influenced vintage men's and women's clothing, plus a more reasonably priced collection of used jeans. Always in stock: your grandpa's cabana wear. But he'd roll over in his grave if he saw what they're charging for it.
691 Broadway (bet. 3rd and 4th Sts.), (212) 420-5980. Open M-Sa 11am-9pm, Su 12pm-8pm. MC, V, AmEx, ❶❷ to 8th St., ❻ to Astor Pl. ♿

Beacon's Closet

Many of the hipsters of Williamsburg are avid thrift shoppers and this is the neighborhood outlet for such diversions. A wide assortment of used clothing fills the racks and it doesn't take too much hunting to find something really nice like a suede jacket or a pair of perfectly worn boot-cut Wranglers. The prices tend to be a little expensive for Brooklyn, but are still about one-third what you'd pay in Manhattan. Plus, they'll buy your unwanted clothes or take them in trade.
110 Bedford Ave. (at North 11th St.), (718) 486-0816. Open M-F 12am-9pm, Sa-Su 11am-8pm. MC, V, AmEx, DC. ❶ to Bedford Ave.

Cheap Jack's

Don't be fooled by the name of this groovy vintage store. The place is anything but cheap. Browse through the vast selection of plain and Hawaiian shirts, one-of-a-kind coats, and vintage-style dresses on the first floor. Head downstairs where the jeans hang. Patience and a keen eye may lead to a heavenly bargain.
841 Broadway (bet. 13th and 14th Sts.), (212) 777-

9564, www.cheapjacks. com. Open M-Sa 11am-8pm, Su 12pm-7pm. MC, V, AmEx, D, ❶❷❸❹❺❻❹❺❻ to Union Sq.-14th St. ♿

Cherry

All the vintage clothing from the '30s to early '80s, is classy, sexy and far out. There is a heavy emphasis on '60s and '70s minimalist styles from swimsuits to nightwear, plus designer pieces by Rudi Gernreich (a radical '60s designer), Gucci and Bob Mackie. You can also find "space-age bio-morphic design" furniture and home accessories such as lamps, phones, speakers and sculpture. *185 Orchard St. (bet. Houston and Stanton Sts.), (212) 358-7131. Open Su-W 1pm-8pm, Th-Sa 1pm-10pm. MC, V, AmEx, D, ❻ to Second Ave.* ♿

INA

This Little Italy clothing store features fabulous designer vintage for both men and women. They carry current collections, but the real treasures are their vintage designer items. *21 Prince St. (bet. Mott and Elizabeth Sts.), (212) 334-9048. Open M-Th,Su 12pm-7pm, F-Sa 12pm-8pm. MC, V, AmEx, ❶❷ to Prince St. ❻ to Spring*

Out of the Closet

Who'd have thought you could find vintage clothing on the Upper East Side? Visit this eclectic second-hand boutique housed in a historic building. Feel better about the prices by reminding yourself that a portion of sales go to AIDS-related charities. *220 E. 81st St. (between Second and Third Aves.), (212) 472-3573. Open Tu-Sa 10:30am-5pm. ❻ to 77th St.*

Screaming Mimi's

You might pass Screaming Mimi's by if not for the window display, which shows off its kooky wares. You'll find some of the most outrageous vintage clothing in the city here, including Elvis suits, pink leisure outfits, leather pants and neon colored patched shirts. The excellent condition of the clothing marks up the prices a bit, but well worth it if you dare to wear. *382 Lafayette St. (4th and Great Jones Sts.), (212) 677-6464.Open M-Sa 12pm-8pm, Su 1pm-7pm. MC, V, AmEx, DC, D. ❻ to Astor Pl., ❶❷❸ to Broadway-Lafayette*

What Comes Around Goes Around

This is quite possibly the largest and most famous vintage store in all of New York, so be prepared to spend a lot of time scouring the store in search of that perfect faded baseball jersey. They have the largest selection of vintage jeans and leather, and will make special orders so that you get exactly what you're looking for. Though it may be slightly overpriced, for the serious shopper it is a worthwhile trip. *351 W. Broadway (bet.*

Grand and Broome), (212) 343-9303. www.nyvintage.com. Open M-Sa 11am-8pm, Su 12pm-7pm. MC, V, AmEx, D. ❶ ❷ to Prince St.

FLEA MARKETS

Annex Antiques Fair and Flea Market,

Saturdays and Sundays, Sixth Avenue from 24th to 27th St. The most famous and the 'original' flea market, the Annex Flea gathers over 500 vendors every weekend in a trio of parking lots that stretch along 6th Ave. While you try to distinguish between trash and treasure, you might stumble upon a celebrity or two - Catherine Deneuve is a fan. *(212) 243-5343 for info. ❶❷ to 23rd St.*

Chelsea Antiques Annex

"The Garage," weekends, 122 W. 25th St. (bet Sixth and Seventh Ave.) Down the street from Annex, this high-scale parking garage sale consists of a multilevel, 23,000-sq. ft. indoor antiques market. *(212)647-0707 for info. Open Sa-Su 7am-5pm*

SoHo Antiques Fair and Flea Market

Weekends, Broadway at Grand St. Not as large or as great for people-watching as the Annex Flea, but that's an advantage if you are strapped for time or are

not a flea market veteran with a great attention span. Find everything from clothing to collectibles and furniture.

COMPUTING

Datavision

Mac owners should stop here first when in need of a spare part. The two-level store is a bit difficult to navigate, but the ubiquitous staff is happy to help with even the most far-out requests. *445 Fifth Ave. (bet. 39th and 40th Sts.), (212) 689-1111. Open M-F 8:30am-8pm, Sa 9am-8pm, Su 9:30am-7pm. MC, V, AmEx, Diners, D, ❹❺❻ to Grand Central*

J&R Music World

Covering an entire block and soaring into the sky, this store carries everything in video, audio, music, and computers. The sales staff aren't all experts so ask for a lot of different opinions before you buy anything. Everything is on display, so customers can fiddle to their hearts' content. *23 Park Row (bet. Beekman and Ann Sts.), 238-9000. Open M-W,F-Sa 9am-7pm, Th 9am-7:30pm, Su 10:30-6:30. MC, V, AmEx, D, ❶❷ to City Hall*

COSMETICS

Face Stockholm

With MAC right up the street, the situation

seems too close for comfort, though this Swedish based company excels at the basics. Personal attention is easy to come by the airy boutique. The $9 nail polish selection makes you wish you had more fingers. A favored stop for fashionistas and actresses, you might even spot a celeb or two.
110 Prince St. (at Greene St.), (212) 334-3900, www.beauty.com. Open M-W 11am-7pm, Th-Sa 11am-8pm, Su 12pm-7pm. MC, V, AmEx, ❶❷ *to Prince St.* ♿ *Additional locations in Manhattan*

Kiehl's

The latest and, many claim, greatest in all-natural skin care and cosmetics. Also available in Barney's and Saks.
109 Third Ave. (at 13th St.), (212) 677-3171. Open M-W,F 10am-6:30pm, Th 10am-7:30pm, Sa 10am-6pm, Su 12pm-6pm. MC,V,AmEx. ❶❷❸❹❺ ❹❺❻ *to Union Sq.-14th St.*

L'Occitane

This small French company has all of the essentials plus skin care. They have a great selection of their own perfumes and candles.
146 Spring St. (at Wooster St.), (212) 343-0109, www.loccitane. com. Open M-Sa 11am-8pm, Su 11pm-7pm. MC, V, AmEx, DC, ❶❷ *to Spring St.*

M.A.C. Cosmetics

Makeup that is cruelty-free, cosmetophiles are more than willing to pay the price for the name and the creamy, metallic signature look. Try the "Diva" lipstick - proceeds go to an AIDS charity. High quality, too.
113 Spring St. (at Mercer St.), (212) 334-4641, www.maccosmetics.com. Open M-Sa 11am-7pm, Su 12pm-6pm. MC, V, AmEx, D, ❶❷ *to Prince St.,* ❶❷❸ *to Spring St. Additional location on Fifth Ave.*

Origins

This cosmetics haven (a subsidiary of Estee Lauder) houses earthy lotions, creams and powders like "clear head shampoo" and "the Zen gardener," infused with essential oils and all natural botanical extracts. The store carries a complete line of devices for de-stressing, including books on reflexology, massage oils and other soothing creams. All the beauty products strive to achieve balance and harmony, Origins' two key words. Oprah is a fan, and they now have a spa at Chelsea Piers.
175 Fifth Ave. (between 22nd and 23rd), (212) 677-9100. Open M-S

10am-8pm, Su 12pm-6pm. ❶❷ *to 23rd St. Additional locations in Manhattan*

Sephora

This French high-scale cosmetics and perfume store is new to America. The sales people keep a hands-off policy: customers can try anything without asking. Run around and try the latest scents and beauty potions from world-renowned designers. This cosmetophile's candy-store holds an endless list of brand-name products arranged in alphabetical order.
1500 Broadway (at 42nd St.), (212) 944-6789. Open M-Su 10am-12am. ❶❷ ❸❹❺❻❼❽ *to 42nd St.-Times Sq.*

GIFTS

Card-o-Mat

This card-filled cubbyhole can come up with a sentimental rhyme or a witty remark for any occasion. Don't miss the "Mr. Bean" fill-in-the-blank birthday cards.
2884 Broadway (at 112th St.), (212) 663-2085. Open M-F 10:30am-7:30pm, Sa-Su 11am-6pm. MC, V, ❶ *to 110th St.* ♿

Dö Kham

Handcrafted Tibetan housewares, gifts and

trinkets at prices that are prone to upset the spiritual balance of even the most calm.
51 Prince St., (212) 966-2404. Open M-Su 10am-8pm. NR6 to Prince St.

E. Rossi & Co.
The king of random Little Italy souvenir shops. Dust-covered merchandise, from huge neon plastic piggy banks to Pope keychains, clutter the store.
191 Grand St. (at Mulberry St.), (212) 966-6640. Open M-F 10am-6pm, Sa 12pm-9pm, Su 12pm-7pm. MC, V, 6 to Spring St.

Exit 9
A great gift selection no matter what you're looking for. There are lovely candle holders and picture frames for tame tastes, funky knickknacks and odd books for strange tastes, and a selection of flasks, cigarette cases, and lighters for self-destructive tastes. Never worry about shopping for them again.
64 Ave. A (bet. 4th and 5th Sts.), (212) 228-0145. Open M-F 12pm-8pm, Sa 11am-8pm, Su 12pm-7pm. MC, V, AmEx, D, FV to Second Ave.

Swiss Army Store
If you're into knives and watches, welcome to paradise. Their first and only store in the heart of SoHo carries their full lines of watches, travel gear, men's apparel and of course, army knives. Reasonably priced for such quality, this is a must for anyone who wants selection and friendly service.
136 Prince St., (212) 965-5714, www.swissarmy.com. Open M-Sa 11am-7pm, Su Noon- 6pm. MC, V, AmEx NR to Prince St.

Our Name is Mud
Paint your own pottery at this cool little store. Up front is a gallery with finished "functional" pieces like mugs, vases, planters, frames and pitchers in bright colors. After a little instruction you can move to the back, pick your own unfinished piece and, for $5 per 1/2 hour, paint it yourself. Perfect for private parties, bridal showers and birthdays. They also offer nine week hand-building courses for $215. Thursdays from 5-10pm is adult night (no kids allowed) where you can bring in your own wine or beer and paint till you drop.
59 Greenwich Ave. (at Seventh Ave.) (212) 647-7899. M-W 11:30am-8pm, Th-F 11:30am-11pm, Sa 11:30am-8pm, Su 11:30am-7pm. MC,V, AmEx, LACE to14th St.
Additional locations in Manhattan

Chelsea Market
Once a Nabisco biscuit factory, Manhattan's largest wholesale and retail food concourse located in the heart of Chelsea offers a multitude of fresh dining options, from fudge to fish and everything in between. The building's brick and terra cotta arches and wood beamed walls provide a haven from the typical urban surroundings while satisfying even the most refined palates.
75 9th Ave. (between 15th and 16th Sts.), www.chelseamarket.com. Open M-F 9am- 10pm, Sa-Su 8am- 8pm ACEL to 14th St.

Confucious Plaza Vendors
Be prepared to wait in long lines for up to twenty minutes at this outdoor market where fresh produce is sold in bulk poundage. Nowhere else, though, could you get two pounds of specialty mushrooms for only $1, or three pounds of broccoli for $1.50.
Bowery (at Division St.), Cash Only, BDQ to Grand St.

Manhattan Mall
A mall! In Manhattan! Its dominating presence highlighted in glass and neon incites feelings of either veneration or loathing. Billed as having the "Largest food court in New York City!" and with Sterns as its anchor store, how could it not incite strong emotions?
33rd St. and Sixth Ave., payments vary with establishment, BDF NQR to 34th St./Herald Square &

A.L. Bazzini
Brazil nuts, pine nuts, peanuts and more. Also find dried fruit and gift baskets and a bunch of other specialties. For cheap fun, stop by for a look around and treat yourself to an ice cream cone.
339 Greenwich St. (at Jay St.), (212) 334-1280. Open M-Su 8:30am-8pm. MC, V, AmEx, 12 to Chambers St. or Franklin St. &

Alleva Dairy, Inc.
Its fourth-generation owner, Bob Alleva, serves up hot and cold sand-

wiches for under $5, authentic enough to keep the idea of Little Italy constant. Mozzarella is made fresh daily at the oldest Italian cheese store in America.

188 Grand St. (at Mulberry St.), (212) 226-7990, 1-800-4-ALLEVA. Open M-Sa 8:30am-6pm, Su 8:30am-3pm. MC, V, AmEx, **L N Q R W 4 5 6** *to Canal St.* &

Balducci's

Heaven for the downtown gourmet. From the appetizers to the desserts, Balducci's has everything you'll need to mix up a delicious meal and impress your friends and family. Wander in just to admire the pastries or salivate over the gourmet delicacies. The best cinnamon raisin bread in history.

424 Sixth Ave. (at 9th St.), (212) 673-2600. Open M-Su 7am-9pm. MC, V, AmEx, **A C E F V S** *to W. 4th St.*

Brooklyn Brewery

New York's closest approximation to a hometown beer is brewed here, and on weekends they open the place up. That means free brewery tours, beer tastings and merchandise for sale. The hats and T-shirts make excellent gifts for any beer lover on your list. They've recently begun using the space as a gallery and performance space as well, making this a perfect day of cheap fun for a variety of different tastes.

North 11th St., Brooklyn (bet. Barry and Wyeth Sts.), (718) 486-7422, MC, V, AmEx, **L** *to Bedford Ave.*

Citarella

With humble beginnings as a small fish market, this gourmet grocer now boasts a full range of fresh fish, meat and pastas. Best known for its extensive selection of fresh local and imported seafood, Citarella also carries a sampling of foie gras, caviar and cheeses for all your dinner party needs both here and in the Hamptons.

2135 Broadway (at 75th St.), (212) 874-0383. Open M-Sa 7am-9pm, Su 9am-7pm. MC, V, AmEx, **1 2 3** *to 72nd St.* **X**

Dean & Deluca

One of New York's most revered specialty food stores, the Zabars of downtown. Stop by for a caffeine break at the stand-up espresso bar, pick up some pate for your next dinner party, and ogle the produce section, full of fruits and vegetables suitable for a still-life. They also offer specialty breads, meats, cheeses, desserts and quality packaged foods.

560 Broadway (at Prince St.), 226-6800. Open M-S

10am-8pm, Su 10am-7pm. MC, V, AmEx, D, **N R** to Prince St., **6** to Spring St.

Di Palos' Fine Foods

Di Palos' has everything you'll need when you're planning an Italian feast. The guys who work here are charming and will help you choose the ingredients: fresh mozzarella, sun-dried tomatoes, sausages, bread, etc. for what is sure to be an unforgettable meal.

206 Grand St. (at Mott St.) 226-1033. Open M-S 9:am-6:30pm, Su 9am-3pm. MC, V, AmEx, **6** to Spring St.

Dynasty Supermarket

One of Chinatown's largest supermarkets, boasting a full herb and medicine counter, an in-

house butcher and fishmonger, a beef-jerky bar, and best of all, weekly sales.

68 Elizabeth St. (at Hester St.), 966-4943. Open M-Su 9:30am-8:30pm. MC, V, **N R** *to Prince St.,* **B D Q** *to Grand St.*

Economy Candy

Calling itself a "nosher's paradise" on the Lower East Side, this is the best discount store in the city for penny candy, imported chocolates, nuts, sweets and gourmet

savories like mustards, chutney, tea and spices. Try their dense, chewy, pistachio-laden Turkish delight, the most authentic this side of Byzantium.

108 Rivington St. (bet. Essex and Ludlow Sts.), 254-1531. Open Su-F 9am-6pm, S 10am-5pm.

MC, V, AmEx, **M** **J** to
Delancey St. ♿

Elk Candy

Resist, if possible, the
urge not to eat the cute,
stylized candies crafted
at this Yorkville land-
mark, renowned for more
than sixty years for its
marvelous marzipan.
*1628 Second Ave. (bet.
84th and 85th Sts.), 650-
1177. Open M-S 9am-
8pm, Su 10am-7pm. V,
MC, AmEx, **4** **5** **6** to
86th St.*

Fairway

"Like no other market"
reads the awning, and
this is indeed the most
popular, largest and low-
est-priced produce and
gourmet market on the
west side. A full deli
counter offers prepared
hot and cold dishes, the
cheese department stocks
an array of imports, and
the bakery sells over a
million bagels every year.
*2328 Twelfth Ave. (at
133rd St.), 234-3883. M-
Su 8am-11pm. **1** to
125th. St. Additional
locations in Manhattan.*

Gourmet Garage

With its original location
a converted garage in
SoHo, Gourmet Garage
was a pioneer in deliver-
ing gourmet goods at
wholesale prices to the
public. The Upper West
Side location offers the
same selection of breads,
cheeses, organic produce,
daily prepared foods, and
a whole Kosher Cellar
downstairs.
*- Upper West Side, 2567
Broadway (at 96th St.),
(212) 663-0656. Open M-
Su 7am-10pm. MC, V,*

*AmEx, D. **1** **2** **3** to
96th St. **X***
*- Soho, 453 Broome St.
(at Mercer St.), (212) 941-
5850. Open M-Su 7am-
9pm. MC, V, AmEx. **N** **R**
to Prince St.*

Hong Kong Supermarket

In a slightly quieter corner of Chinatown, this
supermarket carries a
wide selection of Hong
Kong and Taiwanese ex-
pat foodstuffs. Indulge
your sweet tooth with
selections from the huge
candy aisle, heavily
stocked with fruit tablets,
candies and jellies.
*109 Broadway (at Allen
St.), 227-3388, MC, V, **F**
to East Broadway*

Italian Food Center

An extraordinary Italian
grocery for everything
from sandwiches to the
ingredients you'll need to
imitate your favorite
Italian restaurant's risotto. They offer delivery
throughout Manhattan,
and they cater and have
a mail order catalog ser-
vice.
*186 Grand St. (at
Mulberry St.), (212) 925-
2954. Open Su 8am-6pm,
M-Sa 8am-7pm. MC, V,
AmEx, **6** to Spring St. or
J **M** **Z** **N** **Q** **R** **W** to
Canal St.*

Kalyustan's

Chefs and an internation-
al crowd frequent this
multi-story gourmet eth-
nic food market that
wholesales every kind of
Indian spice imaginable
and features a vast
assortment of Middle
Eastern delicacies. The

small café upstairs stars
falafel that could not be
more authentic.
*123 Lexington Ave.,
between 28th and 29th
Sts., (212) 685-3451.
Open M-S 10am-8pm, Su
11am-7pm.
6 to 28th St.*

Kam Wo Herb and Tea Co., Inc.

Drawers of medicine line
the walls in this apothe-
cary shop, filling the
space with a cloud of
herb smells thick as a
brick. Specialty medicinal
cookware and a library of
health books written by
the boss himself, Dr.
Leung. Herbs, weighed
out on handscales and
wrapped in white rice-
paper envelopes, will
supposedly cure any ail-
ment.
*211 Grand St. (at
Elizabeth St.), (212) 966-
6370. Open M-Su
9:30am-7:30pm. MC, V,
J **M** **N** **Q** **R** **W** **Z** **6** to
Canal St.* ♿

La Maison du Chocolat

As one might guess,
chocolate is this store's
specialty, and it comes in
many shapes and sizes,
none of which even
approach being healthy
or veer far from being
absolutely divine.
*1018 Madison Ave. (bet.
78th and 79th Sts.), 744-
7117. Open M-F 10am-
7pm, S 10am-6pm. MC,
V, AmEx, D, **6** to 77th
Street*

Milano Market

A gourmet Italian deli
and grocery store stocked
from floor to ceiling. In

addition to countless
sandwich combinations,
the store has a pastry
counter full of whole
cakes, pastries and cook-
ies, a gourmet cheese
counter, a fresh fruit
stand, and every-day gro-
cery items.
*2892 Broadway (bet.
112th and 113th Sts.),
(212) 665-9500, M-Su
6am-1am, **1** to 110th St.*

Mondel Chocolates

Florence Mondel
has been cater-
ing to
Morningside
Heights choco-
holics for more
than 50 years. Her
modest store is filled with
homemade fudge and
marzipan, as well as a
dozen different kinds of
truffles.
*2913 Broadway (at 114th
St.), 864-2111. Open M-S
11am-7pm, Su 12pm-
6pm. V, MC, AmEx, **1** to
116th St.*

M. Rohrs House of Fine Teas & Coffee

Satiating the caffeine
addictions of locals for
over 100 years with its
wide selection of refined
tea leaves and coffee
beans, Rohrs is here to
stay. Wooden counters,
aged tea canisters, and
beveled mirrors retain the
shop's original, old-world
charm, an anomaly
among slick coffee bars.
*303 East 85th St. (at
Second Ave.), (212) 396-
4456, www.rohrs.com.
Open Su-Th 7am-9pm, F-
S 7am-10pm. MC, V,
AmEx, **4** **5** **6** to 86th
St.* ♿

Ten Ren Tea and Ginseng Co.

Masters of the ancient but still sophisticated Chinese ritual of tea preparation, the folks at Ten Ren not only sell teas (ranging from $8 to $125 per lb.), they also provide lessons on the proper brewing and enjoying of the venerated green leaf. Superb black teas, jasmine teas and ginger are also sold. *75 Mott St. (bet. Canal and Bayard Sts.), (212) 349-2286. Open M-Su 10am-8pm. MC, V, AmEx,* **J M N R Q W Z 6** *to Canal St.* &

Union Square Greenmarket

"Like visiting a garden or a forest," this oasis amidst the Manhattan mayhem attracts chefs from all over NoHo and SoHo for ultra-fresh exotic ingredients like elephant garlic and verbena, as well as locals from the neighborhood who come for the bargains on vegetables. As you see dozens of vendors selling fresh bunches of every kind of produce imaginable you will forget that you are in New York. *Broadway at 14th St., borders 17th St. and Union Square (Office: 130 E. 16th St., (212) 477-3220), MWFS 8am-6pm.* **4 5 6 L N R** *to Union Square*

Washington Market Park

An open-air farmer's market resplendent with produce, flowers, baked goods and other delicious items. Organic items are aplenty, as are the real-life farmers, who haul their wares from New Jersey and upstate

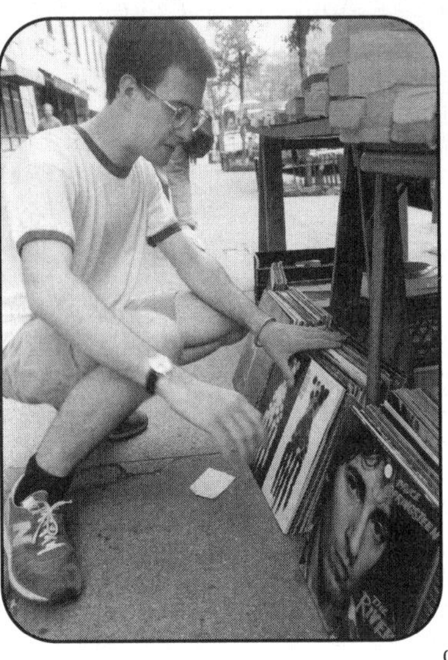

New York. Open Saturdays, 8am-5pm, rain or shine. *Greenwich St. (at Reade St.), Cash Only, June 1-December 1.* **1 2 A C** *to Chambers St.*

Zabar's

A name with impressive cachet in uptown circles, this longtime Upper West Side institution is the prime source for gourmet meats, cheese, breads and produce. Upstairs is an equally well-stocked kitchenware department featuring at least 30 kinds of whisks. The store can get shoulder-to-shoulder crowded on the weekends and during the holidays. *2245 Broadway (at 80th St.), (212) 787-2000. Open M-F 8am-7pm, S 8am-8pm, Su 9am-6pm. MC, V, AmEx,* **1 9** *to 79th St.* &

HOUSEWARES

ABC Carpet and Home

Expect to find ample mother/daughter pairs ooh-ing and aah-ing their way through six floors of housewares, antiques and knickknacks. Although fairly expensive, the store is worth a visit for its creative window displays and extraordinary finds such as a ten-foot tall gilded bird cage. The Parlour Café on the ground floor allows weary shoppers to lounge and lunch on the furniture that they can't afford to buy. *881 and 888 Broadway (at 19th St.), (212) 473-3000. Open M-F 10am-8pm, S 10-6pm, S 11am-6pm. MC, V, AmEx,* **1 N R 4 5 6** *to Union Square* &

Bed Bath and Beyond

An obsessive-compulsive's dream, this moderately priced emporium of all things domestic fits the bill for convenience - a rarity in Manhattan, to be sure. The perfect stop for decorating dorm rooms or first apartments, the convenience of everything in one store sometimes lets you forget you could get what you're buying elsewhere for cheaper. *620 Sixth Ave. (bet. 18th and 19th Sts.), (212) 255-3550, www.bedbathandbeyond.com. Open M-Su 8am-9pm. MC, V, AmEx,* **1 2** *to 18th St.*

Crate and Barrel

For the last minute housewarming party, or largely decorative kitchen paraphernalia, the label delivers the rare combination of style and value. This "upscale Ikea" is ready to equip the urban warrior with the bare necessities, from crème brulée dishes to martini glasses. *650 Madison Avenue (at 59th St.), (212) 308-0011. Open M-F 10am-8pm, S 10am-7pm, 12pm-6pm.* **F N R W** *to 59th St.-Lex. Ave.*

Depression Modern

Plush, beautiful furniture and housewares in retro styles make for great browsing, test-sitting, and daydreaming of a perfectly decorated home for anyone who longs for the era of their grandparents. It's all very expensive, but the people who run it are amiable and tolerant of browsers. *150 Sullivan St., (212) 982-5699. Open W-Su 12pm-6pm. Cash Only,* **1 2 A C E F V S** *to W. 4th St.* &

Dom USA

Need some inflatable furniture for your dorm room? Have a fondness for housewares made of neon-colored plastic? All

that and plenty more for the home at this trendy decorator hot spot, as well as sundry other junk, from pens to pillboxes. Most of it is inexpensive and equally suitable for gift-giving or feeding your personal flair for home decorating.
382 W. Broadway (bet. Spring and Broome Sts.), (212) 334-5580. Open M and W-S 11am-8pm, Su 11am-7pm. MC, V, AmEx, A C E to Spring St., N R to Prince St.

Fish's Eddy

Mix and match from overstocks of commercial dishes and glasses to set a dinner table that no one else will have. Watch the price tags, though. Don't leave without checking out the bins in the back for $1 saucers and the shelves around the sides for $2 wine glasses. Fishes Eddy will leave anyone feeling like a homebody who can set a unique discounted table – that will definitely get your family and guests talking.
889 Broadway (at 19th St.), (212) 420-9020, www.fisheseddy.com. Open M-Sa 10am-9pm, Su 11am-8pm. MC, V, AmEx, L N R Q W 4 5 6 to 14th St.-Union Sq.

Just Bulbs

The name really says it all. Find every variety of light bulb imaginable, including those for decoration, gifts and specific holidays.
936 Broadway (bet. 21st and 22nd Sts.), 228-7820. Open M-F 9am-6pm, T 9am-7pm, S 10am-6pm,

Su 12pm-6pm. MC, V, AmEx, D, Diners, N R to 23rd St.

Mxyplyzyk

Long indispensable to interior designers and the young trend crowd, Mxyplyzyk features relentlessly elegant home furnishings that inspire feelings of mushy love. The merchandise is so original and well selected that it is hard to argue even with the lonely row of slippers. Yes, the prices can skew high-but even the $4 cups are, somehow their own works of art.
123/125 Greenwich Ave. at 13th St., (212) 989-4300. Open M-S 11am-7pm, Su 12pm-5pm. A C E L to Union Square/14th St.

Pottery Barn

A yuppie store that carries everything from beds to plates to sun umbrellas. The perfect place to shop for a new home if you have some money and are into darker colors and sophisticated style and prices. This store is comparable to Crate and Barrel.
*1965 Broadway (at 67th St.), (917) 579-8477. M-S 10am-9pm, Su 11am-7pm.
1 to 66th St.*

Urban Archaeology

The stock is sold both wholesale and retail at this furniture store, which houses a collection of architectural ornaments, artifacts and lighting fixtures in the kitschy retro vein in what was once a four-story candy factory.

143 Franklin St., (212) 431-4646. Open M-F 8am-6pm, S 12pm-6pm. 1 2 to Franklin St.

White Trash

From shiny silver toasters to impressively tacky glassware sets, your own grandmother probably got rid of '50s and '60s junk like this twenty years ago. Nevertheless, it's all hip again and the prices aren't too inflated to be a reasonable and interesting alternative to outfitting your home in department store standards.
304 E. 5th St. (bet. First and Second Aves.), (212) 598-5956. Open T-Sa 2pm-8:30pm, Su 1pm-8pm. MC, V, F to Second Ave., 6 to Astor Pl., N R to 8th St.

Bleecker Bob's

Packed with a huge vinyl selection, including rare albums, Bob's is a hub for DJ's and music collectors alike. Their rock, metal, indie, emo, punk and hardcore CD selection draws everyone else. Other bonuses include the posters, bongs ("for tobacco only") and a body piercing/tattoo shop in the back.
118 W. 3rd St. (bet. MacDougal St. and First Ave.), (212) 475-9677. Open M-Su 12pm-1am. MC, V, AmEx, D, A C E F V S W to 4th St.

Chelsea Second Hand Guitars

Go in and try one on for size: Strats, Les Pauls, Fenders, etc. Vintage gui-

tars for the finger-pick connoisseur.
220 W. 23rd St. (bet. Seventh and Eighth Aves.), (212) 675-4993. Open M-S 12pm-7pm. MC ,V, AmEx, 1 2 to 23rd St., C E to 23rd. St.

Dance Tracks

If you're disappointed in the dance/electronica selection of your neighborhood megastore, look no further. At Dance Tracks you'll discover a wide selection of eurodance, club imports, your favorite DJ's remixes and house. The knowledgeable staff also gives fine recommendations catering to your particular taste, be it techno or trance.
91 E. 3rd St. (at First Ave.), (212) 260-8729. Open M-F 12pm-9pm, Sa 12pm-8pm, Su 12pm-7pm. MC, V, AmEx, D. F V to Second Ave.

Disc-O-Rama

This small chain was serving downtown New York's audio/visual needs before the words "DVD" and "CD" entered our vocabulary. Though they've updated their inventory since then, offering an extensive collection of current music and video releases, Disc-O-Rama still keeps it old school with a vinyl department, and album prices that are always cheaper than a movie ticket. Try finding either of those features in a megastore.
40 Union Sq. E. (bet. 16th and 17th Sts.), (212) 260-8616, ww.discorama.com.

Open M-F 8:30am-6:45pm, Sa 10am-6pm, Su 11am-5:45pm. MC, V, AmEx, **L N R W Q 4 5 6** *to Union Sq.-14th St.* ♿

Fat Beats

Indispensable for hip-hop fans, this well-stocked shop also doesn't do too badly in the acid jazz and reggae departments either. Secondhand bins are an amazing source of classics.
406 Sixth Ave. (bet. 8th and 9th Sts.), (212) 673-3883. Open M-F 12pm-9pm, S 12pm-10pm, Su 12pm-6pm. MC, V, Am Ex, NR to 8th St., **6** *to Astor Pl.*

Generation Records

The best selection of punk, hardcore and underground music in the city. Cheap movie and music posters, T-shirts, used CDs and an extensive vinyl stock soothe the emotional scars inflicted by the glaring staff.
210 Thompson St. (bet. Bleecker and 3rd Sts.), (212) 254-1100. Open M-R 11am-10pm, F-Sa 11am-1am, Su 12pm-10pm. MC, V, AmEx, **A C E F V S W** *to 4th St.*

Kim's Mediapolis

The newest installment of the Kim's stores boasts videos, DVDs, music and books. The video selection remains their strong suit. There's an enormous collection of Hollywood and indie movies. It's difficult to browse, so come with some idea of what you want. The impressive book section overshadows their weaker music selection. Don't expect to get much assistance, either. The staff brings the daydreaming, careless attitude all the way from the Village branches.
Broadway (bet. 113th and 114th Sts.), (212) 864-5321, ww.kimsvideo.com. Open M-Su 9am-12am, **1** *to 116th St.-Columbia University
6 St. Marks Pl. (at Third Ave.), (212) 505-0311. Open M-Su 9am-12am.* **6** *to Astor Pl.,* **L** *to Third Ave.*

Matt Umanov Guitars

Anyone in a band knows this long-time Village institution. Acoustic and electric instruments at reasonable prices, as well as a knowledgeable staff.
273 Bleecker St. (bet. Sixth and Seventh Aves.), (212) 675-2157. Open M-S 11am-7pm, Su 12pm-6pm. MC, V, AmEx, D, **A C E F V S** *to W. 4th St.*

Midnight Records

Calling all spinners, DJs, and jazz heads. Remember those large round disks with deep grooves in them? This dealer of vinyl, with both old and new collectibles, is living proof that albums have not completely gone the way of the dinosaur. Check out their virtual site at www.midnightrecords.com
263 West 23rd St. (bet. Seventh and Eighth Aves.), (212) 675-2768. Open T-S 12am-6pm.

MC, V, AmEx, D, **1 2 C E** *to 23rd St.*

The Music Factory

The latest in contemporary music including hip-hop, gospel, jazz, reggae and soul. Many artists often do in-store signings or performances here to promote their material. Cassettes, vinyl, CD's and even videotapes are available at very affordable prices at this local DJ hang-out.
162-01 Jamaica Ave. (at 162nd St.), Jamaica, Queens. (718) 291-3135. Open M-S 10am-8pm, Su 11am-6:30pm. MC, V, AmEx, D, **E** *to Jamaica Ctr.* ♿

Norman's Sound and Vision

Super friendly and knowledgeable Norman claims his store has the "best selection of jazz in New York." Also browse the vast assortment of rock, punk, indie, Latin and world music. Downstairs features used videos, CDs, vinyl and laserdiscs plus T-shirts and even leather jackets. The eager and unpretentious staff won't make you feel ashamed for buying that No Doubt CD.
67 Cooper Sq. (bet. 7th and 8th Sts.), (212) 473-6599. Open M-Su 10am-11pm. MC, V, AmEx, DC, D, **6** *to Astor Pl.*

Other Music

A well-deserved haven for indie-rock lovers which also offers a full selection of ambient psychedelia, and noise. Keep an eye out for special in-store performances that have already featured Yo La Tengo and Jowe Head.
15 E. 4th St. (bet. Broadway and Lafayette), (212) 477-8150. Open M-F 12pm-9pm, S 12pm-8pm, Su 12pm-7pm. MC, V, AmEx, **N R** *to 8th St.,* **6** *to Astor Pl.*

Sam Ash

Ever want to DJ? Sprawling along 48th Street, these four music shops fulfill almost every music-making need, selling acoustic instruments, recording equipment, MIDI systems, computers and software, DJ equipment, lighting, sheet music, and other items. The staff knows its stuff, and all locations (except for #163) rent and repair instruments and equipment.
155, 160, 159, and 163 W. 48th St. (bet. Sixth and Seventh Aves.), (212) 719-2299. Open M-F 10am-8pm, S 10am-7pm, Su 12pm-6pm. MC, V, AmEx, D, **N R W** *to 49th St. or* **B D F V** *to 47-50 St./Rockefeller Center or* **1 2** *to 50th St.*

Tower Records

New York's first music superstore has been surpassed in size by many others, but still has a strong selection-although it can be hard to find major rock titles here, oddly enough.
-692 Broadway (at 4th St.), (212) 505-1500. Open M-Su 9am-12pm. MC, V, AmEx, **N R** *to 8th St.,* **6** *to Astor Place.
-1961 Broadway (at 66th St.), (212) 799-2500,* **1 2** *to 66th St.-Lincoln Ctr.*

Vinylmania

Specializing in house music and imports. You can listen before you buy. *60 Carmine St. (bet. Seventh Ave. and Bedford St.), (212) 924-7223. Open M-S 11am-9pm, Su 11am-7pm. MC, V, AmEx,* **1 2** *to Houston St.*

Virgin Megastore

Redefining the idea of the megastore, this flashy three-level entertainment complex boasts movie theaters, over one thousand listening booths, and a wide selection of videos, laser discs and CD-ROMs. *1540 Broadway (bet. 45th and 46th Sts.), (212) 921-1020. Open Su-R 9am-1am, F-S 9am-2pm. MC, V, AmEx, D,* **N R S Q W 1 2 3 7** *to Times Square.*
Other locations in Manhattan.

Anbar Shoe Steal

The southeastern corner of TriBeCa is a bargain shoppers paradise, and this is by far the best outlet for great shoe deals. Quality, name brand footwear goes for close-out prices and the selection is remarkably good, especially for those seeking sizes other than a seven or eight. Perfect for finding cheap and stylish accessories to match an end-of season clothes purchase in an unusual color. *60 Reed St. (bet. Church St. and Broadway), (212) 227-0253. Open M-F 9:30am-6:30pm, S 11am-5:45 pm. MC, V, AmEx, D,*

A C 1 2 *to Chambers Street* &

Cole Haan

Shoes of the finest materials and nicest design are available in this Upper East Side foot haven. The store utilizes its space so as to display the merchandise (including other leather goods), quite well. *667 Madison Ave. (at 61st St.), (212) 421-8440. Open M-F 10am-7pm, S 12pm-6pm. MC, V, AmEx, D, 456 to 59th St.,* **N R** *to Lexington Ave.* &

John Fluevog

Possibly the hippest source of shoes in the city, a Fluevog can be spotted a mile away. Chunky platforms, combat-quality boots, and funky, offbeat colors are all well-represented. End-of-the-season sales can yield amazing bargains on the otherwise expensive footwear, usually priced at around $100. *250 Mulberry St. (212) 431-4484. Open M-S 11am-7pm, Su 12pm-6pm. MC, V, AmEx, D,* **N R** *to Prince St. or* **F S V** *to Broadway /Lafayette St.* &

Kenneth Cole – Reaction

Never accused of being right-wing, Kenneth Cole's style is definitely fashion forward. While the pulsating speakers, moderate prices and clean lines are far from innovations, they are welcome diversions from the $124 jeans at neighboring stores. The long lines at the register prove that some things never go out of style. *130 E. 57th (at Lexington Ave.), (212) 688-1670. Open M-S 10am-8pm, Su 11am-6pm.* **4 5 6 F N R W** *to 59th St.-Lex. Ave. Other locations in Manhattan.*

Sacco

Trendy, retro, and classic, this chic shop carries it all. Make this store your first stop for well-made, eclectic women's footwear. Shoes tend to be dressy and relatively expensive, but there are always sale selections. Clearances offer an additional 20 percent off the sale price. *324 Columbus Ave. (bet. 75th and 76th Sts.), (212) 799-5229. Open M-F*

11am-8pm, Sa 11am-7pm, Su 12pm-7pm. MC, V, AmEx, D, **1 2 3** *to 72nd St.* &

Steve Madden – Shoe Biz

A division of Steve Madden, the store has lots of trendy shoes for those who need a lift. Whether stacked or spike heels, platform or wedge, most of the shoes fall somewhere between casual and funky formal. This is a good store for fashion conscious teens and the young at heart who want to walk tall while spending small. *853 Broadway (at 14th St.), (212) 253-8744. Open M-Su 9am-10pm.* **L N R 4 5 6** *to 14th St.). Other locations in Manhattan.*

Trash and Vaudeville

Once this split-level store defined a look that made New York famous. Now merchandise appears trashy and punkish, but the shoe and boot selection in the back is still one of the best in town. *4 St. Mark's Pl. (bet. Second and Third Aves.), (212) 982-3590. Open M-R 12pm-8pm, F 11:30am-8:30pm, S 11:30am-9:30pm, Su 1pm-7pm. MC, V, AmEx, D,* **6** *to Astor Pl.*

Bicycle Habitat

If the quality of a bike store can be determined by counting the number of customers' bikes that

are chained outside, then this is one of the best in the city. Customers here are serious about their bikes and the same people can be found day after day checking out new models, picking up parts or just discussing their obsession.
244 Lafayette St. (bet. Prince and Spring Sts.), (212) 431-3315, www.bicyclehabitat.com. Open M-R 10am-7pm, F 10am-6:30pm, Sa-Su 10am-6pm. MC, V, AmEx, N R to Prince St. or 6 to Spring St.

Blades Boards & Skates

The helpful staff would readily join their patrons on Astor Pl. at one of the wheels-only lunch break congregations. Slick new styles of in-line skates, roller skates and standard skater gear also available at not-so-unconventional prices.
659 Broadway (bet. Bleecker and Bond Sts.), (212) 477-7350, www.blades.com. Open M-S 10am-9pm, Su 11am-7pm. MC, V, AmEx, D, F S V to Broadway-Lafayette St., 6 to Bleecker St.

Gotham Bikes

A good place to buy or rent a bike without being intimidated by a staff of gearheads trying to push an Italian racing model when you just want to ride through the park.
112 W. Broadway (bet. Duane and Reade Sts.), (212) 732-2453, www.gothambikes.com.

Open M-S 10am-6:30pm, S 10:30am-5pm. MC, V, AmEx, 1 2 to Chambers St.

Paragon

Whether the game is badminton, snowboarding or basketball, this sports superstore is sure to have the right gear. The shoe department often has better deals than the chains.
867 Broadway (at 18th St.), (212) 255-8036, www.paragonsports.com. Open M-Sa 10am-8pm, Su 11:30am-7pm. MC, V, AmEx, 1 2 to 18th St.

Patagonia

This trendy sportswear store holds fashionable attire for the mountains, the beach, traveling, surfing, fishing and paddling. Urban types have been wearing Patagonia for even their un-rugged environs. The company is famous for their soft, outdoor fleece jackets. If you want to look stylish on your outward-bound trip, this is the place to shop.
101 Wooster Street (between Prince and Spring Sts.), (212) 343-1776. Open M-S 11am-7pm, Su 12pm-6pm. N R to Prince St, C E 6 to Spring St.

MISCELLANEOUS

Abracadabra

TV stations, movie studios, and theaters are the biggest patrons of this dark and wild costume and statue shop. Those in the "Eyes Wide Shut"

fetish crowd are also fans. Abracadabra will sell you Venician masks identical to those featured in that notorious orgy scene. But if you're not the orgy type, Abracadabra can still give you a Halloween costume without compare, although some of the costumes may have seen better days. The selection can't be beat.
19 W. 21st. (bet. 5th and 6th Aves.), (212) 627-5194. Open M-S 11am-7pm, Su 12pm-5pm. 1 2 to 23rd St.

Aphrodisia

Herbs, spices, and a variety of teas intended to rejuvenate mind and body.
264 Bleecker St. (bet. Cornelia and Jones Sts.), (212) 989-6440. Open M-S 11am-7pm, Su 12pm-5pm. MC, V, AmEx, A C E F V S to West 4th St.

Condomania

Self-explanatory; prophylactics of all shapes, sizes, and flavors. Merely browsing here can be an amusing experience. Condomania even has the latest technology in condoms, including the "reservoir tip" that could fit a baseball, and looks like a light bulb.
351 Bleecker St. (bet. Christopher and W. 4th Sts.), (212) 691-9442. Open Su-R 11am-11pm, F-S 11am-12am. MC, V, AmEx, 1 2 to Christopher Street

FAO Schwarz

Long before Tom Hanks and "Big," F.A.O. has drawn crowds of wide-

eyed youngsters and their equally impressed parents during the holiday season, and it's hard not to get pulled in – the store puts on a helluva show. That said, unless you enjoy triple digit markups, leave the purchases for Toys 'R' Us.
767 Fifth Ave. (at 58th St.), (212) 644-9400, www.fao.com. Open M-W 10am-7pm, R-Sa 10am-8pm, Su 11am-7pm. MC, V, AmEx, D, N R W to 59th St.-Fifth Ave.

Firefighter's Friend

This independently owned novelty store carries New York firefighter and police t-shirts, caps, patches and pins. Though the store is small and cramped, they offer a variety of items and sizes, and much of the proceeds go to the families of the fallen Sept. 11 firemen. They also ship nationwide. The quality is much higher than anything sold on sidewalks, but so are the prices.
263 Lafayette (at Prince St.), (212) 226-3142, www.nyfirestore.com. Open M-Sa 10am-6pm, Su Noon-5pm. MC, V, AmEx, D, N R to Prince St., 6 to Spring St.

House of a Million Earrings

Ethnic-inspired clothing, posters, paintings, crafts and books. Hand-made jewelry, incense and greeting cards are also for sale at this family-owned business. Great place for gifts.
169-17 Jamaica Ave., Jamaica, Queens. (at 169th St.), (718) 297-

7950, MC, V, AmEx, D, **E** to JamaicaCenter/ Parsons/Archer Ave.

Jerry Ohlinger's Movie Store

Shoeboxes of old publicity shots, movie stills, posters and playbills crowd this treasure trove of memorabilia for avid film buffs. Color stills go for around $3.50. Don't miss the autographed pics of Orson Welles and Montgomery Clift by the door.
242 W. 14th St. (bet. Seventh and Eighth), (212) 989-0869. Open M-Su 1pm-7:45pm. MC, V, AmEx, D, **1 2 3 A C E L** *to 14th St.*

Kate's Paperie

Sheaves of fanciful wrapping paper and reams of stationery fill every nook of this location, augmented by paper-related merchandise ranging from kites to hatboxes to desks.
561 Broadway (at Prince St.), (212) 941-9816. Open M-S 10am-7pm, Su 11am-7pm. MC, V, AmEx, **N R** *to Prince St.*

Additional Locations in Manhattan.

Mariposa

New-age music and massive wall displays strive to put this beautiful boutique's butterfly wares into naturalistic context. Lepidopterists can check out the carefully mounted winged specimens in their infinite variety behind clear Plexiglas frames.
South St. Seaport, Pier 17, (212) 233-3221. Open M-S 10am-9pm, Su 11am-8pm. MC, V, AmEx, **A C J M Z 1 2 4 5** *to Fulton Street*

Maxilla and Mandible

Literally filled to the rafters with perfect seashells, fossilized trilobites from exotic locales, authentic antlers and skulls, and insects preserved in amber.
451 Columbus Ave. (at 82nd St.), (212) 724-6173. Open M-S 11am-7pm, Su 1pm-5pm. MC, V, AmEx, **1 2** *to 79th St.*

Pier 17

Three levels of somewhat overpriced tourist shops may not seem like anything special, but at least you can get some great views of the Brooklyn Bridge from the top floor. Also a good place to bring Aunt Martha from Ohio.
South St. (at Fulton St.). Open M-S 10am-9pm, Su 11am-8pm. **A C J M Z 1 2 4 5** *to Fulton St.*

The Pink Pussycat

A Village landmark. All manner of erotica, from lingerie and clothing to, well, other things designed to aid your love life. The store isn't known for its service, so come armed with knowledge. A bag bearing its famous name is bound to create the necessary reaction from any lover.
167 W. 4th St. (bet. Sixth and Seventh Aves.), (212) 243-0077. Open S-R 10am-2am, F-S 10am-3am. MC, V, AmEx, **A B C E F Q** *to W. 4th St.,* **1 2** *to Christopher St.* &

Tents & Trails

Manhattan's low-key place for gearheads. If you're sick of battling it out in E.M.S. and Paragon Sports, this outdoor clothing and equipment store is the place for you. The prices are the best in town.
21 Park Pl. (bet. Church St. and Broadway) (212) 227-1760, MC, V, AmEx, **1 2 A C** *to Chambers St.*

Urban Bird

If you can stand the squawking, visiting this cramped bird shop, chock full of flamboyantly colored parrots, cockatoos and other tropical birds. It is like a free trip to the zoo. If you happen to have a bird, they stock everything you may need for it.
19 Greenwich Ave (bet. 10th and Cristopher Sts.), (212) 352-3332. Open M-F 12pm-7:30pm, S-Su 1pm-8pm. MC, V, AmEx, D, Diners, **A C E F V S** *to W. 4th St.*

Vendors along Canal Street

When you're looking for a Prada knock-off for mom or a cheap pair of shades for yourself, this is the place to go. Prices are always negotiable, no matter how intimidating the vendor appears. If Mom wants that bag to be a Donna Karan instead, no problem—most stands will change the label for you in a jiffy.
Canal St. (bet. Broadway and Elizabeth St.), Cash Only, **J M Z N Q R W** *to Canal St.*

Financial District

Abercrombie & Fitch
Century 21
Dee & Dee
Syms
J & R Musicworld
Mariposa
Pier 17
Tents and Trails

TriBeCa

Anthropologie
Urban Archaeology
Anbar Shoe Steal
Gotham Bikes

Chinatown

Pearl River Mart
Pearl Paint
Confucious Plaza Vendors
Dynasty Supermarket
Hong Kong Supermarket
Kam WO Herb and Tea Co., Inc.
Ten Ren Tea and Ginseng Co.
Vendors along Canal Street

Little Italy

INA
Do Kham
E. Rossi & Co.
Alleva Dairy, Inc.
Di Palos' Fine Foods
Italian Food Center
John Fluevog

Lower East Side

TG-170
Economy Candy

SoHo

555 Soul Inc.
Betsey Johnson
APC
Cynthia Rowley
Living Doll
Stussy
agnes b.
anna sui
Dolce & Gabbanna
Miu Miu
Prada
Alice Underground
SoHo Antiques Fair and Flea Market
Face Stockholm
L'Occitane
M.A.C. Cosmetics
Swiss Army Store
Our Name's Mud
Dean & Deluca
Gourmet Garage
Bicycle Habitat
Patagonia
Firefighter's Friend
Kate's Paperie

East Village

99X
Blue
Patricia Field
Cheap Jack's
Cherry
Kiehl's
Exit 9
White Trash
Dance Tracks
Norman's Sound and Vision
Other Music
Tower Records
Trash and Vaudeville

Greenwich Village

French Connection
Urban Outfitters
Beacon's Closet
Andee's Cheepees
Antique Boutique
What Comes Around Goes Around
A.L. Bazzini
Balducci's
Washington Market Park
Depression Modern
Dom
Bleecker Bob's
Fat Beats
Generation Records
Matt Umanov Guitars
Vinylmania
Blades, Boards, & Skates
Aphrodisia
Condomania
Jerry Ohlinger's Movie Store
The Pink Pussycat
Urban Bird

Gramercy

Empori Armani
Filene's Basement
TJ Maxx
Kalyustan's
Union Square Greenmarket
ABC Carpet and Home
Fishes Eddy
Mxyplyzyk
Disc-O-Rama
Steve Madden-Shoe Biz
Paragon

Chelsea

Sam Flax
Comme des Garcons
Burlington Coat Factory
Daffy's
Loehmann's
Moe Ginsburg
Annex Antiques Fair and Flea Market
Chelsea Antiques Annex
Origins
Chelsea Market
Bed Bath and Beyond
Just Bulbs
Chelsea Second Hand Guitars
Midnight Records
Abracadabra

Midtown

Lee's Art Shop
Gap
H & M
J. Crew
Original Levi's Store
Zara
Bally
Chanel
Gucci
Bergdorf Goodman
Bloomingdale's
Henri Bendel
Macy's
Sak's 5th Ave
Takashimaya
Conway Stores
Strawberry
Datavision
Sephora
Manhattan Mall
Crate and Barrel
Sam Ash
Virgin Megastore
Kenneth Cole-Reactopm

Upper East Side

Calypso
Diesel
Calvin Klein
Givenchy
Barney's
Out of the Closet
Elk Candy
La Maison du Chocolat
M. Rohrs House of Fine Teas & Coffee
Cole Haan
FAO Schwarz

Upper West Side

Banana Republic
Club Monaco
Lord of the Fleas
Citarella
Gormet Garage
Zabar's
Pottery Barn
Tower Records
Sacco
Maxilla and Mandible

Morningside Heights

Card-o-Mat
Milano Market
Mondel Chocolates
Kim's Mediapolis

Harlem

Fairway

Washington Heights

Mister Roger

Queens

Von's School of Hard Knocks
The Music Factory
House of a Million Earrings

Brooklyn

Domsey Warehouse
Brooklyn Brewery

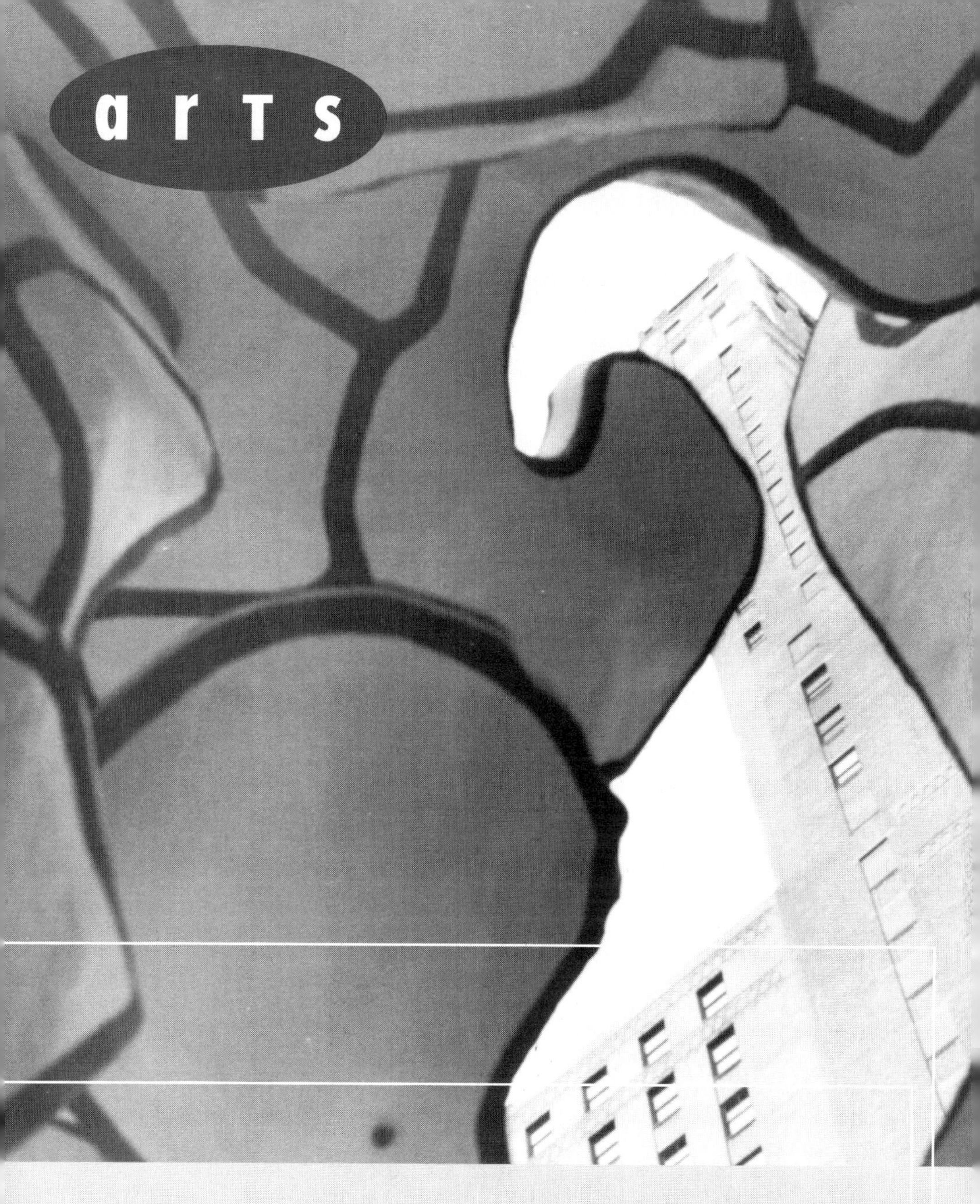

arts

visual
arts
GUGGENHEIM

museums/galleries

The Roots of Museum Culture

New Yorkers take their city's immersion in art for granted—but those new to the city will note that this is taking a lot for granted. The museums are excellent, the galleries exciting and diverse, the breadth of the collections astonishing. Avoid museum burnout by staggering visits, and by selecting museums of different sizes and focus. Most of the major museums now have good—if pricey—cafes, which serve as a perfect way of restoring energy without retreating back onto the streets.

Museums, like everything else in New York, are not cheap. But for the impoverished and the flexible, there's usually a way around entrance fees at the major museums. The Metropolitan Museum, MoMA and the Whitney offer free entry to the public one night a week, usually a weekend night. While museums throughout the city cater to a wide variety of tastes, these three institutions pave the way. Stroll around and be thankful for those great 19th-century robber-barons—most of the collections in the major museums were formerly private. The Metropolitan has benefited from sizable bequests from railroad tycoon Jacob Rogers, as well as from W.C. Bryant and J.P. Morgan. Founded in 1870, additions were made in 1909 by McKim, Mead and White. By 1929, other substantial additions included gifts made by John D. Rockefeller and Louisine Havemeyer. Content with the elitist connotation high art carries, the Met's collection reflects none of the dynamism of the contemporary art scene. The museum balked at Gertrude

Vanderbilt Whitney's 1930 offer of her collection of American paintings and funding to build a wing for it. Since World War II, however, the museum's attitude has been decidedly more open-minded, seeking to exhibit a wider range of art. The Met has since presented more broad-based shows, as well as educational and community programs. Today, with more than a million pieces, the Met is the largest art museum in the western hemisphere. The museum functions on a pay-as-you-wish basis, suggesting, but not enforcing, a donation of $8 for adults. Summers, the roof garden offers museum-goers cocktails and a spectacular view of the mid-town skyline.

Unlike the Met, which was funded

ASHCAN SCHOOL
New York's influence on the course of 20th-century art begins with the Ashcan school, shortly after the turn of the century. New York has emerged as an artistic laboratory in which experimentation is the norm and deviation is embraced. Exchanging the 19th-century's "art-for-art's-sake" sensibilities for what one leader of the movement called "art for life," members of the Ashcan School grew dissatisfied with the academic elitism of contemporary artists. They painted what they saw around them, favoring a Bowery street urchin as a subject over a nude in a studio. Celebrating the vitality that the city provided them, Ashcan artists Maurice Prendergast and George Lukes helped unmoor 20th-century art from its neoclassical foundations.

by a $500,000 tax levied by the city, the Whitney began as one family's private enterprise. Perhaps as a result, the autonomous Whitney has proven tolerant of all genres of American art. Originally housed in four town houses on Eighth Street, the Whitney Museum of American Art committed itself to the promotion of the works of living artists overlooked by other galleries and museums. By 1932, the first of the Whitney's Biennial Exhibitions quickly established the museum as the vanguard showcase of contemporary American painting.

A cultural incubator for many American movements, including Abstract Expressionism and Pop Art, the museum provided an arena in which artists excluded from the mainstream could be celebrated. Equally as important as the breadth of its collection is the contribution the museum has made to the scholarship and legitimization of American art. Due to its enormous appeal, the museum has moved twice in order to accommodate its popularity and the expansion of its collection.

With parts of this collection now on display at its downtown branch and in the lobbies of some of the city's most populous corporate spaces, like the Philip Morris Building, the Equitable Center and the Federal Reserve Plaza, the Whitney encourages prominent presentation of and high regard for American art. *Admission is pay-what-you-wish on Fridays from 1-9pm. Call (212) 570-3676 for more information.*

The Museum of Modern Art is the third of New York's triumvirate of museum powerhouses. Abby Rockefeller established the museum in 1929 with a modest gift of eight prints and one drawing. Shortly thereafter, a generous gift from the wife of Colorado Senator Simon Guggenheim enabled Rockefeller to expand the collection considerably. The MoMA now owns more than 100,000 pieces. Committed from its inception to presenting the visual arts in all its various forms, the museum is responsible for introducing much of the European avant-garde to America.

In addition to the traditional visual arts of painting and sculpture, the MoMA also features furniture design and architecture, prints, illustrated books and photography. The museum's film and video archives, self-described as "the strongest international film collection in the United States," contain all extant negatives from the Biograph and Edison companies.

Apart from the permanent collection, the MoMA runs a special exhibit which changes every few weeks and costs extra to view. The MoMA has recently moved to Queens due to renovations. Until 2005, when it returns to Manhattan, the Summer Concert Series and the Sculpture Garden will remain closed. *Call (212)*

Galleries in the city are exciting places to see new and progressive artwork.

708-9400 for more information or visit www.moma.org. Keep in mind that these are only three of the city's 40-plus museums. The Guggenheim, the Cooper-Hewitt and the Jewish Museum, among others, can be equally rewarding. In Brooklyn, the often-neglected jewel, the Brooklyn Museum, houses an enormous world-class permanent collection and changing exhibits. Living history museums, whose situation in a historic house lends them a more natural feeling, are tucked away in unassuming corners of the city, from the Theodore Roosevelt birthplace in Gramercy to the reputedly haunted Morris-Jumel Mansion in Washington Heights.

The Frick Collection, although it displays works of art in a museum fashion, is set up as a house, avoiding the sterile white-washed look of most city museums. Most museums give special tours and the larger ones often sponsor lectures and movie screenings. Call or stop by for a schedule and information about becoming a member. After all, without the support of their patrons, many museums would go under.

Current Museum and Gallery Culture

From the bright landscapes of Jacob Lawrence to the stark minimalism of Jacob Kline, from Alfred Stieglitz' clean urban angles to the sprawling graffiti Jean-Michel Basquiat, New York has fostered the cutting edge of the art world for decades. While artists like multimedia pioneer Bill Viola and celestial abstractionist Ross Bleckner enjoy one-man shows at the Guggenheim and in swank 57th Street galleries like Mary Boone's, the proverbial struggling artist starts from scratch at galleries like the Lower East Side's Esso, where Parsons, School of Visual Arts and Pratt grads explore the aftermath of pop art. They start at the BoHo paradise Pierogi 2000 and on the walls and sidewalks of the East Village and SoHo, where street-level graffiti artists turn pocked cement into canvas.

Like struggling actors, struggling artists have day jobs. They work in spaces that betray their pursuits, like at Limbo, a perennially popular Avenue A coffeehouse whose rotating installations come across as either pretentious or promising. The Anchorage, a space that opens up beneath the Brooklyn Bridge in the summer, displays intriguing and provocative pieces on its sweeping brick walls and archways. Neophytes should begin with a copy of the Gallery Guide, free in most showrooms, to become familiar with what the city has to offer.

Rising rents have caused many galleries to flee SoHo

*f*ree *a*dmission every*d*ay: pu*bl*ic

Often obscured, overlooked, or dismissed with mild bewilderment, pieces of public sculpture pepper the city; with a little research, it's possible to make sense of the more abstract pieces.

The artistic trends of the '50s and '60s are evident in Isamu Noguchi's "Sunken Garden" sculpture, constructed with granite, glass, and stone in 1961, at the forecourt of One Chase Manhattan Plaza.

The sculptures in Lincoln Center are public pieces of art.

Lying adjacent to the ground floor's banking area and visible from the street-level plaza above, the sculpture was inspired by the raked patterns of Japanese rock gardens from the Uji River in Kyoto. In the '70s, Jean Dubuffet's whimsical "Group of Four Trees" was added to the plaza, pairing its synthetic aluminum and fiberglass frame with the natural stones of Noguchi's piece.

In the mid-'60s at Lincoln Center, sculptures were chosen to represent the urban redevelopment programs which were reshaping the city, and city beautification through sculpture placement was also taking place around the same time downtown, with the Parks department's ambitious program called "Sculpture in Environment." Twenty-nine contemporary sculptures were placed throughout Manhattan, including Astor Place's familiar tilted steel black box, which formally goes by the name "Alamo" but is usually referred to as The Cube. The piece, designed by Bernard Rosenthal in 1967, was one of the first abstract sculptures on city property and has since served as a hangout for pre-pubescent skateboarders.

A few blocks southwest, in the court between the three towers of the residential complex at New York University Towers, Picasso's 1968 "Bust of Sylvette" is a towering presence between Mercer and LaGuardia Place. Critics complain that the piece exemplifies the problems inherent in enlarging a small piece to monumental scale, but that doesn't mitigate local resident's pride in having the 20th-century master's work grace their otherwise empty courtyard.

for Chelsea, the Lower East Side, and Williamsburg, Brooklyn, although there are still devoted daytrippers who crowd into the cast-iron buildings that are central to the art world.

Don't be intimidated by stodgy guards or uppity desk clerks; if you can't get up the nerve, try starting at low-key spots like Wooster Street's The Drawing Center and Broadway's Exit Art, or get your feet wet at one of the city's excellent museums, which consistently launch forward-thinking, provocative exhibits that keep abreast of national and international trends. The ambitious and defiant curators of the Whitney's Biennial, a show occurring in summers of odd-numbered years, never fail to provoke critical and public outcry with their unveilings.

Once you've raised your confidence level, try crashing a well-attended white wine reception, uptown on 57th Street between Madison and Park Avenues, or downtown along West Broadway or Prince Street in SoHo.

L I S T I N G S

MUSEUMS

A

Abigail Adams Smith Museum

John Quincy Adams' daughter wanted to replicate Mount Vernon here, but ended up with this 1799 carriage house. Formerly a hotel with offices for Standard Oil, the museum displays Colonial American memorabilia from the 1820s-40s in reconstructed rooms, which include a tavern, kitchen, bedroom and several parlors. There are lectures regularly, along with live music and an outdoor cafe during the summer months.
421 E. 61st St. (bet. First and York Aves.), (212) 838-6878, Admission: $3, $2 (students), T-Su 11am-4pm, **4 5 6** *to 59th St.,* **N R** *to Lexington Ave.*

African American Wax Museum

Nelson Mandela and Magic Johnson, together at last in life-size wax sculpture. Opened in 1989 by fashion designer and innovative artist Raven Chanticleer, the museum allows tours by appointment only, lending an intimacy to the experience.
316 W. 115th St. (bet. Manhattan and Frederick Douglass Aves.), (212) 678-7818, Cash Only, Suggested Donation $10, $5 (students), Tours: T-Su 1pm-6pm, **B C** *to 116th St.*

Alternative Museum

Founded and operated by artists, this strikingly introspective nonprofit organization features a range of works that compel viewers to examine the relationship between society and art.
594 Broadway, Suite 402 (bet. Houston and Prince Sts.), (212) 966-4444, Admission: $3 suggested, **N R** *to Prince St.*

American Craft Museum

Utilitarian, 20th-century American art, from chairs to teapots, finds a home in this magnificent space. Exhibits in the past have included textiles and intricate weavings.
40 W. 53rd St. (bet. Fifth and Sixth Aves.), (212) 956-3535, Admission: $5, $2.50 (students), T 10am-8pm, W-Su 10am-5pm, **E F V** *to Fifth Ave.* &

American Folk Art Institute

Classes and workshops are offered in all manner of media. Lectures and other panels are also held here. The American Folk Art Institute is actually located across the street from the American Craft Museum.
45 W. 53rd St. (bet. Fifth and Sixth Ave.), (212) 265-1040, Admission $9, $5 (seniors and students), T-Su 10-6pm, F 10-8pm, free on Friday from 6pm-8pm, **E F V** *to Fifth Ave.* &

American Museum of Moving Image

This museum is devoted to the art, history, technique and technology of the visual media and its influence on culture and society. Housed in the old Paramount Studios at the heart of Queens' old movie district, the museum is a treasure trove of movie memorabilia from the '30s and 40's. Regular film series at the Riklis Theater screen over 500 movies a year, which are free with admission.
35th Ave. (at 36th St.), (718) 784-4520, Admission: $8.50, $5.50 (students and seniors), T-F 12pm-5pm, S-Su 11pm-6pm, **R V** *to Steinway St.* &

American Museum of Natural History

A taxidermist's paradise and proud owner of a fantastic new wing packed with dinosaurs. The museum also houses a Hall of Human Evolution and Biology, chronicling human development from ape to homo-sapiens. Eat lunch under the whale.
W. 79th St. (on Central Park West), (212) 769-5100, Admission: $7, $5 (students), M-Su 10am-5:45pm, **B C** *to 81st St.* &

Asia Society

America's pre-eminent organization celebrates Asian cultural awareness with notable film series, lectures, and an art collection featuring sculpture, paintings, ceramics, prints and bronzes from across Asia. Prominent authors and public leaders speak regularly here. Other programs for the public include dance performances, well-attended art exhibits usually gathered from private collections, and receptions involving community and professional organizations. *725 Park Ave. (at 70th St.), (212) 288-6400, Admission: $7, $5 (students and seniors), MC, V, AmEx, T-Su 11am-6pm, F 11am-9pm, free on Friday from 6pm-9pm,* **6** *to 68th St.* &

Asian American Arts Center

As the name suggests, Asian-American artists have top billing at this thriving community arts center, which supports activities ranging from traditional dance performances to the journal on contemporary Asian-American artists, Arts Spiral. In February, the Asia Folk Arts Festival brings traditional arts produced both in the States and abroad for display. *26 Bowery (bet. Bayard and Pell Sts.), (212) 233-2154, Free admission, M-F 12:30pm-6:30pm,* **N R** *to Canal St.*

B

Black Fashion Museum

Both a school and museum of African and black American design and memorabilia since 1979. Visits are by appointment only. *155 W. 126th St. (bet. A.C. Powell and Malcolm X Aves.), Admission: $1.50, $1 (students), M-F 12pm-8 pm by appointment,* **A B C D 2 3** *to 125th St.* &

Bronx Museum of the Arts

Representing the urban experience through photography, sculpture and painting, this community museum pays special attention to the African, Asian and Latino heritage that define the Bronx. Shows change every three months. *1040 Grand Concourse (at 165th St.), (718) 681-6000, Admission: $3, $2 (students), W 12pm-9pm; R-Su 12pm-6pm,* **B D** *to 167th St.- Grand Concourse or 4 to 161st St.*

The Brooklyn Museum

This is a world-class museum with strong permanent collections and impressive special exhibitions. The American paintings are excellent, the Egyptian Wing is outstanding, and there's a lovely sculpture garden as well. Located next to the botanical garden, it's a great way to get away from it all while remaining in the City. *1200 Eastern Parkway (at Washington Ave.), next to Prospect Park, (718) 638-5000, Suggested admission: $6, $3 (students), W-F 10pm-5pm, S-Su 11am-6pm,* **1 2** *to Eastern Parkway*

C

Casa Italiana of NYU

The former home of General Winfield Scott, hero of the Mexican-American War and Chief-of-Staff of the U.S. Army in the 1850s. Call for information about free lectures, films and art exhibits that focus on Italian culture. *24 West 12th St. (bet. Fifth and Sixth Aves.), (212) 998-8730, Free admission, M-F 9am-5pm,* **F V L 1 2 3** *to 14th St.*

Casa Italiana of Columbia University

Ubiquitous in the press

{history}

ABSTRACTIONISM

After Paris fell to Germany in 1940, NY hosted an influx of European avant-guard artists making the city the world's undisputed artistic capital. The influence of émigré artists, such as Mondriaan, Fernand Leger and Max Ernst, precipitated an infusion of expressionism in American art, though their work had been foreshadowed in the homegrown organization American Abstract Artists, which formed in 1936 and included more obscure artists like George L.K. Morris.

The aptly dubbed Abstract Expressionists appended Freud's notion of the subconscious to Surrealism's notion of human-as-automaton and threw in concepts prevalent in mythology and Native American traditions as well. This amalgam, a kind of automatic art analogous to stream-of-consciousness writing, is one popular rationale which would explain the work of Jackson Pollack, Willem De Kooning, and Mark Rothko, whose emphasis on the artistic process led one critic to dub their style "action painting." The movement's first significant museum recognition was not until an immensely popular 1958 exhibit, which eventually traveled to Europe. Other important members of what came to be known as the New York School included Clyfford Still, Robert Motherwell, Lee Krasner, Franz Kline, Elaine de Kooning and Arshile Gorky. America's artistic dominance following the NY School's success led to the founding of an unprecedented number of galleries.

though nowhere to be found on Columbia University's campus, intellectual Umberto Eco is a scholar in residence at this recently remodeled institution, where lectures and events concerned with Italian culture are hosted regularly in the center's mock High Renaissance auditorium. *1161 Amsterdam Ave. (at 118th St.), 854-2306, www.italianacademy.columbia.edu, ❶ to 116th St.* &

Children's Museum of Manhattan

Apartment-bred kids get a taste of nature in the Urban Tree House, see what makes TV tick at the Time Warner Media Center, and read about the life and works of Dr. Seuss at this creative, interactive museum for children of all ages. Lots of wild water fun when the weather gets hot. *212 W. 83rd St. (bet. Broadway and Amsterdam Aves.), (212) 721-1234, www.cmom.org, Admission: $6, W-Su 10am - 5pm, ❶ to 86th St.* &

The Cloisters

A smorgasbord of medieval European glories, not to mention the finest picnicking in the city. The Met has its famed medieval collection here, including the breathtaking Unicorn tapestries, and medieval-themed readings and concerts keep hobbyists and scholars busy. The Cloisters themselves are a collection of European chapels and buildings in the Gothic and Romantic styles disassembled and shipped overseas stone by stone by John D. Rockefeller and George Barnard, then reassembled way uptown. *Fort Tryon Park, (212) 923-3700, Suggested admission: $10, $5 (students), Cash Only for admission, MC, V, AmEx, Diners, D at the gift shop, T-Su 9:30am-4:45pm, Ⓐ to 190th St.*

The Cooper-Hewitt Museum

The Smithsonian's National Museum of Design utilizes its 11,000 square feet to present landmark historic pieces as well as pioneering contemporary designs. Attention is paid to both the one-of-a-kind and the mass-produced. The building itself, once the Carnegie Mansion, boasts an eye-catching ceiling and an intricate staircase. Come free between 5pm and 9pm on Tuesdays. *2 E. 91st St. (at Fifth Ave.), 860-6868, Admission: $8, $5 (students), T 10am-9pm, W-S 10am-5pm, Su 12pm-5pm, ❹❺❻ to 86th St.* &

Czech Center

Exhibits on Czech culture and contemporary art. One recent show included photographs taken by blind children. *1109 Madison Ave. (at 83rd St.), (212) 288-0830, Cash Only, TWF 9am-5pm, R 9am-7pm, ❹❺❻ to 86th St.*

D

Dahesh Museum Inc.

This tiny museum is the only museum in America dedicated to collecting and exhibiting 19th and early 20th century European academic art. Changing exhibitions focus on such aspects of 19th century art as salons, academies and the birth of museums as well as on individual artists, their lives and patrons. *601 Fifth Ave. (at 48th St.), (212) 759-0606, Free admission, T– S, 11 am-6 pm, ❶ to 50th St. or Ⓝ Ⓡ train to 49th St.*

Deutsches Haus

Lecture series by scholars and cultural emissaries, readings by visiting German language authors, and a beautiful gallery space and library with an extensive periodical section are all open to the public. The NYU community enjoys a free film series showcasing everything from Weimar cinema to the contemporary work of artists like Wim Wenders. Ten week German language programs cost $300-400. *42 Washington Place (bet. University Pl. and Fifth Ave.), (212) 998-8660, MC, V, Ⓝ Ⓡ to 8th St* &

The Drawing Center

This nonprofit organization has an extensive collection of works on paper, including lots of drawings by a variety of new and established artists. The operation has been so successful that a second space recently opened across the street. *35 Wooster St. (bet. Grand and Broome Sts.), (212) 219-2166, Cash and Check Only, Ⓐ Ⓒ Ⓔ ❶ ❷ to Canal St.*

Dyckman Farmhouse Museum

A museum of 18th-century farmhouse life, located in one of Manhattan's oldest residences, reminds urbanites that the city did not simply spring from the soil full-grown. Period furnishings and quiet gardens maintain the mood. Benches out front are ideal for catching rays or hanging out with the area's elderly population. *4881 Broadway (at 204th St.), (212) 304-9422, Donations accepted, Cash Only, Ⓐ ❶ to 207th St.*

E

El Museo del Barrio

Originally a project in an East Harlem classroom, the sole American museum of Puerto Rican arts and culture has graduated to Museum Mile. Nearly 8,000 objects span over 800 years of history. The museum recently added more gallery space and celebrated its twenty-fifth anniversary. *1230 Fifth Ave. (at 104th St.), (212) 831-7272, Admission: $5, $3 (students), W-Su 11am-5pm, ❻ to 103rd St.* &

F

Fashion Institute of Technology

Exhibits feature famously fabulous designers, as well as work by talented FIT students.
227 W. 27th St. (at Seventh Ave.), (212) 217-7999, Admission Free, ① to 28th St. &

FIRE Museum

If a field trip to the fire station is a favorite childhood memory, don't miss this chance to relive it. The collection, housed in a renovated Beaux-Arts style firehouse from 1904, is the country's largest. It is full of all standard firehouse trappings, old engines and pump cars, and plenty of intriguing New York City fire history.
278 Spring St. (bet. Houston and Varick Sts.), (212) 691-1303, Admission: $4, free for children, MC, V, AmEx, T-S 10am-5pm, Su 10am-4pm, ① to Houston St. or CE to Spring St. &

Forbes Magazine Galleries

What good is it to merely read Forbes Magazine if you can't fantasize about what to buy once you make the famous "Forbes 500" list? Check out the galleries of "Wall Street's Bible" and ogle the luxe collection of Fabergé eggs, jewelry, toy boats, lead soldiers and fine art. The collection is fit for a czar, although entry is free.
60 Fifth Ave. (at 12th Street), (212) 206-5548, Free admission, T-W 10am-4pm, F-S 10am-4pm, ❺ ❤ to 14th St.

Fraunces Tavern Museum

George Washington gave his farewell address to his troops at this Georgian mansion, which was home to the Departments of Foreign Affairs, Treasury and War during New York's brief spell as a capital city. Now the museum specializes in American history and culture of the 18th and 19th centuries, with plenty of period rooms in which to play pretend. Below is a dark-paneled restaurant.
54 Pearl St. (at Broad St.), (212) 425-1778, Admission: $3, $2(students), TWF 10am-5pm, R 10am-7pm, S 11am-5pm, ❹❺ to Bowling Green or ❷❸ to Whitehall

Frick Collection

Steel kingpin Henry Clay Frick built this mansion with his fine art collection and a future museum in mind. The museum has been realized and now offers a rare chance to view masterpieces displayed in a residential setting. Highlights include portraits by El Greco, Rembrandt and Renoir, with waterscapes by Turner. One of the most soothing spots in the city is the sun-lit, virtually sound-proof indoor courtyard with marble benches and a drizzling fountain. The mail-in procedure for free tickets to Sunday concerts is an ordeal, but no tickets are required to listen in from the courtyard.
1 E. 70th St. (at Fifth Ave.), (212) 288-0700, Admission: $10, $5 (students and seniors), T-S 10am-6pm, Su 1pm-6pm, ❻ to 68th St. &

H

Hayden Planetarium

What is a black hole? Does Planet X exist? Find out at "The 20 Most Asked Questions About the Universe And the Answers," just one of the programs at the astronomy department in the domed building adjacent to the Museum of National History. Weekends find a youngish crowd at the ever-popular 3-D laser light shows. Pink Floyd is an old standby, while a more recent show featuring Nirvana and friends from Seattle ("Laser Grunge") rocks a little harder.
80th St. (bet. Columbus Ave.and Central Park West), (212) 769-5900, order tickets by calling 212-769-5200 or at www.amnh.org, October-June M-F 12:30pm-4:45pm, S-Su 10am-5:45pm, July-September weekends 12pm-4:45pm, ❸ ❻ to 81st St. &

I

International Center for Photography

Founded in 1974, one of the youngest members of Museum Mile showcases over 45,000 photographs and serves as a learning center for budding photographers of all levels.
1133 Sixth Ave. (at 43rd St.), (212) 860-1777, Admission: $9, $6 (students), T-R 10am-5pm, ❺ 19am-8pm, S-Su 10am-6pm, 6 to 96th St.

Intrepid Sea-Air-Space Museum

The former aircraft carrier USS Intrepid, commissioned in 1943, served 31 years in the US Navy. It survived numerous attacks, including seven bombings, five kamikaze assaults and a torpedo. The carrier retired in 1974. It now exhibits naval destroyers, guided-missile submarines, aircrafts and Felix DeWeldon's original Iwo Jima Memorial Statue.
Pier 86 (at Twelfth Ave. and 46th St.), (212) 245-0072. www.intrepidmuseum.org. Call for hours. Admission: $12; $9 for seniors, veterans and students; $2-$6 for children. Ⓐ Ⓒ Ⓔ ❶ ❷ ❸ Ⓝ Ⓡ Ⓠ Ⓦ Ⓢ ❼ to 42nd St.-Times Sq.

Islamic Cultural Center and Mosque

The city's central mosque holds prayer and studies on Sundays, as well as free courses for women on Saturdays on religion and Arabic.
97th St. (bet. First and Second Aves.), (212) 732-5234, ❻ to 96th St.

The Isamu Noguchi Garden Museum

More than 300 works in granite, steel and marble,

including the famous Akari paper light sculptures by Isamu Noguchi, who also designed the twelve galleries and the outdoor sculpture garden. Open April to October. *36-01 43rd Ave (at 36th St.), Queens, (718) 204-7088. Admission $5, $2.50 (students), Cash Only, R-F and M 10am-5pm, S-Su 11am-6pm, shuttle runs from 70th St. and Park Avenue on weekends*

J

The Jewish Museum

The country's largest collection of Judaica, housed in an imperious French Renaissance structure, boasts over 14,000 works in the permanent collection. Works detail the Jewish experience throughout history and feature archeological pieces, ceremonial objects, modern masterpieces by Marc Chagall and Frank Stella, and even an interactive computer program based on the Talmud. Admission is free Thursdays from 5pm-8pm. *1109 Fifth Ave. (at 92nd St.), 423-3200, Admission: $8, $5.50 (students), Su 10am-5:45pm, M-W 11am-5:45pm, R 11am-8pm, ❻ 11am-3pm 11am-5:45pm, 6 to 96th St.*

K

King Juan Carlos I Center

King Juan Carlos the First himself showed up along with Queen Sophia and Hillary Clinton to inaugurate the new hub of Spanish culture in the city. Housed in architect Stanford White's historic 19th century Renaissance-style Judson Hall, the center encourages the study of Spain and the rest of the Spanish-speaking world through lectures, colloquia and conferences with scholars and dignitaries. *53 Washington Square South (Thompson St.and 6th Ave.), (212) 998-3650,*  **Ⓐ Ⓑ Ⓒ Ⓕ Ⓥ Ⓢ** *to West 4th St.*

L

Lower East Side Tenement Museum

Chronicling an era when these streets were the most densely packed in the world, this museum, founded in 1988, is the first attempt the city has made at preserving a tenement. Like most tenements, this building predated existing housing laws. This one dates from 1863. Bedrooms were typically eight square feet, most apartments' largest rooms were a mere twelve by eleven feet, and tenants had no running water, flush toilets or electric lights. Most rooms even lacked windows. Founders Ruth J. Abram and Anita Jacobson strive to recreate the conditions

in this progressive attempt at reclaiming an often overlooked piece of the city's history. *97 Orchard St. (bet. Broome and Delancey Sts.), (212) 431-0233, call for tour reservations and prices. ❻ to Delancey St or*  *❻ ❻ ❻ to Essex St.*

M

The Metropolitan Museum of Art

Where to begin? The Met seems to be as big and sprawling as the city itself, and similarly the trick is finding the hidden (or not so hidden) treasures. Favorites include the spectacular Temple of Dendur, the American Wing Garden Court, the medieval section, and in the summer, the Roof Garden where an older crowd sips white wine and ponders the sculpture (out loud). Don't try to do too much, or to follow a strict plan, since this is the best place to get lost in New York City. *Fifth Avenue (bet. 79th and 84th Sts.), Suggested admission: $10, $5 (students), F-S 9:30am-9pm, S-R 9:30am-5:30pm, closed Monday, ❻ to 79th or 86th St.*

The Morgan Library

The country's largest collection of Mesopotamian cylinder seals now rests where J.P. Morgan used to pad about in slippers, though the appeal of this library and museum is much broader. The library's renowned collection of rare books, manuscripts and drawings contain, as their principal focus, the history, art and literature of Western civilization. *29 E. 36th St. (bet. Madison and Park Aves.), (212) 685-0610, www.morganlibrary.org.*

Open T-R 10:30am-5pm, F 10:30am-8pm, S 10:30am-6pm, Su 12pm-6pm. Cash Only, Admission: $8, $6 (students and seniors), 6 to 33rd St. &

Morris-Jumel Mansion

Down from the remaining farmhouse is the area's extant Georgian mansion, where Washington kept his troops during the Revolution. A choice exhibit displays the obit of Vice President Aaron Burr's wife Elise Jumel, whose early life as a "lady of the night" once scandalized New York society. *160th St. (east of St. Nicholas Ave.), (212) 923-8008, Admission: $3, Cash Only, W-Su 10am-4pm, C to 163rd St.*

The Museum for African Art

Exhibits seeking to facilitate a greater understanding of African art change twice a year at this two-floor showcase, one of two of its kind in the country. Complex exhibits often incorporate elements of folk art, sculpture and more conventional mediums to examine pervasive concepts in the tradition. Past exhibits include "Secrecy: African Art That Conceals and Reveals," and "Face of the Gods: Art and Altars of the Black Atlantic World." Film and video presentations, performance art and interactive, hands-on workshops take place in the newlyopened Educational Department. *593 Broadway (bet. Houston and Prince Sts.), (212) 966-1313, Admission: $4, $2 (students), WR and Su 11am-6pm, F-S 11am-8pm, N R to Prince St.*

Museum of American Illustration

View the work of key illustrators like Norman Rockwell and N.C. Wyeth at the home of the elite Society of Illustrators, which claims a long history of service to none other than the United States Army. Educational opportunities include sketch classes and lectures. *128 E. 63rd St. (bet. Park and Lexington Aves.), (212) 838-2560, Free admission, W-F 10am-5pm, S 12pm-4pm, 456 to 59th St. or N R to Lexington Ave.*

MoMA's Move to Queens

To allow for their current renovation and expansion project at their 53rd St. Manhattan location, the Museum of Modern Art has moved to a temporary new location in Long Island City, Queens and will remain there through the winter of 2004/2005. MoMA QNS, as it is called, houses highlights from MoMA's permanent collection of Modern and Contemporary painting and sculpture by such greats as Picasso, van Gogh and Warhol, as well as new exhibitions focusing on such subjects as MoMA's car collection, contemporary drawing, Avant-Garde architecture and the relationship between Matisse and Picasso. The museum provides a shuttle service from their 53rd St. location (bet. 5th and 6th Aves.) to MoMA QNS called the Queens Artlink and operates Saturday and Sunday from 10:00 am to 5:00 pm. MoMA QNS is also easily accessible by bus or subway from midtown. Directions can be found on MoMA's website. *33rd St.(at Queens Blvd.), (212) 708-9400, www.moma.org. Admission: $12, $8.50 (students and seniors), pay-what you wish Friday from 4pm-7:45pm. S-M and R 10am-5pm, F 10am-7:45pm.*

Museum of Television and Radio

Watch TV all day and still feel cultured. Computer consoles and viewing cubicles access tens of thousands of programs (and you thought cable was overwhelming), though if your tastes are way obscure, you should order ahead of time. A nostalgic display of Kermit the Frog and friends is worth the trip alone. *25 W. 52nd St. (bet. Fifth and Sixth Aves.), (212) 621-6800, Admission: $6, $4 (students), T-Su 12pm-6pm, open until 8pm on Thursday and 9pm on Friday, E V to 53rd St or NR to 50th St.*

Museum of the City of New York

In light of its ego, it's fitting that New York was the first city to get its own museum. Exhibits glorify New York's vast history and include photographs, furniture, costumes and toys. The Sunday concert series and the Big Apple Film make the trip worthwhile. *1220 Fifth Ave. (bet. 103rd and 104th Sts.), (212) 534-1672,*

Suggested admission: $7, $4 (students), Cash Only for Admission, MC, V, AmEx for Gift Shop, W-S 10am-5pm, Su 12pm-5pm, ❻ to 103rd St.

N

National Academy of Design

Founded in 1825 to promote the art of design in America through painting, sculpture, architecture and engraving, the academy still strives to meet its same purpose through training young artists and serving as a fraternal organization for other distinguished American artists. Its permanent exhibit features works by such 19th-century masters as Winslow Homer, John Singer Sargent and Thomas Eakins and such contemporary artists as Robert Rauschenberg, Isabel Bishop and Phillip Johnson.

1083 Fifth Ave. (bet. 89th and 90th Sts.), (212) 369-4880, Admission: $8, $4.50 (students and seniors), W-R 12pm-5pm, F-Su 11am-6pm, 456 to 86th St. &

New York Hall of Science

While designed primarily for kids, this playground of hands-on exhibits appeals to the science nut in everyone. The newly expanded exhibition hall boasts a Technology Gallery, with access to the Internet and a wide range of CD-ROMs. Who can resist entering the Realm of the Atom or the World of the Microbes? Thursdays are free 2pm-

5pm.

47-01 111th Street, Flushing Meadow Park, Queens, (718) 699-0005, www.nyhallsci.org. Admission: $7.50, $5 (students), see website for hours. 7 to 111th St. &

The New York City Transit Museum

While you may consider the turnstiles in subway stations to be antique, the originals are really housed in this authentic 1930s subway station. Vintage subway maps and mosaics comprise the permanent collection, along with exhibitions chronicling the development of rapid transit. Tag along with a school group for a field trip to somewhere great like the Metro-North car-repair facility. The museum is closed for renovations until 2003.

130 Livingston (bet. Boerum Place and Schermerhorn), (718) 330-3060, check website at www.mta.info for information regarding reopening, Admission: $3, $1.50 (students), ❶❷❹❺ to Borough Hall &

New York Historical Society

An imposing building across from Central Park houses both a library and a museum with a wealth of information and images of New York up to the turn-of-the-century. The museum features a permanent installation of 19th century paintings.

2 W. 77th St. (at Central Park West), (212) 873-3400, www.nyhistory.org, T-Su 10am-5pm.

Admission: $5 adults, $3 (students and seniors), ❷ ❸ to 81st St.-Museum of Natural History. &

New York Unearthed

Archaeology and New York may seem like strange bedfellows, but this smallish museum does the juxtaposition justice. Artifacts along the lines of cannon balls and bones, as well as excavation finds, are on display. The Lower Gallery offers the chance to watch conservationists working busily behind glass. Take the New York Systems elevator down for a simulated dig. And you thought this city was just built on top of a bunch of garbage.

17 State St. (at Water St.), 748-8628, Admission free, M-F 12pm-5pm, ❹ ❺ to Bowling Green. X

Nicholas Roerich Museum

Discreetly hidden among a row of brownstones, this museum honors Nicholas Roerich, the artist who designed an international peace symbol during World War II.

319 W. 107th St. (bet. Broadway and Riverside), (212) 864-7752, Suggested contribution, ❶ to 110th St.

P

Police Academy Museum

Ever really wanted to see Al Capone's machine gun? Other police memorabilia and crime-related items are also on exhibit.

235 E. 20th St. (bet. Second and Third Aves.), 2nd Fl., (212) 477-9753, Admission free, ❻ to 23rd St.

P. S. 1

If the name didn't give you a clue, P.S.1. is housed in an old school building, three stories high. The museum has plenty of nooks and crannies, all of which are filled with interesting and enlightening contemporary art exhibits. All of the museum's exhibits are temporary — so you can visit P.S.1. again and again. Summer weekends a fake beach, saunas, good beer and a DJ makes for a party full of hipsters. Until the MoMA relocates back to Manhattan in 2005, P.S. 1 will be affiliated with MoMa QNS.

See information under MoMA listing for further information.

Q

Queens Museum of Art

The must-see exhibit of this small museum, which is located right opposite the Unisphere and housed in the original U.N., is the scale model, the largest of its kind, of New York City. Half-price admission for students.

Flushing Meadows/Corona Park, Queens, (718) 592-9700, Admission: $3, W-F 10am-5pm, S-Su 12pm-5pm, ❼ to Willets Point/Shea Stadium

S

Solomon R. Guggenheim Museum

It's now hard to imagine upper Fifth Avenue without Frank Lloyd Wright's famous spiral of a building, home to one of the most remarkable 20th-century art collections in the world. The controversial new addition, a rectangular tower, was opened in 1992 and houses the permanent collec-

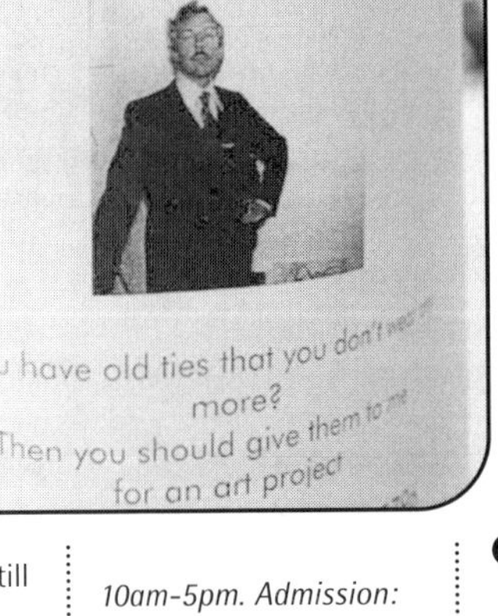

tion. Special exhibits still wind their way down interior ramps. This may not be the best way to view art, but it's surely the most distinctive. Friday evenings are free-bies.
1071 Fifth Ave. (bet. 88th and 89th Sts.), (212) 360-3500, Admission: $12, $8 (students), S-W 9am-6pm, Friday-Saturday, 9am-8pm, ❹❺❻ *to 86th St.* ♿

South Street Seaport Museum

This museum boasts prop-erty on land and water. Here you'll discover detailed exhibits on maritime history in New York's past and present in the museum's gallery, or on their restored ships. Go for the walking tours of Manhattan's many harbors, or see the gallery's collection of watercolors and model ships. The Melville Library also houses impressive archives on port business.
207 Front St., (212) 748-8600, www.southstseaport.org. Open M-W, F 10am-5pm. Admission: $6, $4 (students). Melville Library by appointment only (212) 748-8648. ❹ ❻❶❻❼❶❷❹❺ *to Fulton St.*

Studio Museum in Harlem

From its origins as a rented loft in 1967, this museum has burgeoned into one of the most innovative, focusing on arts from Africa and Black America. The artists-in-residence program gives emerging artists gallery space and the Cooperative School Program puts professional artists in Harlem schools.
144 W. 125th St. (bet. Lenox and Seventh Aves.), Admission: $5, $3 (students), W-R 12pm-6pm, F 12pm-8pm, S-Su 10am-6pm, ❶❶❻❶❷❸ *to 125th St.* ♿

W

The Whitney Museum of American Art

A mother-lode of American avant-garde and post-modern art. Lively, provocative shows are the rule here, including the ever-controversial Biennial, an exhibit of contemporary works held in odd-numbered years that never fails to rile the critics.
945 Madison Ave. (at 75th St.), (212) 570-3676, Admission: $10, $8 (students), T-R 11am-6pm, F 1pm-9pm, S-Su 11am-6pm, ❻ *to 77th St.* ♿

Y

Yeshiva University Museum

The country's oldest Jewish institution of higher learning regularly holds exhibits on both historical and contemporary Jewish themes, such as "The Emergence of the Synagogue in the Ancient World." The space has recently located downtown, moving away from the University's main campus.
15 W. 16th St. (bet. Fifth and Sixth Aves.), (212) 294-8330, Admission: $6, $4 (students), TW and Su 11am-5pm, R 11am-8pm. ❶❶❶❶❶❹❺❻ *to Union Sq.*

GALLERIES

A

Acquavella

Uptown gallery hoppers never overlook this treasure of 19th and 20th century European masters and postwar European and American pieces.
18 E. 79th St. (bet. Madison and Fifth Aves.), (212) 734-6300, M-Sa 10am-5pm, Cash Only, ❻ *to 77th St.*

Annina Nosei Gallery

No video or performance here. The do a brilliant job of featuring the best paintings, drawings, sculpture and photography from all over the world.
530 W. 22nd St. (bet. Tenth and Eleventh Aves.), 2nd Fl. (212) 741-8695, Open T-Sa 11am-6pm, ❶ ❶ *to 23rd St.* ♿

Apex

Off the beaten path of art with a fresh perspective, this is one of the best places to find innovative work. Appreciating it comes easily also, since the staffers are far less aloof than most of their SoHo counterparts. Shows tend to feature a combination of efforts by a few different artists and include both painting and sculpture.

291 Church St. (bet. Walker and White Sts.), (212) 431-5270, T-Sa 11am-6pm, ❶❷ to Franklin St. &

Artist's Space

A testing ground where new artists get the chance to cut their teeth, pay their dues and show their stuff to the gallery world. Shows generally focus on a central theme and contain several new artists with work that fits in. Check out up-and-coming talent in its larval stages.

38 Greene St. (bet. Grand and Broome Sts.), (212) 226-3970, T-Sa 11am-6pm, ❶ Ⓜ Ⓝ Ⓡ ❶❻ to Canal St.

B

Barbara Gladstone

This enormous space has tall ceilings and two levels displaying contemporary and modern art in various media, including rotating painting, sculpture, video installations and photography.

515 W. 24th St. (bet. Tenth and Eleventh Aves.), (212) 206-9300, M-F 10am-6pm, Ⓒ Ⓔ to 23rd St. &

Basilico

One-person shows are the standard at this sprawling showroom where promising newcomers attempt to prove themselves. Pieces are displayed in an unusually manageable fashion.

26 Wooster St. (bet. Grand and Canal Sts.), (212) 966-1831, T-Sa 11am-6pm, Ⓐ Ⓒ Ⓔ to Canal St.

Bullet Space

This "Urban Artist Collaborative" in a deteriorating building showcases city artists known for political and challenging works. The stark gallery also has a musical space, community center and residence for artists. By appointment only.

292 E. 3rd St. (bet. Aves. C and D), (212) 505-8312. S-Su 2pm-5pm, Ⓕ Ⓥ to Second Ave.

C

Christie's

Scope out the goods at the free public viewing five days before the auction at this New York branch of the London legend. 19th and 20th century European art, traditionally favored here, are still strong suits.

20 Rockefeller Plaza, (212) 636-2000, Cash and Checks Only, M-F 9:30am-5:30pm, Ⓑ Ⓓ Ⓕ Ⓥ to 47th-50th Sts.-Rockefeller Ctr. &

Cooper Union

An all-expense-paid college specializing in art, architecture and engineering education, Cooper Union's standards are some of the highest in the country. The school houses the Houghton Art Gallery and the Great Hall, the site of an 1860 speech by Abraham Lincoln.

Copper Sq. (at Seventh St.), (212) 353-4100, ❻ to Astor Place. &

D

Danese

If artists were incomes, those featured here would be upper-middle class. There are some risks but some more established stuff also to keep it safe.

Columbia's generous student bartenders typically tend the wine bar, so a little look-see at openings could be rewarding.

41 East 57th St. (bet. Madison and Park Aves.), (212) 223-2227, Cash Only, Ⓕ to 57th St., 456 to Lexington Ave. &

David Zwirner

A good place for good art. Whatever the well-known featured artist displays, it's done to near perfection, to the delight of critics and other viewers. Even if the style isn't something you find particularly inspiring, the high level of technique demonstrated is easy to admire.

43 Greene St. (bet. Grand

*and Broome Sts.), (212)
966-9074, Cash Only, T-Sa
10am-6pm, **N R** to
Prince St.*

Dia Center for the Arts

Dia opened its main exhibition facility in a four-story renovated warehouse in 1987, dedicating it to large-scale, long-term exhibitions, offering artists the opportunity to develop new work or a focused presentation of work on a full floor of the building.

*548 W. 22nd St. (212)
989-5566, Admission: $4,
$2 (members, students,
and seniors), **C E** to
23rd St.*

Deitch Projects

No stranger to the art world, this gallery has featured the works of George Condo, Keith Haring and Yoko Ono, to name a few. Look for the installation pieces and the attention paid to balancing the quirky exhibits with the more serious and mysterious.

*76 Grand St. (bet.
Wooster and Greene St.),
(212) 343-7300, T-Sa
12pm-6pm, **N R** to
Prince St.*

Dumbbox

Dakota Jackson's new gallery derives its name from its nature—as a dumb box, it has no intrinsic meaning. Rather, it supposedly derives meaning from the party or function it is being used for at the moment. Whatever.

43 Mercer St. (bet.

*Broome and Grand St.),
(212) 925-4994, **N R** to
Canal St.*

E

Esso

If there is a mien that suggests I-just-became-legal-at-a-drinking-establishment, then the artistic counterpart that suggests I-just-finished-art-school reigns at this funky downtown space, where pop art is reworked for a generation that grew up on the Smurfs and Atari.

*221 W. 28th St. (between
Seventh and Eighth
Aves.), (212) 560-9728,
Cash Only, T-F 11am-6pm,
1 2 to 28th St.*

Exit Art

A huge upstairs loft space, complete with a cafe made for lingering when gallery hopping becomes tiresome, and a shop filled with art trinkets. Never stodgy, themed group shows are favored. Past innovations include having the artists move their studios into the gallery and an exhibit of art/paraphernalia from social protest movements. Openings here should not be missed.

*548 Broadway (bet. Prince
and Spring Sts.), (212)
966-7745, Suggested
Contribution of $2, MC, V,
AmEx, T-Sa 12pm-6pm,
N R to Prince St., **4 5**
6 to Spring St.*

F

Feigen Contemporary

This newly opened gallery

is one of many that crops up on the streets of Chelsea hoping their artists (and their rental space) will have some longevity. Past exhibits include digitally tweaked color photo prints of stark interiors and human and bodily oddities.

*535 W. 20th St. (bet.
Tenth and Eleventh Aves.),
(212) 929-0500, T-Sa
11am-6pm, **C E** to 23rd
St.*

G

Gagosian

A vast gallery filled by established artists who are often eager to take advantage of the space. As such, large paintings, three-dimensional pieces and sculpture come into play, and the results can be more absorbing than a similar show executed in a smaller area. Even when the physical potential isn't utilized, the art is usually worth checking out.

*980 Madison Ave. (at
76th St.), (212) 228-2828,
Cash Only, T-Sa 10am-
6pm, **6** to 77th St. &*

Gavin Brown's Enterprise

Join Chelsea's trendiest crowds at this ultra-hip if somewhat pretentious gallery. Nestled in a trendy new spot among old warehouses, Gavin Brown and his "family" of artists have gotten great press coverage. Stop in at the adjoining bar, complete with disco-light floor, after the gallery closes.

*436 W. 15th St. (bet.
Ninth and Tenth Aves.),*

*(212) 627-5258, T-Sa
10am-6pm, **A C E** to
14th St. &*

Greene Naftali Gallery

A western exposure bathes the space in natural light. Works are contemporary and tend to be experimental. Genres range from sculpture and painting to multimedia exhibits.

*526 W. 26th St., Eighth
Floor (bet. Tenth and
Eleventh Aves.), (212)
463-7770, **C E** to 23rd
St.*

Grey Art Gallery

Both foreign and domestic contemporary artists display their work at this offbeat gallery on New York University's main campus.

*100 Washington Square
East (at Waverly Pl.),
(212) 998-6780, Donation
of $2.50, T-F 11am-8pm,
Sa 11am-5pm, **N R** to
8th St. &*

J

Jack Tilton

The artists shown here are respected, but not necessarily for producing expected conventional pieces. Often, the stuff on display requires a second look to see what's really going on. On closer examination, a recent collection of Fred Tomaselli's paintings focusing on birds, leaves and butterflies proved to be elaborate mosaics made up of pills.

*49 Greene St., (212) 941-
1775, Cash Only, **A C E**
to Canal St.*

Jessica Fredericks Gallery

Housed in a brownstone-like building, this smallish space consists of one main viewing room showcasing established and emerging artists.
504 W. 22nd St. (bet. Tenth and Eleventh Aves.), (212) 633-6555, Cash Only, ⓒ ⓔ to 23rd St.

K

Knoedler Gallery

Not to be missed by art historians or art historians in-the-making, the oldest New York-based art gallery, established in 1846, exhibits such modern greats as Nancy Graves, Robert Motherwell, Frank Stella and Robert Rauschenberg.
19 E. 70th St. (bet. Madison and Fifth Aves.), (212) 794-0550, M-F 9:30am-5pm, ⑥ to 68th St.

L

Leo Castelli

Don't want to take a risk? The next best thing to playing it safe at a big museum is found here. The art is all by people who have made a name for themselves, either in the art world or the culture at large. Back in 1958 Castelli hand-picked Jasper Johns for a one-man show, thus launching pop art and minimalism. They even show some Picassos here.
59 E. 79th St. (bet. Madison and Park Aves.), (212) 249-4470, Cash Only, T-Sa 10am-6pm, ⑥

to 77th St.

Linda Kirkland Gallery

Modest in size, but not in vision: the gallery's focus "will be to exhibit art that combines a conceptual bent with a sensual visual form."
504 W. 22nd St., Third Floor, (bet. Tenth and Eleventh Aves.), (212) 627-3930, Cash and Checks Only, ⓒ ⓔ to 23rd St.

M

Marlborough

A good place to see works by relatively well known contemporary and modern artists, this is just one of multiple Marlborough Gallery spaces worldwide. Although their focus is on selling big-ticket pieces from such clients like the estates of Jackson Pollock and Franz Kline, the atmosphere in the gallery is laid back and comfortable.
40 W. 57th St. (bet. Fifth and Sixth Aves.), (212) 541-4900, M-Sa 10am-5:30pm, ① ② Ⓐ Ⓑ Ⓒ Ⓓ to 59th St. - Columbus Circle

Matthew Marks

Marks fills his two downtown spaces, both outposts of his extinct Madison Avenue gallery, with contemporary big names, including Nan Goldin, Brice Marden and Willem de Kooning.
522 W. 22nd St. (bet. Tenth and Eleventh Aves.), (212) 243-0200, T-Sa 10am-6pm, ⓒ ⓔ

to 23rd St. &

Mary Boone Gallery

This longtime SoHo staple recently headed for greener grass up north, and it now carries an elegant address on Fifth Avenue. Many artists, among them Ross Bleckner, who had a solo show at the Guggenheim a couple of years back, came along for the ride.
754 Fifth, Fourth Floor (bet. 57th and 58th Sts.), (212) 752-2929, Cash Only, T-Sa 10am-6pm, Ⓝ Ⓡ Ⓦ to Fifth Ave. &

Miriam and Ira D. Wallach Art Gallery

Columbia's resident gallery presents traveling exhibitions throughout the year, curated by professors and students who ensure an academic tilt to the line-up. Lectures and receptions are often sponsored in conjunction with exhibits.
Columbia University, Schermerhorn Hall, Eighth Fl. (116th Street and Broadway), (212) 854-7288, W-Sa 1pm-5pm, ① to 116th St.-Columbia University &

Momenta Art

The neighborhood's most grown-up gallery, still floating beyond the orbit of the conventional. The focus is on group shows featuring works by many artists reflecting a central, provocative theme, and the execution ranges from competent to brilliant. Well worth the trip for anyone looking for something beyond the SoHo scene.
72 Berry St. (bet. Ninth and Tenth Sts.), Brooklyn, (718) 218-8058, Cash Only, Ⓛ to Bedford Ave.

N

New World Art Center

This "New Renaissance" gallery has an ambitious agenda,
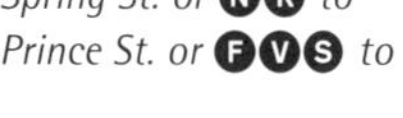
as it seeks to unite fine, graphic, literary, film, video, photographic, designing and performing artists under one roof. The splintered focus keeps exhibits changing monthly.
250 Lafayette St. (bet. Prince and Spring Sts.), (212) 966-4363, MC, V, AmEx, D, ⓒ ⓔ ⑥ to Spring St. or Ⓝ Ⓡ to Prince St. or Ⓕ Ⓥ Ⓢ to

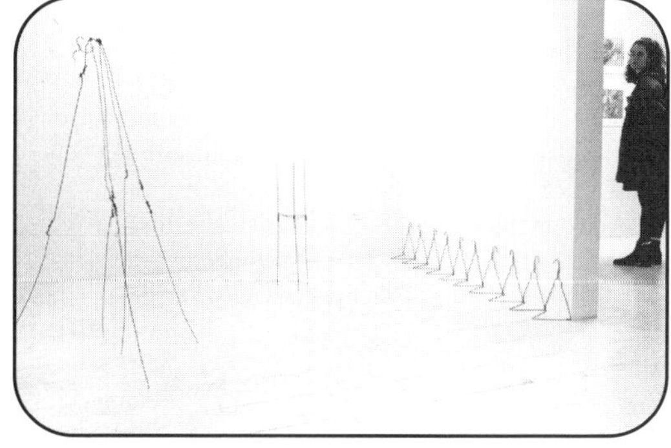

Broadway/Lafayette St.

P

Pace Wildenstein Gallery, Midtown

An old hand at this art thing, this multilevel space hosts somewhat famous names, like Alexander Calder and Chuck Close.
32 E. 57th Street (at Madison Ave.), (212) 421-3292, Cash Only, T-F 9:30am-6pm, Sa 10am-6pm, ⓃⓇ to Fifth Ave. ♿

Pace Wildenstein Gallery, SoHo

A Manhattan art world standard with several outlets throughout the city, the SoHo branch is a testament to the quality that sustains its popularity. Housed in a large and accessible street level space, they offer solo shows by some fine established artists not yet past their prime, such as Elizabeth Murray.
142 Greene St. (bet. Houston and Prince Sts.), (212) 431-9224, T-Sa 10pm-6pm, ⒻⓋⓈ to Broadway/ Lafayette St. ♿

Pat Hearn

Formerly part of the East Village and SoHo scenes, Hearn's Chelsea gallery presents offbeat work by emerging to mid-career Contemporary American and European artists. A veteran of the art scene, she has propelled numerous artists' careers, among them George Condo, Philip Taaffe and Peter Schuyff.
530 W. 22nd St. (bet. Tenth and Eleventh Aves.), (212) 727-7366, T-Sa 11am-6pm, ⒸⒺ to 23rd St. ♿

Paul Morris Gallery

Formerly Morris Healy, Chelsea pioneers Paul Morris and Thomas Healy have gone their separate ways. Healy's space displays contemporary art.
465 W. 23rd St. (bet. Ninth and Tenth Aves.), (212) 727-2752, T-Sa 11am-6pm, ⒸⒺ to 23rd St. ♿

Paula Cooper Gallery

You'll have to squint to read the lettering at this gallery's entrance on the south side of the street. Woodwork in the two rooms resembles a cross between a barn and a church. Tall ceilings in the back room allow for massive installments. Natural light filters through fogged windows.
534 W. 21st St. (bet. Tenth and Eleventh Aves.), (212) 255-1105, Cash Only, T-Sa 10am-6pm, ⒸⒺ to 23rd St. ♿

Peter Blum

Generally on the beaten path in terms of content, with frequent swerves to the odd and obscure. In addition to paintings and sculpture by known artists, architectural sketches and non-Western archeological artifacts have been known to make an appearance in this large, rectangular room.

99 Wooster St., (212) 343-0441, Cash and Check Only, T-F 10am-6pm, Sa 11am-6pm, ⒶⒸⒺ to Spring St. ♿

Phyllis Kind

Since the work of established white male artists still constitutes the majority of what makes it into serious galleries, this deceptively large space often contains shows that challenge this order. Artists like Betty Saar regularly produce some of the most thought-provoking installations you're likely to see.
136 Greene St., (212) 925-1200, MC, V, AmEx, D, T-Sa 10am-6pm, ⒻⓋⓈ to Broadway/Lafayette St., ⓃⓇ to Prince St. ♿

Pierogi 2000

The name reflects the way the traditional Polish flavor of the community melds with the influx of forward-focused artists and others. Like most Williamsburg galleries, the art here is as far outside of the mainstream as the location. The gallery serves as everything from an outlet for resurrections of art treasures unseen for years to a center for lots of the neighborhood's resident artists, many of whom can be found hanging out on its stoop.
167 N. 9th St., Brooklyn, (bet. Bedford and Driggs Aves.), (718) 599-2144, Cash Only, F-M 12pm-6pm, Ⓛ to Bedford Ave.

PostMasters

A challenge to much of what's taken for granted in the art world shows up regularly here. Shows

have included artists working together as a team to produce installations of seemingly ordinary scenes from everyday life, and work questioning directly the idea of art-as-business.
459 W. 19th St. (bet. Ninth and Tenth Aves.), (212) 727-3323, Cash Only, T-Sa 11am-6pm, ❶❷ to 18th St. ♿

PPOW

Started in the 80's in the East Village by two women, this gallery moved here after developing an excellent reputation. The two rooms generally each contain work by a different artist. Women artists are well represented here, as are others with perspectives that don't fit into the old standards, like those of the late well-known AIDS-chronicler David Wojnarowicz, whose estate they own.
476 Broome St. (bet. Wooster and Greene Sts.), (212) 941-8642, T-Sa 10am-6pm, Cash Only, ⓃⓇ to Prince St. ♿

R

Ronald Feldman

Artists with enough talent execute ideas that could easily fall on either side of the thin line dividing success and failure. A Roxy Paine show consisted of 2,200 hand-made mushrooms, each unique, displayed so that they appeared to be sprouting from the floor. Wacky indeed, it got rave reviews.
31 Mercer St. (bet. Grand

*and Canal Sts.), (212)
226-3232, Cash Only, T-
Sa 10am-6pm, **N** **R** to
Canal St.*

S

Salander-O'Reilly Galleries

20th century Modernist
American painters of the
Stieglitz group are exhib-
ited alongside a new gen-
eration of similarly dar-
ing, young artists.
*20 E. 79th St. (bet.
Madison and Fifth Aves.),
(212) 879-6606, Cash
Only (catalogues), M-Sa
9:30am-5:30pm, **6** to
77th St.* &

SoHo Photo Gallery

One of the most well-
established photography
galleries in town, with
shows highlighting many
different styles. They
offer a lot of classes to
the public to educate on
the history and work of
various photographers
and to help people learn
and improve artistic skills.
*Call for schedule infor-
mation. 15 White St. (bet.
6th Ave. and West
Broadway), (212) 226-
8571, Cash Only, Hours
by appointment, **1** **2** to
Franklin St.*

Sotheby's

Don your most expensive
suit or pretend you're an
heir/ess at a viewing at
Manhattan's other lead-
ing auction house.
Collectibles sold here
range from jewels and
vintage wine to decora-
tive and fine arts.
Admission is free, but the
glossy catalog will set
you back about 20 bucks.

*1334 York Ave. (at
72nd St.), (212) 606-
7000, MC, V, **6** to
68th St. or **F** to
Lexington Ave.* &

Staley-Wise

Love photography?
Sorting through the
different styles that
get thrown together,
all involving a cam-
era, and film as
media can be daunt-
ing. This is the place
for those who love
glamorous photogra-
phy, featuring work
ranging from old Life
magazine-style
celebrity photos to
work by today's most
prominent fashion
photographers.
*560 Broadway (at
Prince St.), (212)
966-6223, MC, V, T-
Sa 11am-5pm, **N** **R**
to Prince St.* &

Storefront for Art and Architecture

This international
gallery favors the
abstract, and often orga-
nizes shows along geo-
graphical themes. The
name is derived from the
unique facade.
*97 Kenmare Street (bet.
Mulberry and Lafayette
Sts.), (212) 431-5795,
Open from March to
November, **6** to Spring
St.*

T

Thread Waxing Space

Homage is paid to musi-
cians and pop culture in
this gallery, which has
seen the likes of Beck

Hansen and his grandfa-
ther's mixed-media work.
Space is devoted to music
performances, as well as
performance art featur-
ing intensive audience
interaction.
*476 Broadway (bet.
Broome and Grand Sts.),
(212) 387-2079, T-Sa
10am-6pm, **6** to Astor
Pl.*

303 Gallery

An intimate gallery on a
single floor exhibits contemporary work in many
different media.
*525 W. 22nd St. (bet.
Tenth and Eleventh
Aves.), (212) 255-1121,
Cash Only, T-Sa 10am-*

*6pm, **C** **E** to 23rd St.* &

W

William Secord Gallery

This gallery is known for
its carefully curated and
meticulously selected dog
art. Canine addicts not
satiated by this gallery
alone need not fear. The
Dog Museum, once
directed by Secord as
well, exists in St. Louis.
*52 E. 76th Street, Third
Floor (bet. Park and
Madison Aves.), (212)
249-0075, MC, V, AmEx,
M-Sa 10am-5pm, **6** to
77th St.*

world culture

A

Alliance Française

Brush up on the language of love at Tuesday's $5.50 screenings of French flicks. Dance classes and more than 200 language courses are also available. Members enjoy free films, culinary and wine tastings, travel seminars, art excursions, discounts on French performances around the city, and the use of the multimedia library.
22 E. 60th St. (bet. Madison and Park Aves.), (212) 355-6100, MC, V, AmEx, N R W to Lexington Ave. ♿

The American Academy of Arts and Letters

Recent Initiates, Oliver Sacks and Elie Wiesel, attest to the prestige of this exclusive society created to honor American artists, writers and composers for their accomplishments. Check out samples of honorees' works inside the gallery. For a good look at the neighboring Trinity Church Cemetery, stop by the South Gallery.
633 W. 155th St. (at Broadway), (212) 368-5900, Admission Free, ❶ *to 157th St.*

American Ballet Theatre

Drop-in classes to the tune of 12 dollars a pop ($110 buys ten classes) for aspiring prima donnas at one of the country's premier studios. Alaine Haubert and Diana Cartier teach regularly, though guest instructors from the ABT Artistic Staff occasionally fill in. Advanced dancers should stop by at 10am during the week, while the 6pm weekday classes will best serve intermediates.
890 Broadway, Third Floor (at 19th St.), (212) 477-3030, Cash Only, ❶ *to Union Square.* ♿

The American Numismatic Society

If you had one of those penny books as a kid, this is your chance to see what you may have had if you'd only stuck with it. Numismatics, the study of coins and medals, has been practiced in these hallowed halls since 1858, and their library maintains over 70,000 volumes. Other pursuits include a fellowship program for grad students and museum professionals, publishing monographs and journals and running an annual conference on coinage in America.
617 W. 155th St. (bet. Broadway and Riverside), (212) 234-3130, Admission free, ❶ *to 157th St.* ♿

Americas Society

Inter-American policy issues come up for debate at the conferences and study groups organized by the Society's Western Hemisphere Department. The Cultural Affairs department offers an extensive arts library, lectures in conjunction with special exhibits and concerts with receptions for the white wine crowd.
680 Park Avenue (at 68th St.), (212) 249-8950, Cash Only, ❻ *to 68th St.* ♿

Asia Society

America's preeminent organization celebrates Asian cultural awareness with notable film series, lectures, and an art collection featuring sculpture, paintings, ceramics, prints and bronzes from across Asia. Prominent authors and public leaders speak regularly here. Other programs for the public include dance performances, and well-attended art exhibits usually gathered from private collections, and receptions involving community and professional organizations.
725 Park Ave. (at 70th St.), (212) 288-6400, MC, V, AmEx, ❻ *to 68th St.* ♿

B

Ballet Academy East

Itching to test those dancing shoes? Drop in here and for $11, you can sample one of the jazz, ballet or tap classes.
1651 Third Ave. (bet. 92nd and 93rd Sts.), (212) 410-9140, MC, V, AmEx, ❻ *to 96th St.*

Bronfman Jewish Center

In a townhouse built for Lockwood de Forest, a wealthy exporter, the center presents free lectures focusing on Jewish religious concerns and Israeli politics for an almost exclusive NYU audience. De Forest founded workshops in India to revive the art of woodworking, so the center is replete with the fruits of his labor-original, intricately-carved teak wood imported from India.
7 E. 10th St. (bet. University and Fifth Aves.), (212) 998-4114,

C

China Institute
America's oldest bicultural organization focusing on China promotes awareness of Chinese culture, history, language and arts through semester-long classes in Mandarin, Cantonese, Tai Chi, calligraphy, cooking and painting. Seminars, lecture series and film screenings with Chinese and Chinese-American themes are also regularly scheduled.
125 E. 65th St. (bet. Lexington and Park Aves.), (212) 744-8181, Admission: $5, MC, V, AmEx, **6** *to 68th St.*

E

Ellis Island Immigration Museum
Twelve million immigrants came to Ellis Island between 1892 and 1954. This museum opened in 1990 as a tribute to the journey those people made. Give yourself about three hours to explore the artifacts. If you don't feel like shelling out the $4 or making the trip, take the virtual tour on the website.
Ellis Island, New York Harbor. See www.ellisisland.com (212) 363-3206 for ferry and tour times. Take NR to Whitehall or **4 5** *to Bowling Green, walk through Battery Park to Castle Clinton to pick up tickets.*

G

Goethe Institute
Lovers of German culture visit this multi-story gallery, conveniently located right across the street from the Metropolitan Museum of Art. While the interior is short on feng-shui proportionality, the proprietors constantly rotate the exhibitions to ensure that there's never a dull moment.
1014 Fifth Ave. (bet. 82nd and 83rd Sts.), (212) 439-8700, **6** *to 77th St.*

I

IndoCenter of Art and Culture
Dedicated to the presentation and support of contemporary art and culture of South Asia, the IndoCenter aims to explore the cultural and historical aspects shared by South Asian people of different religions and political views. Exhibitions of paintings, photographs, sculpture and other media by both artists of South Asian origin and artists whose works concentrate on South Asia are complimented by public programming in the visual, performing, film and literary arts.
530 W. 25th St. (bet. 10th and 11th Aves.), (212) 462-4221, Free admission, T-Sa 11am-6pm, **C E** *to 23rd St.*

Instituto Italiano di Cultura
The Italian consulate operates this center for the dissemination of the

country's culture. Concerts, exhibits and lectures occur frequently, or just swing by to flip through Italian mags.
686 Park Ave. (bet. 68th and 69th Sts.), (212) 879-4242, M-F 10am-4pm, **6** *to 68th St.*

J

Jacque Marchais Museum of Art
Housed in a two-story stone building resembling a Buddhist mountain temple and set in a terraced garden overlooking New York Bay, the center features a permanent collection of Tibetan and other Buddhist art and ethnography. Notable past visitors include the Dalai Lama, who came in 1991.
338 Lighthouse Ave., Staten Island, (718) 987-3500, W-Su 1-5pm, Staten Island Ferry to S70 bus.

Japan Society
An all-purpose center of Japanese art and culture, located appropriately enough in Japan House, with exhibitions on the second floor and a stone-lined pool garden on the first floor, complete with bamboo shafts.
333 E. 47th St. (bet. First and Second Aves.), (212)

832-1155, MC, V, AmEx, **E V 6** *to 53rd St.* &

L

La Maison Française
The epicenter of Francophone and Francophile life at New York University. Call for information about free lectures, usually in French, along with conferences and exhibitions which are presented in the center's historic 19th century carriage house.
16 Washington Pl. (bet. Fifth Ave. and University Place), (212) 998-8750, **N R** *to 8th St.*

M

Museum of Chinese in the Americas
No Chinatown experience is complete without a visit to this community-oriented museum, the first ever dedicated to the history of the Chinese in the Americas. The award-winning exhibition, entitled, "Where Is Home?" features a moving collection of memorabilia, photographs, and commen-

tary exploring the diverse identities and experiences of Chinese-Americans. *70 Mulberry St. (at Bayard St.), (212) 619-4785, Admission $1, ⓃⓇ to Canal St.*

N

National Museum of the American Indian

The Old Custom house contains this extensive museum, one of the few Smithsonian institutions outside Washington. The exhibits are fascinating, though the federal architecture and the beautiful rotunda alone merit the trip. There are permanent exhibits of various national dress, culture and art, and visiting exhibits such as photography of the Native American. *One Bowling Green (at the foot of Broadway), (212) 514-3700, Admission Free, M-Su 10am-5pm, ④⑤ to Bowling Green.*

New York Library Society

George Washington, James Fenimore Cooper, Henry Thoreau and Herman Melville all frequented the oldest circulating library in New York, founded in 1754. Nowadays you'll have to fork over $90 ($135 for non-students) for the privilege of perusing literature in the luxurious reading rooms. Non-members are accommodated in the ground floor's reference room.

53 E. 79th St. (bet. Madison and Park Aves.), (212) 288-6900, MWF 9am-5pm, TR 9am-7pm, Cash Only, ⑥ to 77th St.

New York Zendo Shobo-ji

New Yorkers looking to escape urban chaos seek out this serene temple, complete with rock gardens, instructions on correct breathing, meditation, posture, etiquette, and Oriental floor cushions. Hard-core enthusiasts can partake of a purer experience on one of the weekend retreats held at an affiliated monastery in the Catskills. *222 E. 67th St. (bet. Second and Third Aves.), (212) 861-3333, $15 per session, $40 membership for one month, Cash Only, ⑥ to 68th St.-Hunter College*

92nd Street Y

One of New York's most valuable cultural resources serves as an umbrella for a multitude of classes, workshops, and speaking and reading series. The reading series is by far the city's most star-studded, drawing fine poets and authors, both national and international, established and emerging. Tickets run around $5-$7 for students. *1395 Lexington Ave. (at 92nd St.), (212) 415-5500, MC, V, AmEx, ④⑤⑥ to 86th St. ♿*

S

Scandinavia House

You don't have to be Swedish to appreciate this

clean-lined, modern museum, which represents all aspects of modern Nordic culture through temporary art and design exhibits (photography, sculpture, installation), film screenings, lectures and language classes. Children will delight in the cozy playroom and learning center, and visitors of all ages will appreciate a bite at the Café Aquavit and a peek at the avant-garde gift shop. *58 Park Ave. (bet. 37th and 38th Sts.), (212) 879-9779, Admission: $3, $2 (students), M-F 12pm-6pm, ④⑤⑥ to 33rd St. ♿*

Schomburg Center for Research in Black Culture

The Center was founded in 1925 to showcase scholar and historian Arturo Alfonso Schomburg's personal collection of 10,000 items, documenting the development of Black history worldwide. Priceless volumes, photographs, and newspapers are among the five million articles housed here. *515 Malcolm X Blvd. (at 135th St.), (212) 491-2200, www.nypl.org/ research/sc/sc.html. Free admission, see website for specific hours, ⒷⒸ to 135th St. ♿*

The Spanish Institute

Exhibitions acquaint visitors with Spanish culture. Semester-long language classes include the perks of access to both the reference collection and reading room with current publications.

684 Park Ave. (bet. 68th and 69th Sts.), (212) 628-0420, $50 per membership, $20 for students, MC, V, AmEx, D, ⑥ to 68th St.

T

Tibet House

Supporters of the Tibet government in exile, artists, and students make like the Buddha here at this serene cultural embassy. Be forewarned: your state of dharma may be unrooted by celebrity-hounds looking to catch a glimpse at Uma Thurman's father. The gift shop features $625 authentic Tibetan scarves from the man who brought you Hermés, while the most recent annual Tibet House Benefit Concert at Carnegie Hall featured David Bowie, Richard Gere and monks from the notorious Drepung Gomang Monastery. *22 W. 15th St. (between Fifth and Sixth Aves.), (212) 807-0563, ⓁⓃⓆ ⓌⓇ④⑤⑥ to Union Sq.-14th St.*

U

Ukrainian Museum

This small museum features exhibits of contemporary Ukrainian culture and history. Recent exhibitions have included folk art and Easter eggs. *203 Second Ave. (bet. 12th and 13th Sts.), (212) 228-0110, www.ukrainian-museum.org. W-Su 1pm-5pm. Admission: $2-3, ⓁⓃⓆⓇⓌ④⑤⑥ to Union Sq.-14th St. ♿*

performing
arts
NAT KING COLE
WALK
NO PARKING
ANYTIME
APOLLO
AMATEUR NIGHT EVERY WED
HOST MONTERIA IVEY
CELEBRATION JOHN P KEE
SMALLWOOD JUNE 23
LUMSTEIN
Payless

performing arts

At the heart of New York's tourist industry lies the lengendary 42nd Street, whose glittering lights and theaters on Broadway, drawing visitors from all over the world. However, despite the enormous amount of revenue generated by successful shows and high ticket prices, launching a production is among the most expensive and risky of business propositions. As a result of the prohibitive fiscal pressures faced by all new productions, a thriving community has developed away from Midtown's main drag. These off the beaten path theaters are particularly downtown, which originally housed many of the major theaters, resulting in three categories of production: Broadway, Off-Broadway and Off-Off-Broadway.

Roaring New York

The city's professional theater was launched in 1750 with an imported production of Richard III, the first in a succes-

sion of exchanges between the British and American stages that has proved extremely fruitful both for New York and for London's West End.

The New York theater scene as we know it today really got its start around the turn of the century. The city's high society frequented productions by stage luminaries such as Lunt and Fontanne, the Barrymores and the Booths. Meanwhile, the "common folk" packed the city's vaudeville, variety and minstrel theaters located along the Bowery. Vaudeville often fed Broadway during the teens and '20s: before launching their movie careers, performers such as the Marx Brothers graced Broadway stages with their vaudeville circuit reviews.

Edna St. Vincent Millay and her literary friends helped

to launch the Provincetown Playhouse and similar avant-garde theaters in Greenwich Village. The Group Theater featured the works of playwrights such as Eugene O'Neill and Clifford Odets. O'Neill called the city home during this pre-World War I period. His Pulitzer Prize-winning drama Anna Christie was based upon seedy Lower East Side nightlife and was set in the Golden Swan, the saloon frequented by the playwright himself.

The Broadway scene hit its heyday in the late '20s, with literally hundreds of shows opening each year. In a time of such bounty, there were certainly a few bad apples. Critics of the time, such as Robert Benchley, Dorothy Parker and Alexander Wollcott, were never out of work.

Several New York writers, playwrights, actors and critics lunched together regularly at midtown's Algonquin Hotel. These gatherings were vicious and productive, serving as an artistic think-tank in a time of tremendous theatrical activity. George S. Kaufman (along with his myriad of writing partners, such as Moss Hart and Marc Connolly) was very active during this period, penning scores of incredible comedies, several of which were based on the exploits of this group of witty intellectuals.

The World War II and post-war periods were also quite fruitful for New York drama, as two brilliant young playwrights came to make their mark on American theater. Tennessee Williams set new standards with works such as *A Streetcar Named Desire, The Glass Menagerie, Cat on a Hot Tin Roof* and *Camino Real.* Brooklyn-based Arthur Miller gave us the American classics *Death of a Salesman, The Crucible* and *A View from the Bridge.*

Papp and Circumstance

Impresario Joseph Papp founded the Public Theater, producing works such as Hair and A Chorus Line. In addition, Papp founded the New York institution Shakespeare in the Park. Papp's goal for the Public to produce all of Shakespeare's

plays was posthumously met in 1997, when Henry VIII was presented in Central Park. Off-Broadway and Off-Off-Broadway theaters boomed with the works of innovative new groups and artists such as the Open Theater and the Wooster Group. In the late '70s and early '80s, playwrights such as August Wilson and Wendy Wasserstein brought minority voices to Broadway. The mid-'80s witnessed the introduction of a genre of AIDS related plays, such as *The Normal Heart* by Larry Kramer and Tony Kushner's *Angels in America.*

This is a song for Broadway...

The eighties also ushered in the era of the über-musical: theatrical monsters of varying quality that crushed all in their path. These musicals—*Cats, The Phantom of the Opera* and *Les Miserables*—feature extremely high production values and many audience members are attracted by the sheer spectacle.

Large musicals still dominate Broadway, but they have taken on a different quality from the brassy productions of the eighties. Disney's Tony Award winning *Lion King*, directed by Julie Taymor, was hailed by critics and audiences alike. *Rent*, a '90s version of *La Bohéme*, traveled uptown to Broadway from

Downtown's esteemed New York Theater Workshop.

Today, NY theater is more exciting than ever. Exciting performances are opening each day, so treat yourself!

on, *off*, or *way off*?

It's pretty clear what someone's talking about if they mention a Broadway show. But what exactly does the phrase "Off-Off" signify?

Here's a simple guide:
Broadway means the district of theaters clustered around Times Square, usually between 41st and 53rd Streets. Tickets easily cost as much as $75 a pop. Lately shows like *Rent, Cabaret* and *The Lion King* have been drawing huge crowds and enlivening the strip.

Off-Broadway originally meant theaters in Greenwich Village, the majority of which have a seating capacity of 500 or less. Lately, however, this term has come to refer to smaller theaters anywhere in the city. Off-Broadway shows tend to have greater literary and social importance, a wider variety in production quality and cheaper ticket prices (max $40).

Off-Off Broadway is a term used to refer to productions featuring actors who are non-equity, working in theaters of less than 100 seats. Here you can find exciting, daring, performances at shoestring prices. Conversely, of course, there are the occasional painful freak-shows. Conservative theater-goers should perhaps avoid Off-Off-Broadway. The more adventurous who take the risk will find interesting experimental theater in abundance.

R E N T

Throughout the '80s and the early '90s, Jonathan Larsen was a struggling composer living on Greenwich Street—not quite in the Village, and not quite in SoHo. To pay his bills, he worked as a waiter at the Moondance Diner and spent the rest of his time writing and composing. Optimistic and romantic, Larsen embodied the mythical image of the starving artist. He lived in a small apartment and was just able to make ends meet.

In the early '90s, Larsen began work on a modern-day version of the Puccini opera La Bohéme. Relocating the action to the East Village, Larsen spun a relevant and timely portrayal of New York bohemian life. The show tackled problems ranging from AIDS and drug abuse, to housing and unpaid utility bills. More than a vehicle for dramatizing suffering, however, Rent became a celebration of the lifestyle.

Tragically, Larsen passed away on the night before the first preview. The show, however, continued and went on to become a record-breaking success story. Rent opened at the New York Theater Workshop on February 13, 1996. On April 29 of the same year, it opened on Broadway at the Nederlander Theater. Larsen was honored with a posthumous Pulitzer Prize for his work.

cheap tickets

With so many excellent and affordable Off- and Off-Off Broadway venues and so many avenues for obtaining discounted tickets to the Broadway blockbusters, why pay upwards of $60 a seat to furthar fatten the pocketbooks of Cameron Mackintosh and Andrew Lloyd Webber? Here are ways to see great productions for (almost) nothing:

TKTS
This booth sells same-day tickets to Broadway shows at 25-50 percent discounts. Even the best seats are available, but come early or you'll wind up with a "partial view" spot. The wait can be long-up to an hour or so-but is usually enlivened by the delicious chaos of the surroundings.
W. 47th St. at Broadway: branch at Bowling Green, 212-221-0013, ❶❾ to Cortlandt St.

Theater Development Fund
TDF is the best program for college students. A $14 annual fee pays for a spot on the mailing list for Broadway tickets for $17 or less, and TDF's "4-for-$28" voucher program gains admittance to Off-Off Broad-way shows. Send a legal-size, self-addressed stamped envelope for an application and allow six to eight weeks for processing.
1501 Broadway, Room 2110, New York, NY 10036, 221-0013 (recorded information), 221-0885 (operator).

Passport to Off-Broadway
The Alliance of Resident Theaters of NY offers hot seats to Off-and Off-Off Broadway shows at a discount during the spring and fall only.
Call 989-5257 to get on their mailing list.

Standing Room and Rush Tickets
Many shows offer discounts at the box office of the theater a few hours before curtain, generally balcony seats or standing room. Ushers often turn a blind eye while you sneak down to the orchestra and find empty seats.

Two for Ones
Many universities are part of a theater promotion program that offers students coupons known as "twofers": Two tickets to big-budget

productions for the price of one. Visit your school's Student Activities office for information about the program.

Shakespeare in the Park
Productions can be uneven and the star-studded casts underwhelming and overblown, but what better way to spend a balmy summer evening than sitting under the night sky in this intimate theater-in-the-round watching the best dramas by one of the best writers in the Western world? Tickets are free, but regular working folks will have to take a personal day to line up at sunrise to obtain seats to the more popular shows. Weekends can also be sacrificed to the cause. The bigger the stars, the longer the queue. Tickets are distributed the day of the performance beginning at 1pm at the Delacorte and Public Theaters. Show up and hour or two early for the less-hyped productions and many, many hours early for productions like *A Midsummer's Night Dream* in which Patrick Stewart (of *Star Trek* fame) starred a few years ago.
June-September, Delacorte Theater, Central Park (at W. 79th St.), 539-8500, ❷❸ to 81st St.

King's County Shakespeare Festival
The New York Shakespeare Festival's country cousin, staged in the bandshell of Brooklyn's Prospect Park. Their makeshift outdoor productions can produce haphazard, lively, boisterous fun. Named for their Brooklyn homebase, otherwise known as King's County.

A

Actor's Playhouse

Gay-and-lesbian-themed shows command the stage at this Off-Broadway space. Though the seats may be dingy and worn, and the floor may retain a stickiness from a soda from long ago, it is still the best queer and gay theater.

100 Seventh Ave. S. (bet. Christopher and Bleecker Sts.), (212) 463-0060, MC, V, AmEx, D, ❶❷ to Christopher St.

The Afrikan Poetry Theater, Inc.

Fledgling poets, playwrights, directors, and actors all do shows regularly. For those in need of more structured training, various dance, drum and Shakespeare classes are available.

176-03 Jamaica Ave. (at 176th St.), Queens, (718) 523-3312, Cash Only, ❺ to 179th St.

Alvin Ailey American Dance Theater

"The dance came from the people. It should be given back to the people," this theater's namesake once said. He developed the repertoire here with unique pieces often set to music by jazz greats such as Duke Ellington and Wynton Marsalis.

City Center, 131 W. 55th St. (bet. Sixth and Seventh Aves.), (212) 581-1212, MC, V, AmEx, ❶❷❸❹ to 57th St.

Amato Opera House

Head downtown to see the divas of tomorrow paying their dues in an intimate setting. An alternative for opera lovers who lack the funds for nosebleed seats at the Met. One of Amato's goals is to foster opera appreciation by making it more accessible, so many performances are English translations of Italian operas.

319 Bowery St. (at E. 2nd St.), (212) 228-8200, Cash Only, ❶❷❸ to Broadway/Lafayette

American Airlines Theater

The most consistently intelligent indigenous productions and European imports on Broadway proper.

227 W. 42nd St. (bet. Seventh and Eighth Ave.), (212) 719-1300, MC, V, AmEx, ❶❷❸❹❺❶❷❸❹ to Times Square

American Ballet Theater

This dance giant, once led by legends like Lucia Chase, Oliver Smith and Mikhail Baryshnikov, and now headed by former Principal Dancer Kevin McKenzie, continues to stage staggering performances at its home at Lincoln Center. Classical ballet had its first renaissance here, and new works have been commissioned specifically for the ballet by key composers such as Balanchine, Antony Tudor and Agnes de Mille. Call for schedules.

Metropolitan Opera House, Lincoln Center (at W. 64th St. and Columbus Ave.), (212) 362-6000, MC, V, AmEx, ❶❷ to 66th/Lincoln Center

Apollo Theater

Fostering such performers as Josephine Baker, the Supremes and Bill Cosby since it started integrating black audiences and performers in 1935, this multi-use theater is in full swing thanks to a revival effort in the Eighties. The televised "Amateur Night" rages on Wednesdays, and comedians and children's flicks also find space here. The stage even hosted James Brown's post-prison comeback concert.

253 W. 125th St. (bet. Adam Clayton Powell Jr. and Frederick Douglas Blvd.), (212) 222-0992, MC, V, AmEx, D, ❶❷❸❹ to 125th St.

Avery Fisher Hall

Over a hundred virtuosos led by Kurt Masur play Western classics, with an emphasis on European standards and American innovations. Home to the New York Philharmonic.

10 Lincoln Center Plaza (bet. 64th and 65th Sts.), (212) 875-5030, www.lincolncenter.org. ❶❷ to 66th St.-Lincoln Center.

Atlantic Theater

Theater buffs have long insisted that the stage is hallowed ground, but in this case the metaphor rings true. The Atlantic Theater Company, founded in 1985 by David Mamet and William H. Macy, moved into this renovated church in 1991. For a break from tacky musicals, the company proclaims the Atlantic as a place "where great stories are told."

336 W. 20th St. (bet Eighth and Ninth Ave.), (212) 645-1242, ❶❷ to 23rd St.

B

Ballet Academy East

Itching to test those dancing shoes? Drop in here and for $12 you can sample one of the jazz, ballet or tap classes.

1651 Third Ave. (bet. 92nd and 93rd Sts.), (212) 410-9140. Open M-F 9am-9pm, ❻ to 96th St.

Barge Music

Excellent chamber music on the water in moonlight. Bring a date and get all mushy on this converted coffee barge.

Fulton Ferry Landing, Brooklyn, (718) 624-2083, Cash Only, ❶❷ to High St X

Black Spectrum Theater Company, Inc.

Three to five large-scale productions a year, with directors favoring socially conscious works by both emerging and established writers. Kids and teens get in on the action with their own productions.
119 Merrick Blvd. (Corner of 177th and Basley Blvd.), (718) 723-1800, Cash Only, E to Parsons, **Q 8 5** *to Merrick Boulevard X*

Blue Man Group

These "enigmatic" bald— and blue—characters have taken over Manhattan, as well as Boston, Chicago, Vegas and numerous television commercials. Performing an eclectic show comprised of non-related stunts to music generated by their huge custom-made PVC percussion instruments, these blue men begin the show in a stoic manner. By the end, they have the entire audience's participation. Be sure to sit in the "Poncho Section," the first few rows that will inevitably be splattered by paint, Jell-O and other miscellaneous flying objects. Ponchos are provided. Tickets cost range from $55 to $65, but students with I.D. can snag seats Tuesday, Wednesday and Thursday evenings for $25.
Astor Place Theatre, 434 Lafayette St., (212) 254-4370 (tickets/seating), **6** *to Astor Pl.*

Bouwerie Lane Theater

Founded in 1973 by Eve Adamson, this European-style, one-stage theater is one of the few dedicated entirely to producing classics.
330 Bowery St. (at Bond St.), (212) 677-0060, Tickets: $24, $12 (students), MC, V, AmEx, **6** *to Bleecker St.*

Boy's Choir of Harlem

Founded in 1968, this legendary choir has evolved from a small church group to an internationally-acclaimed phenomenon, singing classical, contemporary, spiritual and jazz music at their year-round worldwide performances.
2005 Madison Ave. (bet. 127th and 128th Sts.), (212) 289-1815, Cash Only, **4 5 6** *to 125th St. &*

The Brooklyn Academy of Music

Although the Brooklyn Philharmonic has distinguished itself with its range and a repertoire, running the gamut from European classics to selections from African-American traditions. Its pet projects are clearly those rooted in the avant garde, which are best realized in BAM's provocative yearly New Wave festival that consistently pushes the boundaries of classical music.
30 Lafayette Ave. (at Hanson Pl.), (718) 636-4111 (tickets), (718) 636-4137 (Brooklyn Philharmonic), MC, V, **1 2 4 5** *to Atlantic Ave. &*

C

Carnegie Hall

A century has passed since Tchaikovsky conducted at its inauguration, but this stage keeps abreast of musical trends in their many variations. The Beastie Boys and the Tibetan Freedom Fighters have appeared on the same stage as classical giants like Emanuel Ax. Jazz performers are also frequent guests.
881 Seventh Ave. (at 57th St.), (212) 247-7800, MC, V, AmEx, **A B C D 1 2** *to 59th St. X*

Caroline's on Broadway

Caroline's boasts of "world-reknowned" comedic talent. Good thing, because "reservations" mean clients have to line up an hour before showtime and hope the club's overbooking policy doesn't mean they won't have a seat. Customers are herded like goats into a cramped bar before being seated by numbered ticket. $30 cover charge and two-drink minimum. Stick to wine, champagne, and beer. Headliners include Saturday Night Live, the Chris Rock Show, and BET regulars. Three shows nightly on weekends. *1626 Broadway (bet. 49th and 50th Sts.), (212) 757-4100, M-Su 5:30pm-1am,* **1 2 C E** *to 50th St.*

Castillo Theater

For the last decade, this space has served as a "cultural laboratory" for Artistic Director Fred Newman to practice Developmental Theater, a genre which is predicated on a number of post-modern philosophies but boils down to the idea of psychotherapy for performer and audience members alike. The focus is on black, Latino, gay and international avant-garde theater. This means you can expect anything.
500 Greenwich St. (bet. Spring and Canal Sts.), (212) 941-5800 (corporate office), 1-888-468-7619 (tickets) MC, V, AmEx, D, www.castillo.org, **A C E** *to Canal St. &*

Centerfold Coffeehouse at Church of St. Paul and St. Andrew

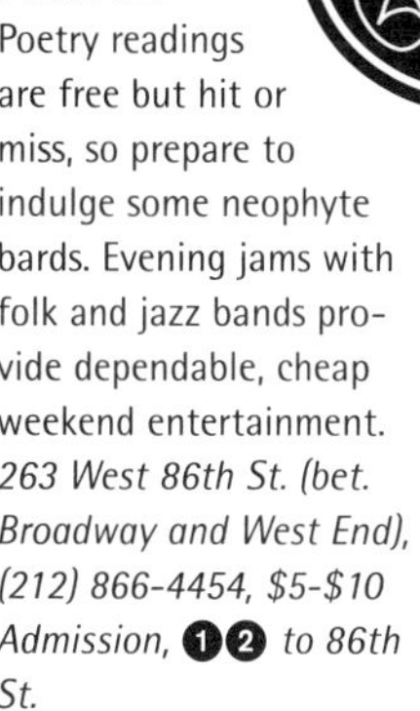

Poetry readings are free but hit or miss, so prepare to indulge some neophyte bards. Evening jams with folk and jazz bands provide dependable, cheap weekend entertainment.
263 West 86th St. (bet. Broadway and West End), (212) 866-4454, $5-$10 Admission, **1 2** *to 86th St.*

Center for the Arts

(College of Staten Island) Many island residents ignore CSI's performance space, favoring Manhattan for theatrical pursuits. This is a true shame considering the 450 seat theater, 9,000 seat concert hall, and art gallery housed within the center. Past well-known acts such as Shawn Colvin and Tito Puente have

graced the concert stage.
*2800 Victory Blvd., (718)
982-2787,* **N** **R** *to
Whitehall St.-South Ferry,
take Staten Island Ferry,
then take S61, S62*

Cherry Lane Theater

Founded in the Twenties
by a literary circle headed
by the poet Edna St.
Vincent Millay, Cherry
Lane's productions are
lead by the best of the
century's avant-garde and
adventurous new pieces.
*38 Commerce St. (bet.
Seventh Ave. and Barrow
Sts.), (212) 989-2020, MC,
V, AmEx,* **A** **C** **E** **F** **V** **S**
to West 4th St.

Chicago City Limits

No alcohol is
served at New
York's best
improv theater, but
you may get a buzz from
the audience participa-
tion. It's generally pricey,
but Thursday's touring
troupe performs for only
ten bucks. Ask about stu-
dent discounts.
*1105 First Ave. (at 61st
St.), (212) 888-5233,
Admission: $20, $15 w/
Student ID, MC, V, AmEx,*
4 **5** **6** *to 59th St.,* **N** **R**
to Lexington Ave.

City Center

The façade of this theater,
a mosque-like panoply of
gold and colorful mosaic,
is a show in itself, with an
equally decadent lobby in
marble and gold. Once
you get past this fanfare,
however, the performance
space itself is fairly modest. Two stages, each of
which seats less than 300
people, display American

dramas and comedies,
popular revivals and bal-
lets.
*131 W. 55th St. (bet. Sixth
and Seventh Ave.), (212)
581-1212. MC, V,*
N **R** **Q** **W** *to 57th St.*
E **B** **D** *to Seventh Ave.*
&

Colden Center For the Performing Arts at Queens College

Classical, pop, jazz, theater, opera and children's
events weekly. Call the
box office for more pre-
cise information.
*6530 Kissena Blvd., (718)
544-2996, MC, V, AmEx,*
7 *to Flushing-Main St.*
&

Collective Unconscious

Every possible configura-
tion of campy art and
anti-art event takes place
at this downtown perfor-
mance space. The hip,
tongue-in-cheek crowd
doesn't take anything
very seriously-especially
not the art world.
Popular open mce at
Reverend Jen's Anti-Slam,
Wednesday nights.
*145 Ludlow St. (bet.
Stanton and Rivington
Sts.), (212) 254-5277, Call
for schedule and show
times, Cash Only,*
F **J** **M** **Z** *to Delancey
St.,* &

The Comedy Garden

This self-declared "laugh
capital of the world" consists of three comedy
venues all located at
Madison Square Garden.
They strive to provide a
variety of comedians and
styles (sketch, stand up or

improv) to satisfy every-
body's sense of humor. To
watch the Knicks game at
the sports bar and enjoy
watching a living legend,
go to the club style stage
(beware of the two drink
minimum), or enjoy the
theater setting (it seats
up to 5,600) and sit in the
balcony where nobody
can tell it is you.
*Theater at Madison
Square Garden, W. 32nd
St. and Seventh Ave.,
(212) 465-6106,
www.comedygarden.com,*
1 **2** **3** **A** **C** **E** *to 34th
St./Penn Station*

Comic Strip Live

New York's most famous
comedy theater regularly
plays host to mainstream
big-name performers and
other crowd-pleasers.
Cheapest of thrills on no-
cover Mondays.
*1568 Second Ave. (bet.
81st and 82nd Sts), (212)
861-9386, MC, V, AmEx,
D, Admission: $12-$15
(weekends) plus 2 drink
minimum,* **4** **5** **6** *to
86th St.*

D

Dance Theater of Harlem

This world-renowned,
neo-classical company,
founded in 1969 as a
school and now one of
the country's most com-
petitive companies dab-
bles in a bit of every-
thing: jazz, tap dance,
modern ballet and sub-
genres. Students of all
ages and at all levels perform in a monthly open
house, usually with
accompanying perfor-
mances by guest artists.

*466 W. 152nd St. (bet. St.
Nicholas and Amsterdam
Aves.), (212) 690-2800,
MC, V, AmEx, D,*
A **B** **C** **D** *to 155th St.*

Dangerfield's

Join out-of-town conven-
tion-goers for new and
established comic talent
in the hyper-Las Vegas
atmosphere of this
uptown club operated
under the auspices of
Rodney Dangerfield.
*1118 First Ave. (bet. 61st
and 62nd Sts.), (212) 593-
1650, Cover: $12-$15,
AmEx,* **4** **5** **6** *to 86th St.*

De La Guarda

Started out of the
Argentine rave scene in
Buenos Aires, De La
Guarda has to be seen to
be believed. Think
Spiderman meets club
kids meets the Cirque du
Soleil. This show is interactive, fun and very
messy. No seats, all
standing, so don't wear
your heels. Get ready to
be strapped into a wild
ride.
*Daryl Roth Theater at
Union Sq. (east side) and
15th St., (212) 239-6200,*
L **N** **Q** **R** **W** **4** **5** **6** *to
Union Sq.*

Don't Tell Mama's

Wrest control of the
microphone away from
fellow exhibitionists at
this extrovert's paradise
where patrons are invited
to sing along with the
waitstaff, the pianist and
the mixed gay-straight
clientele.
*343 W. 46th St. (bet.
Eighth and Ninth Ave.),
(212) 757-0788,
www.donttellmama.com.
Open M-Su 4pm-4am.*

MC, V, AmEx, DC, no cover for piano bar, call for individual cabaret covers, **1 2** *to 50th St.)*

F

The Flea Theater

The home of the Bat Theater Company, you'll be pleased to find both experimental productions of classics and recent, more avant-garde plays. Plays usually run for a week or two, so catch them while you can. You'll also find poetry readings at the theater.
41 White St. (bet. Broadway and Church St.), (212) 226-0051. V, MC, **1** *to Franklin St,* **N R Q W J M Z 6** *to Canal St.* &

G

Gotham Comedy Club

The swanky scene at this genteel Flatiron venue is an enjoyable departure from the cheesy décor of other clubs. While the club attracts some big-name acts, the cost of the cover plus a two-drink minimum is a little less amusing.
34 W. 22nd St. (bet. 5th and 6th Aves.), (212) 367-9000, $7-$15 cover, **F N R 1 2** *to 23rd St.*

H

Harkness Dance Center at the 92nd St. Y

The Upper East Side's cultural mecca hosts professional performances as well informal shows of works in progress or new works. The dance workshops are a good reason for visiting, with programs like Argentine Tango Party, boasting Madonna's instructors, and Israeli folk dancing classes occurring regularly. Call for schedules.
1395 Lexington Ave. (bet. 91st and 92nd Sts.), (212) 415-5552, Tickets: $15, **4 5 6** *to 86th St.* &

HERE

Attractions include unconventional gallery shows of fine art and theater productions of new plays by younger playwrights with some fascinating stories to tell. Not as strange stylistically as what you'll find down on the Lower East Side but definitely Off-Off-Broadway.
145 Sixth Ave. (bet. Spring and Dominick Sts.), (212) 647-0202, MC, V, AmEx, **C E** *to Spring St.* &

I

The Irish Repertory Theatre

Intimate performance space for Irish and Irish-American plays.
132 W. 22nd St. (bet. Sixth and Seventh Aves.), (212) 727-2737, MC, V, AmEx, **F V 1 2** *to 23rd St.* &

J

Jamaica Arts Center

A neo-Italian Renaissance structure built in 1898 houses a non-profit community cultural center dedicated to making all genres of the performing arts accessible to the Jamaica community.
161-04 Jamaica Ave. (at 161st St.), (718) 658-7400, Cash Only, **E J Z** *to Jamaica Center* &

Joyce SoHo

All professional and aspiring dancers are familiar with this branch of the Joyce, the venue of choice for seeing all genres in a setting that's not stiflingly formal. Performances are on Friday and Saturday nights with tickets available thirty minutes before curtain.
155 Mercer St. (bet. Houston and Prince Sts.), (212) 334-7479, Cash Only, **N R** *to Prince St.,* **F S V** *to Broadway-Lafayette*

Joyce Theater

The unlikely successor to a former porno palace, this hotbed of talent inherited a large stage and virtually clear sightlines, which create an ideal setting for performances by top touring companies from around the world. Bookings range from weekly engagements to a month-in-residence with the Feld Ballet and Margie Gillis. The Joyce often subsidizes in-theater production costs. "All Together Different" promotes the seven most promising up-and-coming companies.
175 Eighth Ave. (at 19th St.), 242-0800, MC, V, AmEx, Tickets: $18-$27,

K

The Kraine Theater

One of New York's most eclectic venues, the Horse Trade Theater group manages this "best of the blackbox." With titles such as Vampire Geishas of Brooklyn, the theater may be off-Broadway but the productions are seldom off. Upstairs, the Horse Trade's Red Room houses late night performances.
85 E. 4th St. (at Second Ave.), (212) 777-6088, ❻ to Bleecker, ❺❽❾ to Broadway/ Lafayette

L

La MaMa Experimental Theater

Four small theaters offer new and experimental dance and theater, as well as off-beat performance. The avant-garde nature of the place means shows are hit or miss, but cheap tickets make it worthwhile to test the odds.
74A East 4th St. (bet. Second Ave. and Bowery), (212) 254-6468, MC, V, AmEx, ❺❾ to Second Ave., ❻ to Astor Pl.

Langston Hughes Community Library and Cultural Center

There are year-round readings and performances, as well as a wealth of reference mate-rials in the on-site library.
102-09 Northern Blvd. (at 102nd St.), Queens, (718) 651-1100, ❼ to 103rd St.

Lucille Lortel Theater

Cramped between the music-pumping, glitter merchandise shops of Christopher St. is this supremely immodest performance space, which claims to be New York's foremost off-Broadway theater. A recent success for the theater has been the acclaimed Mrs. Klein, chronicling the life and times of famed psychoanalyst Melanie Klein.
121 Christopher St. (bet. Bedford and Hudson Sts.), (212) 924-8782, MC, V, AmEx, ❶❷ to Christopher St.

M

Manhattan School of Music

Prodigies at one of the country's most prestigious conservatories perform, usually for free. Call ahead for scheduled performances and times.
120 Claremont Ave. (at 122nd St.), (212) 749-2802 or 749-3300, Cash Only at the Box Office, ❶ to 125th St. &

Manhattan Theater Club

Terence McNally, A.R. Gurney and Richard Greenberg are just a few of the playwrights whose work has been featured at MTC, one of the oldest subscription-based theater companies in the city. The company presents a broad range of work, mix-ing audience-pleasers and more challenging pieces on its two stages. MTC received a great deal of media attention in 1998 as the site of McNally's controversial Corpus Christi.
131 W. 55th St. (bet. Sixth and Seventh Aves.), (212) 399-3000, www.mtc-nyc.org. MC, V, AmEx, ❻❽❿ to 57th St. &

Martha Graham Center of Contemporary Dance

Home of the Martha Graham Dance Ensemble, this contemporary dance school trains young dancers in her technique, which is an artistic vision rather than simply a dance system. Sign up for only one class or for 20 (over the course of a month).
27 W. 26th St., 9th Floor (bet. Broadway and Sixth Ave.), (212) 838-5886, ❻❽ to 28th St.

Mark Morris Dance Center

Offering adult and children's dance classes (jazz, modern, and ballet, as well as alternatives such as yoga and pilates) in Fort Greene, Brooklyn, this dance center has gorgeous wood-sprung floors as well as spacious locker rooms. Call Karyn to rent out rehearsal rooms at subsidized rates thanks to a program supported by a grant from the New York State Council on the Arts.
3 Lafayette Ave. (Fort Greene), Brooklyn, (718) 624-8900, ❶❷❹❺ to Nevins, ❼❽❾❿ to DeKalb

Merkin Concert Hall

This modest performance space and new music venue is home to the Festival Chamber Music Society, which strives to provide quality music in a "warm, beginner-friendly environment." Each performance begins with a short lecture about the piece and ends with a champagne reception where audience members can meet the artists.
129 W. 67th St. (bet. Broadway and Amsterdam Ave.), (212) 501-3330. Cash Only ❶❷❸ to 66th St. X

Metropolitan Opera

When the Carnegies were the nouveau riche, Old Money's monopoly on the city's theater boxes frustrated the family so much that they went and built their own opera house. Though the original Met was further downtown, its current location retains a historic stodginess. A safely classical though consistently outstanding repertory.
Lincoln Center (at 66th St. and Broadway), (212) 362-6000 (ticket sales), MC, V, AmEx, ❶❷ to 66th/Lincoln Center

Miller Theater

The student price of $5 buys a consistently impressive line-up, from readings by Pulitzer prize winners like Richard Howard and Louise Glück to performances by established professionals like Yo Yo Ma and Ann Bogart's SITI troupe. Although the stage is

shallow and seating limited, the acoustics are excellent and balcony seats are intimate enough to make the microphones almost superfluous. The theater's curators also present film retrospectives featuring hard-to-find directors and actors.
Broadway and 116th St. (at Columbia University), (212) 854-7799, Cash Only at Box Office, ❶ to 116th St ♿

Minetta Lane Theater

Revues and new plays in a notably comfortable seating. Recent shows include the acclaimed docudrama Gross Indecency-the Three Trials of Oscar Wilde, recounting the legal ordeals that made the artist one of homosexuality's most prominent martyrs.
18 Minetta Lane (bet. Minetta Ln. and MacDougal), (212) 420-8000, MC, V, AmEx ($4 extra charge), ❹❺❻❼ ❶❽❾ to West 4th St. ♿

Minor Latham Playhouse

Once home to legends such as Duke Ellington, this student-run theater hosts productions by both Barnard and Columbia theater groups, who perform works such as the annual Greek drama (performed in the original), as well as works by student playwrights. Tickets are cheap and the seating is quite democratic.
119th St. and Broadway, enter at 117th St. (Barnard Campus), (212)

854-2079, Cash Only, ❶ to 116th St.

N

National Black Theatre

Family values are the focus at this company, founded in 1968 by Broadway star Barbara Ann Teer. Performances take place year-round, and acting workshops are also available.
2033 Fifth Ave. (bet. 125th and 126th Sts.), (212) 722-3800, Check or money order, Tickets: $16-$22, ❷❸ to 125th St.

New Amsterdam Theater

Once you get past the blinding yellow lights, cheesy souvenir stand, and suffocating crowd (all a result of The Lion King's popularity), the interior of the theater is an oasis of art deco elegance with marble friezes, lilac chandeliers, and an enormous, ornate concert hall. Blockbusters like The Lion King, Aida and Beauty and the Beast have shown here.
214 W. 42nd St., (bet. Seventh and Eighth Aves.), (212) 282-2900. ❹❻❼❾❿❽❿❽ ❶❷❸❼ to Times Square ♿

New York City Ballet

Co-founded in part by Balanchine after WWII, this top-notch company produces a particularly breathtaking Nutcracker with champagne galore and lots of three-year-

olds made up like dolls. In residence at the $30 million New York State Theater, the ballet has the largest repertory of any company.
20 Lincoln Center (66th St. and Broadway), (212) 870-5570 (box office), MC, V, AmEx, ❶❷ to 66th/Lincoln Center ♿

New York City Opera

Renews and redefines the soul of opera through stellar, innovative performances of both forgotten and familiar classics. A World Premiere Festival takes the kinds of risks which have made NYCO famous. The theater is smaller, so most seats are more attainable than at the Met and cost less, though the interior belies its origins in its mad, modern reincarnation of the Sixties and Seventies.
Lincoln Center (at 66th St. and Broadway), (212) 870-3570, MC, V, AmEx, ❶❷ to 66th St./Lincoln Center

New York Philharmonic

Over a hundred virtuosos led by Kurt Masur play Western classics, with an emphasis on European standards and American innovations.
Lincoln Center (at 66th St. and Broadway), (212) 875-5030, MC, V, AmEx, ❶❷ to 66th St./Lincoln Center

New York Theater Workshop

This downtown theater staple caters to a hip crowd and often presents work from the farther

corners of the mainstream. It's the original home of Broadway sensation Rent, as well as the rock musical Bright Lights, Big City and The Most Fabulous Story Ever Told. Annual "Just Add Water" festival presents work in development for future seasons. Rush tickets are available for most performances.
79 E. 4th St. (bet. Second Ave. and The Bowery), (212) 780-9037, MC, V, AmEx, DC. ❻❽ to Second Ave. ♿

Nuyorican Poet's Cafe

Founded in 1975 as a gathering and performance space for the Spanish-speaking voices of the New York literary scene, it remains one of the most significant outlets for outsider art because of diversification and even after numerous site changes. In addition to poetry slams and other readings, which helped create the resurgence of poetry as an aspect of cafe culture throughout the country, a night's program often includes theater, a video presentation or a jam session. The Nuyorican Poets have garnered enough respect for their work to sustain several published anthologies and to tour the globe performing. Don't pass up the chance to see them at home.
236 E. 3rd St. (bet. Aves. B and C), (212) 505-8183, Cash Only, ❻❽ to Second Ave.

O

The Ohio Theater

Anything goes here, since the stage is rented out to various freelance performance groups.
66 Wooster St. (bet. Spring and Broome Sts.), (212) 966-4844, Tickets: $10-$15, Cash Only, NR to Prince St., 6CE to Spring St. &

P

Performance Space 122

This small performance space in a converted church serves as a showplace for cutting-edge dance, theater and performance art. Artists range from obscure but talented newcomers to established members of the downtown scene. Runs tend to be short and very popular, so try to get tickets in advance.
150 First Ave. (at 9th St.), (212) 477-5288, MC, V, AmEx, FV to Second Ave.

Pearl Theater

This classic repertoire/resident company sticks to a strict pre-WWI itinerary, with conventional productions of Shakespeare, Moliere, Sophocles and others of their ilk, as well as revived relics. Shows generally run seven weeks. Heterogenous crowd with plenty of local traffic.
80 St. Marks Pl. (at First Ave.), (212) 598-9802, Tickets: never over $30, 6 to Astor Pl., NR to 8th St.

Playwrights Horizons

Long the anchor of Theater Row, this theater company has been premiering innovative and new American plays for the past twenty-five years. The work of Christopher Durang and Wendy Wasserstein was first presented here, as was Stephen Sondheim and James Lapine's Pulitzer Prize-winning musical Sunday In The Park With George. The upstairs Studio Theater presents work by up-and-coming writers.
416 W. 42nd St. (bet. Ninth and Tenth Aves.), (212) 279-4200, www.playwrightshorizons.org. MC, V, AmEx, ACE to 42nd St., NRQWS1237 to Times Sq.

Poets House

This free reading room and resource center houses the largest collection of poetry books in the country. Current poetry and literary periodicals are available for browsing, and Walkmans are provided for listening. Call for information about programs.
72 Spring St. (bet. Crosby and Lafayette Sts.), (212) 431-7920, 6 to Spring St. &

R

Rattlestick Theater

A vehicle for its artistic director, this tiny production company doesn't shy away from risks, an attribute that can cut both ways.
224 Waverly Pl. (bet. Perry and 11th Sts.), (212) 627-2556, ACEL to 14th St., 123 to 14th St.

S

Second Stage

Dedicated to reinventing plays that "didn't get a fair shot the first time around," this unassuming theater of second chances has produced the works of Stephen Sondheim, Edward Albee, August Wilson, Athol Fugard, Mary Zimmerman and Wallace Shawn, to name a few.
307 W. 43rd St. (at Eighth Ave.), (212) 246-4422, www.secondstagetheater.com, MC, V, ACE NQRWS1237 to Times Sq. &

Signature Theatre Company

Under the leadership of visionary artistic director James Houghton, the Signature has carved out a unique mission: highlighting the work of one major playwright each season. Past seasons have included retrospectives and world premieres from Arthur Miller, John Guare, Adrienne Kennedy and Sam Shepard.
555 W. 42nd St. (bet. Tenth and Eleventh Aves.), (212) 244-7529. MC, V, AmEx, ACEQRWS 1237 to Times Sq. &

SoHo Repertory

Home for anything new and compelling, from freshly adapted literary works to personal dramas. Well known for excellent casting choices, the theater generally offers several overlapping runs from which to choose.
46 Walker St. (bet. Church and Broadway Sts.), (212) 334-0962, Cash Only, ACE to Canal St.

St. Clement's Church

A working theater for thirty-five years, this charming little church has hosted some of the best Off-Broadway theater in the city. Episcopal services are still held here Sundays and Wednesday nights. Conveniently located on Restaurant Row and around the corner from the greatest concentration of ethnic restaurants in the city.
423 W. 46th St. (bet. Ninth and Tenth Aves.), (212) 246-7277, ACE to 42nd St./Port Authority

St. Marks Church in the Bowery

A quiet and beautiful cultural oasis in the bustling East Village, this century-old church is home to three excellent arts "projects," including Danspace, Poetry Project and the Ontological Theater. Most notable is the Poetry Project, one of the only programs of its kind, offering special literary events and workshops for budding poets, a forum for both well-known and up and coming poets to read their work.
131 E. 10th St. (at Second Ave.), (212) 674-6377,

St. Paul's Chapel

LeFarge stained glass, tiled ceilings and a 5,347-pipe organ make this the perfect niche for Thursday's midday organ concerts. The Columbia-Barnard Chorus and Gospel Choir perform here regularly, as well as visiting musicians from violinists to vocalists.
1116 Amsterdam Ave. (at 117th St., Columbia University), (212) 854-6625, Cash Only, ❶ to 116th St.

Stand-Up NY

Brett Butler and Dennis Leary cut their teeth here years ago and still swing by to pay their respects when in the neighborhood. The next wave of aspiring comedians hits the stage on Wednesdays for amateur night while Fridays at 11:30pm showcase with the "Comedy in Colors" program, showcasing entertainers of varying ethnicities.
236 W. 78th St. (bet. Amsterdam and Broadway), (212) 595-0850, MC, V, AmEx, D, Admission: $7-$12 (Friday and Saturday), ❶❷ to 79th St .&

Surf Reality

"Anything can happen here" boasts one of the regulars at this zany alternative comedy space. The tiny, makeshift stage hosts acts too silly or outrageous for the mainstream comedy circuit. New York's most bizarre performers turn out for Faceboy's Open Mike, Wednesdays, 8pm-3am,

$3 to sign up and perform. Once a woman pulled an onion out of her body.
172 Allen St., 2nd Floor (bet. Stanton and Rivington Sts.), (212) 673-4182, W-Su two shows nightly at 8pm, 10pm, Cover Varies, ❶❷ to Second Ave.

Symphony Space

Playing host to an incredible range of talent, this spacious theater consistently offers up unique programs, often incorporating disparate genres into a unifying theme. Past line-ups include a Best Films of Our Lives (the curators' lives, which were considerably longer than most of the audience's), which paired movies like Singing in the Rain with Fellini's 8 1/2. Student memberships available.
2537 Broadway (at 95th St.), (212) 864-1414 (program info), MC, V, AmEx, ❶❷❸ to 96th St. &

T

Thalia Spanish Theater

One of New York's hottest stages for established and new Hispanic playwrights, actors, and directors. Three productions yearly, as well as three ongoing showcases in music, dance and special events.
41-17 Greenpoint Ave. (bet. 41st and 42nd Sts.) Long Island City, (718) 729-3880, Cash Only, ❼ to 40th St. X

Theatre for a New Audience

Some of the most innova-

tive, provocative, thoughtful, and coherent productions of Shakespeare and other classics.
154 Christopher St., Suite 3D (bet. Greenwich and Washington Sts.) (venue changes regularly), (212) 229-2819, AmEx, ❶❷ to Christopher St.

TriBeCa Performing Arts Center

Inconspicuously housed in the main building of the Boro of Manhattan Community College, this large venue is easy to miss. That would be a shame since the programming is excellent, offering multicultural music, dance, theater from around the world and urban youth-themed performances consistent with the diverse student population. The college connection means cheap student-rate tickets.
199 Chambers St. (bet. West Broadway and Church Sts.), (212) 220-1460, MC, V, ❶❷❸ to Chambers St. &

V

Variety Arts Theater

The place to go for campy theater and a distorted dose of pop culture. Recent productions have included a new work by writer/drag queen Charles Busch and a musical based on the life of Patsy Cline. Proof that theater doesn't have to be dull, stodgy or squeaky-clean.
110 Third Ave. (bet. 13th and 14th Sts.), (212) 239-6200, MC, V, AmEx, D,

*Diners, ❿❻❻❻❻
❹❺❻ to Union Square &*

W

Williamsburg Art Nexus

This gallery, theater and rehearsal space in-one is located in Brooklyn's trendiest neighborhood. WAX cultivates a supportive environment for contemporary artists in all media and strives to spread art love. WAX features a one-room gallery space and a white walled black box theater available for rent to local artists and performers.
205 N. 7th St., Brooklyn, (718) 599-7997, M-Sa 10 am-6 pm, ❿ to Bedford Ave.

U

Upright Citizens Brigade Theatre

This is improv comedy at its best by the original cast of Comedy Central's Upright Citizen's Brigade and their disciples. In addition to nightly performances in their 74-seat theater in Chelsea, the UCBT provides and intensive "Improv Guerilla Training Center" for wannabe comics. There are multiple performances every night with the original cast. Check the website for show descriptions and times.
161 W. 22nd St. (bet. 6th and 7th Aves.) (212) 366-9176, ❶❷ to 23rd St.

Literature

literature

Almost from its founding, New York has been a literary city. Writers such as Edith Wharton, Willa Cather, Edgar Allen Poe, Langston Hughes, John Cheever, J.D. Salinger, Allen Gingsberg, Jack Kerouac and William S. Burroughs have all called New York home. These authors have used New York's resources for their books, and left the city in a different state after their works were published. New York is regularly depicted in literature as the city where adventures take place, people fall in love and dreams come true—not too far off from the reality of this grand city.

how's the novel coming?

Looking for a writer's workshop? There are a number of different options in the city, ranging from informal groups of writers who gather at coffee shops and people's apartments and critique each other's work, to more formal, structured workshops. The former are mostly found on a word-of-mouth basis, but the latter are easy to find. The most popular is the Gotham Writer's Workshop, which offers workshops in fiction, poetry, screenwriting and a number of other genres at seven different locations in Manhattan. They even have online classes for your convenience—check out their *www.write.org* for pertinent info. Classes meet once a week for three hours and cost about $400 for a ten-week semester. The teachers are widely published writers and have been described as "awesome," "amazing" and "incredible." The Writer's Voice of the West Side Y offers a number of different writing workshops, including nonfiction and literary memoir in addition to a number of discussion groups. They offer one-session intensive courses, which go for $20, weekend-long courses for $190, and the typical ten-week long course rings in at $270. If you are looking for something a little more specific or culturally diverse, check out Other Countries, a black, gay and lesbian organization, and the Asian American Writers' Workshop (AAWW). Unlike its counterparts, the weekly sessions held by Other Countries are free except for a $2 fee for the space. Anyone is welcome to attend and should bring copies of their work to read at the session. This year Other Countries introduced a new, monthly workshop series, including one session titled "Changing Your Inner Underwear." The AAWW offers 6-week long workshops which cost about $125, and feature topics such as poetry writing, fiction-in-progress, how to get published, and screenwriting as well as discussion groups and book clubs.

New Yorkers and tourists alike flock to the Strand, exploring its eight miles of new and used books.

spoken WORD

Spoken word can mean anything from a simple reading to an elaborate performance featuring instruments and props. This art form has recently experienced a surge of popularity as evidenced by sold-out shows, TV performances and CD sales of the spoken-word artist. If you want to check out either a reading or a full-fledged performance, there are many venues throughout the city where both budding talents and venerable members of the literati read their own work and perform the words of others.

The Unterberg Poetry Center at the 92nd Street Y (see Performing Arts, Upper East Side) is the Carnegie Hall of poetry. Everyone from Poet Laureate Rita Dove to W.S. Merwin to Nobel Prize-winner Joseph Brodsky have read here. The city's universities, especially New York University and Columbia, also attract well-known authors. Columbia's resident performing space, Miller Theater (see Performing Arts, Morningside Heights), dabbles in literature and offers $5 student tickets. Though shows are few and far between, they're worth the wait. In the past years, curators of "Theater of the Mind" have sponsored a performance by Yevtushenko, an appearance by Seamus Heaney and a tribute to John Berryman which drew Donal Justice, Richard Howard, Helen Vendler and Louise Gluck. The Columbia Writing Department also brings big names to read on campus. NYU's Master's in Fine Arts program also draws established talent since admission is always free. For writing department readings open to the public, check the "Readings" section of the Voice or NY Press.

The line-up at KGB (see Bars, East Village), which has recently included Karl Kirchway and David Foster Wallace, just keeps getting better. Another downtown social scene that supports poetry is Limbo (see Cafes, East Village), where writers on the cusp read in the quintessential East Village intellectual ambiance. Very refined, and packed with people who love their MTV. More great downtown poetry can be found at the Nuyorican Poet's Cafe (see Performing Arts, East Village), long a mecca for cutting-edge talent.Performances here are never a disappointment as these are not simply readings. The theatrical elements of spoken word are emphasized as much as the poetry, and if someone starts to drag, the audience loudly lets them know it. Over in SoHo, The Drawing Center (see Galleries, SoHo) hosts a readings series entitled "Nightlight" which has featured writers like Sapphire and Gary Indiana. Readings are held one Wednesday a month.

Elitism aside, Barnes and Noble, the enemy of independent booksellers, is a stop on every author's promotion trail and boasts some stellar guests. It's always free, although the folding chairs hardly evoke a salon atmosphere. The Alliance Poets Reading Series at the Educational Alliance (197 East Broadway, (212) 475-6200, FV to East Broadway) hosts one of the most eclectic reading series in the city and is notable for its literary nonpartisanship and willingness to feature rising stars alongside established poets. Symphony Space (see Performing Arts, Upper West Side) is another excellent option. Expect the venerable theater to preserve the classics and to push the avant-garde envelope with "Selected Shorts," readings of short stories by theater and Hollywood actors. The readings are broadcast Sundays on WNYC 93.9, New York's NPR station.

Poetry Slams

A slam is the performance of written poetry with an emphasis on presentation and eloquence. Since its conception in 1984, poetry slamming has become a subculture in every major city. Perhaps the most famous and influential poetry club is the Nuyorican Poets Cafe, on 246 East 3rd Street. This proverbial birthplace of slam has two nights a week that are of note: Wednesday nights are 'Slam Open,' where newcomers emerge onto the scene to test out their work. If they prove themselves, they are invited to the Friday night show, 'Friday Night Slam,' where seasoned professionals are pitted against up-and-comers in a battle judged by audience members. For the grassroots feeling of poetry slamming, Nuyorican is as homegrown as it gets.

Nuyorican Poets Café
(212) 505-8183 w.nuyorican.org, all shows $5

13
Monday nights are open mic at this brightly colored Union Square bar, club and lounge. All shows are $5 and often have featured poets.
35 E. 13th St.
(212) 979-6677
www.bar13.com, $5

Jimmy's Uptown
Tuesday nights are 'Hottest Poets: Poetic Vibes' at this chic Harlem restaurant. Expect to see celebrities, corporate big wigs and a happy poet walking out of the door with the weekly $500 prize.
2207 Adam Clayton Powell Blvd.
(212) 491-4000 $10 plus two-drink minimum

The Poetry Project
Located at St. Mark's Church in the middle of the East Village, the poetry 'project' is a documentation of poetry as well as writing workshops, all of which are possible through government funding.
131 E. 10th St., www.poetryproject.com

Poetry Society of America
They have perhaps the most comprehensive list of poetry readings on their website, www.poetrysociety.org. Though it is a national list, many are in New York. Their program with The MTA offers poets the opportunity to have their words printed out for the public on subway cars.

Unterberg Poetry Center
Not only a forum for poets to perform located at the 92nd Street Y, they also offer writing programs and workshops taught by esteemed writers.
35 W. 67th St. (212) 415-5500

A

A Different Light

The East Coast branch of the largest gay and lesbian specialty book vendor in the country feels refined but homey. A mellow crowd browses through great selections from kitsch to academia and partakes of the small cafe's coffee and sandwiches. The store regularly hosts lectures, musicians and poets.

151 W. 19th St. (bet. Sixth and Seventh Aves.), (212) 989-4850, MC, V, AmEx, ❶❷ to 18th St. ♿

Academy Bookstore

Find used or otherwise discounted books on every subject—especially art, architecture, photography, history and philosophy. The staff will search for out-of-print books.
10 W. 18th St. (bet. Fifth and Sixth Aves.), (212) 242-4848, MC, V, AmEx, ❶❷❸❹❺❻ to 14th St.-Union Sq.

Applause Theatre and Cinema Books

Scripts, books and screenplays. Perfect for the cinephile who has time to browse.
211 W. 71St (west of Broadway), (212) 496-7511, ❶❷❸ to 72nd St.

Argosy Bookstore

Rare books, old maps and lithographs fill this time warp of towering bookshelves and cluttered desks. The only real bargains here are on the outside table.
116 E. 59th St. (bet. Park and Lexington Aves.), (212) 753-4455, MC, V, AmEx, ❹❺❻ to 59th

B

B. Dalton's

A trademark combo of extensive contemporary fiction selection and paltry intellectual offerings. Strong sports section downstairs.
396 Sixth Ave. (at 8th St.), (212) 674-8780, MC, V, AmEx, ❶❷ to Christopher St., ❹❺❻❼❽❾ to W. 4th St.

Bank St. College Bookstore

This store serves the fledgling schoolteachers of the nearby Bank St. College with an extensive selection of children's books and educational theory and planning guides. *610 W. 112th St. (at Broadway), (212) 678-1654, MC, V, AmEx, ❶ to 110th St.* ♿

Barnes and Noble at 82nd St.

This branch was the first of the megastores in Manhattan, now dwarfed by its downtown colleagues but still a nice oasis from the chaos of Broadway. The selection is remarkable, and New York magazine has named the coffee bar on the mezzanine a major West Side singles scene.
2289 Broadway (at 82nd St.), (212) 362-8835, MC, V, AmEx, ❶❷ to 79th St. ♿
Also at:
223-82 Bell Blvd (Bay Terrace Shopping Center), (718) 224-1083, MC, V, AmEx, Diner, D, ❼ to Flushing-Main St., Q28 to Bell Blvd.
1280 Lexington (bet. 86th and 87th St.), (212) 423-9900, ❹❺❻ to 86th St. ♿
33 East 17th St. (Union Square at Broadway), (212) 253-0810, ❹❺❻❹❺❻ to Union Sq., ♿
267 Seventh Avenue (bet. 5th and 6th St.), (718) 832-9066, ❺ to Seventh Avenue

Biography

Muckrakers, voyeurs and fan club presidents come to this high-ceilinged and brick-walled store for the latest on their respective celebs. Also boasts an impressive gay and lesbian section.
400 Bleecker St. (at W. 11th St.), (212) 807-8655, MC, V, AmEx, ❹❺❻❹❺ to 14th St.

Black Books Plus

African and African-American issues are the top priority at this rare find which stocks a number of genres.
702 Amsterdam Ave. (at 94th St.), (212) 749-9632, MC, V, AmEx, ❶❷❸ to 96th St.

Blackout Books

The radical writings available here are required reading for any potential East Village resident. Browsers can educate themselves about global political uprisings, sexual liberation or just have a good laugh. Blackout stocks books, newspapers, magazines and alternative comic books. For the civic-minded, there's a bulletin board in the back noting local meetings and organizations.
50 Ave. B (bet. 3rd and 4th Sts.), (212) 777-1967, ❺❻ to Second Ave.

Book Ark

Relief for those weary of superstores. Fiction offerings are solid, as is the foreign language selection.
173 W. 81st St. (bet. Amsterdam and Columbus Aves.), (212) 787-3914, MC, V, ❶❷ to 79th St.

Bookberries

Coffee table books are the specialty of this store— huge volumes loaded with

pictures, especially along the lines of travel and food. A children's section is located in the rear.
983 Lexington Ave. (at 71st), (212) 794-9400, **4 5 6** *to 68th St.*

Booklink

Come to this shop for quality fiction and children's books. Also a sampling of intellectual and academic periodicals.
99 Seventh Ave. (bet. President and Union), Brooklyn, (718) 783-6067 MC, V, AmEx, Q to Seventh Ave., **1 2** *to Grand Army Plaza*

C

Columbia University Bookstore

The bookstore is the only option for students, with one-stop shopping for all the proper accoutrements of the enthusiastic student, from sweatshirts to pennants. It has a sizable selection of new fiction books as well.
Columbia Campus, entrance at Broadway and 115th St., 854-4131, MC, V, AmEx, **1** *to 116th St.* &

Community Book Store and Cafe

This integral part of Park Slope's social life carries a mixture of current best-sellers and classic fiction, with a wonderful cafe and garden in the back. The owners also coax well-known authors out

for readings, most recently Mary Gordon and Pete Hamill.
143 Seventh Ave. (bet. Garfield and Carroll Sts.), Brooklyn, (718) 783-3075, MC, V, AmEx, **Q F** *to Seventh Ave.*

Complete Traveller

The best store for new and out-of-print books providing information for real trips and fuel for the imagination. The prices reflect the quality and selection. The staff is amiable, erudite and willing to discuss anything from city politics to traveling in sub-Saharan Africa.
199 Madison Ave. (at 35th St.), (212) 685-9007, MC, V, AmEx, D, Diners, 6 to 33rd St.. **B D F V N R Q W** *to 34th St.-Herald Sq.* &

Crawford Doyle Booksellers

Good browsing for high quality fiction.
1082 Madison Ave. (bet. 81st and 82nd Sts.), (212) 288-6300, MC, V, AmEx, **6** *to 77th St.*

D

Dina News Corporation

Though the staff tends to frown upon browsing, try to sneak a peek at this impressive selection of periodicals, including a number of foreign magazines and newspapers.
2077 Broadway (bet. 72nd and 73rd Sts.), (212) 875-8824, MC, V, AmEx, D,

1 2 3 *to 72nd St.*

Doubleday Book Shop

Centrally located on Fifth Avenue, this bookstore caters to more mainstream clientele, stocking their shelves with new titles, best-sellers and travel guides.
122 Fifth Ave (bet. 17th and 18th Sts.), (212) 633-3300, **L N R Q W** **4 5 6** *to 14th St.-Union Sq.*

Drama Bookshop

Drama stocks plays, biographies, acting/directing and writing manuals and much more.
250 W. 40th St (bet. Seventh and Eighth Aves.), (212) 944-0595, **N R Q W S 1 2 3 7** *to 42nd St.-Times Sq.*

E

East-West Books

As the name suggests, the emphasis here is on introducing Western readers to the literature of the East, specializing in religious and philosophical traditions from Mahayana Buddhism to neo-Confucianism. The staff will make special orders.
78 Fifth Ave. (bet 13th and 14th Sts.), (212) 243-5994, MC, V, AmEx, **F L V 1 2 3** *to 14th St..*
Also on the Upper West Side and in Greenwich Village

Ed's Book Exchange, Inc.

Specializing in buying and

selling textbooks, both old and new.
17627 Union Turnpike, Queens, (718) 969-7173, Q46 to St. John's University &

F

Fashion Design Books

Located at the heart of FIT's urban campus, this unique take on the university bookstore stocks a plethora of fashion mags, from the popular to the obscure, and art and design books. In lieu of office accessories, you'll find art and sewing supplies.
234 W. 27th St., (bet. Seventh and Eighth Aves.), (212) 633-9646, MC, V, AmEx, D, **1 2** *to 28th St.* &

Forbidden Planet

Comic book fans seeking everything from superheroes to the latest Eightball cruise the racks to weed out the best of the new and used selection. But the big thing here is science fiction with significant dashes of fantasy and horror.
840 Broadway (at 13th St.), 473-1576, MC, V, AmEx, D, **L N R Q W** **4 5 6** *to Union Square*

G

Gryphon

Crowded shelves of used books climbing almost to

the ceiling and piled on the floor. There are books here that can be found nowhere else in Manhattan. You just have to look real hard.
2246 Broadway (bet. 80th and 81 St.), (212) 362-0706, ❶❷ to 79th St.

H

Hacker Art Books

An eager, knowledgeable staff headed by Pierre, the Parisian owner and conversationalist extraordinaire, can help browsers wade through the initially intimidating selection. The clientele are true art-lovers, not just collectors.
45 W. 57th St. (bet. Fifth and Sixth Aves.), (212) 688-7600, MC, V, AmEx, ❶❶❶❶❹❺❻ to 59th st.

Hotalings News Agency

Walls of magazines, including one of the city's finest selections of foreign-language periodicals.
142 W. 42nd St. (bet. Sixth Ave. and Broadway), (212) 840-1868, MC, V, AmEx, ❶❶❶❶❶ ❶❶❶❶❶❶❼ to Times Sq.

Housing Works Used Bookstore Cafe

Used books SoHo style. No dingy paperbacks with tattered covers and peculiar odors here. Instead, browse through nearly pristine coffee table art books and hardcover fiction with jackets fully intact, all at low used-book prices. There's also a coffee bar.
126 Crosby St. (bet. Houston and Prince), (212) 334-3324 MC, V, AmEx, ❶❶❶ to Broadway/Lafayette, ❻ to Bleecker

K

K & W Books and Stationary

One of the biggest Chinese bookstores, K & W carries Hello Kitty toys and a large selection of books in Chinese and in English on topics like martial arts, bonsai care, and Buddhism .
131 Bowery St., (212) 343-0780, Cash Only, ❶❶❶❶❶❶❶❻ to Canal St.

Kinokuniya Bookstore

Japanese books, some in English translation, with a diverse selection of stationery and gifts.
10 W. 49th St. (at Madison Ave.), (212) 765-7766, MC, V, AmEx, ($10 minimum) ❶❶❶❶ to Rockefeller Center ♿

Kitchen Arts and Letters

With a fabulous selection of over 9,000 cookbooks, the definitive answer to "what's cooking?" for either the novice or the gourmand.
1435 Lexington Ave. (bet. 93rd and 94th Sts.), (212) 876-5550, MC, V, ❻ to 92nd St.

L

Labyrinth Books

Professors and students alike applaud this recent addition to Morningside's healthy population of bookstores, made possible in part by the rare generosity of its landlord (Columbia). Relying on a strong selection of academic titles rather than coffee bars and comfy furniture, Labyrinth is a welcome retreat for hardcore bibliophiles.
534 W. 112th St. (bet. Broadway and Amsterdam Aves.), (212) 865-1588, MC, V, AmEx, ❶ to 110th St. X

The Last Word

Used books in various stages of disrepair, especially those that consistently turn up in the syllabi of Columbia core curriculum classes. Bargain tables outside offer a lot of junk along with the occasional gem.
1181 Amsterdam Ave. (at 118th St.), (212) 864-0013, Cash Only, ❶ to 116th St.

Lectorum Book Store

Spanish and Latin American books in Spanish and Portuguese are dispersed among translations of popular titles by the likes of Stephen King and James Clavell. Bibles, dictionaries and a host of other reference books round out the selection. Check up front for information about lectures and readings.
137 W. 14th St. (bet. Sixth and Seventh Aves.), (212) 741-0220, MC, V, AmEx, ❶❷❸ to 14th St., ❶❶❶ to 14th St.-Sixth Ave. ♿

Liberation Book Store

One of the country's largest and best selections of books about black history and culture. Posters, calendars, and greeting cards are also available.
421 Lenox Ave. (at 131 St), (212) 281-4615, Cash Only, ❷❸ to 135th St. X

Libraire de France

One-stop shopping for French émigrés and Francophiles. New York's largest French-language bookstore sells magazines upstairs and a vast assortment of literature, history and biographies downstairs.
610 Fifth Ave., on the Rockefeller Center Promenade, (bet. 49th and 50 St.), (212) 581-8810, MC, V, AmEx, ❶❶❶❶ to Rockefeller Center

M

Macondo

Pick up an import from either Spain or South America here. The store caters to native speakers

with an excellent selection of literature, plays, and poetry, although prices reflect the import costs.
221 W. 14th St. (bet. Seventh and Eighth Aves.), (212) 741-3108, AmEx, **1 2 3** *to 14th St.*

Manhattan Books

Mainly catering to the textbook needs of students at the nearby college. This can be a good spot to find steals on reference books like dictionaries and style guides. The real attraction is that they'll pay out a small amount of cash for almost any textbook or other academic text, so if something has proven hard to unload, give them a shot.
150 Chambers St. (bet. Greenwich and W. Broadway), (212) 385-7395, MC, V, AmEx, **1 2** *to Chambers St.* ♿

Manhattan Comics and Cards

Action figures gaze down at customers navigating the stacks of comic books. Mags run the gamut. Scavenge through Sunday's half-price bins.
228 W. 23rd St. (bet. Seventh and Eighth Aves.), (212) 243-9349, MC, V, 12 or **C E** *to 23rd St.*

Municipal Art Society Urban Center Books

Books on every architectural topic, from urban design to Freudian interpretations of city planning, line the walls of this cozy nook, complete with a fireplace and library ladders. Enjoy a recent purchase in the courtyard outside.
457 Madison Ave. (at 51st St.), (212) 935-3595, MC, V, **E V** *to Fifth Ave.-53rd St.*

Murder Ink

This specialty bookstore featuring new and used mystery fiction is every sleuth wannabe's dream. Their stock includes many classic whodunits as well as novels featuring elements of espionage and suspense. A mecca for the city's true mystery buffs, this shop has frequent book-signings that draw some big names. The staff knows their stuff.
2486 Broadway (bet. 92nd and 93rd Sts.), (212) 362-8905, MC, V, AmEx, **1 2 3** *to 96th St.*

Mysterious Bookshop

Serving the city's voracious mystery readers, this store stocks out-of-print books plus a healthy number of British imports.
129 W. 56th St. (bet. Sixth and Seventh Aves.), 765-0900, MC, V, AmEx, **N R Q W** *to 57th St.*

N

New York University Bookstore

Lines wind around the block at the beginning of each semester at this academic standard. Students get no special discounts.
18 Washington Pl. (bet. University and Greene Sts.), (212) 998-4678, MC, V, D, **N R** *to 8th St.*

O

Oscar Wilde Memorial Bookstore

For over twenty-five years, New York City's flagship gay bookstore has been offering books for and by gay men and women, as well as videotapes, music, magnets, T-shirts and jewelry. Occasional readings by established authors are scheduled.
15 Christopher St. (at Sixth Ave.), (212) 255-8097, MC, V, AmEx, D, **1 2** *to Christopher St.*

P

Papyrus

Though its hegemony was infringed upon with the opening of Labyrinth, this smallish store stocks a little bit of everything. The literature and travel sections are excellent, as is the selection of textbooks, which often run cheaper than at Columbia University's bookstore.
2915 Broadway (at 114th St.), (212) 222-3350, **1 2** *to 116th St. X*

Partners & Crime

Serving Village mystery aficionados, P&C carries a lot of out-of-print books. The staff will special-order books not in stock. Call for a schedule of readings.
44 Greenwich Ave. (at Charles St.), (212) 243-0440, MC, V, AmEx, **1 2** *to Christopher St.*

Posman Books

Off-season, after January or September, browse through new and used academic titles or rifle through the bins outside for super discounts.
1 University Pl. (at Washington Sq.), (212) 533-2665, MC, V, AmEx, D, **N R** *to 8th St.*

R

Rizzoli

Get lost in this warm store that specializes in beautiful architecture, art, design and coffeetable books. Literature and non-fiction selection is adequate if not inspiring.
31 W. 57th St. (bet. Fifth and Sixth Aves.), (212) 759-2424, MC, V, AmEx, D, **N R Q W** *to 57th St.*

S

Science Fiction, Mysteries and More!

Absurdly named, this sci-fi den is the stomping ground of those whose genre-lust even Forbidden Planet cannot satisfy. New and used paperbacks abound, along with rare editions and collectibles for the very serious. There's also lots of stuff about aliens, occult and conspiracy theories for X-Files types.

140 Chambers St. (bet. W. Broadway and Greenwich Ave.), (212) 385-8798, MC, V, AmEx, Diners, 1 2 3 to Chambers St.

See Hear

Check out the most homemade publications around, with lots of stuff for hardcore and indie-rock fans as well as those who just appreciate irreverent writing that doesn't answer to advertisers.

59 E. 7th St. (bet. First and Second Aves.), 505-9781, MC, V, AmEx, 6 to Astor Pl.

X

Shakespeare & Co.

One of several locations offering a diverse selection of books with the soul of an actual bookstore.

939 Lexington Ave. (bet. 68th and 69th Sts.), (212) 570-0201, MC, V, AmEx, D, 6 to 86th Sts.
Also at:
716 Broadway (at Washington Pl.), (212) 529-1330, MC, V, AmEx, N R to 8th St., 6 to Astor Pl.

SoHo Books

The best sale tables around await outside this bargain book cavern, which offers everything

from slightly outdated editions of Let's Go guides to slick Gen X novels for $1.98 each or three for five dollars.

351 W. Broadway (bet. Broome and Grand Sts.), MC, V, AmEx, (212) 226-3395, N R to Prince St., CE to Spring St.

St. Mark's Books

Why go to a chain when everything you'd ever want can be found in the tall racks of this favorite? Literature, sci-fi, gay lit and mystery are all strong suits. It's just cooler to shop here.

31 Third Ave. (bet. 8th and 9th Sts.), (212) 260-7853, MC, V, AmEx, D, 6 to Astor Pl.

St. Mark's Comics

From "The X Men" to less conventional titles like "Sexy Sushi," there's enough here for any comic book connoisseur.

11 St. Marks Pl. (bet. Second and Third Aves.),(212) 598-9439, MC, V, AmEx, 6 to Astor Pl.

Stowell and Sons Bookstore

Narrow aisles and a certain mustiness lend an authenticity to this bookstore's monthly "Dead Poets" reading series. Check out the back alcove for used books.

33-18 Broadway (bet. 33rd and 34th Sts.), Astoria, Queens, (718) 204-5775, MC, V, N to Broadway

The Strand Bookstore Inc.

Advertising "eight miles of books," The Strand is an awesome sight: two cavernous floors of bookshelves stuffed solid and tables crammed into the space in between. Browse slowly, and with the proper investment of time, you'll turn up books you never dreamed existed.

828 Broadway (at 12th St.), (212) 473-1452, MC, V, AmEx, D, LNRQW456 to 14th St.-Union Sq.
Also at: 25 Fulton St. (at Water St.), (212) 732-6070, MC, V, AmEx, D, A C J M Z 1 2 4 5 to Broadway-Nassau-Fulton St.

Sufi Books

If there were such a thing as a typical neighborhood spiritual bookshop, this would be TriBeCa's. The quiet atmosphere with a soft-spoken staff to match contains a wealth of Eastern religion resources and smaller sections on Judaism and Christianity to feed spiritual quests of any ilk. There's also a large space next door for meditation and yoga classes.

227 W. Broadway, (212) 334-5212, MC, V, AmEx, 1 2 to Franklin St.

T

Tower Video and Books

This counterpart to the Broadway Tower Records has a stellar video selec-

tion downstairs and a bookstore upstairs . *692 Broadway (at 4th St.), (212) 505-1500, MC, V, AmEx, N R to 8th, 6 to Astor Pl.*

W

West Side Judaica

This haven of Judaica supplies music, art and children's educational tools as well as a number of books dealing with Jewish issues. Closes at 3pm on Fridays for Shabbat and doesn't reopen until Sunday.

2412 Broadway (bet. 88th and 89th Sts.), (212) 362-7846, MC, V, 1 2 to 86th St.

Wow Comics

New and old releases from a variety of both mainstream and independent companies are sold alongside baseball cards, action figurines and other memorabilia.

1491 Williamsbridge Rd, Bronx, (718) 829-0461, 2 5 to Pelham Pkwy

Z

Zakka

Insight into the world of the Japanese "manga". Bookstore, boutiques and video palace focusing on Japanese pop culture.

147 Grand St., (212) 431-3961, C E to Spring St.

NYC *film* and *tv* scene.190

a *brief* history of *film* in NYC.191

movie theater listings.192

f i l m + t v

Mae West once told a Hollywood studio executive, "I'm a big girl, from a big town--so don't blow smoke at me, little man." After decades ceding ground to Los Angeles as the film production capital of the country, New York is rebounding as both a location and a production site.

festivals in the city

There are festivals in New York to celebrate every type of film and filmmaker; it's important to keep an eye on the *Times* to find out what's going on at Lincoln Center and at MoMA, which hosts the big-name festivals. **The New York Film Festival** (September and October) has been celebrating American and foreign films for several decades. Tickets for this festival, particularly on opening and closing nights, are snapped up weeks The IFP has been a godsend to filmmakers in New York. Yet the tickets at the Film Market are priced to cater to serious filmmakers, and are expensive, even with the membership discount.

Once summer arrives, films are screened at **Bryant Park Free Film Festival** (Sixth Avenue at 42nd Street) on Mondays at 8:30 p.m. Bring a picnic dinner, a blanket, and a friend- sit back and watch King Kong or Vertigo under the stars. **The Tribeca Film Festival** (at the Tribeca Film Center, tickets are available at *www.ticketmaster.com*) runs in the second week in May and has international, indie and short films for only $10 a pop, or you can buy an all-day pass (unlimited screenings and after-parties) starting at about two grand. The tenth annual **Gay and Lesbian Film Festival** will be held June 4th-14th at the Joseph Papp Public Theatre (for updates and info. call (212) 260-2400). During the first week of August, enjoy air-conditioned splendor and affordable ticket prices at the **Harlem Week Black Film Festival** at the Adam Clayton Powell Jr. State Office Building (call (212) 749-5298 for information). The Angelika at (212) 995-2000 has festivals of its own, year-round.

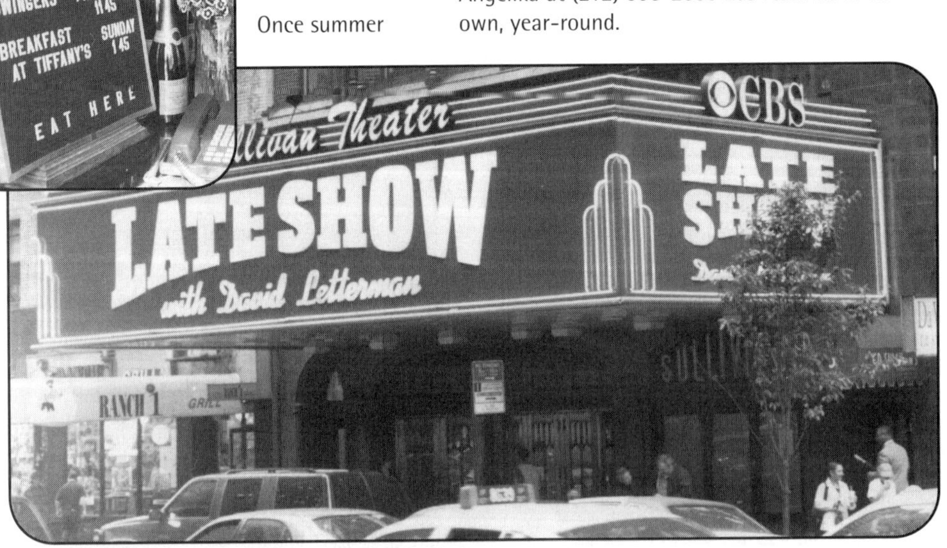

1900-1940

At the turn of the century, budding filmmakers shot footage of the city's vaudeville and theatrical shows and other sites. Even footage of buildings under construction was popular with audiences. After perpetual sunshine had drawn the studios to California, agents and executives still scanned New York stages for talent, realizing, in the late '20s, that many of the stunningly beautiful silent-screen stars had squeaky speaking voices and needed to be replaced by Broadway actors.

In the early '30s stage diction was the rage and actors imitated the accent of the English upper-class. Straight-talking Humphrey Bogart, however, had his big break on Broadway in *The Petrified Forest*. Bogart impressed his co-star (the hugely popular Leslie Howard) so much that Howard refused to appear in the film version unless Bogart also reprised his Broadway role. Barbara Stanwyck and Joan Crawford both started out as Broadway "hoofers."

1940-1990

In the '40s, neo-realism, film noir and avant-garde filmmaking deepened the power and complexity of image on film. NYC, with its combination of grit and glamour, was the perfect setting for noir classics like Billy Wilder's *The Lost Weekend*. In the '50s when Hollywood was focusing on teenyboppers and Technicolor, New York television and filmmakers found increasing meaning in realism. *On The Waterfront* was a revolutionary combination of method acting and on-location shooting whose stark simplicity stood out from the over-elaborate productions of the dying studio system.

Realism in Film Depiction

Realism merged with pageantry in the 1972 production of *The Godfather*, which marked the beginning of a decade of great American films, most of them reflections on the American Dream-New York style. Coppola and Pacino, Scorcese and DeNiro united to present the world with defining images of New Yorkers, images which still form an international perception of this city and its people. With hindsight, it now seems clear that, in 1986, when Spike Lee scraped together funding for his second feature-length film, *Do the Right Thing*, he was setting the stage for a surge of independent films which would revolutionize the business.

Independent Films

Independent films continue to provide a much needed alternative to blockbusters, while also allowing the art and business of filmmaking to be passed on to the next generation. On any given day in Manhattan (and the four boroughs), there are any number of films in production. Theatres like the Angelika, Lincoln Plaza and The Film Forum offer the world's best cinema-and countless organizations like The Independent Feature Project are nurturing and networking with the filmmakers of tomorrow.

---

to the budding filmmaker,

New York is filled with auteurs-to-be filming low-budget projects of enormously varying quality. The good news is it's surprisingly easy to break in--on a low level. All you have to do is work for free. The Independent Feature Project at (212) 465-8200 requires volunteers year-round. Work a few hours and you can attend the rest of a weekend seminar or festival for free.

Also, be sure to buy the publications: Screenwriter and The Independent Filmmaker are good, and Backstage is essential--film students advertise there for actors. Call them up and volunteer to do anything. Film is a hugely social business, so the more people you meet, the more chance you have of ending up with paid work. Going to film festivals is not cheap. The Mayor's Office of Film, Theater, and Broadcasting (212) 489-6710 was created to aid with such productions.

Students or professionals go to the office to get special permits and even police help to accommodate filming in New York. When you've got that short-film shot and edited, you'll have the hot calling card of the nineties. And hopefully, you'll already have schmoozed with a few distributors--because distribution is the major challenge in this business.

A

American Museum of the Moving Image
See Museums

Angelika Film Center
This independent film multiplex offers cappuccino and gelato from the well-stocked café and there is always the possibility of running into celebrities like Bono or Brad Pitt.
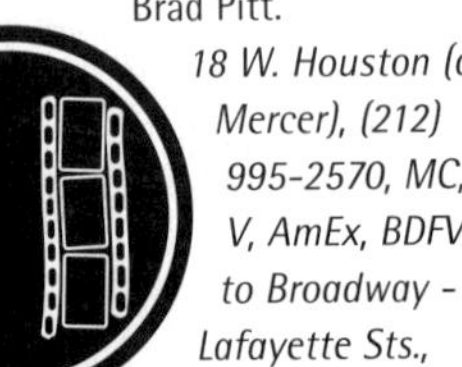
18 W. Houston (at Mercer), (212) 995-2570, MC, V, AmEx, BDFV to Broadway - Lafayette Sts., NR to Prince St., 6 to Bleecker St.

Anthology Film Archives
Started in 1970 as a museum devoted to avant garde cinema, this institution has since become a mecca for aspiring artists seeking inspiration and hardened film buffs. With a vast library and programming designed to showcase it, an excellent opportunity is provided to see rare foreign films, early works by now-established directors, and legendary but rarely seen stuff like Warhol flicks.
32 Second Ave. (at 2nd St.), (212) 505-5181, Cash Only, 6 to Bleecker St., FV to Second Ave.

C

Cinema Village
The single movie screen may have a reputation for hosting questionable flicks of the porn persuasion, but it actually accommodates a far wider array of independent films with themes ranging from gay and lesbian to kung fu action to African Diaspora.
22 E. 12th St. (bet. University Pl. and Fifth Ave.), 924-3363, Cash Only, LNRQW 456 to 14th St.-Union Sq.

Clearview's Chelsea West
333 W. 23rd St. (bet. Eighth and Ninth Ave.), (212) 989-0061, MC, V, AmEx, CE12 to 23rd St.

Clearview's Waverly Twin
Your basic two-theater movie house, which vacillates between mainstream and art films. This can lead to interesting juxtapositions, such as Godzilla and The Ice Storm.
323 Sixth Ave. (at 3rd St.), (212) 929-8037, MC, V, AmEx, ACEFVS to West 4th St.

City Cinemas Village East
By all indications this seems to be just another many-screened showplace for big-budget Hollywood productions, but within the nondescript exterior lies the preserved interior of the old Yiddish Theater complete with original adornments and multi-tiered theater-style seating. So for a real treat, buy a ticket for whatever is showing in Theater Number One and get there early to check out this historical landmark.
189 Second Ave. (at 12th St.), (212) 529-6799, MC, V, AmEx, LNRQW 456 to 14th St.-Union Sq.

F

Film Forum
Two programs run in this classic setting. Program One has first-run independent and foreign feature films as well as some excellent documentaries. Program Two screens revivals including reissues of individual classics as well as film series featuring everything from the complete works of great, if sometimes obscure, directors to genre films.
209 W. Houston St. (bet. Sixth Ave. and Varick St.), (212) 727-8110, Cash Only, 12 to Houston St.

K

Kim's Video and Audio
Less pedantic than their East Village counterparts, the staff here still knows what's up and has no qualms about either helping you sift though a bunch of out-there directors, or matching your trivia on obscure Weimar actresses. Foreign film selection here also beats the East Village locations.
144 Bleecker St., (212) 260-1010, MC, V, AmEx, D, Diners, 6 to Bleecker.

Kim's Video
The most interesting and comprehensive selection of videos in town including everything from the typical new releases to the most esoteric art-house, foreign and genre flicks. Be forewarned, most everything is arranged by director or some odd category so come well-informed with something in mind or deal with the staff, who are knowledgeable but a little overeager to prove it.
85 Ave. A (at 5th St.), (212) 529-3410, MC, V, AmEx, NR to 8th St., 6 to Astor Pl.

L

Lincoln Plaza Cinemas
Down the street but still in the shadow of its titan neighbor Sony, this small-ish theater doesn't want to do the big-budget Hollywood schtick anyway, preferring foreign and independent film festival standouts and a few surprises.
1886 Broadway (bet.

62nd and 63rd Sts.), (212) 757-2280, MC, V, AmEx, ❶❷ *to 66TH St.-Lincoln Center* ♿

M

The Movie Place

Avoid the weekend hordes at Blockbuster and that migraine-inducing light too. Comparable selection here, and more importantly, they deliver to your doorstep. The staff loves movies, which is more than you can say for a movie chain.
237 W. 105th St. (and Broadway), (212) 864-4620, MC, V, AmEx, ❶ *to 103rd St.*

N

NYU Cantor Film Center

By the students, for the students, and offered at the oh-so student-friendly rate of two dollars a pop. The theater's screen spans a minimal width and metallic fold-up chairs do little to keep viewers comfortable, but the cash saved can readily be shoved into a back pocket for extra padding.
36 E. 8th St. (at University Pl.), (212) 375-8116, Cash Only, ❷❸ *to 8th St., 6 to Astor Pl.*

P

The Paris

Highbrow European first runs and revivals show at this tony midtown movie house behind the Plaza Hotel. Very civilized.

4 W. 58th St. (at Fifth Ave.), (212) 688-3800, ❹❺❻ *to Fifth Ave-59th St.*

Q

Quad Cinema

As can be expected with most theaters, which run primarily independent flicks, the movie screens here are smaller here than in first-run theaters. But the film selections, which include many foreign and revival series, are so choice that screen size is the last thing considered. Tucked away from heavy street traffic on 13th St., and with only four screens hosting its wares, there's little chance the intimate, neighborhood appeal of this movie house will be mainstreamed any time soon.
34 W. 13th St. (bet. Fifth & Sixth Aves.), (212) 225-8800, ❼❽❾ *to 14th St.*

S

The Screening Room

The place to catch independent and foreign film hits after they leave the Angelika/Film Forum/the Quad, or classics like *Breakfast at Tiffany's* shown every Sunday. The non-traditional seating makes it feel as comfy as a Blockbuster night, without the Bud Light and the remote. Diners at the restaurant next door get seated first for shows, so with a dinner-and-movie date, you can score a loveseat.

54 Varick St. (at Laight St.), (212) 334-2100, MC, V, AmEx, ❶❷ *to Canal St.* ♿

Sony IMAX at Lincoln Center

By far Lincoln Center Multiplex's coolest attraction: nature films, which are always amusing for their close-ups of bug eyes, have given way a bit to plot-oriented pieces. The show on New York's history is a crowd-pleaser.
1992 Broadway (at 68th St.), (212) 336-5000, MC, V, AmEx, ❶❷ *to Lincoln Center* ♿

Sony Theaters Lincoln Square

Perhaps the city's glitziest theater where sweeping murals depicting stars of the Thirties and Forties and higher-than-average ticket prices try to suggest a larger-than-life cinematic experience. It's really just a lot of escalators, a screen or two the size of Kansas, and the videos playing at the concessions stand that try to prompt salivating by actually panning over the candy selection. The big-budget box-office hits are as predictable as ever.
1992 Broadway (at 68th St.), (212) 336-5000, MC, V, AmEx, ❶❷ *to 66th St.* ♿

W

Walter Reade Theater/Film Society of Lincoln Center

Since 1985, the luxurious Walter Reade Theater has

been the home of New York's elite film club, which screens everything from Jim Carrey to Godard, with an emphasis on the latter end of the spectrum. New Directors/New Films, in conjunction with the MoMA, has premiered work by such directors as Pedro Almodovar and Peter Greenaway, while film festivals sport titles like Rendezvous With French Cinema Today. Overall, rich in retro and avant-garde classics, just avoid the post-film talk if you fear pretension.
165 W. 65th (bet. Broadway and Amsterdam Aves.), (212) 875-5600, Cash Only at box office, ❶❷ *to Lincoln Center*

Z

The Ziegfeld Theater

This elegant, immaculate old show palace, one-time home of the Ziegfeld Follies, restores some of the glamour and sense of occasion to the typical movie-dinner date. The biggest and best screen in town to see blockbuster new releases and re-mastered old ones like *Vertigo, Lawrence of Arabia* and the *Star Wars* trilogy.
141 W. 54th St. (bet. Sixth and Seventh Aves.), (212) 765-7600, ❸❻ *to Fifth Ave.*

Want to advertise to 30,000
students and young professionals?

dining
coffee house
955

restaurants + cafes

Dining in this city simply has no comparison. It's like buying an infinitely condensed greatest hits album of world cuisine wrapped up in a soft corn taco and served on a rainbow tray with silverware and chopsticks. No other place can compete. New York has the best chefs and the greatest variety in the world. Yet, the character of NYC dining is sometimes hard to define. After all, what does it mean to have a New York Strip Steak or a Manhattan Clam-Chowder?

Most people define this city by its diversity. In a sense, this is the characteristic that ties New York City together and gives it a feeling of homogeneity. While it is true that no single cuisine, in isolated form, could be called "New York", when together, this adjective seems to qualify for anything and everything. Whether it's Indian, Russian, Moroccan, Brazilian, or Korean, in New York, it's New York cuisine.

One way to locate New York's dining diversity is to visit some of the city's famous cultural enclaves. Although Wok 'n' Rolls and Ollie's chain restaurants can serve up Chinese as fast a McDonald's Big Mac, the best place for authentic Chinese cuisine is Chinatown. If you're looking for some good old-fashioned meatballs, your best bet is crossing over into Little Italy. There are also smaller enclaves such as "Little India" on 6th street between 1st and 2nd avenues. This is where curry chicken and tuna bindi are king. Likewise, the Ukranian Diners of the East Village serve Borscht and pierogi combos like burgers and fries. Watch out - the drinks aren't free.

Although the various enclaves lend cultural dining a deep degree of authenticity, authentic diversity is not confined to them. Choose any neighborhood in New York and discover a wide selection of delicious cultural cuisine. From Restaurant Row on 46th between 8th and 9th in the theater district to the moderately priced bistros that line the village, New York City offers dining delight to everyone.

They don't call it the "Big Apple" for nothing. One bite of NYC will send the most pious man into utter depravity. With over 10,000 restaurants to choose from, New York City is dining heaven. However, in a place of such prodigious size, it is important to choose wisely when dining in New York. This guide will give you the most tender section of the beef. When all is said and done it should be clear why the finest strip steak and the tastiest soup are both preceded by the densely packed adjective, New York.

Deli Capital of the World

New York is home to the most famous delis in the world. From the Carnegie Deli to the Second Avenue Deli to Katz's on the Lower East Side, Manhattan is, for all practical purposes, the Deli Capital of the world. The original meaning of the word "deli" derives from German. Delicatessen can literally be translated as "delicate meal" or "delicacies".

New York became this way during the late 1800's when delis began to open under German and Alsatian immigrants. In time, deli fever spread to the flourishing Jewish community in response to a lack of kosher alternatives. The new trend, kosher-style delis, became associated with this group of immigrants. Delis have since become associated with small grocery stores and sometimes sit-down restaurants. In other parts of the world, such as Jakarta, Tokyo, and Hamburg, "New York Style Delis" are typically sandwich shops that offer a variety of Jewish specialties such as Matzoh ball soup, gefilte fish, stuffed cabbage, chopped liver and more.

In recent times, however, the New York Deli Style has branched out to include more than just Jewish foods. Rupert Jee, a man of Asian descent, is the manager of the "Hello Deli" on 53rd and Broadway. Thanks to David Letterman's popular skit, Rupert's hole-in-the-wall is now a New York institution.

Mr. Pink's *guide to tipping*

Tipping in NYC, like anywhere else, is an unwritten law. So, how do people learn how to tip? The ordinary New Yorker learns through experience. He gets a smile when he has tipped well, an angry pejorative when he has not. The purpose of this segment is to spare you, the friendly foreign reader, from the painful experience of tipping poorly in NYC. Let's learn from the example of Mr. Pink:

Mr. Pink: *"I don't tip. I don't believe in it."*
Answer: It is standard to tip your server 15 to 20 percent of the check's total. An easy way to calculate the tip is to double the sales tax which appears below the subtotal on the check. Whether you believe in it or not, you must tip while in New York City. Or, like Mr. Pink, you might end up dead.

Mr. Pink: *"I don't tip because society says I gotta. I tip when somebody deserves a tip. When somebody really puts forth an effort, they deserve a little something extra."*
Answer: Although this is the custom in many European cultures, this is not the custom in New York. Here, it is customary to always tip a server.

However, one may indeed vary the size of the tip in accordance with the server's performance. If the server is outstanding, it may be a nice gesture to exceed the 20 percent cap. Likewise, if the performance is unpleasant (which, unfortunately, is sometimes the case due to the number of overqualified wait staff who would rather be making their living on Broadway), the tip you leave can be indicative of your displeasure.

It should also be noted that certain restaurants will add a gratuity to the bill for parties of more than six people. So, if you're with a group, it's wise to make sure your total doesn't already include the tip.

Mr. Pink: *"I'm gonna tip. Normally I wouldn't."*
Answer: Good boy Pink. Now you're a bonafide New Yorker (Bronx cheer).

The Paul Shaffer sandwich and the Biff Henderson on wheat are two of the best in all of New York.

Naming sandwiches after celebrities, however began at the Stage Deli in the theater district where one could order sandwiches named after their favorite celebrities. This trend has spread throughout New York and across the globe. It shows up in other New York delis such as Hamilton in Morningside Heights. Funny names for deli sandwiches are just another symptom of the New York pride.

So, if you like turkey on sour dough, chicken cutlet on a roll, or corned beef on rye, New York City serves up the best in the world. And, if they forget the pickle, you have a right to yell and scream. That's what being in New York is all about.

LISTINGS

RESTAURANTS

Bridge Cafe

Even if you're not a part of the city's political machine, the attentive staff will provide you with reliable standards at this adorable eatery just south of City Hall, one of former mayor Ed Koch's favorite haunts. Mostly a middle-aged crowd of spin doctors and other politicos.
279 Water St. (at Dover St.), (212) 227-3344, www.bridgecafe.com. Open Su-M 12pm-10pm, T-Th 12pm-11:00pm, F 12pm-12am, Sa 5pm-12am, MC, V, AmEx, Entrées: $12-$24, ❹❺❻ *to Brooklyn Bridge-City Hall.* ♿

14 Wall St.

Join stockbrokers and investment bankers carrying on the legacy of J.P. Morgan by puffing cigars and sipping scotch in his old library, the closest thing to a private dining room in the city. The breakfast room overlooks the Harbor.
14 Wall St. (bet. Broadway and Broad St.), (212) 233 2780, www.14wallstreetrestaurant.com. Open M-F 12pm-3pm, 5pm-8pm. MC, V, AmEx, DC, D. Entrées: $20-$25, ❷❸ *to Wall St.* ♿

Harbour Lights

The food is second to the view here. Go on a beautiful day and give your eyes a treat while your legs rest after exploring South Street Seaport all day. It may be overpriced, and a little touristy, but the view makes it seem worthwhile.
South St. Seaport, Pier 17, 3rd fl. (at Fulton St.), (212) 227-2800, www.harbourlts.com. Open M-Th 11am-1am, F 11am-2am, Sa 10am-2am, Su 10am-1am. MC, V, AmEx, DC, D, Entrees: $25-$40, ❹❺❻ *to Fulton St.* ♿

Harry's at Hanover Square

If you're in the mood for suits, cigars, and meat, this Wall St. hangout is the place. Order a martini and scan the great wine list as you enjoy one of Harry's excellent steaks. Not known for its feminine touches, it's not the place for "ladies who lunch." Like the stock market, it's closed on weekends.
1 Hanover Sq. (bet. Pearl and Stone Sts.), (212) 425-3412. Open M-F 11:30am-10:30pm. MC, V, AmEx, DC, D, Entrées: $14-$30, ❿Ⓡ *to Whitchall St.* ♿

Mangia

Gourmet Mediterranean cuisine and friendly waitstaff at this restaurant make it a culinary hotspot for the surrounding working worlds of businesses, galleries and museums. Mangia's diverse array of pastas, sandwiches, and entrées — including an "antipasto table," with a wonderful selection of foods ranging from paella to rare tuna — is sure to quench anyone's desire for a gastronomic thrill. In a rush? Stop at the café downstairs for equally delicious take-out dining. They deliver, and do they ever.
40 Wall St. (bet Nassau and Broad Sts.), (212) 425-4040. Open M-F 7am-10pm. MC, V, AmEx, DC, D, Entrées: $11-$15, ⓃⓇ *to Rector St.* ♿

Wave

Enjoy this Japanese restaurant's outdoor terrace. The stunning views of New York Harbor and the Statue of Liberty are the perfect backdrop for some of the finest sushi around. With the breeze off the water, and shade from the trees, there's no better place to chill on a hot summer day.
21 South End Ave. (at Battery Park), (212) 240-9100. Open M-F 11:30am-10:30pm, Sa-Su 12:30pm-10:30pm. MC, V, AmEx, DC, Entrées: $7-$18, ❶ *to Rector St.* ♿

CAFES

Seaport Café

The menu at this open-air café features fresh pastas, sandwiches, wraps, gourmet coffees and desserts. It's perfect for casual diners who don't want generic fast food or a high tab. The outdoor table area is great for people-watching, ensuring that diners won't miss any of the action on the lively pier area.
89 South Street (at Pier 17), (212) 964-1120. Open Su-Th 7am-2am, F-Sa 7am-3am. MC, V, AmEx, DC, D, ❿Ⓜ❼❷❸❹❺ *to Fulton St.*

RESTAURANTS

Bouley Bakery

Reserve well in advance for what many consider to be "the perfect meal." The white walls, curved ceiling, and green stone floors all work to create an ambiance that is both elegant and casual. Bouley Bakery maintains its cachet by using the finest regional ingredients, and taking great care with each meal served. The wait staff will help you order, so sit back and relax.
120 W. Broadway (bet. Duane and Reade Sts.), (212) 964-2525. Open M-Su 11:30am-3pm, 5:30pm-10:30pm. MC, V, AmEx, Entrées: $28-$35, ❶❷❸ *to Chambers St.* ♿

Bubby's

Forego the fancily-named sandwiches, which don't merit their prices, in favor of the sturdier fare like quesadillas served with great salsa. Gorgeous ceiling-high windows afford people-watching, and the wooden floor and benches evoke the comfort level of an unpretentious, rather rustic, cafe. Great brunch.

carts with *heart*

The pace of life is faster in New York than any-where else in the world. Even at the strangest hours, the sidewalks rush with crowds of hun-gry people burning off their energy. Demand is always high for the quick, the cheap, and the easily edible. Namely, hot dogs.

Although street vendors can be found in most world cities, New York has a top claim to mobile food vendors, especially hot dog carts. National suppliers call their carts "New York Hot Dog Carts" and tourists from the farthest stretches of the globe line up to eat New York style hot dogs.

There are over 3,000 hot dog vendors here. In certain busy areas, like the corner of Centre and Hogan Street, eight carts can be found in two city blocks. Usually vendors are found at street corners and near subway stops.

Although hot dogs are New York City's most characteristic fast-food product, they are by no means the only option available. Over the span of a few blocks in almost any part of the city, one will come across kiosks, honeyed nut stands, ice cream trucks and coffee carts. Kiosks are great for a quick drink, a candy bar, or a cigarette. Nut stands like "Nuts 4 Nuts" offer honey-roasted peanuts, coconuts, almonds and cashews. During the winter, a hot chestnut always hits the spot. Ice cream trucks like the "Good Humor truck" offer chilled deserts, from snow cones to choco-tacos. Coffee carts usually serve egg on a roll, bagels, buttered rolls and other breakfast foods along with that coffee.

In the busiest city in the world, street vendors serve an important function. From 6 am to 6 pm, they are the most convenient way to dine. So, if you're in the city, eat a hot dog and slurp some Joe. It's only $1 and the heartburn is worth it.

---

120 Hudson St. (at N. Moore St.), (212) 219-0666, www.bubbys.com. Open M-Th 8am-4pm, 6pm-11pm, F 8am-4pm, 6-12am, Sa 9am-4:30pm, 6pm-12am, Su 9am-4:30pm. MC, V, AmEx, Entrées: $7-$15, **❶❷** to Franklin St. &

Café Noir

A trendy spot for late-night dining, the bar is generally inundated with well-dressed, air-kissing types looking for fun. The atmosphere and food are Spanish-Moroccan. Eschew the more expen-sive entrées in favor of lighter fare like sandwich-es and tapas, which com-bine simple ingredients to perfection. Use the differ-ence in price to splurge on a good bottle of wine from their extensive list of French vintages.
32 Grand St. (at

Thompson St.), (212) 431-7910. Open M-Su 12pm-4am. AmEx,Entrées: $12-$18, **❹❻❸** to Canal St.

Casa La Femme

This Egyptian restaurant screams "Romantic," with Arabian Nights tents lined up along the walls, gauzy fabric that will effectively shelter your party from prying eyes. The hookahs aren't filled with opium, but are so much fun you won't notice. Check out the belly dancers on weekends. Try not to choke over the bill when it comes.
150 Wooster St. (bet. Houston & Prince Sts.), (212) 505-0005. Open Su-W 5pm-12am, Th-Sa 5pm-4am. NR to Prince St., 6 to Spring St., **❺** *to Broadway-Lafayette*

Chanterelle

One of the city's most highbrow restaurants, serving elegant cuisine in a lovely high-ceilinged dining room. The prix fixe lunch is superb, and the most affordable option.
2 Harrison St. (at Hudson St.), (212) 966-6960, www.chanterellenyc.com. Open M 5:30pm-11pm, T-Sa 12pm-2:30pm, 5:30pm-11pm. MC, V, AmEx, DC, D, Entrées: $20-$30, **❶** *to Franklin St.* &

Duane Park Café

For quiet conversation and delicious food in a relaxed atmosphere, this place can't be beat. The soft shell crabs and roast-ed Bartlett pear are musts. Best of all, you can actually get a table without a reservation.
157 Duane St. (bet.

Broadway and Hudson St.), (212) 732-5555, Open M-R 12pm-2:30pm, 5:30pm-10pm, F 12pm-10:30pm, Sa-Su 6pm-10:30pm, MC, V, AmEx, DC, D, CB, Entrees: $15-22, **❶❷** to Chambers St.

Edward's

Formerly the Odeon Bar, Edward's is a mellow bar and restaurant where locals don't fear being deluged by TriBeCa celebrities. With mellow lighting, friendly staff and decent food, Edward's is a keeper.
136 W. Broadway (bet. Duane and Thomas), (212) 233-6436, Open M-Th 8am-12am, F-Su, 8am-3am , MC, V, AmEx, DC, D, CB, Entrees: $8 - 18, **❶❷❸** *to Chambers St.*

Layla

For authentic food from a trendy restaurant with beautiful decor, this is as good as it gets. The menu is a mix of standards like tabouleh and new creations centered around fish and lamb. Even when the food isn't incredible, the beautiful setting is enough to compensate. *211 W. Broadway (at Franklin St.), (212) 431-0700, www.myriadrestaurantgroup.com. Open M-Th 5:30pm-10:30pm, F-Sa 5:30pm-11:30pm. MC, V, AmEx, Entrées: $19-$27, ❶ to Franklin St.* &

Nobu

One of the hottest and best restaurants in the city, offering exquisite L.A.-style Japanese cuisine served in a pristinely decorated, lofty and uncluttered space. Be prepared to spot the rich, famous and gourmands. Reservations must be made 30 days in advance, leaving you plenty of time to eagerly anticipate the meal. *105 Hudson St. (at Franklin St.), (212) 219-0500, www.myriadrestaurantgroup.com. Open M-F 11:45am-2:15pm, 5:45pm-10:15pm, Sa-Su 5:45pm-10:15pm. MC, V, AmEx, DC, Entrées: $20-$30, ❶ to Franklin St.* &

The Odeon

After many years, this place remains one of the most stylish eateries around. Its secret lies in maintaining a classically stylish, rather than trendy decor, and serving excellent brassiere food for the late-night dining crowd. More suitable for making the scene with a group than an intimate dinner for two. DeNiro is a frequent visitor. *145 W. Broadway (bet. Duane and Thomas Sts.), (212) 233-0507. Open M-Th 11:45am-2am, F 11:45am-3am, Sa 11:30am-3am, Su 11:30am-2pm. MC, V, AmEx, DC, D, Entrées: $15, ❶❷❸ to Chambers St.* &

TriBeCa Grill

This flagship of the DeNiro restaurant empire is a haven for those who like to enjoy a little celebrity watching with their meal. Movie big shots from the nearby TriBeCa Film Center can be found sharing the spacious, darkwood and brick dining room with plenty of other notables and, of course, some commoners, all there to enjoy New American cuisine. Yum yum all around. *375 Greenwich St. (at Franklin St.), (212) 941-3900, www.myriadrestaurantgroup.com. Open M-Th 11:30am-5pm, 5:30pm-11pm, F 11:30am-5pm, 5:30pm-11:30pm, Sa 5:30pm-11:30pm, Su 11:30am-5pm, 5:30pm-10pm. MC, V, AmEx, Entrées: $18-$28, ❶ to Franklin St.* &

CAFES

Yaffa's Tea Room

Alice in Wonderland stumbles out of the rabbit hole and finds herself in New York. Burgundy velvet and antique crystal chandeliers make you feel like a cosmopolitan Queen of Hearts sipping her tea. Reservations required for high tea ($20), served Monday through Saturday 2pm-5pm.

353 Greenwich St.), (212) 274-9403. Open M-Su 9-11:30. MC, V, AmEx, DC, ❶❷ to Franklin St. &

Chinatown

RESTAURANTS

Bo Ky

Seafood variations served over rice and noodles are the staples of the Chinese menu. The central location attracts both tourists and locals on a lunch break. Efficient service moves patrons in and out in a hurry. *80 Bayard St. (at Mott St.), (212) 406-2292. Open M-Su 8pm-9:30pm. Cash Only, Entrées: $5-$13. ❿ⓙⓜⓝⓡⓩ❻ to Canal St.* &

Funky Broome

This Little Italy restaurant wants to be a better-lit, hipper version of its bargain Chinese cousins down the street south of Canal. The food is standard, the prices good, the clientele are a mix of Chinatown locals and SoHo regulars. The décor runs heavy on fish tanks with live lobsters and such. During the day, it's somber, at night, it's bright bright. *176 Mott St. (Broome St.), (212) 941-8628. Open Su-Sa 11:30am-12am. ❻ to Spring St.*

Golden Unicorn

Cleaner and more polished than most Chinatown dim sum houses, this chandeliered restaurant has become especially popular among tourists and local businessmen hosting lunch meetings. Delicious dim sum (7 days a week, 9am-3:30pm) is served Hong-Kong style, stacked on metal carts piloted by vigorous employees. Many claim it's dim sum and then some. *18 East Broadway (at Catherine St.), (212) 941-0911. Open Su-Sa 8:30am-10:30pm. MC, V,*

AmEx, DC, D, Entrées: $8-$11, **B D Q** *to Grand St.*

Joe's Shanghai

Joe's crabmeat buns are deservedly famous, and tourists, locals and suburban Chinese flock here year round for them. Friendly service and the savory food keep customers coming back for more. Try the soup dumplings, filled with juicy crabmeat and pork in a flavorful broth.
9 Pell St. (bet. The Bowery and Mott St.), (212) 233-8888. Open Su-Sa 11am-11:15pm. Cash Only, Entrées: $5-$18,
J M N R Z 6 *to Canal St.*

New York Noodletown

Away from the tourist center of Chinatown lies this affordable and cozy restaurant where you're guaranteed to find a dish to excite your taste buds. In-season seafood specials, the crab in particular, are a definite must-try, as is the barbecued chicken/duck/pork combo. The ultra-accommodating service will make sure that you leave both full and fully satisfied.
28 Bowery (at Bayard St.), (212) 349-0923. Open M-Su 9am-3:30am. Cash only, Entrees: $8-12,
B D Q *to Grand St.*

Onieal's Grand Street

A turn-of-the-century tavern, rumored to have been frequented by Teddy Roosevelt during his tenure as police commissioner. Onieal's retains its old-world charm for the bankers, architects, models and celebrities who come for the flavorful

dishes. New American with Italian overtures, it also features a traditional Irish breakfast, while at night it transforms into a popular late night lounge.
174 Grand St. (bet. Baxter and Mulberry Sts.), (212) 941-9119. Open M-Sa 11:30pm-4am, Su 4:30pm-4am. MC, V, AmEx, DC, Entrées: $17-$25, **B D Q** *to Grand St.,* **J M N R Z 6** *to Canal St.*

Pongsri Thailand Restaurant

Practically adjacent to the municipal courthouses, Pongsri delights jury-duty sufferers with its tasty and affordable lunch specials. Standard noodle and curry dishes are all fabulous, if sometimes ultra spicy.
106 Bayard St. (at Baxter St.), (212) 349-3132. Open M-Su 11:30am-11:30pm. AmEx, Entrées: $5-$10,
J M Z N R Q W 6 *to Canal St.* ♿

Vietnam Restaurant

A basement location nestled in the crook of elbow-shaped Doyers Street, Vietnam Restaurant would be hard to find if it were not for the blazing sign above the doorway. The menu is hit-or-miss, but when it hits, it hits hard. The daily specials continue to astonish, as do the fish sour soups, caramel pork and the strange-sounding but absolutely delicious "shrimp paste grilled on sugar cane."
11 Doyers St. (bet. The Bowery and Pell St.), (212) 693-0725. Open Su-Th 11am-9:30 pm, F-Sa 11am-10:30pm. AmEx, Entrées: $4-$8, **B D Q**

to Grand St., **J M Z** *to Bowery.*

CAFES

Chinatown Ice Cream Factory

If chocolate and vanilla make you groan with boredom, this tiny café will satiate your jaded taste buds. Lick away at flavors like red bean, green tea, taro and lychee. The ginger is divine. There's usually a line around the block on weekends.
65 Bayard St. (bet. Mott and Elizabeth Sts.), (212) 608-4170. Open M-Su 11am-11pm, Cash Only,
J M Z N R Q W 6 *to Canal St.* ♿

Tai Pan Bakery

The pastries at this extremely popular bakery merit its long weekend lines. Custard tarts and pearl milk tea drinks are sure to please. Fish burgers are for the adventurous.
194 Canal St. (212) 732-2222. Open M-Su 7:30am-8:30pm. MC, V, Amex **J M Z N R Q W 6** *to Canal St.*

RESTAURANTS

Buona Notte

Attractive space with seating choices in the front, dining room and garden. Plenty of mirrors, so you can detect the fettuccine between your teeth before your date does. Nice presentation and delicately seasoned dishes.
120 Mulberry St. (bet. Canal and Hester Sts.), (212) 965-1111. Open M-

Su 12pm-11pm. MC, V AmEx, Entrees: $11-24,
J M Z N R Q W 6 *to Canal St.,* ♿

Cafe Gitane

France approaches the border of Little Italy, armed with authentic bistro menu and aloof waiters. Perfect ambience for flipping through fashion mags, drinking cappuccinos and posing.
242 Mott St. (bet. Houston and Prince Sts.), (212) 334-9552. Open M-Su 9am-12am. Cash Only, Entrées: $7-$10, **N R** *to Prince St.)*

Luna's Ristorante

Come join The Family at this neighborhood hideaway in the heart of Little Italy where the decor is non-pretentious. The aroma of fresh garlic sizzling in olive oil more than compensates for the lack of hyped-up atmosphere and perfunctory service. Still one of the best buys in Little Italy.
112 Mulberry St. (bet. Canal and Hester Sts.), (212) 226-8657. Open Su-Th 12am-12pm, F-Sa 12pm-2am. MC, V, AmEx, **J M Z N R Q W 6** *to Canal St.* ♿

Positano Ristorante

The slender space and subdued décor make Positano seem less raucous than its Mulberry Street neighbors. A peaceful meal in the heart of Little Italy.
122 Mulberry St. (bet. Canal and Hester Sts.), (212) 334-9808. Open M-Su 12pm-12am. MC, V, AmEx, **J M Z N**

R Q W 6 *to Canal,* ♿

Puglia

Like Pasta? Like Elvis? Then you're in luck — spend your time at large communal tables, chugging wine with new friends as an Italian Elvis works his magic on a little Casio keyboard in the corner. By the time you leave, you'll feel less lonely.
189 Hester St. (bet. Mott and Mulberry Sts.), (212) 226-8912, www.littleitalynyc.com/puglia. Open M-Su 12pm-1am. MC, V, AmEx, DC, Entrées: $5-$10, **J M N R Z 6** *to Canal St.* ♿

CAFES

Ferrara Bakery and Café

America's oldest espresso bar, Ferrara's has been around since 1892 and has been owned by the same family ever since. Everything is homemade! This is the best cannoli this side of Palermo.

195 Grand St. (bet. Mulberry and Mott Sts.), (212) 226-6150, www.ferraracafe.com. Open Su-F 8am-12am, Sa 8am-1am. MC, V, AmEx, DC, D, **J M Z N R Q W 6** *to Canal St.*

Lower East Side

RESTAURANTS

Castillo de Jagua

A homely but decent Dominican dive in the heart of Loisaida, this place pleases with rice & beans, fried plantains, cafe con leche and fresh squeezed O.J. served to the beat of loud Caribbean music.
113 Rivington St. (bet. Ludlow and Essex Sts.), (212) 982-6412. Open M-Su 8am-12am. Cash Only, **F J M Z** *to Delancey St.* ♿

Grilled Cheese

All kinds of combinations of grilled cheese imaginable here, and they're all priced to go. The place is very small, but how long does it take to make and eat a grilled cheese, anyway?
168 Ludlow St. (bet. Houston and Stanton Sts.), (212) 982-6600. Open M-Su 11am-12am. Cash only, Entrees: $2-$8, **F V** *to Second Ave.* ♿

Katz's Delicatessen

Steaming pastrami, corned beef sandwiches and other artery-clogging delicacies await at this cavernous, superior (non-Kosher) delicatessen, where yellowing paint and curling posters tell patrons to "Send a salami to your boy in the army." Nothing much has changed here in the last 50 years. A dollar tip to one of the gruff, portly attendants behind the counter will beget a sandwich big enough to feed a family of five. Take a ticket when you go in.
205 E. Houston St. (at Ludlow St.), (212) 254-2246. Open Su-T 8am-10pm, W-Th 8am-11pm, F-Sa 8am-3am. MC, V, AmEx, Entrées: $5-$15, **F V** *to Second Ave.* ♿

Le Pere Pinard

This charming French restaurant in the Village might very well have been transported from the south of France, wait staff and all. Bare wooden tables and eclectically decorated stucco walls add to the rustic, French country ambience but hardly hint at the sophisticated food to come. Especially delicious are the Raw Tuna and Ginger in Soy Sauce, the Shrimp, Mango and Asparagus Salad, and the delightfully gooey Chocolate Valrona Cake with coconut sorbet.
175 Ludlow St. (bet. Houston and Stanton Sts.), (212) 777-4917. Open M-Th 5pm-12am, F-Sa 11am-1am, Su 11am-11am. AmEx, Entrees: $12-$18, **F V** *to 2nd Ave.*

Oliva

Oliva – a Spanish gem of a restaurant, where waiters greet regulars with a peck on the cheek – is the perfect spot to dine with a date or an intimate friend. Expect romantic ambience with slow groovy music, chosen by the manager (a local DJ). The food is impeccably presented and savory: choose from an excellent daily selection of seafood and paella on Sundays and Mondays, as well as the sinfully sweet dessert wines. You might leave with your wallet a bit lighter, but you'll be smiling.
161 E. Houston St. (at Allen St.), (212) 228-4143.

Open M-F 5:30pm-12am, Sa-Su 11am-1am. AmEx, Entrées: $10-$20, **F** **V** *to Second Ave.*

Ratner's

Ratner's has lost its completely kosher menu, but patrons still come for the friendly atmosphere. In its heyday, Ratner's was the place to eat gefilte fish and matzoh balls. Today, you'll find hamburgers alongside tasty cheese and pineapple blintzes. For a taste of the original menu, sample the appetizer platter with eggplant and whitefish. The vegetarian cutlet is also worth a taste. Do expect heaping portions of everything.
138 Delancey St (bet. Suffolk and Norfolk), (212) 677-5588. Open Su-F 8am-8pm, MC, V, AmEx, D, Entrées: $8-$15, **F** **J** **M** **Z** *to Delancey St.*

Sammy's Romanian

This bustling and lively restaurant hosts rich meals and a loud Yiddish band. Locals and other New Yorkers, none of whom are dieting, frequent the place. Red meat is a featured menu item. Chopped liver, and lots of vodka are popular as well.
157 Chrystie St. (at Delancey St.), (212) 673-0330, Open M-Th 4pm-10pm, F-Sa 4pm-11pm, Su 4pm-9:30pm, MC, V, AmEx, Entrées: $20-$27, **F** **V** *to Second Ave.*

Tonic

Natural light pours in through the skylights of this cavernous space as patrons feast on cheap, eclectic café fare. A former Lower East Side kosher winery, Tonic has a performance space in back, encircled in red velvet. Avant-garde and experimental films are played on Monday nights. The most endearing feature is the downstairs cocktail lounge with circular booths built within 2,500-gallon hardwood wine casks.
107 Norfolk St. (bet. Delancey and Rivington Sts.), (212) 358-7503, www.tonic107.com. Open Su-W 8am-12am, Th-Sa 8am-4am. Cash Only, Entrées: $5-$12, **F** **J** **M** **Z** *to Delancey St.)*

Triple Eight Palace

After taking the escalator to the threshold of this Hong Kong extravaganza, you understand how they derived the "palace" part of the name. The multi-roomed restaurant assumes the air of a circus, with families chattering over fried and steamed noodles, shrieking toddlers playing chicken with rolling dim sum carts, and tables of heated woks threatening diners with third-degree burns. The dumplings, buns and shellfish are all excellent.
88 E. Broadway (under the Manhattan Bridge), (212) 941-8886. Open M-Su 8:30am-9:30pm. MC, V, AmEx, DC, D, Entrées: $10-$18 **F** *to East Broadway.*

SoHo

RESTAURANTS

Baluchi's

Named after Pakistan's Balochistan province, this bonafide Indian restaurant does justice to the sultry opulence for which the region is known. Numerous options will satisfy vegetarians, including pallak paneer and Basmati rice. Check out the half-priced dinners.
193 Spring St. (bet. Thompson and Sullivan Sts.), (212) 226-2828. Open M-Su 12pm-3pm, 5pm-11pm, MC, V, AmEx, DC, Entrées: $10-$14, **C** **E** *to Spring St. X f*

Bistro Margot

A French treasure hidden in SoHo, gourmet enough to satisfy the upper-crust, older patrons who don't mind the bloated prices. A surplus of two-person tables and seductive lighting emphasize its potential as a date restaurant.
26 Prince St. (bet Mott & Elizabeth St.), (212) 274-1027, Open M-Th 11am-11pm, F-Sa 11-12, AmEx, Entrées: $5-$13, **F** **S** **V** *to Broadway-Lafayette St.* &

Blue Ribbon Sushi

Let the simple yet elegant modern Japanese decor draw you into this fashionable SoHo sushi haven and you shall be rewarded with yellowtail and tuna of melt-in-your-mouth freshness. Closed Mondays, the restaurant is open for dinner until 2am but accepts no reservations, so weekend waits can be long, especially taking into consideration its diminutive dimensions.
119 Sullivan St. (bet. Prince and Spring Sts.), (212) 343-0404. Open T-Su 12pm-2am. MC, V, AmEx, DC, D, Entrées: $20-$30, CE to Spring St. &

Café Habana

This café has been the slummin' it restaurant of choice with the swishy SoHo crowd for a while now. The food is solid, the prices good but overall not worth the sometimes long wait. It's not hard to make Cuban food taste great: try the Cuban sandwich and fried plantains. Habana has a sister takeout café next door.
17 Prince St. (at Elizabeth St.), (212) 625-2001, Open M-Su 9-12, MC, V, AmEx, **F** **V** *to Second Ave.*

The Cupping Room Cafe

A wonderful spot with an ambitious, if slightly pricey, brunch. Even at peak hours, there's plenty of space in the large, airy, main room, so the wait is never too long. Portions are generous. Try the delicious Eggs Florentine and the variety of pancake options.
359 W. Broadway (at Broome St.), (212) 925-2898, www.cuppin-groomcafe.com. Open Su-Th 7:30am-12am, F-Sa 24hrs. MC, V, AmEx, Entrées: $7-$15, **A** **C** **E** *to Canal St.* &

Fanelli's

One of the last remnants of pre-gentrification SoHo. Everything about this place is unpretentious, from the spare decor to the sturdy pub-style food, which is what keeps it going strong as an alternative to all the other too chic and trendy restaurants in the neighborhood. Be prepared to wait. On weekends they're often packed for hours.

94 Prince St. (at Mercer St.), (212) 226-9412. Open M-Th 10am-1am, F-Sa 10-4, Su 11am-1am MC, V, AmEx, Entrées: $10-$12, **N** **R** *to Prince St.*

Jerry's

A longtime crowd pleaser, Jerry's still has a line out the door for weekend brunch. Try a plate of stellar tuna salad or citrus-marinated chicken. This hot lunch spot draws a huge artiste crowd and plenty of celebrities while maintained down-to-earth if snooty service.
101 Prince St. (bet. Greene and Mercer Sts.), (212) 966-9464. Open M-W 8:30am-11pm, Th-F 8:30am-11:30pm, Sa 10:30am-11:30pm, Su 10:30am-5pm. MC, V, AmEx, Entrees: $9-$13, **N** **R** *to Prince St.*

Kin Khao

Don't be surprised to see a supermodel sitting down the bench from you here. This place is very trendy. However, the atmosphere isn't prohibitive to normal people and once you get inside, the wait staff is unpretentious and the decor beautiful and comfortable. The food is Thai, and the quality isn't all that consistent. To be safe, stick to one of the noodle dishes that are always delectable.
171 Spring St. (bet. W. Broadway and Thompson St.), (212) 966-3939. Open Su-W 5:30pm-11pm, Th-Sa 5:30pm-12am. MC, V, AmEx, Entrées: $11-$19, **C** **E** **6** *to Spring St.*

Kitchen Club

Turquoise curtains, a huge checkered tile floor, and French doors which open out onto the street give Kitchen Club its unique atmosphere. Serving up Continental cuisine with a Japanese twist, this "friendly little place" is as eccentric on your tongue as it is on your eyes.
30 Prince St. (at Mott St.) (212) 274-0025. Open T-F 12pm-3:30pm, T-Su 6pm-11:30pm. MC, V, AmEx, Entrées: $16-$22, **N** **R** *to Prince St.,* **F** **S** **V** *to Broadway-Lafayette*

Le Pain Quotidien

The smell of freshly baked bread welcomes you to this cozy Belgian bakery/café featuring a giant communal wooden table and some of the flakiest croissants this side of the Atlantic. Everything from rustic baguettes to country loaves, for which European flour is specially imported, is masterfully prepared and baked on the premises in batches throughout the day. A delicious array of breakfast and lunch dishes are also served.
100 Grand St. (at Mercer St.), (212) 625-9009, www.painquotidien.com. Open M-F 7:30am-7:30pm, Sa-Su 8am-7:30pm. Cash Only, **A** **C** **E** *to Canal St.*

The Mercer Kitchen

At this cafe specializing in American provincial food, you can sit under the sidewalk on a Soho street in a glass encased dining room and watch people walking above. The celebrity-spotting is fabulous, the prices impressive.
99 Prince St. (at Mercer St.), (212) 966-5454.

Open M-Su 7am-12am, MC, V, AmEx, DC, Entrées: $25-$30, **N** **R** *to Prince St.*

Palacinka

"It's anything you want it to be," says co-owner Tariq, but really this BYOB café specializes in serving tired and trendy SoHo shoppers delicious French-style crepes as a light meal or dessert. It's worth a visit just for the unusual, but obviously trendy décor. This includes a smattering of random antiques amid metal tables and chairs that can be easily positioned for a romantic meeting over a cup of coffee. Be prepared to sit a while.
28 Grand St. (bet. Sixth Ave. and Thompson St.), (212) 625-0362, Open Su-W 10:30am-11pm, Th-Sa 10:30am-12am, Cash Only, Entrees: $6-$8, **A** **C** **E** *to Canal St.*

Penang Malaysia

This lively, decked out Malaysian eatery is usually packed on weekends and rightfully so; the food is innovative and tasty and the crowd generally young and hip. To avoid a wait, try eating in the bar downstairs which features a lounge and live music.
109 Spring St. (bet. Greene and Mercer Sts.), (212) 274-8883, www.penangnyc.com. Open M-Th 12pm-12am, F-Sa 12pm-1am, Su 1pm-12am. MC, V, AmEx, DC, Entrées: $11-$20, **6** *to Spring St.*

Rialto

First-time visitors are consistently wowed. The understated SoHo ambience and first-rate Continental food entice stunning neighborhood types time and again. Feast on the Chef's Tasting Menu (a 3, 5 or 8 course meal), which includes a potato leek soup infused with roasted garlic, served in a demitasse cup. The staff shuffles back and forth to the magnificent garden out back.
265 Elizabeth St. (bet. Houston and Prince Sts.), (212) 334-7900. Open M-Su 11am-1am, MC, V, AmEx, DC, Entrées: $8-$18, **F** **S** **V** *to Broadway-Lafayette X*

Rice

This tiny, cramped healthy Asian joint has crowds around the block. It's cheap, cash only but usually worth the wait. Light on the waistline, too.
227 Mott St. (bet. Prince & Spring Sts.), (212) 226-5775, Open M-Su 12am-12pm, Cash Only, **N** **R** *to Prince,* **6** *to Spring (Additional location in Brooklyn)*

Spring Street Natural

Despite the copious offerings of twigs and figs on the menu, there's plenty of chicken and fish to offer those not as health fully inclined. The breads are unusual, the water is get-it-yourself, the staff somnolent. But the food is worth the wait, and the prices are good. The wide windows are good for people watching.
62 Spring St. (at Lafayette St.), (212) 966-0290, MC,V, AmEx, DC, Open Su-Th 11:30am-12am, F-Sa 11:30am-1am, **6** *to Spring St.*

Woo Lae Oak

This Korean import has barbecue and eye candy to die for. You know you're not in Benihana when Kate Hudson, Edward Norton or Kevin Spacey float by your table. Try grilling table-side the filet mignon, black tail shrimp or ostrich, or order the cod in a spicy garlic sauce. Every dish looks and tastes like a million bucks - spicy and subtle. The digs and music are very LA, sleek metal and pulsing beats, lots of model types reposing at the bar. One of the city's best Asian.
148 Mercer St. (bet. Houston & Prince Sts.), (212) 925-8200, MC, V, AmEx, DC, Entrees: $14-24, Su-Th 12:00pm – 11pm, F-Sat: 12:00pm-11:30pm, ⓃⓇ to Prince Street

Zoë

About as good as SoHo gets: attentive waitstaff, elegant decor, and intricate yet subtle food all await you at this SoHo hot spot. The crowd is a pleasing mixture of downtown denizens and suited professionals on their way home from work. The crowd does get funkier as the evening wears on. Perfect for a romantic date.
90 Prince St. (bet. Broadway and Mercer St.), (212) 966-6722. Open T-R 12pm-3pm, 6pm-10:30pm, F 12pm-3pm, 6pm-11pm, Sa 11:30am-3pm, 5:30pm-11pm, Su 11:30am-3pm, 5:30pm-11pm. MC, V, AmEx, Entrées: $18-$28, NR to Prince St. &

CAFES

Ceci-Cela

Homemade sorbet and café au lait evoke La Cote d'Azur at this charming patisserie perched on the edge of Little Italy. The chat room in back is oh-so-perfect for nibbling on petit-fours and playing post-structuralist salon. The chocolate gateau and croissants are famous all over the city. Just don't bring your pooch, no animals allowed.
55 Spring St. (bet. Mulberry and Lafayette Sts.), (212) 274-9179, Open M-R 7am-7pm, F-Sa 7am-10pm, Su 8am-7pm. MC, V, ⑥ to Spring St, NR to Prince. &

Once Upon A Tart

Delectable pastries, both savory and sweet, at lower prices than the standard coffeecakes served up by Manhattan's corporate chain espresso bars. Everything is made in their own bakery. Try a special that includes a tart and choice of salads. The crowd here is very loyal, brunch is packed.
135 Sullivan St. (bet. Houston and Prince Sts.), (212) 387-8869. Open M-F 8am-8pm, Sa 9am-8pm, Su 9am-6pm, MC, V, AmEx, D, ⒸⒺ to Spring St. &

RESTAURANTS

Angelica Kitchen

A vegetarian's paradise as well as an introductory course for vegan-phobic carnivores, offering tangy soups, tofu and pesto sandwiches and tofu-lemon "cheesecake." Portions are generous and very moderately priced.
300 E. 12th St. (bet. First and Second Aves.), (212) 228-2909. Open M-Su 11:30am-10:30pm. Cash Only, Entrées: $6-$12, Ⓛ to First Ave. &

Around the Clock

There's not much to recommend during the day, but the late-late-night crowd qualifies as a revealing cross-section of the East Village. Depending on how far the hands are past midnight when you swing by, you'll spot either bleary-eyed club kids with the munchies are killing time or else the harried waitstaff is halfheartedly trying to oblige the grumpy, early-morning regulars.
8 Stuyvesant St. (at Third Ave.), (212) 598-0402. Open M-Su 24hrs. MC, V, AmEx, DC, D, Entrées: $5-$10, ⑥ to Astor Pl. &

Bendix Diner

Patrons have been congregating at this casual hot-spot in such numbers that owners have been forced to expand. Greasy spoon prices mean the American-Thai fusion dishes leave no room for guilt.
167 First Ave. (bet. 10th and 11th Sts.), (212) 260-4220. Open M-Su 8am-12pm, MC, V, AmEx, Entrées: $6-$18, Ⓛ to First Ave. &

Bereket Turkish Kebab House

This 24-hour hot

spot, right down the street form Orchard Street's cheap leather boutiques, provides greasy Middle Eastern food. The best time to go is drunk, sometime after midnight when it's packed and the only people louder than the patrons are the staff. *187 E. Houston St. (at Orchard St.), (212) 475-7700. Open M-Su 24hrs., Cash only, Entrees $5-8,* **F V** *to Second Ave,* ♿

Boca Chica

Great for anyone who likes to have fun when paying to eat out. The atmosphere is decidedly festive and colorful, a perfect match for the South American and Caribbean food they serve. Best bets are the pork or seafood dishes, staples of the cuisine that you've probably never tasted before, which should definitely be accompanied by one of their exotic margaritas.
13 First Ave. (at 1st St.), (212) 473-0108. Open M-Su 5:30pm-11pm, Su 12pm-4pm (brunch). MC, V, AmEx, D, Entrées: $8-$17, **F V** *to Second Ave.*

Café Pick Me Up

With a view of bustling Tompkins Square Park, Café Pick Me Up serves as a prime people-watching locale, particularly if you're fortunate enough to secure an outside table. In addition to its delicious beverages, Pick Me Up offers a wide array of tasty morsels to help refuel the weary traveler. *145 Avenue A (corner of 9th St), (212) 673-7231. Open Su-Th 6:30am-*

1:30am, F-Sa 6:30-2:30, **L** *to 1st Ave.* ♿

Cafe Gnocco

On a warm night, step through the cozy asymmetrical dining room into the back garden. Tucked in between apartment buildings, the outdoor space has a European feel. Candlelight, ivy and good wine make this the ideal place for a romantic dinner and quiet conversation.
337 E. 10th St. (bet. A and B Aves.), (212) 677-1913. Open M-F 4pm-12am, Sa-Su 12pm-12am. Cash Only, Entrées: $8-$17, **L** *to First Ave.* ♿

Cyclo

You can't miss this East Village eatery, what with the cyclo parked out front. Though the noise volume is high and the tables a bit cramped, the light, fresh Vietnamese cuisine more than compensates. The jellyfish and shrimp salad in a chili lime dressing is one of the more unusual appetizers, and the oxtail broth with noodles, sliced beef, scallions and fresh herbs with fill you up without bogging you down.
203 First Ave. (bet. 12th and 13th Sts.), (212) 673-3975. Open Su-Th 5pm-11pm, F-Sa 5pm-12am, MC, V, AmEx, Entrees: $9-$14, **L** *to First Ave.* ♿

Dojo

The American and Japanese influenced dishes really only please fans of macrobiotic fare, but the dirt-cheap prices and a frisky social scene are enough to lure NYU undergrads away from their meal plans.
24 St. Marks Pl. (bet. Second and Third Aves.),

(212) 674-9821. Open Su-Th 11am-12:30am, F-Sa 11am-1:30am. Cash Only, Entrées: $4-$8, **6** *to Astor Pl,* **N R** *to 8th St. (Additional locations in Manhattan)*

First

Show a date you're hip by eating at this swanky, late night crowd pleaser. Martinis come in several sizes, shapes and flavors while the seasonal menu offers an unusual mix of incredible dinners. The candle lit tables and low lighting may make you feel like you have entered a black & white movie.
87 First Ave. (bet. 5th and 6th Sts.), (212) 674-3823. Open M-Th 6pm-2am, F-Sa 6pm-3am, Su 11am-4pm, 6pm-1am. MC, V, AmEx, Entrées: $18-$22, **F V** *to Second Ave.)*

Global 33

This low-lit lounge/restaurant remains true to its name with a menu of international tapas-style dishes and an interior reminiscent of a 60s airport lounge. The petite dishes are artfully presented and delicious: Tart ceviche is heaped into a martini glass, cool roasted beets are served with warm goat cheese. Global also has a full menu of swanky cocktails, highlighted by some of the best Cosmopolitans around. Rotating DJs add to the festive feel (and the noise level).
99 Second Ave. (bet. 5th and 6th Sts.), (212) 477-8427. Open M-Sa 5:30pm-12am, Su 11:30am-5pm, 6pm-2am. MC, V, AmEx, Entrées: $4-$12, **F V** *to Second Ave.* ♿

Kate's Joint

Kate's serves cheap vegan cuisine in a diner atmosphere, complete with fake bacon and tofu mayo. They serve some nice salads and veggie burgers that fill that greasy need the night after drinking. *58 Ave. B (at 4th.) (212) 777-7059. Open Su-Th 9am-12am, F-Sa 9am-2am, MC, V, AmEx, DC, D, Entrées: $4-$13,* **F V** *to Second Ave,* **N R** *to 8th St.,* **6** *to Astor Pl.*

Khyber Pass

With Persian rug place mats, subdued lights of red and blue, ceiling drapery like the inside of a genie bottle and a choice of authentic floor-style seating, Khyber Pass offers a unique cultural experience. From Baulanee Kadu, a spiced pumpkin turnover served with yogurt dip, to the Kabuli and Shireen Palow, which are lamb and Cornish hen dishes, Afghan cuisine is served at its finest. Best of all, it is inexpensive and smack in the center of the trendiest part of New York. (Trendy/Romantic) *34 St. Marks Place (bet. Second and Third Ave.), (212) 473-0989, Open M-Su 12pm-11pm, Amex, MC, Visa, Entrees: $6-12,* **6** *to Astor Pl.*

Lanza's

Authentic Italian food sans gimmicks or fancy perversions. The clientele is large and loyal, filling the restaurant nightly for both the classy old-style ambiance and superior food at bargain prices. Thankfully it's neither trendy nor cutting-edge. *168 First Ave. (bet. 10th and 11th Sts.), (212) 674-7014. Open M-Su 12pm-*

11pm. MC, V, AmEx, DC, Entrées: $11-$17, **6** to Astor Pl., **L N R Q W 4 5 6** to 14th St.-Union Sq., &

Le Tableau

An unusual reprieve from typical East Village flamboyance, this adorable French restaurant offers high quality food and wonderful service to a casual mix of clientele. The daily rotating specials menu should encourage you to make repeat visits, but be sure you make a reservation Friday or Saturday nights for parties of five and up to enjoy the live jazz band (and remember, a full band in a popular restaurant makes for cozy dining!). *511 E. 5th St. (bet. A and B Aves.), (212) 260-1333. Open M-Th 5pm-11pm, F-Sa 5pm-12pm, Su 5pm-10pm. MC,V, AmEx, Entrées: $10-$18.* **F V** *to Second Ave.* &

Life Cafe

Featured in the Broadway play Rent, this eclectic source of nutritious Cal-Mex is an East Village landmark of laid-back creativity. Check out the rotating exhibits by local artists, preferably during the weekday happy hour (5pm-9pm). *343 E. 10th St. (at Ave. B), (212) 477-8791, www.life-cafenyc.com. Open Su-Th 11am-1am, F-Sa 11am-3am, MC, V, D, Entrées: $7-$12,* **L** *to First Ave.)* &

Mamas Food-Shop

Mama is, in fact, a man who cooked so much food for his friends that his space evolved into a

restaurant. All the food is homestyle excellence, and the portions are huge. Try the grilled salmon and don't miss the awesome mac-and-cheese. Across the street, get soup and sandwiches at *Stepmamas, a spin-off. 200 E. 3rd St. (bet. Aves. A and B), (212) 777-4425. Open M-Sa 11am-10pm. Cash Only, Entrées: $6-$8,* **F V** *to Second Ave.* &

Mamlouk

The prix-fixe menu changes monthly at this Middle Eastern, vegetarian-friendly restaurant, but you can always expect six delicious courses. After your meal, enjoy a hookah the size of a small child with rose or strawberry tobacco as you lounge on the couches. *211 E. 4th (bet. Aves A and B), (212) 529-3477. Open T-Su for seatings at 7pm and 9pm, MC, V, AmEx, Prix-fixe: $30,* **F V** *to Second Ave.,* &

Mekka

People of all types are drawn to the excellent Southern and Caribbean food at this urban hip-hop restaurant. Difficult as it is to resist, don't devour too much of the complementary cornbread, or you may find yourself incapable of walking at the end of the night, or worse yet, you won't have room for the peach cobbler, which is a must. *14 Ave. A (bet. Houston and 2nd Ave.), (212) 475-8500, www.mekkarestaurant.com. Open Su-W 5pm-11pm, Th 5pm-12am, F-Sa 5pm-1:30am, Su 11am-11pm, MC, V, AmEx, D, Entrées: $14,* **F V** *to Second Ave.*

Mitali East

The stretch of 6th Street between 1st and 2nd Avenues is overrun with mediocre Indian food joints – Mitali isn't one of them. Most of the chicken dishes here are quite tasty and not too greasy, and they give you a lot of bang for your buck. *334 E. 6th St. (bet. First and Second Aves.), (212) 533-2508, Open M-Su 12pm-12am. AmEx, MC, V, Entrees: $7-$10,* **F V** *to Second Ave*

Nino's Pizza

There must be a thousand different slice joints in this city, but this is without a doubt one of the very best. In addition to making great pizza, the place looks out on Tompkins Square Park and keeps hours as late as any bar. A plain slice is always a safe bet, but the more adventuresome shouldn't miss the white pizza with fresh tomatoes. *131 St. Marks Pl. (at A Av.), (212) 979-8688, Open M-Su 11am-4am, Cash Only, Entrées: $10,* **6** *to Astor Pl.* &

Odessa

One of the hippest of the East Village's Eastern European diners, open 24 hours. Everything from standard diner food to potato pancakes and other regional fare finds its way onto the menu. The location makes it perfect for a food break while cruising the Ave. A bar scene, and to continue drinking you need only walk next door to their lounge, where the cheapest gin and tonics in Manhattan are served by a surly, old Russian lady. *119 Ave. A (bet. 7th and 8th Sts.), (212) 253-1470,*

Open M-Su 24hrs, MC, V, AmEx, Entrées: $6-$12, FV to Second Ave., **L** *to First Ave. X)* &

Old Devil Moon

East Village restaurant specializing in southern food with a cool and funky atmosphere and big portions. *511 E. 12th St. (bet. Aves. A and B), (212) 475-4357. Open M-Th 5pm-11pm, F 5pm-12am, Sa-Su 10am-4pm, 5pm-12pm. MC, V, AmEx, DC, Entrées: $12,* **L** *to First Ave.* &

Paquito's Restaurant

Think California taquerias – fast, cheap, and incredibly tasty Mexican food – transported to NYC. Paquito's has all the prerequisite items like burritos, enchiladas and tacos, but is a step above most of the New York joints that dare to call themselves Mexican. It's a tiny place, but everyone devours their food so quickly that you can usually get a table without much of a problem. *143 First Ave (bet St. Mark's Pl. and 9th St.), (212) 674-2071, Open M-Su 11am-11:30pm, MC, V, AmEx, Entrees: $2-$7,* **F V** *train to Second Ave.,* **6** *train to Astor Pl.*

Pommes Frites

Nothing to expect at this cramped spot except for Belgian fries in a paper cone. There's only one type of fry to be had here, but try one of several toppings, including mustard, ketchup, peanut sauce, and some spicier condiments. The service

is quick, and you probably won't spend more than five bucks or five minutes as you grab your fries and go on your way.
123 Second Ave. (at St. Marks Pl.), (212) 674-1234. Open Su-Th 11:30 am-1am, F-Sa 11:30am-2 am, Cash only, **6** *to Astor Pl,* **N R** *to 8th St.*

Shabu Tatsu

This authentic Japanese version of cook-it-your-self soups is fun, messy and healthy. With lots of succulent meat and veg-etables, you can boil your own meal then dip it into the yummy sauce and top it off with rice. Unpretentious.
216 E. 10th St. (bet. 1st & 2nd Aves.), (212) 477-2972, Open M-Su 5pm-1am, MC,V, AmEx, **6** *to Astor Pl.*
(Additional locations in Manhattan)

Step Mama's

Right across the street from Mama's is this sandwich, soup, salads, and dessert shop. Step in and order one of their large, tasty chicken or meatloaf sandwiches, or maybe just one of the big cookies on your way home from work. It's cheap take-out food (you can eat in, too) that hits the spot.
199 3rd St. (bet A and B Aves.), (212) 228-2663, Open M-Sa 11am-10pm, Cash only, Entrees: $5-$8, **L** *to First Ave.,* **F V** *to Second Ave.*

Time Cafe

Around mealtimes there are rarely many free tables in this vast, lofty space, and it's no wonder, since this is one of the better places around. Health-conscious organic food and an extensive menu with selections like fancy tuna sandwiches and pan roasted penne are sure to satisfy nearly any craving. Check out their jazz club downstairs.
380 Lafayette (bet. Great Jones and 4th Sts.), (212) 533-7000, www.time-cafenyc.com. Open M-Th 8am-12am, F 8am-1am, Sa 10am-1am, Su 10:30am-12am, MC, V, AmEx, Entrées: $12-$22, **6** *to Astor Pl.*

Two Boots Restaurant

Two Boots spe-cializes in Cajun-Creole fare, creative pizzas with kitschy names like "The Divine" and "Mrs. Peel", and lots of vegan options. In other words, it's for the coolest kids in town. And as a bonus, the food's really good too. Just eye the slices before you buy, some-times they hang around a little too long.
42 Ave. A (at 3rd St.), (212) 505-2276, Open Su-Th 11:30pm-1am. F-Sa 11:30-2. MC, V, AmEx, D, Entrees $8-10, **F V** *to Second Ave,*
(Additional locations in Manhattan)

CAFES

Alt.coffee

The comfy couches are here because you'll be sit-ting awhile, checking the hotmail and figuring out where you'll go tonight. The staff is as handy with the latte maker as they are with any of your Internet questions.
139 Ave. A (bet. St. Marks Pl. and 9th St.), (212) 529-2233, Open M-F 7am-1:30am, Sa-Su 10am-2am, Cash Only, **L** *First Ave.* &

Cafe Orlin

Blend in by ordering an espresso and whipping out some sort of portfo-lio. Leave it open on the table and enjoy a smoky omelet or a slice of chocolate cake. Most reg-ulars are artsy East Village chain smokers cum aspir-

ing directors. The low-angle view allows a glimpse of the shoes passing by on St. Marks Place.
41 St. Marks Pl. (bet. First and Second Aves.), (212) 777-1447, Open Su-Th 9am-2am, F-Sa 24hrs, MC, V, **6** *to Astor Pl.*

Casa Adela

This café was started by the proprietor Luis Rivera's mother, and has been around for over 20 years. Its cooking is clas-sic, its décor clean and bright. You can't go wrong with the chicken and rice. Adela may be the epitome of boricua cooking. You might feel out of the loop not speaking Spanish, but the welcome is just as warm in English.
66 Avenue C (bet 4th and 5th Sts.), (212) 473-1882, Open M-Su 7am-8pm, Cash Only, Entrees: $6-8, **F V** *to Second Ave*

Masturbakers

The most popular item at this appropriately titled bakery, housed in the Old Devil Moon restaurant, is the penis cake. Their breast cake, bearing the words "Breast Wishes," runs a close second. With moist devil's food cake, rich frosting and naughty details, their bakery lives up to their motto: "tasty but tasteless."
511 E. 12th St. (bet. Aves. A and B), (212) 475-0476. Open M-F 10am-5pm (M-Su 10am-10pm for pick-up only). MC, V, AmEx, **L** *to First Ave.* &

Veniero's

Whether you just broke up with someone or are looking for a place to chat for hours, Veniero's fits the bill. Either way try the scrumptious pastries and great drinks. One of the best cafes in the city. *342 E. 11th St. (bet. First and Second Aves.), (212) 674-7070, www.homedelivery.com. Open Su –Th 8am-12am, F-Sa 8am-1am. MC, V, AmEx, D, ❶ to First Ave.* ♿

Veselka

This upscale Ukrainian has good service, fun décor and great prices. Try the kasha, the pierogies and the sausage. Always packed with students and artistes. The brunch is fab, try the crepes. *144 Second Ave. (at 9th St.), (212) 228-9682, Open M-Su 24 hours, MC, V, AmEx, ❻ to Astor Pl.*

Yaffa Cafe

East Village funkadelic café with reasonably priced sandwiches, salads, pastas, omelets, and crepes, as well as a handsome selection of vegetarian items and unbelievable desserts. Enjoy the kitschy decor and sit outdoors when weather permits to observe the goings-on at St. Marks Pl. Open 24 hours. *97 St. Marks Pl. (bet. 1st St. and Ave. A), (212) 677-9001. Open M-Su 24hrs. MC, V, AmEx, ❻ to Astor Pl.*

Greenwich Village

RESTAURANTS

Anglers and Writers

No longer home to the Paris Review crowd, but the soups and stews are probably better now than they were in the good old days. There will often be a wait for Sunday brunch.

420 Hudson St. (at St. Luke's Pl.), (212) 675-0810, Open M-Sa 9-12, Su 10am-10pm, MC, V, AmEx, Entrées: $8-$14, ❶❷ *to Houston.* ♿

Cornelia Street Cafe

The leisurely ambiance of soothing lights coupled with a background jazz and blues blend complements the similarly unforced take on simple New American cuisine. Venture downstairs after dinner to catch nightly theater, jazz and poetry performances in the cabaret. *29 Cornelia St. (bet. Bleecker and W. 4th Sts.), (212) 989-9318, Open Su-Th 10am-12am, F-Sa 10am-1am, MC, V, AmEx, DC, Entrées: $12-$15, ACEFVS to West 4th St.,* ❶❷ *to Christopher St.* ♿

Corner Bistro

Locals lament the marathon waits at this immensely popular burger-and-beer joint, but they still throng despite the slow service. It's the prime territory to see and be seen. It is the basic, effortlessly funky version of the neighborhood haunt made palatable to yuppie Villagers by virtue of its enduring cachet and steady stream of televised college basketball games. Tables long ago marked by penknives crowd the middle, though intimate space may be free in back. *331 W. 4th St. (bet. 12th and Jane Sts.), (212) 242-9502. Open M-Su 11:30am-4am. Cash Only, Entrées: $4-$6,* ❶❷❸❹ *to 14th St.* ♿

Cowgirl Hall of Fame

Before riot-girls there were cowgirls, and at this Greenwich Village fave, owner Sherry Delamarter won't let gringos forget. Come for the history lesson and eclectic Chuckwagon dishes like eggplant fritters and Frito pie. Its mostly lesbian clientele revel in the place's unabashed homage to the cowgirls of yesteryear, right down to the gift shop full of cowgirly souvenirs. Check out the suit of armor as you go through the doors. *519 Hudson St. (at 10th St.), (212) 633-1133, Open Su-Th 5pm-11pm, F-Sa 5pm-12am. MC, V, AmEx, Entrées: $8-$15,* ❶❷ *to Christopher St.* ♿

Florent

Fanciful bistro fare is available at all hours on weekends for a sophisticated gay and straight crowd in the hip Meat-Packing District. Housed in an old diner, the space is cool and understated. Dishes are a mix of French and American classics. *69 Gansevoort St. (bet. Greenwich and Washington Sts.), (212) 989-5779, Open Su-W 9am-5am, Th-Sa 24hrs, Cash Only, Entrées: $6-$16,* ❶❷❸❹ *to 14th St.,* ❶❷❸ *to 14th St.* ♿

Garage Restaurant & Café

Suburban steak house meets Greenwich Village panache at this sprawling multi-leveled village favorite. Its famous weekend jazz brunch offers both top-notch music and a mean eggs benedict. During the week, come

for the music but stay for the unforgettable mussels, or their hearty sandwiches and raw bar. *99 Seventh Ave. S. (at Grove St.), (212) 645-0600, Open Su-Th 12pm-1am, Fr-Sa 12am-3am, MC, V, AmEx, Entrées: $8-$25,* ❶❷ *to Christopher St.* ♿

Gotham Bar and Grill

Architecturally brilliant entrées like Atlantic salmon with ramps, morels, sweet peas, and chervil, betray the hand of one of the city's finest gourmets, Alfred Portale, and his kitchen team of all-star chefs, who've made Gotham's New American cuisine a staple for New York connoisseurs. Entrées bypass typical meats for rabbit, pheasant, and a couple so rare they're probably endangered. Sample it all with a $19.99 prix fixe lunch in the spacious, angular dining room. Don't pass up the most divine warm chocolate cake in all of New York. *12 E. 12th St. (bet. Fifth Ave. and University Pl.), (212) 620-4020, Open M-F 12pm-2:15pm, 5:30pm-10:15pm, Sa 5pm-11:30pm, Su 5pm-10pm, MC, V, AmEx, DC, Entrées: $25-$40,* ❶❷❸❹❺❻❹❺❻ *to Union Sq.-14th St.* ♿

The Grange Hall

The coziest corner in the Village is home to one of its very finest restaurants. One of Uma Thurman's haunts, this classy outpost of European refinement and American-style roasts and chicken dishes dis-

plays excellent taste without being ostentatious. Great for cocktails, the Hall is also famed for brunch.
50 Commerce St. (bet. Bedford and Hudson Sts.), (212) 924-5246, Open M-R 12pm-3pm, 6pm-11:30pm, F 12pm-3pm, 5:30pm-12am, Sa 11am-3pm, 5:30pm-12am, Su 10:30am-3:30pm, 6pm-10:30pm. MC, V, AmEx, Entrées: $12-$25, **①②** *to Christopher St.* &

Home

The name conjures up the American iconography of mom and apple pie, but despite the low pretension and familiar line-up of pork chops and chocolate pudding, this refined Village eatery is a bit too urbane to qualify as a suburban transplant. Chefs may not infuse the catfish with mom's love, but they are committed to resisting the strong French trends in New American cuisine, instead steering culinary attention toward hometown faves. Home's homemade ketchup proves again why classics never go out of style.
20 Cornelia St. (bet. Bleecker and W. 4th Sts.), (212) 243-9579. Open M-F 9am-4pm, 5pm-11pm, Sa-Su 10:30pm-4:30pm, 5:30pm-11pm. AmEx, Entrées: $13-$19, **ⒶⒸⒺⒻⓋⓈ** *to West 4th St.* &

John's of Bleecker Street

This thin, coal oven baked pizza is preceded by its well-deserved reputation. A good place for groups to hang out. No slices, only whole pies, the mark of an excellent pizzeria.
278 Bleecker St. (bet. Sixth and Seventh Aves.), (212) 243-1680. Open M-TH 11:30am-11:30am, F-Sa 11:30am-12:30am, Su 12pm-11:30am. Cash Only, Entrées: $12, **ⒶⒸⒺⒻⓋⓈ** *to West 4th St.* &

Le Café Bruxelles

One of a number of Belgian joints now open on the West Side, this is perhaps the most consistent. The staff is authentically ethnic, the setting cozy, and the food — mussels, fabulous frites, and beers brewed at monasteries — is très, très bon.
118 Greenwich Ave. (at 13th St.), (212) 206-1830, Open M-Th 12pm-11:30pm, F-Sa 12pm-12am, Su 12pm-10:30pm. MC, V, AmEx, DC, Entrées: $12-$18, **ⒶⒸⒺⓁ** *to 14th St.* &

Les Deux Gamins

French-inspired omelets, salads and rich entrées consistently attract crowds at this endearing, perennially popular bistro. Brunch goes down perfectly with cafe au lait or cocoa in warmed bowls on a lazy Sunday morning. Service can be harried, though the crowd of low-key locals in their late 20s is tolerant.
170 Waverly Pl. (at Grove St.), (212) 807-7357, Open M-Su 8am-12pm. AmEx, Entrées: $14-$23, 12 to Christopher St., **ⒶⒸⒺⒻⓋⓈ** *to W. 4th St.* &

Mi Cocina

Mexican cuisine, West Village-style: haute, pricey, and with a generous supply of liquor. The most savory south-of-the-border dishes here may not be authentic, but the place is chic.
57 Jane St. (at Hudson St.), (212) 627-8273. Open M-Th 4:30pm-10:45pm, F-Sa 4:30pm-11:45pm, Su 4:30pm-10pm. MC, V, AmEx, DC, Entrées: $13-$22, **ⒶⒸⒺⓁ** *to 14th St.*

Monte's

Existent since 1918, the charm of this amicable basement trattoria will remain long after the taste has slipped away. The menu spares no calorie, so go all the way and try the zabaglione served cold with strawberries.
97 MacDougal St. (at 3rd St.), (212) 228-9194, Open Su-M, W-R 12pm-11pm, F-Sa 12pm-11:30pm, MC, V, AmEx, DC, D, Entrées: $7-$13, **ⒶⒷⒸⒹⒺ** **ⒻⓆ** *to W. 4th Street*

Moustache

Nestled on a peaceful back street in the West Village, Moustache transports you to a more pleasant time and place, a feeling intensified by the delicious food, from traditional fare such as the merguez sandwich to their innovative "pitzas." Also try Moustache's East Village location at 265 E 10th St, famed for its garden.
90 Bedford St. (bet. Grove and Barrow Sts.), (212) 229-2220, Open M-Su 12pm-12am. Cash only, Entrees: $5-$12, **①②** *to Christopher St.*

One if by Land, Two if by Sea

Don't be fooled by the unassuming exterior of this converted 200-year-old carriage house once owned by Aaron Burr. With an extensive wine list and an exquisite tasting menu, this gem of colonial history provides for the ultimate in romantic dining experiences. The Bluefin Tartare is incredible and the superb Beef Wellington is rightfully called the house specialty. The friendly and knowledgeable wait staff is more than happy to talk about the restaurant's history or unassumingly help you choose which utensil is appropriate for the next course.
17 Barrow St. (bet. Seventh Ave. and W. 4th St.), (212) 228-0822, Open Su-Th 5:30pm-10pm, F-Sa 5:30pm-11:15pm. MC, V, AmEx, DC, Entrees: $41-$60. **①②** *to Christopher St.* **ⒶⒸⒺⒻⓋⓈ** *to W. 4th St.* &

Pão!

When dinning at Pão! watch motorcycles zoom by and taxis clatter up the street. Huge framed menus feature delicious Portuguese seafood dishes, but the steak, topped with garlic and spicy cream sauce, is their specialty. A small bar inside.
322 Spring St. (at Greenwich St.), (212) 334-5464, Open M-F 12pm-2:30pm, 6pm-11pm, Sa-Su 6pm-11pm, MC, V, AmEx, Entrées: $14-$17, **ⒸⒺ** *to Spring St.* &

Peanut Butter & Co.

As the name suggests, this cozy little take-out café serves peanut butter in all forms, ranging from classic Fluffernutters and peanut butter pie to unorthodox PB&J shakes. Prices are high ($6.50 for most sandwiches), but that doesn't keep NYU students and local businessmen from packing the place at lunchtime. *240 Sullivan St. (bet. Bleecker & W. 3rd Sts.), (212) 677-3995, Open Su-Th 11am-9pm, F-Sa 11am-10pm. MC, V, AmEx, DC, D, Entrees: $5-7,* **A C E F V S** *to W. 4th St.*

Petite Abeille

Scads of Tintin paraphernalia and tasty Belgian bites make this a popular feature of Little Belgium. Absolutely divine fries and mussels. *400 W. 14th St. (bet. Ninth and Tenth Aves.), (212) 727-1505, Open M-Th 7am-11pm, F 7am-11:30pm, Sa 9am-11:30am, Su 9am-11pm, Cash Only, Entrées: $10-$12,* **A C E L** *to 14th St.* *Additional location on Hudson St., (212) 741-6479)*

Pó

So popular that it is not uncommon to require reservations a month in advance, this charming little West Village Italian draws in customers with its warm atmosphere, reasonable prices and generous portions. Whether the quality of the food lives up to the restaurant's reputation is debatable, it nonetheless makes for a trendy evening out. *31 Cornelia St. (bet. Bleecker and W. 4th Sts.), (212) 645-2189, Open T-Th 11:30am-2:30pm, 5:30pm-11pm, F-Sa 11:30am-2:30pm, 5:30pm-11:30pm, Su 11:30am-2:30pm, 5pm-10pm, AmEx, Entrées: $15,* **A C E F V S** *to W. 4th St.,* **1 2** *to Christopher St.*

Quantum Leap

Handpicking the best in natural dishes that Mexico, Japan, and the Middle East have to offer, this healthy kitchen excels at weekend breakfasts which include whole grain, buckwheat, or blue corn waffles and/or pancakes smothered with organic maple syrup. Not exactly the ascetic way, but better than bacon. *88 W. 3rd St. (bet. Thompson and Sullivan Sts.), (212) 677-8050, Open M-F 11:30am-11pm, Sa 11am-11pm, Su 11am-10pm. MC, V, AmEx, Entrées: $5-$10,* **A C E F V S** *to W. 4th St.* &

Sammy's Noodle Shop and Grill

Hurried urbanites took their time in warming up to this noodle shop's flavorful fare, though now it's an indispensable lunch fixture, with an annexed bakery serving fresh desserts. Try the roast meat soups and dumplings. *453 Sixth Ave. (bet. 10th and 11th Sts.), (212) 924-6688, Open M-Su 11:30am-12am, MC, V, AmEx, D, DC, Entrées: $10-$12,* **A C E F V S** *to W. 4th St.* &

Souen

Downtown New Yorkers may delight in their manufactured indulgences, but this unassuming, primarily macrobiotic restaurant has been helping them get in touch with their earthier side for twenty years. The Japanese influenced menu specializes in dishes featuring tempeh, seitan, and organic vegetables, and the sugar-free futomaki and tempeh croquettes are noteworthy. *28 E. 13th St. (bet. University Pl. and Fifth Ave.), (212) 627-7150, Open M-Su 10am-11pm, MC, V, AmEx, DC, D, Entrées: $8-$16,* **L N R Q W 4 5 6** *to Union Sq.-14th St.*

Surya

This chic West Village Indian offers a unique array of tastes several notches above its counterparts in the East Village. Fresh seafood glazed with a subtle date sauce, perfectly spiced basmati and creamy deserts with a hint of cardamom. Wash it down with a "Tajamopolitan" or other unique specialty drinks. *302 Bleecker St. (bet. Seventh Ave. S. and Grove St.), (212) 807-7770, Open M-F 12pm-3am, 5:30pm-11pm, Sa-Su 12pm-3:30am, 5pm-12am. MC, V, AmEx, DC, D, Entrées: $16-$24,* **1 2** *to Christopher St.* &

Tartine

There's nothing more pleasant on a Sunday morning than brunch at Tartine with the sun shining through the floor-to-ceiling windows and birds chirping. The menu is standard and portions are hardly generous, but the staff has orange juice on the table by the time patrons sit down. Alas, by noon the wait outside is 45 minutes, but here's a tip. They actually open at 9am for coffee, not the posted 10:30. *253 W. 11th St. (at W. 4th St.), (212) 229-2611. Open T-F 9am-10:30pm, Sa-Su 10:30am-4pm, 5:30pm-10pm. Cash Only, Entrées:* *$8-$14,* **1 2** *to Christopher St.,* **A C E L** *to W. 14th St.* &

Tavern on Jane

This tavern serves much more than pub food, but at pub food prices. While the fish and chips is a reliable delight, customers go crazy for the grilled leg-of-lamb with sour cherry sauce, potatoes au gratin and garlic spinach; the Moroccan tuna, served with saffron, lemon and garlic couscous; and wilted watercress. The atmosphere is cozy and inviting— regulars are bound to strike up a friendly conversation over a pint of beer. Simply put, you know a place is great when the staff hangs out there on their nights off. *31 Eighth Ave. (at Jane St.), (212) 675-2526, Open M-Sa 12pm-1am, Sa-Su 11am-1am. MC, V, AmEx, Entrées: $7-$15,* **A C E L** *to 14th St.* &

Wok 'n Roll

They don't kick you out till 3am on weekends, and you'll never significantly alter the level of your water glass at this airy dumpling house, where the polished wood decor and predictable noodle and dumpling fare feels like a friend's mom's dinner you can always count on. Fair prices keep it packed with NYU kids. *169 Bleecker St. (at Sullivan St.), (212) 260-6666, Open Su-Th 11am-4am, F-Sa 11:30am-3am. MC, V, AmEx, Entrées: $7-$13,* **A B C D E F Q** *to W. 4th St.*

Ye Waverly Inn

One of the vestiges of 19th century Village life, this former carriage house exudes a quaint colonial feel with wooden ceiling beams and old fashioned offerings from both north and south, like Yankee pot roast and southern fried chicken, with excellent puddings and muffins. Occasionally, local celebs drop by.
16 Bank St. (at Waverly Pl.), (212) 929-4377, Open Su-R 11:30am-3:30pm, 5pm-10:30pm, F-Sa 11:30am-3:30pm, 5pm-11:30pm, MC, V, AmEx, DC, Entrées: $12-$17, ❶❷❸ *to 14th St.* &

CAFES

Café Milou

Named after Tintin's dog, this bistro is a breath of fresh air in the midst of trendy theme-oriented eateries on Seventh Ave. Opened by Abraham Merchant, of Merchant's, with a menu created by an ex-Windows on the World chef.
92 Seventh Ave. S. (bet. Bleecker and Grove Sts.), (212) 414-9824, Open M-W 12pm-12am, Th 12pm-1am, F-Sa 12am-2am, Su 12am-12am, MC, V, AmEx, DC, ❶❷ *to Christopher St.* &

Caffe Danté

Famous both for its Buffalo mozzarella and espresso, this space may be small but it is well arranged. If your stomach is craving a larger meal, check out the trattoria next door, which is under the same management.
79-81 Macdougal St. (bet.

Bleecker and Houston Sts.), (212) 982-5275, Open Su-R 10am-2am, F-Sa 10am-3am, Cash Only, ❶❷❸❹❺❻ *to W. 4th St.* &

Caffe Reggio

The standard by which Village cafés are measured, Caffe Reggio's charm makes it popular among students, hipsters and aging bohemians. The dark interior is suitable for curling up with a book or your significant other. Prices respect the starving artist's pocketbook.
119 MacDougal St. (bet. Bleecker and 3rd Sts.), (212) 475-9557, Open Su-R 9am-2am, F-Sa 9am-4am, Cash Only, ❶❷❸❹❺❻ *to West 4th St.* &

French Roast

Art nouveau dominates the decor at this airy, bustling café. Brunch and lunch available. Try the consistently delicious soups.
458 Sixth Ave. (at 11th St.), (212) 533-2233, Open M-Su 24hrs, MC, V, AmEx, ❶❷❸❹❺❻ *to W. 4th St.* &
(Additional locations in Manhattan)

Go Sushi

This newcomer capitalizes on both the sushi trend and the still burgeoning coffee bar culture: sleek stools and tattered copies of Paper meet sushi samples of fatty tuna and salmon prepared fresh around-the-clock by an in-house chef. Wash it all down with Go's own freshly brewed ginger ale.
3 Greenwich Ave. (bet. Sixth Ave. and 8th St.), (212) 366-9272, Open M-Su 11:30am-11:30pm, MC,

V, AmEx, ❶❷❸❹❺❻ *to West 4th St.*

The Grey Dog's Coffee

Bring a novel, your laptop or your friends to this warm rustic café where sunlight pours in through the open French windows and casts shadows on the pressed tin ceilings above. Order a big chunk of fresh-baked bread, a terrific cup of coffee and amble back to one of the artsy tables with apples, fish, or chili peppers painted on top. At night the lights dim and the place becomes a casual wine bar.
33 Carmine St. (bet. Bleeker and Bedford Sts.), (212) 462-0041, Open Su-R 7am-11:30pm, F-Sa 8am-12:30am, Cash Only, ❶❷❸❹❺❻ *to West 4th St., 19 to Houston St.* &

Taylor's

One of the best things about the West Village is this bakery, which has several other locations in downtown Manhattan. A fabulous selection of pastries, cakes and other decadent desserts, as well as soups, sandwiches and typical beverages. TYou should get there early or your choices will be limited.
523 Hudson St. (bet. 10th and Charles Sts.), (212) 378-2890, Open M-Su 6am-9pm. Sa-Su 7am-9pm, Cash Only, 12 to Christopher St.

Gramercy

RESTAURANTS

Bachue

Vegans: just picture in

your head delicious (eggless) pancakes and waffles, as well as a fine selection of bean, pasta, seitan, tempeh, tofu and vegetable dishes.
36 W. 21st St. (bet. Fifth and Sixth Aves.), (212) 229-0870, Open M-F 8am-10:30pm, Sa 10am-10:30pm, Su 11am-7pm. MC, V, AmEx, D, Entrées: $5-$13, ❻❼ *to 23rd St.,* ❽❾ *to 23rd St.* &

Blue Water Grill

With everything from live jazz to an oyster bar, this delightful seafood café will keep you happy whether you're looking to eat or simply people-watch. This Grill is perpetually crowded, beautiful and hip. The food can be nouveau cuisine, heavy on the seafood, but consistently good. The high-ceilinged restaurant will remind you this was once a bank. Check out the jazz playing downstairs. Try to reserve a sidewalk table.
31 Union Square W. (at 16th St.), (212) 675-9500, Open M-Sa 11:30am-12am, F-Sa 11:30am-1am, Su 11:30am-12am. MC, V, AmEx, Entrées: $15-$25, ❶❷❸❹❺ ❻❼❽ *to 14th St.-Union Sq.* &

Bolo

Food Network favorite Bobby Flay's version of "Fantasy Spanish" cuisine doesn't miss a beat at this relaxed Flatiron restaurant. Sangria, rabbit on roasted pea risotto and sautéed wild mushrooms with chile oil are only a few of Mr. Flay's playful gastronomic creations. A comprehensive selection of fine wines and ports are perfect complements to a meal that is the stuff

dreams are made of.
*23 E. 22nd St. (bet.
Broadway and Park Ave.
S.), (212) 228-2200, Open
M-Th 12pm-2:30pm,
5:30pm-10pm, F 12pm-
2:30pm, 5:30pm-11pm, Sa
5:30pm-11pm, Su
5:30pm-10pm, MC, V,
AmEx, DC, D. Entrées:
$25-$30,* **N R 6** *to 23rd
St.* &

Cal's

A striking open loft space
gives you ample elbow
room and surprising pri-
vacy while dining, yield-
ing an unusually relaxed
atmosphere for this
trendy neighborhood. The
food is good, the risotto
is standout and the wait-
staff is stand up.
*55 W. 21st St. (bet. Fifth
and Sixth Aves.), (212)
929-0740, www.cal-
srestaurant. com. Open
M-F 11:30am-5pm, 5pm-
12am, Su 5pm-10:30pm.
MC, V, AmEx, dc, Entrées:
$16-$22,* **F** *to 23rd St.,*
N R *to 23rd St.* &

Chango

Pinks, yellows, blues,
couch-style seating, bam-
boo dividers, and finished
terra cotta – if Mexico hit
oil, its future would be
Chango. From the tri-
colored tortillas and guacamole to the over-sized
margaritas to the cut-
away cove-lit ceiling to
the ceramic serving
plates, this trendy hot-
spot is a non-stop fiesta.
Bring a date who doesn't
mind the sound of chat-
ter or the competition of
a gorgeous wait-staff and
you'll find a perfect
choice in both taste of
food and stunning décor.
*239 Park Ave South (bet.
19th and 20th Sts.), (212)
477-1500, M-W 12pm-
11pm, R-S 12pm-12am,
Su 12pm - 10pm, MC, V,*

*Amex, DC, Entrees: $14-
25,* **6** *to 23rd.*

City Crab

Surf and turf your way
into City Crab for an
enormous selection of
underwater delights.
Everything on the menu,
from steamers to lobster
to Alaskan King-Crab, is
fresh from the Fulton Fish
Market and prime for
good hearty eatin'. The
service is quick and the
small-town feel is a nice
contrast to the sophisti-
cation of Park Avenue
South. It's a great place
to bring a big group of
friends for a messy, but
delightful, meal.
*235 Park Ave South (at
19th St.), (212) 529-3800,
Open M-R 11:30am-11pm,
F 11:30pm-12:00am, Sa
12pm-12am, Su
12:00pm-11:00pm, MC, V,
AmEx, Entrees: $17-30,*
L N R Q W 4 5 6 *to
14th St.-Union Sq.*

Coffee Shop

This shop is not really a
coffee shop, but rather an
upscale Brazilianish
restaurant with a fabu-
lous bar in back. An
episode of Sex and the
City has been filmed here.
The drinks and the crowd
are consistently gorgeous,
the food good but a bit
beside the point. Try to
get an outside table, and
enjoy the views.
*29 Union Sq. W. (16th
St.), (212) 243-7969,
Open M 7am-2am, T
7am-4am, W-F 7am-
5:30am, Sa 8am-5:30am,
Su 8am-2am, MC, V,
AmEx,* **L N R Q W 4
5 6** *to 14th St.-Union
Sq.*

Eleven Madison
Park

This upscale hotspot

serves New York seasonal
cuisine with a French
influence. Along with the
regular menu they have a
fine à la carte. Go just for
the grandeur of the
space, which it shares
with another creation by
the same restauranteur —
Tabla.
*11 Madison Ave. (at 24th
St.), (212) 889-0905,
Open M-F 11:30am-2pm,
5:30pm-10:30pm, Sa
12pm-2pm, 5:30pm-
11pm, Su 5:30pm-10pm,
MC, V, AmEx, DC, D,
Entrées: $21-$32,*
6 N R *to 23rd St.* &

Ess-A-Bagel

Ess (Yiddish for "eat") is
the real deal for bagels.
Its pumpernickels are
chock-full of raisins, its
cream cheese always
fresh, the lines always
long. If you're on a diet,
don't bother.
*359 First Ave. (21st St.),
(212) 260-2252, Open M-
Sa 6:30am-9pm, Su
6:30am-5pm, MC, V,
AmEx,* **6** *to 23rd St.,* **L**
*to First Ave.
(Additional location in
Midtown)*

Friend of a
Farmer

Only in Gramercy could
you find a Vermont snug-
ness more convincing
than anything in the
Green Mountain State
itself. While dinner is
hearty and well-prepared,
featuring stick-to-your-
ribs specialties like shepherd's and chicken pot
pies, the crowded brunch
is the best feature.
Another plus is that
you've possibly seen simi-
lar prices in Montpelier.
*77 Irving Pl. (bet. 18th
and 19th Sts.), (212) 477-
2188. Open M-F 8am-
10pm. Sa 9:30am-10pm,
Su 9:30am-9:30pm, MC,*

*V, AmEx, DC, D, Entrées:
$8-$22,* **L N R Q W 4
5 6** *to 14th St.-Union
Sq.* &

Galaxy

This dark, cozy, Irving
Plaza neighbor has a ceiling spattered with twin-
kling stars and swirling
blue planets. After sam-
pling hemp-infused dishes
like soba noodles, tiger
shrimp and garden burger,
you might feel like you're
dining on cloud nine. For
your non-culinary needs,
they also sell a complete
line of hemp products,
from lip balm to textiles.
*15 Irving Pl. (at 15th St.),
(212) 777-3631,
www.galaxyglobaleatery.c
om, Open M-R 8pm-4am,
F 8pm-3:30am, Sa 11am-
3:30am, Su 11am-1:30am,
MC, V, Entrées: $8-10,*
L N R Q W 4 5 6 *to
14th St.-Union Sq.* &

Gramercy
Tavern

Don't be fooled
by the rustic
decor: Prices
reflect the all-
star clientele at
this hotspot for
hobnobbing and net-
working. Stargazers may
be willing to pay the price
for a chance at sharing
lunch with Johnny Depp.
*42 E. 20th St. (bet.
Broadway and Park Ave.
S.), (212) 477-0777, Open
M-R 12pm-2pm, 5:30pm-
10pm, F 12pm-2pm,
5:30pm-11pm. Sa
5:30pm-11pm, Su
5:30pm-12am, MC, V,
AmEx, DC, D, Entrées:
$18-$25,* **6 N R** *to 23rd
St.* &

Les Halles

Authentically Parisian,
down to the boucherie by
the front door, this

bustling brasserie is well known for its memorable steak frites and onion soup. Cramped tables mean people-watching and eavesdropping are favored diversions. Made famous by the tell-all book, Kitchen Confidential.
411 Park Ave. S. (bet. 28th and 29th Sts.), (212) 679-4111, Open M-Su 12pm-12am, MC, V, AmEx, Entrées: $14-$22, **6** *to 28th St.* &

Madras Mahal

Vegetarian Kosher Indian food attracts an eclectic crowd, ranging from vegetarian Indians to Orthodox Jews. The atmosphere is friendly and service staff is dedicated.
104 Lexington Ave. (bet. 27th and 28th Sts.), (212) 684-4010, www.madras-mahal.com, Open M-R 11:30am-3pm, 5pm-10pm, F-Sa 12pm-10:30pm, Su 12pm-10pm, MC, V, AmEx, D, DC, Entrées: $7-$12, **6** *to 28th St.* &

Mesa Grill

Bobby Flay's limitless imagination has bestowed upon the city Southwestern flavors served in a light, airy space that pulses with festivity. A New York favorite, this restaurant is an eye-opener for those yet unacquainted with the exuberance of Flay's cuisine.
102 Fifth Ave. (bet. 15th and 16th Sts.), (212) 807-7400, www.mesagrill.com, Open M-F 12pm-2pm, 5:30pm-10pm, Sa-Su 11:30am-230pm, 5:30pm-11pm,. MC, V, AmEx, D, Entrées: $18-$39,

L N R Q W 4 5 6 *to 14th St-Union Sq.* &

Park Avalon

Sink back and soak up the high self-esteem of this crowded, gothic hot spot, where the pleasure is in the seeing as much as in the eating. In spite of its popularity, claustrophobia is unlikely due to the spacious interior. The Mediterranean-American food, by the way, isn't shabby either.
225 Park Ave. S. (bet. 18th and 19th Sts.), (212) 533-2500, Open M-R 11:30am-12am, F-Sa 11:30am-1am, Su 10:30am-4:30pm, 5pm-11:30pm. MC, V, AmEx, D, Entrées: $14-$20,

L N R Q W 4 5 6 *to Union Sq.-14th St.* &

Patria

Professionals give way to cover girls as the sky darkens and the scene heats up in the multi-tiered dining area, lights streaming through the huge windows. The menu includes Latin American cuisine from countries ranging from Brazil to Mexico and comes out meticulously styled, like tamales cradled in corn husks. There is a prix fixe dinner every night for $54 a person.
250 Park Avenue S. (at 20th St.), (212) 777-6211, Open M-R 12pm-3:30pm, 5:30pm-11pm, F 12pm-3:30pm, 5pm-12am, Sa 5pm-12am, Su 5:30pm-10:30pm, MC, V, AmEx, DC, Entrées: $19-$29,

L N R Q W 4 5 6 *to 14th St.-Union Sq.* &

Pongal

The best Indian restaurant on the strip of the best Indian restaurants in New York. Pongal's South Indian vegetarian dishes have made it a time and review tested institution that shows no sign of closing or changing.
110 Lexington Ave. (bet. 27th and 28th Sts.), (212) 696-9458. Open M-F 12pm-3pm, 5pm-10pm, Sa-Su 12pm-10pm. MC, V, D, Entrées: $15-25, **6** *to 28th St.*

Steak Frites

For the best Steak Frites in New York, sally down to Union Square for this romantic French Bistro. Sparkling with the culture of the "Rive Gauche", both the exotic and the ordinary are served with flare and artistry. The only drawback is the paralyzing grin you might get from the waitress if you don't order in French.
9 East 16th (bet 5th and Union Sq. West), (212) 463-7101, Open M-R 11:30am-11:30pm, F-Sa 11:30am-12:30am, Su 11:30am-10:30pm, Amex, MC, Visa, Entrees: $15-22, **L N R Q W 4 5 6** *to 14th St.-Union Sq*

Tabla

One of the few restaurants where you can get American food infused with Indian spices. Be aware that your choices are prix fixe, à la carte, or a tasting menu. All are delicious.
11 Madison Ave. (at 25th St.), (212) 889-0667, www.tablanyc.com, Open M-F 12pm-2pm, 5:30pm-10:30pm, Sa-Su 5:30pm-10:30pm. MC, V, AmEx, DC, D, Entrées: $52, **N R 6** *to 23rd St.* &

Tamarind

Memphis-based Raji Jallepalli rocks the house with some of the best Indian food in NYC. The focus is on regional Indian dishes at this spacious restaurant, where waiters are numerous and attentive and the food is delicious. It's quite pricey, but well worth it.
41-43 E. 22nd St. (bet. Broadway and Park Ave. S.), (212) 674-7400, Open Su-R 11:30am-3pm, 5:30pm-11:30pm, F-Sa 11:30pm-3pm, 5:30pm-12:30am, MC, V, AmEx, Entrees: $31-40, **6** *to 23rd St.*

Union Square Cafe

Five times this restaurant has been voted most popualr restaurant by critics. The food is gourmet, but not the intimidating kind that makes you think your holding your fork wrong. Union Square Cafe is a landmark, whose great food and friendly service are here to stay.
21 E. 16th St. (bet. Fifth Ave. and Union Sq. W.), (212) 243-4020, Open M-R 12pm-2:30pm, 6pm-10:15pm, F-Sa 12pm-2:30pm, 6pm-11:15pm, Su 5:30pm-9:45pm. MC, V, AmEx, DC, D, Entrées: $25-$35, **L N R Q W 4 5 6** *to Union Sq.-14th St.* &

Zen Palate

This mostly-vegan, mostly-Asian restaurant serves up mostly excellent food at moderate prices, ensuring its continuing popularity with the coveted 18-34 demographic. No alcohol, unfortunately. Try the tempeh and tofu – some of it tastes like meat.
34 Union Sq. E. (at 16th St.), (212) 614-9291, Open M-R 11:30am-11pm, F-Sa 11:30pm-12am, Su 11:30pm-10:30pm. MC,

V, AmEx, DC, Entrees: $12-20, **①❶❷❸❹ ❹❺❻** *to Union Sq.,* ♿

CAFES

Java N Jazz

Java N Jazz is working hard to prove that they can do the coffee bar thing better than their mega chain counterparts, and it shows. Though they claim to be a relaxing place, so much is going on in and around this tiny café that you feel like everyone there has exceeded their daily caffeine limit. The walls are decked with art exhibits from neighborhood artists, they have live jazz on Friday and Saturday nights. You can even grab a box lunch to take back to work, or to bring over for a picnic in nearby Union Square Park.
868 Broadway (bet. 17th and 18th Sts.), (212) 473-4200, www.java-n-jazz.com. Open M-R 6:45am-10pm, F-Sa 7:30am-12am, Su 8am-10pm. MC, V, AmEx, D, **①❶❷❸❹❺❻** *to 14th St.-Union Sq.* ♿

Chelsea

RESTAURANTS

Amin Indian Cuisine

Dinner here avoids the circus-like pitfalls of Sixth Street's outfits. Curries, kebabs, and kormas are spicy enough to satisfy natives, and will only set you back about $10. Combo platters allow for both gluttony and variety.
155 Eighth Ave. (bet. 17th and 18th Sts.), (212) 929-7020, Open M-R 12pm-11pm, F-Sa 11:30am-

11:30pm. MC, V, AmEx, Entrées: $7-$19, **❶❷❸❹** *to 14th St. X f*

Cutting Room

Opened in December of '99, The Cutting Room is quickly establishing itself as one the hippest venues in the city. It's a restaurant, a lounge, a theater and a cabaret all wrapped up into one. The atmosphere is darkly lit and the stage has showcased performers from Sheryl Crow and David Bowie to Janeanne Garofalo and performance art sword-swallowers. The Cutting Room is an exciting place and promises a fun evening if you like don't mind the lack of conversation caused by the loudness of the entertainment.
19 W. 24th St. (bet. Broadway and Sixth Ave.), (212) 691-1900, Open T-F 5pm-4am, Sa 8pm-4am. MC, V, AmEx, Entrées: $12-17, **❶❷** *to 23rd St.*

Empire Diner

Featured in the opening montage of Woody Allen's Manhattan, this 24-hour eatery boasts an upscale dinner menu, complemented by a jazz pianist. It's a great club-hopping pit stop; staying up for prix-fixe brunch is well worth the sleep deprivation. Don't go à la carte, as the prices soar.
210 Tenth Ave. (at 22nd St.), (212) 243-2736, Open M-Su 24 hours, MC, V, AmEx, Entrées: $5-$18, **❶❷** *to 23rd St.*

Eugene

This lounge/restaurant is both a great place to be seen and a great place to be incognito. The almost hidden couch-style sur-

roundings are darkly lit, while the open spaces are filled by roaming models. Art-deco décor evokes a sense of snapping fingers and prohibition era snickers. The food is expensive but satisfying.
27 W. 24th St. (bet. 5th and 6th Aves.), (212) 462-0999, Open W-Sa 6pm-4am, MC, V, AmEx, Entrées: $22-$28, **❶❷** *to 23rd St.,* **❶❷** *to 23rd St.*

Le Madri

Le Madri blends homey and chic in a spacious restaurant featuring modern dishes rooted in Italian tradition. Conventional creations, like French fries and fried calamari, come off surprisingly well, but best are the house-made pastas, anything from the wood-burning oven, the seafood, and the popular osso buco. Desserts deserve special mention, truly Italian in their subtlety and simplicity. Try a real tiramisu. There's also the extra perk of a possible celebrity spotting, and valet parking.
168 W. 18th St. (at Seventh Ave.), (212) 727-8022, Open M-R 12pm-3pm, 6pm-10:30pm, F-Sa 12pm-3pm, 6pm-11:30pm, Su 12pm-3pm, 6pm-10:30pm, MC, V, AmEx, DC, Entrées: $13-$32, **❶❷** *to 18th St.*

Merchants, NY

At this downtown branch of a trio of sleek establishments of the same name, some actually order food here to go with their martini or cosmopolitan. Check out the downstairs sofa scene for ultimate cushiness. The appetizer and dessert menus are excellent.

112 Seventh Ave. (bet. 16th and 17th Sts.), (212) 366-7267, Open M-Su 11:30am-4am. MC, V, AmEx, D, Entrées: $10-$18, **❶❷❸❹** *to 14th St.*

Rocking Horse Cafe Mexicano

One of a string of Mexican restaurants along Eighth Ave., this is the most upscale, with fresh food, a perky waitstaff, and a popular brunch. Interesting twists on traditional fare include variations with crab and lobster, but the old standards are excellent as well.
182 Eighth Ave. (bet. 19th and 20th Sts.), (212) 463-9511, www.rockinghorse-cafe.com, Open Su-R 10am-11pm, F-Sa 10am-12am, MC, V, AmEx, Entrées: $14-$20, **❶❷** *to 23rd St.,* **❶❷** *to 23rd St.*

Tonic

The glamorous sister of the famous downtown Tonic. Authentic bar in front, beautiful dining room in back, and attractive French waiters make it well-worth the steep prices.
108 W. 18th St. (bet. Sixth and Seventh Aves.), (212) 929-9755, Open M-T 12pm-3pm, 5pm-10:30pm, W-Sa 12pm-3pm, 5pm-11pm, MC, V, AmEx, D, Entrees: $20-$25, **❶❷** *to 18th St.*

Viceroy

Come to this trendy spot for "see-food" — Chelsea's bold and beautiful are on display from the inside or out, with floor to ceiling windows providing a free

peek. Viceroy features some great dishes (and the food's not half-bad either). This cool, comfortable place makes for a glam time.
160 Eighth Ave. (at 18th St.), (212) 633-8484, Open M-R 11am-12am, F 11am-1am, Sa 9am-1am, Su 9am-12am, MC, V, AmEx, DC, D, Entrées: $10-$20, 12 to 18th St., Ⓐ Ⓒ Ⓔ Ⓛ to 14th St. &

CAFES

Big Cup

Day-glo colors and paisley patterns recall the '60s. Lounge all day in comfy chairs, sip a mocha, and watch the city pass you by. A major gay singles scene.
228 Eighth Ave. (bet. 21st and 22nd Sts.), (212) 206-0059, Open M-F 7am-1am, Sa-Su 8am-2am, Cash Only, Ⓒ Ⓔ to 23rd St. &

Emack and Bolios

Looking for something sweet and delicious? Look no further. For delicious gourmet ice cream, yogurt, and smoothies, Emack and Bolios cannot be beat.
56 Seventh Ave. (bet. 13th and 14th Sts.), (212) 727-1198. Open M-Su 12pm-12pm. Cash Only, Entrees: $2-$3, 123 Ⓣ Ⓞ 14th St.

Midtown

RESTAURANTS

44 Restaurant at the Royalton Hotel

Dining at this restaurant is a special treat. Its ultra-trendy ambience and Phillip Starck-designed interior make its European-American food seem even better than it is. The customers are a glamorous, black-clad crowd, often admiring themselves in the restaurant's giant mirrors. It's quite expensive but worth it if you like classic steak and fish dishes in a fancy spot.
44 W. 44th St. (bet. Fifth and Sixth Aves.), (212) 944-8844. Open M-Su 7am-11am, 12pm-3pm, 5:30pm-10:30pm. MC, V, AmEx, Entrees: $22-36, Ⓐ Ⓒ Ⓔ Ⓝ Ⓡ Ⓠ Ⓦ ① ② ③ ⑦ to 42nd St. &

Abigael's

Whether it's mouth-watering portobello mushrooms with balsamic drizzles, cedar-plank prepared salmon, or the most tender ribs and steak, Abigael's will be a hit even if you're not kosher. Serving primarily meat dishes, this place will knock you off your feet with great service and terrific food. Abigael's is also known for their fabulous deserts to cap off a fun night of kosher feasting. (Kosher)
1407 Broadway (at W. 39th), (212) 575-1407, abigaels.com. Open M-R 12pm-2:30pm, 5pm-10pm, F 12pm-2:30, Sa 8pm-12am, Su 4:30pm-9:30pm. MC, V, AmEx, Entrees: $22-30, Ⓐ Ⓒ Ⓔ Ⓝ Ⓡ Ⓠ Ⓦ ① ② ③ ⑦ to 42nd St.-Times Sq.

Asia de Cuba

If only all of NYC were as good looking and stylishly-dressed as this crowd. You might have to wait upwards of an hour for a table at prime-time even if you have a reservation, but the delicious food and sophisticated atmosphere make it worth the wait. Enjoy one of their excellent mixed drinks to help fan out the burning hole in your wallet.
237 Madison Ave. (bet. 37th and 38th Sts.), (212) 726-7755. Open M-W 12pm-11:00pm, R-F 12pm-12am, Sa 5:30pm-12am, Su 5:30pm-11pm. MC, V, AmEx, DC. Entrees: $17-$30. ④ ⑤ ⑥ ⑦ Ⓢ to Grand Central Station.

B. Smith's

This upscale soul food place has a sister restaurant in Union Station, Washington, DC, and is known to be a draw for the expense account crowd. Owner Barbara Smith, once a model, sure knows how to decorate but the food isn't consistently fabulous. Try the greens and salads, skip the fried items.
320 W. 46th St. (bet. 8th & 9th Aves.), (212) 315-1100. Open Su 11:30am-10pm, M 5pm-10:30pm, T 5pm-11:30pm, W 11:30am-11:30pm, R 5pm-12am, F 5pm-12:30am, Sa 4pm-12:30am. Ⓐ Ⓒ Ⓔ Ⓝ Ⓡ Ⓠ Ⓦ ① ② ③ ⑦ to 42nd St.-Times Sq.

Bread from Beirut

Simple ingredients cooked in a variety ways create an eclectic and authentic menu of Lebanese delights. Though offerings are mostly vegetarian, meat-eaters will get a kick out of the Kebbeh, a ball of meat wrapped up in wheat. The patrons are a well-rounded mix of young professionals, high-school kids, and families. Bread from Beirut is a fun, inexpensive place for everybody and anybody. (Lebanese) *24 W. 45th Street (bet 5th and 6th), (212) 764-1588. Open M-Su 7am-10pm. MC, V, AmEx. Entrees: $8-14.* Ⓐ Ⓒ Ⓔ Ⓝ Ⓡ Ⓠ Ⓦ ① ② ③ ⑦ *to 42nd St.-Times Sq.,* Ⓝ Ⓡ *to 49th St.*

Broadway's Jerusalem II Kosher Pizza

The most popular Kosher pizza joint in Manhattan. Lots of students from the nearby Stern College for Women drop by for a slice, as do Jewish office workers or tourists heading out to a Broadway show. Delivery is available to almost anyone, anywhere in the world. *1375 Broadway (bet. 37th and 38th Sts.), (212) 398-1475, www.flyingpizzas.com. Open M-R 7am-12am, F 7am-4pm, Sa 7am-10:30pm, Su 11am-10:30pm. Cash Only. Entrees: $5-$15.* ① ② ③ *to 34th St.* ♿

Bryant Park Grill

Nestled up against the backside of the main branch of the Public Library, a restaurant would be hard-pressed to be more picturesque, especially in spring. This Grill has the distinction of being the only restaurant located in the unexpectedly beautiful midtown Bryant Park. The food and service are uneven, the window views fabulous and the crowds crushing. The bar, partic-

ularly when it moves outdoors in the summer, is known as a primo meat market. Brunch is excellent. *25 W. 40th St. (bet. Fifth and Sixth Aves.), (212) 840-6500, www.arkrestaurants.com. Open M-Su 11:30am-3:30pm, 5pm-10pm. MC, V, AmEx, Entrées: $14-$24,* Ⓑ Ⓓ Ⓕ Ⓠ *to 42nd St.,* ⑦ *to Fifth Ave.* ♿

Burritoville

This Mexican chain has great prices, low on ambience and big on quantity. The burritos won't win any awards, but for a quick bite with or without heartburn, Burritoville fits the bill. Beware the fresh salsa. *625 Ninth Ave. (44th St.), (212) 333-5352, Open M-Su 11-12, MC, V, AmEx,* Ⓐ Ⓒ Ⓔ *to 42nd St. (Multiple Locations in Manhattan)*

Café Centro

Popular with the expense account set, this midtown Mediterranean is high on service and the food is consistently good. This café has taste to spare, an oasis in midtown for those looking for a good restaurant. Lunch is jam-packed. *200 Park Ave. (45th St. & Vanderbilt Ave.), (212) 818-1222. Open 11:30am-3:30pm, 5pm-10:30pm. MC, V, AmEx, Diners.* ④ ⑤ ⑥ ⑦ *to Grand Central Station.*

Café Un Deux Trois

Though a little strenuous on the wallet, this busy, touristy spot is perfect for a bowl of savory French onion soup or a delectable dish of crème

brulée. Avoid the high prices by sitting at the bar. If you're up for a full meal, sit table-side for a plate of steak and pomme frites and let your imagination run wild as you design your own table cloth with a cup full of crayons. *123 W. 44th St. (bet. Sixth Ave. and Broadway), (212) 354-4148. Open M-F 12pm-12am, Sa-Su 11am-12am. MC, V, AmEx, DC, Entrees: $15-24,* Ⓐ Ⓒ Ⓔ Ⓝ Ⓡ Ⓠ Ⓦ Ⓢ ① ② ③ ⑦ *to 42nd St.-Times Sq.* ♿

Carmine's

Come with a group of friends and order up a storm of family-style Italian. Seating is slow, so a visit to this enormous darkwood institution happily mandates a stop at the lovely bar. *200 W. 44th St. (bet. Broadway and Eighth Ave.), (212) 221-3800. Open Su-M 11:00am-11pm, T-Sa 11:00am-2am. MC, V, AmEx, Entrées: $15-$25,* Ⓝ Ⓡ Ⓢ ① ② ③ ⑦ *to 42nd St.-Times Sq.*

Chef Ho's

Chef Ho's is a solid Chinese that delivers late. Its dishes aren't too oily, and it's hard to find a bad dish. The seafood and eggplant are particularly good, the service just okay. *1720 Second Ave. (bet. 89th & 90th Sts.), (212) 348-9444. Open M-Su 11am-12am. MC, V, AmEx.* ④ ⑤ ⑥ *to 86th St.*

Churrascaria Plataforma

Plataforma is New York's swankiest Brazilian bar-

beque joint, where the all-you-can-eat meatfest will have you dieting for the rest of the week. The lighting and clientele are beautiful, the lime-based drinks divine, and the salad bar a work of art. The prices aren't cheap, but for a memorable evening, it can't be beat. *316 W. 49th St. (bet. 8th & 9th Aves.), (212) 245-0505. Open 12pm-12am.* Ⓐ *to 50th St.*

Cosi

This upscale lunch joint boasts a unique salty pressed bread and a made-to-order sandwich toppings bar. The brick oven at the front of every restaurant churns out the bumpy-looking flatbread, and patrons snatch up the scraps left in a large bowl left at the middle of the line. The sandwiches aren't cheap or simple, but always yummy. Think tandoori chicken or grilled eggplant with red peppers. Cosi's now has breakfast, with square bagels. *165 E. 52nd St. (bet. Lexington & 3rd Aves.), (212) 758-7800. 38 E. 45th St. (bet. Madison & Vanderbilt Aves.), (212) 949-7400. 11 W. 42nd St. (bet. 5th & 6th Aves.), (212) 398-6660. 60 E. 56th St. (bet. Madison & Park Aves.), (212) 588-0888. 1633 Broadway (51st St.), (212) 397-2674. 61 W. 48th St. (bet. 5th & 6th Aves.), (212) 265-2674. 3 E. 17th St. (bet. B'way & 5th Ave.), (212) 414-8468. 202 W. 36th St. (bet. 7th & 8th Aves.), (212) 967-9444.*

685 Third Ave. (bet. 43rd & 44th Sts.), (212) 697-8449.
841 Broadway (13th St.), (212) 614-8544.

Daily Soup

This soup chain has over a dozen types of soup, hot in winter and some cool soups in summer. The décor is strictly steel Spartan, but the lunchtime crowd is usually in and out anyway.
41 John St. (bet. Dutch & Nassau Sts.), (212) 791-7687.
325 Park Ave. S. (bet. 24th & 25th Sts.), (212) 531-7687.
134 E. 43rd St. (bet. Lexington & 3rd Aves.), (212) 949-7687.
241 W. 54th St. (bet. B'way & 8th Ave.), (212) 765-7687.
55 Broad St. (Beaver St.), (212) 222-7687.
780 Third Ave. (bet. 48th & 49th Sts.), (212) 828-7687.

Dallas BBQ

This barbecue joint may not be authentic, but it is fun. It is big on sauce, and will do just fine for New Yorkers not from Texas or Tennessee. Don't wear white.
1265 Third Ave. (bet. 72nd & 73rd Sts.), (212) 772-9393.
27 W. 72nd St. (bet. Columbus Ave. & CPW), (212) 873-2004.
21 University Pl. (8th St.), (212) 674-4450.
132 Second Ave. (St. Marks Pl.), (212) 777-5574.
132 W. 43rd St. (bet. B'way & 6th Ave.), (212) 221-9000.
3956 Broadway (166th St.), (212) 568-3700.

Dish of Salt

Giant wooden parrots and colorful banners cater to the exotica stereotype, but the greasy and decidedly Americanized Chinese food is safe enough for the after work and pre-theater crowds.
133 W. 47th St. (bet. Sixth and Seventh Aves.), (212) 921-4242, www.dishofsalt.com. Open M-F 11am-10:30pm, Sa 4pm-11pm. MC, V, AmEx, Entrées: $18-$27, **N R** *to 49th St.*

Don Giovanni

For a slice of the neighborhood, sit outside at a table and enjoy a pie at Don Giovanni. Made in a brick oven, with thin crust, fresh mozzarella and a sweet tomato sauce, this pizza is bound to please. Be forewarned: delivery takes at least an hour.
358 W. 44th St. (bet. Eighth and Ninth Aves.), (212) 581-4939, www.dongiovanni-ny.com. Open Su-R 12pm-12am, F-Sa 12pm-2am. MC, V, AmEx, Entrées: $7-$22, **A C E** *to 42nd St.* &

Firebird

This Russian restaurant is caviar heaven, where you will be pampered head to toe. From the bar to the restaurant, from the jazz lounge to the upstairs bar, Firebird has a high staff to diner ratio. Even the chef revolves into the dining room to see what's going on. In two former renovated townhouses, Firebird recreates St. Petersburg of 1910, replete with Cossack costumes and vintage paintings from a former era. The vodkas are to die for, and the dumplings, chicken Kiev and lamb are scrumptious. The owner's late wife was the granddaughter of the mayor of St. Petersburg. The prices, too, will be worthy of royalty.
365 W. 46th St. (bet. 8th & 9th Aves.), (212) 586-0244. Open M-Sa 11:45am-2pm, 5pm-11pm, Su 5pm-11pm. MC, V, AmEx. **A C E** *to 42nd St. or 50th St.*

Four Seasons

If you want to spot Henry Kissinger, Ranan Lurie or other old school New York power broker, the Pool Room is the place. Call it stuffy, call it pretentious Continental, but the Four Seasons is still the place to beat for wheeling and dealing. The food is fabulous, the wine list spectacular, the service stellar. They know what they are doing, so know your wines before you go.
99 E. 52nd St. (bet. Lexington & Park Aves.), (212) 754-9494. Open 12pm-2pm, 5pm-9:30pm. MC, V, AmEx. **6** *to 51st St.*

The Flame

Better known as a neighborhood icon than for its food, The Flame nonetheless ably serves up the expected diner menu, from omelets to burgers to gyros. The business crowd converges around 1pm for lunch, but otherwise there is ample seating and rarely (if ever) a wait. A good place to chat without having to fork over lots of dough.
893 Ninth Ave. (at 58th St.), (212) 765-7962. Open M-Su 6am-12am. MC, V, AmEx, D, Entrées: $4-$12, **A B C D 1 2** *to 59th St.-Columbus Circle.* &

Fresco Tortilla Grill

Times Square's best – or arguably, only – secret is this tiny Mexican hole-in-the-wall. A great place to satisfy your hunger for good food and New Yorker credibility for less than five bones.
125 W. 42nd St. (bet. Broadway and Sixth Ave.), (212) 221-5849. Open M-Su 11am-9pm. Cash only, Entrees: $3-5, **A C E S N R 1 2 3 7** *to 42nd St.-Times Square.*

Go Sushi

This sushi factory is short on ambience, but long on cheap prices and plentiful fish. Don't expect the freshest sushi in Manhattan, but for sushi dishes on the go, Go hits the fast lane.
3 Greenwich Ave. (6th Ave.), (212) 366-9272.
982 Second Ave. (52nd St.), (212) 593-3883.
756 Ninth Ave. (51st St.), (212) 459-2288.
511 Third Ave. (bet. 34th & 35th Sts.), (212) 679-1999.

Hale & Hearty Soups

H&H, like the Daily Soup, offers dozens of 'homemade' soups along with salads and other healthy fare. A favorite with men and women in suits unafraid of spilling their lunch, H&H is especially popular in the winter when a warm meal is just the ticket. The prices and lunchtime crush might make some pause before venturing in.
849 Lexington Ave. (bet. 64th & 65th Sts.), (212) 517-7600.
75 Ninth Ave. (bet. 15th

& 16th Sts.), (212) 255-2400.
55 W. 56th St. (bet. 5th & 6th Aves.), (212) 245-9200.
22 E. 47th St. (bet. 5th & Madison Aves.), (212) 557-1900.
462 Seventh Ave. (bet. 35th & 36th Sts.), (212) 971-0605.
49 W. 42nd St. (bet. 5th & 6th Aves.), (212) 575-9090.
32 Court St. (Remsen St.) Brooklyn, NY, 11201 (718) 596-5600.
685 Third Ave. (bet. 43rd & 44th Sts.), (212) 681-6460.

Hangawi

Just for fun, bring someone really square and uptight to this sublime, all-vegan Korean restaurant. By the third course, he'll be so seduced by the otherworldly calm that he won't even notice he's eating a lemon stuffed with mushrooms.
Midtown, 12 E. 32nd St. (bet. Fifth and Madison Aves) (212) 213-0077. Open M-F 12pm-3pm, 5pm-11pm, Sa 1pm-11pm, Su 1pm-10pm. MC, V, AmEx, DC, Entrees: $15-20, NR to 28th St.

Houlihan's

This all-American chain is long on comfort food and short on ambience. When the family visits from Omaha and you need any old standby, Houlihan's will fit the bill.
677 Lexington Ave. (56th St.), (212) 339-8858.
380 Lexington Ave. (42nd St.), (212) 681-8409.
350 Fifth Ave. (34th St.), (212) 630-0339.
196 Broadway (bet. Fulton & John Sts.), (212) 240-1280.
1900 Broadway (63rd St.), (212) 339-8862.

729 Seventh Ave. (49th St.), (212) 626-7312.
2 Penn Plaza (33rd St.), (212) 630-0348.

Houston's

Pronounced "How-ston's," this chain restaurant is popular with New Yorkers looking to remind themselves of home, wherever that used to be, with appetizers like spinach dip. It's a cut above most chains.
153 E. 53rd St. (enter at 54th St. & 3rd Ave.), (212) 888-3828.
378 Park Ave. S. (27th St.), (212) 689-1090.

Joe Allen

Upscale thespians, including bonafide Broadway celebs in search of some post-performance relaxation, come to this dark and elegant but unpretentious eatery to fill up on gourmet meatloaf and hot fudge pudding cake. On Sunday nights 8pm to closing, fifteen percent of every check goes to Broadway Cares/Equity Fights AIDS.
326 W. 46th St. (bet. Eighth and Ninth Aves.), (212) 581-6464, www.joeallen-orso.com. Open Su-R 11:30am-12am, F-Sa 12pm-12am. MC, V, Entrées: $10-$21, A C E to 42nd St. &

Joe's Shanghai

This is an authentic Chinese for the crowd that knows its Asian food. Try the soup dumplings, filled with delectable crab and pork, lots of juice to spare. The service won't bowl you over, but the food will. The prices are good, too.
24 W. 56th St. (bet. 5th & 6th Aves.), (212) 333-3868. Open 11am-10:30pm. MC, V, AmEx, D.

E V to 53rd St.

Kiiroi Hana

This authentic sushi joint is long on authenticity, short on imagination and décor. Try some inside out rolls, or the eggplant appetizer in miso sauce. Usually fresh, good for lunch.
23 W. 56th St. (bet. 5th & 6th Aves.), (212) 582-7499. Open M-Su 11am-2:30pm, 5:30pm-10:30pm. E V to 53rd St.

Kyma

The authentic Greek fare and unpretentious atmosphere attracts locals interested in food, not hype. Preparing the food before you in an open kitchen, the portly chef expertly unfolds filo dough as he greets the regulars and offers recommendations. You may be tempted to stuff yourself on the abundant entrées, such as the striped bass baked with feta cheese, but leave room for the baklava and other homemade desserts.
300 W. 46th (at Eighth Ave.), (212) 727-8886. Open M-Su 11:30-11:30pm, MC, V, AmEx, DC, Entrées: $15-$22, A C E to 42nd St., N R Q W S 1 2 3 7 to 42nd St.-Times Sq.

La Bonne Soupe

An authentic French bistro, right down to the waiters' thick accents and the creamy chocolate mousse. Red-checkered tablecloths and colorful paintings add to the homey, rural atmosphere. Start with a glass of wine and some fondue or the Paysanne soup, then try the duck platters, and end the meal with crème

caramel. It'll be one "bonne" meal under $25...tres bien!
48 W. 55th St. (bet. Fifth and Sixth Aves.), (212) 586-7650, www.labonnesoupe.com. Open M-Su 11:30am-12am. MC, V, AmEx, D, Entrées: $10-20, N R to 57th, E V to 53rd.

Le Cirque 2000

Set in the historic Villard Houses and attached to the New York Palace Hotel, Le Cirque combines the refinement of the past with giddy designs of the future. It is unfortunate, though, that the decorations have covered up the elegant wall paintings. Every detail at Le Cirque has been planned to the fullest extent, from the signature plates that have monkeys on them to the extremely attentive waitstaff that is always trying to give you another fork. The food is spectacular, and the crème brulée is a must-have for dessert.
455 Madison Ave. (bet. 50th and 51st Sts.), (212) 303-7788, www.lecirque.com. Open M-Sa 11:30am-2:30pm, 5:30pm-10:30pm, Su 5:30pm-10:30pm. MC, V, AmEx, DC, Entrées: $30-$40, 6 to 51st St., E V to Lexington Ave. &

Mangia

Gourmet Mediterranean cuisine and friendly waitstaff at this lunch restaurant make it a culinary hot-spot for the surrounding working worlds of businesses, galleries and museums. Mangia's diverse array of pastas, sandwiches, and entrées — including an "antipasto

table," with a wonderful selection of foods ranging from paella to rare tuna — is sure to quench anyone's desire for a gastronomic thrill. In a rush? Stop at the café downstairs for equally delicious take out dining.
50 W. 57th St. (bet. Fifth and Sixth Aves.), (212) 582-5554. Open M-F 6:30am-8:30pm, Sa 8:30am-5pm. MC, V, AmEx, DC, D, Entrées: $11-15, **N R B Q** *to 57th St.*
16 E. 48th St. (bet Fifth and Madison Aves.), (212) 754-0637. Open M-F 11:30am-4pm. MC, V, AmEx, DC, D, Entrées: $11-15, **6** *to 51st St.*

Michael Jordan's Steakhouse

This upscale steakhouse is part of Grand Central's makeover. Stop by for dinner before grabbing the Metro North upstate, or make the trip to this gorgeous station to enjoy a martini at the end of the day. The steaks are good.
Grand Central Station (on the W. balcony), 23 Vanderbilt Ave. (bet. Park and Lexington Aves.), (212) 655-2300. Open M-Sa 12pm-11pm, Su 1pm-10pm. MC, V, AmEx, Entrées: $17-$32, **S 4 5 6 7** *to 42nd St.- Grand Central Station.*

Milos

By-the-pound pricing. A Greek piscatory/restaurant where the fish are laid out for you to pick. Fresh fish too, cooked for you in Mediterranean sauces. Nothing compares to the seafood at Milos, it floats somewhere above, an ideal not to be touched.
125 W. 55th St. (bet. Sixth and Seventh Aves.), (212) 245-7400. Open M-Sa 12pm-3pm, 5:30pm-11:30pm, Su 5pm-11pm. MC, V, AmEx, DC, Entrées: $40-$60, **N R** *to 57th St.*

Norma's

This brunch, all day, all the time, is a good-feeling, good-lucking restaurant you wouldn't expect in Le Parker Meridien Hotel. With fabulous chocolate or Rice Crispy French Toast for kids, and smothered eggs or eggs benedict for adults, Norma's has something for everyone. Even Martha has dined here, among other entertainment types. Don't expect starched linen, this place is refreshingly low-key. They don't even take reservations. The décor is airport-like, all sleek metal and orb-like lighting cut into the walls, but the feeling is warm and the eavesdropping, priceless. Try the Wa Zaa, a waffle smothered in a berry brulee. Norma's isn't normal, thankfully.
On weekends come early. 118 West 57th Street (in Le Parker Meridien Hotel), (212) 708-7435, **A B C D 1 2** *to 59th St.*

Orso

With an un-impressive Italian menu, the post theater crowds and sometimes star-studded clientele make Orso more exciting for its atmosphere than cuisine. The service is stuffy and the meals are oily or just "okay". If you're a people watcher, you've come to the right place. If you like food, leave now.
322 W. 46th St. (bet. Eighth and Ninth Aves.), (212) 489-7212, www.orsorestaurant.com. Open M-Su 12pm-11:30 pm. MC, V, **A C E S N R 1 2 3 7** *to 42nd St.-Times Square.*

Osteria del Circo

Tuscany goes to the circus in this Italian offshoot of Le Cirque 2000. The menu runs heavy on tasty fish and pasta, nothing too ingenious or pretentious - especially when the signature dessert is a crème-filled Italian donut. Unlike its upscale French cousin, Osteria just wants to have fun. The circus theme runs from the trapeze ladders draped from wall to wall or the flame-colored metal juggler and musician sculptures perched on the back wall.
120 W. 55th St. (bet. Sixth and Seventh Aves.), (212) 265-3636, www.osteriadelcircio.com. Open M-Sa 9am-2:30pm, 5:30pm-11pm, Su 5:30pm-11pm. MC, V, AmEx, DC, Entrées: $30-$40, **N R** *to 57th St.*

Pamir

Savory pilaf complements the well-executed lamb and chicken dishes, from kebabs to quabilli palaw, at this cozy uptown enclave of Afghan cuisine adorned with hand-tooled metalwork and bright Afghan rugs. Denim-clad patrons will feel self-conscious in the upscale atmosphere.
1065 Second Ave. (at 58th St.), (212) 644-9258. Open M-Su 5pm-11pm. MC, V, AmEx, Entrées: $11-$16, **6** *to 77th St.*

Pietrasanta

A Hell's Kitchen neighborhood secret where the chef actually comes out of the kitchen to ask how customers are enjoying their meals. For an appetizer, try the succulent scallops in a rich pesto sauce, and order the pumpkin ravioli in sweet pepper sauce as an entrée. Delish.
683 Ninth Ave. (at 47th St.), (212) 265-9471. Open Su-M 12pm-10:30pm, T 12pm-11pm, W 11am-11pm, R 12pm-11am, F 12pm-12am, Sa 11:30am-12am. MC, V, AmEx, Entrées: $8-$16, **C E** *to 50th St.*

Planet Hollywood

The food here is worse than Hard Rock Café, but the movie star memorabilia is one-of-a-kind. Check out the spacesuits, autographed pictures and goofy costumes. Packed with tourists.
1540 Broadway (45th St.), (212) 333-7827. Open Su-R 11am-12am, F-Sa 11am-1am. MC, V, **A C E** *to 42nd St.*

Ruby Foo's

Fun, cool, hip pan-Asian with everything from dim sum to sushi and a popular Sunday brunch. Ruby Foo's is known for its over-the-top and ostentatious decor and sometimes snooty service.
1626 Broadway (at 49th St.), (212) 489-5600. Open M-Su 11:00am-11pm, T-R 11am-11:30pm, F-Sa 11am-12:30am. MC, V, AmEx, Entrées: $25, **C E** *to 50th St.*

Seppi's

Alsatian isn't just a pet anymore. This classy casual restaurant in the belly of the Parker Meridien redefines French cuisine from the region

bordering Germany. No sauerkraut here, just succulent lamb shanks, crawfish ravioli, buffalo carpaccio and eau de vie to wash it all down. Try the hot banana tart with the chocolate crust and ice cream filling. Not cheap, but good for the family and theatre crowds - the low lighting and real French prints will put anyone at ease. The $28 prix-fixe is a good deal. *123 W. 56th St. (in Le Parker Meridien Hotel), (212) 708-7444,* **Ⓐ Ⓑ Ⓒ Ⓓ ❶ ❷** *to 59th St.*

Shallots NY

Shallots NY is the city's most chic kosher establishment. Hidden away in the Sony building, it has a private feel and an upscale ambience. Unlike most kosher restaurants, Shallots offers rarities such as sweetbreads, veal-bruschetta, morels, and truffles as well as normal meat dishes alongside fish and vegetarian options. It's a little pricey but well worth the rabbi's blessing. *550 Madison Ave (bet. 55th and 56th Sts.), (212) 833-7800. MC, V, AmEx,* **Ⓝ Ⓡ** *to Lexington Ave. (kosher)*

Soup Kitchen

While Seinfeld fanatics are bemoaning the end of an era, one remnant lives on. The lines at this pop-culture landmark are unreal at lunchtime, but have you noticed how smoothly it moves along? Patrons have made up their minds what to order by the time they reach the counter of this famous take-out. Otherwise it's "No soup for you!" *259-A W. 55th St. (bet. Eighth Ave. and Broadway), (212) 757-7730. Open M-F 12pm-6pm. Closed for the summer. Cash Only, Entrées: $6-$8,* **Ⓝ Ⓡ** *to 57th St.*

Sparks Steak House

One of the best steakhouses in New York City. Come with a full wallet and an empty stomach for incredible meat and seafood. *210 E. 46th St. (bet. Second and Third Aves.), (212) 687-4855. Open M-R 12pm-11pm, F-Sa 5pm-11:30pm. MC, V, AmEx, DC, Entrées: $22-$35,* **❹ ❺ ❻ ❼** *to 42nd St.-Grand Central.* ♿

Tao

Trendsetters would swear that the newly-opened Tao is a religious experience. After walking in under what looks like a huge golden cocoon above the door, diners enter a murky enclave of cool dominated by a backlit three-story golden Buddha. The food is a fabulous Asian fusion, although some diners complain that the disco-sounding music is too loud to talk over. This place is always packed, so come with a reservation in hand. *42 East 58th St. (bet. Madison & Park Aves.), (212) 888-2288. Open M-T 11:00am-12am, W-F 11:00am-1am, Sa 5pm-1am, Su 5pm-12am. MC, V, AmEx, DC, Entrees: $16-25, 456 to 59th,* **Ⓝ Ⓡ** *to 59th and Lexington Ave.*

TGI Friday's

TGI's is a national chain known for its Buffalo wings, burgers and brews. Don't expect much else, just a taste of home, wherever that was. *47 E. 42nd St. (bet. Madison & Vanderbilt Aves.), (212) 681-8458. 1680 Broadway (bet. 52nd & 53rd Sts.), (212) 767-8326. 21 W. 51st St. (bet. 5th & 6th Aves.), (212) 767-8352. 761 Seventh Ave. (50th St.), (212) 767-8350. 484 Eighth Ave. (34th St.), (212) 630-0307. 47 Broadway (Exchange Pl.), (212) 483-8322. 604 Fifth Ave. (bet. 48th & 49th Sts.), (212) 767-8335. 1552 Broadway (46th St.), (212) 944-7352.*

Toledo

The cherry wood, archways and courtly dining hall of this midtown Spanish restaurant evoke the elegance of a bygone century. Ask, and the retinue of waiters will proudly point you to the best dishes. Or try the authentic paella prized for its fresh seafood and savory saffron rice. The sangria is almost too delicious for your own good, and after a few glasses you'll sing its praises.
6 E. 36th St. (bet. Fifth and Madison Aves.), (212) 696-5036. Open M-F 11:30pm-10:30pm, Sa 12pm-11pm. MC, V, AmEx, DC, Entrées: $22-$26, **B D F N Q R** *to 34th St.* ♿

Topaz Thai Restaurant

This spot may be cramped and a bit hard to find, but the food's tasty and, judging by the constant flux of diners, happy on the budget. Upon your arrival, a smiling, speedy waiter will seat you at a table three inches from your neighbors on all sides. However, the delicious curried entrees and Thai iced tea will make you forget the cramped quarters.
127 W. 56th (bet. Sixth and Seventh Aves.), (212) 957-8020. Open M-Su 12pm-11pm. MC, V, AmEx, D, **B D Q 1 2 3** *to Columbus Circle.*

Trattoria Dell'Arte

Tons of well-heeled Manhattanites dine here on their way to a show, but the decor is the biggest celebrity at this huge modern Italian restaurant opposite Carnegie Hall. Busts of famous noses, enormous paintings of close-up body parts, and electric-colored walls make the space happening. This chic spot also boasts polished service and the tastiest bread in New York.
900 Seventh Ave. (at 57th St.), (212) 245-9800. Open M-Sa 11:45am-2:45pm, 5pm-11:30pm, Su 11:45am-2:45pm, 5pm-10:30pm. MC, V, AmEx, D, Entrées: $17-$38, **N R** *to 57th St.*

Turkish Kitchen

Turkish music brings to mind the minarets of Istanbul silhouetted across the Golden Horn, and shockingly red wallpaper coupled with a laundry list of kebabs strives to maintain exotic authenticity. Don't be afraid to experiment; just about anything with lamb is sure to be good.
386 Third Ave. (bet. 27th and 28th Sts.), (212) 679-1810, www.turkishkitchen.com. Open M-F 12pm-3pm, 5:30pm-11pm, Sa 5pm-11:30pm, Su 5pm-10:30pm. MC, V, AmEx, DC, D, Entrées: $10-$18, **6** *to 28th St.*

Uncle Nick's Greek Cuisine

Serving enormous kebobs, salads brimming with stuffed grape leaves and olives and huge wedges of flaming saganaki cheese, Uncle Nick's Greek Cuisine won't leave you hungry. The bustling atmosphere, attentive waitstaff, and speedy service make this restaurant great for pre-theater dining.
747 Ninth Ave. (bet. 50th and 51st Sts.), (212) 245-7992. Open M-Su 12pm-11pm. MC, V, AmEx, D, Entrées: $9-$15, **A C E** *to 50th St. X*

Uncle Vanya

Delicious, inexpensive, authentic — what more could you possibly want? To top it off, the vodka flows freely, the food is hardy (the Russian dumplings are out of this world), and there's often live music, a pleasant folk singer, incomprehensible to non-russophones. In fact this place is so authentic the whole staff is hard to understand they are so Russian. Dasdarovya.
315 W. 54th St. (bet. Eighth and Ninth Aves.), (212) 262-0542. Open Su-R 12pm-11pm, F-Sa 12pm-12am. Cash Only, Entrées: $8-$12, **C E** *to 50th St.*

Via Brasil

This Little Brazil fave is full of jazz, palms and fabulous food. The waiters are nice, the appetizers as good as the entrees. Try the lime drinks, fish casserole and piping hot coffee. Lots of Brazilians come here too.
34 W. 46th St. (bet. 5th & 6th Aves.), (212) 997-1158.

Victor's Café

This classic Cuban is full of plaintains, meats and fawning service. Live music on certain nights. The brunch is nice and relaxed. A great place to go before the theatre.
236 W. 52nd St. (bet. B'way & 8th Ave.), (212) 586-7714. Open 12pm-12am. MC, V, AmEx, **C E 1 2** *to 50th St.*

CAFES

Columbus Bakery

For everything from yummy breakfast pastries to salads and sandwiches, this midtown spot can provide you with a variety of delicious treats. You can sit inside for a break from the streets, or, when it's warm enough, sit outside to watch the passers-by s you snack.
957 First Ave. (bet. 52nd and 53rd Sts.), (212) 421-0334, www.arkrestaurants.com. Open M-Su 7:30am-9pm. MC, V, AmEx, D, Entrees: $3-$7, **6** *to 51st St. X*

Cupcake Cafe

A quaint bakery with pink walls and tin ceilings on the raunchiest stretch in Hell's Kitchen. Great donuts, waffles, and (duh) cupcakes, with a few tables for immediate consumption. The location is unfashionable for a food pilgrimage, but come for old-fashioned sweets.
522 Ninth Ave. (at 39th St.), (212) 465-1530. Open M-F 7am-7pm, Sa 8am-7pm, Su 9am-5pm. Cash Only, **N R Q W S 1 2 3 7** *to 42nd St.-Times Sq.*

Emack and Bolios

By the time you get to the fourth floor of Macy's, you'll need a break. Look no further than Emack and Bolios for sandwiches and sweeter goodies. Then pick up your bags and start again, rejuvenated by your sweet tooth fix. This upscale ice cream joint is the cream of choice for native New Yorkers, especially in the age of homogenized Ben & Jerry's.

Macy's, 151 W. 34th St., 4th Floor, (212) 494-5853. Open M-Su 10am-8pm. MC, V, AmEx, Entrees: $4-$6, **1 2 3** *to 34th St.,* **N Q R W B D** *to 34th St.-Herald Square.*

Ferrara Bakery and Café

America's oldest espresso bar has been a Little Italy staple since 1892. If you can't make the trip all the way downtown, visit this midtown location to satiate yourself until your next visit. Everything is homemade! Ferrara's has been serving up cannoli for many moons, and is a perennial favorite for New Yorkers looking to have coffee and dessert after the show or trip to another restaurant. *195 Grant St., (212) 226-6150, www.ferrara-cafe.com. Open Su-F 8am-12am. Sa 8am-1am. MC, V, AmEx,* **W Q N R M J Z 6** *to Canal St.*

Krispy Kreme

A southern import, these donuts melt in your mouth so fast and taste so good that it's impossible to eat fewer than three. With the best donuts in Manhattan, KK has even seasoned Manhattanites glued to its windows, watching glossy fried confections lurch off its conveyer belt. If you want to be a hit in your office or dorm, pick up a dozen. *2 Penn Plaza, Amtrak Level (bet.. 32nd and 33rd Sts.), (212) 947-7175, www.krispykreme.com. Open M-Su 6am-10pm. Cash Only, BDFGNR1 to 34th St.-Herald Sq. Port Authority Bus Terminal, Eighth Avenue (bet.. 40th and 41st Sts.), (212) 290-8644,*

www.krispykreme.com. Open M-F 6am-9pm. Cash Only, **A C E N R S 1 2 3 7 9** *to Times Square-42nd St.*

The Palm Court

Lovely, if overpriced, for desserts and tea in the Plaza Hotel. You can sit back and sip your tea while you watch the privileged but touristy walk in and out of the hotel. Then browse through The Plaza yourself; there's logic behind its fame. *The Plaza Hotel, 768 Fifth Ave. (at Central Park S.), (212) 759-3000. Open M-Sa 6:30am-2:30pm, Su 10:30am-3pm, Tea served M-Sa 3:45pm-6pm, Su 4pm-6pm. MC, V, AmEx, D, Entrees: $19-$30,* **N R** *to Fifth Ave.* &

RESTAURANTS

Benihana of Tokyo

This kitschy restaurant, known for its knife-throwing chop-chop chefs who display their talents tableside, has been around for many moons. With a reputation for drawing tourists rather than locals, Benihana is a retro alternative to Manhattan chic. *120 E. 56th St. (bet. Lexington & Park Aves.) (212) 593-1627. Open M-R 5pm-10:30pm, F-Sa 5pm-11:30pm, Su 4pm-10:30pm.* **E V** *to 53rd St.*

The Comfort Diner

This retro-hip diner takes itself pretty seriously, if the slightly bitter menu offers any clues - "Sorry,

Mom, but we don't remember yours tasting this good," reads the meatloaf description. To their credit, it really is pretty good meatloaf. *142 E. 86th St. (at Lexington Aves.), (212) 426-8600. Open Su-W 8am-11pm, R 8am-12am, F-Sa 8am-2am. MC, V, D, Entrees $8-10,* **4 5 6** *to 86th St.* &

Daniel

Another one of New York's finest: amazing food, beautiful setting, and, of course, prices to match. *60 E. 65th St. (bet Park and Madison Aves.), (212) 288-0033, www.daniel-nyc.com. Open T-Sa 12pm-2am, M-Sa 5:45-11pm. MC, V, AmEx, DC, Entrées: $40-$60,* **4 5 6** *to 68th St.-Hunter College.* &

Elaine's

A magnet for A-list hometown celebs often featured in gossip columns. This popular hangout serves up standard American fare. Quality blows hot and cold (mostly cold), but coming here for the food is like living in New York for the weather: it just shouldn't be a priority. Regulars include Woody Allen, Barbara Walters and George Plimpton. *1703 Second Ave. (bet. 88th and 89th Sts.), (212) 534-8103. Open M-Su 6pm-2am. MC, V, AmEx, DC, D, Entrées: $15-$35,* **4 5 6** *to 86th St.* &

Harry Cipriani

Throw on the Chanel suit and relax because your trust fund's paying for this meal, like it does everything else. If you can stand the attitude, come

to look for celebrities and feel like one yourself. *781 Fifth Ave. (bet. 59th and 60th Sts.), (212) 753-5566. Open M-Su 7:30am-10:30am, 12pm-3pm, 6pm-11pm. MC,V, AmEx, DC, D, Entrées: $40,* **N R 4 5 6** *to 59th St.-Lexington Ave.* &

La Gouloue

Sure the food's great, but this is a snobby place. If you don't fit into the snobby mold you will be treated like second-rate cheese. Try the skate fish, and guffaw at all the people being told there's a two hour wait on all of the empty tables. *746 Madison Ave. (bet. 64th and 65th Sts.), (212) 988-8169. Open M-Sa 12pm-4 pm, 6pm-11pm, Su 12pm-4pm, 6pm-10:30pm. MC, V, AmEx, D, Entrées:$20-$35* **6** *to 68th St.* &

Lipstick Café

Lipstick, in what is known as the lipstick building (for its shape, narrowing at the top) is a consistent crowd-pleaser with great salads and specials. The prices aren't cheap, but the crowd is always lively and the location is great, in a building lobby surrounded by windows and people in motion. Only Monday thru Friday for breakfast and lunch. *885 Third Ave. (bet. 53rd & 54th Sts.), (212) 486-8664.*

The Lobster Club

Chef/owner Anne Rosenzweig made headlines years ago when she stormed the citadel of all-male chefs at the city's top rated restaurants. Indulge in one of her signature dishes like corn cakes with crème fraîche and caviar, or chocolate-bread pudding swimming in brandy-custard sauce; in all her cooking, Rosenzweig expertly combines French technique and American heartiness. *24 E. 80th St. (bet. Madison and Fifth Aves.), (212) 249-6500. Open M-Sa 11:30am-11pm, Su 11:30am-10pm. MC, V, AmEx, DC, Entrées: $18-$29, ❻ to 77th St.*

Sant Ambreous

Famous for the cakes you'll see displayed in the windows, this Upper East Side café is infamously overpriced. Rumor has it the cakes are prettier than they are tasty anyway. Still, there's no shortage of patrons at this Northern Italian cafe, where the cappuccinos and gelati are to die for. Think of it as a taste of Italy on the Upper East Side. *1000 Madison Ave. (bet. 77th and 78th Sts.), (212) 570-2211. Open M-F 7:30am-7pm, Sa 9am-7pm, Su 10am-6pm. MC, V, AmEx, D, Entrees: $20-$30, ❻ to 77th St. ♿*

Le Bilboquet

Chain-smoking Eurotrash crowds people this diminutive French bistro. Models can't appreciate the menu, but don't let that stop you from taking advantage of the well-executed bistro fare. *25 E. 63rd St. (bet. Madison and Park Aves.), (212) 751-3036. Open M-Su 12pm-11pm. MC, V, AmEx, Entrées: $17-$24, ❶❷❹❺❻ to 59th St.-Lexington Ave.*

Le Pain Quotidien

The smell of freshly baked bread welcomes you to this cozy Belgian bakery/café featuring a giant communal wooden table and some of the flakiest croissants this side of the Atlantic. Everything from rustic baguettes to country loaves, for which European flour is specially imported, is masterfully prepared and baked on the premises in batches throughout the day. A delicious array of breakfast and lunch dishes are also served. *1311 Madison Ave. (bet. 84th and 85th Sts.), (212) 327-4900, www.painquotidien.com. Open M-Su 7:30am-7pm. Cash Only, Entrées: $8-$12, ❹❺❻ to 86th St.*

Manana Restaurant

Delicious and reasonably-priced Mexican food lies behind this otherwise unassuming First Avenue facade. The atmosphere is cute, if a little cheesy, but the main draw here is the food. Everything is good across the board, but the Yucatan-style carnitas are worth a trip all by themselves. *1136 First Ave. (between 62nd and 63rd Sts.), (212) 371-8023. Open M-F 11:30am-11pm, Sa-Su 12pm-11pm. MC, V, Amex. Entrees: $8-$16, ❹❺❻ to 59th St.*

Maya

Excellent cuisine, excellent service, and a comfortable atmosphere make dining at this "Gourmet Mexican" truly a euphoric experience. The food is that good. Colorful and flavorful, the dishes are inventive with surprising combinations. Try the mango margaritas and the guacamole with fresh chips. *1191 First Ave. (at 64th St.), (212) 585-1818. Open M-Su 5pm-11:30pm. MC, V, AmEx, Entrées: $17-$27, ❶❷❹❺❻ to 59th St.-Lexington Ave. X*

Merchants, NY

The East Side branch of a trio of sleek establishments of the same name, some actually order food here to go with their martini or cosmopolitan; check out the downstairs sofa scene for ultimate cushiness. The appetizer and dessert menus are excellent. *1125 First Ave. (at 62nd St.), (212) 832-1551. Open M-Su 11:30am-4am. MC, V, AmEx, DC, Entrées: $13-$19, ❶❷❹❺❻ to 59th St.-Lexington Ave.*

Mocca Hungarian

Throw your doctor's cholesterol warnings to the wind and dig into peasant staples like goulash and stuffed cabbage. The decor takes its cues from Communist functionalism. *1588 Second Ave. (bet. 82nd and 83rd Sts.), (212) 734-6470. Open M-Su 11:30am-10:00pm. Cash Only, Entrées: $7-$14, ❹❺❻ to 86th St. ♿*

Pamir

Savory pilaf complements the well-executed lamb and chicken dishes, from kebabs to quabilli palaw, at this cozy uptown enclave of Afghan cuisine adorned with hand-tooled metalwork and bright Afghan rugs. Denim-clad patrons will feel self-conscious in the upscale atmosphere.

1437 Second Ave. (bet. 74th and 75th Sts.), (212) 734-3791. Open M-Su 5pm-11pm. MC, V, AmEx, Entrées: $11-$16, ❻ to 77th St. ♿

Payard Patisserie and Bistro

Payard's two-tiered restaurant, dim lighting and French service create an elegant, Upper East Side atmosphere. With an impressive wine list, traditional French cuisine and impeccable service, your meal will be well worth the bill. If you're not in the mood for big spending, skip straight to the dessert menu; their pastries truly melt in your mouth and most are under $10. The best dessert in New York. *1032 Lexington Ave. (bet. 73rd and 74th Sts.), (212) 717-5252, www.payard.com. Patisserie Open 7am-11pm. Bistro open M-SR 12pm-10:30pm, F-Sa 12pm-11pm. MC, V, AmEx, DC, D, ❻ to 77th St.*

Penang Malaysia

This lively, decked out Malaysian is usually packed on weekends and reasonably so; the food is innovative and tasty, the crowd generally young and hip, and there's live music and a lounge in the bar downstairs. Try eating down there to avoid the wait upstairs. *1596 Second Ave. (at 83rd St.), (212) 585-3838, www.penangnyc.com. Open M-R 12pm-12am, F-Sa 12pm-1am, Su 12pm-11:30pm. MC, V, AmEx, DC, Entrées: $11-$20, ❹❺❻ to 86th St. ♿*

Rosa Mexicano

A well-heeled clientele sips pomegranate margaritas at the crowded bar while waiting for a taste of well executed classics. Guacamole is prepared table-side and desserts like the tamal en cazuela dulce, a sweetish, warm cornmeal swirled with a chocolate sauce, make this a must.
1063 First Ave. (at 58th St.), (212) 753-7407. Open M-Su 5pm-11:30pm. MC, V, AmEx, DC, D, Entrées: $17-$26, **N R 4 5 6** *to 59th St.-Lexington Ave.*

CAFES

DTUT

Ever want to hang out in a coffeehouse reminiscent of Central Perk? Here's your chance. With deep couches, delicious coffee, and yummy goodies, you can spend hours just chatting with pals at this Upper East Side café. Be sure not to miss the do-it-yourself s'mores.
1626 Second Ave. (bet. 84th and 85th Sts.), (212) 327-1327. Open Su-R 8am-12am, F-Sa 8am-2am. Cash Only, Entrees: $5-$12, **4 5 6** *to 86th St.*

Lexington Candy Shoppe

Its antique malt-mix dispenser and shake machine have been churning since 1925, making a meal at this old-fashioned soda fountain and diner a historical event. Pay homage by ordering one of the burgers sizzling on a small griddle and a complicated dairy concoction.
1226 Lexington Ave. (at 83rd St.), (212) 288-0057. Open M-Sa 7am-7pm, Su 9am-6pm. MC, V, AmEx, Entrées: $6-$8, **4 5 6** *to 86th St.*

Serendipity 3

Famous for their frozen hot chocolates and ice cream sundaes that go on forever, leave your diet at the door when you visit. Though a bit overpriced for the quality of the entrees, most concede that it's worth it when they taste the desserts.
225 East 60th St. (bet. Second and Third Aves.), (212) 838-3531, www.serendipity3.com. Open Su-R 11:30am-12am, F 11:30am-1am, Sa 11:30am-2am. MC, V, AmEx, DC, D, Entrees: $12-$17, **N R 4 5 6** *to 59th St.- Lexington Ave.*

RESTAURANTS

Tavern on the Green

Only the well-connected score the best seats, but the crystal chandeliers and tranquil setting are impressive, if garish. This legendary Central Park outpost is a popular destination for tourists and grannies. The prices may overwhelm you, the food may underwhelm. Check out the mind-boggling wine list, now the best in New York. In winter, twinkling lights on the surrounding trees make for quite a Yuletide scene.
Central Park West (at 67th St.), (212) 873-3200, www.tavernonthegreen.com. Open M-R 11:30am-3pm, 5pm-9pm, F-Su 10am-3:30pm, 5pm-1am (limited menu after 11pm). MC, V, AmEx, D, Entrées: $13-$25, **B C** *to 72nd St.*

RESTAURANTS

Ayurveda Café

Upper Westsiders swear by this quaint Indian restaurant with a daily prix-fixe menu. The food is vegetarian and based on the Hindu philosophies of Ayurveda. What that boils down to is simple, healthful, holistic food that satisfies without being too filling.
706 Amsterdam Ave. (bet 94th and 95th Sts.), (212) 932-2400. Open M-Su, 11:30am-11pm, MC, V, AmEx, D, Entrees: $9-16, **1 2 3** *to 96th St.*

Benihana of Tokyo

This kitschy restaurant, known for its knife-throwing chop-chop chefs who display their talents tableside, has been around for many moons. With a reputation for drawing tourists rather than locals, Benihana is a retro alternative to Manhattan chic.
47 W. 56th St. (bet. 5th & 6th Aves.), (212) 581-0930. Open Su-R 12pm-11pm, F-Sa 12pm-12am. MC,V, AmEx, **F** *to 57th St.*

Boulevard

A fun family restaurant with Sesame Street-style murals and all-you-can-eat specials on Monday nights. Screaming babies covered in mashed potatoes, platefuls of enormous dinosaur ribs, and the Maryland crabcakes are all part of the charm. You'll have to request the aptly named "Liquid Hell" barbecue sauce, which is kept hidden in back.
2398 Broadway (at 88th St.), (212) 874-7400. Open M-F 11:30pm-11pm, Sa-Su 11am-12am. MC, V, AmEx, Entrées: $7-$18, **1 2** *to 86th St.*

Bruculino

Sicilian seafood cooked to perfection is served in the soothing wood and wave interior of this West Side culinary treasure. Dishes are inventive and colorful. Outdoor seating is available on the terrace. Try the specials of the evening and leave room for coffee and dessert.
225 Columbus Ave. (at 70th St.), (212) 579-3966. Open M-Sa 11am-11pm, Su 11am-10pm. MC, V, AmEx, Entrées: $10-$20, **B C** *to 72nd St.*

Cafe Des Artistes

You'll feel glamorous at this classic New York restaurant. Don't get addicted to that feeling though, because visiting this romantic rendezvous too often will clean out your wallet as seductively as it filled you up.
1 W. 67th St. (bet. Columbus Ave. and Central Park West), (212) 877-3500, *www.cafedesartistes.com. Open M-F 12pm-2:30pm, 5:30pm-10:30pm, Sa 11am-2:30pm, 5:30pm-11pm, Su 10am-2:30pm, 5:30pm-10:30pm. MC, V, AmEx, DC, Entrées: $30-$40,* **1 2** *to 66th St.-Lincoln Center.*

Carmine's

Come with a group of friends and order up a storm of family-style

Italian. Seating is slow, so a visit to this enormous darkwood institution happily mandates a stop at the lovely bar.
2450 Broadway (bet. 90th and 91st Sts.), (212) 362-2200. Open Su-R 11:30am-11pm, F-Sa 11:30am-12am. MC, V, AmEx, D Entrées: $15-$25, ❶❷❸ to 96th St. &

Columbus Bakery

This family staple has consistently good pastries, pizzettes and other bakery-style food. With nice interiors and consistently packed brunches, Columbus is a great place to hang out on a lazy afternoon – if you can get a table. Beware the stroller wars at the door.
474 Columbus Ave. (bet. 82nd & 83rd Sts.), (212) 724-6880. Open M-Su 8am-10pm.

Deli Kasbah

Orthodox patrons fill the dining room, while takeout satisfies folks of all faiths with amazingly fresh meats and stellar entrées, like the jumbo pastrami burger. The menu has a Middle Eastern slant, with lots of hummus, babaganoush, and falafel. Sample all three of them in the Kasbah Combination.
251 W. 85th St. (bet. Broadway and West End Ave.), (212) 496-1500. Open Su-R 12pm-10pm. MC, V, D, Entrées: $8-$20, ❶❷ to 86th St.

Fine and Schapiro

One of the finest sitdown delis in Manhattan, F&S sparkles with homey friendliness. Diner-style meals are served up alongside a delightful brand of old-fashioned Jewish humor. The menu contains every kosher favorite from matzoh ball soup and stuffed cabbage to an array of gourmet sandwiches. The only drawback is the pervading guilt that you'll be sent to your room if you don't finish your food. (Kosher)
138 West 72nd Street (bet. Broadway and Columbus), (212) 877-2874. Open M-Su 10am-10pm. MC, V, AmEx, D, Entrees: $8-17, ❶❷❸ to 72nd St.

French Roast

This restaurant with a French twist is known for its burgers and being able to hang out for hours with just a coffee on your check. The service is laidback, but this isn't the Upper East Side. The outside tables are great for people-watching. The salads are nice, burgers and omelettes even better. A mellow French restaurant for a mellow West Side crowd.
2340 Broadway (85th St.), (212) 799-1533. Open 24 hours. MC, V. ❶❷ to 86th.

Gabriel's

Among the crème de la crème of the bevy of restaurants around Lincoln Center, the combination of casual and class here is just about perfect. Beautiful decor, an astonishing, seasonal menu (order the delectable butternut squash ravioli), and a refined yet informal staff all account for why this is one of New York's hottest spots for dinner. Come after 7:45 pm to avoid the preconcert crowd.
11 W. 60th St. (bet. Broadway and Columbus Ave.), (212) 956-4600. Open M-R 12pm-3pm, 5pm-11pm, F 12pm-3pm, 5pm-12am, Sa 5pm-12am. MC ,V, AmEx, D. Entrées: $25-$27, ❶❷ ❸❹❶❷ to 59th St.-Columbus Circle.

Gabriela's

One of the best homestyle Mexican restaurants in New York, Gabriela's is a family-friendly, low-key place, where the waiters won't make guacamole tableside but will cheerfully seat you at one of its many booths. Loud and colorful, Gabriela's is a mainstay of the Upper West Side.
685 Amsterdam Ave. (93rd St.), (212) 961-0574. Open M-Su 12pm-12am. MC, V, AmEx. 123 to 96th St.
311 Amsterdam Ave. (75th St.), (212) 875-8532. Open M-R 11am-11pm, F-Sa 11am-12am, Su 11am-10pm. MC, V, AmEx. ❶❷❸ to 72nd St.

Gennaro

Native Italian chef Gennaro Picone graced several upscale Manhattan establishments before opening his own place where he serves unpretentious, truly Italian (not Italian-American) dishes in a tiny, unassuming space. The decor may seem a little rough around the edges, but the food is most definitely not (try the gnocchi), and the prices are so reasonable that they impose a $20 minimum. But be warned, the waits are long and the space is cramped.
665 Amsterdam Ave. (bet. 92nd and 93rd Sts.), (212) 665-5348. Open Su-R 5pm-10:30pm, F-Sa 5pm-

*11pm. Cash Only, Entrées:
$8-$15, ❶❷❸ to 96th
St.*

Good Enough to Eat

The line to get into this popular brunch spot can often be seen from a few blocks away (no reservations accepted). Those who stick it out choose from ample portions of old-fashioned favorites and enjoy the warm, cozy atmosphere. "Just like Mom used to make" specialties include Cinnamon Swirl French Toast ($8.50) and Lumberjack breakfast ($8.00). Dinner is served nightly.
483 Amsterdam Ave. (bet. 83rd and 84th Sts.), (212) 496-0163. Open M-R 8am-4pm, 5:30pm-10:30pm, F 8am-4pm, 5:30pm-11pm, Sa 9am-4pm, 5:30pm-11pm, Su 9am-4pm, 5:30pm-10pm. MC, V, AmEx, Entrées: $18-$21, ❶ to 86th St. ❷ ❸ to 79th St.-Natural History Museum. &

Gray's Papaya

Gray's resembles its lowbrow cousin, Papaya King, offering lots of cheap hot dogs, papaya juice and other heartburn fare. A hit with bankers slumming it during lunch hour, to penniless students, to out-of-work types, Gray's is a New York institution. Don't expect Julia Child, but for $3 you too can fill up with comfort food.
*2090 Broadway (72nd St.), (212) 799-0243.
402 Sixth Ave. (8th St.), (212) 260-3532.
535 Eighth Ave. (37th St.), (212) 904-1588.*

Jean Georges

Undoubtedly one of the best in New York. The food's like a narcotic in your blood stream meaning you don't realize how good the food is until later when no other food compares. Sublime is the word. Be warned: despite the three dining areas, it is still hard to get in. Trump International Hotel, 1 Central Park West (bet. 60th and 61st Sts.), (212) 299-3900, *www.jean-georges.com. Open Su-W 7am-11am, 12pm-3pm, 5:30pm-10pm, R-Sa 7am-11am, 12pm-3pm, 5:30pm-11pm. MC, V, AmEx, DC, Entrées: $24-$32, ❹❺ ❻❼ to 59th St.-Columbus Circle.* &

La Caridad

This Dominican chain isn't known for its healthy fare, but is for its greasy food, large portions and authentic service. Try the chicken and rice and beans. Try out your Spanish.
2197-2199 Broadway (78th St.), (212) 874-2780. Open M-Sa 11am-12am, Su 11am-10:30pm. Cash and Checks only. ❶ ❷ to 79th St.

Le Monde

Le Monde is a Columbia fave, serving some of the best coffee in the area. The food gets mixed reviews, but if you stick to the basics like burgers and omelettes, you can't go wrong. You may have to be aggressive to get good service here.
2885 Broadway (bet. 112th & 113th Sts.), (212) 531-3939. Open M-R 11:30am-12:30am, F 11:30am-1:30am, Sa 10:30am-1:30am, Su 10:30am-12:30am. MC, V, AmEx, Entrees: $15-25, ❶❷ to 116th St.

Lemongrass Grill

Lemongrass is a consistent Thai restaurant that is heavy on the lemongrass and light on the ambience. There isn't much to complain about, particularly the prices. A good take-out option, too.
*2534 Broadway (bet. 94th & 95th Sts.), (212) 666-0888.
80 University Pl. (11th St.), (212) 604-9870.
37 Barrow St. (7th Ave. S.), (212) 242-0606.
61A Seventh Ave. (bet. Berkeley & Lincoln Pls.), Brooklyn, (718) 399-7100.
110 Liberty St. (Church St.), (212) 962-1370.
53 Ave. A (4th St.), (212) 674-3538.
138 E. 34th St. (bet. Lexington & 3rd Aves.), (212) 213-3317.*

Le Pain Quotidien

Le Pain may have the only communal seating arrangement in Manhattan, which can get crowded, especially near the Metropolitan Museum of Art. A long butcher block table filled with butters, jams and breads can be fun, but only if you're in a good mood. The food is consistently good, nice salads and hot food too.
50 W. 72nd St. (bet. Central Park W. & Columbus Ave.), (212) 712-9700. M-F 7:30am-7pm, Sa-Su 8am-7pm. MC, V, AmEx, DC, ❶❷ ❸ to 72nd St.

Niko's Mediterranean Grill and Bistro

Nearly always crammed to capacity, this tavern offers a range of delicacies that take cues from all over the Mediterranean, particularly Greece and Lebanon. Noteworthy are the stuffed grape leaves and the rodos yuvetsi, a lamb stew. Afterwards, choose from among the array of authentic honey-drenched desserts.
2161 Broadway (at 76th St.), (212) 873-7000, www.nikosgrill.com. Open Su-R 9am-11:30pm, F-Sa 9am-12:30am. MC, V, AmEx, D, Entrées: $10-$18, ❶❷❸ to 72nd St. &

Ollie's

Ollie's is a substandard Chinese restaurant located in suprastandard locations: next to Columbia University and Lincoln Center, for instance. There are rumors of health code violations, and consistent complaints about bad service. But it looks good, and the food comes fast.
*200B W. 44th St. (bet. B'way & 8th Ave.), (212) 921-5988.
1991 Broadway (bet. 67th & 68th Sts.), (212) 595-8181.
2315 Broadway (84th St.), (212) 362-3712.
2957 Broadway (116th St.), (212) 932-3300.*

Ozu

Though prompt seating can be a problem, this small, Japanese macrobiotic, near-organic restaurant wins points for its creative tofu, grain, noodle, tempura and vegetable dishes. The ambitious side orders will transport you to new levels of sensual awareness, especially the three-root sesame salad with carrot, burdock root, and daikon radish.

566 Amsterdam Ave. (at 87th St.), (212) 787-8316. Open M-Su 11:30am-10pm. MC, V, Entrées: $7-$12, ❶ ❷ to 86th St.

Penang Malaysia

This lively, decked out Malaysian is usually packed on weekends and rightfully so. The food is innovative and tasty, the crowd generally young and hip, and there's live music and a lounge in the bar downstairs. Try eating down there to avoid the wait upstairs.   The Chinatown location is cheaper.
240 Columbus Ave. (at 71st St.), (212) 769-3988, www.penang nyc.com. Open M-R 12pm-12am, F-Sa 12am-1am, Su 12pm-11pm. MC, V, AmEx, DC, Entrées: $11-$20, ❸ ❸ to 72nd St.

Pizzeria Uno Chicago

This chain isn't authentic and will certainly blow your diet. The deep dish pizza crust is buttery for a reason, and the ambience pure fast food. But for a good time in a relaxed atmosphere, it can't be beat.
*220 E. 86th St. (bet. 2nd & 3rd Aves.), (212) 472-5656.
432 Columbus Ave. (81st St.), (212) 595-4700.
55 Third Ave. (bet. 10th & 11th Sts.), (212) 995-9668.
391 Sixth Ave. (bet. 8th St. & Waverly Pl.), (212) 242-5230.
89 South St. (Pier 17), (212) 791-7999.
39-02 Bell Blvd. (39th Ave.), Queens, (718) 279-4900.
107-16 70th Rd. (bet.*

*Austin St. & Queens Blvd.), Queens, (718) 793-6700.
9201 Fourth Ave. (92nd St.), Brooklyn, (718) 748-8667.*

Popover Cafe

New England charm meets New York savvy at this convivial spot, one of the most popular brunch venues in the neighborhood. Feast upon gourmet omelets and excellent griddle specialties — and don't forget the popovers.
551 Amsterdam Ave. (at 87th Sts.), (212) 595-8555. Open M-F 8am-10pm, Sa-Su 9am-10pm. MC, V, AmEx, Entrées: $13-$22, ❶ ❷ to 86th St. ♿

Rain

Delicious pan-Asian fusion cuisine and a vibrant, attractive crowd make this one of the Upper West Side's hottest dining spots. On Friday and Saturday nights, the bar overflows with 20-somethings trying to get a table, but the Asian canopy and exotic beers make it worth the wait.
100 W. 82nd St. (at Columbus Ave.), (212) 501-0776. Open M-R 12pm-3pm, 6-11pm, F 12pm-3pm, 6pm-12am, Sa 12pm-4pm, 5pm-12am, Su 12pm-4pm, 5pm-10pm. MC, V, AmEx, D, Entrees $12-22, ❶ ❷ to 79th St. ♿

Rikyu

The freedom to choose can be mind-boggling for early-bird diners taking advantage of the $9.95 prix fixe, with 17 dinner options. You can't go wrong with remarkably fresh sushi or any combination involving tempura, teriyaki or cooked fish.

483 Columbus Ave. (bet. 83rd and 84th Sts.), (212) 799-7847. Open M-Su 12pm-11pm. MC, V, AmEx, D, Entrées: $10-$17, ❶ ❷ ❸ to 72nd St. ♿

Ruby Foo's

Fun, cool, hip pan-Asian with everything from dim sum to sushi and a popular Sunday brunch.
2182 Broadway (at 77th St.), (212) 724-6700. Open Su-W 11:30am-11:30pm, R-Sa 11:30am-12:30am, MC, V, AmEx, Entrées: $25, ❶ ❷ to 79th St. ♿

Saigon Grill

One of the tastiest and best-priced Vietnamese restaurants in the city and a favorite of Upper West Siders. Not much elbow room, so go early to avoid the crowds. You'll be craving the fresh summer rolls for days afterward.
2381 Broadway (at 87th St.), (212) 875-9072. Open M-Su 11am-12am. MC, V, AmEx, D, Entrées: $7-$13, ❶ ❷ to 86th St.

Sarabeth's

This cheerful, yellow cafe is brimming with old-fashioned goodness. Sarabeth's serves hearty breakfasts and light, sophisticated lunches, but for a special treat, drop in for afternoon tea between 3:30 and 5:30. You'll feel like the Queen of England as you sip tea and nibble on finger sandwiches, cookies and scones.
423 Amsterdam (bet. 80th and 81st Sts.), (212) 496-6280. Open M-Su 8am-10:30pm. MC, V, AmEx, ❶ ❷ to 79th St. ♿

Time Cafe

Around mealtimes there are rarely many free tables in this vast, lofty space, and it's no wonder, since this is one of the better places filling the niche between greasy coffee shop and fancy restaurant. Health-conscious organic food and an extensive menu with selections like fancy tuna sandwiches and pan roasted penne are sure to satisfy nearly any craving.
2330 Broadway (at 85th St.), (212) 579-5100. Open Su-R 10am-12am, F-Sa 10am-1am. MC, V, AmEx, Entrées: $12-$22, ❶ ❷ to 86th St. ♿

Under the Stairs

This bar/restaurant has been around for as long as anyone in the neighborhood can remember, and they still pack them in for happy hour. Come for the lively crowd, the loud jazz on weekends, and Wednesday's bargain shrimp night.
688 Columbus Ave. (bet. 93rd and 94th Sts.), (212) 663-3103. Open Su-W 11am-12am, R-Sa 11am-2am. MC, V, AmEx, Entrées: $10-$25, ❸ ❸ to 96th St. ♿

CAFES

Café Con Leche

Cramped or cozy, depending on how tolerant you are of the neighboring conversation, this Cuban café pulses with upbeat salsa music and chatter. Standard dishes are perfectly prepared, from empañadas to "filet de pollo al limon." This café has bright, fun décor and serves up its dishes with visual flair. The portions aren't typical Latin gar-

gantuan, and neither are the prices. Leche is a good deal, but you won't be stuffed when you leave. You can, however, linger over your café con leche or dinner for hours without the staff harassing you.
424 Amsterdam Ave. (bet. 80th and 81st Sts.), (212) 595-7000, www.cafecon-leche.com. Open Su-W 8am-11pm, R-Sa 8am-12am. MC, V, AmEx, 1 2 to 79th St. X
726 Amsterdam Ave. (bet. 95th and 96th Sts.), (212) 678-7000, www.cafecon-leche.com. Open M-R 11am-12am, F 12pm-12am, Sa 10am-12am, Su 11am-11pm. MC, V, AmEx, ❶❷❸ to 96th St. ♿

Cafe Lalo

This bright and lively European café serves night owls until 2am Sunday through Thursday, and until 4am on weekends. Come for the vast menu of decadent drinks and desserts; Sunday brunch available.
201 W. 83rd St. (bet. Broadway and Amsterdam Ave.), (212) 496-6031, www.cafe lalo.com. Open M-R 8am-2am, F 8am-4am, Sa 9am-4am, Su 9am-2am. Cash Only, ❶❷ to 86th St.

Cafe Mozart

A slice of Europe on the Upper West Side, perfect after a show or for late morning paper perusal.

154 W. 70th St. (at Broadway), (212) 595-9797. Open Su-R 8am-1am, F-Sa 8am-2am. MC, V, AmEx, ❶❷❸ to 72nd St.

Drip

This coffee bar also has its liquor license so you can speed on caffeine, then come down with a micro-brewed beer. Singles can leaf through binders chock full of bios while sipping lattes and nibbling on oversized Rice Krispies treats. Atmosphere is casual, friendly, and relaxed unless, of course, you do find a match!
489 Amsterdam Ave. (bet. 83rd and 84th Sts.), (212) 875-1032, www.dripcafe.com. Open M-R 8am-1am, F 8am-2am, Sa 9am-3am, Su 9am-1am. MC, V, ❶❷ to 86th St. ♿

H&H Bagel

To certain New Yorkers, these bagels are good

enough to qualify as a delicacy. The poppy and everything varieties go quickly, but the basic plain sourdough is something special, too. Call 1-800-NY-BAGEL to have mail orders delivered anywhere in the world. Not cheap, either.
2239 Broadway (at 80th St.), (212) 595-8003, www. hhbagel.com. Open M-Su 24hrs. Cash Only, ❶❷ to 79th St. ♿

RESTAURANTS

107 West

This restaurant's eclectic menu and décor waffle between southwestern, Italian and New York chic themes, but the food is consistently good (especially the rigatoni with chicken and capers). A cozy interior and glassed-in porch provide the classy atmosphere for a perfect date, without incurring the debilitating costs often associated with fine dining.
2787 Broadway (at 107th St.), (212) 864-1555, Open M-R 5pm-11pm, F 5pm-12pm, Sa 11am-12pm, Su 11am-10:30pm, MC, V, Amex, D, Entrees $8-18, ❶ to 110th St.

Alouette

This intimate bi-level French bistro serves up savory and inventive cuisine in a rich, warm atmosphere — an

anomaly for the Upper West Side. Wearing red velvet drapery and lace-curtained windows, Alouette is a romantic option in West Side dining. The prices are great in exchange for this culinary and atmospheric decadence.
2588 Broadway (bet. 97th and 98th Sts.), (212) 222-6808, www.alouettenyc.com, Open M-Sa 5:30pm-11pm, Su 5:30pm-10pm, MC, V, AmEx, DC, Entrées: $16-$22, ❶❷❸ to 96th St. ♿

Amsterdam Café

Friendly neighborhood feel with a good menu of classic bar items and pastas. Their weekend brunch for $4.95 is the best deal in the area.
1207 Amsterdam Ave. (bet. 119th and 120th Sts.), (212) 662-6330, Open M-F 10am-4am, Sa-Su 9am-4am. MC, V, AmEx, DC, D, Entrées: $7-$10, ❶ to 116th St.-Columbia University. ♿

Awash

Ethiopian restaurants aren't exactly ubiquitous, so it's a thrill just to find one, especially one as decent as Awash. Order any of the numerous meat or vegetable dishes and learn to eat Ethiopian-style, using a piece of injera (a thin teff pancake) to pick up your food. If you're brave try the kitfo, a delicious mix of raw ground beef and exotic spices.
947 Amsterdam Ave. (bet. 106th and 107th Sts.), (212) 961-1416, Open M-R 1pm-12am, F-Su 12pm-12am, MC, V, AmEx,

Entrées: $7-$13, ❶ ❷ *to 103rd St.* ♿

Caffé Pertutti

Bright and breezy, with a hard-tiled floor and marble-topped tables, this neighborhood café hosts intellectual tête-à-têtes while serving up Italian standards which hardly merit their above-average prices. The salads, however, are enormous and tasty, and the desserts usually taste as good as they look.
2888 Broadway (bet. 112th and 113th Sts.), (212) 864-1143, Open M-Th 10am-1am, F-Sa 10am-2am, Su 11am-12am, Cash Only, Entrées: $7-$12, ❶ ❷ *to 110th St.* ♿

Caffé Taci

Crowds of Columbia students eat adequately prepared Italian basics in the mock-ruin interior of this popular, dimly-lit eatery. Manhattan School of Music students sing live opera on Wednesday, Friday and Saturday nights; due to slow service, diners can theoretically hear one in its entirety.
2841 Broadway (at 110th St.), (212) 678-5345, Open Su-R 10am-1230am, F-Sa 10am-1am, Cash Only, Entrées: $5-$14, ❶ ❷ *110th St.* ♿

Camille's

Named after the owner's mother, this cozy Columbia magnet is reliably good. Pizzas are a bargain at $4.25, and the hearty pasta dishes are topped with light and flavorful sauces. It's difficult to eat this well for less money; breakfast is a particularly cheap alternative to bacon 'n egg grease-balls at area diners.
1135 Amsterdam Ave. (at 116th St.), (212) 749-2428, Open M-F 7:30am-8pm, Sa 8:30am-5pm, MC, V, AmEx, Entrées: $3-$9, ❶ *to 116th St.-Columbia University*

Famous Famiglia's

Come for the photos of celebrities on the wall, the jocular service, and the delicious and greasy pizza. The 'hood's finest garlic twists and the pizza's garlicky tomato sauce will keep the vampires away.
2859 Broadway (at 111th St.), (212) 865-1234, www.famousfamiglia.com, Open M-Su 10am-2am, MC, V, AmEx, D, Entrées: $14.50, 1 to 110th St. ♿

Jerusalem Restaurant

Step off the grungy street and into Jerusalem's Arab quarter in this small Middle Eastern hot spot. Amidst the cook's frantic Arabic exclamations and the sultry music you'll find some of Manhattan's best shawarma and falafel - the perfect spot for a sumptuous late night meal or a snack on the run.
2715 Broadway (bet. 103rd and 104th Sts.), (212) 865-2295, Open M-Su 10am-4am. Cash only, Entrees $3-9, ❶ ❷ *to 103rd St.* ♿

Mama Mexico

The food isn't out of this world, but evenings it's packed, with a giant mariachi band blaring boleros to hungry diners. Ask for a tequila shot, and you'll think an alarm went off in the back of the restaurant. Service suddenly picks up, and, a couple of shots later, the owner's pouring booze down your throat. Expect long waits.
2672 Broadway (bet. 101st and 102nd Sts.), (212) 864-2323, Open Su-R 12pm-12am, F-Sa 12pm-2am, MC, V, AmEx, Entrees: $10-20, ❶ ❷ *to 110th St.* ♿

Metisse

Ooh la la! With this rich, delicious, reasonably priced food, you might blink and think you've found Paris in New York.
239 W. 105th St. (bet. Broadway), (212) 666-8825, Open Su-R 5:30pm-10:30pm, F-Sa 5:30pm-11pm, MC, V, D, Entrées: $12.50-$18.50, ❶ ❷ *to 103rd St.* ♿

Metro Diner

Unique to the world of diners, this veggie-friendly establishment offers all the standard diner fare — only fresh! — with a splash of Mediterranean dishes including a variety of salads and vegetarian plates. Grab a booth and soak in its streamlined train car decor. A great post-movie hangout.
2641 Broadway (at 100th St.), (212) 866-0800, Open M-Su 6am-1am. MC, V, AmEx, Entrées: $10-$14, ❶ ❷ ❸ *to 96th St.* ♿

Miss Mammie's Spoonbread Too

How do you want your soul food: barbecued, blackened, deep-fried, smothered in sauce? It's all here. Save room for some banana bread pudding, coconut pineapple cake or sweet potato pie. The laid-back staff, who take just long enough to make you appreciate your meal, will be more than happy to serve you any of the above. Some dishes greasy, most great.
366 W. 110th (bet. Columbus and Manhattan Aves.), (212) 865-6744, Open M-Sa 12am-10:30pm, Su 11am-9pm, MC, V, AmEx, Entrees: $10-17, ❷ ❸ *to 110th St.*

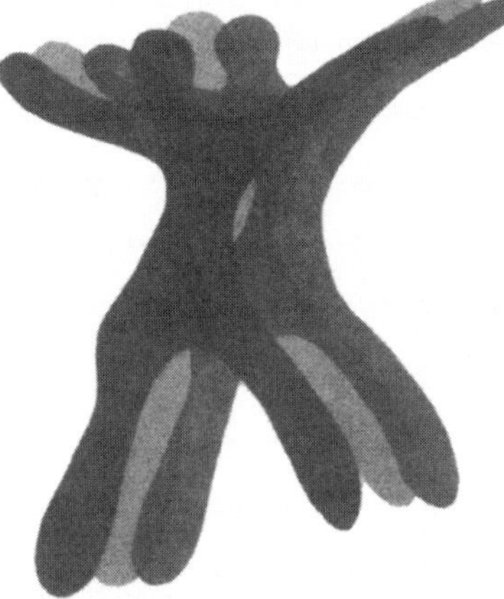

The Heights

This slick restaurant-bar now has a rooftop garden which is heated in the cooler months. Potent margaritas, fresh salsa with tricolored chips, and an eager waitstaff make this a favorite among Columbia students. Start early by slurping $2.50 margaritas during happy hour between 5pm-7pm and 12am-1am.
2867 Broadway (at 111th St.), (212) 866-7035, Open M-F 11:30am-4am, Sa-Su 11am-4am, MC, V, AmEx, D, Entrées: $8-$15, ❶❷ *110th St.*

La Rosita

For years, New Yorkers have claimed that this place serves the best cup of coffee. The service is well-paced (read "slow") so that food usually arrives as you're about to crack, but devouring your meal is always worth the wait. Probably the most authentic cooking and definitely the best Latin food in the neighborhood. *2809 Broadway (bet. 108th and 109th Sts.), (212) 663-7804, Open M-Su 7am-12am. MC, V, AmEx, D, Entrees: $3-15,* ❶❷ *to 110th St.* ♿

Saji's Kitchen

This hole-in-the-wall is one of Morningside Heights' hidden gems. Behind a tiny counter that blares rock music lies uptown's best Japanese food at amazingly low prices. This is mainly a take-out/delivery place, but the food is so good that going anywhere else seems like a waste. *256 W. 109th St. (at Broadway), (212) 749-1834, Open M-F 11:30am-10:30pm, Sa-Su 12pm-10:30pm, Cash only, Entrees: $2-11,* ❶ ❷ *to 110th St.* ♿

Sophia's Bistro

Downtown style has been creeping into the local neighborhood during the last year. This little bistro leads the onslaught, offering hip, romantic dining. Pale yellow and red brick, flickering candlelight, and wine-colored drapery create a laid-back atmosphere. *998 Amsterdam Ave. (bet. 108th and 109th Sts.), (212) 662-8822, Open M-F 4pm-12am, Sa-Su 4pm-2am, MC, V, AmEx, Entreés: $6-$10,* ❶❷ *to 110th St.* ♿

Terrace

The exquisite view of upper Manhattan from this upscale dining room may finally convince your parents that living next to Harlem isn't so bad, or it may impress your date by revealing your uncanny ability to find romance in the most unexpected places. After trying the house risotto or grilled salmon, visit the rooftop garden. The open air and a much-needed cocktail will help you recuperate from the bill. *400 W. 119th St. (bet. Amsterdam Ave. and Morningside Dr.), (212) 666-9490, Open T-R 12pm-2:30pm, 6pm-10pm, F 12pm-2:30pm, 6pm-11pm, Sa 6pm-11pm, MC, V, AmEx, DC, D, Entrées: $25-$38,* ❶ ❷ *to 116th St.-Columbia University.* ♿

Tomo

Enjoy good sushi and Japanese fare in this upbeat Morningside

Heights eatery. The place tends to fill up quickly and the tables are packed close together, but the prices are reasonable, though not cheap. *2850 Broadway (bet. 110th and 111th Sts.), (212) 665-2916, Open M-Sa 12 pm-11:30pm, Su 12pm-11pm. MC, V, AmEx, Entrees: ($6-$14),* ❶ ❷ *to 110th St.* &

Tom's Restaurant

Once you push through the occasional crowd from a Kramer's Reality tour (the southern façade serves as a cutaway shot in Seinfeld), you'll be surprised to see what the fuss is all about. Though recent renovations have jacked the prices up a bit be sure to find huge platters, late hours, and thick "Broadway" shakes that keep kids coming back to this greasy spoon. *2880 Broadway (at 112th St.), (212) 864-6137, Open Su-W 6am-1:30am, R-Sa 24hrs. Cash Only, Entrées: $3-$10,* ❶ ❷ *to 110th St.* &

Turkuaz

With the restaurant's artistically draped fabric ceiling that evokes a breezy Ottoman tent and the waiters' red satin balloon pants, you might think you've stepped into a tale from the Arabian nights. Enjoy the traditional dishes and desserts at this Upper West Side Turkish delight, which offers both Turkish and Western style food. Almond pudding is especially good. Forget the drinks. *2637 Broadway (at 100th St.), (212) 665-9541, Open Su-Th 11am-11pm, F-Sa 11am-12am, MC, V, AmEx, D, Entrees: $10-15,* ❶ ❷ *to 103rd. St.*

CAFES

Hamilton Deli

The true New York experience awaits at this popular deli. Hefty heroes with names like "The Lewinsky" are served up dripping with onions and mustard by a whirlwind staff of no-nonsense locals. Grab a drink or candy bar from the convenience store in the back and you're ready to go. The coffee runs a bit weak, however. *1129 Amsterdam Ave. (at 116th St.), (212) 749-8924, Open M-F 6am-12am, Sa-Su 7am-9pm, Cash only,* ❶ ❷ *to 116th St.*

The Hungarian Pastry Shop

The cafe's enduring reputation as Columbia University's intellectual hangout par excellence has suffered somewhat since the citywide smoking ban. Still the place of choice, however, to ostentatiously discuss Fellini or Godard, or write that dissertation on the hermeneutics of the Marquis de Sade while sipping chamomile tea and nibbling on a linzer torte. *1030 Amsterdam Ave. (bet. 110th and 111th Sts.), (212) 866-4230, Open M-F 7:30am-11:30pm, Sa 8:30am-11:30pm, Su 8:30am-10:30pm, Cash Only,* ❶ ❷ *to 110th St.*

Nussbaum & Wu

Not your ordinary coffee stop — a Chinese pastry shop and deli collided to form this one. Well-lit with a great wrap-around counter, you just may decide to stay a while. Fresh sandwiches and yummy pastries, both Asian and non, are available here, not to mention bagels and, of course, coffee too. *2897 Broadway (at 113th St.), (212) 280-5344. Open M-Sa 6am-12am, Su 6am-11pm, MC, V, AmEx,* ❶ ❷ *to 110th St.*

Harlem

RESTAURANTS

Amy Ruth's

Menu offerings like the Rev. Al Sharpton Chicken and Waffle special give new meaning to the concept of soul food. The traditional southern food is nothing to write home about, but hearty portions ensure you won't leave hungry. *113 W. 116th St. (bet. Seventh & Lennox Aves.), (212) 280-8779, Open M-Su 7:30am-11 pm, MC, V, AmEx, Entrees: $9-18,* ❷ ❸ *to 116th St.* &

Café Largo

This intimate, dimly lit restaurant has a trendy feel to it, but the crowd remains diverse. Ask for the orange glazed steak, a worthwhile special that doesn't appear on the menu. *3387 Broadway (bet. 137th and 138th Sts.), (212) 862-8142, Open M 5pm-12am, T-F 12pm-12am, Sa-Su 11am-12am, MC, V, AmEx, Entrees: $10-24,* ❶ *to 137th St.*

Copeland's

A rich and varied menu offers everything from braised oxtails and gumbo to grain-fed catfish and shrimp Creole. The atmosphere is for serious eating; Sunday's gospel brunch is among the neighborhood's finest. *547 W. 145th St. (bet. Broadway and Amsterdam Ave.), (212) 234-2357, Open Su-R 8am-11pm, F-Sa 8am-12am, MC, V, AmEx, D, Entrées: $9-$25,* ❶ *to 145th St.* &

Jimbo's Coffee Shop

This tiny greasy spoon is always crowded and confused with people clamoring for the phenomenal, $3 bacon cheeseburger. *1345 Amsterdam Ave. (bet. Hancock and 127th Sts.), (212) 865-8777, Open M-Su 6am-10pm, Cash only, Entrees: $3-5,* ❶ *to 125th.*

Londel's

Owner Londel Davis greets customers at the door of his sophisticated new Strivers Row supperclub, a harbinger of gentrification in this quickly changing neighborhood. Harlem's hottest restaurant serves delicious, painstakingly prepared Southern food like smothered pork chops and pan-seared red snapper to the neighborhood's most upwardly mobile. *2620 Frederick Douglass Blvd. (bet. 139th and 140th Sts.), (212) 234-6114, Open T-Sa 11:30am-12am, Su 9am-5pm, MC, V, AmEx, D, Entrées: $9-$20,* ❶ ❷ ❸ *to 135th St.)* &

Miss Maude's

Newly opened by the owners of Miss Mammie's on 110th, Miss Maude's is bigger and better. You can't find better soul food for a lower price. Summers, it's a great place to sip lemonade and get fat; winters, it's a great place to sip something warmer and stay fat.
547 Lenox Ave. (bet. 137th and 138th Sts.), (212) 690-3100, Open M-Sa 11:30pm-10pm, Su 11am-10pm, MC, V, AmEx, Entrees: $10-17, ❷❸ *to 135th St.* &

Perk's Fine Cuisine

"Every third person's a gangsta and the other two are buppies," said one Harlemite about this Harlem hangout. Savor succulent baby back ribs while vocalist Robert Fox serenades the ladies with his super-slick renditions of "Me and Mrs. Jones" and other R&B standards. Terrific bar menu; gracious waitstaff in the plush, expensive dining room downstairs.
553 Manhattan Ave. (at 123rd St.), (212) 666-8500, Open M-Sa 4pm-4am, MC, V, D, Entrées: $13-$22, ❶❷❸❹ *to 125th St.* &

Slice of Harlem

Darn, they're good, and they know it. Hailed as some of the best pizza in New York, Slice has innovative combinations, lots of toppings and prices a notch above Domino's. Try the veggie pizza, even broccoli-haters will love it.
308 Lenox Ave. (bet. 125th & 126th Sts.), (212) 426-7400, Open M-R 9-10, F-Sa 9-11, Su 12-10, MC, V, AmEx, ❷❸ *to*

125th St.

Sylvia's

Although the most venerable soul food restaurant in New York, Sylvia's succeeds on more than reputation. The crispy and flavorful fried chicken is good, but some of the sides could use reviving. Come Sunday for the after-church gospel brunch. And don't forget to leave space for sweet potato pie.
328 Lenox Ave. (bet. 126th and 127th Sts.), (212) 996-0660, Open M-Sa 11am-10:30pm, Sa 8am-10:30pm, Su 11am-8pm, MC, V, AmEx, D, Entrees: $9-$18, ❷❸ *to 125th St.*

CAFES

Krispy Kreme

A southern import, these donuts melt in your mouth so fast and taste so good that it's impossible to eat fewer than three.
280 W. 125th St (on Eighth Ave.), (212) 531-0111, www.krispykreme.com. Open M-Su 6am-10pm, MC, V, AmEx, ❶❷❸❹ *to 125th St.*

Washington Heights

RESTAURANTS

Bleu Evolution

The food and setting will justify the trek uptown. There's a lovely garden to eat in and a lounge that stays open long after the kitchen closes. Despite its out-of-the-way location, this place is undeniably hip. Some say it's the best part of the neighborhood.
808 W. 187th St. (at Fort Washington Ave.), (212) 928-6006, Open M-Su 11am-3pm, 5pm-11pm, MC, V, AmEx, D, Entrees: $12-$15, ❶ *to 191th St.* &

Coogan's Restaurant

Latinos and Irish congregate at this upscale pub to partake of classics such as shell steak, shrimp scampi, French onion soup and roast beef au jus. Karaoke nights on Tuesdays and Thursdays enhance the eclecticism of this popular local hangout, just down the street from the Columbia Presbyterian Medical Center.
4015 Broadway (at 168th St.), (212) 928-1234, www.coogans.com, Open M-Su 11am-12am. MC, V, AmEx, DC, Entrées: $9-$17, Ⓐ Ⓒ❶ *to 168th St.-Washington Heights.* &

Bronx

RESTAURANTS

Bellavista

Riverdale has a bunch of good restaurants, but most residents enjoy this one. It's got a warm environment with a menu of your basic basic Italian fare--pizza and pasta. The sort of basic Italian fare that never did anybody wrong.
554 W. 235th St. (bet. Oxford and Johnson

Aves.), Riverdale, (718) 548-2354, Open M 5pm-10pm, T-Su 12pm-10pm. MC, V, AmEx, DC, D, Entrees: $12-$24, ❶ to 231st St. ♿

Dominick's

There's a reason for the Sunday evening wait, this grandfather of Bronx restaurants is the blueprint for all of the Bronx's other Italian restaurants. There's no menu, just be patient while the waiter tells you exactly what it is you need.
2335 Arthur Ave. (at 187th St.), East Tremont, (718) 733-2807, Open M, W, Th, Sa, 12pm-10pm F 12pm-11pm, Su 1pm-9pm, Cash only, Entrees: $15-$30, ❷ ❹ to 182nd-183rd Sts. ♿

Il Boschetto

The place to see huge portions of food on big ass plates. Bring the beano and an appetite. Bring a bunch of friends too. Forget the conversation, just concentrate on the large portion of food in front of you and proceed to hurt yourself.
1660 E. Gun Hill Rd. (at Tiemann Ave.), Baychester, (718) 379-9335, Open T-Su 12pm-10pm, MC, V, AmEx, DC, D, Entrees: $25-$35, ❺ to Gun Hill Rd. ♿

Jimmy's Bronx Café

After just four years in the Bronx, this "Latin Restaurant and Entertainment Complex" has become the nucleus for nightlife in the borough's Latino community. Upstairs, seafood is served into the wee hours as patrons watch boxing and baseball on the large TVs. Downstairs, the dance floor resembles a hotel ballroom, built for high capacity. As at other Latin clubs, there's no such thing as overdressing, though casual seems prevalent. Salsa dancing on Tuesday nights.
281 W. Fordham Rd. (at Major Deegan Expressway), Fordham, (718) 329-2000, www.jimmysbronxcafe.com, Open Su-R 10am-2am, F-Sa 10am-4:30am, MC, V, AmEx, Entrées: $8-$18, ❶ to 207th St. ♿

Le Refuge Inn

You'll be tempted to stay the night at this bed and breakfast. Whoever thought the words, "I think I'd like to live in the Bronx" would cross your mind. Well they will when you sit down to the delicious French food and great service, staring the whole time at the stairs leading to the rooms above.
620 City Island Ave. (at Sutherland St.), City Island, (718) 885-2478, Open W-Sa 6pm-10pm, Su 10-12, AmEx, Entrées: $45-$55, ❻ to Pelham Bay Park. ♿

Lobster Box

Though not what it used to be, the Lobster Box still provides the amazing view of the water it's always boasted. The lobster's great, the fish mediocre. What it

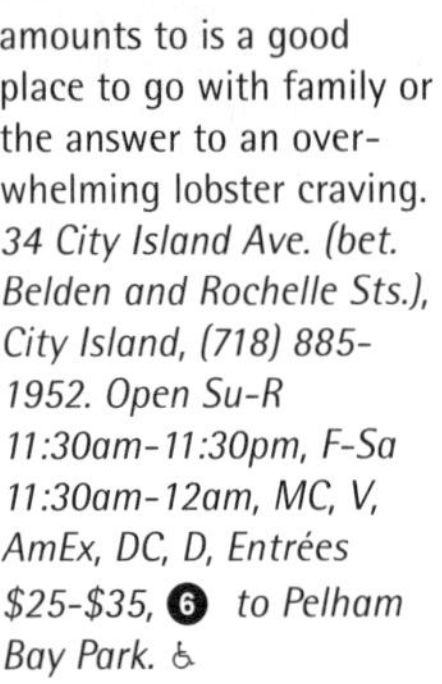

amounts to is a good place to go with family or the answer to an overwhelming lobster craving.
34 City Island Ave. (bet. Belden and Rochelle Sts.), City Island, (718) 885-1952. Open Su-R 11:30am-11:30pm, F-Sa 11:30am-12am, MC, V, AmEx, DC, D, Entrées $25-$35, ❻ to Pelham Bay Park. ♿

Mario's

After visiting the Botanical Gardens a lot of people amble over to this Arthur Avenue institution that's been around since 1919. A near oppressive amount of tourists mingles with locals, but it's worth the pasta.
2342 Arthur Ave. (bet. 184th and 186th Sts.), East Tremont, (718) 584-1188, Open Su, T-R 12pm-10pm, F-Sa 12pm-11:30pm, MC, V, AmEx, DC, Entrées: $16-$25, ❷ to Pelham Pkwy

Queens

RESTAURANTS

Annam Brahma Restaurant

The eclectic menu's only unifying thread is that everything is prepared sans meat, meaning everything from Indian ratia to tofu omelets to chapatti roll-ups may grace your table. Thursdays the cooks rally around pasta for Italian day; Tuesdays put Chinese vegetarian mainstays center stage. Check out the books, tapes, and other items for sale in the back of the restaurant.
84-43 164th St. (at Eighty Fifth Ave.), Jamaica, (718) 523-2600, Open M-T, R-Sa 11am-10pm, W 11am-4pm, Su 12pm-10pm, Cash Only, Entrées: $4-$8, F to Parsons Blvd. ♿

Carmichael's

Wizened locals fill up on soul food after Sunday's sermon at this slightly derelict, though cozy, neighborhood favorite. The fried chicken is amazing.
117-08 Guy R. Brewer Blvd. (at One Hundred Eighteenth Ave.), Jamaica, (718) 723-6908, Open M-Su 6am-8:30pm, Cash Only, Entrées: $6-$10, ❺ to Jamaica Center-Parsons/Archer.

Dante Restaurant

Mature crowds of businessmen and nearby St. John's University profes-

sors and athletes visit this dimly lit Italian bistro and bar. After hours it's a good place for big hair and big fun.
168-12 Union Turnpike (bet 168th & 169th Sts.), Flushing, (718) 380-3340, Open T-F 12pm-10pm, Sa 2pm-10pm, Su 1pm-9pm, MC, V, AmEx, D, Entrées: $9.95-$19.95, ❷❻ to Union Turnpike-Kew Gardens. ♿

Manducatis

Wine buffs and locals alike frequent Manducatis, a friendly family-run restaurant with fresh ingredients and a vast wine cellar reflecting serious dedication to Italian imports. Fireplaces and lavender tablecloths dress up the exposed brick walls. The menu standards astound, particularly the homemade pasta, but if nothing appeals, you can create your own dish.
13-27 Jackson Ave. (at Forty Seventh Ave.), (718) 729-4602, Open M-F 12pm-3pm, 5pm-10pm, Sa 5pm-10:30pm, Su 2:30pm-7:30pm. MC, V, AmEx, DC, D, Entrees: $8-$19, ❼ to 21st St. (Van Alst), ❼ to Vernon Blvd.-Jackson Ave. ♿

El Sitio de Astoria

Set the mood for truck-stop romance with your table's jukebox, although deals like the bandejas completas — a massive serving of meat, rice, beans, plantains, and croquettes —aren't among the wisest first-date choices. Getting a little tipsy on the sangria should take care of this.
35-55 31st St., Long Island City, (718) 278-7694, Open Su-R 8:30am-11pm, MC, V, AmEx, Entrées: $7-$13, ❷❼ to Thirty Sixth Ave. (Washington Ave).

Elias Corner

You'll have to read the reviews on the wall or point at fish in the glass case — there are no menus — but either way Elias Corner will stuff you silly. Across the street from its old location, this seafood pleasure house features rough charm and primitive décor, but no matter: Delicious red snapper, octopus, and squid, along with bottles of cheap but effective wine make this completely worth the trip to Astoria.
24-02 31st St. (at Twenty Fourth Ave.), Astoria, (718) 932-1510, Open M-Su 4pm-12am. Cash Only, $8-$16, ❷ to Astoria Blvd. (Hoyt Ave.). ♿

Girassol Churrascaria

A churrascaria is a fancy word for barbecue, and if you enter these doors be prepared to be rolled out. This is all-you-can eat, and this place will put any kind of meat or sausage on a spit and serve it up to you sizzling. Beware: not for the faint-hearted or vegetarians. Don't wear a belt.
33-18 28th Ave (bet 34th & 35th Sts.), Astoria, (718) 545-8250, Open M-Su 11am–12am, Amex, MC, Visa, D, Entrees: $12-22, ❷❼ to 30th Ave.

Jackson Diner

This is the most famous Indian restaurant in New York, and it's not even in New York. Jackson Heights is a short trip on the F train. The popularity of this place has led even cynical Manhattanites to trek out here to partake of the homestyle portions. The place has been extensively renovated since its humble beginnings, but the food and surrounding neighborhood remain true to form.
37-47 74th St. (bet. Roosevelt & 37th Aves.), (718) 672-1232, Open Su-R 11:30am-10pm, F-Sa 11:30am-10:30pm, Cash only, ❸❻❼❽❾❼ to 74th St.-Roosevelt Ave.

Joe's Shanghai

Tourists, locals, and suburban Chinese flock here for the juicy crabmeat buns for which Joe's is deservedly famous. Friendly service and the savory quality of the rest of the fare keeps customers coming back for more.
136-21 Seventh Ave. (bet Main and Union Sts.), (718) 539-3838, Open Su-R 11am-11:00pm, F-Sa 11am-12pm, Cash Only, Entrées: $5-$18, ❼ to Main St.

Los Arrieros Restaurant

Steamed beef tongue, anyone? This Colombian place has everything from tripe, to oxtail, to beef liver. Come with an appetite, although an entire platter won't cost you more than $10. Don't expect Julia Child, but for these prices, who cares? (Columbian)
76-02 Roosevelt Ave. (at 76th St.), Jackson Heights, (718) 898-3359, Open Su-R 11am-9:30pm, F-Sa 11am-10:30pm, Cash only, Entrees: $5-8, ❸❻❼❽❾❼ to 74th St.-Roosevelt Ave.

Pollos a la Brasa

This restaurant is chicken heaven. Every way to cook, fry, or broil chicken, they have found it here. This Ecuadoran restaurant also has the corn cakes with cheese known as arepas. (Ecuadoran)
81-01 Roosevelt Ave. (at 81st St.), Jackson Heights, (718) 639-5555, Open M-Su 24 hours, MC, V, AmEx, D, Entrees: $12-18, ❼ to 82nd St.

Rib Shack

This venue's offerings of sweet potato pie, collard greens, and fried chicken will move the hearts of devoted soul food lovers. The employees are so friendly that they regularly garner tips, a wow considering that customers are only allowed to order take-out.
157-06 Linden Blvd. (bet. Sutphin and Guy Brewer Blvds.), Jamaica, (718) 659-7000, Open Su-R 11am-12pm, F-Sa 11am-12:30am, MC, V, AmEx, Entrées: $6-$8, ❸❿❽ to Jamaica Blvd.-Archer Ave., ❻ to Sutphin Blvd.

Terra Brasil

Terra is mainly take-out, but has the basic Brazilian marinated beef dishes, but their claim to fame is a salad and meat bar from $3.99 a pound that draws locals in like flies to honey. They also have delicious little chicken or shrimp tartlets and cheese bread to go. (Brazilian)
33-04 36th Avenue, Long Island City, (718) 609-1367, Open M-Sa 11am-9pm, Su 11am-7pm, V, Entrees: $5-8, ❷❼ to 36th Ave.

Zum Stammtisch

While German cuisine hardly qualifies as in vogue to chic Manhattan critics, its heartiness goes over well with the locals in this quiet neighborhood. Stained glass windows and dim lights bring to mind stodgy 19th century German intellectuals debating Hegel over steins.
69-46 Myrtle Ave. (at Cooper Ave.), Glendale, (718) 386-3014, Open Su-R 12pm-10pm, F-Sa 12pm-11pm, MC, V, AmEx, Entrées: $7-$16.

CAFES

Cafe Kolonaki

The fun and cozy split-level coffee shop is fairly new to the Steinway shopping area. The decor is contemporary.
33-02 Broadway (at 33rd St.), Astoria, (718) 932-8222, Open M-Su 8am-1am. MC, V, AmEx, D, **N W** *to Broadway* &

Omonia Café

Enjoy a piece of Greece at Astoria's best liquor, coffee, and pastry bar. Lounge at a table among a multilingual crowd, or choose what to order from the vast selection of standard and exotic pastries behind the glass counter up front including five shelves of different kinds of baklava.
32-20 Broadway (at 33rd St.), (718) 274-6650, Open M-Su 6am-4am, MC, V, AmEx, D, **N W** *to Broadway* &

Brooklyn

RESTAURANTS

Bar Tabac

This relaxing and moderately priced French Bistro features magnificent duck, confit cigars, luscious desserts, and an attentive waitstaff. You could spend several hours lounging around the back room - designed to resemble the inside of a fin de siecle Paris subway train - as you sip wine and sample savory selections like mouth watering steak frites and scrumptious sea bass.
128 Smith St. (at Dean St.), Carroll Gardens, (718) 923-0918, Open M-F 11:30am-1am, Sa-Su 11am-1am, AmEx, Entrees: $11-$16, **F G** *to Bergen St.*

Coco Roco

You might someday ask yourself, where can I get tasty Peruvian food in Brooklyn? Here it is, equipped with spicy Peruvian chicken and amazing sangria. It's also a fun, sprightly place that hustles and bustles.
392 Fifth Ave (bet 6th and 7th Sts.), Park Slope, (718) 965-3376, Open Su-T 12pm-10:30pm, F-Sa 12pm-11:30pm, MC, V, Amex, **F** *to 4th Ave,* **R** *to 9th St.*

Cucina

One of the best restaurants in New York and it's not even in Manhattan. Everything is great here, but the risotto is what people rave about. The antipasto is the best this side of Tuscany and the wine and dessert menus are superb. Plus there is valet parking on weekends. In a word: perfect.
256 Fifth Ave. (bet. Garfield Pl. and Carroll St.), Park Slope, (718) 230-0711, www.cucinarestaurant.com, Open T-R 5:30pm-10:30pm, F-Sa 5:30pm-11pm, Su 5pm-10pm. MC, V, AmEx, DC, D, Entrées: $15-$28, **M N R** *to Union St.*

The Downtown Brooklyn Diner

It's late and you're lost somewhere between the gas station and the party you were going to, driving around Brooklyn. Chances are you are on Atlantic Ave. and a good suggestion is stopping at this 24 hour diner, ordering breakfast, lunch or dinner, and figuring out where the hell you are.
515 Atlantic Ave. (at Third Ave.), (718) 243-9172, Open M-Su 24hrs, MC, V, AmEx, Entrées: $6-$8, **M N R Q W 1 2 4 5** *to Pacific St.-Atlantic Ave.*

Giardini Pizza and Restaurant

Some of the best pizza and straight up Italian food in New York, which is no small feat considering there's a pizza joint on every corner. This place delivers (literally, too) with great plain and topping slices and a nice array of the old standards - spaghetti, stuffed shells, parmigianas and big, tasty heroes. It's cheap, fast, and deeply satisfying.
363 Smith St. (at Carroll St.), Carroll Gardens, (718) 596-5320, Open M-Su 10am-10pm, F 10am-11pm, Cash only, Entrees: $1.25-9.00, **F G** *to Carroll St.*

Grimaldi's

Every New Yorker claims to know the best pizzeria in the city, but Grimaldi's may be the real thing. Old Brooklyn ambiance is enhanced by Sinatra and Bennett crooning as you savor crisp, thin-crust pizza that will satisfy even the most discriminating pizza lovers.
19 Old Fulton St. (bet. Water and Front Sts.), Fulton Ferry Landing, (718) 858-4300, Open M-R 11:30am-11pm, F 11:30am-12am, Sa 12pm-12am, Su 12pm-11pm, Cash Only, Entrées: $12-$20, **A C** *to High St., F to York St.* &

Junior's

Sample "New York's Best Cheesecake" (don't confuse it with the cheese pie!) or just about anything else you can imagine at this monster diner/bar, open till 2am on weekends. Busy bar, with eclectic group of patrons. Speedy service, but sometimes a wait for a table on weekends. It's been around for ages, and any Brooklyner worth his or her salt will stop here from time to time. The food is solid, the prices good and the ambience, pure old school Brooklyn.
386 Flatbush Ave. (at DeKalb Ave.), (718) 852-5257. Open Su-W 6:30am-12:30am, R 6:30am-1am, F-Sa 6:30am-2am. MC, V, AmEx, DC, D, Entrées: $10-$28, **M N Q R** *to DeKalb Ave.* & *(Additional location in Manhattan)*

New Prospect Café

A diminutive cutie, the light menu here features

some excellent seafood
vegetable dishes and nice,
reasonably priced wine.
Not for New York's night
owls, the kitchen closes
by 10pm; on the other
hand, brunch is excellent
and always crowded.
*393 Flatbush Ave. (bet.
Plaza St. and Sterling Pl.),
Prospect Heights, (718)
638-2148, Open M 5-10,
T-R 12-10, F 12-11, Sa11-
11, Su 11am-10pm, MC, V,
AmEx, Entrées $9-$16, 12
to Grand Army Plaza, Q
to Seventh Ave.* &

Oznot's Dish

This quirky restaurant has
become a premiere site
for nouveau ethnic cui-
sine, combining
Mediterranean flavors and
French presentation. With
bright mosaics covering
the walls and a year-
round sunroom, Oznot's is
elegantly hip: the wait-
staff is down-to-earth
but knowledgeable, the
ambience laid back but
classy, and the food superior but moderately
priced. The expansive
menu, offering outra-
geous meat dishes as well
as vegetarian delights,
boasts a selection of 300
wines.
*79 Berry St., (at N. 9th
St.), Williamsburg, (718)
599-6596, Open M-F
11am-4:30pm, 6pm-
11:15pm, Sa-Su 10am-
4:30pm, 6pm-12am, MC,
V, Entrées: $11-$18, L
to Bedford Ave.* &

Patois

This French restaurant
joins a host of new ven-
tures on Smith Street and
doesn't disappoint with
favu leek and goat cheese
tart, tasty duck breast,
and excellent grilled
salmon served over lentils.
Good wines compliment
most of the food,

whether it be the tripe
stew or beer-drenched
mussels.
*255 Smith St. (bet.
Degraw and Douglas
Sts.), Carroll Gardens,
(718) 855-1535, Open T-R
6pm-10:30pm, F-Sa 6pm-
11:30pm, Sun 11am-3pm,
5pm-10pm, MC, V, AmEx,
Entrees: $12-18, F G to
Bergen St.*

Peter Luger Steak House

Simply the best steak-
house in New York City.
Not for the faint of heart
(and definitely not for
vegetarians), the menu is
limited to steak, salmon,
and lamb chops, as well
as an amazing array of à
la carte side-dishes.
Informal, given the price
of a meal, a reservation
on a Friday or Saturday
can be weeks in the wait-
ing. Worth the wait,
worth the cost, just plain
worth it!
*178 Broadway (between
Bedford Ave. and Driggs
St.), Williamsburg, (718)
387-7400, www.peter-
luger.com, Open M-R
11:45am-9:45pm, F-Sa
11:45-10:45pm, Su
12:45pm-9:45, Cash Only,
Entrées: $50-$60, J M
Z to Marcy Ave.* &

Petite Crevette

Ignore the decor, which is
in transition, and step
inside this roomy
Brooklyn Heights restau-
rant where a friendly and
comfortable ambience is
promoted by the staff
and patrons alike. For the
best bites, ask waiter
Lynn, who runs the dining
room like "a big dinner
party," for a suggestion
from the fish, stews, or
pastas and sit back to
enjoy some of the fresh-
est fish available. FYI, it's

BYOB.
*127 Atlantic Ave. (at
Henry St.), Brooklyn
Heights, (718) 858-6660,
Open M-R 11:45am-
10pm, F-Sa 11:45am-
11pm, MC,V, AmEx,
Entrées $8-$19, M N R
1 2 4 5 to Court St.-
Borough Hall* &

Queen Italian Restaurant

Downtown Brooklyn's
pasta of choice for local
suits and shoppers; try
anything on the menu
since it's difficult to go
wrong, especially with the
spicy, crisp pizza.
*84 Court St. (bet.
Livingston and
Schermerhorn Sts.), (718)
596-5954, Open M
11:30am-10:30pm, T-F
11:30am-11pm, Sa 4pm-
11pm, Su 4pm-10pm, MC,
V, AmEx, Entrées: $15-
$25, M N R 1 2 4 5
to Court St.-Borough
Hall.* &

Red Rail

Come one, come all to
this busy and popular
breakfast/lunch spot and
enjoy a nice prix fixe
brunch that includes cof-
fee, tea, and all the
mimosas you can handle.
Try the big, nicely pre-
sented omelets, grilled
squid salad with basil, red
onion and tomato, or
tasty avocado salad with
tomatoes and goat
cheese. If the architec-
ture appears familiar, you
may remember it from a
heated romantic spat
between Nicolas Cage and
Cher in Moonstruck.
*502 Henry St. (at Sackett
St.), Carroll Gardens, (718)
875-1283, Open M-R
9:30am-3:30pm, 5:30pm-
10:30pm, F 9:30am-
3:30pm, 6pm-11pm, Sa
9:30am-3:30pm, 6pm-
11pm, Su 9:30am-3:30pm,*

*5:30pm-10pm, MC, V,
AmEx, F G train to
Carroll St.*

Rose Water

Vegetarian cuisine coming
at ya, loaded with organic
seasonal ingredients that
combine to make delec-
table, low-priced meals.
Get the fine cheese plate
accompanied by slices of
pears, black grapes, and
squishy (in a good way)
bread, or try the seared
diver scallops with roasted butternut squash.
*787 Union St. (at Sixth
Ave.), Park Slope, (718)
783-3800, Open M-T
5:30pm-10pm, W-R
5:30pm-10:30pm, F-S
5:30pm-11pm, Sun 11am-
3pm, 5:30pm-10pm, MC,
V, AmEx, M N R train to
Union St.*

Sotto Voce

Cool Décor fills this tiny
neighbor restaurant,
which is always
hopping with
happy diners
eating crab
cake antipasto,
homemade fet-
tuccine in rose-
mary cream sauce,
and veal medallions.
Great for the meat lover
in you. If you've got
room, go for the delicious
cheesecake with straw-
berries. You won't regret
it.
*225 Seventh Ave. (at 4th
St.), Park Slope, (718)
369-9322, Open M-R
12pm-11pm, F 12pm-
12am, Sa 10am-12am, Su
10am-11pm, Cash only,
Entrees: $10-$22, F to
Seventh Ave.*

Tom's Diner

"I came, I sat, I wrote"
reads a note from
Suzanne Vega on the wall
of this venerable lun-

cheonette, suggesting that it is this Prospect Heights favorite, not Tom's on 112th St. in Manhattan, immortalized in Vega's "Tom's Diner." Worthy of immortality, Tom's is a charmer, founded in 1936 with prototypical Brooklyn fare, great egg creams, and terrific service. Closes at 4pm.
782 Washington Ave. (at Sterling Pl.), Prospect Heights, (718) 636-9738. Open M-Sa 6am-4pm. Cash Only, Entrées: $3-$8, ② ③ to Eastern Pkwy.-Brooklyn Museum. ♿

CAFES

Fall Cafe

Settle into a cushy couch and finish a physics problem set or dig into your debut novel. Sustenance comes at starving student prices: $3 or less for soups, and a small coffee for less than $1.
307 Smith St. (bet. President and Union Sts.) Carroll Gardens, (718) 403-0230, Open M-F 7:30am-9pm, Sa 8:30am-9pm, Su 9am-8pm, Cash Only, ❶ ❷ to Carroll St. ♿

L Café

The food - standard American café fare - is mediocre, but the eclectic crowd will hold your attention as you wine and dine inside this tiny brick enclave or in the sunny, outdoor garden.
189 Bedford Ave. (bet N. 6th and N. 7th), (718) 302-2430, Open M-W 9am-11:30pm, R-F 9am-12am, Sa-Su, 10am-12am, MC, V, AmEx, ❶ to

Bedford Ave.

Omonia Café

You won't be sorry when you come here for dessert or a sweet snack. With delicious cakes and coffees, and two locations in Queens and Brooklyn, these cafes are lovely places to sit and savor yummy pastries and delicious coffees late into the evening.
7612 Third Ave. (bet. 76th and 77th Sts.), (718) 491-1435, Open M-Su 8am-4am, MC, V, AmEx, Entrees: $12-$16, ❶ to 77th St. ♿

Sweet Melissa Patisserie

A reasonably priced café for sweets, salads, and French food. It's becoming increasingly popular among local residents, with a building reputation for good food. The place may be small, but as the name promises, it's sweet.
276 Court St. (bet. Butler and Douglass Sts.), (718) 855-3410, Open Su-R 8am-10pm, F-Sa 8am-12am, Cash Only, Entrees: $4-$6, ❶ ❷ to Bergen St. ♿

Staten Island

RESTAURANTS

Aesop's Tables

There's a lot you can do with the metaphor here. Aesop's Tables. Are the stories in the variations of new American food Aesop's Tables offers? Or, are the stories at your table where the décor provides hours of speculation. The moral-worth it if your in town, but don't go out of your way otherwise.

1233 Bay St. (at Maryland Ave.), (718) 720-2005, Open T-R 5:30pm-9:30pm, F-Sa 530-1030, Su 5pm-9pm, MC, V, AmEx, Entrees: $11-$17, ❶ ❷ to South Ferry, 51 bus to Hylan Blvd/Bay St. ♿

Basilio Inn

Housed in a 19th century stable imbued with a Tuscan rustic flavor, the Inn serves up incredible Italian — the red snapper Livornese is divine.
2-6 Galesville Court, (718) 447-9292, Open M-F 12pm-3pm, 5pm-10pm, Sa 5-10, Su, 1-8, AmEx, Entrées: $12-$14, ❶ ❷ to South Ferry, Train to Grasmere ♿

Denino's Pizzeria and Tavern

As much a Staten Island institution as the ferry, if not more so. Denino's has been around since 1937, owned by the same family and serves some of the best thin crust pizza and fried calamari in the city. The sort of place you go to with a big group, order a lot and get ugly.
524 Port Richmond Ave. (bet. Hooker Pl. and Walker St.), (718) 442-9401, Open Su-R 12pm-11pm, F-Sa 12pm-12am, Cash Only, Entrees: $8-$15, ❶ ❷ to South Ferry, Train to New Dorp ♿

Parsonage

The priest is gone, but this 150-year-old house of a priest serves food that is as close to divine as it gets on Staten Island. The food's American with twists-cherry peppers here, bunch of Italian stuff there. The ambience com-

pletes the experience. Two floors of antiques in an antique house. And on your plate recipes so time tested they'll be around as long as the house you're eating them in.
74 Arthur Kill Rd. (at Clark Ave.), (718) 351-7879, Open M 5pm-10pm, T-R 11:30am-10pm, F-Sa 11:30am-11pm, Su 1pm-9pm, MC, V, AmEx, D, Entrees: $16-$30, ❶ ❷ to South Ferry, 54 or 74 bus to Arthur Kill Rd. ♿

CAFES

Carol's Café

Arguably the best restaurant in Staten Island, the worst thing about Carol's Café is that it's only open four days a week. Though the eclectic fare may take a while to get to your table, you'll concede that it was worth the wait.
1571 Richmond Rd. (bet. Four Corners Rd. and Seaview Ave.), (718) 979-5600, Open W-F 11:30am-3pm, 6pm-12am, Sa 5pm-12am, MC, V, AmEx, D, Entrées: $14-$35, ❶ ❷ to South Ferry, Train to Dongan Hills ♿

Cargo Cafe

Just a stone's throw from the Staten Island Ferry terminal, this modern, trendy spot is hard to miss. A youngish local crowd congregates on the terrace in summer for delectable fresh fish specials like pan-seared tuna. Local artists often showcase their works and live jazz cooks up Thursdays.
120 Bay St. (at Flosson Terrace), (718) 876-0539, Open M-Su 12pm-2am, MC, V, AmEx, D, Entrées: $10-$18. ❶ ❷ to South Ferry, Located near Ferry Pier ♿

nightlife
ya can't stand da beatz...

New York offers what no other American city can: limitless ways to get your groove on. If you've got the cash, time and friends, there's no town more dynamic than this one. $3 beers and $15 Manhattans trickle down neighboring throats, and pumped-up partiers can move from the underground dance floor of Nell's to mingle sweat at Webster Hall. You can still find jello shots here, but New York's drinks and venues are constantly changing to fit the tastes of a fickle and transient party population. Keeping up with the shifting fortunes of clubs here is a full-time job.

Some New Yorkers are out to pick up or be picked up. Others want major attention after all those hard workouts, or to catch a glimpse of celebrity. This is why people come to New York: to bask in reflected evening glamour in the city that never sleeps. Nowhere else save perhaps Miami can a woman pull out her most outrageous dress and heels, and no one bats an eye.

New York's nightlife drives many New Yorkers through the long workdays with the promise of excitement and escape. There's no such thing as "a weeknight" in this town. Here, the weekend starts on Monday. From hotspots like Black Betty and Galapagos in Williamsburg to mellow clubs like The Knitting Factory and new-age palaces like Tao, New Yorkers can visit a new club every night

for a year and never touch down twice.

The bar and club crowds start late and end even later. That's not to say you can't toss down a few beers as a warm-up during the prized happy hour. But for most regulars, going out means only hitting the streets around 11 pm, when the bars and lounges in places like SoHo and the East Village really pick up. People still flock to underground hangouts like the Astor Lounge on Bleecker and Bowery on the star-studded Belmont Lounge in Gramercy. These are popular for pre- and post-clubbing.

Students from area schools pack night venues all over the city, and there are plenty of bars and clubs that cater to younger tastes. Classic spots like the Bitter End and Café Wha? in Greenwich Village, and jazz dens like Smoke and Soundz Bar near Columbia bring students out to socialize after studying—or not studying.

In Harlem, old standbys like St. Nick's and Lenox Lounge keep cranking out the sounds and the strong drinks. And on Amsterdam around the 80s, the saloons and late night ethnic eateries keep

locals out late.

Each neighborhood of New York feels like a city in itself, and once you find the night spots that suit you—whether they're the mellow, post-industrial digs in Chelsea or the funky lounges on the Lower East Side—getting familiar with a distinct part of town and its nightlife is one of the pleasures of coming to know this city. Only here can salsa dancers swivel next to country western saloons and hip-hop plays down the street from folk music. And at the end of your evening, no matter how wild you've been, you won't ever need to drive home as cabs roam the streets of New York at all hours.

New Yorkers aren't like other bar-goers. Here, people go to bars where nobody knows their name. For the most part, no one wants to. Most people travel to different bars constantly looking for the latest and greatest in human décor. Whatever people's preference, the quantity and style of bars that link the streets of New York make it almost impossible to avoid a drink after work.

New York has plenty of the rougher stuff too. Irish pubs abound in New York, such as Dublin House and Paddy Reilly's. So do college and sports bars, which tend to attract a predominantly male crowd. In hangouts like Pete's Candy Store in Williamsburg and 288 in the Lower East Side, crowds get together by the hundreds. New York features plenty of downscale places like Yogi's on Broadway in the West 70s, a country saloon where clients exhale heavy clouds of smoke and guffaw over Budweisers. Finally Fred's, a bar/music joint on Lower West Side, is loud for those looking to shed a polite veneer.

A more lofty bar life exists in New York as well, like the cabarets, piano and hotel bars that are part of a long tradition of metropolitan elegance. Bar clientele usually self-select, and if you don't belong you will know it soon enough. For the bourgeois-inclined, there are plenty of classy clubs to choose from like the tame, relaxed atmosphere in CoZ on East 6th St.

Get to know a neighborhood and its various watering holes, and they could become your home away from home. You'll probably spend more time there than in your apartment, anyway.

Pool and dart halls in New York add a competitive edge to the drinking scene. Most New Yorkers associate pool and dart halls with baseball-capped, plaid-shirted fraternity boys. However, in some places, the hipper-than-thou set has discovered the glory of competition while simultaneously downing Cosmopolitans.

Regular gatherings around the pool table at the Stoned Crow in Greenwich Village are complemented by a jukebox, dart board, and a virtual reality race car video game. Morningside Heights' 1020 Bar also features a rather pool-playing crowd. In Gramercy, Revival, a low-key bar, provides a much more laid-back approach to the game of pool. The Dive Bar, located on Amsterdam Avenue at 96th Street, is a tame spot. There is never a line for the free darts and even the resident pool sharks won't intimidate. The Tapas Lounge on First Avenue at 59th St. boasts that its customers can graze on

tapas and sip sangria while playing backgammon.

At Max Fish on Ludlow Street a fishy decor provides the backdrop for numerous pool games. Some bars are frequented solely for their pool tables. The ultimate game room--darts, pinball, video games--can be found at the Ace Bar on East 5th Street between Avenues A and B. The SoHo Billiards on Mulberry Street at Houston Street is a smoky hangout hosting a ton of pool tables and '80s music.

Though playing and drinking at the same time can be pricey, some spots offer discounts. Located on West 21st Street between Fifth and Sixth Avenues, Chelsea Billiards offers pool tables at half-price on Thursdays. Amsterdam Billiards, on Amsterdam Avenue and 77th Street, allows four people to play from 11pm to 3am for $19 on Sundays-Thursdays.

clubs

The New York club scene has something for every body: Goth, salsa, reggae, thrash, techno, whatever. New York's clubs go from hot to not in a matter of weeks. Given that few have to drive home afterwards, and the subway is open virtually 24 hours, the options are unlimited.

You have to keep up with publications like The Village Voice and Time Out to keep abreast of who's dancing where. There are relatively few clubs, such as Vinyl, that have longstanding DJs on weekends who keep the crowds coming month after month. Clubs here often have theme nights so that you never have to dress the same way twice. One has a cyberfetish party (have you ever wanted to dress up as a submissive computer mouse?). Another has a drag queen review.

Many bars in New York have earned the title of "club" because DJs fill the bar with dancing pairs. But these smaller places, like Baraza on the Lower East Side and Happy Ending in SoHo, must close at 4 a.m. because they don't have cabaret licenses, sprinkler systems or multiple exits.

Not only does the music vary around New York, but also the digs. Mega-dance clubs like the Tunnel, Life, System and Speed pump in strobe lights and lots of smoke on the dance floor and use a velvet rope to separate the in-crowd from the out.

Wear with Flair

At high-profile places, a high standard of dress is required. Don't even dare show up at a club in ripped jeans and sneakers, there's nary a club in town that would let you in. Think black, think very dressed up minus the big hair or mullet 'do of other cities.

Dressed to Kill and Charged to Death

NY clubs charge high covers, upwards of $40, because they know people will pay. When New Yorkers go out on the town, they carry plenty of cash for the multiple drinks, taxis and entrance fees that await them. It is easy to blow $300 a night. Dress codes and prices vary from venue to venue, just like the club scene varies from the hip-hop royalty at Justin's to Chelsea's wildest dance warehouses. So between your outfit, your shoes, your drinks and your cover, you could be eating ramen till next paycheck.

house rules

To make it past the velvet rope in NY, you will need the wiles of a coyote. Here are a few rules that should prepare even the most unseasoned partygoer for NY's sometimes unruly club scene, and then how to get lucky once you get in (maybe).

Dress up, way up. Lose the gum, the big hair, the heavy make-up, the cheap cologne. Don't wear anything dry-cleanable because once you enter the darkened sanctum of the club the smoke will forever soak your threads.

Do order "the" drink. No sissy drinks in New York, do your research what the house drink is, or ask. Be forewarned: water costs just as much as an alcoholic drink most of the time.

Be ready to start and end late. The party won't truly start till 11 pm or so on a good night.

Case the club, find out where the action is, and keep moving. New Yorkers don't stay put long; it gets boring.

Be ready for some serious body contact. Most clubs are wall-to-wall people, and you will have various bodily fluids and drinks rubbed or splashed you before the night is over.

Whatever you do, don't scream or pick a fight. Get over it.

Women, never ever accept a drink from a man who has carried it to you himself. Always get your drinks straight from the bartender, and watch them as they mix it. Then, never accept a ride home from a stranger – the danger is not worth it.

Finally, at 4 am when you're ready to go, sip some Joe with your friends. There are plenty of diners open. People come from all over the world to party like this, all night and all the way. So stay up. Because you can.

grin and... *beer* it

Beers have never poured so plentifully at the pubs, lounges and clubs that link the streets of New York. A combination of Brooklyn micro-breweries and bottled imports have made this town a mecca for exotic, sweet-tasting ambers and fine lagers from around the globe. And of the thousands of drinking holes, several venues offer the best beer for your buck.

The Swift Hibernian Lounge has gained a foothold on the market for fine, foreign beer selections in the East Village. This Irish-style pub was named after Jonathan Swift, author of *Gulliver's Travels* and *Hibernae*. A mural on the wall opposite the bar depicts Swift himself, six-feet tall, holding a frothy mug of Guinness in his hand.

On the liquor shelves behind the bar, ancient empty bottles of beer-Pure Brewed Samuel Smith, Oatmeal Stout, Salvator, India Ale and others set the tone for a serious beer drinking experience. A chalkboard above the bar introduces a few of the 40 bottled beers and 20 additional brews served here on draught. And each month, one or two "guest beers" grace the Swift menu. However, it's no secret that many of Swift's customers hover here because the pub serves "the best Guinness downtown."

According to one of the waitresses here, Belgian and German beers are the strongest-"for real beer drinkers." But have no fear, those of you looking for lighter options. Swift's also carries brands from Japan, Jamaica, Mexico and Australia, with flavors like peach, raspberry or currant.

On tap at Swift's, you can choose from lagers, ales, stouts, wheat beers, white beers, cream ales and ciders. The brew comes in foot-tall glasses, so be prepared to toss down a meal in its entirety. Flavored, strong beers like Lindeman's, come in 20oz. Pints and cost $10, while normal brews run $5. Some specialty malts, however, like the Belgian Delirium Tremens Chimay Grand Reserve, pours at $18 for a 25oz. slug. Other numbers like Doc Otis Hard Lemonade and Harpoon Hibernian Ale (not to mention the ever-popular Magic Hat No. 9) fetch decent prices. *34 E. 4th St. (bet. the Bowery and Lafayette Sts.), (212) 227-9348,* **F V S** *to Broadway-Lafayette St.*

Zum Schneider, a German-style beer pub replete with a black forest atmosphere of fake vines growing from fake trees, offers loud soccer-hungry fans liter-sized mugs of lager to pour down their throats. The Bavarian Bierhaus crowds, mostly professionals in their 30s, enjoy the open air, patio feel of Zum's in the summertime.

They have a dozen German beers to choose from, like Weltenburger Kloster, Hacker Pschorr (Munich Lager), Panlaner (also Munich beer), Schneider Weisse and Spaten. Brews range from $5 to $7 a pint, double for giant liter mugs. To help digest the beers at Zum's, guests choose from a menu that offers German pub food like Wiener Schnitzel ($15), Bratwurst ($12) or Baked Bavarian Meat Loaf ($10). *598 Ninth Ave (bet. 42nd and 43rd Sts.), (212) 598-1098,* **A C E N R Q W S 1 2 3 7** *to 42nd St. - Times Square.*

Interested in more good drinking? Here are some other New York breweries:

Brooklyn Brewery
N. 11th St., Brooklyn
(718) 486-7422

Chelsea Brewing Company
Pier 59, Chelsea Piers
(212) 336-6440

Heartland Brewery
Union Square
(212) 645-3400

Typhoon Brewery
E. 54th St. (at Madison Ave.)
(212) 754-9006

Like everything in New York, music comes in every flavor, and evolves so quickly that even die-hard music fans have a hard time keeping up with what's hot now.

Live music venues have sprung up all over the city, especially in the East Village and Lower East Side, where singer-songwriters and their bands increasingly get their start. Lou Reed, Bob Dylan, Paul Simon, RUN DMC and the Beastie Boys all got their start.

The Harlem jazz scene is flourishing with regular shows at the Lenox Lounge, St. Nick's, the historic Apollo Theater and Smoke club, and it offers Columbia locals a deep, dark jazzy experience. Soundz Bar, on the northern edge of Morningside Heights, has become one of the best music lounges on the Upper West Side.

For those who want to hear big-name players, the Bowery Ballroom on Delancey is a good place to start. The Beacon Theatre and Madison Square Garden bring in some of the best talent and Carnegie Hall and Lincoln Center host the high-profile performances of classical favorites like Yo-Yo Ma.

a short history of jazz in NYC

When you think "jazz," you might think "Harlem Renaissance" and the huge outgrowth of musical talent that flourished here in the first half of the century. Virtually every jazz great, from James P. Johnson to Fats Waller, played in places like The Cotton Club.

By the 1950s, 52nd Street was a solid wall of sound: legendary clubs like the Downbeat, the Hickory House, Jimmy Ryan's, Kelly's Stable and Birdland converged on "Swing Street" to host the likes of Count Basie and Dizzy Gillespie.

Jazz also began the next revolution. Jazz greats such as Ellington and Basie collaborated with Big Joe Turner to create a new style that was dubbed Rhythm and Blues, first broadcast in 1954. DJ Alan Freed was called it "rock and roll."

Also in the 1950s, American and Latin jazz melded, and the result was a danceable beat known as "mambo," played widely in Cuban and Puerto Rican clubs like the Copacabana. This era was memorialized in the book "The Mambo Kings Sing Songs of Love," by Oscar Hijuelos.

At the same time, John Coltrane was developing what would be known as modal jazz, experimenting at the Village Vanguard. This new style eventually led to freestyle in the late '60s, personified by Thelonious Monk and Ornette Coleman.

Jazz regained popularity in the '90s with the revival of downtown clubs like the Blue Note and the Village Vanguard. Now the city is home to active jazz clubs such as Sweet Basil Smalls, and The Time Cafe/Fez.

gay nightlife

Gay life in New York has shifted mightily in the past fifty years. Once, Greenwich Village was the epicenter of gay life. In a then-conservative America, many gay men after Stonewall felt free to take ownership of their neighborhoods and mold them into what many felt were ideal neighborhoods. In the 1980s, gay neighborhoods began to incorporate parts of Chelsea and the Meat Packing District in the West 20s, due to rising rents in the Village.

In the 90s, Chelsea experienced the emergence of more fine restaurants, gentrified apartment buildings and safer communities. The gay population was credited with cleaning up Chelsea's image. Companies like Banana Republic and Hugo Boss soon set up shop there. Now, many gay clubs and bars have migrated to Clinton to the north. Formerly known as Hell's Kitchen, the neighborhood between 42nd and 57th Sts. and 8th and 10th Aves., has become one of the newest, fastest-growing gay communities in New York. The party scene remains as wild as ever, and you don't have to live here to party well.

A sampling of the gay club scene: SBNY, or the Splash Bar, at 50 W.17th Street (call (212) 691-0073), boasts evenings like Same Sex Saturday, replete with live shows, DJs and midnight videos. For less tame fun, check out the always-packed Roxy, at 515 W.18th St., a half block from Chelsea Piers (call (212) 645-5156)). Also try Mother, a long-running club on W.14th St. at Washington. Jackie 60 offers theme nights that draw party-going crowds all through the week (located at 111 E. 19th St., (at Irving Pl.), (212) 929-6060, ❹❺❻ⓁⓃⓇⓆⓌ to Union Sq.). And the posh environs of the G Lounge on W.19th Street between 7th and 8th Aves. host a professional gay crowd (call (212) 929-1085).

Stonewall, at 53 Christopher St. (call (212) 463-0950), isn't the original, which was next door, but its proximity reminds patrons of that night many years ago when a spontaneous act of solidarity galvanized the gay rights movement. Patrons are diverse in age, with some neighborhood folk mixing with out-of-towners and guys rock to a jukebox of wildly divergent musical styles at The Bar (68 Second Ave, (212) 674-9714).

Womyn's World

Although there aren't as many gay clubs for women here, the lesbian crowd is big business. The Clit Club is ever-popular, at 327 Bowery (bet. 2nd and 3rd Sts., Cover: $5). Cowgirl Hall of Fame boasts a gift shop, restaurant and décor full of cowgirl kitsch, located at 519 Hudson St., (212) 633-1133. Meow Mix is an old standby at 269 E. Houston St, (212) 254-0688. It is fast becoming the né plus ultra-hip scene. Or try Henrietta Hudson, at 438 Hudson St., (212) 924-3347, Julie's at 305 E. 53rd St. (between 1st and 2nd Aves., (212) 688-1294) or Wonder Bar at 505 E. 6th St, (212) 777-9105. Go on the weekends for a fun, racially-mixed crowd at Crazy Nannies, 21 Seventh Ave. South, (212) 366-6312.

some hot spots...

Barracuda, 275 W. 22nd St., (212) 645-8613
Big Apple Ranch, 39 W. 19th St., (212) 807-0802
Boiler Room, 86 E. 4th St., (212) 254-7536
Break, 232 8th Ave., (212) 627-0072
Dick's Bar, 192 2nd Ave., (212) 475-2071
Dugout, 185 Christopher St., (212) 242-9113
Duplex, 61 Christopher St., (212) 255-5438
G, 233 W. 19th St., (212) 929-1085
Hangar, 115 Christopher St., (212-627-2044
Julius, 159 W. 10th St., (212) 929-9672
King, 579 6th Ave., (212) 366-5464
Lure, 409 W. 13 St., (212) 741-3919
Monster, 80 Grove St., (212) 924-3557
Spike, 120 11th Ave., (212) 243-9688
Stonewall Inn, 53 Christopher St., (212) 463-0950

LISTINGS

Financial District

Clubs
New York Dolls

Dolls hails itself as the strip bar for the average man looking for the approachable woman. You won't find any former Playmates of the Month here, and the bumping and grinding on stage is more music video than Demi Moore in Striptease, but this is definitely a place for the average guy who doesn't want to feel intimidated by dressed-up yuppies.
59 Murray St. (bet. Warren St. and Park Pl.), (212) 227-6912, Open M-Sa 12pm-4am. MC, V, AmEx, Cover: $10 after 8pm, ❶❷Ⓐ❻ *to Chambers St.*

Music
Orange Bear

A good after-work bar. Most performers are unknown locals working on their acts. On Sundays, the space is used as an art gallery and for poetry readings.
47 Murray St. (bet. Church St. and Broadway), (212) 566-3705. Open M-F 11am-4am, Sa 5pm-4am. MC, V, AmEx, Cover: free-$5, ❶❷ *to Chambers St.,* Ⓝ Ⓡ *to City Hall.*

Tribeca

Bars
Bubble Lounge

The banking and "Beemer" set explains the bar's selection of champagnes and sparkling wines, arguably the city's best. The posh interior provides a great setting to impress a first date with some champagne and caviar, so long as you don't mind dropping mucho dinero.
228 W. Broadway (at White St.), (212) 431-3433. Open M-Sa 5pm-4am. MC, V, AmEx, D, ❶❷ *to Franklin St.* ♿

Church Lounge

One bartender described it confidently as the "cultural, sexual, cocktail center of Tribeca." Yet, it seems more like a tourist stop in "I'm cool, I Swearville." Ironically, you'll be laughed at if you order a Cosmopolitan (they're so over!). Drinks are expensive, too: martinis cost $12.
In the Tribeca Grand Hotel, 2 Sixth Ave. (at White St.), (212) 519-6678. Open M-Su 7am-3am. MC, V, AmEx, DC, D, Ⓐ❻Ⓔ *to Canal St.*

Grace

A sophisticated, corridor-like watering hole where young professionals en route to the clubs stop to schmooze. The dining room in back serves up tasty dishes until 4am.
114 Franklin St. (bet. W. Broadway and Church St.), (212) 343-4200, grace.citysearch.com. Open M-Su 11:30am-4am. MC, V, AmEx, ❶❷ *to Franklin St.*

Liquor Store Bar

Huge front windows, an oak bar and sidewalk seating render this bar irresistible. The charming, slightly motley group of locals welcomes newcomers as a fresh victims for their stale jokes. Heaven for any true bar lover.
235 W. Broadway (at White St.), (212) 226-7121, www.liquorstore.net. Open M-Su 12pm-4am. Cash Only, Ⓐ❻Ⓔ *to Canal St.* ♿

Lush

Lush is a lounge with upscale standards: the crowd and staff are extremely well-dressed and good looking. Everyone exudes a sort of frosty air that goes well with the cold cosmo they are sipping. The music is chill, too.
110 Duane St. (bet. Church St. and Broadway), (212) 766-1275, lush.citysearch.com. Open T-F 5pm-4am, Sa 8pm-4am. MC, V, AmEx ❶❷ Ⓐ❻ *to Chambers St.*

Rubber Monkey

Velvet curtains frame a mini cabaret stage with a lush multi-level seating area, while the downstairs houses a secondary bar and dance floor.
279 Church St. (at White St.), (212) 625-8220. Open M-W 11:30 am-3am, R-F 11:30am-9pm, Sa-Su 10pm-4am. MC, V, AmEx, D, Ⓐ❻Ⓔ *to Canal St.*

Music
Knitting Factory

If you don't mind the dank, minimalist aesthetic of The Knitting Factory, you can enjoy funy music venues like it all over the city. Musical acts range from alternative to avant-garde, blues to punk, and jazz to rock.
74 Leonard St. (bet. Broadway and Church St.), (212) 219-3006, www.knittingfactory.com. Open: M-F 5pm-3am, Sa-Su 6pm-3am. MC, V, AmEx, Cover: $6-$30, ❶❷ *to Franklin St.*

Shine

It would be tough to tell someone which night to show up at this eclectic venue. The Tuesday night drum and bass party? The Wednesday night DJ cook-off? The weekly Friday and Saturday late night freakouts, with, for example, fire jugglers, trapeze artists, burlesque and cabaret? Maybe you should just catch an early band and go from there. Musical acts range from alternativeto hip-hop and percussion to rock, with occasional R&B

285 W. Broadway (at Canal St.), (212) 941-0900 www. shinelive.com. Open M-Su 9:30pm-4am. MC, V, AmEx, Cover: $8-$15, **A C E** to Canal St. & 21+

Chinatown

Bars
Double Happiness
Friendly bartenders and an excellent mix of happy house and organic grooves attract a hip, young and unpretentious crowd nightly to this basement bar. With ample floor space for dancing, and hidden, candle-lit alcoves, Double Happiness is perfect either for that first date or for a night on the town with a group of friends. The bar menu features pan-Asian cuisine with an Italian accent.
173 Mott St. (bet. Broome and Grand Sts.), (212) 941-1282. Open M-Su 6pm-4am. MC, V, **6** *to Spring St.*

Winnie's
So what if it's a dark, low-ceilinged dive with baleful-looking dishes of chips and peanuts scattered across the bar? The big video-karaoke screen in back is where the action is. Come watch locals singing Asian chart-toppers. A dollar will buy you a song but one caveat: these folks are serious karaoke artists and won't hesitate to mock your braying.
104 Bayard St. (bet. Mulberry and Baxter Sts.), (212) 732-2384. Open M-Su 8pm-4am. Cash Only,

J M Z N R Q W 6 *to Canal St.* &

Clubs
Fun
Everything it claims to be, Fun is packed with enough dazzling gee-gaws to make you woozy. Movie clips and live-feed video from the bathrooms project onto the walls. Cocktail waitresses are shuttled to the upper level in a lucite hydraulic lift. Using hidden microphones, the DJs sample crowd voices into their mix. On Tuesdays, hipsters come by to play video games on the 20-foot screen.
130 Madison St. (at Pike St.), (212) 964-0303. Open M-Su 10pm-4am. MC, V, AmEx, Cover: None, **F** *to East Broadway.* &

Little Italy

Bars
Mare Chiaro Tavern
Gape at the huge photo of Frank Sinatra. Then go get yourself a drink at one of Little Italy's last genuine bars. Also known as "Tony's" in case you want to feel like a real local.
176 Mulberry St. (bet. Grand and Broome Sts.), (212) 226-9345, Open M-Su 10am-2am. Cash Only, **6** *to Spring St.* &

Vig Bar
Owner Russell has kept this lounge from getting too pretentious. Friendly bartenders and great DJs are Vig's greatest draws, and the dimly lit lounge areas are an added bonus. A pick-up scene on weekends.
12 Spring St. (bet. Elizabeth St. and The Bowery), (212) 625-0011. Open M-Su 5pm -4am. MC, V, AmEx, DC, D, **6** *to Spring St.*

Lower East Side

Bars
Angel
Late on weekends, cloud nine it isn't. The bouncers are mean, the lines big. Inside, it's all hip-hop. The lounge upstairs is a good place to break commandments. Weekdays it's slower and more a bar between bars than a place to stay.
174 Orchard St. (bet. Houston and Stanton Sts.), (212) 780-0313. Open Su-R 7pm-3am, F-Sa 7pm-4am. MC, V, **F** *to Second Ave.* &

Baraza
Part tropical bungalow, part industrial warehouse, this dim-lit bar hosts waiters with dreadlocks and a DJ who plays reggae beats while couples and youngish trios cluster at the bar and around small tables in back. A green steel door greets you on the street, so unless you know what you're looking for, this rasta hip-hop venue may go unnoticed. A chilling place for those Alphabet Citizens.
133 Ave. C (bet. 7th and 8th Sts.), (212) 539-0811,

CoZ

Techno and house music thump out of this sexy, clean-cut dive in the heart of the Lower East Side. A glittery disco ball rotates overhead, the bartenders speak French and the owners are Cypriots, giving this place an exotic je ne sais quoi. An excellent drink here is the caiphroska, which blends the caipirinha with vodka, using blond sugar cane, fresh orange juice and lime. Also try the Cypriot sausage and smoked kasseri cheese, which might make you want to pack your bags and head for the Mediterranean. *511 E. 6th St. (bet. Aves. A and B), (212) 995-8889. Open M-Su 6pm-4am,* **6** *to Astor Pl.*

DBA

On Sundays, enjoy complimentary bagels with lox and cream cheese. Everyday, enjoy one of the most extensive beer selections in the city. Hand-pumped ales and a wide variety of tequilas make this a popular hangout for regular East Siders, and there's a beer garden in back for those who crave fresh air. *41 First Ave. (bet. 2nd and 3rd Sts.), (212) 475-5097. Open M-Su 1pm-4am,* **6** *to Bleecker St.,* **F V S** *to Broadway-Lafayette St.*

Esperanto

Crowds fill this tropical restaurant/bar on Monday and Wednesday evenings to hear Cuban bands and boleros play. A pan-Latin menu of food and drinks combines Brazilian with Cuban, Caribbean and other South American cuisines. Customers choose from items like Paella Bahiana, the standard Brazilian fare of feijoada (bean stew) or seafood ceviche. Meals cost from $13 to $16, and drinks like mojitos run $6 to $8. *145 Ave. C (at 9th St.), (212) 505-6559. Open M-R 6pm-12am, F-Sa 6pm-1am, Su 6pm-11pm. Sunday Brunch 11am-4pm,* **L** *to First Ave.,* **6** *to Astor Pl.*

Good World Bar

Tucked away, Good World is a true neighborhood bar in an unlikely setting. It draws a mixed crowd from Chinatown and the Lower East Side. *3 Orchard St. (bet. Division and Canal Sts.), (212) 925-9975. Open M-Su 11am-4am. MC, V, AmEx,* **F V** *to E. Broadway.*

Idlewild

Its airplane-fuselage design has gawking crowds flocking in. The gimmick gets old, but, in its favor, the music is eclectic, the atmosphere is loungy and a DJ spins nightly. *145 E. Houston St. (bet. First and Second Aves.), (212) 477-5005. Open T-Su 4pm-indefinite. MC, V,* **F V** *to Second Ave.* ♿

Industry

One of the most chic bars in the Lower East Side. All the décor is custom-made, from the amber-colored stained glass bar top to the leather/suede sofa seating, poly-carb glass roof and atmospheric lighting. Owner Chris Eddy thinks of his place as an antidote to the cold, isolated atmosphere of New York bars towards a warmer, client-

friendly environment. The chef serves up specialty dishes like fresh gazpacho in the summer and lobster bruschetta."
*509 E. 6th St. (bet. Aves. A and B), (212) 777-5920. Open M-Sa 6pm-1am, **6** to Astor Pl.*

Kush

This relaxed, Middle Eastern-tinged lounge is a good place to meet someone new. Try the olives.
*183 Orchard St. (bet. Houston and Stanton Sts.), (212) 677-7328. Open T-Sa 6pm-4am, Su-M 8pm-4am. **F V** to Second Ave.*

Lansky Lounge

A 20s gangster theme complete with zoot-suited doormen leading you down a long corridor and through two doors so you feel like you're in speakeasy. Martinis are the size of a baby's head and there's pretty good food to boot.
104 Norfolk St. (bet. Delancey and Rivington Sts.),(212) 677-9489, *lanskylounge.citysearch.com. Open M-Su 6pm-4am. MC, V, AmEx,* **J M Z F** *to Delancey St.*

Louis

For people who prefer good conversation to yelling over loud music, this Alphabet City jazz bar is cool and laid-back. You can fritter away your time sipping inexpensive but carefully selected French and Italian wines or imported beer with live jazz four nights a week. While nibbling on olives and goat cheese at the

hand-crafted art deco bar, you can feel at home and out on the town at the same time - just be sure to observe the no cell phone rule. Closed on Mondays.
*649 E. 9th St., (212) 673-1190. Open T-R, Su 7pm-12am, F-Sa 7pm-2am, **L** to First Ave.*

Ludlow Bar

This dependably cool bar stakes all its seating on minimalist couches. The pick-up scene, however, is most robust around the pool table.
165 Ludlow St. (bet. Houston and Stanton Sts.), (212) 353-0536. Open M-F 8pm-4am, Sa-Su 8pm-4am. MC, V, AmEx, **F V** *to Second Ave.*

Luna Lounge

Lively swarms of boho kids populate this cavernous bar. The front room is eminently nondescript, but if you can push through the back room you have a pretty good chance of catching a local rock act.
Lower East Side, 171 Ludlow St. (bet. Houston and Stanton Sts.), (212) 260-2323, www.lunalounge.com. Open M-Su 4pm-4am. Cash Only, **F V** to Second Ave.

Max Fish

Hipsters live it up at this bright and lively Ludlow standard, once a hotspot, now comfortably cool. Play pool with the regulars or spend a week's wages on pinball while enjoying local artists' work hanging on the

walls.
178 Ludlow St. (bet. Houston and Stanton Sts.), (212) 529-3959, *www.maxfish.com. Open M-Su 5:30pm-4am. Cash Only, **F V** to Second Ave.*

Meow Mix

Cool cats of all persuasions are welcome at this campy and casual bar. A hub of the queer art scene, it hosts everything from comedy to poetry to performance art. Pick up a calendar.
*269 E. Houston St. (at Suffolk St.), (212) 254-0689, www.meowmix-chix.com. Open M-R 7pm-4am, F 5pm-4am, Sa-Su 3pm-4am. Cash Only, **F V** to Second Ave. (see Womyn's World sidebar)*

Motor City Bar

"Professional creative types" too old to be carded flock to this unlikely Detroit-themed bar. The vehicular bric-a-brac adorning the walls may strike some as a little corny. Slicker and a little less funky than other joints in these parts, Motor City is favored by locals "cuz there's elbow room."
*127 Ludlow St. (bet. Rivington and Delancey Sts.), (212) 358-1595. Open M-Su 4pm-4am. Cash Only, **J M Z F** to Delancey St.*

Swim

There's not much seating or, for that matter, much space at all. Still, Swim's crowd of benign hipsters and good music (check out the Tuesday night

party) make it worth a visit.
*146 Orchard St. (bet. Rivington and Stanton Sts.), (212) 673-0799. Open M-Su 5pm-4am. MC, V, AmEx, DC, **F V** to 2nd Ave.*

Tile Bar/WCOU Radio

They may serve good martinis, margaritas and hot sake, but sitting down at an old-school bar across from huge wood-framed mirrors, you're going to want a long cool pint. Looking around at the trappings of old New York, it is no surprise the owner is fond of antiques. Check out the vintage black and white photographs of the old neighborhood that adorn the walls. Whether your musical taste runs toward Stan Getz or the Beastie Boys, you're sure to find something on the eclectic jukebox glowing against the back wall. Happy Hour 5-8, seven days a week, and Sundays from midnight to 4 am.
*115 First Ave. (at 7th St.), phone number unavailable. Open M-Su 5pm-4am, **6** to Astor Pl.*

Welcome to the Johnson's

Decorated like the Brady Bunch's rec room, WTTJ's is where the shabby-chic go to meet each other. There are strong drinks at the bar, more for the whiskey-sour set. The jukebox, stocked with classic rock and funk, is one of the city's best.

123 Rivington St. (bet. Essex and Suffolk Sts.), (212) 420-9911. Open M-Sa 3pm-4am, Su 1pm-4am. Cash Only, ⓙⓜⓩ ⓕ *to Delancey St.*

Zum Schneider-Bavarian Bierhaus

An essential German-style beer pub, this place has become a must-drink for locals. The soccer crowd gathers here to watch from a handful of TV screens and drink beer from 10-inch-tall liter mugs of Weltenburger Kloster, Kacker Pschorr, Panlaner, Schneider Weisse and Spaten, to name a few. $5-7 for pints, double that for liters, and accompanied by menu items like Wiener Schnitzel ($15), Bratwurst ($12) and Baked Bavarian Meat Loaf ($10).
107 Ave. C (at 7th St.), (212) 598-1098. Open M-R 5pm-1am, F 4pm-2am, Sa-Su 9pm-4am, ⓛ *to First Ave.*

Clubs
The Sapphire Lounge

Drink before coming to this claustrophobic den. Sweaty fun awaits anyone who can shove their way to the middle of the dance floor. It's deserted on weeknights, though.
249 Eldridge St. (at Houston St.), (212) 777-5153. www.sapphire nyc.com. Open M-Su 7pm-4am. Cash Only, Cover: $3-$5, ⓕⓥ *to Second Ave.* ♿

Music
Arlene Grocery

Arlene has established itself as one of the premiere showcases for many New York-based independent labels. The bands play for free here to build a fan base, and the sound is great. Think acoustic, pop, rock and ska.
95 Stanton St. (bet. Ludlow and Orchard Sts.), (212) 358-1633, www.arlenegrocery.com. Open 6pm-4am. Cash Only, No Cover, ⓕⓥ *to Second Ave.* ♿

East Village

Bars
Ace Bar

Have a beer and play darts or pool in this cavernous neighborhood bar. Take a look at the old lunchboxes you used to own when you were in grade school. It's never too loud or too crowded.
531 E. 5th St. (bet. Aves. A and B), (212) 979-8476. Open M-Su 2pm-4am. MC, V, AmEx, ⓕⓥ *to Second Ave.*

Angel's Share

House rules border on the Draconian: no loud conversation, no parties bigger than four and no standing. But the ambience is intimate, the drinks professionally mixed and the floor-to-ceiling windows offer an excellent view of Stuyvesant Street. Bring a date.
8 Stuyvesant St. (at Third Ave.), (212) 777-5415. Open M-Su 7pm-2am. MC, V, AmEx, DC, 6 to Astor Pl.

Barmacy

Owner Deb Parker (of Beauty Bar fame) welcomes private functions, film shoots, photo shoots and "anything else you'd like to shoot except drugs" at her establishment. It's not reserved most nights when stylish downtowners crowd the place for generously-poured drinks.
538 E. 14th St. (bet. A and B Aves.), (212) 228-2240. Open M-Su 4pm-4am. MC, V, ⓛ *to First Ave.* ♿

B Bar and Grill

Formerly the Bowery Bar, this gives the impression of a place too cool for its own good. It specializes in delightfully strong apple martinis, and the three bars-including an outdoor courtyard and a back-room dance floor-keep customers entertained. Tuesday is gay night and Saturday brings in a young Wall Street crowd. Weekend brunches stay generally mellow.
40 E. 4th St., (212) 475-2220. Open M-F 11:30am-4am, Sa-Su 10:30am-4am, ⓝⓡ *to 8th St.,* ⓺ *to Astor Pl.*

Beauty Bar

Sparkling walls glitter and vintage hair dryers function as lounge chairs at this beauty salon-turned-bar. The owner's own collection of '40s hairpins and pomade ads add to the deliciously kitschy mood. Wednesday afternoon manicure and drink specials are a must.
231 E. 14th St. (bet.

Second and Third Aves.), (212) 539-1389. Open M-F 5pm-4am, Sa-Su 7pm-4am. MC, V, ⓛⓝⓡⓠ ⓦ⓸⓹⓺ *to Union Sq.-14th St.* ♿

Box Car Lounge

They have a cool glass and metal bar area at the front and a lounge area at the back. Box Car Lounge has great specials, especially the sake martinis. It also has an airy garden and happy hour bargains.
168 Ave. B (bet. 10th and 11th Sts.), (212) 473-2830. Open M-R 6pm-4am, F-Su 4pm-4am. MC, V, AmEx, DC, ⓛ *to First Ave.*

Cherry Tavern

It's small. It's cheap. It's got a pool table and a good jukebox, but on weekends it can be suffocatingly packed and smoky.
441 E. 6th St. (bet. First and A Aves.), (212) 777-1448. Open M-Su 6pm-3:45am. Cash Only, ⓺ *to Astor Pl.*

The Cock

The name says it all. Bring your earplugs and surgical masks, because this classic gay bar is not for the faint of lungs or ears. On Saturday nights the party is called Foxy, where anything can and usually does go. On Sundays it's Sperm, where, obviously, only boys dare to tread.
188 Ave. A (at 11th St.), (212) 777-6254. Open M-Su 9.30-4am. Cash Only. ⓛ *to First Ave.*

Coyote Ugly

For all those not in the

know, a coyote ugly is when you get so loaded that you wind up going home with someone and waking up to find that they are singularly unattractive and you would rather cut off your arm than wake them up. It's not pretty and neither is this East Village standard. But dive bars are supposed to be ugly, just don't expect Tyra Banks to be dirty dancing on the bar.
153 First Ave. (bet. 9th and 10th Sts.), (212) 477-4431. Open M-R 2pm-4am, F 1pm-4am, Sa-Su 12:30pm- 4am. MC, V, ❻

to Astor Pl., ❶ *to First Ave.*

Decibel
Go early and with a small group, because this small, beautiful sake bar gets packed fast. Hipsters

descend on it because it's cave like and mellow, great for dates. If you want something more fast-paced, check out its spawn Megadecibel.
240 E. 9th St (bet. Second and Third Aves.), (212) 979-2733. Open M-Su 8pm-3am. MC, V, AmEx. ❻ *to Astor Place.*

Dempsey's Pub
A slightly snobby bar that serves well drinks for $2 and happy hour half-pints for $1.50, don't confuse this place with the more happening Jack Dempsey's bar in Chelsea. This hole looks something

like an old-fashioned German beer hall. Books line the walls and NYU students fill up here on weekends. A neighborhood bar for classics like Irish Amber and Murphy's Stout.
61 Second Ave., (bet. 3rd

and 4th Sts.), (212) 388-0662. Open M-Su 11am-4am. MC, V, AmEx,* ❺❻ *to Second Ave.*

Doc Holiday's
"I'm trapped in here with the convicts who love me," said one bartender about the regulars. On weekends, this country-western joint swarms with hell-raisers who come to admire the wild animal pelts on the walls and the even wilder staff who can often be found dancing on the bar. Try the homestyle BBQ food.
141 Ave. A (bet. 8th and 9th Sts.), (212) 979-0312.

Open M-Su 12am-4am. Cash Only, ❶ *to First Ave.* &

11th Street Bar
Locals fleeing the influx of Avenue A tavern tourists find asylum. Narrow in front at the

crowded bar, it opens up in the back with a handful of tables large enough to fit all your roommates or new friends.
510 E. 11th St. (bet. Aves. A and B), (212) 982-3929. Open M-Su 4pm-4am. MC, V, AmEx, ❶ *to First Ave.* &

Fuel at Phebe's
Last year, a brooding New Yorker named Wolfgang converted this once college-age, pool-shooting dive into a sleek corner bar on the Bowery. The dim-lit venue has a plush, ocean-like lounge in back, with blue, purple and green sofa chairs. At the shiny bar counter in front, they serve out generous pints of Original Sin cider, Magic 9 Lager from Vermont, Boddington's Ale and Stella Artois. Good for the 20s crowd, with DJs on the weekends and Sunday heavy metal nights.
Bowery (at 4th St.), (212) 473-9008. Open M-Su 5pm-2am. MC, V, AmEx, ❿❽ *to 8th St.,* ❻ *to Astor Pl.*

International Bar
Cheap drinks can make you dizzy and claustrophobic at this small dive. You'll have to squeeze past the long bar to the small back part where, if you're lucky, you can get a seat. It's got a mixed crowd and a decent jukebox-and did we mention the cheap drinks yet?
120 First Ave. (bet. 7th and 8th Sts.), (212) 777-9244. Open M-Su 2pm-4am. Cash Only, ❺❻ *to*

Second Ave.

Joe's Pub

This elegant but cozy lounge hosts some of the city's best live music, from hip-hop to cabaret, and acts are nearly always followed by a DJ. The drinks may be expensive but the waitstaff makes up for the prices by being so genial you want to hug them. Live acts are consistently good, so come by even if you have never heard of the musicians.
425 Lafayette St. (bet. East 4th and Astor Pl.), (212) 539-8777, www.joespub.com. Open M-Su 6pm-4am. MC, V, AmEx, Cover: $5-$20, ❻ to Astor Pl.)

KGB

Old Soviet paraphernalia give this small upstairs barroom an illicit feel, which is reinforced by the regular poetry readings and theater downstairs. It's perfect for bringing out your inner subversive artist with a good stiff drink.
85 E. 4th St. (bet. Second and Third Aves.), (212) 505-3360. Open M-Su 7:30pm-4am. Cash Only, ❶❹ to Second Ave.

Lakeside Lounge

Come prepared to wait for your drinks since this hipster haunt is packed even on nights the bartender calls "real slow." Lots of live bands, too.
162 Ave. B (at 10th St.), (212) 529-8463, www.lakesidelounge.com.

Open M-Su 4pm-4am. MC, V, AmEx, ❶ to First Ave. &

Manitoba's

Owned and operated by "Handsome" Dick Manitoba, frontman for NYC's legendary punkers the Dictators, Manitoba's pours some of the East Village's strongest drinks. Dick books live music ranging from country to rock seven nights a week.
99 Ave. B (bet. 6th and 7th Sts.), (212) 982-2511. Open M-Su 4pm-4am. MC, V, AmEx, ❶❹ to 8th St., 6 to Astor Pl. &

Mars Bar

A rowdy and boozy bunch fill this tattered shoebox of a bar at all hours. Possibly the dumpiest, most dishevelled bar on the planet but charming nevertheless.
25 E. 1st St. (at Second

Ave.), No Phone. Open M-Su 12pm-4am. Cash Only, F to Second Ave. &

Mona's

Punk rock lives - in the jukebox at Mona's. It's a favorite place for East Village squatter kids who come here with their mangy dogs and multiple tattoos and piercings.
224 Ave. B (bet. 13th and 14th Sts.), (212) 353-3780. Open M-Su 3pm-1am. Cash Only, ❶ to First Ave.

M & R Bar

A simple combination of good drinks and classic American food have kept the M & R in style, despite increased competition from Orchard and Ludlow Streets. Open for brunch on Saturdays.
264 Elizabeth St. (bet. Houston and Spring Sts.), (212) 226-0559. Open M-Su 5pm-2am. MC, V,

AmEx, ❶❹ to Prince St., ❻ to Bleecker St. &

Niagara

Niagara puts a hip spin on nostalgia. From the bartenders in their silk, hand-painted ties to the bamboo-walled tiki lounge downstairs, Niagara pays homage to America's innocent years. The tiki lounge features a full range of tropical drinks.
112 Ave. A (bet. 7th and 0th Sts.), (212) 420-9517. Open M-Su 4pm-4am. MC, V, AmEx, ❶❹ to Second Ave.

No Malice Palace

Be careful. You might walk right past this signless black hole in the wall. Inside you will find a comfortable dark hideaway to lounge your body and lubricate your tonsils. The drinks tend to be on the pricey side.
197 E. 3rd St. (bet. A and

B Aves.), (212) 254-9184. Open M-Su 7:30pm-4am. Cash Only, ❶❷ *to Second Ave.*

Starlight

A long, dark bar with an open couch-filled area in the back, Starlight is a crowded gay bar that caters to lesbians on its massively popular Sunday night party.
167 Ave. A (bet. 10th and 11th Sts.), (212) 475-2172. Open M-Su 6pm-4am. Cash only. ❻ *to Astor Pl.*

Swift Hibernian Lounge

Beneath the dreamlike painting that stretches the length of the long beer hall, drinkers at Swift's encounter sweating mugs of beers imported from all over the world, which they toss down in in the loud company of friends from the neighborhood. The dim-lit, cavernous back room has long oak tables and separates itself from the bar, physically and atmospherically, with a purple velvet curtain.
34 E. 4th St. (bet. Lafayette St. and the Bowery), (212) 260-3600. Open M-Su 12pm-4am. MC, V, AmEx, ❶❷ *to 8th St.,* ❻ *to Astor Pl.*

288

This bar stocks colorful pottery behind the bar. A jukebox bangs out country and classic rock, and artists and filmmakers in their 20s and 30s make this a regular drinking hole on weeknights. Guinness ranks highly here, and Wisconsin folks are particularly welcome (Packers game every Sunday on the TV).
288 Elizabeth St. (at E. Houston), (212) 260-5045. Open M-Su 12pm-8pm. Cash Only. ❶❸❷ *to Broadway-Lafayette St.,* ❻ *to Bleecker St.*

Clubs
Guernica

Guernica makes up for its tameness with a gourmet late night menu and some top house and bass DJs.
25 Ave. B (bet. 2nd and 3rd Sts.), (212) 674-0984, www.guernicanyc.com. MC, V, AmEx, Cover: free-$5, ❶❷ *to Second Ave.* &

Webster Hall

This is one of the city's biggest nightclubs. Four spacious floors spin disco, reggae and techno. You can even shoot a game of pool. Don't miss out on the flying trapeze show in the wee hours. Lots of bridge a nd tunnel types.
125 E. 11th St. (bet. Third and Fourth Aves.), (212) 353-1600. Open R-Sa 10pm-5am. MC, V, AmEx, D, Cover: $20-$30, ❶❷ ❸❹❺❻ *Union Sq.-14th St.*

Music
Bowery Ballroom

The Bowery Ballroom is one of the premiere venues in the city. It consistently gets good acts. The space is simultaneously cavernous and cozy, and the coat check line moves. With acoustic, country, eclectic, hip-hop, Latin and pop shows.
6 Delancey St. (bet. the Bowery and Chrystie St.), *(212) 533-2111, boweryballroom.com. Hours depend on show times. MC, V, Cover: $10-$20,* ❶❷ *to Second Ave.* &

Brownies

One of the best places to catch bands who are not quite commercial. Sunday shows are for all ages. With blues and rock shows.
169 Ave. A (bet. 10th and 11th Sts.), (212) 420-8392, browniesnyc.com. Open 7pm-3am. MC, V, AmEx, Cover: $6-$10, ❶❷ *to Second Ave.,* ❸ *to First Ave.* &

CBGB

A legend, CBGB's has been a mecca for artists and punks since the 70s, helping to launch acts like Blondie, the Ramones and Patti Smith. You can still catch local and national acts every night of the week. With alternative, pop and rock shows.
315 Bowery (at Bleecker St.), (212) 982-4052, www.cbgb.com. Open 7pm-4am. Cash Only, Cover: $3-$12, ❻ *to Bleecker St.* &

CB's 313 Gallery

The kinder, gentler sibling of CB's. It boasts a superior sound system and staff, and some of the best acoustic-based music in town. A downstairs lounge, with DJ, serves brick oven pizza. With acoustic, electronica, folk and rock shows.
313 Bowery (at Bleecker St.), (212) 677-0455, www.cbgb.com, Open M-Su 12pm-4am. MC, V, *AmEx, DC, D, Cover: $5-$8,* ❶❷ *to Second Ave.,* ❻ *to Bleecker St.* &

Continental

Everybody from Patti Smith to The Ramones to Guns n'Roses has played this famous club. There's an indoor ATM for the cash-strapped. With hard rock and ska shows.
25 Third Ave. (at St. Marks Pl.), (212) 529-6924, www. nytrash.com/continental. Open 4pm-4am. Cash Only, Cover: Free-$10, ❻ *to Astor Pl.,* ❶❷ *to 8th St.* &

Fez (Time Cafe)

Originally the site of Sticky Mike's, a Warhol hangout, now housing hip singer-songwriters like Ellis Paul, Peter Mulvey and Jennifer Kimball. This unique room has mirrored columns and sparkly vinyl booths, and every so often the room vibrates from the subway train passing underneath. Hidden treasure: the Mingus Big Band every Thursday night. Full menu, full bar. With acoustic, comedy, jazz, rock and singer-songwriter shows.
380 Lafayette St. (at Great Jones St.), (212) 533-2680, www.time-cafenyc.com. Cash only, Cover: $8-$20, ❶❷❸ *to Broadway-Lafayette St.* &

Sidewalk Cafe

Before moving to the backroom of the Sidewalk Cafe, the Fort was an

after-hours club on the Lower East Side. It still retains its underground appeal, centered around manager Lach's Anti-Folk Anti-Hoot on Mondays, which is an open mic. Sidewalk Cafe features one of the cheapest breakfast specials in NYC, as well as a full menu and bar. With folk, anti-folk and rock shows.
94 Ave. A (at 6th St.), (212) 473-7373. Open M-F 8pm-4am, Sa-Su 24 hours. MC, V, AmEx, Cover: $3, F V to Second Ave. ♿

Irving Plaza
Mostly a venue for national touring acts with major record label backing and a fair amount of radio play. It's a place to come for the music, not the atmosphere. A long, narrow design causes the crowd to crush at the front.
17 Irving Pl. (at 15th St.), (212) 777-6800, www.irvingplaza. com. Open 1 hr before showtime. AmEx,, L N R 4 5 6 to Union Sq.-14th St. ♿

Mercury Lounge
Once a headstone shop, the Mercury Lounge has established itself as a premiere venue for "just-breaking" bands. High stage, excellent sound system and standing room only for three to five acts per night. With acoustic, alternative and rock shows.
217 E. Houston St. (bet. Essex and Ludlow Sts.), (212) 260-1214, www.mercuryloungenyc.

com. *Open 8pm-12am. MC, V, Cover: $7-$12, F V to Second Ave.* ♿

Nightingale Bar
The Nightingale has a reputation for being the favorite late night jam spot for many now-famous acts. You can see local acts here seven nights a week. Happy hour from 1pm-8pm daily. With pop and rock bands and the occasional soloist.
213 Second Ave. (at 13th St.), (212) 473-9398. Open M-Sa 1pm-4am, Su 7pm-4am. Cash Only, Cover: free-$5, L to Third Ave. ♿

Nuyorican Poets Cafe
The Nuyorican has made a name for itself as a center for experimental music and spoken word art in NYC. Besides its performances, visitors can see visual art exhibits and film retrospectives. Best value: the Friday night poetry slam, with NYC's nationally competitive team. No food, but wine and beer available. With acoustic, experimental, hip-hop, latin, jazz, salsa and spoken word shows.
236 E. 3rd St. (bet. Aves. B and C), (212) 505-8183, www.nuyorican.org. Call for schedule and showtimes. Cash Only, Cover: $5-$15, F V to Second Ave. ♿

Greenwich Village

Bars
Absolutely 4th
This small, snazzy little

lounge is valiantly holding out against the NYU menace. A slightly older, slightly calmer crowd relaxes at the jewel-toned bar, oblivious to the underage debauchery outside.
228 W. 4th St. (at Seventh Ave.), (212) 989-9444. Open M-Su 5pm-3am. MC, V, AmEx, D, 1 2 to Christopher St. ♿

Automatic Slim's
When it gets late - very, very late - dancing on the bar is allowed, one might even say encouraged.
733 Washington St. (at Bank St.), (212) 645-8660. Open M-Su 5pm-4am. MC, V, AmEx. A C E L to 14th St., 1 2 to Chistopher St.-Sheridan Sq. ♿

Bar d'O
Arguably the place that initiated the lounge craze. Tuesdays, Saturdays, and Sundays, DJs host the all-night festivities.
29 Bedford St. (at Downing St.), (212) 627-1580. Open Su-R 7pm-3am, F-Sa 7pm-4am. Cash Only, 1 2 to Christopher St.-Sheridan Sq.

Blind Tiger Ale House
With 24 micro-brews on tap and bottled beers from 12 countries, this haunt satisfies just about anyone's taste for brew. The crowd is strictly white-collar, after-work and non-Budweiser.
518 Hudson St. (at 10th St.), (212) 675-3848, www.blindtigeralehouse.com. Open M-Su 12pm-

4am. MC, V, AmEx, D, 1 2 to Christopher St.-Sheridan Sq.

Boots and Saddle
Urban and rural cowboys flock to this Western-style veteran, proving that denim is friendlier than leather. Happy hour Monday through Friday 3-9pm and Saturday and Sunday Beer Blasts with $1.50 drafts and $2.50 bottles.
76 Christopher St. (at Seventh Ave.), (212) 929-9684. Open M-Sa 8am-4am, Su 12pm-4am. Cash Only, 1 2 to Christopher St.

Cedar Tavern
Pay tribute to Willem de Kooning with a visit to this spacious tavern that the famous abstract expressionist frequented. The patrons are no longer the counterculture scenesters of the '60s, but the Tiffany lighting and the monumental 19th century bar remain.
82 University Pl. (bet. 11th & 12th Sts.), (212) 741-9754. Open M-Su 11:30pm-4am. MC, V, AmEx, DC, D, L N R Q W 4 5 6 to 14th St.-Union Sq. ♿

Crazy Nanny's
Go to this lesbian bar on the weekends for a fun, racially mixed crowd.
21 Seventh Ave. South (at Leroy St.), (212) 366-6312. Open M-F 4pm-4am, Sa-Su 3pm-4am. MC. V, AmEx, 1 2 to Houston St.

Cubbyhole
Favored by friendly college-aged women of vari-

ous sexual persuasions, this small, dark rendezvous spot lives up to the double entendre in its name. The bar has a $5 cover on Saturday nights from 8:30pm to 10pm.
281 W. 12th St. (bet. 7th and 8th Aves.), (212) 243-9041. Open M-R 4pm-2am, F 4pm-4am, Sa 2pm-4am, Su 2pm-2am. Cash Only, ❶❷❸Ⓐ©Ⓔ❶ *to 14th St.*

Down the Hatch

Down the Hatch is pretty straightforward about its essential nature: its a rowdy, fun college bar with busy foosball tables and Christmas lights. Attracting a lot of NYU students and a few older passersby, it attracts a good mix of people for a fun night out.
179 W. 4th St. (bet. 6th and 7th Aves.), (212) 627-9747. M-Su 4pm-3am. MC, Ⓐ©Ⓔ©❶Ⓢ *to W. 4th St.*

Hell

Only in Hell will one find a mix of straight and gay twenty-somethings partying together. Some are on their way to nearby fetish clubs; others are content sipping a fiery martini in Hell's comfy lounge. The drinks are stiff (but stay away from the nightly specials.
59 Gansevoort St. (bet. Washington and Greenwich Sts.), (212) 727-1666. Open Sa-R 7pm-4am, F 4pm-4am. MC, V, AmEx, Ⓐ©Ⓔ ❶ *to 14th St.-8th Ave.*

Henrietta Hudson

This is the internationally-renowned, number-one women's bar in NYC.
438 Hudson St. (at Morton St.), (212) 924-3347. Open M-R 4pm-4am, F-Su 1pm-4am. MC, V, AmEx, ❶❷ *to Christopher St.-Sheridan Sq.*

Nowbar

Intimate without being cramped, the downstairs dance floor is complemented by an upstairs lounge. Creative, indirect lighting renders the festive straight and gay singles crowd visible.
22 Seventh Ave. South (at Leroy St.), (212) 293-0323. R-Sa 10pm-4am. MC, V, AmEx, ❶❷ *to Houston St.*

Off the Wagon

While most of the bars on or near Bleecker strive towards trendy, Off the Wagon insists that just being a bar where people come to get smashed is enough. The name pretty much says it all, and if obliteration is your goal, you've definitely come to the right place.
109 MacDougal St. (bet. Bleeker and 3rd Sts.), (212) 533-4487. M-R 2pm-4am, F-Su 12pm-4am. MC, V, Amex, D Ⓐ ©Ⓔ©❶Ⓢ *to W. 4th St.*

Polly Esther's

Kitsch by the truckload here. Psychedelia, beaded curtains and the requisite Brady Bunch and Sonny and Cher homages will satisfy every Gen-Xer's fantasy of Flower Power and free love. The prices aren't retro, however.
186 W. 4th St. (bet. Sixth and Seventh Aves.), (212) 924-5707, www.pol-lyesthers.com. Open R-Sa 8pm-4am. MC, V, AmEx, DC, D, Cover: $8. ❶❷ *to Christopher St.-Sheridan Sq.* ♿

The Slaughtered Lamb

This is one of the Village's best-known pubs. Tourists flock to this horror-film theme bar for the shocker movies and overpriced drinks.
182 W. 4th St. (bet. 6th and 7th Aves.), (212) 627-5262. Open Su-R 6pm-2am, F-Sa 6pm-4am. MC, V, AmEx, DC, D, Ⓐ©Ⓔ

©©Ⓢ *to West 4th St.-Washington Sq.* ♿

Stonewall

On the night that Judy Garland died in 1969, cops raided the gay bar Stonewall for the umteenth time, and this time the patrons fought back, starting a riot that started the gay rights movement. Now you can swing your hips to loud dance music and maybe even find that Mr. Right for the night too.
53 Christopher St. (at Seventh Ave.), (212) 463-0950. Open M-Su 2:30pm-4am. Cash Only. ❶❷ *to Christopher St. See Gay Nightlife.*

Off the Wagon

109 MacDougal Street
(between West 3rd and Bleecker Sts.)
(212) 533-4487

Kitchen and Bar Open Daily:
2pm-4am Monday - Friday
12pm-4am Saturday-Sunday

Happy Hour
Monday - Friday 4pm-8pm
Half Price Drinks

Monday 8pm-Close
$1 Drafts, $7 Domestic Pitchers
Tuesday 8pm-Close
1/2 Price 1/2 Yards
Wednesday 8pm-Close
◆LADIES' NIGHT◆
$2.50 Flavored Vodka Drinks $1 Drafts
Thursday 8pm-Close
$7 and $10 Pitchers $2 House Shots
Saturday and Sunday 12pm-7pm
$7 and $10 Pitchers   1/2 Price Buffalo Wings
Sunday 8pm-Close
$3 Sundays

POOL TABLE ❖ FOOSBALL TABLE ❖ DARTS
Catch all your favorite sporting events here
Available For All Types of Priviate Functions

The White Horse Tavern

A Village landmark, reputed to be the place where Dylan Thomas drank himself to death. But the poets are long gone, supplanted by a pedestrian twenty-some-thing crowd. Dinner essentials are served, including good burgers. *567 Hudson St. (at W. 11th St.), (212) 243-9260. Open Su-R 11am-2am, F-Sa 11am-4am. Cash Only.* **❶❷❸** *to 14th St.*

The Village Idiot

You go to the Idiot and you get drunk. Their mission is made clear the moment you walk in. It's loud-no-conversation-loud, trashy-country-music loud. The bar-tenders dance on the bar periodically and force shots on anyone naive enough to ask for a glass of water. The beer is cheap. *355 W. 14th St. (at Ninth Ave.), (212) 989-7334. Open M-Su 12pm-4am. Cash Only,* **❶❸❺❶** *to 14th St.* ♿

Clubs
Bowlmor Lanes

Mondays herald the Night Strike: How much do heavy house, drum and bass and disco improve your bowling technique? With glow-in-the-dark pins and shoes after 10pm and lights out, a strike or two are ought to happen. *110 University Place (bet. 12th and 13th Sts.), (212) 255-8188. Open M and F 10am-4am, T-W 10am-1am, R10am-2am, Sa 11am-4am, Su 11am-1am. MC, V, AmEx, Cover: $7 per game per person, $3 shoe rental. Cash Only.* **❶❶❷❹❺ ❻** *to 14th St.-Union Sq.*

The Lure

Leather-bound S&M boys manifest their darkest fantasies. Not exactly for the faint at heart. Thinks weights, clamps, and chains. *409 W. 13th St. (bet. Ninth Ave. and Washington St.), (212) 741-3919. Open M-F 8pm-4am, Sa-Su 3pm-4am. Cash Only, Cover: $0-$5.* **❶❶ ❶** *to 14th St., L to Eighth Ave.*

Spa

If you can get into this club, you are obviously elite. The security is tight and temperamental, and the patrons (many celebs) are a lucky bunch. Décor is bright and clean, drinks are exceptional, DJs are of the highest caliber. *76 E. 13th St. (bet. Broadway and Fourth Ave.), (212) 388-1060. Open T-Sa 10pm-4am. MC, V, Amex* **❶❶❶❶ ❶❹❺❻** *to 14th St.*

Music
Acme Underground

All cleaned up and ready to get dirty: this low-frills basement stage got a makeover and a brand new sound system for its spruced-up lineups. Have ID ready. With alternative rock shows.
9 Great Jones St. (bet. Broadway and Lafayette St.), (212) 420-1934, Open 7pm-4am. Cash Only, Cover: $5-$10. **❶❶** *to 8th St.,* **❶❶❶** *to Broadway-Lafayette St.*

The Baggot Inn

A darkly-lit venue in the heart of the Village. It's a great place to see some of your acoustic singer/songwriters, with plenty of table seating and dollar draft happy hours. With acoustic, pop and rock. *82 W. 3rd St. (bet. Thompson and Sullivan Sts.), (212) 477-0622. www.thebaggotinn. com. Open M-Sa 11am-3am. MC, V, AmEx, Cover: free-$5,* **❶❶❶❶❶❶** *to West 4th St.*

The Bitter End

Opened 40 years ago, The Bitter End has seen countless performers rise to stardom, including Bob Dylan, Joni Mitchell, Tracy Chapman and Jackson Browne. With blues, folk, funk, R&B and rock. *147 Bleecker St. (bet. Thompson St. and LaGuardia Pl.), (212) 673-7030, www.bitter end.com. Open Su-R 7pm-3am, F-Sa 8pm-3am. MC, V, AmEx, DC, D. Cover: $5-$10,* **❶❶❶❶❶❶** *to West 4th St.*

Blue Note

Though the regular fea-tures are an assault on the pocketbook, the five dollar after-hours shows on Fridays and Saturdays are a real bargain. If you

have the money to spend, see some of the national jazz acts that come through that you won't see anywhere else. Full continental menu, full bar. With jazz.
131 W. 3rd St. (bet. MacDougal St. and 6th Ave.), (212) 475-8592, www.bluenote.net. Open Su 12pm-6pm and 7pm-2am, M-Th 7pm-2am, F-Sa 7pm-4am. MC, V, AmEx, Cover: $25 and up, **ⒶⒸⒺⒻⓈⓋ** *to West 4th St.*

Bottom Line

One of New York's oldest and most celebrated venues, beloved by performers and audiences alike. Welcomes local and national acts ranging from '70s artists Jimmy Webb, John Hiatt and Paul Simon to contemporary faves Dan Bern, Jill Sobule and David Wilcox. Full kitchen, full bar.
15 W. 4th St. (at Mercer St.), (212) 228-6300. Call for schedule and showtimes. Cash Only, Cover: $15-$25, **ⓃⓇ** *to 8th St.,* **❻** *to Bleecker St.* &

The Duplex

This piano bar right off Sheridan Square has been providing live show tunes for years. A mature contingent lingers here, so tweed is more prevalent than muscle-tees. Large and elegantly decorated, the legendary space offers cabaret upstairs. Shows are varied and frequent, so make reservations.
61 Christopher St. (at Seventh Ave. South),

(212) 255-5438, www.theduplex.com. Open M-Su 4pm-4am. Cash Only, Cover: $3-$15, **❶❷** *to Christopher St.-Sheridan Sq.*

Elbow Room

A long, spacious room with comfy couches along the wall. It's got a hip vibe, but it's rapidly becoming a tourist trap thanks to a rash of celebrity sightings. With pop and rock.
144 Bleecker St. (bet. Thompson St. and La-Guardia Pl.), (212) 979-8434. Open 6pm-4am. MC, V, AmEx, Cover: $5-

$15, **ⒶⒸⒺⒻⓈⓋ** *to West 4th St.*

Kenny's Castaways

One of the landmark bars in the West Village. It's a good place to have a beer and see some up-and-coming local bands. You can listen to the music from the cozy upper level if you want to get away from the crowd. With blues and rock.
157 Bleecker St. (bet. Thopson and Sullivan Sts.), (212) 473-9870. Open 1pm-4am. MC, V, AmEx, Cover: $5-$10, **ⒶⒸⒺⒻⓈⓋ** *to West*

4th St. &

SOB's

Though the name stands for "Sounds Of Brazil," that doesn't even begin to cover the scope of the first world beat club in New York. A bastion of world rhythm, groove and hip-hop, it's like stepping into a different country every night as African, Middle Eastern, Celtic, Caribbean and Latin American artists use this club as a home base for national tours.
204 Varick St. (at W.

Houston St.), (212) 243-4940, www.sobs.com. Open M-Sa 6:30pm-3am. MC, V, AmEx, Cover: $10-$25, ❶❷ to Houston St. &

The Village Vanguard

With regulars like Woody Guthrie and Pete Seeger, this 64-year-old club was renowned as a center for folk before it became a legend as a jazz club in the fifties. Some of the most important jazz recordings in the world, from Coltrane to Davis to Rollins to Evans, were created within these hallowed walls. You can still catch the top quality mainstream and avant-garde jazz acts each night.
178 Seventh Ave. So. (bet. 11th St. and Waverly Pl.), (212) 255-4037, www.villagevan guard.net. Open Su-R 8:30pm-1am, F-Sa 8:30pm-2am. Cash Only, Cover: $15-$20, ❶❷❸ to 14th St.

SoHo

Bars
Bar 89

A stylish crowd and pricey drinks are nothing unusual in this neck of the words. What's special about Bar 89 is the fabulous unisex bathrooms where the technology boggles the noodle. The clear glass doors suddenly turn opaque upon closing.
89 Mercer St. (bet. Spring and Broome Sts.), (212) 274-0989. Open M-Su 12pm-2am. MC, V, AmEx, ❻ to Spring St. &

Botanica

Botanica's Afro-Cuban decor and snappy but friendly bartenders make this one of the neighborhood's most comfortable places to get sloppy. There's a full bar and a decent selection of draft beers, but don't ask for anything too complicated or silly unless you're prepared to take the heat.
47 E. Houston St. (bet. Mulberry and Mott Sts.), (212) 343-7251. Open M-F 5pm-4am, Sa-Su 4pm-4am. Cash Only, ❺❻❼ to Broadway-Lafayette St.

The Cub Room

Business attire is the unwritten dress code for the young and affluent who enjoy expensive cocktails and a serious pick-up scene, while lounging on the comfy furniture.
131 Sullivan St. (at Prince St.), (212) 677-4100, www.cubroom.com. Open M-Su 12pm-2am. MC, V, AmEx, ❻❼ to Spring St. &

Ear Inn

This place used to be a brothel. These days it's just a homey bar that attracts a hip, yuppie crowd. Ask about their seasonal poetry readings.
326 Spring St. (bet. Greenwich and Washington Sts.), (212) 226-9060, www.earinn.com. Open M-Su 12pm-4am. MC, V, AmEx, ❻❼ to Spring St., ❶❷ to Houston St. &

ñ

Savor pitchers of sangría while admiring the Wednesday night flamenco dancers, and don't even try to resist the tapas. It's tiny, though, so stake out a place early and camp out all night.
33 Crosby St. (bet. Broome and Grand Sts.), (212) 219-8856. Open Su-R 5pm-2am, F-Sa 5pm-4am. Cash Only, ❿❾❽ ❼❻❺ to Canal St. &

Pravda

Pravda embodies neither post-Soviet mayhem nor hard-core proletariat boozing. Still, the eighty flavors of vodka (including the bourgeois mango and raspberry), caviar and rust-tinted decor almost justify the name. High-class SoHo-ites eschew communism for black market prices.
281 Lafayette (bet. Prince and Houston Sts.), (212) 226-4696. Open M and W 5pm-1am, T and R 5pm-2:30am, F-Sa 5pm-3:30am, Su 6pm-1am. MC, V, AmEx, ❻ to Bleecker St. &

The SoHo Grand Bar

This hotel bar is growing ever more popular for their martinis, yet sophisticated neighborhooders head here for their "nightcaps".

310 W. Broadway (bet. Canal and Grand Sts.), (212) 965-3000. Open M-R 12pm-1am, F-Sa 12pm-3am. MC, V, AmEx, D, **A** **C** **E** *to Canal St.* &

Veruka

This is a hot spot for celebrities and the trendy SoHo crowd that loves them. It's noisy and busy every night of the week. More a place for dancing and mingling with hot-shots than hanging out with friends. Every Tuesday the DJ spins progressive house and hip-hop.
525 Broome St. (bet. Thompson St. and Sixth Ave.), (212) 625-1717. Open M-Su 8pm-4am. MC, V, Amex **6** **C** **E** *to Spring St.*

Void

A great free film series is the heart of this nightspot. Find out what the event is ahead of time and be prepared to appreciate it. There's no other social scene, just people lining the walls, mesmerized by the big screen.
16 Mercer St. (at Howard St.), (212) 941-6492, www.voidltd.com. Open T-R 8pm-2am, F-Sa 8pm-3am. Cash only, **N** **R** **Q** **W** **J** **M** **Z** **6** *to Canal St.*

Clubs
Culture Club

This is the place for the ultimate '80s escape, with Reagan-era pop served up in this two-story club. It boasts a casual atmosphere, murals of your favorite '80s artists and even a Delorean that

Michael J. Fox would envy.
179 Varick (bet. King and Charlton Sts.), (212) 243-1999. Open W-Sa 9am-5pm. MC, V, AmEx, D, Cover: $15-$20, **1** **2** *to Houston St.* &

Don Hill's

This clubhouse is consistently crowded with crazy college kids, especially on Wednesday nights for the Beauty party, when kids come out to groove '80s style, and Hot Fudge Sundays, which features soul and hip hop music, and the Famous Squeeze Box on Friday nights: a gay rock drag queen party.
511 Greenwich St. (at Spring St.), (212) 219-2850. Open M-Su 9pm-4am. MC, V, AmEx, D, **C** **E** *to Spring St.,* **1** **2** *to Canal St.* &

Gramercy

Bars
Belmont Lounge

The Belmont Lounge is a dark and comfy spot to enjoy a cigar and drinks with friends after a concert at Irving Plaza. Weekends tend to get a bit crazy, as the Lounge hosts DJs that pack 'em in on Fridays and Saturdays to the tune of a $5 cover.
117 E. 15th St. (bet. Irving Pl. and Park Ave.), (212) 533-0009. Open M-Su 4pm-4am. MC, V, AmEx, **L** **N** **R** **Q** **W** **4** **5** **6** *to Union Sq-14th St.* &

Heartland Brewery

Take the pulse of the after work crowd at this hip Union Square bar.

Patrons move fast, talk fast and drink fast, enjoying the award winning house brews while communing with cell phones, PDAs and sometimes even each other. Plenty of seating is always available.
35 Union Square West (at 17th St.) (212) 645-3400. Open M-Su 12pm-12:30am. MC, V, AmEx, DC, **L** **N** **R** **Q** **W** **4** **5** **6** *to Union Sq.* &

Live Bait

Located on Madison Square Park, curious passerby and neighborhood locals find it hard to resist this urban rendition of the Louisiana bayou. Force your way past the boisterous happy hour crowd to the tables in back in order to sample the Cajun shrimp or the mesquite BBQ.
14 E. 23rd St. (bet. Broadway and Madison Ave.), (212) 353-2400. Open Su-W 11am-1am, R-Sa 11am-2am. MC, V, AmEx, **N** **R** *to 23rd St.* &

Metronome

Slightly more polished and pricey than the other Gramercy bars, Metronome draws an older, professional crowd. There's dancing on Saturday nights and live jazz Wednesday through Saturday.
915 Broadway (at 21st St.), (212) 505-7400. Open T-Sa 5pm-11pm. MC, V, AmEx, DC, **N** **R** *to 23rd St.* &

Paddy Reilly's Music Bar

The world's first and only

all-draught Guinness bar. That's pretty much their deal. They have traditional Irish music seven days a week. Celebrities love the bar, maybe because it's quiet and you can get a seat.
519 Second Ave. (at 29th St.), (212) 686-1210. Open M-Su 11pm-4am. MC, V, AmEx, **6** *to 28th St.* &

Pete's Tavern

Pete's has been a local hangout for ages. Although it's mostly a bar, the Italian menu is more than adequate.
129 E. 18th St. (at Third Ave.), (212) 473-7676. Open Su-T 10:30am-1:30am, W-Sa 10:30am-2:30am. MC, V, AmEx, **L** **N** **R** **4** **5** **6** *to Union Sq.-14th St.*

Red Room at the Gershwin Hotel

The newly renovated Gershwin Hotel's Red Room bar is fast becoming one of the Flatiron District's hottest hangouts. The bar serves only beer and wine, but that doesn't seem to stop the young and pretty mid-twenties crowd from packing the place on weekends. Tuesday nights feature stand-up comedy.
7 E. 27th St. (bet. Fifth and Madison Aves.), (212) 545-8000. Open M-Su 7pm-3am. Cash Only, **6** *to 28th St.* &

Rodeo Bar & Grill

Don't expect cowboy hats and big belt buckles at this cozy Wild West watering hole, but then

again, don't let the giant stuffed buffalo above the bar surprise you. The menu is limited, but live rockabilly bands keep the place swingin'.
375 Third Ave. (at 27th St.), (212) 683-6500, www.rodeo bar.com. Open Su-R 6pm-12:30am, F-Sa 6pm-4am. MC, V, AmEx, DC, D, **6** *to 28th St.* &

Rocky Sullivan's
The owner of this bar is the lead singer of an Irish band named Schanechia (Gaelic for "Storytelling"), which plays here often. This is primarily a Guinness crowd, with a hard-core constituency of Irish males that cluster in the simple, brick-walled beer hall downstairs on Lexington Avenue. 129 *Lexington Ave. (at 28th St,), (212) 725-3871. Open M-Su 4pm-43am.* **6** *to 28th St.*

Music
OHM Nightclub
Latin music and live bands on Wednesdays as well as savory Spanish cooking draws a crowd that is young, mixed and attractive. Free admission for ladies before 9pm. With dance, hip hop, house, funk and R&B. *16 W. 22nd St. (bet. Fifth and Sixth Aves.), (212) 229-2000, www.ohmnyc.com. Open: R-Sa 8pm-4am. MC, V, Am Ex, Cover: $10-$20,* **N R** *to 23rd St.* &

Bars
Barracuda
Dark and cruisy in front, with a funky lounge complete with lava lamps, attracting a young crowd of good-looking men and a smaller crowd of equally hip and attractive women interested in chatting. *275 W. 22nd St. (bet. Seventh and Eighth Aves.), (212) 645-8613. Open 4pm-4am. Cash Only.* **C E** *to 23rd St.,* **1 2** *to 23rd St.* &

Bongo
Famed for their New England-stylelobster rolls, and authentic 50's furniture, this comfortable lounge encourages a low-key atmosphere. *299 Tenth Ave. (bet. 27th and 28th Sts.), (212) 947-3654. Open M-W 5pm-2am, R-Sa 5pm-3am. MC, V, AmEx, DC, D.* **C E** *to 23rd St.*

Ciel Rouge
Can we say, "Date Place"? Sexy and swanky, with all the illicit glamour of a Prohibition-era speakeasy, this retreat offers sophisticated drinks. Hide in the scarlet lounge complete with plush chairs and a baby grand , the ultimate in retro chic. *176 Seventh Ave. (bet. 20th and 21st Sts.), (212) 929-5542. Open Su-R 7pm-2am, F-Sa 7pm-4am. Cash Only.* **1 2** *to 23rd St.*

Dusk
With cracked mirror walls and a bathroom so dark you can't check your make-up, this bar makes it clear that appearances are not the point, so relax and have a drink. The pool table in the front is always busy and the bar further back serves the mostly local crowd killer cosmopolitans and margaritas. *147 W. 24th St. (bet. Sixth and Seventh Aves.), (212) 924-4490. Open M-W 6pm-2am, R-Sa 6pm-4am. MC, V, AmEx, DC, D,* **1 2 3** *to 23rd St.*

"g"
Casual elegance is the key here. The subtly-lit bar is surrounded by lounges galore, and the back features coffee and gourmet juices. *223 W. 19th St. (bet. Seventh and Eighth Aves.), (212) 929-1085. Open M-Su 4pm-4am. Cash Only,* **1 2** *to 18th St.*

Lava
Lava is known for its sweet vodka drinks like the Lava Flow, Blue Lagoon and Purple Haze, all served in gigantic tiki bowls designed to get six people trashed. If you'd like, the bartenders will set them afire. Faux lava flows down the walls and trees. *28 W. 20th St. (bet. Fifth and Sixth Aves.), (212) 627-7867. Open W-Sa 5pm-4am. MC, V, AmEx,* **N R F V** *to 23rd St.* &

Passerby
The signless door front and flashing red, yellow and blue checkered floor suggest another trendy bar. But with nary a martini glass in sight, this low-key watering hole favors locals over supermodels any day. Stick to beer and chat with the ever-changing crowd of gallery employees, yuppies, geeks, artists and loners. *436 W. 15th St. (bet. Ninth and Tenth Aves.), (212) 206-7321. Open M-Su 6pm-2am. MC, V, AmEx,* **A C E L** *to 14th St.*

Slate
The former Chelsea Billiards has been revamped as New York's swankest pool hall. Low blue lighting lends the place a vaguely amniotic effect. There's surprisingly little attitude for this part of town, and the new restaurant, featuring Mediterranean fusion cuisine, is fantastic. *54 W. 21st St. (bet. Fifth and Sixth Aves.), (212) 989-0096. Open M-Su 11am-4am. MC, V, AmEx, DC, D,* **L N R Q U** *W456 to 14th St.-Union Sq.*

Clubs
Centro-fly
This hot spot is filled with all kinds, from club kids to seriously beautiful people. Complaints abound about the attitude factor, but, at least for the time being, Centro-fly is enjoying its time in the limelight. *45 W. 21st St. (bet. Fifth and Sixth Aves.), (212) 627-7770. Open R-Sa 10pm-4am. MC, V, Amex, D, Cover: $10-$20.* **N R F V 1 2** *to 23rd St.*

Cheetah

Most clubs get involved in some Faustian pact: they get real popular for a few months, but then they start to gasp for air. Cheetah avoided this fate. It's never been white-hot, but it's always been respected for its plush interior, beautiful crowd and great hip-hop.
12 W. 21st St. (bet. Fifth and Sixth Aves.), (212) 206-7770. Open M 11pm-4am, W 7pm-4am, R-Su 10pm-4am. MC, V, AmEx, D, F V N R to 23rd St.

Nell's

Three rooms on two floors offer an eclectic mix of music ranging from reggae, hip-hop, jazz, Latin, funk and disco. The elegance of the spacious upstairs room calls for a sophisticated drink from the well-stocked bar. Downstairs, relax in a more intimate lounge or move to house, R&B or classics aimed at a stylish mix of "tourists, regulars and DJs."
246 W. 14th St. (bet. Seventh and Eighth Aves.), (212) 675-1567, www.nells.com. Open T, R-Su 10pm-4am, M 7pm-1am, W 9pm-3am. MC, V, AmEx, Cover: $10-$15, A C E 1 2 3 L to 14th St.

Park

This sleek spot in the far west of Manhattan, one block from Chelsea Piers, brings in models and a generally upscale '30s and '40s set in an elegant, spacious setting. The outdoor garden has leafy trees, fuel-heated lamps and yellow light bulbs overhead. The interior feels industrial with a Zen touch, like the Japanese paper lanterns and the brick walls that pad the heavy music beat. Park can be a little confident in its clean-cut atmosphere. Special plates include mussels and chorizo ($12), fois gras ($18), steak tartare ($13), and larger numbers such as pan seared salmon and couscous ($21), paella ($25) and the delicate duck sandwich ($13).
118 Tenth Ave. (bet. 17th and 18th Sts.), (212) 352-3313. Open M-Su 6pm-12am. A C E L to 14th St.

Roxy

Almost always crowded, the place hosts nonstop dancing. The crowd is different every night. Saturday packs in the Chelsea boys.
515 W. 18th St. (bet. Tenth and Eleventh Aves.), (212) 645-5156. www.roxy.com. Cash Only, Cover: $10-$25, C E to 23rd St.

Serena

A low ceiling, red walls, and curious tin chandeliers lend a cozy atmosphere to this basement lounge under the Chelsea Hotel. Perch yourself atop one of the seats surrounding the gargantuan U-shaped bar, or sink, drink in hand, into a couch lining one of the adjacent rooms and dig the foxy clientele.
222 W. 23rd Street (bet. Seventh and Eighth Aves.), (212) 255-4646. MC, V, AmEx, Cover: None. C E to 23rd St.

Bars

Campbell Apartments

With lush oriental carpeting, comfy lounge chairs, and an arabesque ceiling, Campbell Apartments is more than just a cozy spot for Wall-Streeters to throw back a few before hitting the Metro-North. Be forewarned, drinks are pricey and the place closes around midnight.
15 Vanderbilt Ave. (at Grand Central), (212) 953-0409. Open M-Sa 3pm-1am, Su 3pm-11pm. MC, V, AmEx, S 4 5 6 7 to 42nd St.-Grand Central.

Carnegie Club

This two-floor cigar kingdom attracts the usual white-collar crowd. No smoking jackets spotted here, but patrons do enjoy feeling literary among bookshelves while sipping fabulous martinis. Live jazz rounds out the ambience on weekends.
156 W. 56th St. (bet. Sixth and Seventh Aves.), (212) 957-9676. Open M-Sa 4:30pm-1am. MC, V, AmEx, N R Q W to 57th St.

Danny's Skylight Room at the Grand Sea Palace

While it claims to have one of the best sound and lighting systems in the city, most people go to this reasonably priced bar for the skylight.
346 W. 46th St. (bet. Eighth and Ninth Aves.), (212) 265-8130, www.danysgrandpalace.c om. Open M-Su 12pm-12am. MC, V, AmEx, DC, D, A C E N R S Q W 1 2 3 7 to 42nd St.

Hannah's Lava Lounge

A small but cozy hideout, Hannah's serves a wide range of drinks and has live music every night. Most sip martinis on antique couches in the back room.
923 Eighth Ave. (between 54 & 55th Sts.), (212) 974-9087. Open M-Su 12pm-4am, C E to 50th St.

Hudson Bar

Take a fluorescent green escalator to reach this trendy bar with shiny floors, bright lights, translucent gel cushions on Louis XV chairs and a main bar that glows from within. But this hip place also has overpriced drinks and a pretentious staff. Guys coming alone will have a difficult time making it past the velvet rope.
356 W. 58th St. (bet. Eighth and Ninth Aves.), (212) 554-6343. Open M-Su 4pm-4am. MC, V, AmEx A B C D 1 2 to 59th St.

Jimmy's Corner

Escape the giddiness of the Theater District at this easy-going local dive, the site of some scenes in Raging Bull. Owner Jimmy Glen subsidizes his career as a boxing trainer and manager with the revenues from this hopping bar. An eclectic crowd of boxing fanatics, literateurs, grad students and the occasional movie star. *140 W. 44th St. (bet. Sixth and Seventh Aves.), (212) 944-7819. Open M-Su 11am-4am. MC, V, AmEx,* **A C E N R S Q W 1 2 3 7** *to 42nd St.*

La Nueva Escuelita

One of those rare places that manages to be popular without pretension, LaNueva Escuelita is a pseudo-salsa, heavily gay club that opts for mayhem over slickness. Best known for sheer fabulosity and salsa nights. *301 W. 39th St. (bet. Eigth and Ninth Aves.), (212) 631-0588. Open R-Sa 9pm-2am, Su 8pm-1:30am. MC, V, AmEx, D,* **A C E N R S Q W 1 2 3 7** *to 42nd St.*

Le Madeleine

This brick-walled French bistro hosts guests with a pretty courtyard and a glass roof.
Free chips are served at the bar counter, and French-style dishes run from about $15 up-perfect for a cozy dinner after a Broadway show. *403 W. 43rd St. (bet. 10th and 11th Aves.), (212) 246-2993. Open M-Su 12pm-12am.* **A C E N R S Q W 1 2 3 7** *to 42nd St.*

Monkey Bar

It's hip, hopping and hot. This Art Deco masterpiece has a glamorous older crowd sipping cocktails and flaunting Chanel. The bar is named after a glamorous '40s style actress living at the hotel who always brought her monkey down with her. The epitome of swank. *Hotel Elysée, 60 E. 54th St. (bet. Madison and Park Aves.), (212) 838-2600. Open M-R 12pm-2am, F 12pm-3am, Sa 5:30pm-3am, Su 5:30pm-12am. MC, V, AmEx, DC,* **6** *to 53rd St.* &

The Oak Room

One of two lounges at the Algonquin Hotel where Dorothy Parker's wit presided over a legendary circle of writers and critics in the '20s. Dress up to fit in with the stylish crowd soaking up late-night cabaret performances in this stylish English tearoom. *59 W. 44th St. (bet. Fifth and Sixth Aves.), (212) 840-6800. Open M-Su 7pm-4am. MC, V, AmEx,* **B D F V** *to 42nd St.* &

O'Flaherty's Ale House

Here, you'll find the only pub in NY with a tree growing right through the middle of the bar. In the back, discover a private garden away from the Midtown bustle. Live music, great beer and plenty of dancing keep everyone busy. *334 W. 46th St. (bet. Eighth and Ninth Aves.), (212) 581-9366. Open M-Su 12pm-4am. MC, V, AmEx, Entrees: $21-$30. DC, D,* **1 2** *to 50th St.,* **N R** *to 49th St.*

O'Lunney's Times Square Pub

This late night spot with a bit of a cult following serves food until 3 am.
Expect Irish and American cuisine and a rowdy post-theatre crowd. The selection of food is basic, but the beers are exceptional. Service can be lacking, but the ambiance is generally fun and the moderate prices on the menu will keep you in your seat. *151 W. 46th St. (bet. Broadway and Sixth Ave.), (212) 840-6688, www.olunneys.com. Open M-Su 11am-4am. MC, V, AmEx, DC, D,* **A C E N R S Q W 1 2 3 7** *to 42nd St.*

Parnell's Pub

Outfitted with a dark wood bar and plenty of Irish pride, this bar/restaurant serves traditional dishes along with the famous Guinness. *350 E. 53rd St. (bet. First and Second Aves.), (212) 355-9706. Open M-Su 11am-4am. MC, V, AmEx,* **E V 6** *to Lexington Ave.-51st St.* &

Revolution

Yuppies gather around the fireplace, smoke long cigarettes and trade jokes at this watering hole that is unusually hip and upscale for Hell's Kitchen. A basic upscale bar. *611 Ninth Ave. (bet. 43rd and 44th Sts.), (212) 489-8451. Open M-Su 5pm-3am. MC, V, AmEx, DC, D,* **A C E N R S Q W 1 2 3 7** *to 42nd St.* &

Les Sans Culottes

An authentic country-style French restaurant that fills up with the theater crowd until 8 p.m. A range of French courses are available for $20.95
with a wide selection of French wines. *347 W. 46th St., (212) 247-4284. Open M, T, R, F 12pm-12am, W, Sa 11:30am-12am, Su 12pm-11pm.* **A C E N R S Q W 1 2 3 7** *to 42nd St.*

The Townhouse Club

An extremely professional gay bar catering to well-dressed men with big bank accounts and the fellows who love them. A piano bar in back augments the somewhat pretentious ambience. *236 E. 58th St. (bet. Second and Third Aves.), (212) 754-4649. Open M-Su 4pm-4am. Cash Only,* **N R W F 4 5 6** *to Lexington Ave.*

Siberia

Literally a hole in the wall, Siberia is small, dark, and revels in its trashiness. Siberia attracts a diverse crowd, from actor/waiters to yuppies. Their jukebox is among the best in town, and they host DJs and film screenings weekly. *250 W. 50th St. (bet. Eighth and Ninth Aves.), (212) 333-4141. Open M-Su 3pm-4am. Cash Only,* **1 2** *to 50th St. .*

Clubs
Exit

Exit's is the Wal-Mart of the New York club scene. The scene is mostly young people, people on ecstasy or both. While it's not as hip as Spa or Saci, it has much less attitude. *610 W. 56th St. (bet. Tenth and Eleventh Aves.), (212) 582-8282. Open F-Sa 10pm-6am.*

MC, V, AmEx, D, **①②ⒸⒺ** to 50th St.

Saci

Saci is a pretentious warehouse . The crowd is generally attractive and well-dressed but guys without ladies will have to wait a long time to get in. The dance music is not the latest and a good drink is extremely expensive (and comes in a plastic cup no less.)
135 W. 41st St. (bet. Sixth Ave. and Broadway), (212) 278-0988. Open R-Sa10pm-4am. MC, V, AmEx, DC, **ⒶⒸⒺⓃⓇ ⓈⓆⓌ①②③⑦** *to 42nd St.*

Music
Carnegie Hall

Still the reigning champ of bourgeois nightlife, this legendary institution is the artist's Valhalla. Concerts usually take place every night of the week except July-August, when the Hall is closed for the season. The majority of acts are classical, but you still may catch the occasional Joan Baez or David Bowie if you're lucky. Adjoining restaurant and bar serves American cuisine. With classical, pop, and special events.
881 Seventh Ave. (at 57th St.), (212) 247-7800, www.carnegie hall.org. Call for schedule and showtimes. MC, V, AmEx, Cover: $16-$150, **ⓃⓇⓆⓌ** *to 57th St.* ♿

Connolly's

You can't be Irish in New York if you haven't heard of Black 47, the Dublin rock band. Black 47 plays at Connolly's every Saturday, with other acts occasionally playing the odd night. Full menu, full bar (of course).
14 E. 47th St. (bet. Fifth and Madison Aves.), (212) 867-3767, www.conollysnyc.com. Open M-Sa 11am-4am, Su 12pm-4am. MC, V, AmEx, Cover: $10, **ⒺⓋ** *to Fifth Ave.* ♿

Don't Tell Mama

This authentic piano bar off the Broadway theater district provides any kind of music upon request, both in the front room and in the back. Happy hour runs between 4 and 7 p.m., half price for drinks.
343 W. 46th St.(bet. Eighth and Ninth Aves.), (212) 757-0788. Open M-Su 4pm-4am. **ⒶⒸⒺⓃⓇⓈⓆⓌ ①②③⑦** *to 42nd St.*

Downtime

Plenty of seating at the bar and at tables makes this a comfortable room to listen to emergent New York bands. One of the best open mic nights in town (Thurs.). No food, full bar. With hip-hop, pop, and rock.
251 W. 30th St. (bet. Seventh and Eighth Aves.), (212) 695-2747. Open M-Su 5pm-4am. MC, V, Cover $5-$10, **①②** *to 28th St.* ♿

Hammerstein Ballroom

Opened in 1906 by Oscar Hammerstein, the ballroom is the setting for a number of national tour-ing acts as well as television broadcasts and corporate events. Music may be an eclectic roster from Hanson to Manson. No food, several bars. With ethnic, hip-hop, metal, pop, punk, rhythm, and rock.
311 W. 34th St. (bet. Eighth and Ninth Aves.), (212) 485-1534. Call for schedule and showtimes. Cash Only, Cover: $20-$60, **ⒶⒸⒺ①②③** *to 34th St.-Penn Station.* ♿

Iridium

This large music lounge has been relocated from the Lincoln Center to the heart of the tourist area in Midtown. Big-name bands play here every week, bringing in both the local hardcore jazz fans and curious foreign tourists. Drinks run $7 to $10 and food entrees average around $20 each.
1650 Broadway (at 51st St.), (212) 582-2121. Open Su-R 5pm-12am, F-Sa 7pm-2am, **①②ⒶⒸ** *to 50th St.*

B. B. King Blues Club & Grill

A prestigious place for New York musicians , this venue lodged between Broadway's musical theaters combines a restaurant with a music hall and attracts both locals and tourists. Music ranges from blues, jazz and rock to soul and hip hop, featuring big-name artists like B.B. King himself.

Some 500 people can pack this luxurious music hall and enjoy good American food and drink over a wonderful evening of live music. Then again, few come for the food. *237 W. 42nd St. (bet. Seventh and Eighth Aves.), (212) 997-4144. Call for schedules and showtimes. MC, V, AmEx,* **A C E N R S Q W 1 2 3 7** *to 42nd St.*

Roseland

It started as a popular ballroom in the 1930s, and the newly renovated Roseland is still one of the more frequented venues in town. Large enough to draw a sizable crowd but small enough to retain some of that club charm, these days expect to find the bigger names in alternative acts. No food, full bar. With alternative rock, dance and pop. *239 W. 52nd St. (bet. Broadway and Eighth Ave.), (212) 777-6800, www.roselandballroom.com. Call for schedule and showtimes. Cash Only, Cover: $15-$20.* **1 2 C E** *to 50th St.*

The Supper Club

As one of New York's more elegant venues, be prepared to dress up for a night of dinner and dancing on the town. Historically a ballroom, The Supper Club is the center of the swing scene every Friday and Saturday night. During the rest of the week, catch a live band under the sparkling

chandelier and painted gold stars. French and American Continental served from 5:30pm-12:30am. With '40s lindy-hop, jump, swing, occasional private rock and pop concerts. *240 W. 47th St. (bet. Broadway and Eighth Ave.), (212) 921-1940, www.supperclub.city-search.com. Open F-Sa 5:30pm-4am. MC, V, AmEx, Cover: $20-$25,* **1 2** *to 50th St.,* **N R** *to 49th St.*

Swing 46 Jazz and Supper Club

Rocking with swing music on a dance floor by the dining hall, this venue serves a three-course dinner at a fixed price of $18.95 every day of the week. A dressy code is required, no jackets necessary. *349 W. 46th St. (bet. Eighth and Ninth Aves.), (212) 262-9554. www.swing46.com. Open M-Su 5pm-3am. MC, V, AmEx,* **A C E N R S Q**

W 1 2 3 7 *to 42nd St.*

W. Bank Café's Laurie Beachman Theatre

W. Bank Café's cabaret room is just below the restaurant and bar. It's a place for a nice dinner followed by a relaxing evening downstairs. Great for entertaining out-of-town business clients. *407 W. 42nd St. (bet. Ninth and Tenth Aves.), (212) 695-6909. Open M-Sa 11:45am-1am, Su 11:30am-3pm, 4pm-12am. MC, V, AmEx, call for cover charges for individual shows,* **A C E N R S Q W 1 2 3 7** *to 42nd St.*

Upper East Side

Bars
American Spirits

This dive is popular with the mid-20s set, probably due to karaoke on Tuesday and Thursday nights, and an epic daily happy hour. *1744 Second Ave. (at 91st St.), (212) 289-7510. www.americanspiritsnyc.com. Open Su-T 3pm-4am, F-Sa 12pm-4am. MC, V, AmEx, DC, D,* **4 5 6** *to 86th St.*

American Trash

Bikers and bankers meet without colliding at this East Side dive. Its subtitle -"professional drinking establishment" - suggests democracy. *1471 First Ave. (bet. 76th & 77th Sts.), (212) 988-9008. Open M-Su 12pm-4am. MC, V, AmEx,* **6** *to 77th St.*

Amsterdam Billiard Club

More genteel than most pool halls, the ABC is the kind of place that's full of old men and dark wood. Weekends can get feisty, but mostly the scene is laid-back, with lots of regulars, such as director/owner Paul Sorvino. *210 E. 86th St. (bet. Second and Third Aves.),*

*(212) 570-4545.
www.amsterdambilliards-
club.com. Su-W 12pm-
2am, R-Sa 12pm-3am.
MC, V, AmEx, D,* **④⑤⑥**
to 86th St.

Auction House

Mature customers popu-
late this pricey, baroque
lounge, a microcosm of
the Upper East Side. *300
E. 89th St. (bet. First and
Second Aves.), (212) 427-
4458. Open M-Su 8pm-
4am. MC, V, AmEx, DC, D,*
④⑤⑥ *to 86th St.* ♿

Big Sur

If the shenanigans of the
young working crowd
enjoying rock music in
comfortable seating does-
n't suit you, check out
the alternate social scene
near the unisex bath-
rooms.
*1406 Third Ave. (at 80th
St.), (212) 472-5009.
Open M-W 4:30pm-11pm,
R-Sa 4:30pm-12am, Su
4:30pm-10pm. MC, V,
AmEx, DC,* **⑥** *to 77th St.*
♿

Brother Jimmy's

Anyone from below the
Mason-Dixon line will
feel at home in this
southern bar. Post-colle-
giate pre-professionals
come for the generous
bartenders and Sunday
special: $18.95 for unlim-
ited beer and all the ribs
you can stomach.
*1485 Second Ave. (bet.
77th and 78th Sts.), (212)
288-0999, Open M-F
5pm-2am, Sa-Su 12pm-
4pm. MC, V, AmEx,* **⑥** *to
77th St.* ♿

The Cocktail
Room

Painted in neon colors

and furnished with
'60s mod dinettes,
the Cocktail Room
looks like some-
thing out of "A
Clockwork
Orange." Instead,
enjoy an impres-
sive array of
extremely well-
made cocktails.
The prices are a bit
steep, but the
pours are gener-
ous. Light tapas
menu available.
*334 E. 73rd St.
(bet. First and
Second Aves.),
(212) 988-6100.
Open M-F 5pm-
4am, Sa 7pm-4am.
MC, V, AmEx, D,*
④⑤⑥ *to 72nd
St.* ♿

Hogs &
Heifers
North

While a little tamer than
its downtown cousin,
Hogs East is still a
raunchy, good-times
country & western bar.
The beers are always cold
and cheap, and the music
is always live, whether
there's a band playing or
just a bunch of drunks
singing along to Willie
Nelson on the juke box.
*1843 First Ave. (at 95th
St.), (212) 722-8635.
Open t-W 3pm-2am, R-
Sa 3pm-4am. Cash Only,*
⑥ *to 96th St.* ♿

Lexington Bar and
Books

This pricey, high-class
cigar bar offering great
ambience and fantastic
martinis is a nice place to
pretend you're all grown
up with the white-collar
types. Proper attire is

required. Live jazz on
Fridays and Saturdays.
*1020 Lexington Ave. (at
72nd St.), (212) 717-3902.
Open Su-R 4:30pm-2am,
F-Sa 4:30pm-4am. MC, V,
AmEx, DC,* **⑥** *to 68th St.*

Subway Inn

It's right across the way
from Bloomingdale's, but
you'll seldom see shop-
pers take a load off their
Blahniks at this perfect
dive bar. Dark, smelly,
dirty and cheap, Subway
is heroically antithetical
to the glittering, retail
stores surrounding it.
Drink up and then tumble
down the conveniently
proximate subway
entrance.
*143 E. 60th St. (at
Lexington Ave.), (212)
223-8929. M-Sa 8am-
4am, Su 12pm-4am. Cash*

Only, **FNRW④⑤⑥**
*to 59th St.-Lexington
Ave.* ♿

Music
The Sun Music
Company

A new version of
the famous but
recently-
defunct Fast
Folk Cafe, The
Sun Music
Company is more
for the performer than
the audience. Weekend
shows regularly feature
touring artists and indie-
label acts, and Mondays
host a workshop series on
things such as guitar
playing, songwriting,
vocal technique and
music business issues.
Wine, beer and snacks are
available.
340 E. 71st St. (at First

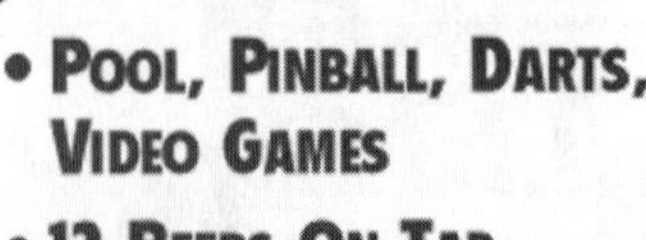

Ave.), (212) 396-9521. Open 8:30pm-12am. Cash Only, Cover: $10, ❻ to 68th St.-Hunter College. ♿

Central Park

Bars

Loeb Boathouse

It's the only place to get a cocktail in Central Park. Luckily, it's a gorgeous one. Come and pass an afternoon at one of the outside tables and watch city slickers haplessly plying the oars on rental dinghies. Hours vary with the season (and weather) and rarely extend past nine, so call ahead. Adjacent cafe serves food. Central Park, Central Park Lake (at 74th St.), (212) 517-2233. Open W-Sa 6pm-10pm, Buffet Brunch Sa-Su 11:00am-3:00pm. MC, V, AmEx, DC, D, ❷❸ to 72nd St. ♿

Upper West Side

Bars

420 Bar and Lounge

This swank member of the Amsterdam scene, populated with the requisite professionals and well-heeled single malt sippers, could teach the SoHo lounges a thing or two. Local scenesters, spared the cab fare downtown, don't seem to mind the pricey cocktails. 420 Amsterdam Ave. (at 80th St.), (212) 579-8450. Open M-Su 5pm-4am MC, V, AmEx, DC, D, ❶❷ to 79th St. X)

The All State Cafe

Once the Upper West Side's best singles bar, the All State is still a great place to grab a steak or a beer. The menu features hearty American offerings, and the draughts run cool with several good ales. The regular clientele is a mixed bag of young professionals and old-timers. 250 W. 72nd St., (bet. West End Ave. and Broadway), (212) 874-1883. Open M-Su 11:30am-2am. Cash Only, ❶❷❸ to 72nd St.)

Blondies

Mounted televisions playing sporting events run continuously above the batenders, whose blonde coifs explain this boisterous sports bar's name. Try the "world-famous atomic wings." 212 W. 79th St. (bet. Broadway and Amsterdam Aves.), (212) 362-4360. Open M-Su 110:30am-4am. MC, V, AmEx, DC, ❶❷ to 79th St. ♿

The Boat Basin Café

This open-air drink scene feels like a medieval courtyard with the sweet smell of barbecue. A clean-cut 30s crowd languiushes on three separate levels under a Romanesque ceiling and thick stone pillars. Look out over the Hudson and the lights of New Jersey and enjoy tasty oddities like the smoked chicken and spinach salad with apples and toasted walnuts. But dress to kill-this place is for groups out to have fun and singles looking for action. W. 79th St. at the Hudson River, (212) 496-5542. M-Su 11am-10pm, ❶❷ to 79th St.

Bourbon Street

Show up here to find athletic women dancing on the bar (especially Friday and Saturday nights) and kick back. Lots of neighborhood sport teams love to frequent this bar and take in a few brews. Make sure to have a potent frozen hurricane or two. 407 Amsterdam Ave. (at 79th St.), (212) 721-1332, Open M-Su 12pm-4am, M, V, AmEx, ❶❷ to 79th St., http://www.bourbon-streetnyc.com.

Dive Bar

Sure, it's got dive written all over it, literally, but this haunt is actually quite tame. Even the resident pool sharks won't intimidate. Chug till 4am every day and don't overlook a strong menu. 732 Amsterdam Ave. (at 96th St.), (212) 749-4358. Open M-Su 11am-4am. MC, V, AmEx, ❶❷❸ to 96th St., ❷❸ to 96th St.

Dublin House

While not a traditional Irish bar, the Dublin House is nevertheless a blessing to the Upper West Side. Its unpretentious atmosphere and straight-up bar attract the authentic old-timer and college student alike. Even the expat Irish come here.
225 W. 79th St. (bet. Broadway and Amsterdam Ave.), (212) 874-9528. Open M-Su 8am-3:30am. Cash Only, ❶❷ *to 79th St.* ♿

The Evelyn Lounge

This spacious bar that is crowded most days of the week. It's sort of romantic, with fireplaces and comfortable chairs and couches in the back rooms. On the other hand, it's kind of cheesy. Evelyn is a singles scene with men outnumbering women about 3 to 1. There is live music several nights a week but not enough room to dance.
380 Columbus Ave. (at 78th St.), (212) 724-5145. Open Su-R 5pm-2am, F-S 5pm-4am. MC, V, AmEx, DC, ❶❷ *to 79th St.*

The Gin Mill

Tasty shots with silly names abound, and there is never a Jaegermeister shortage. Don't categorize the Gin Mill as a sports bar, but rest assured you can always catch the Sunday game here. A great place to chill, have food, and drink.
442 Amsterdam Ave. (bet. 81st and 82nd Sts.), (212) 580-9080. Open M-F 11am-4am, Sa-Su 12pm-4am. MC, V, AmEx, ❶❷ *to 79th St.* ♿

Jake's Dilemma

This bar steals attention from other bars along the Amsterdam bar strip in the West 80s. With three levels, a young, hip crowd, pool tables, and good looking bartenders, Jake's only dilemma is what drink to order next.
430 Amsterdam Ave. (bet. 80th and 81st Sts.), (212) 580-0556. Open M-F 5pm-4am, Sa-Su 1pm-4am. MC, V, AmEx, ❶❷ *to 79th St.* ♿

Parlour

This Irish bar has good drinks and especially fine Guinness for the Upper West Side. The traditional Irish ambiance keeps the yuppie Upper West Siders at bay. Jeans are okay here even on the weekends. The ample seating and downstairs dance area provide for a relaxed night with friends.
250 W. 86th St. (bet. Broadway and Riverside Dr.), (212) 580-8923. Open M-F 12pm-4am, Sa-Su 11am-4am. MC, V, AmEx, ❶❷ *to 86th St.*

The P & G

You may know the P&G from its cameo roles in *Taxi Driver, Seinfeld* or *Donnie Brasco*, but it's still an unassuming place. An old neighborhood bar dating back to the 1940s, the P&G is the real deal, filled with locals and old-timers drinking to tunes from the classic rock jukebox.
279 Amsterdam Ave. (at 73rd St.), (212) 874-8568. Open M-Sa 10am-4am. Su 12pm-2am. Cash Only, ❶❷❸ *to 72nd St.* ♿

Potion

Potion has cool décor, with an outside wall marked by portholes of blue bubbles. Their special drinks called "potions" are decent but also, at $10, expensive. It is frequently crowded with young yuppie types, and there are too few places to sit. Also, the bouncers and the bartenders can be obnoxious.
370 Columbus Ave. (bet. 77th and 78th Sts.), (212) 721-4386, www.potion lounge.com. Open T-Sa 7pm-4am. MC, V, AmEx, ❶❷ *to 79th St.*

Prohibition

This bar is good for hanging out with friends. There is little style and the live music is often amateurish, but the atmosphere is not pretentious. There is plenty of seating and a pool table.
503 Columbus Ave. (bet. 84th and 85th Sts.), (212) 579-3100. Open M-Sa 5:30pm-4am, Su 5:30pm-3pm. MC, V, AmEx, DC, D, ❶❷❸❻ *to 86th St.*

Raccoon Lodge

You'll get just what you'd expect from a bar with this name-it's a dive. The patrons are not your typi-

cal Upper-West Siders; men with cowboy hats and motorcycles frequent this bar. Maybe it's the video and electronic poker games. There is little seating and what there is resembles picnic tables. The alcohol is cheaper than the average for the neighborhood, which is a plus.
480 Amsterdam Ave. (at 83rd St.), (212) 874-9984. Open M-F 11am-4am, Sa-Su 1pm-4am. MC, V, AmEx, D, ❶❷ to 86th St.

Shark Bar

A well-known, upscale hangout. Low lighting and polished wood accents make this hideaway a romantic alternative to other more raucous bars. You might need to ward off the post-collegiate singles hovering around the bar.
307 Amsterdam Ave. (bet. 74th and 75th Sts.), (212) 874-8500, www.sharkbar.com. Open Su-T 5pm-1:30pm, W 12pm-12am, R 12pm-12:30am, F 12pm-1:30am, Sa 5pm-1:30am. MC, V, AmEx, ❶❷❸ to 72nd St. ♿

Time Out

For the true sports fanatic: know your stats and be ready to talk some serious trivia. The crowd of cheering, jeering, thirty-something men ignores the pool table in favor of the twenty-three televisions. This is New York's home to the Celtic's soccer supporter club, so know what you mean when asking about the "football" game.
349 Amsterdam Ave. (bet. 76th & 77th Sts.), (212) 362-5400. Open M-F 5pm-3am, Sa-Su 12pm-3am. MC, V, AmEx, D, DC, ❶❷ to 79th St. ♿

Yogi's

An old-fashioned country saloon like this one provides a stark contrast to the new age eateries and standard pubs that line Broadway and Amsterdam in the 70s. Bras dangle behind the bar and the jukebox is stacked with hits by Credence, Willie Nelson, Johnny Cash and Dolly Parton. Enjoy $8 pitchers of Bud under a big American flag and a bear's head, alongside shouting sports fans.
2156 Broadway (bet. 75th and 76th Sts.), (212) 873-9852. Open M-Su 11:30am-4am, ❶❷❸ to 72nd St.

Bars
1020 Bar

While most of the bars in Morningside Heights pretend to be something they are not, 1020 is just a bar, and quite content that way. During the week, come with a good friend to throw back a few in peace. On the weekends, watch the artsy kids take their first fumbling steps towards skankiness at a nascent pick-up scene. The drinks are okay and prices are friendly.
1020 Amsterdam Ave. (bet. 110th and 111th Sts.), (212) 531-3468.

Open M-Su 4pm-4am. MC, V, AmEx, ❶❷ to Cathedral Parkway (110th St.) ♿

Abbey Pub

Both the food and the atmosphere are comforting at this ideal neighborhood bar where older locals mingle easily with the collegiate (and younger) crowd. A perfect spot to meet for beers and a shared basket of fish 'n chips.
237 W. 105th St. (bet. Broadway and Amsterdam Ave.), (212) 222-8713. Open M-F 4pm-2am, Sa-Su 4pm-3am. MC, V, AmEx, ❶❷ to 103rd St.

Amsterdam Café

This local favorite, espicially of AEPi, is a great place to visit, especially the padded bar. Columbia students and locals alike come for cheap pitchers, pub grub and sports TV in a relaxed restaurant atmosphere.
1207 Amsterdam Ave. (bet. 119th and 120th Sts.), (212) 662-6330. Open M-Su 9am-4am. MC, V, D, AmEx, DC, ❶❷ to 116th St.-Columbia University.

Eden

This new bar near Columbia is a perfect place to settle down on one of the many comfortable couches. With lots of space to enjoy the intimate setting, you'll find tasty drinks at reasonable prices. Make sure to try the "Naked". Mostly for couples and mid-20-somethings looking to relax in a unique

Morningside Heights venue. *2728 Broadway (between 104th and 105th Sts.), (212) 865-5565. Open M-Su 5pm-4am. MC, V, D. ❶❷ to 103rd St.*

The Heights

A favorite spot for Columbia undergrads and grads alike, stop by for their famous $3 frozen margaritas during happy hour (5 p.m. - 7 p.m., 11:30 p.m.- 12:30 a.m.). Make sure to arrive before happy hour if you want a seat, otherwise you'll be standing in the packed bar. A great place to chill with friends and enjoy the strong margaritas.
2867 Broadway (bet. 111th and 112th Sts.), (212) 866-7035, Open M-Su 11am-4am. MC, V, D, ❶❷ to 110th St.-Cathedral Pkwy.

Mo's Cantina

Taking over what used to be the What Bar, Mo's prides itself on being a college bar. Featuring Ricky, the pyromaniac bartender, the place entertains groups of friends with shockingly good tasting, flaming shots. Bar food is reasonably priced here, especially the 35-cent wings on Monday nights. Make sure to stop by for $2 beers during happy hour, 5 p.m.-8 p.m.
110th St. and Amsterdam Avenue, no phone. ❶❷ to 110th St.-Cathedral Pkwy.

Nacho Mama's

Featuring both outdoor and indoor seating, come

here for a laid-back (some say tame) atmosphere. You'll find a large number of college students, but some older folks as well. Try their pitchers of sweet sangria for something a little different. Drinks here are okay, but nothing too special.
2893 Broadway (between 112th and 113th Sts.), (212) 665-2800. Open M-Su 11:30am-4am. MC, V, D, AmEx, ❶❷ to 110th St.-Cathedral Pkwy.

SoHa Bar & Lounge
Weekends witness a hedonistic pick-up scene at SoHa, with coeds often dancing on the bar. Weeknights are more relaxed, good for sinking into a couch with a

Cosmo and surveying the room.
998 Amsterdam Ave. (bet. 108th and 109th Sts.), (212) 678-0098. Open M-Su 4pm-4am. MC, V, AmEx, ❶❷ to 110th St.-Cathedral Pkwy.

The West End
Hanging out at the West End is a rite of passage for Columbia freshmen with bad fake IDs. It's gone downhill since the days when Kerouac and Ginsberg made this their haunt, now attracting a loyal clientele of frat boys in cologne. It is owned by a Columbia Journalism School alum.
2911 Broadway (bet. 113th and 114th Sts.), (212) 662-8830. Open M-Su 11am-3am. MC, V, AmEx, DC, D, ❶❷ to

116th St.-Columbia University. ♿

Music
Postcrypt Coffeehouse
Located in the basement of St. Paul's chapel on the Columbia University campus and seating only fifty, the Postcrypt is one of the most unique rooms in the city. No electronic equipment is allowed on the stage and the only lighting is from candles stuck in wine bottles and chandeliers. Suzanne Vega played her first gig here when she was a student at Barnard College across the street. Snacks and bottled beer available. With acoustic, country, folk and jazz.
St. Paul's Chapel at Columbia University (at

117th St. and Broadway), (212) 854-1953, Open F-Sa 9pm-12am (during school year only). Cash Only, Cover: free, ❶❷ to 116th St.-Columbia University.

Smoke
This is the classiest bar in the neighborhood, and one of the best places for good, intimate jazz. Smoke made a name for itself with jazz acts like George Coleman, Slide Hampton, Cecil Payne, Leon Parker, Eric Alexander and a legendary cameo by George Benson. Don't miss the Wednesday Blues night. You'll find, well, lots of smoke.
2751 Broadway (bet.

105th and 106th Sts),
(212) 864-6662,
www.smokejazz.com.
Open: 5pm-4am. MC, V,
Cover: $8-$15 ($10 drink
minimum), **①②** to 110th
St.-Cathedral Pkwy.

Harlem

Bars
Lady Luci's Cocktail
This spacious neighborhood lounge brings in an older crowd with live jazz most nights.
Monday nights are the best, when a 17-piece big band takes the stage. 2306 Frederick Douglass Blvd. (bet. 124th and 125th Sts.), (212) 864-8760. Open M-Su 7pm-4am. Cash only, **Ⓐ Ⓑ Ⓒ Ⓓ** to 125th St. &

Lenox Lounge
There's live jazz most nights, and, with recent renovations, it looks as cool as it sounds. 288 Lenox Ave. (bet. 124th and 125th Sts.), (212) 427-0253. Open M-Su 12pm-4am. MC, V, AmEx, DC, D, **②③** to 125th St.) &

Showman's
Everything is copacetic at this laid-back haunt, according to the Copasetics, a brotherhood of tap dancers, which makes this popular club its headquarters. Come for the live jazz Wednesday through Saturday. 375 W. 125th St. (bet. Morningside and St. Nicholas Aves.), (212) 864-8941. Open M-Sa 12pm-4am. MC, V, AmEx, 2 drink minimum. **①** to 125th St. &

Music
Cotton Club
A Harlem legend since before you were born, the Cotton Club is still kicking. Show times vary widely and you must call for reservations. The "don't miss": $25 gospel brunches every weekend. Full Southern menu and full bar. 656 W. 125th St. (bet. Broadway and Riverside Dr.), (212) 663-7980, www.cottonclubnewyork.com. Call for schedule and showtimes. MC, V, Cover: $15-$30, **①** to 125th St.

Washington Heights

Bars
Coogan's
Coogan's, whose layout recalls the set of "Cheers," hosts a bustling, after-work crowd from Columbia Presbyterian Medical Center, as well as a loyal and mixed neighborhood clientele. The atmosphere is always festive, especially on karaoke nights (Saturday and Tuesday). It also serves food from an extensive menu. 4015 Broadway (bet. 168th and 169th Sts.), (212) 928-1234, www.coogans.com. Open M-Sa 11am-4am. MC, V, AmEx, **Ⓐ Ⓒ ①** to 168th St. &

Goldbrick Inn
This vaguely posh pub is a little bit out of place in the neighborhood. They seem to know this, though, closing around one many nights. 1965 Amsterdam Ave. (bet. 157th and 158th Sts.), (212) 281-8171. Open M-R 12pm-2am. Cash only. **①** to 155th St.

Irish Brigade Pub
A feisty female bartender serves a much older crowd interested in letting loose. Beers start at $1.50, pitchers at $6. Sometimes as a special treat, there's a DJ.

4716 Broadway (at Arden St.), (212) 567-8714. Open M-Su 10am-4am. Cash Only, Ⓐ to Dyckman St.-200th St.

Rose of Kilarney Bar

This dive is beloved by Columbia Med students for its friendly, down-to-earth atmosphere and starving-student prices. *1208 St. Nicholas Ave. (bet. 170 and 171st Sts.), (212) 928-4566. Open M-Su 8am-3am. Cash only. ❶ⒶⒸ to 168th St.-Washington Heights. ♿*

Queens

Bars
Bohemian Hall and Park

Come for the beer. Stay for atmosphere. This European-style beer garden (complete with polka stage) will fool you into thinking that you didn't just step off the N train after all. This place is legendary for a reason. *Astoria, Queens, 29-19 Twenty Fourth Ave. (bet. 29th and 31st Sts.), (718)728-9776. Open M-F 5pm-2am, Sa-Su 12pm-2am. Cash Only, ⓃⓌ to Astoria Blvd. ♿*

Cafe Bar

This is one of those places that will become a favorite the first time you walk in. The funky decor and laid-back atmosphere make it a good place to spend hours over coffee, dessert or a drink. It's especially good for people watching on Friday and Saturday nights when the old country locals mix

with club kids. *Astoria, Queens, 32-19 36th St. (bet. 32nd and 33rd Sts.), (718) 204-5273. Open Su-R 9:30am-3am, F-Sa 9:30am-4am. Cash Only, ⒼⓇⓋ to Steinway St., ⓃⓌ to Broadway. ♿*

Irish Rover

The Irish Rover draws a mean pint of Guinness and makes a pretty good shepherd's pie for its mostly local clientele. As one might guess, the regulars are mostly Irish, but the crowd is always mixed. Occasional live performances liven up the joint. *Astoria, Queens, 37-18 Twenty Eighth Ave. (bet. 38th and 37th Sts.), (718) 278-9372. Open M-Sa 8am-4am, Su 12pm-4am. Cash Only, ⒼⓇⓋ to Steinway St. ♿*

Clubs
Krash

No doubt its parent club in San Juan would be proud of the Latin music this cavernous dance emporium serves up Mondays, Thursdays, Fridays and Saturdays. Worth the token if you crave this beat. *Astoria, Queens, 34-48 Steinway St. (at Thirty Fifth Ave.), (718) 937-2400. MC, V, Cover: $1-$10, ⒼⓇⓋ to Steinway St.*

Bronx

Clubs
The Warehouse

A gay dance club in the Bronx is somewhat anachronistic. The

Warehouse reflects its roots by laying the focus on the dancing, not on profiling, and offering an ecstatically blue-collar menu of fried meat by-products. *The Bronx, 141 E. 140th St. (bet. Walton Ave. and Grand Concourse Rd.), (718) 992-5974. Open Sa 11pm-7am. Cover: $15; cash only. ❷❹❺ to 149th St.-Grand Concourse*

Brooklyn

Bars
Black Betty

Black Betty dishes up cool live music and North African cuisine to a young crowd of new Brooklynites seven days a week. The jazz, world music and trip-hop acts booked by the "Professor" have helped to make this one of Williamsburg's most popular nightspots. Be sure to call ahead for reservations. *Brooklyn, 366 Metropolitan Ave. (at Havemeyer St.), (718) 599-0243. Open M-F 5pm-4am, Sa-Su 7pm-4am. MC, V, AmEx, Ⓛ to Bedford Ave., Ⓖ to Metropolitan Ave.*

Boat

Great jukebox, good drinks, friendly staff, nice design and layout. What more could you want of a neighborhood bar in Brooklyn? Located right off the F train, this place is usually busy early in the week, gets the nightcap crowd on the weekends and is a "Cheers" kind of place for the

locals. *Carroll Gardens, Brooklyn, 175 Smith St. (bet. Wyckof and Warren Sts.), (718) 254-0607. Open M-Su 5pm- 4am. MC, V, AmEx, ❻Ⓖ to Bergen St.*

Carriage House

Home away from home for Park Slope's cable-deprived in need of a Knicks fix. Had enough sports? Amuse yourself at the pool table or come by on karaoke night. *Park Slope, Brooklyn, 312 Seventh Ave. (bet. 7th and 8th Sts.), (718) 788-7747. Open M-Su 4pm-4am. MC, V, AmEx, D, ❻ to Seventh Ave.-Park Slope. ♿*

Excelsior

Darkness shrouds this neighborhood gay bar until you step outside onto the cute veranda and descend the stairs into the even cuter large garden. Mostly, although not exclusively, men are there to appreciate all this cuteness. *Park Slope, Brooklyn, 390 Fifth Ave. (bet. 6th and 7th Sts.), (718) 832-1599. Open M-F 5pm-4am, Sa-Su 2pm-4am. Cash Only ⓂⓃⓇ❻ to Fourth Ave.*

Frank's Lounge

Frank's is the friendly neighborhood lounge in this part of Brooklyn. Come in and you'll be greeted with smiles and the sounds of smooth DJing. It gets crowded on weekends, but you can always expect to see regulars and quality mixed

drinks.
Fort Greene, Brooklyn, 660 Fulton St. (at S. Eliot St.), (718) 625-9339. Open Su-R 4pm-2am, F-Sa 4pm-4am. Cash only C to Lafayette, G to Fulton St., ❶❷❹❺ to Nevins Ave.

Last Exit

Last Exit is an oasis of cool in the sometimes-stuffy bar wasteland that is Brooklyn Heights. The low-key lounge serves delicious martinis and strong mixed drinks to a young, fresh clientele. A friendly staff, comfy couches and unpretentious crowd also await.
Brooklyn, 136 Atlantic Ave., (bet. Henry and Clinton Sts.), (718) 222-9198. Open M-Su 12pm-4am. MC, V, AmEx, DC, D, ⓂⓃⓇ❶❷❹❺ to Borough Hall, ❺Ⓖ to Bergen St.

Mugs Ale House

Baffled by so many good beers on tap, most people never investigate the vast selection of bottled imports. The colorful local contingent and a decent jukebox explain why Manhattanites schlep out here for a drink. Join 'em.
Williamsburg, Brooklyn, 125 Bedford Ave. (at N. 10th St.), (718) 486-8232. Open M-Su 10am-3am. MC, V, AmEx, D, Ⓛ to Bedford Ave.

Pete's Candy Store

Only locals, cool Brooklynites and "those who know" visit this venue, which offers bingo on Tuesdays, Quiz-O on Wednesdays and jazz quartets on Thursdays,

with DJs and a neighborhood bar feel the rest of the week. Toasted panini accompany a drink list packed with dark and stormy "Mac Daddys" and all the usual cocktail suspects.
Williamsburg, Brooklyn 709 Lorimer St. (between Frost and Richardson Sts.), (718) 302-3770. Ⓖ to Metropolitan Ave., Ⓛ to Lorimer.

Rising Café

A local place for gay women. It's good if you're sick of travelling into Manhattan to visit the standard haunts. On Saturdays a DJ spins as the dance floor swells. On Wednesdays, Fridays and Sundays, the stage is ceded to local singer-songwriters and other performers.
Park Slope, Brooklyn, 186 Fifth Ave. (at Sackett St.), (718) 789-6340. Open M-Su 9am-2am. Cash Only, ⓃⓇ to Union St., ❶❷ to Bergen St.

Sparky's Ale House

24 cold taps and four hand drawn casks filled with micro and macro brews from all over the world, poured along side such old favorites such as Guinness, Harp, Brooklyn and Stela. The pool table, dartboards and jukebox help the popularity.
Carroll Gardens, Brooklyn, 481 Court St. (bet. Nelson and Luquer Sts.), (718) 624-5516. Open M-F 4pm-4am, Sa-Su 2pm-4am, ❺Ⓖ to Carroll St.

Teddy's

The best bar food in

Brooklyn. Try a burger or go for dessert. There's plenty of drinks to wash it down, too. Teddy's is of the few places offering pitchers of really good beer.
Williamsburg, Brooklyn, 96 Berry St. (at N. 8th St.), (718) 384-9787. Open Su-W 11:30am-2am, R-Sa 11:30am-4am. MC, V, Ⓛ to Bedford Ave. ♿

Clubs
Galapagos

Local artists from Williamsburg and Greenpoint come to hear house quartets and watch dance, theater and a variety of film series at this hip performance space the first stop out of Manhattan. $3.50 for beers and $5 for well drinks makes it ideal for those light in the wallet. Check out New Year's Eve here, when bottles of champagne descend from the ceiling at midnight with glasses tied to them.
70 N. 6th St. (between Kent and Wythe Aves.), (718)782-5188. Open Su-R 6pm-2am, F-Sa 6pm-4am. Cash Only, Ⓛ to Bedford Ave.

Bars

Cargo Café

The décor is a bit perplexing: the solitary distraction on the ceiling, for

example, is a forlorn-looking tuba. But the kitchen is open late and they have a nice pseudo-outdoors room, so the mostly local, older crowd doesn't mind too much.
Staten Island, 120 Bay St. (at Slosson Ave.), (718) 876-0539. Open M-Su 12:30pm-2:30am. MC, V, AmEx, DC, ❹❺ to Bowling Green, then to South Ferry Terminal. ♿

Ruddy & Dean

Patrons enjoy a great view of Manhattan from the patio.
Staten Island, 44 Richmond Terrace (bet. Day and Wall Sts.), (718) 816-4400. Open M-R 11:30pm-4am, Sa-Su 12pm-4am. MC, V, AmEx, DC, ❹❺ to Bowling Green, then to South Ferry Terminal. ♿

Sidestreet Saloon

High-schoolers in shiny pants pack this dive. Most nights a DJ spins hip-hop, but once a month there's an '80s party.
Staten Island, 11 Schuyler St. (bet. Richmond Terrace and Styvasen St.), (718) 448-6868. Open M-Su 11:30am-4am. MC, V, AmEx, DC, ❹❺ to Bowling Green, then to South Ferry Terminal. ♿

leisure

leisure

New York is often stressful, and people who work hard want to play even harder. In a city known for its shopping and theater, New York has an amazing amount of outdoor life. For New Yorkers, some of the many perks of the city are its lesser-known forms of recreation. Whether you want a serious workout or a break from the metropolis, there is something for you, no matter what shape you're in.

People-watching in the city's parks is the ultimate New York spectator sport.

Central Park is where the outdoor sports meet-Ultimate Frisbee, softball, Capture the Flag, soccer, ice skating. Central Park is also filled with rollerbladers, bikers, runners, skateboarders and sunbathers. For those looking for a less traditional urban escape, Central Park offers the adventurous New Yorker canoe rentals, a carousel, a zoo, a marionette theater, a castle and many playgrounds.

Of course, if you are looking for a less physically enervating release, New York's professional sports teams are legendary. Both NFL teams, the Giants and the Jets, play at home at Giants Stadium in New Jersey. The New York/New Jersey MetroStars also have their soccer games at the Meadowlands in New Jersey. There are three NHL teams serving the area - the New Jersey Devils, the New York Islanders, and the New York Rangers. New York boasts two baseball teams. Yankee Stadium, the "House that Ruth Built," is in the Bronx. The Mets' Shea Stadium is in Queens - in Flushing Meadow, alongside the US Tennis Association complex, where the US Open is held. If you're curious about cricket and want to get jiggy, wicket-style, head up to Van Cortlandt Park at 242nd Street on a weekend afternoon.

When looking for the ultimate escape from the city, many New Yorkers will opt to take day or weekend trips to areas easily accessible from the metro area. Take a hike across the Brooklyn Bridge. The views of Manhattan are phenomenal. For a break from the urban jungle, sample some of the natural beauty of Long Island. Head for the beaches; they run for miles. If wilderness sounds better, then venture upstate. Check New York out - all of it.

parks

Beyond the asphalt jungle, a tranquil oasis can be found all over. On a gorgeous Saturday afternoon in June, gather a blanket, picnic basket and a bottle of suntan lotion and forget about what awaits on Monday morning. Whether enjoying the squirrels fighting over an acorn or simply watching the sometimes freaky assemblage of parkgoers, New York City has parks to suit any taste.

Central Park

Central Park, designed by Frederick Law Olmstead around 1859, runs from 59th to 110th Streets and is bordered by Central Park West and Fifth Avenue. Olmstead wanted to create a park where New Yorkers of all classes could relax in a life-sized reflection of what he considered to be pastoral England. Only in the early days, you had to wear your Sunday best to even get into the Park. Jogging shorts would not have fit the bill.

Central Park is created from raw stuff: 843 acres of 270,000 trees, shrubs, and vines and ten million cartloads of rock. None of it was here when Olmstead started and it's testament to New York's tenacity that they created such an artful imitation of nature with the same facility as fellow architects were giving to building early skyscrapers. The park took sixteen years to

build and cost the modern equivalent of $20 million.

Central Park is visited by 20 million people a year and provides a welcome relief from the expense and expanse of the rest of the city. While the antique castle carousel costs a dollar per ride, almost all of the Park's attractions and events are free, including Belvedere Castle, the Swedish Cottage Marionette Theater, The Conservatory Garden and Shakespeare in the Park.

By 1965, the park was declared a national historic landmark, and as part of urban renewal and countercultural movements during the 60s, the park hosted rock concerts and "be-ins." Deterioration during the 1970s led to a revival by the Central Park Conservancy in the 1980s, reinstating the park as the public respite it was constructed to be. Twenty years ago the park was home to more drug dealers than yuppies.

In Sheep's Meadow, near the southeastern edges of the park, picnickers, Frisbee players and sunbathers share the expanse beneath the watchful eyes of the midtown skyline. For the more dramatic, the Delacorte Theatre at 81st Street houses the renowned Shakespeare-in-the-Park series, with performances under the stars, for those lucky enough to get tickets. Tickets are distributed on the day of the show at the Box Office beginning at 1pm. They are free, but working folks will have to take a personal day to line up at sunrise to obtain seats to the more popular shows. With names like Kevin Kline and Helen Hunt on the showbill, who wouldn't?

Under the watchful eye of the Dakota, John Lennon's former abode, Strawberry Fields gives the music lover a place to sit back, relax, and contemplate life. After George Harrison's death, thousands of fans converged here and spent hours holding hands and singing songs. Enter the Park at 72nd Street on the West Side to experience nature as John himself would have liked it. At the center of 161 plants (representing the 161 nations of the world), a circular

Italian mosaic with the word "Imagine" can be found. Be sure to attend the numerous free summer concerts that are held on the SummerStage, near 96th Street. Central Park SummerStage is New York's premier free performing arts festival. Throughout the summer expect events from all genres. Check out their web page, www.summerstage.org, for listings.

Battery Park

Located from State Street to the New York harbor, this park provides picnic-perfect promenades. The park has been completely renovated since Sept. 11. Misty breezes from the Atlantic Ocean, the East River, and the Hudson River combine to add the final refreshing touch to an amazing view of the lower Manhattan skyline. New York offers itself to you with panoramic visions of Governors Island, Staten Island, the Statue of Liberty, Ellis Island and the intricate span of the Verrazano Narrows Bridge. Soak it all in while munching, lounging and chatting on the green.

Washington Square Park

Known more for voyeuristic spectacle than quiet seclusion, this park showcases Greenwich Village's activity. Street musicians, acrobats, NYU students, flame swallowers and players of Go, an ancient Chinese board game, animate this park. The visual centerpiece is the Arch, designed by Stanford White, marking the 100-year anniver-

sary of George Washington coming to New York. Many New Yorkers don't know that the park was formerly used as a cemetery and people enjoying the park are really dancing on the graves of over 10,000 bodies. In the northwest corner, the notorious Hanging Elm stands as a reminder of the public executions that happened in the early 1800s. Still, the eerie history does not deter picnickers. Pack some popcorn too and watch the show.

The Cloisters

Fort Tryon boasts lush, grassy lawns, landscaped terraces, footpaths, and flower gardens for the emotionally spent city dweller. Come here after an educational tour of the medieval museum exhibits known for their collections of tapestries, illuminated manuscripts, stained glass and precious metal work. Bask in the self-satisfaction of culture as you relax on a sun-drenched hill south of the museum, perfect for relaxing. At the end of the day, watch a

romantic sunset and check out the superb views of the towering Palisades across the Hudson River

Fort Tryon Park, (212) 923-3700. Tuesday through Sunday 9:30am-5:15 pm. Subway: Ⓐ to 190th St.

sweat sweat sweat sweat sweat

pumping iron and climbing stairs

Gyms aren't just gyms anymore. In New York, they are, in the words of The New York Health and Racquet Club, "a way of life." The fitness craze of the 90's brought gym facilities to all parts of the city, and they attract people from all walks of life. All the spandex and muscle at these places can be intimidating, but don't give up. Many gyms pride themselves on a non-judgmental, laid-back policy. Shop around since most facilities allow trial periods on a no-strings-attached basis.

The Gyms

New York's generic gym is **New York Sports Club**. Always clean, always sterile, these clubs offer what the average gymgoer needs - equipment that works and TV screens that deliver up to 10 channels. This gym has the most branches throughout New York and the outer boroughs. *Check www.nysc.com for gym locations and more information.*

Crunch is the New York antidote to the thong-wearing aerobics devotees. They offer funky décor and even funkier classes. If you've ever wanted to sweat with a drag queen dishing up dirt, or take a spinning class in a room that would double for a hot disco replete with dramatic lighting, or a striptease exercise class, then this is the gym for you. Always experimental, always edgy, Crunch is expanding thanks to a buyout by Bally's, but promises to keep its flava. *Check www.crunch.com for gym locations and more information.*

New York Health and Racquet Club is the solidly middle class and usually middle-aged gym. They offer not just a gym, but also "a lifestyle." Their gyms are clean if cluttered, and all boast a bathroom attendant with sundry cosmetics and hairsprays. They have monthly boat cruises, and seem to be trying to get more singles interested in their gyms. They have more pools than any other New York chain. *Check www.hrcbest.com or call (800) HRC-BEST for gym locations and more information.*

Equinox Fitness Club is the Queen Bee of NYC gym chains. With New Age music piped into its dressing rooms, to the pulsing rhythms of its exercise floors, to the consistently high quality of its popular instructors, Equinox is the gym of choice for well-heeled New Yorkers looking to look good while they sweat. *Check www.equinoxnyc.com for gym locations and more information.*

LA Sports/Reebok bring a more Los Angeles flavor to the New York fitness scene. Their classes are known as trailblazers, and many classes start here that end up hitting the big time elsewhere (including, reportedly, spinning). The rates are daunting, but with an all-star clientele these two gyms are looking to be the most exclusive gym in town. *Call (212) 362-6800 for gym locations and more information.*

Gold's Gym is New York's working class gym. With few Gold's here, it is largely the domain of the outer boroughs. You'll find a broad mix of clients here, and you'll never feel underdressed. *Check www.goldsgym.com for gym locations and more information.*

Dolphin Fitness is a homegrown, bargain-basement gym. Don't expect many amenities, but the rates can't be beat if you don't mind exercising in sometimes cramped quarters. *Check www.dolphinfitnessclubs.com for gym locations and more information.*

Bally's is the nation's marketing extravaganza gym chain. The rates are super cheap, but so is the corporate sponsorship that runs nonstop ads on its TVs and strings promotional materials through the dressing rooms and hallways. Some say you get what you pay for with Bally's, but the monthly fee is cheaper than almost anywhere in town. *Check www.ballyfitness.com for gym locations and more information.*

See sports/recreation listings for more detailed information.

Beaches

Escape the hellish heat and humidity of Gotham's concrete jungle and head to the beaches for some urban purification. The rush of bright bikinis, sun and skin offers welcome relief for most city dwellers. Jocks can show off their muscles at the numerous basketball and tennis courts and the social set can try their hand at miniature golf or shuffleboard. Lounge lizards can relax and dream away the sounds of honking horns on the

sand and picnic areas. For music lovers there are the diverse sounds of outdoor concerts set against the backdrop of crashing surf. Nature trails keep the environmentalist inspired.

Jones Beach State Park

With 6.5 miles of sand and surf, beach diehards will find a slice of heaven in this granddaddy of beaches. West Bathhouse, Central Mall and East Bathhouse comprise the three most famous of the eight sections that make up this Long Island haven for hedonists.

People mostly flock to the Central Mall section because of its many landmarks, like the famous 200-foot water tower and the Boardwalk Restaurant, where everything from a down-to-earth hamburger deluxe to a sophisticated grilled North Atlantic salmon. Because of its popularity, Central Mall does get crowded with the scantily clad, so for tranquil moments head for the other sections.

East Bathhouse could be the best sanctuary for mediators and peace seekers with its picturesque Zach's Bay. With its sacred expanse of green, Parking Field 10 is also a good bet for a quiet picnic. Further east along the beach, things get a little less mainstream with nudists, bongo drummers and gay sunbathers. Make sure to check out the many top-name concerts at the 11,200-seat outdoor theater near the park entrance. *Wantagh, L.I. Call (516) 679-7222 for information. Long Island Railroad to Freeport, Babylon Branch. Call (516) 822-LIRR for schedules. $9.50 round-trip off-peak, $14 round-trip peak period.*

Sandy Hook

Since the ten beach sections of Sandy Hook stretch over several miles of widely spaced roadways, navigating can be limited without wheels. As a barrier peninsula, this New Jersey beach is visually stunning. At the northern tip, bring the sunblock and check out the panoramic views of the Twin Towers and the Verrazano Narrows Bridge.

For the active, daring bunch, whip out the wind-surfing gear and head for the cove area. After a refreshing wipeout, sample refreshing drinks and relish the ambiance at the full-service concession stand and bar within a mile and a half of the beach's entrance. Not only do surf and sand dominate the landscape, but also 250 historic sites keep visitors coming, including the nation's oldest operating lighthouse. Also legendary is the clothing-optional stretch of beach located in area G. *Highlands, NJ. (908) 872-5900. Academy Bus Line from Port Authority to Highlands Bridge. $12.75 round-trip.*

Coney Island Beach

Even more famous than the Coney Island hotdog is the beach. Enjoy the amusement park, which features the quintessential rollercoaster, the Cyclone. Despite the 2.9 mile shoreline, the rides are what keep this beach the most popular. By late evening, the thrill seekers leave-and leave behind their refuse. With the help of heavy machinery, crews tidy up the sand for another day of fun.

To avoid the herds, head toward the boardwalk by the New York Aquarium, between West 8th Street and West 5th Street. For body traffic, head toward the area between Steeplechase Pier at West 17th Street and West 8th Street.
On the Atlantic Ocean, between West 37th Street and Ocean Parkway (718) 946-1350. Subway: B D F N to Stillwell Avenue/Coney Island; D F to West 8th Street/NY Aquarium.

See sports/recreations listings for more information.

Long Island

Long Island has long served as a playground for New Yorkers. The Island, as it is lovingly known, is easily accessible by the Long Island Railroad and offers a variety of recreational possibilities. In the summer, celebrities, society notables and others willing to rent a room in a house crowded with strangers and empty kegs, head out to the Hamptons, a conglomeration of small towns on the island's eastern end. They spend the warmer months in enormous private mansions on the shore, and their presence creates a flurry of business in the normally quiet towns. Tourists come as well, and not just for a glimpse

of the rich and famous. The beaches in the Hamptons are beautiful, and some are relatively deserted. There are trendy shops and galleries to browse through in town, and for a real guilty pleasure, walk or drive through the residential blocks and stare at the mansions.

To the west lies the largely suburban Nassau county, and to the east, the livin' large Hamptons. By car, take the Long Island Expressway to exit 70, then right for three miles to Route 27 (Sunrise Highway) that leads directly into Southhampton-albeit in heavy traffic. More easily accessible by the Long Island Railroad from Penn Station or the Hampton Jitney shuttle bus, the Hamptons can be a welcome vacation from the city's frenetic pulse.

Out on a Limb

The East End of Long Island is famous for succulent tomatoes, serene beaches and the decadent lifestyle of its summer residents. The playground of famous and infamous celebrities, the Hamptons serve as backdrop to both the garden parties of Martha Stewart as well as the shenanigans of Sean "P. Diddy" Combs. Nonetheless, the polarized nature of Hamptons vacationers does not change the fact that it is still the place to see, and be seen.

However, most tourists do not visit the Hamptons just to stargaze. The beaches in the Hamptons are beautiful and

some are relatively deserted. In addition, charming shops and galleries attract browsers along the main thoroughfares of many of the towns. For a real treat, take a scenic drive

through the residential areas and admire the mansions that pepper the coastline. In Southhampton, Meadow and Gin Lanes, which run parallel to the ocean, are prime spots to scope Hampton real estate. In Bridgehampton, don't miss out on antiquing and the Candy Kitchen for some homemade ice cream.

South Hampton is equally charming, but the presence of Cartier and Armani mean that the village is far less bohemian. Still, the artisan bakers at Tate's turn the chocolate chip cookie into a work of art. Lastly, don't miss rubbing elbows with the bluebloods at the Hampton Classic (www.hampton classic.com), an annual horse show that takes place during the last week in August.

For a trek off the beaten path, take a day trip to Shelter Island, a secluded and peaceful place nestled between the north and south forks of Long Island's east end. Shelter Island is about 12 square miles and can only be reached by ferry, so it's obviously not a huge hub

for tourism. Rent a sailboat and go fishing, or hike over the varied terrain and enjoy the peace and quiet. *The Shelter Island website, at ww.shelter-island.org, contains information about the island, transportation, places to stay and restaurants.*

For more mansions and spectacular views closer to Manhattan, check out the North Shore, or the Gold Coast. Old Westbury Gardens (71 Old Westbury Road, Old Westbury, 516-333-0048) and peruse the replica of a Charles II English mansion, the former estate of the Phipps Family. The beautifully manicured gardens (open from April to October) were also featured in the 1999 film, Cruel Intentions.

The Sands Point Park and Preserve (Middleneck Road, Port Washington, 516-571-7900) is the site of Castlegould and Hempstead House, two impressive estates of Howard Gould. Falaise, a mansion built by Harry F. Guggenheim, can be visited by bus or walking tour. To get there take the LIRR to Port Washington.

For a bit of contrast, Stonybrook, another village on the North Shore, is a town with a colonial heritage. The town is filled with Colonial style homes and other remnants of early American culture - the peaceful harbor and an 18th century grist mill top it all off. To get there, take the Long Island Expressway to exit 62, then proceed north to Nicholls Road and turn left onto Route 25A that will take you to the center of town. Also on 25A is Oyster Bay, another charming and rustic town which has two main attractions: Sagamore Hill (Cove Neck Road, Oyster Bay, 516-922-4447), former home of Teddy Roosevelt, and the Planting Fields Arboretum (Planting Fields Road, 516-922-9200). There is a 65-room Tudor Mansion on the grounds of the estate, as well as a rose garden and over 600 species of rhododendrons and azaleas. Visit during spring and enjoy the display.

Long Island has a number of public beaches, but the most popular by far is Jones Beach (Ocean Drive, Wantagh, 516-785-1600, see Beaches section), which can be reached by the LIRR. The beach is saturated with sun-worshipers on summer weekends, so get there early. Long Island's most famous boardwalk is found here and it offers such amenities as 1920's bathhouses, outdoor eateries, miniature golf and swimming pools. Also during the summer is the Jones Beach Concert series, a very popular event for many talented musicians. *Call (212) 713-6300 or see www.ticketmaster.com.*

The island has a number of lovely parks and Eisenhower Park (take Hempstead Turnpike to East Meadow, 516-572-0348) is surely the prettiest. The park offers facilities for everything from golf, to jogging, to cricket as well as a boating lake and an upscale restaurant. The swimming facilities are world class, and hosted the Goodwill Games in 1998.

Upstate NY

Saratoga Springs, is a legendary resort town. Located just north of Albany, Saratoga Springs is famous for its healing mineral springs. It's also the site of America's oldest and most beautiful racetracks. The racing season attracts bluebloods and tourists alike, as does the summer entertainment. From June until August, the Saratoga Performing Arts Center has something going on almost every night. Saratoga State Park has two beautiful golf courses, four swimming pools, a dozen picnic areas and several tennis courts. Reserve a spot at the Roosevelt and Lincoln Bathhouses (518-584-2011) well in advance and enjoy the fizzy mineral baths and famous massages that made the town famous. Take Amtrak (from Penn Station; see Resources section) or Greyhound (from Port Authority) to Saratoga.

Some miles away from Saratoga Springs is Albany, the state capital. Visit in the fall and enjoy the colorful foliage. Albany is the home of the New York State Museum, which chronicles the development of New York State and its cities. There are, among other things, full-size replicas of Manhattan stores, buses and government offices. The Museum is housed in a 98-acre complex in the heart of downtown Albany known as Empire State Plaza, which was a gift from the late Governor Nelson Rockefeller. There is an art collection and a 42nd-floor observation deck, along with an enormous assortment of stores. Visit the Albany Urban Cultural Park Visitor's Center to learn more about the city and its unique history. Take Amtrak to Albany. The tracks run along the Hudson River, so it's bound to be a scenic trip.

For a more spectacular view of the Hudson River, travel along

its east bank. Enormous mansions line the shore and the Catskill and Shawangunk mountains provide an incredible backdrop. Most of the historical estates are open to the public now, so spend a weekend hopping from mansion to mansion. The town of Rhinebeck is a good starting point. It's home to the oldest hotel in America (see Bed and Breakfasts, this section). Tour the old homes of FDR and painter Frederic Edwin Church, among others. Contact Hudson River Heritage (P.O. Box 287, Rhinebeck, NY 12572) for more information on the estates. Take Amtrak to Rhinecliff, which is three miles from Rhinebeck.

To experience the scenery of the mountains in peace and quiet, try a less frequented town like Woodstock. Set against a mountain, the town affords spectacular views. Take a scenic drive up Mead's Mountain to enjoy the vantage point from Overlook Trail. Travel to the town of Phonecia nearby for more dramatic view of the wilderness. Esopus Creek, which follows the road (Route 28), for many miles, and is a favorite for fly fishing and tubing. Ride the Catskill Mountain Railroad for unobstructed views of the waterway. If skiing is on the agenda, try Hunter Mountain. It is just a short drive from Phonecia. From the ski-lift, there is a 360-degree view of the surrounding mountains. Belleayre Mountain also has excellent skiing. For more information, contact the Woodstock Chamber of Commerce (P.O. Box 36, Woodstock, NY 12498). Take the Adirondack Trailways Bus (967-2900, or 800-858-8555) to Woodstock and Phonecia.

New Jersey

On the other side of the city lies New Jersey, accessible by the PATH ((212) 234-7284) for only a dollar. Make a beeline for Hoboken, Frank Sinatra's birthplace. Maxwell's on Washington Street books acts rivaling those of New York's best rock clubs. Exploring the rest of the city

can be a hit-or-miss affair, but some worthwhile shops, thrift stores, bars and restaurants can be found along and just off of Washington Street. Venture across the state to the Jersey border on the Delaware River, where a small group of towns offer some excellent shopping. Lambertville in particular is a choice place for antiques, and the town has some lovely restaurants and inns as well. Enjoy the nearby shopping in Princeton and cruise the magnificent university campus. There is a major outlet center in Flemington, which includes names like Calvin Klein and Adidas. Reach these areas via the New Jersey Turnpike (the Flemington Princeton exit), or take the Trans-Bridge Lines bus to Lambertville.

Atlantic City is a hotbed of glitz and conspicuous consumption. All the major hotels, casinos, and shops line the famous boardwalk; straying from it might be dangerous at night. Call the Atlantic City Convention Center and Visitor's Bureau for travel information. Get there by bus from the Port Authority in Manhattan (see the Resources section). Spend all the winnings at the Paramus Park Mall (in Paramus) or the Roosevelt Field Shopping Mall (in Garden City, 516-742-8000). Both are spectacular examples of the suburban ideal. Clothes are tax-free in New Jersey, so hop a bus at the Port Authority and stock up.

For outdoor fun, take a New Jersey Transit shuttle bus to the beautiful New Jersey shoreline. Ocean Grove's wide, clean beach is complemented by the surrounding Victorian architecture, while Bayhead is reminiscent of New England, with fine sand, rough seas, and Cape Cod-style houses. Spring Lake boasts fine sandy beaches, tree-lined streets, mansions, cottages, and shops. Point Pleasant Beach is home to a boardwalk filled with cruising teens, while Belmar supports the majority of the shore's nightlife.

For the ultimate in outdoor thrills, visit New Jersey's best amusement park, Six Flags Great Adventure. For a special retreat, visit Cape May, the nation's oldest seaside resort. The whole town was declared a historic landmark. There are over 600 gingerbread Victorian houses within the city limits. It's most appealing at the tail end of summer, just after Labor Day. Have tea at the Mainstay Inn (see Bed and Breakfasts section) and stroll down the beach promenade. Cape May Point State Park boasts one of the country's oldest lighthouses. *Contact the Greater Cape May Chamber of Commerce (P.O. Box 109, Cape May, NJ 0824) for more information.*

How to Leave NY

Long Island Railroad
(516) 822-LIRR
New Jersey Transit
(800) 582-5946
Port Authority Bus Terminal
(212) 564-8484
Amtrak
(800) USA-RAIL
Metro North Railroad
(212) 340-3000

The Statue of Liberty

Long the quintessential New York landmark, the Statue is bowed but not beaten in the wake of Sept. 11. No longer can you climb up her long arm into the belly of the torch. No longer can you walk around her pedestal. And no longer can you visit her island without viewing the gaping hole in the New York skyline.

But regardless of the reminders of that awful September day, visitors still flock to see her by ferry. The ferry, which leaves regularly from Clinton Castle in Battery Park and Liberty Park, New Jersey, requires an advance-purchase ticket. Expect long lines and a dingy ferry that has seen better days. Few notice.. Kids especially dig the view, having seen the Statue in one too many history lessons and cartoon caricatures. Run by the National Park Service, the Statue is a national monument and it runs an information center, guided tours and a gift shop.

Contact (212) 363-3200 for more information. Hours: 9 am - 5pm. Fees: Adults $10, Seniors over 62 and Children under 12 $4, Children under 4 free.

Looking for something a little less tame?
Recreation for the Adventurous

Extreme sports are not for the feeblehearted, and skydiving ranks up there as one of the most fear-inducing sports around. Since the Brooklyn Bridge doesn't allow bungie jumping, you'll have to settle for Skydive Sussex (973-702-7000) in New Jersey or Skydive Long Island (631-208-3900).

This is what will happen, roughly. First, you'll need to go on a nice day when visibility is fabulous. Then, you'll sign lots of forms that say if you crash, bash or otherwise kill yourself, they are not responsible. You'll wait around while your chute is packed, and be introduced to the gentleman who will hold your life in his hands. Since beginners are not let out of the plane alone, you will have a man strapped to your back, who will make sure the rip cord is pulled on time. You will be given a lengthy safety instruction, and it is to your benefit to listen carefully. Unlike in a commercial airplane, this is one ride where you are definitely making a run for it. You will be briefed in all manner of straps, belts, altimeters, and crash landings. They will laugh at your doofy jokes. You'll be told how to hold your hands and feet when you are aloft, and how to watch for the exact moment you're supposed to pull your ripcord after freefalling for about one exhilarating minute.

Then you go up and you'll be tempted to forget everything you've ever been told, as your rickety Fokker or Cessna airplane wobbles and dips its way up to 10,000 or so feet and you realize you're really going to jump out that tiny window into...nothing. Your guide will most likely be cracking jokes with the pilot and you'll wonder what is so funny. Then comes the moment, and you'll ease up to the door, look down and...the rest is up to you.

Bed and Breakfasts usually conjure up images of sleeping in canopied four-poster beds and waking up to the gentle ringing of Vermont cowbells and the scent of freshly brewed coffee. This gentrified picture is not as out of place as you would imagine in the tri-state area. The following accommodations not only provide a place to sleep for a night, but rather a refuge into a simpler lifestyle. For good deals, prices at B&B's can't be beat. So go indulge and take a mini-vacation. We won't tell your boss.

Abingdon Guest House

Find no perky, air-kissing inn owners or gratuitous socialization over fruit salad in this quaintly furnished nine-room house. Seclusion and independence are usually the norm. In the mornings, wake up to a complimentary continental breakfast provided by Brew Bar. *13 Eighth Ave. (bet. 12th and Jane Sts.), (212) 243-5384, $135-$150.*

Akwaaba Mansion

Enchanting and a return to bygone elegance is what visitors call a stay in this Stuyvesant Heights bed and breakfast. As a restored 1860s Italianate villa with an Afrocentric soul, this antique-furnished home has eighteen suites featuring different themes. Choose from the Regal Suite, a room with deep burgundy colors and rich textiles surrounding a Victorian style bed; the Black Memorabilia Suite, a retreat that combines the ambiance of a noble ancestral past with the liberating free-spirit of youth. Finally, the Jumping the Broom Suite, a retreat into romance complete with a canopy bed draped in gauzy tulle and a complementary gift of champagne, strawberries and fresh whipped cream. After spending a night in these luxurious rooms, enjoying a drink on the wrap-around porch, getting cozy by the fireplace, receiving a massage, day-dreaming in the fairytale gardens. *347 MacDonough Street, Brooklyn, (718) 455-5958, $135-$150.*

Baisley House

Velvet drapes heavy with fringe, elegant silk-moiré wallpaper, and a delicately hand-painted ceiling of clouds give this cozy Carroll Garden row house a divine, ethereal atmosphere lifted from a page of an Edith Wharton novel. The feel of genteel New York pervades this bed and breakfast. During warm weather, guests are invited outside by Henry Paul, the interior decorator and landscape designer, for dessert and coffee at Victorian tables and chairs amidst a vivid rose garden. *294 Hoyt Street between Union and Sackett Streets, Carroll Gardens, Brooklyn, (718) 935-1959, $95-$245.*

Bed and Breakfast on the Park

By Prospect Park, a bigger version of the Baisley House, this B&B offers seven bedrooms and garden-level suites. Inside, the patrons get spoiled with elaborately carved moldings, lush, ankle-skimming oriental carpets, and beds fit for kings and queens. The guilt-free decadence extends to the dining hall where guests eat sumptuously while brilliant light filters through stained-glass windows. *113 Prospect Park West (bet. 6th and 7th Sts.) Park Slope, Brooklyn, (718) 499-6115, $125-$300.*

Inn at Irving Place

In the heart of Gramercy, this small Victorian B&B is exactly

what comes to mind when one considers elegance and distinction. The rooms are furnished with hardwood floors and canopy beds, and are a perfect getaway from the hustle and bustle of daily city life. Downstairs at Cibar, the inn's bar and lounge, sip a blackberry cosmopolitan as you sit at a dimly lit table.
56 Irving Place (bet. 16th and 17th Sts.), (212) 533-4600, $325-$495.

Foy House

In the heart of historic Park Slope Brooklyn, this bed and breakfast brownstone built in 1894 still holds most of its late 19th century furnishings in pristine condition. An aura of authenticity and classicism permeate the three rooms and garden apartment. The large wood silver holders in the dining hall and the love seat in the lower level are original pieces. For the real, homey bed and breakfast experience, come here.
819 Carroll St. (bet. Eight Avenue and Prospect Park West), Park Slope, Brooklyn, (718) 636-1492, $120-$200.

Hotel Alternatives...

Visitors to Manhattan will thank you for directing them to these accommodation services that offer lodging more charming and less expensive than their chain-hotel counterparts. Whether you're searching for a cozy bed and breakfast for a weekend visit or an entire furnished apartment for an extended stay, these agencies can book you into fabulous apartments during your time in New York. Breakfast is usually provided, but check with the agency for details.

Hospitality Inc.
(212) 965-1102, fax: (212) 965-1149, www.acompanies.com
Bed, Breakfast and Books
(212) 865-8740

Outward Bound...

Three Village Inn

Picture old, white Colonial homes, a Melville-esque harbor packed with fishermen, kids chasing a trail of ducks to ponds, 18th-century grist mills and suddenly this Early American style of bed and breakfast comes to mind. Once the home of Captain Jonas Smith, a NY ship builder who became Long Island's first millionaire, it evolved from being a tea service to being one of the most charming inns in the area. Relax in one of the seven rooms upstairs in the main house or one of the peripheral cottages tucked into pretty landscaping out back. For traditional, early-American food try the chicken pot pie and Yankee pot roast served as Continental fare in the flowery dining hall and at the almost 300-year-old Country House located in the village. Then take a walk down the colonial-influenced Main Street for a real time-warp experience into the past.
150 Main St., Stony Brook, Long Island, (631) 751-0555, $159-$179.

Mainstay Inn

Go to Cape May, a historic seaside retreat town for the most authentic sampling of Victorian living. Otherwise known as the "Victorian Mansion," this bed and breakfast is the centerpiece of the 600 prize Victorian homes within the 2.2 square miles of heaven. Graceful 14-foot ceilings, tall mirrors, ornate plaster moldings, bejeweled chandeliers and cupola with ocean views treat guests to more than just an innocuous getaway. Come in October and bring the cameras and corsets for the Victorian Week extravaganza complete with house tours, period fashions shows and lectures on period art.
635 Columbia Avenue, Cape May, New Jersey, (609) 884-8690, $110-$395.

Centennial House

Hollywood potentates and posh NY society converge in the lush precincts of the Hamptons. For a captivating, high-styled getaway come here. Socialites flock to Southampton, while writers and artists look for inspiration in the monastic seclusion of the East Hamptons. None of these things? Go anyway, because the beaches here are the some of the most gorgeous and the numerous historical sites, mostly Colonial-style homes, are a summer's stroll away from this three-bedroom bed and breakfast. Built in 1876, this charmer offers an intimate flavor with its exquisitely decorated rooms with fabrics and prints adorning the walls. For more pampering, take a dip in the inn's swimming pool.
13 Woods Lane (Route 27), East Hampton, (631) 324-9414, $295-$780.

Perhaps in response to the daunting challenge of maintaining a human form while working a desk job, New Yorkers pursue physical activity with an almost pathological fervor. The gym social set and company softball teams trying to salvage their blood pressure are just the most obvious examples of a serious subculture of exercise.

The cult of the body, coupled with an almost burdensome desire to have fun, may drive yuppies to the racquetball court, but it is possible to utilize the city's manifold resources as opportunities of true, uncomplicated relaxation time without letting the muscled and Spandex-ed masses kill your runner's high. Hit off-peak hours at the gym. Venture into the outer boroughs for expansive, serene parks, and take advantage of any private spaces to which you may have access through affiliation with a university.

RUNNING

The opportunities afforded by the city are accompanied by precautions unique to the area that even the most seasoned athlete should note. Some of the most scenic jogging paths, like those in Riverside Park on the Upper West Side, provide very poor support for knees and ankles, so if you plan on running regularly, invest in high-quality shoes which absorb the impact of concrete. Always be aware of your surroundings, including other runners, bikers, rollerbladers, cars, kids, strollers or pedestrians.

Runners seeking camaraderie should contact the New York Road Runner's Club at (212) 860-4455, headquartered near the Jackie O. Reservoir at the eastern entrance to the park on 90th Street. The club's activities include twice-nightly runs in Central Park at 6:30pm and 7:15pm, a weekend jog at 10am, a marathon prep, a New Year's Eve run, and a Central Park Safety Patrol. During summer evenings, traffic is closed off in the Park.

Riverside Park is a beautiful place to run for those who don't mind the pavement, since the infrequent strips of dirt are ill-maintained and subject to ruts and mud. The best place to veer down towards the riverside path, where a small houseboat community docks and optimistic fishermen occasionally cast their lines, is at 86th Street. A quarter of a mile track is maintained at 72nd Street. Further north, on top of the 145th Street incinerator, there's another quality track.

Also in Manhattan, a jogging path follows the East River from Sutton Place all the way down to Gracie Mansion. Down in the Village, the Westside Highway Path is a newly refurbished strip for downtown joggers, bladers, and bikers that can seem as circus-like as the boardwalk on Coney Island on busy days.

When traffic is cut off on Saturdays and Sundays in Prospect Park, the roughly two-and-a-half-mile route looping around the park makes a good jog. For post-jog relaxation, the interior path offers shady groves and gaggles of swans.

RUNNING CLUBS
New York Road Runners Club
(212) 860-4455 or
www.nyrrc.com for more information.
Achilles Track Club
A nation-wide club for athletes with disabilities ranging from blindness to epilepsy to heart disease.
(212) 354-0300
Central Park Track Club
For information, visit www.centralparktc.org.

Front Runners

A gay and lesbian running group.

(212) 724-9700

Moving Comfort

Ladies only, but you've got to be able to do 10K in forty minutes.

(212) 737-4702 or www.movingcomfortny.org.

CYCLING

Riding a bike in Manhattan is an excellent and inexpensive means of transportation and exercise, but it can get a bit wild so observing the following precautions can help you to avoid falling prey to cabs and MTA bus drivers:

✓ Claim space in a lane so as to avoid pedestrians and opening car doors. Many major avenues have bike paths as well. Always ride on the right with traffic. D rivers don't always watch out for obstacles to their left side, which is where you'll be when riding against traffic.·

✓ Wear a helmet without fail.

✓ When in Central Park path or on other bike paths, don't hang a U-turn.

✓ For clearly defined bike paths, all the running paths mentioned above suffice as well as specific bike trails like the one-mile Brooklyn Bridge bike lane across the East River. If you have a couple hours to kill, try the Ocean Parkway bike path which begins in Prospect Park Church Avenue and ends up at Coney Island. It's perfectly permissible to take your bike on the subway (you'll get buzzed through the door after depositing a token), though the commuter trains require a pass for bikes.

CYCLING CLUBS

Five Boroughs Bicycle Club

www.bikenewyork.org or (212) 932-2300 ext. 115

New York Cycle Club

(212) 828-5711

Sundance Outdoor Adventure Society

For gays and lesbians.

(212)598-4726

SOFTBALL

The Sheep Meadow in Central Park, closed in winter, overflows in summer with loads of scantily-clad sunbathers, Frisbee players and picnickers. Regulation-sized softball and baseball diamonds are located around 100th Street on the eastern side of the park. The Heckscher fields around 64th Street are well-maintained but often claimed by amateur, fiercely territorial leagues known more for mild spectator value than for open field policies, since most harken from the high-strung cubicles of nearby Midtown. There are huge, underutilized Astroturf fields atop the 145th Street incinerator in Riverside that are a good alternative to the Central Park melee.

Five softball diamonds and two baseball diamonds, accessible from the 9th Street and Park West entrance, are well-maintained at Prospect Park and a bit friendlier than their Manhattan counterparts.

MANHATTAN

Batting Cages at Chelsea Piers

23rd Street at the Hudson,

(212) 336-6500

Hackers, Hitters and Hoops

123 West 18th Street, (212) 929-7482

To reserve a field in a city park of any borough:

Manhattan: (212) 408-0309

Bronx: (718) 822-4282

Queens: (718) 520-5933

Brooklyn: (718) 965-8919

Staten Island: (718) 816-6172

ROLLERBLADING & ICE-SKATING

Some words of wisdom: Central Park, in particular on weekends and in the spring and summer, is packed with people who have not yet perfected maneuvering on blades, so don't assume they'll honor the right-of-way or even be able to brake. Other parks, where it's not such a social scene, are a little less like a circus.

In-line skaters can attempt the advanced shalom courses in

Central Park by the Bandstand and west of the Great Lawn by the restaurant Tavern on the Green, where on weekends experienced skaters do informal exhibitions for a large crowds of spectators. Watch and learn, but if you've just fitted your knee-pads for the first time, you may be better accommodated on The Dead Road, from about 66th to 69th Streets in the middle of the park.

CENTRAL PARK SKATING
Wollman Rink
Mid-park at 63rd St., (212) 439-6900, www.wollmanskatingrink.com
Lasker Rink
Near 110th St. and Lenox Ave. (212) 534-7639, Winter Ice Skating: Adults $4, Skate Rental: $3.50, In-Line Skating: Adults: $4 in the rink, $15 for two hours in the park, $25 for all day

World's Fair Rink in Flushing Meadows–Corona Park
(718) 271-1996
Abe Stark Rink at Coney Island
On Boardwalk (at West 19th St.), (718) 946-3135, Admission: $7 (adults); Skate Rental: $4 (weekends only)

SWIMMING

Two city pools are particularly clean and accessible although invariably crowded on weekends and especially during the sweltering summer months: Carmine Street Pool (Seventh Ave. South at Clarkson St.), (212) 242-5228, and John Jay Park (E. 77th St. and Cherokee Pl.), (212) 794-6566.

New York City beaches are open from Memorial Day through Labor Day weekends from 10am to 6pm. The main ones are all found in the outer boroughs.

INDOOR POOLS

MANHATTAN
Luye Aquafit
310 E. 23rd St. (212) 505-2400
McBurney YMCA
215 W. 23rd St. (212) 741-9210
Asphalt Green
555 E. 90th St., (212) 369-8890
Doug Stern's
700 Columbus Ave. (at 95th St.), (212) 222-0720
Harlem YMCA
181 W. 135th St. (212) 281-4100
92nd Street YMCA
1395 Lexington Ave.(at 92nd St.), (212) 415-5729

OUTDOOR POOLS

Hamilton Fish
128 Pitt St. (at Houston St.), (212) 387-7687
Dry Dock
E. 10th St. (bet. Aves. C and D)
John Jay Park Pool
E. 77th Street and Cherokee Place, (212) 794-6566
Lasker Pool
W. 110th St. (at Lenox Ave.), (212) 534-7639
Thomas Jefferson
E. 112th St. and First Ave., (212) 860-1372
Jackie Robinson
Bradhurst Ave. and W. 146th St., (212) 234-9606
Highbridge
Amsterdam Ave. and W. 173rd St., (212) 927-2400

INDOOR/OUTDOOR POOLS
MANHATTAN
Asser Levy
Asser Levy Pl. (at East 23rd St.), (212) 447-2020

Carmine Street Pool
Clarkson St. (at 7th Ave. South),
(212) 242-5228

BRONX
Claremont
170th St. and Clay Ave.,
(718) 901-4792
Crotona
173rd St. and Fulton Ave.,
(718) 822-4440
Mapes
E. 180th St. (bet. Mapes and
Prospect), (718) 364-8876
St. Mary's
St.Anne's Ave. and E. 145th St.,
(718) 402-5155
Van Cortlandt
W. 242nd St. and Broadway,
(718) 548-2415

QUEENS
Astoria
19th St. and 23rd Dr. (718) 626-8620
Fisher
99th St. and Thirty-Second Ave.,
(718) 779-8356
Liberty
173rd St. and106th Ave.
(718) 657-4995
Roy Wilkins
119th St. and Merrick Blvd.,
(718) 276-4630

BROOKLYN
Brownsville
Linden Blvd. and Christopher
Ave., (718) 485-4633
Bushwick
Flushing Ave. and Humbolt St.,
(718) 452-2116
Commodore Barry
Flushing and Park Aves., Navy
and North Elliot Sts., (718) 243-2593

Howard
Glenmore and Mother Gatson
Blvd., East New York Avenue,
(718) 385-1023
St. Johns
Prospect Pl. (bet 10th and 11th
Sts.), (718) 771-2787
Sunset
7th Avenue (bet. 41st and 44th
Sts.), (718) 965-6578

STATEN ISLAND
Faber Street and
Richmond Terrace
(718) 816-5259
Lyons
Pier 16 and Victory Blvd.,
(718) 816-9571
Tottenville
Hylan Blvd. and Joline Ave.,
(718) 356-8242
West Brighton
Henderson Ave.(near Chappet
St.), (718) 816-5019

BEACHES

Orchard Beach
(718) 885-3273, **6** *to Pelham*
Bay Pk.
Coney Island and Brighton
Beach
(718) 946-1350, **D Q** *to*
Brighton Beach, **B D F** *to*
Stillwell Ave./Coney Island
Rockaway Beach
(718) 318-4010, **A S** *to*
Rockaway Park Beach/116th St.
South and Midland Beaches
Located on Staten Island
(718) 987-0709

TENNIS

If you have an affiliation with a
university you will most likely
have access to courts. If you
prefer to search out city courts,
Central Park's mid-area around
93rd St. are among the most
happening, though only those
with season permits can reserve
a court in advance. Call (212)
280-0205. However if you don't
mind the wait, join the others
waiting to plunk down five
bucks to play on an unreserved
court for an hour. Bring a deck
of cards and join the others in
line in a game of bridge or
poker. Riverside Park's clay
courts near 96th St. are well-
maintained by neighborhood
volunteers. If you don't mind
the trek to Queens, tennis
courts abound at the prestigious USTA National Center
(718) 592-8000), the site of the
US Open.

ALL BOROUGHS
Parks and Recreation
General Information
(800) 201-PARK

MANHATTAN
New York Health and
Racket Club
Piers 13 and 14 (at Wall St.),
(212) 422-9300
NYHRC Tennis Courts
60 W. 23rd St., (212) 989-2300
Central Park Tennis
Center
West 93rd St. and
Central Park West, (212)
280-0205
Tower Tennis
1725 York Ave. (at 89th St.),
(212) 860-2464
Riverside Park
96th St. and Riverside Dr. (212)

496-2006, 119th St. and Riverside Dr., (212) 486-2103

Harlem Tennis Center
143rd St. (bet Lenox and 7th Aves.), (212) 283-4028

Riverbank State Park
145th St. and Riverside Dr.,
(212) 694-3600

Fred Johnson Playground
151st St. and Seventh Ave.,
(212) 234-9609

Columbia Tennis Center
575 West 218th Str. at Seaman Ave. (behind Baker's Field), (212) 842-7100

BRONX
Stadium Tennis Center in Mullaly Park
11 East 162nd St. (718) 322-4191, (718) 293-2386

QUEENS
Alley Pond Tennis Club
79-20 Winchester Blvd., Queens Village. (718) 468-1239
Long Island City Indoor Tennis
50-01 Second St., (718) 784-9677
The U.S.T.A. National Center
Flushing Meadows Corona Park, (718) 583-8000

BROOKLYN
Breakpoint Tennis Club in Bensonhurst
9000 Bay Parkway, (718) 372-6878
Prospect Park Tennis Center
305 Coney Island Ave. (at Parkside), (718) 438-1200

HORSEBACK RIDING

While the only horses you may ever see are pulling moneyed tourists through Central Park, the serious equestrian can seek out several options for horse-back-riding within the city limits, though costs are often high. Central Park has a bridle path for experienced riders, and Van Cortlandt Park has a fairly extensive riding center.

By far the best option for horseback-riding is the newest addition to the sleek recreation supercenter Chelsea Piers. The members-only full riding facility is geared toward the serious urban rider who before now didn't have the option of staying in the city to pursue such passions as jumping, dressage and polo. Offering classes to the novice as well as to the seasoned equestrian, the center is a private club where the distinguished, long-established world of horseback-riding teams up with the new world of educational and entertaining multimedia equipment to further the sport that doubles as a recreational pastime for the wealthy. Thanks to huge glass doors along the east and west of the building, both indoor and outdoor arenas sport exquisite views of the Hudson River in a 30,000 sq.-ft. space.

Definitely a stylish addition to a burgeoning waterfront, though avid riding enthusiasts will have to plunk down $2500 as an initial membership fee, and $250 a month thereafter.

Chelsea Piers
63 North River, Pier 63 (at 23rd St. and the West Side Highway), (212) 367-9090
Claremont Riding Academy
175 West 89th St., (212) 724-5100

BRONX
Pelham Bit Stable
9 Shore Road, (718) 885-0551
The Riverdale Equestrian Center
West 254th Street and Broadway, (718) 548-4848

Lynne's Riding School
88-03 70th Rd., (718) 261-7679
Dixie Dew Stables
*88-11 70th Rd., (718) 263-3500
ear, $325 for 3 months*

RECREATION CENTERS

Membership in this city-run Manhattan Recreation Centers costs $25 a year for adults from 18 to 50 years, $10 for youths 13-17, and is free for those 12 years and under. Most have locker rooms and showers, but patrons must bring their own locks, towels, and toiletries. The centers have gyms, weight rooms, aerobics classes, and pools. Call for particular programs.

In Midtown, the Manhattan recreation centers located on 54th Street between First and Second Avenues and on West 59th Street between Tenth and Eleventh Avenues offer indoor swimming running, aerobics, weightrooms, and all the basics, and the member ship fee will only set you back $25! The 168th Street Armory offers one of the finest track and field facilities in the city. *Call (212) 281-9376 for information.*

In the outer boroughs, world-class gyms, weightrooms, basketball courts and pools are available for a fee that's often cheaper than in Manhattan.

MANHATTAN
Alfred E. Smith
Catherine St. (bet. Cherry and Monroe Sts.), (212) 285-0300
Asser Levy
Asser Levy Place (Ave. A and E. 23rd St.), (212) 447-2020
Carmine Street
Clarkson St. and Seventh Ave. South, (212) 242-5228
West 59th
West 59th St. and Tenth Ave., (212) 397-3166
Hamilton Fish
128 Pitt St., (212) 387-7687
Hansborough
West 134th St. (bet. Fifth and Lenox Aves.), 234-9603
Highbridge
Amsterdam Ave. (at West 173rd St.), (212) 27-2400
Jackie Robinson
*Bradhurst Ave. (at West 146th St.), (212) 234-9606
North Meadow Central Park (at 97th St.), (212) 348-4867*
Pelham Fritz
Mount Morris Park West, (at West 122nd St.), (212) 860-1380
Thomas Jefferson
E. 112th St. and First Ave., (212) 860-1372

BRONX
Crotona
East 173rd and Fulton Sts., (718) 822-4272
Saint Mary's
East 145th St. and St. Anne's Ave., (718) 402-5155

QUEENS
The Lost Batallion Hall
93-29 Queens Blvd., (718) 263-1163
Roy Wilkins
177th St. and Baisley Blvd., (718) 276-4630
Sorrentino
Beach 19th St. and Cornaga Ave., (718) 471-4818

BROOKLYN
Brownsville
Linden and Mother Gaston Blvds. (at Christopher St.), (718) 485-4633
Red Hook
Bay and Henry St, (718) 722-3213
Sunset Park
44th St. and Seventh Ave., (718) 965-6578

STATEN ISLAND
Cromwell
Pier 6 and Murray Hulbert Ave., (718) 816-6172

BOATING

Genteel dreams of whiling away the afternoon in a trim rowboat can be realized in the Loeb Boathouse that also rents canoes for those inclined to the wilderness aesthetic.

MANHATTAN
Loeb Boathouse in Central Park
East Drive (at 74th St.), $10 for the first hour, $2.50 for each additional hour, and a $30 refundable deposit, (212) 517-2233.

BRONX
Crotona Lake
East 173rd St.and Crotona Park, (718) 822-4440

BROOKLYN
Kate Wollman Rink in Prospect Park
Between Lincoln and Parkside,

pedalboats for four people at $12 per hour, $10 refundable deposit required

PROFESSIONAL SPORTS

Watching others expend their energies in athletic pursuits can be just as satisfying. New York boasts several notable arenas hosting our beloved home teams.

Although the house that Ruth built has a tentative date with a wrecking ball scheduled for sometime in the early 21st century, **Yankee Stadium** (See the Bronx) remains, after nearly seventy-five years of witnessing baseball history, the most scenic and historic venue the city offers for viewing professional sports.

Shea Stadium, home of the Mets, has served as baseball's other home in the city since its 1964 opening brought National League baseball back after the Dodgers ignominious departure in 1957. While Shea and the Mets lack the tradition and lore of the Yankees, its more accessible location and the revitalization of the team in the '00 World Series help keep Shea packed with higher attendance.

Madison Square Garden, New York City's primary indoor arena, located above Penn Station, has been an exciting place to go lately with both the Knicks and the Rangers enjoying strong teams and exciting playoff runs through the nineties. Although the '96-'97 seasons failed to produce a championship for Ewing's Knicks or Messier's Rangers, optimism remains high this fall. At the spacious Garden, fans can see the floor even from the worst seats, and the crowd is often raucous enough to qualify as a secondary attraction. Other events at the Garden include Rangers games, college basketball, ice shows, dog shows, tennis tournaments and big-name concerts.

Yankee Stadium
(718) 293-6000, Tickets: $6-$21, ❹ ❻ ❼ *to 161st St./ Yankee Std.*

Shea Stadium
126th St. and Roosevelt Ave. (718) 507-8499, Tickets: $7-$19, ❼ *to Willis Point/Shea Stadium*

Madison Square Garden
Knicks, (212) 307-7171, Tickets: $25-$425
Rangers, (212) 465-6741, Tickets: $22-$125, ❶ ❸ ❺ ❶ ❷ ❸ *to 34th St.- Penn Station*

HIKING AND CAMPING

Sometimes one must embrace the raging animal within and get off this face-paced, soul-sucking island. These clubs can help you resurrect the serenity you lost during your last subway ride.

Appalachian Mountain Club
(617) 523-0636

Hudson River Watertrail Association
www.hrwa.org

New York/New Jersey Trail Conference
(201) 512-9348

Campers' Group
www.panix.com/~levner/camping/

SOCCER CLUBS

During the 1998 World Cup, the UN lobby was crowded with diplomats cheering on their favorite teams. The Cosmopolitan League can help you find places to play the beautiful game.

The Cosmopolitan Soccer League: *(212) 355-6700*

WALKING CLUBS

Pedestrians unite! Racewalkers can find kindred spirits by calling the following:

Park Racewalkers
(212) 628-1317

MISCELLANEOUS

Lazer Park Entertainment Center
Located in Times Square, this entertainment is the ideal place to relax and be a kid again. Play lazer tag with a group of friends or colleagues, throw someone a birthday party or just go because you're bored. Be prepared to wait if you decide to go on a Friday or Saturday night, but fear not- there are legions of video games to entertain you as you wait.

1560 Broadway (46th Street), (212) 398-3060

Six Flags Theme Park
A little over two hours away from the city, this NJ branch recently opened their wildlife safari, a 350-acre park with over 1,200 animals. The "great adventure" park has all that you'd expect; park food, stage shows, rides and restaurants. Be sure to take a ride on Nitro, the "most explosive coaster on the planet," which reaches speeds of 80 m.p.h. But only before lunch, please.

Route 537, Jackson, New Jersey,
www.sixflags.com/parks/ great
adventure
(732) 928-1821

Chelsea Piers

Whether you are looking for batting cages, driving ranges, some Hudson River kayaking, or an indoor soccer league, the Chelsea Piers Sports and Entertainment Complex, between 17th-23rd Streets, is the ultimate stop for all of your recreational desires. Located on 30 acres of waterfront, the piers include a golf club, a health club, two ice rinks, a roller rink/extreme park, a field house, a bowling alley, a maritime center and dance studios. If none of these seem to be quite the right release, then visit the Origins Spa next door and have someone else relieve your stress for you. Price gouging at its finest, Chelsea Piers is a bit cavernous and makes up for what it lacks in charm with an impressively eye-pleasing clientele. It may cost a bit more than your first car to purchase a membership here, but its resources are worth it. In addition to the recreational facilities, the Piers house Silver Screen Studios, an enormous center for film and television production, including You've Got Mail, Everyone Says I Love You, Law and Order and Spin City.

Russian and Turkish Baths

The Tenth Street Baths and Health Club (a.k.a. the Russian Turkish Baths) may be one of the best places in New York City to visit for some relaxation. It is certainly not the place to visit if you desire a fruity facial, but if you are looking for a Dead Sea Salt Scrub or simply to let out some steam, then there is nowhere in the city better suited for your needs.

There is actually only one large communal bath in the three-story facility, which is the 45 degree Fahrenheit destination of bathers leaving the one of two saunas or the Russian Radiant Steam Room. Radiant, however, doesn't even begin to describe the intensity of the sauna-or the extreme pleasure felt after a few minutes spent wrapped up in its eucalyptus haze.

The bath is coed-except on Wednesday and Saturday mornings, when women and men, respectively, shed the shorts required during coed hours, and plunge their nude, sweaty bodies into the water.

The bathers themselves range from the hip residents of the Village to the old Russian men. In addition to its bathing facilities, the club offers massages and skin enhancing treatments, a Swedish shower, a sundeck, as well as an inexpensive restaurant serving authentic home-style Russian cuisine. Borscht, anyone? $22 a day includes access to all facilities, robes, slippers, towels, soap, and razor. The baths are certainly one of the most exciting-and oldest (since 1892) - escapes within the city. *268 E. 10th St. (bet. First Ave. and Avenue A), (212) 473-8806*

moving + storage

Nearly all recent transplants to the city move frequently during the first few years they are here, so a number of industries thrive on the desperation that accompanies the undertaking of such a feat in the midst of the urban melee. The luxury of a private car is accessible only to those with dutiful friends or relatives in the vicinity, leaving most prospective movers with that omnipresent resource, the U-Haul (562 West 23rd, at Eleventh, (212) 620-4177). Note the emphasis on "U": if you are carting heavy boxes and/or furniture, movers are an additional investment, easy to come by and worth the expense provided you're not transporting Czech crystal. Do not hire other people to pack for you. Most universities have connections with moving and storage companies, as well as shipping companies, that allow you to leave your boxes at some check-off point near campus, saving you the trouble of trekking across town with a thousand pounds of books in tow.

There are several places throughout the city where you can stock up on boxes and other moving supplies if you plan in advance: boxes are relatively cheap at Moving Supplies & More ((212) 223-3555, phone orders only), where advice about how to pack, how much you should pay for movers, and more, comes along free with your purchase; free delivery with a $25 purchase. Another option is Robert Karp Container Corp. 618 West 52nd Street, bet. Eleventh and Twelfth Avenues, (212) 586-4474) which stocks picture and mirror boxes along with the standards, and offers free delivery for orders over $100.

When to Move

Take advantage of street-cleaning days to get closest to your building. Moving in the early morning or late at night is clearly a better choice, since traffic isn't as bad and, if you're moving out of a dorm, you may just get a shot at the elevator. Summer weekends are the best times to move into the city. In many sections of Manhattan, residents flee New York's steamy weather and traffic within the city is relatively light during these time periods. Weekends can be a problem, however, if you are using a U-Haul, since vans are only rented out for six hours then. Those moving into or out of apartment buildings should call supers in case there are times when you aren't allowed to move, especially if you will involve doormen or elevators.

If you plan on utilizing a cab, definitely move late at night or in mid-morning, since drivers get surly and unhelpful it they feel they're wasting time with you instead of picking up more fares at a peak time. Even better than a cab is a car service, since drivers have huge cars with body-bag sized trunks, and are a bit more helpful with loading and unloading. Be sure to agree on a price before getting into the car. If a driver helps unload and load boxes, make sure to tip well, since they are going above and beyond the call of duty. Moving in a taxi or Gypsy Cab is okay with a few boxes; with large boxes and breakables, invest in a van, especially since within the city, a U-Haul cargo van only costs $19.95 a per day.

ANIMALS

ASPCA Humane Organization
(212) 876-7700
Center for Animal Care and Control
1-888-LOST123, Open 24 hours daily.

CHILDCARE

Babysitter's Guild
It's best to call a day ahead.
60 East 42nd St., (212) 682-0227, www.babysittersguild.citysearch.com, 9am-9pm daily
Columbia University Career Services
Call in with a semi-permanent position, and they will post it on the part-time employment board. Students call for more information and to negotiate a babysitting rate.
116th St. and Amsterdam Ave., (212) 854-5609, Fax: (212) 854-5640
Town & Country's Gilbert Child Care
For children over nine months, the hourly rate is $7.25 with a four hour minimum; it's about a $1-$2 more for children under nine months. Same-day service is possible, but definitely call ahead for weekends.

157 West 57th St., (212) 245-8400 (reservation office), M-F, 9pm-5pm
Parents League
Join for $35 a year and gain access to the League's baby-sitting service, which includes sitters age thirteen to eighteen who attend one of the member schools. Check out the sitters' files, arranged by neighborhood, on the premises.
115 East 82nd St., (212) 737-7385, M, W, R 9am-4pm, T 9am-6pm, F 9am-12pm, ❹❺❻ to 86th St.

CONSUMER RESOURCES

Better Business Bureau
(212) 533-7500, M-F, 9am-5pm
New York City Department of Consumer Affairs, Complaints Department
(212) 487-4444
New York State Consumer Frauds Helpline and Protection Bureau
1-800-771-7755
Small Claims Court/ Civil Court
You don't need a lawyer to file a suit to claim

under $3000; over 60,000, New Yorkers go to Small Claims Court every year, though winning in court doesn't mean you will necessarily get the money due to poor enforcement mechanisms.
(212) 791-6000

COPY SERVICES

Chelsea Copy and Printing
255 West 23rd Street (bet. Seventh and Eighth Aves.),(212) 924-4953
Kinko's
Notorious among college students for catering to those last-minute needs, Kinko's is open 24 hours. Some services include: copying, faxing, computer use and enlargements.
*118-10 Queens Boulevard (at 70th Ave.), (718) 286-7700, MC, V, AmEx, D, Diners, ❸❻ to Union Tpke ♿
(Additional locations in Manhattan)*
Village Copier
Reasonable rates; conveniently located to Columbia.
601 West 115th Street (bet. Broadway and Riverside Drive), (212) 666-0600, MC, V, AmEx, ❶❾ to 116th St. ♿

CRISIS LINES, HOTLINES AND MEDICAL NUMBERS

Bellevue Hospital Rape Crisis Service
Free medical treatment for rape victims, as well as counseling referral.
(212) 562-3435, M-F 9am-5pm
Crime Victims Hotline
Victims of any personal crime, including domestic violence, rape, and theft, as well as legal advice.
(212) 577-7777, Open 24 hours daily
St. Luke's/ Roosevelt Hospital Rape Crisis Center
Trained volunteers talk victims through dealing with rape, both legally and emotionally.
(212) 523-4728, M-F 8am-7pm
Sex Crimes Report Line
A female detective from the NYPD handles reports of all sex crimes, child victimization, hate crimes against gays, send an ambulance, provide counseling referrals, and set up an interview with a Sex Crimes Squad detective; you may request to be interviewed in your home.
NYPD Sex Crimes

CUTTA

Columbia University Tutoring & Translating Agency

Complete tutoring and translating services to meet all your
scholarly, academic, and legal needs

* Tutoring, translating, interpreting, transcribing, proofreading
* All European and Asian Languages
* Native speakers and specialists with unique language skills
* Notarized translations of diplomas, transcripts, certificates, etc.
* Competitive rates with volume discounts
* Rush service, fastest turn around in the business
* Convenient on-campus location
* All media - print, audio, video and digital

Location & Delivery Address:
70-74 Morningside Drive
between 118th & 117th Sts.

Mailing Address:
2960 Broadway MC 5727
New York, NY 10027

(212) 854-4888 Fax: (212) 663-9398

Email: cutta2000@hotmail.com
www.columbia.edu/cu/ccs/cutta/

Unit, (212) 267-7273,
Open 24 hours daily

Domestic Violence Helpline

Trained social workers offer advice and use of shelter space, though working women pay a fee.
(800) 621-4673, Open 24 hours daily, English and Spanish

New York State Child Abuse and Maltreatment Register

Call to report suspected child abuse.
(800) 342-3720, Open 24 hours daily

New York State Domestic Violence Helpline

Information on legal options and referrals to local programs and shelters.
(800) 942-6906, Open 24 hours daily, (800) 621-4673 (Spanish), M-F, 9am-5pm

The Samaritans

Volunteers help those suffering from depression, thoughts of suicide, and alcoholism.
(212) 673-3000, www.samaritansnyc.org, Open 24 hours daily

Suicide Prevention

Trained volunteers help talk people through thoughts of suicide.
(212) 532-2400 (interpretation service), www.helpline.org, 9am-10pm daily

DAYCARE AND OTHER RESOURCES

Agency for Child Development

Pre-school and referral information, as well as a free directory of daycare services.
(718) 523-6826

Child Care Inc./ The Pre-School Association

This nonprofit group offers parents telephone counseling, information of day care and early childhood programs, and names of day care providers in your neighborhood.
275 Seventh Ave, 15th fl.,
(212) 929-7604, ❶❷ to 28th street

The New York Public Library's Early Childhood Resource Center

There is an entire floor devoted to resource materials for parents, and appropriately enough, a playroom for kids.
66 Leroy St. (at Seventh Ave.), (212) 929-0815, ❶❷ to Houston St.

DISABILITY INFORMATION

Although New York City may appear daunting at first, armed with information and determination, any disabled individual can take advantage of most of what the City has to offer. The best resources on accessibility can be found at:

Hospital Audiences, Inc. (HAI)
(212) 575-7676
Mayor's Office for People with Disabilities
(212) 788-2830
New York City Transit Authority Travel Information Center
(718) 330-1234

Lighthouse Incorporated
Information on resources for the blind
111 East 59th St. (bet. Park and Lexington Aves.), (212) 821-9200, (800) 829-0500,
M-F, 9am-5pm,
N R *to Lexington Ave.*
New York Society for the Deaf
Information on resources for the deaf.
817 Broadway (at 12th St.), (212) 777-3900, M-F 9am-5pm, **N R 4 5 6** *to Union Sq.*
Andrew Heiskell Library for the Blind and Physically Handicapped
(212) 206-5400

DRY CLEANERS

Joe Far Laundry
Fast and efficient, this inconspicuous laundry is the cheapest in Morningside.
B'way and 112th St., (212) 666-3440, cash only, **1**

to 116th St.
M+N Cleaners
Speedy and organized and they offer delivery.
292 Eighth Avenue (bet. 25th and 26th Sts.), (212) 675-8966, **1 2** *to 23rd St.*
Piermont Cleaners
Pick up that suit en route to the show.
845 Seventh Avenue (at 54th Street), (212) 582-0919, MC, V.

ENTERTAINMENT

Cultural Affairs Department Line
(212) 643-7770
Parks and Recreation Department
Special events: (212) 360-8146; Summer Stage: (212) 360-2777

GAY AND LESBIAN

Gay and Lesbian Switchboard
A good resource for visitors to get advice about the city.
(212) 777-1800, 10am-12am daily
Gay Men's Health Crisis Hotline
Advice for people concerned about HIV/AIDS.
(212) 807-6655, M-F 10am-9pm, S 12:00pm-3pm
Lesbian and Gay Community Services Center
(See sidebar in the Gay Feature for more information.)
208 West 13th St. (at

Eighth Ave.), (212) 620-7310, 9am-11pm daily, **F L 1 2 3** *to 14th St.*
New York City Gay and Lesbian Anti-Violence Project
647 Hudson St. (at Gansevoort St.), (212) 807-0197, M-R 10am-8pm, F 10am-6pm, Hotline open 24 hours daily, **F L 1 2 3** *to 14th St.*

GOVERNMENT OFFICES

Birth Records
(212) 788-4520
Department of Motor Vehicles
516 and 914 area codes: (800) DIAL-DMV, Manhattan: (212) 645-5550,
Outer Boroughs: (718) 966-6155
Directory Assistance
Outer Boroughs: (718) 555-1212
Manhattan: 411
Immigration And Naturalization Service
(212) 206-6500
Passport Agency
630 Fifth Ave., Room 230, (212) 206-3500, M-F 7:30am-4pm.
United States Postal Service Zip Code Information
(212) 967-8585

HAIRCARE

Aveda
Haircuts that would normally set you back $65 are free in the training

class. Expect to wait a month. No coloring.
233 Spring Street (bet. Varick and Prince Sts.), (212) 807-1492, Call for specific times, by appointment, **C E** *to Spring St.*
Bumble and Bumble
Leave a message explaining what you want done, and they'll get back to you if they think they can use you for the training class.
146 E. 56th St. (bet. Third and Lexington Ave.), Call for specific times and appointment, 521-6500, Cut: $10, Color: $20, 456 to 59th St. or **N R** *to Lexington Ave.*
Crisca Hair Salon
Stop in for a moderately priced haircut with no appointment necessary.
21 E. 51st St. (bet. Fifth and Madison Aves.), (212) 759-4743, MC, V, **E V** *to Fifth Avenue*
Headlines
This busy salon that does the basics from hair to manicures. First-time walk-in clients can take advantage of a $15 cut if someone's free. Otherwise, cuts start at $26.
220 Eighth Ave. (bet. 20th and 21 Sts.), 243-0533, MC, V, **1 2** *to 23rd St.*
Jacques Dessange
By appointment only.
505 Park Ave. (bet. 59th and 60th Sts.), (212) 308-1400, Cut: $10, Color: $20, 456 to 59th St. or **N**

R *to Lexington Ave.*

Jean Louis David

Moderately priced, but cuts are hit or miss unless you latch onto a regular stylist. Check out their training center for great deals on M, T, and W.
Broadway (bet. 73rd and 74th Sts.), (212) 873-1850, cash only, **1** **2** *to 79th St.*

Jeffrey's Manhattan Eyeland

Small selection of unique frames. Check out the window displays.
Broadway (bet. 87th and 88th), 787-3232, MC, V, AmEx, **1** **2** *to 86th St.*

Saks Fifth Avenue Beauty Salon

Same procedure, but if you have the patience you'll end up with a free cut.
611 Fifth Ave., 9th floor, (bet. 49th and 50th Sts.), Call for specific times, (212) 320-4700, **E** **V** *to Lexington/Third Aves.*

J. Scott

Columbia students pamper themselves with professional cuts, colors, and massages.
2929 Broadway (bet. 114th and 115th Sts.), (212) 666-6429, MC, V, **1** *to 116th St.* &

The Service Station

Bodies in need of a tune-up, look toward the twelve-foot Gulf sign. Cuts start at $40. The shop offers an array of body tweakings, including manicures, tanning, and electrolysis.
137 Eighth Ave. (bet. 17th and 18th Sts.), (212) 243-7770, **1** **2** *to 18th St.*

Vidal Sassoon

You can't get scheduled till they take a look at your hair. Twenty percent off the already cut-rate prices for students.
90 Fifth Ave. (bet. 14th and 15th Sts.), (212) 229-2000, by appointment, **L** **N** **R** **4** **5** **6** *to Union Square*
730 Fifth Ave. (bet 56th and 57th Sts.), (212) 535-9200.

HEALTH

Bailey House

Deals with emergency situations for people with AIDS/HIV.
275 Seventh Ave. (at 25th St.), (212) 414-1428, M-F 9:30am-5:30pm, **N** **R** *to 28th St.*

Emergency Dental Associates

(800) 439-9299, 9am-7pm daily

Fire Department and Emergency Medical Service

Report problems, including delayed service, poor treatment, or no-shows.
(718) 416-7000

Herpes Hotline and Advice Center

Advice and treatment run by a private medical practice.
(212) 213-6150, M-R 9am-6:45pm, F 9am-3pm, (212) 684-7455

Mental Health Counseling Hotline

Therapists will talk you through any emotional problems and issue referrals.
(212) 734-5876, Open 24 hours daily

New York City AIDS Information Hotline

(212) 447-8200, 9am-9pm daily

New York University Student Dental Plan

Affordable, one-fee yearly dental care for college or university students.
David B. Kriser Dental Center, 345 E. 24th St. (at First Ave.), (212) 998-9870

Poison Control Center

Call with questions.
(212) 764-7667

HOTELS

New York City boasts more hotel rooms than any other city in the world, barring Las Vegas. That doesn't, however, make finding an affordable hotel in New York an easy process. While in Midtown and the Financial District, hotels seem a dime a dozen, outside these districts lodgings are significantly harder to come by, and no matter where you are, hotels will milk you for all you're worth. Space is often at a premium, and the city also gets in on the action by levying a hefty "hotel occupancy tax" of 13.25% making an under-$200-a-night deal a bargain. If you foresee a trip in high season, for example during December, book well in advance since rooms go quickly.

Upper End ($200+)

Four Seasons Hotel

Don't let the grand walk up from the lobby to the reception desk intimidate you, and forget all those models and celebrities milling around the lobby bar, too; if you've got the funds to sign on as a guest, the service is warm and welcoming without being obsequious. You could fit several average New Yorkers' apartments into the coolly elegant rooms with impressive cityscape views to boot. A list of premium amenities could fill pages. Everything here is state-of-the-art and sophisticated, down to the Magrittes and Kandinskys distributed liberally throughout. Drawbacks? This luxurious experience comes at a very hefty price.
57 E. 57th St. (bet. Madison and Park Aves.), (212) 758-5700, Rooms start at $500, MC, V, Am Ex, D, **N** **R** **Q** **W** **F** **4** **5** **6** *to 59th-Lexington* &

Hilton Rockefeller Center

As large and impersonal as convention centers go, this one does the job with

finesse. While the enormous lobby can make locating the concierge a bit of a problem, the rooms are reliably comfortable. Nice location, too, although the name is a bit misleading since Rockefeller Center is six blocks away.
1335 Sixth Ave. (bet. 53rd and 54th Sts.), (212) 586-7000, MC, V, Am Ex, D, Diners, Rooms start at $280, 🅱🆅 *to Fifth Ave.*

Loews

With jacuzzis, personal trainers at your request, and a concierge on two levels to direct you to all the sights and stores the hotel rests in the center of, Loews has big city accommodations with a friendly staff ready to make you feel right at home.
569 Lexington Ave. (at 51st St.), (212) 752-7000, MC,V,AmEx, Weekend Rates: around $240, 🅴🆅 *🄶 to 51st-Lexington*

Peninsula

A neophyte in the parade of luxury properties along the spine of upper Fifth Avenue, the Peninsula was born with a silver spoon in its mouth, namely a million-dollar location. Fantastic views abound from the renowned rooftop bar, the Pen-Top, and the outlook from the opulent day spa on the 21st floor is far from shabby. Though small and a bit minimalist, rooms are nice, and for the money, views should be better than an air shaft. Still, the Peninsula is a classy place, and the well-heeled visitors who stay here can attest to that.
700 Fifth Ave. (at 55th St.), (212) 956-2888, Rooms start at $390, MC, V, Am Ex, D, 🅵🆅 *to Fifth Ave.*

Plaza

The stuff of legends, the epitome of old New York, where every middle-American dreams of staying. Tons of movies, from *Home Alone II* to *Plaza Suite,* pay homage to the Edwardian romance of this classic. The parkside hotel seems dedicated to preserving this mystique, from its opulent lobby to the delicate splendor of the Palm Court restaurant. This vision of elegance is marred somewhat by the scores of gawking halter-topped tourists from Iowa, though if you escape to your room, old-style sinks and marble fireplaces will re-orient you in the hotel's tradition. Overall, it's steeped in style and short on coziness.
Central Park

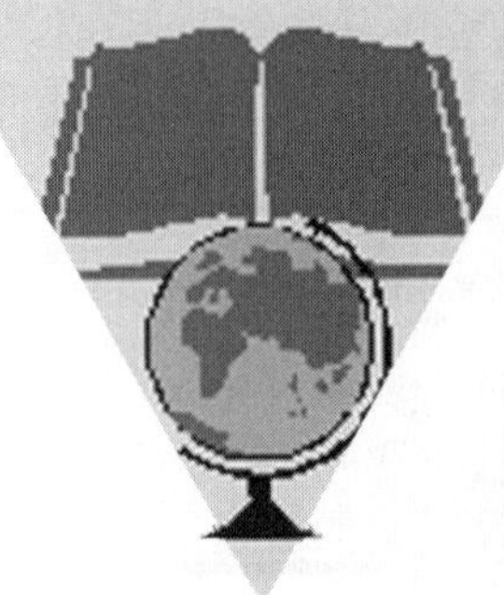

Columbia University Center for Career Education

❖ CCE can assist you in beginning your career development process early and help you in discovering your interests, values and skills.

❖ Register with CCE at http://www.cce.columbia.edu. You'll gain access to current programming and services, work-study information, internships on- and off-campus employment opportunities.

❖ Visit CCE; speak with a Career Advisor to help you map out your present and future career goals.

❖ Participate in Career Fairs and Career Week and gain early exposure to current employers and industries.

EXPLORE YOUR CAREER OPPORTUNITIES EARLY!

Center for Career Education

East Campus, Lower Level / (212) 854-5609
www.cce.columbia.edu cce@columbia.edu

South (at Fifth Ave.), (212) 759-3000, Rooms start at $290, MC, V, Am Ex, D, Diners, **F V** to Fifth Ave. ♿

SoHo Grand
Currently the hottest hotel in New York, this newcomer made headlines and angered neighborhood residents as the first hotel in SoHo. Everything is in sync with the neighborhood: artsy, avant-garde types walk through the cutting-edge industrial lobby to their custom-designed digs. You can request a black goldfish to accompany you during your stay. In keeping with the cyber-sexy image, you can even make reservations on their website:
http://www.SoHoGrand.com
310 West Broadway (at Canal St.), (212) 965-3000, Rooms start at $250, MC, V, AmEx, D, Diners, **A C E 1 2** to Canal St.

UN Plaza-Millennium Hotel
Often overlooked by tourists, this pleasant Hyatt outpost is a good bet in Midtown East. Directly across from the United Nations and the East River, all of the rooms have incredible views. The mood, evoked by an abundance of mirrors, brass, marquee lights, and dark walls, is subdued, even stodgy, but who wants to complain when the rooms are this comfortable? People who stay here tend to be quiet, or foreign, or both. One UN Plaza 43th St. (bet. First and Second Aves.), (212) 758-1234, Rooms start at $225, MC, V, AmEx, D, **S 4 5 6 7** to 42nd St./Grand Central Station ♿

Mid-Range ($100-$200)

Gramercy Park Hotel
Pre-war in more than simply architecture, this established outpost on Gramercy Park also attracts a largely pre-war clientele. Charm abounds here, and the neighborhood is an interesting one to explore, but more importantly, visitors here will be the secret envy of every New Yorker: the hotel holds a coveted key to private Gramercy Park, a privilege for which many neighborhood residents would kill.
2 Lexington Ave. (at Gramercy Park, 21st St.), (212) 475-4320, MC, V, Am Ex, D, Diners, Rooms start at $145, **6** to 23rd St. ♿

Marriott Marquis
Look for the garish yellow Hertz billboard and you

won't miss this Times Square staple for theater-bound tourists and other visitors who equate flashiness with luxury. With two thousand rooms, a revolving rooftop restaurant, an ultra-glitzy lobby, and its own Broadway theater, the Marquis dispenses with the need to even leave the premises for a taste of overwrought glamour.
1535 Broadway (at 45th St.), (212) 398-1900, Rooms start at $200, MC, V, Am Ex, **N R Q W S** **1 3 7** *to Times Square*

Paramount

Cheap by New York standards, this snazzy hotel offers reasonable prices for well-appointed rooms, trendy clientele, and smart chic. Designed by master hotelier Phillipe Starck, everything here is too cool: the lobby decor looks like Dr. Seuss himself moonlit as the interior decorator, while bathrooms have funky, pyramid-shaped aluminum sinks. Expect showbiz types (guests of "Saturday Night Live" stay here) who don't mind being shoehorned into microscopic rooms.
235 West 46th St. (bet. Broadway and Eighth Ave.), (212) 764-5500, Rooms start at $145, MC, V, Am Ex, D, Diners, **A C** **E** *to Port Authority,* **N** **R Q W S 1 2 3 7** *to Times Sq.*

Wales Hotel

An anomaly among the luxury properties of the Upper East Side, this homey, attractive hotel in venerable Carnegie Hill provides very nice rooms in an unexpectedly charming atmosphere. Its proximity to Museum Mile and Madison Avenue shopping is an added bonus.
1295 Madison Avenue (bet. 92nd and 93rd Sts.), (212) 876-6000, Rooms start at $199, MC, V, Am Ex, **4 5 6** *to 86th St.* &

*Budget
(under $100)*

The De Hirsh Residence (at the 92nd St. YMCA)

Dormitory style residence hall where one can stay by the day (minimum 3-day stay), or apply to stay by the month for up to a year. The activities available at the Y are open to De Hirsh residents.
1395 Lexington Ave. (at 92nd St.), (212) 415-5650, Rooms are $35/doubles (apiece), $49/singles, **6** *to 86th St.*

East Campus Hotel

Columbia University guest accommodations offers rooms for visitors.
Columbia University, (212) 854-2946, MC, V, Rooms are $75/single, $90/double, **1** *to 116th St.* &

Herald Square Hotel

One can get a "very small single" with a shared bathroom for just $50 a day; add $25 for a private shower.
19 West 31st St. (bet. Broadway and Fifth Ave.), (212) 279-4017, MC, V, Am Ex, D, Rooms start at $55, **1 2 3** *to 34th St.*

New York International House AYH-Hostel

Vistors can stay in large ten-to-twelve-person bedrooms. Members get a better deal. Maximum stay is one week.
891 Amsterdam Ave. (at 103rd St.), (212) 932-2300, MC, V, Rooms are $27/$24 (members), **1** *to 103rd St.*

NYU Guest Accommodations

Accommodations are available for guests, call for special deals at nearby hotels.
636 Greenwich St., (212) 443-4700, MC, V, Am Ex, Rates vary by hotel

Park West Studio Hotel

Extended stay prices are the best deal at $165/wk.
465 Central Park West (bet. 106th and 107th St.), (212) 866-1880, Cash Only, Rooms start at $50, **B C** *to Cathedral Pkwy.*

Pickwick Arms

No frills, but it's often the best bet for savvy budget travelers who appreciate the warm lobby and the safe neighborhood and don't mind the forgettable rooms. The rooftop garden overlooking the skyscrapers makes this place an even bigger bargain.
230 East 51st Street (bet. Second and Third Aves.), (212) 355-0300, Rooms start at $60, MC, V, Am Ex, **E V 6** *to Lexington-51st St.*

Washington Square

Experience the quintessential trade-off of a resident New Yorker: location vs. space. Shoebox rooms at the only hotel in the Village, but in return, you're within walking distance of Washington Square Park, which beats the sleaze of Times Square any day.
103 Waverly Pl.(off Washington Sq. Park), (212) 777-9515, Rooms start at $110, MC, V, AmEx, **A C D F V S** *to W. 4th St.*

The Outer Boroughs

There arEn't very many choices for lodging in Brooklyn, Bronx, Queens, and Staten Island. There are a few motels and inns sprinkled throughout, although they usually tend to be located along the major expressways out of town. Luxury options are pretty much confined to bed and breakfasts. Here is a partial listing.

Le Refuge Bed and Breakfast
620 City Island Ave., City Island, (718) 885-2478

Best Western City View Motor Inn
33-17 Greenpoint Ave., (718) 392-8400

Marriott LaGuardia Airport
102-05 Ditmars Blvd., (718) 565-8900

Comfort Inn Brooklyn
8315 Fourth Ave., Bay Ridge, (718) 238-3737

Staten Island Hotel
1415 Richmond Ave., (718) 698-5000

HOUSING

Housing Complaints (general)
(212) 960-4800
Rent Stabilization Association. (owners)
(212) 214-9200
Rent Stabilization Association. (tenants)
(212) 961-8930
Division of Housing and Community Renewal
(212) 240-6010

INSTITUTIONAL LIBRARIES

Andrew Heiskell Library for the Blind and Physically Handicapped
(212) 206-5400

Archive of Contemporary Music
54 White St., (bet. Broadway and Church Sts.), (212) 226-6967
Baha'i Center and Library
53 E. 11th St. (bet. University Pl. and Broadway), 674-8998
Donnell Library Center
(212) 621-0618
Frick Art Reference Library
10 E. 71st St., (212) 288-8700

Gilder-Lehrman Library
(212) 481-6299
Hampden Booth Theatre Library
(212) 228-7610
Jewish Theological Seminary of America
(212) 678-8000
Morgan Library
29 E. 36th St. (bet. Madison and Park Aves.), (212) 685-0008
New York Law Institute
120 Broadway (bet. Cedar and Pine Sts.), (212) 732-8720

LEGAL SERVICES

Community Action For Legal Services
Government-funded referral service.
(212) 431-7200
Legal Aid Society
Free advice on legal matters and referrals, but you must live below 34th Street in order to qualify.
(212) 577-3300, M-F

9am–5pm

LIBRARIES

Queens Central Library
(718) 990-0778 (also extensions, 0779, 0781, 0700)
New York Public Library
(212) 340-0849
The New York Public Library For The Performing Arts
(212) 870-1630
Science, Industry and Business Library (NYPL)
(212) 592-7000
Brooklyn Central Library
(718) 230-2100
Bronx Central Library
(718) 579-4200
Telephone Reference Service
Librarians are extremely helpful about answering reference questions; they will refer you to the department with the most data.
Manhattan: (212) 340-0849
Bronx: (718) 220-6576
Brooklyn: (718) 780-7700
Queens: (718) 990-0714

MOTOR VEHICLES

Alternate Side of the St. Parking Regulations
(212) 442-7080
Parking Violations Help Hotline (NYC Dept. of Transportation)

(212) 477-4430
Towed-Away Cars (NYC Bureau of Traffic Operations)
(212) 971-0070

OPTICIANS

Columbia Opticians
Fittings and frames.
1246 Amsterdam Ave. (at 119th Street), (212) 316-2020, MC, V, ❶ to 116th St.
Confucius Plaza Optical
One of the least expensive vision alternatives in this area.
17 Bowery, (212) 431-4910, MC, V, AmEx, ❶❶ to Second Ave.
Jeffrey's Manhattan Eyeland
Small selection of unique frames.
2391 Broadway (bet. 87th and 88th Sts.), (212) 787-3232, MC, V, AmEx, ❶❷ to 86th St.
Ocean-View Optical
Stylish specs, but be prepared to pay the high-end prices.
Union Square East bet. 16th and 17th St., (212) 477-9515, MC, V, AmEx, ❶❹❺❻NR❷❶ to Union Sq.-14th St.

PHOTO SERVICES

Fotorush
One-hour processing, also passport photos, video transfer, and slide transfers.
2889 Broadway (at 113th Street), (212) 749-0065,

MC, V, ❶ to 110th St.

POST OFFICES

US General Post Office
Twenty-four hour postal service, except for money =orders and registered mail, in the famous McKim, Mead, White masterpiece of design. Call to find out which branch is closest to you.
380 West 33rd St. (at Eighth Ave.), (800) 275-8777 (Info Line), ❶❷❸ *to Penn Sta.*

RENTALS

Furniture:
Cort-AFR Furniture Rental
711 Third Ave. (at 44th St.), (212) 377-1501, M-Sa, First month's rental plus a two-month security fee is required.
International Furniture Rentals
345 Park Ave. (bet. 51st and 52nd Sts.), (212) 421-0341, M-Sa, One-and-a-half month's rent required as deposit.

Air Conditioners:
AABCO
1594 York Ave., (212) 585-2463, MC, V, AmEx, Average cost during the hot season (May through October) is $200.
Ace Air Conditioning Service Corp.
24-81 47th St., Astoria, Queens, (718) 726-7120, MC, V, Room size determines price.

Bicycles:
Bicycles Plus
1400 Third Ave., (212) 794-2929
Metro Bicycles
1311 Lexington Ave. (at 88th St.), (212) 427-4450; 360 W. 47th St., (212) 581-4500; 231 W. 96th St., (212) 663-7531; 417 Canal St., (212) 334-8000; 546 Avenue of the Americas (at 15th St.), (212) 255-5100; 332 East 14th St. (at First Ave.), (212) 228-4344
Pedal Pusher Bike Shop
1306 Second Ave. (at 69th St.), (212) 288-5592.
Stuveysant Bicycle
349 W. 14th St., (212) 254-5200

Roller Blades:
Blades Board and Skate
160 East 86th St., (212) 996-1644; 105 West 72nd St., (212) 787-3911, Open 7 days a week.
Manhattan Sports
2188 Broadway (at 78th St.), (212) 580-4753; 2901 Broadway (at 113th St.), (212) 749-1454, Rents and Repairs.

SANITATION

New York City Department of Sanitation
(212) 219-8090
Environmental Action Coalition (recycling)
(212) 677-1601

New York City Bureau of Highways (potholes)
(212) 768-4653
New York City Bureau of Electrical Control (street lights)
(212) 669-8353
New York City Department of Environmental Protection (water mains and sewers)
(718) 699-9811

SHOE REPAIR

Ambassador Luggage and Leather Goods
Repair of all types of leather goods.
371 Madison Ave. (bet 45th and 46th Sts.), (212) 972-0965, MC, V, AmEx; ❹❺❻❼Ⓢ *to 42nd St./Grand Central Station* &
Drago
Shoe shine, repairs, shoe polish, and other shoe needs.
2851 Broadway (bet. 110th and 111th),(212) 663-7060, MC, V, ❶ to 110th St.

STORAGE

Access Self Storage
Open 7 days a week, Access has 24-hour security, ample free parking, insurance and exceptional clean service for their customers.
29-00 Review Avenue (at 29th St.), (718) 729-0442, MC, V, AmEx, D, ❼ to Hunter's Pt
Chelsea Moving &

Storage Inc.
300 W. 23rd St. (bet. Seventh and Eighth Aves.), (212) 243-8000, ❶❷ *to 28th St.*
Chelsea Mini Storage
224 Twelfth Avenue, (212) 564-7735, ❶❷ *to 28th St.*
Guarantee Storage Centers Inc.
531 W. 15th Street, (212) 645-2943, ❶❷ *to 23rd St.*

SUBSTANCE ABUSE

Alateen Information Center
(212) 941-0094, Open 24 hours daily
Alcoholics Anonymous
(212) 647-1680, 9am-10:30pm
Pills Anonymous
(212) 874-0700, Open 24 hours daily

THE CITY ON THE NET

Guides to New York:
www.insideny.com
www.columbia.edu/~hauben/nyc.guides.html
www.citysearch.com
www.ny.yahoo.com
www.sidewalk.com
Museums/Libraries:
Metropolitan Museum of Art:
www.metmuseum.com
American Museum of Natural History:
www.amnh.org
New York Public Library:

www.nypl.org

Nightlife:

Playbill Online:
www.playbill.com
New York City Ballet:
www.nycballet.com
New York City Opera:
www.interport.net/nyc-opera
New York Philharmonic:
www.nyphilharmon.org
MovieLink:
www.777film.com
Village Voice Essentials
Guide to New York at
Night:
www.villagevoice.com/e/
nighttit.html
ClubNYC:
www.clubnyc.com
Metrobeat:
www.metro.com

Food:

Zagat's Dining: pathfind-er.com/Travel/Zagat/Dine
New York Food:
www.nyfood.com
Kosher Restaurant data-base:
www.shamash.org/kosher/
\krestqquery.html
New York City Beer
Guide: www.nycbeer.com

Transportation:

Subway Navigator Site:
metro.gaius.fr:1001/bin/se
lect/english/usa/new-york
Metropolitan Transit
Authority:
www.mta.nyc.ny.us

Sports:

Knicks:
www.nba.com/
knicks
Yankees:
www.yankees.com
Giants:
www.nfl.com/

giants
Jets: www.nfl.com/ jets
Government

NYC government:

www.ci.nyc.by.us
Public Advocate's Office:
www.pubadvocate.nyc.gov
/~advocate
New York City Council
Homepage: www.coun-cil.ny.us
United Nations:
www.un.org

Parks and Recreation:

Central Park: www.cen-tralpark.org
Parks and Recreations
Special events:
www.user.interport.net/~j
erdugal/nycpark.spe-cialevents.html

TOURS

**Adventures
on a Shoestring**

Walking tours through
Greenwich Village, SoHo,
Chinatown, the Lower
East Side, and other
neighborhoods according
to demand. Guides are
committed to helping the
low-budget explorer and
refuse to raise their rates,
which have remained at
five bucks a tour for the
thirty-five years of the
organization's existence.
*(212) 265-2663, $5 per
tour*

**Architectural Tours
through the 92nd St. Y**

Tours of Manhattan's his-toric cast-iron districts in
Gramercy and SoHo, and
other architecturally
interesting spots in the
city, are led by experts

Joyce Mendelsohn, Barry
Lewis, and Andrew
Dolkart.
*92nd St. Y, 1395
Lexington Ave. (at 92nd
St.), (212) 415-5500,* ❹
❺ ❻ *to 86th St.*

Backstage on Broadway

Get a group of twenty-five together to tour
behind the scenes of a
Broadway theater; tours
led by actors, directors,
and stage managers. Call
for reservations.
*228 West 47th St. (bet.
Broadway and Eighth
Ave.), (212) 575-8065, $8
(students), Cash Only,* ❶
❷ ❸ *to 42nd St.*

**Big Onion
Walking Tours**

A group of Columbia
University graduate stu-dents in American History
gives tours of New York's
ethnic neighborhoods.
Find out why New York
City used to be called the
big onion.
(212) 439-1090, Tour: $7

Harlem Your Way Tours

Tours of Harlem tailored
to your particular inter-est-historical or current.
(212) 690-1687, Tour: $25

Oscar Israelowitz Tours

Guided tours of the Lower
East Side, as well as boat
tours of Jewish NY.
Lecture programs as well.
(718) 951-7072

Urban Park Rangers

Rangers take you around
the city's parks. What you
see all depends on what
you're interested in,
whether it be bird-watch-ing, fishing or Native

American history.
*1234 Fifth Ave. (at 104th
St.), (212) 360-2774,
9am-5pm Daily,* ❻ *to
103rd St.*

WIRE SERVICES

MoneyGram

Fifty offices throughout
the city.
(800) 926-9400

**Credit Union National
Association**

(800) 358-5710

Western Union

(800) 325-6000 for near-est location.

UTILITIES

**Con Edison
Emergency Line**

Call to report problems.
*Gas, electrical, or steam
emergencies: (212) 683-8830, Open 24 hours*

**Public Service
Commission
Emergency Hotline**

If your gas or electricity is
cut off because you
haven't paid the bills,
they will give advice.
*(800) 342-3355, M-F
7:30am-7:30pm*

YMCA's

Harlem
(212) 281-4100

McBurney
(212) 741-9210

Prospect Park
(718) 768-7100

Vanderbilt
(212) 756-9600

West Side
(212) 875-4100

INDEX